The middle years of the twentieth century marked a particularly intense time of crisis and change in European society. During this period (1930-1950), a broad intellectual and spiritual movement arose within the European Catholic community, largely in response to the secularism that lay at the core of the crisis. The movement drew inspiration from earlier theologians and philosophers such as Möhler, Newman, Gardeil, Rousselot, and Blondel, as well as from men of letters like Charles Péguy and Paul Claudel.

The group of academic theologians included in the movement extended into Belgium and Germany, in the work of men like Emile Mersch, Dom Odo Casel, Romano Guardini, and Karl Adam. But above all the theological activity during this period centered in France. Led principally by the Jesuits at Fourvière and the Dominicans at Le Saulchoir, the French revival included many of the greatest names in twentieth-century Catholic thought: Henri de Lubac, Jean Daniélou, Yves Congar, Marie-Dominique Chenu, Louis Bouyer, and, in association, Hans Urs von Balthasar.

It is not true — as subsequent folklore has it — that those theologians represented any sort of self-conscious "school": indeed, the differences among them, for example, between Fourvière and Saulchoir, were important. At the same time, most of them were united in the double conviction that theology had to speak to the present situation, and that the condition for doing so faithfully lay in a recovery of the Church's past. In other words, they saw clearly that the first step in what later came to be known as *aggiornamento* had to be *ressourcement* — a rediscovery of the riches of the whole of the Church's two-thousand-year tradition. According to de Lubac, for example, all of his own works as well as the entire *Sources chrétiennes* collection are based on the presupposition that "the renewal of Christian vitality is linked at least partially to a renewed exploration of the periods and of the works where the Christian tradition is expressed with particular intensity."

In sum, for the *ressourcement* theologians theology involved a "return to the sources" of Christian faith, for the purpose of drawing out the meaning and significance of these sources for the critical questions of our time. What these theologians sought was a spiritual and intellectual communion with Christianity in its most vital moments as transmitted to us in its classic texts, a communion that would nourish, invigorate, and rejuvenate twentieth-century Catholicism.

The *ressourcement* movement bore great fruit in the documents of the Second Vatican Council and has deeply influenced the work of Pope John Paul II.

The present series is rooted in this renewal of theology. The series thus understands *ressourcement* as revitalization: a return to the sources, for the purpose of developing a theology that will truly meet the challenges of our time. Some of the features of the series, then, are a return to classical (patristic-medieval) sources and a dialogue with contemporary Western culture, particularly in terms of problems associated with the Enlightenment, modernity, and liberalism.

The series publishes out-of-print or as yet untranslated studies by earlier authors associated with the *ressourcement* movement. The series also publishes works by contemporary authors sharing in the aim and spirit of this earlier movement. This will include any works in theology, philosophy, history, literature, and the arts that give renewed expression to Catholic sensibility.

The editor of the Ressourcement series, David L. Schindler, is Gagnon Professor of Fundamental Theology and dean at the John Paul II Institute in Washington, D.C., and editor of the North American edition of *Communio: International Catholic Review,* a federation of journals in thirteen countries founded in Europe in 1972 by Hans Urs von Balthasar, Jean Daniélou, Henri de Lubac, Joseph Ratzinger, and others.

RETRIEVAL & RENEWAL

Ressourcement

IN CATHOLIC THOUGHT

THE NUPTIAL MYSTERY

Angelo Scola

Translated by

Michelle K. Borras

WILLIAM B. EERDMANS PUBLISHING COMPANY
GRAND RAPIDS, MICHIGAN / CAMBRIDGE, U.K.

Originally published as
Il mistero nuziale. 1. Uomo-donna — 2. Matrimonio-Famiglia
by Pul-Mursia, Rome, 1998-2000

English translation © 2005 Wm. B. Eerdmans Publishing Co.

Wm. B. Eerdmans Publishing Co.
255 Jefferson Ave. S.E., Grand Rapids, Michigan 49503 /
P.O. Box 163, Cambridge CB3 9PU U.K.
www.eerdmans.com

Printed in the United States of America

09 08 07 06 05   7 6 5 4 3 2 1

ISBN 0-8028-2831-0

The current translation of *The Nuptial Mystery* was prepared by Michelle Borras, who made use of the following previous translations: Chapter 1, sections 1-3, translated by Margaret McCarthy, appeared in *Communio* 25 (spring 98); Chapter 5, translated by David Louis Schindler Jr., et al., appeared in *Communio* 25 (winter 98); Chapters 14 and 16 were translated by Linda Cicone; Appendix 4 appeared in *Communio* 24 (spring 97).

Contents

II. The Nuptial Mystery:
A Theological Perspective

Contents

III. The Nuptial Mystery and Cultural Changes: The Tasks of Marriage and the Family

Contents

IV. The Nuptial *Mystery:*
Marriage and the Family in the Light of the Christian *Mysteries*

Contents

Contents

Preface to the English Edition

"Love is not love / Which alters when it alteration finds, / Or bends with the re-mover to remove" (Shakespeare, Sonnet 116). Only poetic genius can express so keenly and synthetically the content of every man's elementary experience. Gratuity and perpetuity are dimensions of love that it cannot give up without ceasing to be itself. Love is love only insofar as it is indomitable in affirming the other — always and no matter what.

The publication of *The Nuptial Mystery* in English gives me an opportunity to stress once more the deep-rooted conviction that has guided my reflection on the body, the sexual difference, the man-woman relation, marriage, and the family over the years: the Christian proposal *fits* the men and women of our time. *It fits,* in other words, it corresponds deeply to what the fascinating interweaving of freedom and reason known as the human heart yearns for; it corresponds to what man seeks, more or less consciously, in everything he does. In the climate of disincarnate spiritualism and androgynism that defines the temper of first-world societies — and what we are facing today is not simply the latest version of human weakness, but a thought-out, persistent proposal that is at the antipodes of Christian thought! — Paul's words *"Woe to me if I do not preach the Gospel"* (1 Cor. 9:16) sound with special urgency in the ears of the Christian people. The theology presented in this book therefore understands itself as serving Christian proclamation.

For this reason, I would like to thank the faculty and students of the North American session of the Pontifical John Paul II Institute for Studies on Marriage and the Family — in the persons of its vice president, Carl Anderson, and of its dean, Professor David Schindler — for the common work of these last few years, which is also at the root of the English edition of this book. My thanks also to Michelle K. Borras, one of my students at the Rome campus of the Institute, who has translated the work with such great care and dedication. Finally, I am grateful to my publisher, William B. Eerdmans, whose generosity and helpfulness have made it possible to bring this enterprise to completion.

ANGELO SCOLA
Patriarch of Venice
Venice, March 5, 2003
Ash Wednesday

Preface

"None of the great thinkers or poets have ever found an answer to the question, 'What is love?' . . . If one imprisons the light, it slips through the fingers."[1] Evdokimov expresses a conviction which belongs to fundamental human experience: in a certain sense, nothing is more instantaneous for man than the recognition of love, when he is surprised by it. Before the radiant smile of an infant toward his mother, the consuming desire of a young man in love, the knowing tenderness of an elderly couple, the radical dedication of men and women in the miserable slums of many cities, or the luminosity radiated by certain persons dedicated to God, the affirmation is spontaneous: There is love! And yet it is not at all easy to respond to Evdokimov's question. Nor is it necessary to point to the heedlessness of modern times, with its libertine behavior, to explain this inability to define love. Notwithstanding the times, love lets itself be recognized when it arises. The difficulty is tied, rather, to the very nature of the phenomenon of love, which goes beyond spatial and temporal circumstances even as it is colored by them.

Can, then, this unique nature of love justify the use of the term "mystery"? I believe it can, under two conditions. First, mystery must not be equated with the unknown (the not-yet-known); it refers, rather, as Scheeben explains in his unsurpassed masterpiece, *The Mysteries of Christianity*, to the personal and kindly way in which Being addresses us, calling us to affirm our objective and dramatic partaking in him. Secondly, we must treat as a unity the plurality of meanings, at first glance so diverse, to which fundamental human experience refers when we speak of "love." C. S. Lewis notes with great

1. P. Evdokimov, *The Sacrament of Love* (Crestwood, N.Y.: St. Vladimir's Seminary Press 1995), 105.

perceptiveness that the term "love" covers a spectrum that runs from *venere* (carnal lust) to that perfection with which the three Persons love each other in the one God. We thus pass from one term of the analogy to the other, preserving a common denominator of all these forms of love, according to the exclamation of William of St. Thierry: "O amor, a quo omnis amor cognominatur etiam carnalis ac degener!" (*Super Cantica,* preface).

It is precisely in the category of *nuptial mystery* — as the inseparable intertwining of sexual difference, love, and fruitfulness — that we discover a way adequately to describe (though certainly not define) the phenomenon of love. This is the fascinating hypothesis this work will attempt to verify.

Beginning with the original "datum" of man and woman, discussed above all in the first two sections, our exploration of the nuptial mystery will move on to the (essential) study of marriage and the family. Properly speaking, it is only in the reality of marriage and the family that we find the full countenance, or expression, of man and woman.

This volume contains some articles which have not been edited and others which have been previously published. These latter have been substantially reworked with an eye to both the rethinking and presentation of the contents. Some themes are repeated throughout, but not casually. Certain key categories, indicated in the analytical index — here rather an index of main ideas — surface more than once. These repetitions, which depend in part on the analogical progression of the theme, allow for the better treatment of certain nuances. Nuances, in a topic such as the nuptial mystery, are not always irrelevant.

As this work draws to a close, I feel the need to thank again all the students and professors of the Pontifical John Paul II Institute for Studies on Marriage and the Family. In saying *all,* I do not refer only to those I have met in Rome in these past twenty years, but also to all those who frequent the many realities which, on the various continents (in the United States, Mexico, Brazil, Benin, India, the Philippines, Australia, Spain, Ireland, and Austria), make up, in a plurality of sessions, the one John Paul II Institute. As president of the Institute, I have in recent years had the singular gift of being able to lecture in all the various sessions. I have also had the opportunity to get to know the Institute's many professors. What I have received is priceless!

How can I not include in my thanks those who have helped, in concrete ways, in the final preparation of this text? I refer particularly to Father Gabriel Richi Alberti, Michela Pirola, and Carla Gianella. Without their help this manuscript would not yet be in the hands of its publisher, to whom I also extend my thanks. I also thank those who in their presentations, reviews, or more simply by letter or in person commented on the first (Italian) volume of this text upon its publication. These have offered me, even through more or less justified criticisms, the possibility of penetrating a little bit more into the mysterious nuptial rhythm from which is woven the gift which — I am ever more convinced — is the stuff of every being. In the end, every being is a gift of him who, as John affirms in a manner both simple and moving, *"is love"* (1 John 4:16).

ANGELO SCOLA
Lateran, April 24, 2000
Monday of the Octave of Easter
Holy Year

To the Reader

The publication of *The Nuptial Mystery* (*Man and Woman* and *Marriage and the Family*) in a single volume allows me to make several clarifications, prompted by the precious stimuli provided by several reviews of the original editions.[1]

A few words are needed regarding the object of our study, the *nuptial mystery*. The term "nuptial" — which we prefer to the perhaps more common "spousal" — highlights the *relational* character of love. Following the biblical theme of the wedding feast of the Lamb (cf. Rev. 19:7-9), this term reveals love's capacity to bring into play the dimensions of the *one*, the *other*, and the *unity of the two*. The prerogative of nuptiality is maintained in all of love's inflections, but the theme of love is so wide that it could be investigated in any number of other directions. Our own investigation will limit itself to love's nuptial character. Obviously, many things will be said about love in the course of our work, but all will be from this precise perspective.

The mysteriousness of love does not mean that love is something unknown — to the contrary, it is a constitutive factor of fundamental human experience well known to every person! Rather, because love is the essential way in which the personal freedom of every human being enters into relation with its foundation, love participates in the nature of mystery proper to this foundation. This foundation cannot be seized; it remains ultimately ungraspable. To be aware of its existence and attributes does not mean that

---

1. Cf. G. Cottini, in *Studi Cattolici* 446 (1999): 901-2; J. S. Botero Giraldo, in *Studia Moralia* 37 (1999): 516-18; A. Miralles, in *Annales Teologici* 13 (1999): 630-33; M. Calipari, in *Medicina e morale* 49 (1999): 608-9; F. Ardusso, in *Famiglia oggi* 22, no. 8/9 (1999): 87-88.

we thereby possess it, even conceptually: *"si comprehendis non est Deus."* In the end, the face of love is that of the trinitarian mystery.

To briefly restate the content of the nuptial mystery, one cannot but take as a starting point *fundamental human experience,* an experience that is, thus, proper to every human being.[2] We find nuptiality inscribed in this fundamental experience as an inseparable intertwining of three factors: sexual difference, love in its proper sense (relation to the other, gift), and fruitfulness.

As the place in which the "I," as *corpore et anima unus,*[3] encounters the objective presence of the other, sexual difference opens the possibility of relation between the two and reveals the human being's proper and intrinsic (loving) orientation to *gift.* This exchange between the two always bears fruit *(fecundity).* The dual unity of man and woman is the necessary starting point for a description of the phenomenon of the nuptial mystery. It constitutes this mystery's *horizontal dimension.*

At this point a series of decisive questions arises: Why does this dual unity of man and woman exist and what is the reason for it? Why this nuptial character of love and where does it come from?

To respond to these questions, our study, sifting through equalities and differences, will try to trace out the nuptial character present in all the manifestations of love, from the most elevated to the most base. Through the use of analogy, we will treat the various expressive modes of the single concept of *love* in such a way that these will shed light on one another and both facilitate and deepen our understanding of the phenomenon of love. The three factors of the nuptial mystery (difference, love as gift, fruitfulness) are present — obviously with the necessary differences, which cannot be stressed enough! — in all the analogous forms of love. The *vertical dimension* of the nuptial mystery passes through man and woman to the *other* in general, and ultimately to God himself. In a certain sense, however, it also opens onto other levels of living beings (animals) and, according to the classical sensibility, even to inanimate being — for instance, in the Thomistic notion of *amor naturalis.*

If we keep in mind that our reflection begins with the *phenomenon* of nuptial love to then involve *all* the elements of love, there is no reason not to extend our gaze as far as the light that Christian revelation brings to bear on the subject. Without confusing the natural and supernatural dimensions, and with the opportune distinctions of method (reason and faith; philosophy and theology), the *Christian mysteries* of the Trinity, Jesus Christ, the Church, and the sacraments reveal important aspects of the nuptial mystery. They consti-

2. Cf. A. Scola, *Questioni di Antropologia Teologica* (Rome, 1997), 164-65, 201-11.
3. Cf. *Gaudium et Spes* 14.

tute a "place" where our knowledge of this mystery can be greatly deepened. After all, spousal language is used throughout the sacred Scriptures!

It is opportune to situate the analytical presentation of the content of this work in its historical context: the contemporary world, the dominant mentality of which has obscured the features of that human experience which we indicate with the expression *nuptial mystery*, to the point of rendering them unrecognizable. This obscuration intensified in the years following the promulgation of *Humanae Vitae*. The early attempts to separate the unitive and the procreative dimensions of the conjugal act introduced a pernicious relativism into ethics. A more accurate ethical and anthropological reflection was called for in order to enable dialogue with the dominant culture, which, for all its rejection of certain essential traits of the Christian vision of marriage and family, was still incapable of doing away with the ultimate coordinates of this vision. However, in the 1990s two factors began to erode the frame of reference of the cultural sensibility, a structure that had previously held firm even in the midst of heated debate. These factors were the separation of ethics from larger questions of meaning and the growing perception of the irrelevancy of the moral magisterium. In response, a regeneration of a Christian subjectivity conscious of the reasons for God's design for person, marriage, and family demanded a theological and anthropological development of ethics based on the principle that only in the incarnate Word do persons discover the truth about themselves.[4]

At the turn of the century, however, we observe yet another radical change of mentality, an *anthropological mutation* that undermines not only the ethical frame of reference but the very grammar and syntax of the human person and of authentic community, thus threatening what Lewis calls the "abolition of man." The dominant "androgynism," which has its source in the Promethean claim to separate the inseparable — sexuality, love-gift, and procreation (the nuptial mystery) — gives rise to a disincarnate spiritualism and to a pernicious dualism between the personal and social spheres. Primary relations are seriously compromised, if not completely changed. What is required now is no longer simply the regeneration of the Christian subject. What is required is even more fundamental: giving back the form of humankind as such to human reason. Such an undertaking requires the courage to return to fundamental human experience, in which the original structure of being shines forth. The nuptial character of love, offered in our study first under the aspects of marriage and the family, is a dimension particularly capable of revealing the features of fundamental human experience. This study, pur-

---

4. Cf. *Gaudium et Spes* 22.

sued from the viewpoint of Christian revelation, also demonstrates that nuptiality is an essential part of God's plan. This latter gives reality its true consistency.

Discovering, accepting, and deepening our understanding of this mystery in order to then propose it to the freedom of each human being is a choice full of realism. It is *fitting,* capable of revealing the good reasons behind the Christian faith, a faith that exalts the *humanum.* It is this that the present work proposes to do, in treating the theme of the nuptial mystery.

But first, a brief word to clarify what the reader ought *not* to seek in this work. This book is not a comprehensive treatment of the Christian mysteries (the Trinity, Christ, etc.), nor of the sacramental or moral theology of marriage and the family; nor is it an investigation of the ethical questions necessarily tied to the theme of man and woman and marriage and family. Nor should the reader seek in this study, which may rightly be attributed to the area of theological anthropology, a full treatment of that subject.[5]

At this point what is *offered* in the various treatises collected in this work should emerge with clarity. This "offer," as shown by the positive reception enjoyed by the first volume of the Italian edition, extends beyond the circle of those involved in academics (both professors and students). What this book proposes is an inquiry into love, carried out by following the "guiding thread" of nuptiality.[6] This in turn allows for a unified and deepened understanding of God's design for the person, marriage, and the family.[7]

---

5. Such an attempt can be found in the manual by A. Scola, G. Marengo, and J. Prades, *La persona umana. Manuale di antropologia teologica* (Milan: Amateca, 2000).

6. I have thought it opportune to add to these chapters seven appendices that may help the reader to enter more fully into the book's theme. These are essays tied to specific circumstances: the declarations regarding the non-admissibility of women to the ministerial priesthood (Appendix 1); a reading of several articles of St. Thomas's *De Passionibus* on *affectio* and *amor* (Appendix 2); a commentary on *Donum Vitae* regarding the theological principle of procreation (Appendix 3); a reflection on the importance of the theme of sexual difference in priestly and theological formation (Appendix 4); some reflections of the content of the teaching of *Humanae Vitae,* a prophetic defense of that level of fundamental human experience that I have termed the "nuptial mystery" (Appendix 5); some useful notes taken from a conversation on the theme of the engagement period (Appendix 6); and a reflection on the nuptial mystery as a perspective for systematic theology (Appendix 7). These texts, in spite of their definite limits, are not extraneous to our central theme, and they can be a source of further light.

7. "The further investigation of God's plan for the person, marriage, and the family should be the task in which you are engaged, with renewed vigor, at the beginning of the third millennium. I would like to suggest a few perspectives for this research. The first concerns the foundation in a strict sense, that is, the Mystery of the Holy Trinity, the very source of being and thus the ultimate reference point of anthropology. In the light of the mystery of the Trinity, sexual difference reveals its full nature as the expressive sign of the whole person. The second perspec-

I highlight the importance of the adjective "unified." The mystery of love is by its very nature inseparable from the burning questions of life (including those of genetic engineering), from death (which, in view of the link between generation and dying, introduces the problem of intergenerational relations), and from education. I am convinced that the sometimes radical incomprehension of the depth of this mystery flows from an ignorance of love's nuptial character. This incomprehension depends in its turn on the twofold process of *separation* and the pretended *abolition of difference* (difference is insuperable and postulates the identity that founds equality) which has characterized Western thought from modernity onward.

This inability to think in a unified way about the phenomenon of love has led, on the basis of the possibilities revealed by science and technology, to the separation of those factors which are constitutive of the nuptial mystery (difference, love-gift, and fruitfulness). If, however, we were to return to things as they are (and, says Husserl, we must have the humility to return to things as they are!), these factors would appear indissolubly connected.

The voice of the church, and of the magisterium in particular when it intervenes on these subjects, resounds as one "crying out in the wilderness" (Matt. 3:3). The church is heard, more often than not, as an antiquated or obsolete intrusion into the consciences of today's men and women, in whom it does nothing but sow fear (with all its "no's") — fear, if not angst. In reality this is not the case: such a reaction depends on the fact that the dominant culture does not help people to *think* in terms of the nuptial character of love. (As a side note, this is one of the reasons why this study gives some attention — which certainly does not claim to be exhaustive — to certain macroscopic historical-cultural quandaries in which we live.)

Rather, it is precisely by virtue of nuptiality that there shines forth the extraordinary diffusive capacity of being which, in its trinitarian foundation, is pure gift (love). In all of its manifestations, love, when it is really love, does

---

tive which I would like to submit to your study involves the vocation of man and woman to communion. This, too, has its roots in the Trinitarian mystery; it is fully revealed in the incarnation of the Son of God — in whom the divine and human natures are united in the Person of the Word — and is historically inserted into the sacramental dynamism of the Christian economy. The nuptial mystery of Christ the Bridegroom of the Church is expressed in a singular manner through sacramental marriage, a fruitful community of life and love. In this way, the theology of marriage and the family — and this is the third point I would like to offer you — is inserted into the contemplation of the mystery of the One and Three, who invites all mankind to the wedding feast of the Lamb, accomplished at Easter and perennially offered to human freedom in the sacramental reality of the Church." John Paul II, "Discourse of the Holy Father to the Participants in the Encounter Promoted by the Pontifical John Paul II Institute for Studies on Marriage and the Family," no. 5, in *L'Osservatore Romano,* August 28, 1999.

not cease to offer to each human being forms of beauty that propel him or her toward the truth (beauty is always the "splendor of the truth"!). Why, then, should we not seek, through the nuptial mystery, "all the truth" (John 16:13) about love? Along the paths of love, the "whole truth" will make us "free indeed" (cf. John 8:36).

ANGELO SCOLA

PART I

Categories of the Nuptial Mystery:
Two Original Theses of *Mulieris Dignitatem*

CHAPTER 1

A Theological Sketch of Man and Woman

1.1. A Constant Concern

John Paul II, from the very beginning of his pontificate,[1] unfolds the anthropological and theological foundations of the man-woman pair, and he returns to this important topic with noteworthy frequency. At least two very important documents have been dedicated specifically to this reflection — *Mulieris Dignitatem (= MD)* (1988) and the *Letter to Women* (1995) — and it has appeared with analytical comprehensiveness in catecheses, talks, addresses, homilies, etc. Moreover, with respect to the teaching of previous pontiffs,[2] such teaching marks a considerable advance, both qualitatively and quantitatively.[3]

1. Already on April 29, 1979, John Paul II took up the question in an audience granted to the participants of the Tenth National Congress of Italian Domestic Workers. Cf. "Woman's Dignity," *Origins* 9, no. 2 (May 31, 1979): 31-32.

2. See, e.g., John XXIII, "Discorso nella solenne apertura del Concilio Vaticano II," in *Enchiridion Vaticanum* (Bologna, 1985), 55; *Gaudium et Spes* 9, 29, 31, 40, 60; *Apostolicam Actuositatem* 9, 32; *Ad Gentes* 17; Paul VI, "Presentare all'uomo contemporaneo il messaggio cristiano nella sua integralità," in *Insegnamenti di Paolo VI*, vol. 11 (Vatican City, 1974), 630-42. For a bibliography of the feminine question in the magisterium, see *La femme dans l'enseignements des Papes* (Abbaye St. Pierre de Solesmes, 1982); *La donna nel magistero di Paolo VI* (Rome, 1980); *Les enseignements pontificaux: Le problème féminin (1878-1958)* (Tournai, 1965); A. Aluffi, *Il privilegio di essere donna nella documentazione del Vaticano II* (Rome, 1967); M. Alcala, *La mujer y los ministerios en la Iglesia del Vaticano II a Pablo VI* (Salamanca, 1982); L. Antinucci, "La Chiesa e la nuova coscienza femminile. Una lettura del Magistero del postconcilio," in *La donna nella Chiesa a nel mondo* (Naples, 1988), 285-313; G. Bragantini, *Le donne nel Concilio Vaticano II* (Rome, 1984); G. Cazora Russo, *Il ruolo della donna nei documenti pontifici da Leone XIII a Paolo VI: Ricerca sullo status sociale della donna*, vol. 2 (Rome, 1975), 752-826; R. Harahan, *The Vocation of Women: The Teaching of the Modern Popes from Leo XIII to Paul VI* (Rome, 1983).

3. Obviously we cannot pretend to provide a complete list of all the contributions of John

In the apostolic letter *Mulieris Dignitatem* we find the most organic expression of the pope's thought on this subject. It therefore constitutes our primary point of reference. In its turn, *Mulieris Dignitatem* is to be read in the context of the celebrated Wednesday catecheses on the theology of the body, apart from which the richness of the letter would not be fully apparent. In *Mulieris Dignitatem* John Paul II, referring to the Synod of Bishops in Octo-

---

Paul II on the question which concerns us. We must, however, cite the more important documents and, above all, show with a few examples the diversity of occasions on which the pope has taken up this question. The major documents are fundamentally three: in the first place the encyclical letter *Redemptoris Mater* (March 25, 1987), in which the pope introduces the views informing his most important contribution on women: the apostolic letter *Mulieris Dignitatem* (August 15, 1988), whose themes have been taken up again in the *Letter to Women* (June 30, 1995). To these documents must be added the cycles of Wednesday catecheses, two in particular: the one on human love, brought together in *The Theology of the Body: Human Love in the Divine Plan* (Boston: Daughters of St. Paul, 1997), and the one dedicated precisely to women (some of them tied to the reflection on Mary): June 22, 1994; July 6, 1994; March 15, 1995; September 6, 1995; November 29, 1995; December 6, 1995. In 1995, together with the celebration of the United Nations conference on women in Beijing, the pope dedicated many talks to the subject of women during the Sunday Angelus: June 25; July 9, 16, 23, 30; August 6, 13, 15, 20, and 27; September 3 and 10; December 8. John Paul II addressed himself on different occasions to international organizations, making the question concerning women a fundamental part of his talk, for example: *To the XXV Conference of the Food and Agriculture Organization* (November 16, 1989); *To the Secretary of the International Conference on Population and Development* (March 18, 1994); and with reference to the conference in Beijing: *To the Secretary General of the IV Conference of the UN* (May 26, 1995). Another series of talks that seems significant to us includes homilies and talks about women saints; in these the pope refers to the dignity and vocation of women, for example: November 5, 1979; September 11, 1984; June 10, 1987; April 9 and 30, 1989; June 20, 1993; April 24, 1994; January 19 and 20, 1995; February 5, 12, 19, and 26, 1995; May 10, 1995; October 1 and 29, 1995. Other than these talks, John Paul II has tackled the theme of women in reference to the following questions: family, work, feminism, conferences of women's associations, world days of women, the theme of the priesthood reserved only to men, *ad limina* visits of bishops. For more complete documentation of all the contributions of the pope on the subject of women, cf. P. Vanzan and A. Auletta, *L'essere e l'agire della donna in Giovanni Paolo II* (Rome, 1996). Other titles on the subject include: *Dignità e vocazione della donna: Per una lettura della "Mulieris dignitatem"* (Vatican City, 1989); M. Farina, "La *Mulieris dignitatem*: il progetto di Dio appella una nuova autocoscienza femminile. Approccio teologico-fondamentale," *Rivista di Scienze dell'educazione* 27 (1989): 11-24; Farina, "La questione donna: un'istanza critica per la teologia," *Ricerche Teologiche* 1 (1990): 91-120; S. Maggiolini, ed., *Profezia della donna: Lettera apostolica "Mulieris dignitatem." Testo e commenti* (Rome, 1988); A. Serra, "La 'Mulieris dignitatem.' Consensi e dissensi," *Marianum* 53 (1991): 512-88; D. Tettamanzi, *Grandi cose ha fatto con me l'onnipotente: Meditando con il Papa la "Mulieris dignitatem"* (Rome, 1988); M. Toso, ed., *Essere donna: Studi sulla lettera apostolica "Mulieris dignitatem"* (Turin, 1989); P. Vanzan, "'Mulieris dignitatem': reazioni, contenuti e prospettive," *La Civilta Cattolica* 139, no. 4 (1988): 255-58.

ber 1987 on the vocation and mission of the laity in the church and the world, affirms:

> One of the recommendations [of the synodal fathers] was for a further study of the anthropological and theological bases that are needed in order to solve the problems connected with the meaning and dignity of being a woman and being a man. It is a question of understanding the reason for, and the consequences of, the Creator's decision that the human being should always and only exist as a woman or a man. It is only by beginning from these bases, which make it possible to understand the greatness of the dignity and vocation of women, that one is able to speak of their active presence in the Church and in society. *This is what I intend to deal with in this document.* (*MD* 1)

In this text the pope offers us a basic methodological premise for our reflection: only by beginning from the proper foundations can one grasp the depth of the dignity and the mission of women. In fact, only by going to the root of the personal being of man and of woman, which implies identity and difference,[4] is it possible to consider woman as a being who is "other," and not just "another thing."

In this chapter I intend to present the theological foundations of the man-woman pair in the teaching of John Paul II. In the context of a brief but systematic overview of the pope's reflection on this subject, the novelty of the two anthropological theses contained in *Mulieris Dignitatem* can emerge more clearly. These theses will provide the subject matter for our further study; for convenience' sake we will mention them both here. They both refer to the theme of the *imago Dei.*

The first establishes an (in a certain sense direct) analogy between the dual unity of man and woman and the relations between the three persons in God. Developing the classical analogy between the individual person and God, inasmuch as man is created in his image, the pope holds that the *imago Dei* also includes man's communional quality. He discerns an analogy between man's existence in dual unity and God's existence in the relations of the Trinity. The second thesis, strictly connected to the first, affirms that human sexuality is an integral part of the *imago Dei* (cf. *MD* 6). Both affirmations, which remain in continuity with the church's perennial teaching, expand this teaching in an original way and open up a fascinating field of research.

---

4. Cf. A. Lobato, "La mujer y el varón. El problema de la diferencia," *A Ordem* 89 (1997): 89-121; A. Ruiz Retegui, "El tratamiento diferencial de la sexualidad en la Carta Apostólica *Mulieris dignitatem,*" *Scripta Theologica* 22 (1990): 881-97.

Before entering into the question to be addressed here, I must make two important clarifications: First, our point of departure is pontifical teaching and not the extensive debate about this thematic as it has developed in the fields of theology, philosophy, and the human sciences, as well as in the cultural and social arena. Obviously, this does not mean that we have disregarded the relevant literature, or that we have not considered the challenges of feminist thought.[5] It means, rather, that our discussion will not on this occasion enter *directly* into the cultural debate by way of examining the positions of others, but will present some suggestions for a fundamental reflection on the theme.[6] Our choice should, however, allow for an adequate response to the legitimate claims of "feminism" and, at the same time, a calm critique of specific feminist positions that are irreconcilable with Catholic doctrine.[7]

In the second place, it belongs to the nature of the magisterium to enunciate Christian doctrine by affirming its contents and by marking its parameters. The magisterium directs itself, therefore, to all the people of God, and becomes a point of departure for further reflection. The avenues opened by the pope in his teaching on women beg to be probed critically and systematically, by the appropriate theological method. We will develop our reflection in three parts. In the first place, we will inquire into the anthropological foundation of the man-woman pair. Secondly, we will point to the christological context into which this is inserted. Finally, we will address its ecclesiological and Mariological foundation.

1.2. The Anthropological Foundation: The Dual Unity of Man and Woman

One of the preeminent aspects of the anthropology implied in John Paul II's teaching consists in his reflection on the relation between man and woman.[8]

5. Cf. F. Martin, *The Feminist Question: Feminist Theology in the Light of Christian Tradition* (Grand Rapids: Eerdmans, 1994), with an extensive bibliography.

6. For bibliographical references on this subject, see P. Cavaglia, M. Cirianni, and M. P. Manello, "Indicazioni bibliografiche sul tema 'donna'," *Rivista di Scienza dell'Educazione* 35 (1997): 453-79.

7. Cf. J. Burggraf, "Dignità e ruolo della donna nella chiesa e nella società," *Annales theologici* 1 (1987): 39-50. For a historical perspective, see E. dal Covolo, *Donna e matrimonio alle origini della Chiesa* (Rome, 1996); J. I. Saranyana, *La discussion medieval sobre la condición femenina. Siglos VIII al XIII* (Salamanca, 1997), with an extensive bibliography.

8. See G. Chantraine, *Uomo e donna* (Parma, 1986); C. Giuliodori, *Intelligenza teologica del*

The pope begins with a series of considerations on the two accounts of creation in Genesis (1:27 and 2:18-25), which converge in the affirmation that man is made "in the image and likeness of God," an affirmation the Holy Father calls "the basis of all Christian anthropology" (*MD* 6). *Mulieris Dignitatem* asserts in section 7 that "man cannot exist 'alone' (Gen 2:18); he can exist only as a 'unity of the two,' and therefore in relation to another human person. . . . Being a person in the image and likeness of God thus also involves existing in a relationship, in relation to the other 'I'" (*MD* 7). The man-woman pair appears, in this way, to be the expression of the ontological principle of dual unity, according to which, unity always presents itself in a contingent reality within an intrinsic polarity (this also holds true for soul and body, and individual and community).[9]

We will limit ourselves to itemizing, almost by a list of headings, four essential features of the meaning of the man-woman pair.

a. Man exists always and only as a masculine or feminine being. There is not a single man (or woman) who can by himself alone be the whole of man. He always has before himself the other way of being human, which is to him inaccessible. In this way we discover in the relation of man and woman the contingent character of the human creature: the "I" needs the other and depends upon the other for his fulfillment.[10] The duality of masculine and feminine "gender" thus presents itself at once as internal and external to the "I." Or rather, the "I" registers a lack within himself that opens him to one "outside of himself." It is in this context that the reflection on the principle of a helpmate (understood not unilaterally but reciprocally) arises.[11] This contingence identifies not only man's limits, but also his capacity for self-transcendence in the discovery of the other-than-himself as positive for himself. In this sense contingence reveals that man, like every creature, is a sign: he is not only an individual (identity) but also a person (relation/difference). Accordingly, the

---

maschile e del femminile (Rome, 1991); A. Scola, "*L'imago Dei* e la sessualità umana," *Anthropotes* 1 (1992): 61-73; Scola, "Maria modello del cristiano e della donna," in *Profezia*, 148-58; Scola, "La visione antropologica del rapporto uomo-donna: il significato dell'unita dei due," in *Dignità e vocazione*, 91-103.

9. Cf. A. Scola, *Hans Urs von Balthasar: A Theological Style* (Grand Rapids: Eerdmans, 1995), 84-100.

10. On this subject John Paul II affirms: "the meaning of man's original unity, through masculinity and femininity, is expressed as an overcoming of the frontier of solitude. At the same time it is an affirmation — with regard to both human beings — of everything that constitutes man in solitude" (John Paul II, *Theology of the Body,* 45).

11. John Paul II, *Letter to Women* 7.

pope says: "Being a person in the image and likeness of God thus also involves existing in a relationship, in relation to the other 'I'" (MD 7).

b. At the same time, we can characterize the relation between masculine and feminine as a relation of identity and difference.[12]

The question of identity is easily traced back to the absolute equality of the two (of man and woman) in their being as persons and in everything that derives from this. The conciliar text constantly recalled by the pope to illustrate this claim is taken from the constitution Gaudium et Spes (= GS): "If man is the only creature on earth whom God has desired for its own sake, man can fully discover his true self only in a sincere giving of himself" (GS 24). In this sense the pope joins with the Western philosophical tradition expressed in the definition of Boethius: "persona est naturae rationalis individua substantia" [a person is an individual substance of a rational nature].[13]

The question about difference is more complicated. In fact, to think about sexual difference is the very thing that appears problematic today. In any case, sexual difference is not reducible simply to a problem of roles; it must be understood ontologically. Dual unity, in this sense, is a phenomenological sign of that which Thomas called the distinctio realis, and Heidegger, ontological difference: even in the relation of man and woman, as in the relation between being and ens, is expressed the call of Being, addressed, through reality (which is its sign), to human freedom.

It is for this reason that the dual unity of sexual difference does not mean an irenic and symmetrical reciprocity as Aristophanes supposed in Plato's Symposium. Man and woman are not two halves destined to merge so as to regenerate a lost unity. This is evident even at the phenomenological level of the states of life. Man lives relations not only of a spousal sort, but also of paternity, maternity, fraternity, etc.

On the other hand, the reciprocity of man and woman "can stand as a paradigm of that community dimension which characterizes man's entire nature."[14]

There is another aspect linked to the question of sexual difference that we cannot fail to mention. I am referring to how it is that dual unity inevitably imposes an ulterior and more acute awareness of one's own original depen-

12. Cf. A. Scola, Identidad y diferencia (Madrid, 1989).
13. Liber de persona et duabus naturis, III: PL, 64:1343. This is taken up by Thomas in the Summa Theologiae Ia, q. 29, a.1.
14. H. U. von Balthasar, Theo-Drama II: Dramatis Personae: Man in God, trans. Graham Harrison (San Francisco: Ignatius, 1990), 365.

8

dence. By virtue of his sexual nature, in fact, man discovers death as mediated through his connection with generation. Dual unity places the "I" within the circle of human generations, which follow one upon the other relentlessly. In this way the species itself is preserved, but the individual is exposed to death.

c. From a more theological point of view, human sexuality, and therefore the difference of the sexes, belongs to man's being as image of God.[15] This statement helps us avoid, in any attempt to define the human being, every move to confine him within the intracosmic (and thereby to reduce sexuality to the level of animality). On the other hand, sexual difference helps us understand that the image cannot be reduced to some purely spiritual element. Moreover, the inclusion of sexual difference in the *imago Dei* allows us to speak — under precise conditions, to be sure — of a certain analogy between the relation of man and woman and the trinitarian relations. *Communio* as an essential dimension of man is part of his being in the image of God.

d. What we have said thus far allows us to see in spousal love the *analogatum princeps* of every kind of love[16] and, at the same time, to consider it a privileged metaphor for man's relation with reality.[17] On this subject the pope affirms: "The nature of one and the other love (virginity and marriage) is 'conjugal,' that is, expressed through the total gift of oneself. Both types of love tend to express that conjugal meaning of the body which from the beginning has been inscribed in the personal makeup of man and woman."[18]

These four elements, which characterize the meaning of the relation of man and woman, allow us to conclude that sexuality is an original, and not derivative, dimension of man. One cannot construct an anthropology apart from the human being's sexual nature. Were sexual difference not essential to the consideration of the person, the relation to the other would be established independent of such difference. Sexuality in that case would be a purely accidental fact. Does not this sort of disincarnate anthropology, so to speak, end in a negation of the woman as a personal subject of "desire," with the risk of reducing her purely to an object of masculine desire? Similarly, any position

---

15. We have shown this in Scola, "*L'imago Dei* e la sessualità umana."

16. This is an intuition dear to Soloviev. Cf. V. Soloviev, *The Meaning of Love*, trans. Jane Marshall (London: Geoffrey Bles, Centenary Press, 1946).

17. Scheeben uses the relation between man and woman to define the relation between faith and reason. Cf. M. J. Scheeben, *The Mysteries of Christianity* (London: Herder, 1946), 762-96.

18. John Paul II, *Theology of the Body*, 277-78.

that understands the personal dignity of the woman not as its essential premise but rather only as one of its consequences, would end up compromising
the value of maternity and virginity.

The affirmation of human sexuality as an integral part of the *imago Dei*,
as we have said above, also allows us to establish a radical differentiation of
human sexuality from animal sexuality, with which it obviously maintains
solid bio-instinctual connections. Against every Gnostic temptation we must
affirm the fully human, that is, personal, character of sexuality. In this sense
the body expresses the person,[19] and expresses it even in its being masculine
and feminine. Every attack upon the dignity of the body (and here unfortunately the woman is more exposed than the man) is an attack upon the dignity of the person.

Another consequence of this conception of the dual unity is the radical elimination of every exclusionary counterposition between man and woman.
Rather, only in their reciprocal dependence is their personal character fulfilled. This implies the simultaneous affirmation of their identity and difference. The exclusive exaltation of one of the poles over the other cannot help
but rupture the original dual unity willed by the Creator. Therefore it will not
be possible to promote the dignity and the rights of women if this characteristic is not respected. On the other hand, it is obvious that every form of
"chauvinism" contradicts the creative design. Thus the fact that the current
debate on the question of women is posed in terms of *reciprocity*, having
evolved from its earlier forms of *emancipation and separation*, is something
positive.[20] Without entering here into the merits of particular questions, it is
beyond all doubt that the search for equality (or, as we would prefer to say,
identity), with respect to sexual difference or diversity, better corresponds to
the Christian vision of life.[21]

The work in favor of the dignity and mission of women in the church and
in the world can be eminently creative by defending all dimensions of the
woman's being, those she shares with the man by virtue of their common
identity and those proper to her by virtue of her being woman.

19. Cf. John Paul II, *Theology of the Body*, 61.
20. Cf. Farina, "La questione donna," 111-12.
21. Cf. Scola, *Hans Urs von Balthasar*, 92-93.

1.3. The Christological and Trinitarian Context of the Dual Unity of Man and Woman

The anthropological affirmation of the dual unity of man and woman is decisive. However, it needs to be deepened. We cannot, in this place, even hint at the philosophical foundation of dual unity, which would require us to articulate the terms of an adequate ontology for the anthropology underlying our discussion. We will rather pause for a moment on its theological foundation, which, starting with the data of revelation, provides a better explanation as to why God wanted us as man and woman.

For this task we must fix our gaze upon the fullness of revelation, and therefore upon Jesus Christ: "The eternal truth about the human being, man and woman — a truth that is immutably fixed in human experience — at the same time constitutes the mystery which only in 'the Incarnate Word takes on light . . . (since) Christ fully reveals man to himself and makes his supreme calling clear,' as the Council teaches" (*MD* 2). In the revelation of the Son of God incarnate, we should therefore be able to shed light on dual unity, even the dual unity of man and woman.[22]

In the event of the incarnation a new, definitive relation between God and man is established. In fact, through the hypostatic union the person of Jesus Christ constitutes the place of the encounter between God and humanity. This encounter can be read as a spousal union; indeed, it constitutes the new spousality: "Only the supreme act of God's love who, emptying himself of his divinity, gives himself entirely, opens the possibility of a renewed union."[23] The dual unity of man and woman is remade in the hypostatic union of Christ, which becomes its foundation. "Through the union of the two natures in Christ the global plan of God is manifest, that plan which, beginning with the one flesh of Adam and Eve, through the one flesh of the Redeemer, reaches the one flesh of the Mystical Body within which, through the travail of the Paschal Mystery, man and woman reach the perfection of their likeness to God."[24]

Everything we have said so far concerning the christological foundation of dual unity begs for further clarification in turn. In fact, the incarnation of the Son can be conceived only from within the trinitarian relations. It is within the dynamic of the divine life, within the relation between the Father and the Son and the Spirit, within the so-called "processions," that we must look for the possibility of the incarnation. Otherwise stated, the Word's be-

---

22. For this reflection we draw inspiration from Giuliodori, *Intelligenza teologica*, 163-74.
23. Giuliodori, *Intelligenza teologica*, 166.
24. Giuliodori, *Intelligenza teologica*, 168.

coming flesh presupposes his eternal procession from the Father and that procession, common to the Father and the Son, of the Spirit; it presupposes the intratrinitarian life as a unity of nature and a trinity of persons. The mystery of the Trinity, therefore, is the ultimate foundation of dual unity.

The relations between Trinity and dual unity, however, are not simply the final outcome of a complex theological reflection. There is an aspect that makes them truly accessible, and it is this: in dual unity we find an analogy of the trinitarian communion. In fact, as the Holy Father suggests in *Mulieris Dignitatem*, man is not only image of God on account of his being free and rational, but also because he is a being who is fulfilled in communion, as relation (cf. *MD* 7). The image of God is completed in interpersonal communion.

However much these considerations may appear inaccessible, they are far from abstract, for they possess a determinative relevance for human life in its concreteness. In the first place — and this point seems to me particularly important — we must admit that a culture that does not accept the revelation of the trinitarian God ultimately renders itself incapable of understanding sexual difference in a positive sense. It is this that prevents us from calmly accepting the personal identity of the diverse two, of man and woman. Not for nothing does the open acceptance of homosexuality belong both to classical paganism and to the paganism of the present day. If, from the beginning, there is no possibility of a difference that does not alter identity, as occurs in the full sense in the life of the triune God from whose loving design man originally comes forth as a sexually differentiated being, any subsequent difference will be seen as the result of a fall or as the fruit of violence. For this reason a society that loses its reference to the personal triune God, to the Other, is unable to understand sexuality as original to man. In fact, such a society cannot avoid lapsing into a negative vision of sexuality. Sexuality either becomes an object of taboo or it is trivialized, having been assumed to be something self-evident, because it is tied exclusively to those characteristics that belong to man as an "animal." In any case, it remains marginal to serious discussion. The result of all this will be the censure or the insignificance of sexuality.

Another consequence of lack of understanding of the trinitarian and christological foundation directly concerns the institution of the family, founded on marriage. In fact, to speak about trinitarian unity and the hypostatic union as the ultimate foundation of the dual unity of man and woman shows us that difference, without confusion and without separation, is something positive, something that exalts, not destroys, unity. This enables us to see that unity is the full meaning of difference. Difference, or alterity, is a path to a more complete unity. This alone suffices to explain why, in the sacrament of marriage, through which the woman constitutes with man *one flesh,* the salvific will of the God of Jesus Christ is expressed, the will of him who asks man not to separate what God has united. Indissolubility constitutes the destiny and the very core of the relation of man and woman in marriage. It is for this reason that indissolubility lies at the heart of the vocation of marriage. In fact, marriage is a vocation, in the true sense of the word, precisely on account of indissolubility. Here spousal love approaches its summit, and the vocation of marriage displays its greatest dignity.

Allow me to offer one final and very general remark. The retrieval of christological and trinitarian reflection as the foundation for anthropology can only help to deepen the notion of person, all too often identified erroneously with that of the "individual" or of the "spiritual subject."[25] Certainly the notion of the person, rightly understood, supplies the adequate tools for a critique of both the liberal and collectivist system, by supplying the basis for a correct relation between state and civil society.

1.4. The Ecclesial-Marian Foundation of the Dual Unity of Man and Woman

Up to this point we have concerned ourselves with the anthropological foundation of the dignity and mission of the woman (dual unity), and its theological root (both christological and trinitarian). In this third and final part of our argument we must take up the ecclesial foundation of the theme.

Let us begin with a statement from Balthasar concerning the mystery of man and woman: "the fullness of mystery is only attained in the mystery of Christ and his Church (Eph 5:27, 33)."[26] One can see in fact that the Christ-church pair presents itself as the original pair. The man-woman pair is in a certain sense derived from it. And it is derivative according to a well-known classical principle, according to which the end, or destiny, of a reality is included in its origin.[27] Dual unity finds its definitive archetype in the marriage

---

25. Cf. Scola, *Hans Urs von Balthasar,* 77-78.

26. H. U. von Balthasar, *Theo-Drama III: Dramatis Personae: Persons in Christ,* trans. Graham Harrison (San Francisco: Ignatius, 1992), 289.

27. On this note Balthasar affirms: "the difference is part of the *imago Dei:* 'Let us make man in our image and likeness. . . . In the image of God he created them. Male and female he created them' (Gen 1:26-27). If this were not so, Christ could neither have pointed to the relationship of the sexes to describe his mysterious union with the Church, nor have given to the sacrament of marriage the power and the real possibility of symbolizing this perfect relationship in the relationship of the sexes" (H. U. von Balthasar, *The Christian State of Life,* trans. Sr. Mary Frances McCarthy [San Francisco: Ignatius, 1983], 103).

between the crucified and risen Lord and his body which is the church (cf. *MD* 23-27).

The Pauline image of the church as bride of Christ (cf. Eph. 5:25-32) follows the history of salvation. In that history Yahweh elects the Hebrew people, whose complement, in the fullness of time, is constituted by the new people of God. This spousal dimension of the relation between the God-man and the church is well expressed by Augustine: "all of the Church in fact is the spouse of Christ and its principle and first fruit is the flesh of Christ."[28]

The Pauline image enables us to assert that the church places us before God as his feminine interlocutor, and from him receives all its fruitfulness.[29] The Lord, in fact, loves his people as his spouse and for its salvation offers his own life. From the sacrifice of the cross flows the obediential love of the church, which is also the *forma humanitatis*. In this spousal relation

> The man-woman polarity is linked to the mystery of the Christ-Church relationship (Eph 5), where nuptial love not only reaches its fullest form, but where at the same time its connection with death through the closed circle of generations for the sake of the species is broken. This is so not only because death is conquered in Christ, but also and more precisely because Christ inaugurates a new form of fruitfulness which is not identical to human procreation. This is a fecundity for the kingdom, which becomes the eschatological sign of the marriage between Christ and the Church; it is a virginal fecundity or nuptiality which is not at all asexual.[30]

The principal way to grasp the spousal bond between Christ and the church in all its profundity is the figure of Mary.

1.4.1. Mary, the Ecclesia Immaculata

When in Ephesians 5:27 Paul affirms that Christ established for himself a church "without stain," an *"Ecclesia immaculata,"* as Balthasar loved to say in the last years of his life,[31] it must be recognized that this title in its strict sense can be applied only to Mary. She was without sin in order to conceive and

---

28. Augustine, *In epistulam Joannis ad Parthos tractatus* 2.2.

29. Cf. H. U. von Balthasar, "Who Is the Church?" in *Explorations in Theology II: Spouse of the Word* (San Francisco: Ignatius, 1991), 143-91; Balthasar, *Man in History: A Theological Study,* trans. William Glen-Doepel (London: Sheed and Ward, 1968), 306-14; Balthasar, *Elucidations,* trans. John Riches (London: SPCK, 1975), 64-72.

30. Scola, *Hans Urs von Balthasar,* 98.

31. Cf. H. U. von Balthasar, *La realtà e la gloria* (Milan, 1988), 45-47, 101-5.

give birth to the Son of God, to be the Theotokos, or God-bearer. In this sense Mary is the prototype of the church.

The Marian dimension of the church, which does not lose sight of the Petrine-apostolic ministry, constitutes the humus in which John Paul II elaborates his reflections on woman in *Mulieris Dignitatem*. The document begins with a parallel between woman and the Mother of God (*MD* 3-5), because the dignity and mission of woman is fully illumined by the singular dignity of the Theotokos. And the capstone which holds the figure of woman and that of her archetype together is the Pauline formula of the letter to the Galatians: "When the fullness of time had come, God sent forth his son, born of woman" (Gal. 4:4; cf. *MD* 3).

Within this first parallel between woman and the Mother of God, the archetypical comparison with Mary will be taken up again in the characteristic spiral progression of John Paul II's thought, in a parallel between Eve and Mary (*MD* 9-11), and again, in a certain sense, in the theme of the church as the bride of Christ (*MD* 23-27), since Mary is the prototype of the church. We can add to these considerations the theme of virginity and motherhood (*MD* 17-22), also analyzed from within a Marian perspective, and thus see to what extent the figure of Mary represents the warp on which the pontiff weaves his reflections on woman. Among all these levels of interpretation contained in the apostolic letter, the parallel between woman and the Mother of God is the most fundamental. We will attempt to analyze this more closely.

> Thus the "fullness of time" manifests the extraordinary dignity of the "woman." On the one hand, this dignity consists *in the supernatural elevation to union with God* in Jesus Christ, which determines the ultimate finality of the existence of every person both on earth and in eternity. From this point of view, the "woman" is the representative and archetype of the whole human race: she *represents the humanity* which belongs to all human beings, both men and women. On the other hand, however, the event at Nazareth highlights a form of union with the living God which can *only belong to the "woman,"* Mary: *the union between mother and son.* The Virgin of Nazareth truly becomes the Mother of God. (*MD* 4)

This lengthy citation is a concentration of theological anthropology which merits attentive examination. In contemplating the great dignity of Mary, whom Paul calls "woman," the pope gathers two essential facts. This first involves the predestination of every human being in Christ to be a child of God (*filii in Filio*).[32] This predestination is not considered in and

---

32. Cf. G. Biffi, *Tu solo il Signore. Saggi di teologia inattuale* (Casale Monferrato, 1987), 42-67.

for itself, but in reference to its preeminent realization in Mary. But all that is fulfilled in Mary and in the mysteries of her life is fulfilled with an eye to her being the Theotokos. As Theotokos, Mary realizes, preeminently among all men, this predestination in Christ. She is the paradigm of every human being, man and woman. Woman, so to speak, becomes the "type" of the person who adheres to the decision of the Father to predestine all men in Christ, of the human being who is fully such when his freedom acknowledges Christ.

The second fact, of fundamental importance, reveals that within the supernatural elevation to union with God which flows from predestination in Christ, the Theotokos realizes a particular form of union which consists precisely in being the Mother of God. This union is singular, unique, and nonrepeatable. With a view to this union, Mary is certainly filled with grace from on high, that is, from the Spirit, but this does not deprive her of freedom. To the contrary, her fiat expresses the full participation of her personal and feminine "I" in the mysterious event of the conception and birth of the Son of God: "Grace never casts nature aside or cancels it out, but rather perfects and ennobles it. Therefore the *fullness of grace* that was granted to the Virgin of Nazareth, with a view to the fact that she would become *Theotokos,* also signifies the fullness of the perfection of 'what is characteristic of woman,' of 'what is feminine.'* Here we find ourselves, in a sense, at the culminating point, the archetype, of the personal dignity of women" (*MD* 5).

In investigating the parallel between woman and the Mother of God, the pontiff unveils two fundamental themes of Christian anthropology: Mary is the model of man (the human being) as such and, in a particular way, she is the model of women. The two themes are intimately connected, as the apostolic letter shows well. In order to exalt the dignity and vocation of women, the letter begins with an anthropological condition willed by the Creator: the unity of the two, by which the human being exists "always and only . . . as a woman or a man" (*MD* 1).

1.4.2. Mary, Sexual Difference, and Woman

Properly speaking, Mary is the model of every human being, because it is she who eminently realizes the supernatural predestination of all men to be sons and daughters in the Son. This predestination is not in reality different from the gratuitous, supernatural, universal, and infallibly efficacious will with which God decides to make of every human being his son in Jesus

Christ, so that the only-begotten becomes also the firstborn. For this reason every member of mankind is raised to this supernatural end.[33] On this basis the Council affirms that Jesus Christ "fully reveals man to himself" (cf. GS 22). The infallible efficacy of predestination in Christ requires, however, man's free adherence. Not every man is saved, but every man in Christ is saved. He who extricates himself from that gratuitous grasp by which God makes us his children — he who does not live, as Saint Paul says, "in Christ"[34] — condemns himself. Mary lives her whole life in Christ; all the great mysteries that surpass her while simultaneously involving her in the closest way possible take their light and their strength from Christ, the only-begotten Son of God who by his death and resurrection has become the firstborn of many brethren. Mary thus fulfills her predestination in Christ in a preeminent way, because she is free of sin and remains freely faithful to her mission, notwithstanding the sword that pierces her, until her assumption in glory.

The expression "Mary, model of Christians" must not therefore be seen as limiting but rather as including all that is human. She is the model of the Christian and thus of every human being. The Holy Father rightly affirms, "Do we not find in the Annunciation at Nazareth the beginning of that definitive answer by which God himself 'attempts to calm people's hearts'?" (MD 3). The figure of Mary in the history of the time of the church, which is eschatological time, thus remains the model of every Christian, precisely because she is at the same time the mother of the Head and the mother of each member of the church. A mother does not cease pointing out to her children the center of all things: her Son Jesus Christ.

As we have seen, the mystery of the Theotokos, the encounter between the power of the Spirit and the virginal fiat of Mary, lies at the heart of the pope's argument for the connection between woman and Mary. Within the great salvific event which begins with the predestination of Jesus Christ, Mary appears as copredestined to realize her union with God in a preeminent fashion, because she becomes his mother. Moreover, since she is "full of grace" with a view toward this event and through her freedom, the Spirit accomplishes "great things" in her, exalting her whole person and thus also her being woman. Her femininity is exalted because being man or woman — being of a particular sex — represents a constitutive dimension of the "I" (cf. MD

33. On predestination in Christ, see I. Biffi, Identità cristiana. Essere uomini in Gesù Cristo (Casale Monferrato, 1988).

34. On the anthropological and ethical meaning of being "in Christ," see Scola, Questioni di antropologia teologica (Rome, 1997), 76-77; G. Chantraine and A. Scola, "L'événement Christ et la vie morale," Anthropotes 3 (1987): 5-23.

7). The mystery of the Theotokos as a mystery of perfection means that in Mary one sees the perfection of that which is proper to women.

Upon this Mariological core of the doctrine of Mary as the archetype of women,[35] the pope places another element essential to understanding the first in all its meaning: the relation between Eve and Mary. The figure of Eve, also archetypical, allows us to arrive at the roots of the theme from at least three directions. In the first place, Eve, in an interpersonal relation with Adam, is at the origin of human history. She is created, with Adam, in the image and likeness of God inasmuch as she is a rational animal, but also because she is endowed with a communional quality which allows her to live reciprocity and difference by virtue of the "unity of the two" (cf. MD 6-7). Secondly, Adam and Eve, independently of the distribution of roles, are at the origin of man's original sin, on which depends the darkening of the image and its grave consequences for the reciprocal gift of self: "your desire shall be for your husband, and he shall rule over you" (Gen. 3:16). Lastly, it is in reference to the first woman, Eve, that the other woman, she of the Protoevangelium, appears on the scene: "I will put enmity between you and the woman, between your seed and her seed; he shall bruise your head, and you shall bruise his heel" (Gen. 3:15). All three directions of this reflection on Eve lead to Mary, whom the Fathers rightly called the "new Eve." She who is full of grace, in whom the Spirit has worked "great things," is a daughter of Eve in all things except sin, so that woman as such finds her fulfillment in Mary. And the path of her fulfillment becomes the paradigm and model of the realization of the feminine.

In Mary, model of women, we find, first of all, elements which have to do with the feminine identity and which therefore concern every woman. It is to these which the Holy Father primarily refers. Obviously these elements cannot be reduced to mere roles, and they must not be interpreted as rigid structures. To the contrary, they are constitutive "givens," without which the dignity and vocation of each woman could never be realized, and they find their most sublime fulfillment in Mary. These fundamental dimensions cannot be interchanged with roles, as is often done by a certain type of contemporary feminism which does not realize that in so doing, it is destroying the possibility of an authentic liberation of women. But neither can it be denied that the dominant culture of a society can reduce these profound dimensions of being woman to rigid and formal roles that destroy women's freedom. True liberation will lie in finding and promoting, in full freedom, the authentic meaning of these dimensions.

In brief, it seems to me that the Holy Father indicates three of these di-

---

35. Cf. John Paul II, *Letter to Women* 10-11.

mensions as fundamental in women: nuptiality, motherhood, and the "prophetic genius."[36]

If man exists as a dual unity, then woman represents the other "I" whom God places beside man as a person equal in dignity. In the unity of the two, the nuptial nature of the human being is made manifest: in identity and through difference, man and woman can give themselves to each other in marriage. It is impossible for either man or woman to realize themselves outside of this nuptial dimension. For this reason it is deeply mistaken to conceive of the struggle for women's liberation as the abolition of a difference which, more than biopsychological, is ontological. The abolition of difference coincides with a misunderstanding of the profound meaning of human sexuality, even beyond its nature as a sign of the possibility of encountering another with a view to fulfillment in communion, through a spousal gift of self. It is a sign of man's contingence and of his dependence on his Creator. It is important to specify that for the Holy Father this spousal nature is not only realized in the choice for marriage.[37] It can also be fulfilled in the choice for virginity, in a dedication to Christ the Bridegroom: "There exist many reasons for discerning in these two different paths — the two different vocations of women — a profound complementarity, and even a profound union within a person's being" (*MD* 21). The spousal dimension of women is fully actualized in Mary, Virgin, Bride, and Mother.

The reciprocal gift of self which man and woman actualize in marriage opens itself to new life. The one born is not simply an individual of the human species; he is a person, singular, unique and unrepeatable, made in the image of God. The woman participates in the generation of this life in a particular way, because maternity is tied to the constitutive nature of woman's being and to the personal dimension of the gift. The exclamation of Eve, the mother of all living, "I have gotten a man with the help of the Lord" (Gen. 4:1), is repeated each time a child comes into the world, and "expresses the woman's joy and awareness that she is sharing in the great mystery of eternal generation" (*MD* 18).

Spiritual maternity is connected to physical maternity, corresponding to the fact that nuptiality is an intrinsic dimension both of virginity and marriage. The virginal motherhood of Mary becomes, once again, the paradigmatic element: her "let it be done to me according to your word" contains the

---

36. Cf. C. Basevi, "Il carisma profetico delle donne nella Prima Lettera ai Corinti, *Annales Theologici* 6 (1992): 35-53.

37. Cf. A. Scola, "Spiritualità coniugale nel contesto culturale contemporaneo," in *Cristo sposo della Chiesa sposa*, ed. R. Bonetti (Rome, 1997), 52-54.

most complete openness to the welcoming of life and letting oneself be completely disposed of by the Lord. Mary, her heart pierced as she stands under the cross, is the sublime witness of this abandonment.

Lastly, to woman and to her genius, which the Holy Father does not hesitate to call "prophetic" (MD 29-30), is particularly entrusted that "order of love" which, according to the Christian faith, has primacy in the lives of men. And in a certain sense every human being is entrusted to woman. The pope recognizes in the "feminine genius" a particular capacity to defend the dignity of the person, willed by God for his own sake, and to impede those things which darken the light of the face of God which shines in every man (cf. Ps. 4:7).

CHAPTER 2

Sexual Difference and the Meaning
of the "Unity of the Two"

In *Mulieris Dignitatem* the Holy Father goes beyond restating the traditional doctrine — taken from Augustine and John Damascene — of the human person as the image of God insofar as he is a rational creature,[1] and introduces two important innovations of an anthropological character.

The first can be formulated concisely in the following question: Does human sexuality belong to the *imago Dei* (cf. *MD* 6)? We will deal with this question in the following chapter. The other innovation, which is the subject of the present chapter, refers to the thesis by which the "*creation of man is also marked by a certain likeness to the divine communion ('communio'),*" which is expressed in the "unity of the two." The communion of love which man and woman live in the sincere gift of self is an image of the "communion of love that is in God, through which the Three Persons love each other in the intimate mystery of the one divine life" (*MD* 7).

The theme of the "unity of the two" had already made its appearance in the celebrated Wednesday catecheses on human love.[2] In *Mulieris Dignitatem* the theme is taken up again and deepened within a unitary and dynamic anthropological vision. Though the great classical bases of the Christian conception of the person are not abandoned, they are developed with the help of the category of relation, specifically the relation between man and woman. In fact, the profound meaning of sexuality is not seen as

1. Cf. H. U. von Balthasar, *Theo-Drama II: Dramatis Personae: Man in God,* trans. Graham Harrison (San Francisco: Ignatius, 1990), 316ff.
2. Cf. John Paul II, *The Theology of the Body: Human Love in the Divine Plan* (Boston: Daughters of St. Paul, 1997), 42-48.

merely an accidental element of the person, who is already fully defined as a composite *(synholon)* of body and soul. Rather, it is considered to be one of the constitutive characteristics of the human being, which dynamically contributes to explaining both his personal nature and his being a creature made in the image of God.

In this chapter we will attempt to deepen our understanding of the contents of the formula, the "unity of the two," in order to seek out the foundations of such an anthropological vision.

2.1. The "Unity of the Two"

In the Wednesday catecheses John Paul II already gives a precise definition for the expression "the unity of the two": "Following the narrative of Genesis, we have seen that the 'definitive' creation of man consists in the creation of the unity of two beings. Their unity denotes above all the identity of human nature; their duality, on the other hand, manifests what, on the basis of this identity, constitutes the masculinity and femininity of created man."[3] This unity is within a common humanity, but is a "unity of the two" (cf. *MD* 6). Thus we find, in synthesis, the human creature characterized according to the famous verse of Genesis: "God created man in his own image, in the image of God he created him; male and female he created them" (Gen. 1:27). This anthropological revelation gives rise to three fundamental problems: the meaning of the "double incarnation" of man in male and female; the man-woman relation as the fruit of identity and difference; and the relation between sexuality and being in the image of God. These three elements, strictly interconnected, shed light on one another and allow for a clear reading of the anthropological dimensions at play in human sexuality. Ultimately, this is "a question of understanding the reason for and the consequences of the Creator's decision that the human being should always and only exist as a woman or a man" (*MD* 1).

2.1.1. Man Exists as Male and Female

We have already mentioned that in order to understand the meaning of human sexuality we must let the data, both phenomenological and ontological, speak. That is, no man (and no woman) can be by himself alone all of man;

---

3. John Paul II, *Theology of the Body*, 45.

he always has before him the other way of being human, which is to him inaccessible. The human being is distinguished by an alterity which is difference, because of his sexual nature. And within this aspect of his nature, human contingence is inevitably manifest.

Sexual difference bespeaks the derived nature of the human being, and his constitutive limit.[4] Not for nothing does the Genesis account of the creation of woman describe how Adam perceives Eve's "otherness" and her difference. Inasmuch as the woman is similar to him ("flesh of my flesh"), Adam cannot dominate her, because God drew her out of his rib and placed her beside him as another "I," as an interlocutor which Adam could not have given himself. Thus, there remains even in this likeness which is the fruit of a common humanity an irreducible difference: sexual difference. The two are identically persons, but are sexually diverse. They are, in a certain sense, a "unity of two."

This account reveals the structural experience of *lack* which, from Adam on, is constitutive of all human beings and all peoples. Because of this "void," as Blondel calls it, human reason registers a radical dependence inexorably urging it to seek out that *quid* which represents the ultimate meaning of being. Without a doubt, the human being's sexual nature represents one of the *original loci* in which he experiences his own contingence. This nature, which makes its presence known by imposing on the consciousness an "other" different from the self, indicates finitude, but more precisely ontological dependence. In the Christian tradition all of this necessarily leads us back to creation.[5] One can thus argue that the human being's ontological, creatural dependence on God is inscribed even in his sexual nature.

There is an important consequence of this truth: in a world which seeks to eliminate God, it becomes impossible to consider sexual difference. This provides a parameter which ought to make us think when we analyze the macroscopic problems regarding sexuality in our culture.[6]

The experience of creaturely contingence found within sexuality makes itself evident also in the essential end of the sexual tendency: procreation.[7] As

---

4. Cf. Balthasar, *Theo-Drama II,* 374ff. Chrysostom's affirmation is very expressive: "Where there is death, there is marriage; where there is no marriage, neither is there death" (*De virginitate* 14.6).

5. Cf. *Catechism of the Catholic Church (= CCC)* 279ff.

6. Cf. A. Scola, ed., *Quale vita? La bioetica in questione* (Milan, 1998), with contributions from D. Bijou-Duval, S. Grygiel, L. Melina, P. Morandé, A. Scola, R. Colombo, G. Zuanazzi, M. Hendickx, H. Hude, J. Laffitte, D. Schindler, and W. Waldstein.

7. Cf. K. Wojtyla, *Love and Responsibility,* trans. H. T. Willetts (San Francisco: Ignatius, 1993), 30. On the relationship between sexuality and procreation see infra, pp. 110-37.

has been observed since ancient times, the problem of generation is linked in a singular reciprocity with the problem of death. Augustine's affirmation which portrays newborn children turning to their parents with this spirited expression is famous: "Away with you! It is time that you think about moving on; we also must do our part."[8] We need not turn to Hegel's analysis on the relation between the individual and the species to see how much death is implied in human reproduction.[9] Death is already contained within sexual procreation and birth, because these are connected to the closed circle of generations which implacably succeed one another.

From this point of view, too, sexuality bespeaks contingence, a contingence in which finitude makes all its weight felt. This is true to the point that Balthasar, who reflected seriously on the nature of human sexuality, defined it as one of the constitutive tensions of anthropology, ultimately insoluble *in naturalibus.*[10] The tension between man and woman, beginning with the constitution of the different sexes in a common humanity, is the emblem of the human being's incessant movement toward a "thou" he can never possess, because freedom, in its constitutive otherness, can never be dominated. The tension between parents and children flows from the reciprocity between procreation and death. On the natural and pre-Christian plane, this reciprocity exposes human sexuality to the closed circle of the intracosmic law of the individual and the species, hence risking a dichotomy between the spiritual and the sexual in which the latter is left to itself as something vile, if not demonic.

In the light of revelation we know that because of original sin, this tension is more than a tension;[11] it is a flaw which obscures and diminishes the image and likeness of God in man (cf. *MD* 9-10).

---

8. Augustine, *Enarrationes in Psalmos* 127.15.

9. Cf. G. W. F. Hegel, *Enciclopedia delle scienze filosofiche in compendio* (Milan, 1996), 625: "The species is preserved only through the decline of individuals, which fulfill their destiny in the process of coupling and, in the measure in which they have no higher destiny, thus encounter death."

10. Cf. Balthasar, *Theo-Drama II,* 355: "When man thus eventually steps forth and becomes a question to himself, however, he takes himself along, together with all his constant attributes. For he is spirit and body, man and woman, individual and community. These constants are part of his nature, his essence, which does not mean that they solve his riddle; in fact, they render it more profound and more pressing. In all three dimensions, man seems to be built according to a polarity, obliged to engage in reciprocity, always seeking complementarity and peace in the other pole. And for that very reason he is pointed beyond his whole polar structure. He is always found crossing the boundary, and thus he is defined most exactly by that boundary with which death brutally confronts him, in all three areas, without taking account of his threefold transcendence."

11. Cf. *CCC* 399-401.

2.1.2. Man and Woman: Identity and Difference

Within this original meaning of sexuality, understood as an expression of that creaturely contingence in which one of the constitutive tensions of the "I" is made manifest, it is easier to grasp the meaning of the reciprocity between man and woman as objectively contained in the "unity of the two."[12]

In fact, the experience of contingence does not impede but rather urges on the finding of the self in the discovery of the other: "This at last is bone of my bones and flesh of my flesh" (Gen. 2:23). This passage points primarily to the identity of the personal being of man and woman, because the two are created in a common humanity. On the other hand, difference is documented here in a manner just as radical. In fact, if the identity of the two in a common humanity is manifest even in their somatic constitution, just as transparent in that same constitution is the fact that the male body is male and the female body female to the last cell. Precisely this — identity in difference — gives rise to the reciprocity between man and woman which, in the pontifical document, opens the way to interpersonal communion (cf. *MD* 7). Rightly is it said that the reciprocity between man and woman "can stand as a paradigm of that community dimension which characterizes man's entire nature."[13] Its profound meaning lies in this being-for-one-another that the Holy Father, taking up a conciliar theme dear to him, defines beginning with the idea of the gift of self (cf. *GS* 24). Thus the entrustment of both of the two to the other, expressed by the very structure of sexual reciprocity — and this precisely because it persuades man of his contingence — opens man wide to the sincere gift of self that allows him to find himself.

Such an affirmation leads to a necessary consideration of the two factors which constitute this reciprocity, identity and difference. It is by these factors that man is created as a "unity of the two."

The absolute equality of the two in their being persons and in all that derives from this forms the basis of identity. *Mulieris Dignitatem* reiterates this throughout: the two necessarily have humanity in common, and this is the basic condition for the gift of self ("a helper similar to him," Gen. 2:20).

It is more difficult to consider difference, which within the common humanity of the two allows for the reciprocal gift of self. The fact that discrimination against women in history has arisen precisely at this point of difference bears witness to this difficulty. The papal document makes two comments on the subject. On the one hand, it affirms that the personal resources of feminin-

---

12. On the asymmetrical character of this (sexual) reciprocity, cf. infra, pp. 116-21.
13. Balthasar, *Theo-Drama II*, 344.

ity are certainly not less than those of masculinity; they are simply different (cf. *MD* 10). On the other hand, the document warns women against the risk of seeking equality with men through a sort of masculinization of themselves, which would end in abolishing difference and thus in deforming their own richne§s (cf. *MD* 10). The question of difference cannot be reduced to a simple problem of roles, but needs to be thought out ontologically.

In this perspective, difference allows itself once more to be led back to the question of that "otherness"[14] which bespeaks creaturely contingence and at the same time, because there is equality in a common humanity, founds the reciprocal gift of self — that is, the spousal dimension of the human being.

The phenomenological consideration of the existence of man and woman suggests that "otherness" be recognized as a difference which means contingence, and likewise the consideration of otherness as contingence reveals itself to be the decisive point for the identification of sexual reciprocity and of the nuptial character of the human person. If this is the case, we must now attempt to approach that mystery of the other on which, in concrete human existence, this difference depends.

2.2. The Foundation of the "Unity of the Two"

The first step toward this approach is clearly indicated from the beginning of the document, and consists in the identification of the *imago Dei* as a constitutive factor of the God-man relation, which revelation itself places at our disposition (cf. *MD* 6-8).

2.2.1. *Human Sexuality and Interpersonal Communion*

The problem seems to be that of determining whether human sexuality is a part of man's being in the image of God, and how this sexuality is configured in a manner qualitatively different from that of animals, with which it nevertheless shares certain characteristics and elementary bio-instinctual dynamisms. This possibility clears a path toward the stabilizing of the tension present within sexuality, and toward breaking through the closed circle of individual and species; in this way human fruitfulness is freed from the mechanical reciprocity of birth and death.

---

14. Cf. A. Ruiz Retegui, "El tratamiento diferencial de la sexualidad en la Carta Apostólica *Mulieris dignitatem*," *Scripta Theologica* 22 (1990): 893ff.

Beyond the rigorous interpretations of modern-day textual criticism, not always in agreement amongst themselves, it must be recognized that Genesis 1:27 — "in the image of God he created him; male and female he created them"— with its close juxtaposition, leads us to think that human sexuality is part of the image.[15]

On the other hand, an integral understanding of the doctrine of the *imago Dei* cannot but take into account the systematic elaboration that this theme has received in the great Christian tradition, with its two-thousand-year history. The classical Augustinian-Thomistic tradition cannot be ignored, which locates the *imago Dei* ultimately in the *mens*, understood as the seat of the intelligence and the will, and thus in the properly rational nature of man. However, man must also be considered in his entirety, as *corpore et anima unus* (cf. *GS* 14), and insofar as he is created from the beginning as man and woman.

With the presupposition that human sexuality is part of the *imago Dei*, it is possible to clearly affirm sexuality's destination to communion, as regards both the man-woman relation and the relation between parents and children. Properly speaking, man is not the image of God, because his likeness stands within an abysmal "non-likeness" (cf. *MD* 8); he is only *ad imaginem Dei*, "to the image of God." This "movement to place" indicates that the image of God in man is a dynamism leaning on ontological bases *(corpore et anima unus)* that are necessary but not closed in upon themselves, open to a fulfillment which comes about precisely in relation. Theologically speaking, man, a spiritual subject who is metaphysically well defined but contingent, lives *from* and *in* relation to God through his very creation. He is called to realize this constitutive relation, which is already communional, in every relation which is given to him, beginning with the most "primordial." And since the creation of man posits him in being as a "unity of two," the relation between man and woman — as well as those of paternity, maternity, and sonship to which it gives rise — can represent the revelatory nucleus of the horizontal dimension of communion.

Secondly, the participation of human sexuality in the *imago* appropriately identifies the principle of human procreation, differentiating it from that of animals. The fruit of the conjugal communion of love is not simply an individual of the human species, but is, properly speaking, another man, *this man* or *this woman*, an image of God: "This image and likeness of God, which is essential for the human being, is passed on by the man and woman, as spouses and parents, to their descendants: 'Be fruitful and multiply, and fill the earth and subdue it' (Gen 1:28)" (*MD* 6).

---

15. Cf. infra, pp. 32-52, where this theme is developed.

The anthropological tension which characterizes sexuality *in naturalibus* finds, in this understanding of man created in the image of God, the path toward a solution. The sexual sphere does not in fact relegate man to the animal and intracosmic sphere, such that in order to find himself he must pursue an ascesis centered on the spiritual dimension of his own person in antithesis to his sexuality. Rather, human sexuality, though reflecting the microcosmic nature of the human being and thus his unique structure as a bridge between the intra- and hyper-cosmic, possesses a *sacramental* destination as the "language of the body" which reveals the "I" in its personal integrity.[16] This is so because sexuality is a constitutive part of man's being in the image of God.

2.2.2. *The Unity of the Two and Trinitarian Communion*

The anthropological depth of *Mulieris Dignitatem* does not stop here. The document pushes us as far as establishing a connection between the reciprocity of man and woman and the reciprocity of the Trinity. *Gaudium et Spes* already points to this link (cf. *GS* 24), and the Holy Father develops it further:

> The fact that man "created as man and woman" is the image of God means not only that each of them individually is like God, as a rational and free being. It also means that man and woman, created as a "unity of the two" in their common humanity, are called to live in a communion of love, and in this way to mirror in the world the communion of love that is in God, through which the Three Persons love each other in the intimate mystery of the one divine life. The Father, Son, and Holy Spirit, one God through the unity of the divinity, exist as persons through the inscrutable divine relationship. Only in this way can we understand the truth that God in himself is love (cf. 1 Jn 4:16). (*MD* 7)

This significant development is connected to an anthropological conclusion, identified from the beginning of our reflection as a real innovation of the papal document: "This 'unity of the two,' which is a sign of interpersonal communion, shows that the creation of man is also marked by a certain likeness to the divine communion *('communio')*. This likeness is a quality of the personal being of both man and woman, and is also a call and a task" (*MD* 7). With a view to this important affirmation, the pope says in a passage just prior to this that by penetrating to the depths of the truth about the image

16. Cf. John Paul II, *Theology of the Body*, 61.

and likeness of God, "we can understand even more fully what constitutes the personal character of the human being" (*MD* 7).

From this long but necessary citation emerges a truth: the human person possesses a communional "quality." It can be said that every human being is a "communional person," ontologically open to communion with the other, because he is ontologically dependent on communion with his Creator. We must now investigate this anthropological datum in a vertical direction, in order to shed further light on the meaning of human sexuality.

The communion between man and woman, as the primordial expression of every possible communion between human beings, realizes the *imago Trinitatis* when founded on the love of the divine Good, which is the love of charity. In the Trinity the three persons are united in the love of a single divine Good, identical in each one. The "children of God" who live in communion actuate this dimension of the *imago Trinitatis* (cf. *GS* 24), which is eminently fulfilled in the conjugal communion (cf. *GS* 12).

To this important analogy between communion and the trinitarian life and its reflection in the conjugal communion between man and woman, we could perhaps add another element not made explicit in itself in the apostolic letter except by way of an important reference to the "communional quality" of the person. Certainly it is not easy to establish an analogy between the man-woman relation and the trinitarian relations as such, which are pure relations of origin, so great is the abyss of dissimilarity between the two terms of the analogy. And yet if we understand the man-woman relation (the "unity of the two") as the final datum of the creative act of God, then an objective and convincing connection between the two terms can come to light.[17]

The thesis of Bonaventure and Thomas on the trinitarian principle of creation is well known.[18] If there is a production of the *dissimilar*, one must necessarily recognize a preexisting production of the *similar*, since inequali-

---

17. Cf. B. Castilla Cortázar, "La Trinidad como familia. Analogía humana de las procesiones divinas," *Annales Theologici* 10 (1996): 381-416; P. Coda, "Familia y Trinidad. Reflexión teológica," *Estudios Trinitarios* 29 (1995): 187-219; S. del Cura Elena, "Dios Padre/ Madre. Significado e implicaciones de las imagines masculinas y femininas de Dios," *Estudios Trinitarios* 26 (1992): 117-54; S. Giuliani, "La famiglia è immagine di Dio," *Angelicum* 38 (1961): 166-86; Giuliani, "La famiglia è immagine della Trinità," *Angelicum* 38 (1961): 257-310; M. Hauke, "La discussion sobre el simbolismo feminine de la imagen de Dios en la pneumatología," *Scripta Theologica* 24 (1992): 1005-27; B. de Margerie, "L'analogie familiale de la Trinité," *Science et Esprit* 24 (1972): 77-92; A. Orbe, "La procession del Espíritu Santo y el origen de Eva," *Gregorianum* 46 (1964): 103-18.

18. Cf. G. Marengo, *Trinità e creazione* (Rome, 1990).

ties can arise only from equalities.[19] For this reason Thomas will say that the processions in God are the principle of order of the processions of creatures from God.[20] Developing this doctrine, Gerken, and following him, Balthasar arrive at the affirmation that a nontrinitarian God could not be a creator.[21]

Once the Mystery has revealed himself by pure grace, otherness in perfect equality gives a reason for the existence of otherness in difference. This otherness in difference is singularly documented in the reciprocity of man and woman. The otherness of the absolutely identical sheds light on the meaning of the otherness of the different. And created man's "difference" with respect to God reaches as far as his being sexual, to his existing as man and as woman. Studies are not lacking which follow this line of thought and show how fruitful a trinitarian logic and ontology can be for the understanding of man.

The fact that the fruit of this otherness in difference, in the unity of the two, is a new man created in the image of God, shows what a depth of mystery is always involved in every sexual act. This stands against every banalization of that act and, especially, against the choice of breaking the objective tie between the unitive and procreative aspects that characterize it.[22] Are not our bodies "temples of the Spirit" (cf. 1 Cor. 6:19)?

2.2.3. Man and Woman, Christ and the Church

A final consideration which sheds further light on the meaning of human existence in a "dual unity" of male and female is suggested by chapter 7 of the apostolic letter, in which, among other things, the "beginning" of Genesis is reinterpreted according to the celebrated text of Ephesians 5:21-32.

When the Holy Father develops the symbolic dimension of the "great mystery," he affirms that the symbol of the Bridegroom, referred to Christ, is masculine and expresses the spousal character of the love between God and

---

19. Cf. Bonaventure, *Collationes in Hexaëmeron* 11.9: "The production of the similar necessarily precedes the production of the dissimilar, which can be seen in the following way: the similar is related to the dissimilar as the identical to the diverse, and as the one to the many; but the identical necessarily precedes the diverse just as the one precedes the many: hence, the production of the similar precedes the production of the dissimilar."

20. Cf. Thomas Aquinas, *Summa Theologiae* I, q. 45, a. 6 co: "et secundum hoc processiones Personarum sunt rationes productionis creaturarum, inquantum includunt essentialia attributa, quae sunt scientia et voluntas."

21. Cf. H. U. von Balthasar, *Theo-Drama V: The Last Act*, trans. Graham Harrison (San Francisco: Ignatius, 1998), 61.

22. Cf. infra, pp. 110-37.

the church. The church, on the other hand, is the bride, and through her all human beings — men and women — are called to be the feminine "symbol" (cf. *MD* 25).

Because of this spousal dimension, the relationship between Christ and the church is analogous to that between man and woman. The conjugal covenant between man and woman explains the spousal character of the relationship between Christ and the church, and this latter in turn founds the sacramental nature of the relationship between man and woman. We could ask ourselves, which of these two couples is the original, such that it encompasses the other and explains its full meaning?

Great theologians such as Barth and Balthasar have not hesitated to say that the dual unity of male and female receives its full meaning precisely in view of the relationship between Christ the Bridegroom and the church his bride. This relationship is visible under the veil of the sacrament of the Eucharist, in which the slain Lamb celebrates his nuptials as the Bridegroom. In the memorial of his death and resurrection, Christ in fact "makes" his body, the church, which is his bride. But this will above all be clear in heaven, as the book of Revelation anticipates with its final invitation: "Come, I will show you the Bride, the wife of the Lamb" (Rev. 21:9). In Christ Jesus and in his relationship with the church, "the first account of creation is over-fulfilled . . . for in the mind of God the incarnate Word has never existed without his Church (Eph 1:4-6)."[23]

Without wanting to transfer, at all costs, all that has been said thus far into a rigid theological system, the great spousal symbolism of the union between Christ and his church contributes to fully explain the meaning of that nuptial mystery by which man exists as a "unity of the two," as man and woman. In any case, we find here the foundation of an ethos which allows for the realization of the true dignity of every man and every woman, as well as of their spousal dimension. More than a few consequences flow from this principle (cf. *MD* 17-22 and 28-30).

23. Cf. Balthasar, *Theo-Drama II*, 413.

CHAPTER 3

Human Sexuality and the Imago Dei

A closer examination of the relation between sexuality and the *imago Dei* reveals that the theme has ever been present in Christian thought, prompted by
the lapidary affirmation of the book of Genesis: "God created man in his own
image, in the image of God he created him; male and female he created them"
(Gen. 1:27). A little further on in Genesis, we find the same theme taken up
again: "When God created man, he made him in the likeness of God. Male
and female he created them, and he blessed them and named them Man when
they were created" (5:1-2). Yet the question of whether or not human sexuality
participates in the *imago Dei* is, on many counts, still open. Would not the
fact that human beings share their sexual nature with many animal species
discount such a hypothesis? Ought we not, therefore, as the tradition has in
substance done,[1] limit the image to the rational nature of man inasmuch as
he is a spiritual subject? In short, can the connection between the image of
God and sexual difference (male-female) be sustained on solid exegetical and
dogmatic bases?

Without pretending to give an exhaustive answer to this open question,
we will in this chapter propose a contribution to the research being carried

---

1. With the important exception of Irenaeus. On this topic see A. Orbe, *La teologia dei secoli
II e III* (Casale Monferrato, 1995), 261-73, in particular 273: "The two ideologies — those of
Origen and Irenaeus — seem to justify in equal measure the dignity of man, made by God the
Father with the help of the Son and the Holy Spirit. In reality, they are separated by an abyss.
Origen defends the dignity of the pure intellect, almost as if the *nous* alone could have been cre-
ated in a Trinitarian manner, without an explanation of the dignity of the body or flesh of Adam
which is not created in the image and likeness of God. Irenaeus is silent about the *psyche* (or in-
tellect) so as to attribute dignity to the human 'clay,' created in itself in the image and likeness."
See also J. Fantino, *L'homme image de Dieu chez Irénée de Lyon* (Paris, 1983).

out on the subject. We will proceed in two steps. In the first place, we will examine the teaching set forth in *Mulieris Dignitatem,* within the context of John Paul II's catecheses on spousal (nuptial) love. Secondly, we will add some considerations of a biblical and theological character.

3.1. Human Sexuality, the "Beginning" and the *Imago Dei*

Part 3 ("The Image and Likeness of God"), paragraph 6 of *Mulieris Dignitatem* directly confronts our theme. The paragraph presents a synthetic examination of the two creation accounts in Genesis. From the first account (Gen. 1:1–2:4a) the pope draws a teaching regarding the personal character of the human being,[2] both of man and of woman: *"Man is a person, man and woman equally so,* since both were created in the image and likeness of the personal God" (*MD* 6).

From the second account (Gen. 2:4b-25) the pope affirms the thesis at the heart of our inquiry: "The text of Genesis 2:18-25 helps us to understand better what we find in the concise passage of Genesis 1:27-28. At the same time, if it is read together with the latter, it *helps us to understand even more profoundly* the fundamental *truth* which it contains *concerning man* created as man and woman in the image and likeness of God." Further on in the text he adds, "The woman is another 'I' in a common humanity. From the very beginning they appear as a 'unity of the two.'" Sexual difference is placed in immediate relation to the *imago Dei.* The paragraph concludes with an affirmation that the destination of the two to marriage can be attributed, according to Genesis, to the difference between man and woman, with a view to the "transmission of life to new generations, the transmission of life to which marriage and conjugal love are by their nature ordered" (*MD* 6).

These three facts (man and woman are persons because they are created in the image of a personal God; they are the image of God as man and woman, that is, as a unity of the two; and, as such, they are ordered to procreation) together constitute a doctrine that, though basing itself on the classical thesis of man as *imago Dei* inasmuch as he is a personal subject, widens into a recognition of sexual difference as a constitutive part of the *imago.* This recognition occurs by virtue of the original "unity of the two" and their procreative destination.

It cannot be disputed that even in the conciseness of its formulation,

---

2. Cf. C. Caffarra, "La persona umana: aspetti teologici," in *A sua imagine e somiglianza?* ed. A. Mazzoni (Rome, 1997), 76-90.

paragraph 6 of *Mulieris Dignitatem* contains a most interesting anthropological evaluation of human sexuality. This last is no longer condemned to the intracosmic, as is animal sexuality, or forced into a numinous *(theion)* and cosmogonic sexual exchange between heaven and earth. Without negating its similarity on the bio-instinctual level with animal sexuality, human sexuality is elevated to the level of the *imago Dei*. This cannot but have enormous consequences. Though remaining in continuity with the tradition, the magisterium proposes an important innovation.

In order to understand John Paul II's thesis better, we must take into account other important texts of his magisterium, in which the theme of man and woman has already been elaborated. We refer to the celebrated Wednesday catecheses on human love,[3] and particularly to the first part of these.

The scope of the pope's analysis is the search for the "beginning."[4] This "beginning" is identified in the first place by means of a commentary on Matthew 19:3-9, the passage which recounts the dialogue between Christ and the Pharisees about marriage, with reference to the two creation accounts contained in Genesis.[5]

---

3. A compilation of the texts of these catecheses can be found in John Paul II, *The Theology of the Body: Human Love in the Divine Plan* (Boston: Daughters of St. Paul, 1997). In this chapter we refer to the first cycle, begun on September 5, 1979, and concluded on April 2, 1980. We cite the titles of the catecheses of this first cycle as an indication of the development of the pope's thought: (1) "The Unity and Indissolubility of Marriage"; (2) "Analysis of the Biblical Account of Creation"; (3) "The Second Account of Creation: The Subjective Definition of Man"; (4) "The Boundary between Original Innocence and Redemption"; (5) "The Meaning of Man's Original Solitude"; (6) "Man's Awareness of Being a Person"; (7) "The Alternative between Death and Immortality Enters the Definition of Man"; (8) "The Original Unity of Man and Woman"; (9) "By the Communion of Persons: Man Becomes the Image of God"; (10) "In the First Chapters of Genesis, Marriage Is One and Indissoluble"; (11) "The Meaning of Original Human Experiences"; (12) "The Fullness of Interpersonal Communication"; (13) "Creation as a Fundamental and Original Gift"; (14) "The Nuptial Meaning of the Body"; (15) "The Human Person Becomes a Gift in the Freedom of Love"; (16) "The Mystery of Man's Original Innocence"; (17) "Man and Woman: A Gift for Each Other"; (18) "Original Innocence and Man's Historical State"; (19) "Man Enters the World as a Subject of Truth and Love"; (20) "Analysis of Knowledge and of Procreation"; (21) "The Mystery of Woman Is Revealed in Motherhood"; (22) "The Knowledge-Generation Cycle and the Perspective of Death"; (23) "Marriage in the Integral Vision of Man."

4. On the category of "beginning" in the thought of John Paul II, see I. Biffi, *Amore personale: Note di filosofia e di teologia della sessualità* (Casale Monferrato, 1986); P. G. Pesce, "Nel mistero della creazione," in John Paul II, *Catechesi sul matrimonio* (Rome, 1980), 27-43.

5. Cf. John Paul II, *Theology of the Body*, 25-27. See also I. de la Potterie, "Antropomorfismo e simbolismo nel linguaggio biblico sulla relazione uomo-donna," in *Dignità e vocazione della donna: Per una lettura della "Mulieris dignitatem"* (Vatican City, 1989), 110-16; A. Tosato, "Magistero pontificio e Sacra Scrittura (due pagine di storia)," *Anthropotes* 8 (1992): 239-72.

Genesis 1:1–2:4 is the first account of creation and is attributed to the priestly tradition.[6] It is considered to have been redacted after Genesis 2:5-25,[7] called the "Yahwist" account. This latter is more fully comprehensible, as it includes Genesis 3–4:1 (the account of original sin).

The analysis of these two accounts, which occupies the whole first part of the catecheses, demonstrates their objective correspondence.[8] The second and more ancient account possesses — one might say — a subjective or psychological character, in which we see for the first time a certain human self-understanding and self-knowledge.[9] To this corresponds the more "objective" character of the first and more recent account. This latter possesses a

---

6. For the reader's benefit, we cite the entire passage of Gen. 1:26-31: "Then God said, 'Let us make man in our image, after our likeness; and let them have dominion over the fish of the sea, and over the birds of the air, and over the cattle, and over all the earth, and over every creeping thing that creeps upon the earth.' So God created man in his own image, in the image of God he created him; male and female he created them. And God blessed them, and God said to them, 'Be fruitful and multiply, and fill the earth and subdue it; and have dominion over the birds of the air and over every living thing that moves upon the earth.' And God said, 'Behold, I have given you every plant yielding seed which is upon the face of the earth, and every tree with seed in its fruit; you shall have them for food. And to every beast of the earth, and to every bird of the air, and to everything that creeps on the earth, everything that has the breath of life, I have given every green plant for food.' And it was so. And God saw everything that he had made, and behold, it was very good. And there was evening and there was morning, a sixth day."

7. Gen. 2:18-25: "Then the LORD God said, 'It is not good that man should be alone; I will make him a helper fit for him.' So out of the ground the LORD God formed every beast of the field and every bird of the air, and brought them to the man to see what he would call them; and whatever the man called every living creature, that was its name. The man gave names to all cattle, and to the birds of the air, and to every beast of the field; but for the man there was not found a helper fit for him. So the LORD God caused a deep sleep to fall upon the man, and while he slept he took one of his ribs and closed up the place with flesh; and the rib which the LORD God had taken from the man he made into a woman and brought her to the man. Then the man said, 'This at last is bone of my bones and flesh of my flesh; she shall be called Woman, because she was taken out of man.' Therefore a man leaves his father and his mother and cleaves to his wife, and they become one flesh. And the man and his wife were both naked, and were not ashamed."

8. There have been numerous attempts to separate them and to read one independently of the other, or even one against the other. We refer not so much to a certain Greek patristic tradition that hypothesizes a double creation, to which we will return further on, but rather to the various Gnostic interpretations of the theme which have succeeded one another in history. Cf. C. Colpe, *Die religionsgeschichtliche Schule. Darstellung und Kritik ihres Bildes vom gnostischen Erlösermythus* (Göttingen, 1961); H. M. Schenke, *Der Gott Mensch in der Gnosis* (Göttingen, 1962); E. Benz, *Adam: Der Mythus vom Urmenschen* (Munich, 1955) (this last deals with fairly recent periods in the history of Gnosticism).

9. Cf. John Paul II, *Theology of the Body,* 29-32.

theological nature,[10] to which is connected precise metaphysical and ethical implications.

The "beginning" thus coincides with the life of the original man, from the moment of creation to the moment of original sin. Moreover, this "beginning" is definitively illumined precisely by its relation to original sin. Sin is seen as the discriminating factor between the two very distinct situations of original innocence *(status naturae integrae)*[11] and original culpability *(status naturae lapsae).*[12]

Christ's reference in Matthew 19 to the two accounts of creation appears, in the light of the above, as an invitation, filled with ethical consequences, to recognize an essential continuity between the historical state of sin, proper to man in every age, and the (in a certain sense) "prehistorical" state of innocence:

> Christ's words, which refer to the "beginning," enable us to find in man an essential continuity and a link between these two different states or dimensions of the human being. The state of sin is part of "historical man," both the one whom we read about in Matthew 19, that is, Christ's questioner at that time, and also any other potential or actual questioner of all times of history, and therefore, naturally, also of modern man. That state, however — the "historical" state — plunges its roots, in every man without exception, in his own theological "prehistory," which is the state of original innocence.[13]

10. Cf. John Paul II, *Theology of the Body,* 27-29.

11. To situate the pope's considerations in the context of theological reflection on original sin, see G. Colzani, *Antropologia teologica* (Bologna, 1988), 265-87; G. Gozzelino, *Il mistero dell'uomo in Cristo. Saggio di protologia* (Turin, 1991), 419-25. Still useful is A. Michel, "Justice originelle," in *Dictionnaire de théologie catholique,* VIII/2, 2021-42. Cf. moreover Denzinger-Schönmetzer, *Enchiridion symbolorum,* 1511 (hereafter DS); *CCC* 374-79.

12. Cf. Colzani, *Antropologia teologica,* 337-90; L. Ladaria, *Antropologia teologica* (Rome, 1986), 152-202. For a study of the Tridentine decree on original sin, see the contribution of A. Vanneste, "La préhistoire du décret du Concile de Trente sur le péché originel," *Nouvelle Revue Théologique* 86 (1964): 355-68; Vanneste, "Le Décret du Concile de Trente sur le péché originel. Les trois premiers canons," *Nouvelle Revue Théologique* 87 (1965): 688-726; Vanneste, "Le Décret du Concile de Trente sur le péché originel. Le quatrième canon," *Nouvelle Revue Théologique* 88 (1966): 581-726.

13. Cf. John Paul II, *Theology of the Body,* 32. We stress that the use the pope makes of the terms "historical" and "theological pre-history" does not imply a position taken in the controversies regarding the "historical" character of original sin. On this subject it has been affirmed that the Catholic theologian can consider the narrative of original sin to be a typical case of "historical etiology": "Etiology can also be, however, the establishment of a historical cause in a concrete, objectively possible, and justified manner. This cause is drawn out of a present situa-

However serious the rupture operated by the sin of origin, it is impossible to understand historical man without rooting him in his revealed theological prehistory.[14]

On the other hand, the "beginning" to which Christ refers objectively implies the redemption. In the Yahwist text, after the fall, man is placed in the redemptive perspective of the Protoevangelium: "I will put enmity between you and the woman, and between your seed and her seed; he shall bruise your head, and you shall bruise his heel" (Gen. 3:15). Paul expresses this in the celebrated passage of Romans 8:22-23: "We know that the whole creation has

---

tion which comes to be better understood thanks to an explanation of its origin; thus the real cause and the present consequence are seen in a single perspective. In this sense, the degree to which the real historical cause is concretely conceived can vary a great deal. Even the manner of presenting this cause, made explicit by its very existence, can be more or less related to symbology, which in itself is not that of the antecedent event, but has its origin in the experience of the etiologist. This does not, however, mean that the object under consideration must be merely the object of a mythological etiology. Rather, this etiology should be called a historical etiology. . . . Catholic theology, in conformity with the teaching of the Church (DS 3862ff; 3898ff) holds that such affirmations, in what they properly express, involve singular, truly historical facts, which occurred in a determined point in time and space. However, theology also has the possibility of interpreting these observations as historical etiology, that is, as affirmations made by man from his successive historical-salvific and non-salvific experiences of himself in his relationship with God, since through and in these experiences he can recognize how things must have been at 'the beginning' of the human condition. If we exactly and perfectly determine the starting point of this etiology and prudently qualify what is affirmed, we can in fact accept that what is properly affirmed in such narratives can be seen as the result of just such a historical etiology. This is, at the very least, possible with the help of the Spirit of God" (K. Rahner, "Considerazioni fondamentali per l'antropologia e la protologia nell'ambito della teologia," in J. Feiner and M. Löhrer, *Mysterium Salutis*, vol. 2/2 [Brescia, 1970], 28-29).

14. With regard to this, Giuseppe Colombo affirms, "The hypothesis of sin, in its 'theological' sense, must be placed at the origin of the divine plan, in the sense that man's sin, as the possibility inherent in created freedom but correlatively in direct reference to the original will of God/the Trinity 'revealed' in Christ, cannot be considered as unforeseeable, and thus as unforeseen by God/the Trinity. . . . It was in fact 'Adam,' the biblical man 'created in Christ' and therefore 'in grace' — according to the formulations of theology — who sinned. His action obviously could not upset or modify the plan of God/the Trinity and in so doing destroy man's reference to Christ. To the contrary, man's sin could only bring this plan into relief in its characteristic of event, and thus of dependence on created freedom — in any case, as already included in the original plan of God/the Trinity 'revealed' in Christ" (G. Colombo, "Tesi sul peccato originale," *Teologia* 15 [1990]: 265). The historical continuity between the original and the lapsarian states must be sought in the single supernatural end of man: "From all eternity all men were thought and willed in Christ the Redeemer, modeled from the beginning on him, reaching their end in him, placed in radical connection to him" (G. Biffi, *Approccio al cristocentrismo* [Milan, 1994], 85-86). Cf. moreover A. Scola, *Implicazioni antropologiche di una catechesi matrimoniale e prematrimoniale* (Rome, 1984).

been groaning in travail together until now; and not only the creation, but we ourselves, who have the first fruits of the Spirit, groan inwardly as we wait for adoption as sons, the redemption of our bodies." Paul understands man's yearning as a yearning for the redemption of his body. Theological reflection is thus illumined by experience, and between experience and revelation we find a surprising convergence. Without a doubt, the redemption of the body of which Paul speaks is a content of revelation which cannot be deduced from experience; yet it is precisely the concrete experience of every man which appears to correspond to the revealed "given."[15] Thus the search for the "beginning" is further defined as a search for the beginning of the theology of the body, through new levels of interpretation of the Genesis texts.

The first of these urges us on to an understanding of the meaning of man's "original solitude." This solitude, which is anterior to the man-woman relation (even if this "anterior" is not to be understood chronologically), refers, upon examination of the wider context of Genesis 2, to man's humanity. By nature man is *alone,* even before being a masculine human being who is lacking the woman.[16]

That man works the soil (cf. Gen. 2:5), dominates the earth (1:28), and gives names to all the animals (2:19) are motives and circumstances that shed light on the meaning of solitude as a search for man's own subjectivity. Man stands before God poised to recognize his own identity. He discovers himself to be *alone* because he is irreducibly different from the other animals: this is the first moment of self-knowledge attained by man, and passes through his knowledge of the world. Through self-knowledge and self-determination the human subject recognizes himself as a person (the anthropological definition of the Yahwist text). On the other hand, his original solitude reveals to him that his humanity places him in a unique, exclusive, and nonrepeatable relation with God himself (the theological definition of the Priestly text).[17]

But how does man come to recognize his original solitude and the meaning inscribed in this? Through his body. By means of his body man perceives that he is part of the visible creation, and yet he simultaneously perceives his difference from the other animals. Original solitude, with its very significant content, is thus placed in relation to the meaning of the body. That meaning, as we have seen, implies in the first place the capacity to work, permanent activity, and in the second place the alternative between death and immortality, that unmistakable sign of man's structural dependence on God (that is, of his contingence).

---

15. Cf. John Paul II, *Theology of the Body,* 32-34.
16. Cf. John Paul II, *Theology of the Body,* 35-37.
17. Cf. John Paul II, *Theology of the Body,* 37ff.

Only after having discovered the original meaning of his body,[18] and thus of his solitude, does man grasp his sexual character and understand the value of the second level of solitude, relative to the man-woman relation.[19]

It is precisely in the creation of man as male and female that solitude becomes a possible path to original unity. In the same moment that the question "Who am I?" springs from original solitude, awakening an anthropological consciousness, the discovery of sexuality through the body indicates the path out of solitude: personal communion between man and woman. The possibility of a *communio personarum* between man and woman explains God's decision to give Adam a "helper," who finds her fullness in the fact of existing as a *person* for the *person.*

Man is not the image of God only by virtue of his humanity. He becomes image, too, by virtue of the *communio personarum* between man and woman.[20] In other words, what visibly makes man and woman similar persons is their body, inasmuch as the body manifests their integral humanity. The body thus reveals man to himself. Masculinity and femininity lead him to a full recognition of his own body as a principle of reciprocal enrichment. The unity through which man and woman become "one flesh" possesses, from the very beginning, the character of a choice. In this choice, in the reciprocal self-gift of persons, is granted a particular knowledge of the body that leads man and woman back to the original mystery of creation. The body permits the perception of original solitude and is the instrument of an *anthropological discovery;* this precludes the elaboration of an anthropology, and a theological anthropology in particular, that does away with sexuality as an original "given" and as part of the *imago Dei.* Such an anthropology would not give an adequate account of man.

The theology of the body traced out by the Holy Father is further enriched through the attentive study of another substantial element contained in the Yahwist text: original nakedness.[21] This element is in turn clarified in

18. Important interpretative keys and discussions of the Christian understanding of the body can be found in B. M. Ashley, *Theologies of the Body: Humanist and Christian* (St. Louis: Pope John Center, 1985).

19. The pope affirms that "[T]he fact that man is a 'body' belongs to the structure of the personal subject more deeply than the fact that in his somatic constitution he is also male or female. Therefore, the meaning of 'original solitude,' which can be referred simply to 'man,' is substantially prior to the meaning of original unity. The latter is based on masculinity and femininity, as if on two different 'incarnations,' that is, on two ways of 'being a body' of the same human being created 'in the image of God' (Gen 1:27)" (*Theology of the Body,* 43).

20. Cf. John Paul II, *Theology of the Body,* 45ff.

21. Cf. John Paul II, *Theology of the Body,* 51-54.

relation to the event of original sin; before sin nakedness did not generate shame. In Genesis 2:25 we contemplate original innocence, which opens onto the profound meaning of the common union *(communio personarum)* between man and woman, realized according to the measure of their being in the image of God.

Original innocence depends on the mystery of grace contained in creation, which enables man and woman to exist from the beginning in a reciprocal relation defined by the disinterested gift of self.[22] In this self-gift we glimpse the authentic meaning of the nuptial meaning of the body,[23] that font of original happiness which maintains its value even in historical reality.

At this point in our itinerary we must try to understand the tie proposed by the catecheses between the state of original innocence and the historical state *(status naturae lapsae simul et redemptae).*[24]

In the original state, innocence radiated in a certain sense from the bodily nakedness of man and woman, without the fear that a concupiscent gaze of one upon the other might arise. There was no concupiscence in Eden; love would have been fruitful in a manner different from the one we know. Because of sin the natural powers of the body *(virtutes)*, analogously to the natural powers of the soul (the intellect and the will), are emancipated from one another. A unified use of his powers is no longer possible for man. Thus love is betrayed by disobedience: the sin of origins, in disfiguring man's freedom, disfigures the exercise of his sexuality.[25]

In this way the destination and the original meaning of sexuality are changed according to the modality to which the biblical text bears witness: "To the woman he said, 'I will greatly multiply your pain in childbearing; in pain you shall bring forth children, yet your desire shall be for your husband, and he shall rule over you'" (Gen. 3:16). In the first place, because of the sin of origins, sexuality is connected to pain and death: through the propagation of the species, sexuality is linked more strongly to death, which, after the origi-

22. Cf. *CCC* 374-79.

23. John Paul II, *Theology of the Body*, 54-57, 60-63.

24. Cf. John Paul II, *Theology of the Body*, 72-74.

25. In this sense the *Catechism of the Catholic Church* states, "Although it is proper to each individual, original sin does not have the character of a personal fault in any of Adam's descendants. It is a deprivation of original holiness and justice, but human nature has not been totally corrupted: it is wounded in the natural powers proper to it; subject to ignorance, suffering, and the dominion of death; and inclined to sin — an inclination to evil that is called 'concupiscence.' Baptism, by imparting the life of Christ's grace, erases original sin and turns man back toward God, but the consequences for nature, weakened and inclined to evil, persist in man and summon him to spiritual battle" (405).

nal fall, can no longer be thought of as an innocent and natural passage.[26] Secondly, the violence of the affective powers emerges in fallen man. Without the light and sustenance of reason and freedom created in grace, sexuality is no longer lived according to the freshness of the original dynamic of oblation. Rather, it is transformed into an expression of the will to power of man over man, which can reduce the person to the status of an object.

In revealing the spousal value of the body, original innocence, on the other hand, indicates to historical man that the ethos of the body is the ethos of the gift,[27] an ethos which allows one to receive the other as a subject. The body thus becomes, in a certain sense, a primordial sacrament because, in rendering visible masculinity and femininity, it transmits the mystery of truth and of love, the mystery of the divine life in which man participates.

It is precisely in being conscious of this primordial sacrament[28] that man can discover and deepen the biblical meaning of "knowledge," connected as it is to matrimonial cohabitation.[29] After the fall, in the union of man and woman, the meaning of maternity and paternity takes form as a further discovery of the meaning of the body. Although profound differences exist between the state of original innocence and the state of sinfulness inherited by man, the image of God constitutes a basis for continuity between the two states. Thus it is that in generation man can still give the name of "man" to one like him: "Now Adam knew Eve his wife, and she conceived and bore Cain, saying, 'I have gotten a man with the help of the LORD'" (Gen. 4:1).[30] However, this "possession," profoundly different from that of original innocence, is marked by suffering and death.[31]

In what we have described so far, it is clear that each human being coming into the world carries with him "this beginning [which] . . . is the first inheritance of every human being in the world, man and woman. It is the first attestation of human identity according to the revealed word, the first source of man's vocation as a person created in the image of God himself."[32]

The evidence offered by experience that human sexuality is a constitutive (and not derivative) factor of the *imago Dei* finds an authoritative foundation in the texts of the papal magisterium cited above. At this point in our discussion, we will consider the findings of biblical and dogmatic theology as well.

---

26. Cf. DS, 1510-16.
27. Cf. John Paul II, *Theology of the Body,* 63-69.
28. Cf. John Paul II, *Theology of the Body,* 75-77.
29. Cf. John Paul II, *Theology of the Body,* 77-80.
30. Cf. John Paul II, *Theology of the Body,* 80-83.
31. Cf. John Paul II, *Theology of the Body,* 83-86.
32. John Paul II, *Theology of the Body,* 86.

3.2. Is Human Sexuality Part of the *Imago Dei?*

We will now take up the question from a different perspective: What does it mean that human sexuality is part of the *imago Dei?* Any further exploration in this direction must once again take as its starting point the celebrated passage of the book of Genesis attributed to the Priestly school: "Then God said, 'Let us make man in our image, after our likeness; and let them have dominion over the fish of the sea, and over the birds of the air, and over the cattle, and over all the earth, and over every thing that creeps upon the earth.' So God created man in his own image, in the image of God he created him; male and female he created them" (Gen. 1:26-27).

3.2.1. Suggestions from the Area of Biblical Studies

Even if we were to limit our research to the last two or three decades, the volume of exegetical literature produced concerning these two verses is of such proportions that we could not give a detailed account of it here. Upon consideration, the outcome of this body of work nevertheless reveals itself, even to the untrained eye, to be far from monolithic; more often than not it seems contradictory. Insofar as it touches upon the issue at hand — whether human sexuality belongs to the *imago Dei* — we can formulate a number of brief observations.[33]

First, the *imago Dei* cannot be limited to man's rational nature, but must be extended to the totality of the human being, *corpore et anima unus.*[34] This necessarily implicates man's existence always either as male or female.[35] Sec-

33. A detailed examination of the abundant literature on this subject up until 1989, on which I have based my conclusions, can be found in M. F. Harper, "Whether the Image of God Can Be Extended to Human Sexuality: Analysis of Biblical and Dogmatic Studies of Genesis 1:26-27" (licentiate thesis in manuscript form, Pontifical John Paul II Institute for Studies on Marriage and the Family at the Pontifical Lateran University, Vatican City, 1989). See also C. Miller, "Genesis 1:26," *Review and Expositor* 87 (1990): 699-703; A. Soggin, *Genesi 1–11* (Genoa, 1991); L. Ruppert, *Genesis. Ein kritischer und theologischer Kommentar. 1 Teilband: Genesis 1:1–11:26* (Würzburg, 1992); W. Gross, "Die Gottenbildlichkeit des Menschen nach Gen 1:26-27 in der Diskussion des letzten Jahrzehnts," *Biblische Notizen* 68 (1993): 35-38; M. Navarro, *Barro y aliento. Exégesis y antropología de Génesis 2–3* (Madrid, 1993).

34. Cf. DS, 800; CCC 362-68.

35. Cf. T. C. Vriezen, "La création de l'homme d'après l'image de Dieu," *Oudtestamentische Studien* 2 (1943): 87-105, especially 99; G. von Rad, *Genesi 1–12* (Brescia, 1969), 67. The second volume of this last work (Italian edition, ed. O. Soffritti) contains a complete bibliography on the subject. See also G. Ravasi, "'Nella sua mano è il respiro dell'uomo di carne.' Sacralità della vita nel linguaggio biblico," in *A sua immagine e somiglianza?* 33-43.

ondly, the human person, insofar as he is predestined and created in Christ, must be understood as a protagonist in a covenant with God. Creation is already part of this covenant. Now, since the human being is created always and only as man or as woman, his diverse identity cannot but take its place, on a more or less elevated level, in that relation which constitutes the covenant.[36]

In the third place, biblical Wisdom literature suggests the idea that the *imago Dei* in man is realized according to a gradual itinerary, with the help of God's wisdom.[37] The man-woman relation can therefore be seen as that singular experience in which the impossibility of man's realizing the *imago Dei* on his own, outside of a relationship with the other, appears most evident.[38] Insofar as he is man-woman, man is called to participate in the task of restoring friendship with God, allowing for the continuity of the salvific lineage destined to fill and subdue the Promised Land.[39] Hence, beginning with biblical Wisdom literature, man and woman can be seen as a reflection of that plurality of plenitude characteristic of the creativity of God ("and God said, 'Let us make man . . .'"). Far from being solely a trait man shares with the animals, sexual difference is somehow a reflection of the mode in which God himself creates.[40]

In the fourth place, keeping in mind the sensibility of the Jewish people, the man-woman relation, insofar as it is part of the *imago Dei*, must be considered in strict relation to the blessing and command of Genesis: "increase and multiply." The exegetes themselves point out that this relation derives not only from the obvious textual juxtaposition, but also from the nature of marriage, which in the Jewish tradition could never be considered separately from the vocation to motherhood and fatherhood.[41] By virtue of the paternal-filial relation existing between Yahweh and Israel,[42] *Adam,* as man and woman, is more the image of God the more he imitates the Father, be-

36. C. Westermann, *Genesis 1–11,* Biblischer Kommentar des Altes Testament, vol. 1/1 (Neukirchen-Vluyn, 1974), 217-18, with an extensive bibliography.

37. Cf. F. Festorazzi, "Modelli interpretative della salvezza nella Bibbia," *Rivista biblica italiana* 3 (1977): 245-67, especially 259.

38. Cf. Festorazzi, "Modelli interpretative della salvezza nella Bibbia," 259.

39. Cf. Festorazzi, "L'uomo imagine di Dio (Gen 1:26-27) nel contesto totale della Bibbia," *Bibbia e Oriente* 3 (1964): 105-18, especially 112; Festorazzi, "Gen 1–3 e la Spaienza di Israele," *Rivista biblica italiana* 27 (1979): 41-51, especially 49-50.

40. Cf. G. F. Hasel, "The Meaning of 'Let Us' in Gen 1:26," *Andrews University Seminary Studies* 13 (1975): 58-66; A. Feuillet, *Jésus et sa Mère* (Paris, 1974), 208.

41. Cf. A. Tosato, *Il matrimonio nel Giudaismo Antico e nel Nuovo Testamento* (Rome, 1976), 54; Tosato, "L'istituto famigliare dell'antico Israele e della Chiesa primitiva," *Anthropotes* 13 (1997): 109-74.

42. Cf. T. C. Vriezen, *An Outline of Old Testament Theology* (Oxford, 1970), 172.

coming himself the father of children who are ordered to the covenant. This becomes explicit in the book of Genesis (5:1-5), when *Adam* (obviously man and woman) generates Seth in his image and likeness, to continue the salvific genealogy.[43]

The human vocation to maternity and paternity becomes more clear in the light of the *una caro* ("one flesh"; cf. Gen. 2:24). Since the Priestly text presupposes this union, the blessing "increase and multiply," even if at first glance similar to that addressed to the animals (cf. Gen. 1:22), cannot have only a functional significance. Rather, the "one flesh" becomes more fully evident if seen as a participation of man and woman in the *imago Dei*.[44] To Adam and Eve — the historical and concrete "face" of the man-woman relation — is given the command to fill the earth, and for this they are constituted as a "house," for the sake of a great lineage.[45] In the light of the faith of Israel, this original couple prefigures the "house" that Yahweh has built in Israel and will build again, at the time of the new Jerusalem, when he will marry the virgin Israel and make her the mother of many children who will come from all the ends of the earth.[46] The idea of the woman whose husband has built her into a "house," generating from her many children, is a soteriological idea which makes the original couple participants in building up the house of Yahweh.

In the fifth place, according to the New Testament, and for Saint Paul in particular, man and woman are seen as part of the *imago Dei*, in the sense that from the beginning the man-woman relation represents Christ, who, in union with the church, fills the earth with his *pleroma*,[47] incorporating into his bride all men, both Jews and Gentiles.[48] The union between Christ and

43. Cf. Vriezen, *An Outline*, 174. See also H. Cazelles, *La vie de la Parole de l'Ancien au Nouveau* (Paris, 1987), 103-6.

44. Cf. Tosato, *Il matrimonio*, 63.

45. Cf. L. Ligier, *Péché d'Adam et Péché du monde*, vol. 1 (Paris, 1960), 223 n. 55, 243.

46. The theme is present in Jer. 31:4-8: "Again I will build you, and you shall be built, O virgin Israel! Again you shall adorn yourself with timbrels, and shall go forth in the dance of the merrymakers. Again you shall plant vineyards upon the mountains of Samaria; the planters shall plant, and shall enjoy the fruit. For there shall be a day when watchmen will call in the hill country of Ephraim: 'Arise, and let us go up to Zion, to the LORD our God.' For thus says the LORD: 'Sing aloud with gladness for Jacob, and raise shouts for the chief of the nations; proclaim, give praise, and say, 'The LORD has saved his people, the remnant of Israel.' Behold, I will bring them from the north country, and gather them from the farthest parts of the earth, among them the blind and the lame, the woman with child and her who is in travail, together; a great company, they shall return here." See also Isa. 54:5, 11b-13.

47. Cf. Eph. 1:23: "which is his body, the fullness of him who fills all in all."

48. Cf. Eph. 2:12-19.

the church thereby reveals, in creation, the "mystery hidden for long ages"[49] of uniting all things in Christ, making all human beings children of the one Father.[50] The man-woman pair is for Paul the prophetic harbinger of this mystery: the union between Christ and the church. This indicates the great dignity to which man is called, inasmuch as, male and female, he is part of the *imago Dei.*[51]

In summary, notwithstanding the many exegetes who are skeptical of such a reading of Genesis 1:26-27, claiming it to be anachronistic, there are more than a few facts provided by exegetes themselves which allow us to affirm, already at this stage, the implication of man and woman (that is, sexual difference) in the *imago Dei.*

3.2.2. Clues from Dogmatic Theology

If there are many exegetical studies on the *imago Dei* tied to the methodology of modern criticism, the dogmatic studies produced on the subject are downright innumerable. The theme has a history of over two thousand years. The daunting volume of these studies can be somewhat reduced if we restrict ourselves to our specific area of research (human sexuality and the *imago Dei*). Notwithstanding that reduction, it would still be impossible to trace out here, even in general outline, the theological evolution of our problem. We are inevitably limited to drawing a few significant positions here and there from the precious coffers of the history of theology.

Since we are preoccupied with critically documenting the conviction that a connection exists between the *imago Dei* and sexual difference, it is first of all necessary to point out that the authors who are convinced of the unfoundedness of such a position are not few. We limit ourselves here to a brief mention of the reason they adopt to sustain their thesis: the link between sexuality and the *imago Dei,* they affirm, is an unbecoming — if not downright deviant — theological elaboration of the biblical idea of the *imago Dei.*[52]

In confronting this problem we must consider more attentively the sort

---

49. Cf. Eph. 3:9: "and to make all men see what is the plan of the mystery hidden for ages in God who created all things."

50. Cf. Eph. 1:5: "He destined us in love to be his sons through Jesus Christ"; Eph. 3:14-15.

51. Cf. A. di Marco, "*Mysterium hoc magnum est . . .* (Eph 5:32)," *Laurentianum* 14 (1973): 43-80, especially 66-67.

52. H. Doms's *Sessualità e matrimonio* is important in this regard, and contains numerous bibliographical references. In J. Feiner and M. Löhrer, *Mysterium Salutis,* vol. 4 (Brescia, 1970), 409-64, especially 421-22.

of reading of the creation accounts begun by Philo of Alexandria and contin-ued in Gnostic and Manichean circles, both because this approach to the texts influenced some of the Greek Fathers and because, particularly in its conse-quences, the approach surfaces again today in the cyclic reappearance of "re-vised editions" of gnosticism. In positing a "double creation," this reading radically calls our thesis into question.

Dividing and, in a certain sense, opposing the two creation accounts and stressing the fact that in the second account Eve is taken out of the side of the sleeping Adam, this position hypothesizes a "double creation." The first is ideal, in a certain sense asexual or androgynous, and the second is what now concretely exists (i.e., sexual).

Philo affirms that the first account refers to the "ideal" or "celestial" man, an asexual man conformed to the full image of humanity, while the second account refers to "animal" or fallen man. Consequently, man would have been in the image of God only in his first, celestial condition. The *imago Dei* as such is asexual, beyond the division into male and female.[53]

Several of the Greek Fathers — Gregory of Nyssa, Origen, Maximus the Confessor, and John Damascene — took up this thesis and reelaborated it, re-proposing it in orthodox terms as they sought to explain original sin. For Gregory of Nyssa, Adam is the image of the totality of humanity and includes the archetype of this humanity realized in its fullness — that is, Jesus Christ.[54] Sexuality appears in relation to original sin, while Adam, in and for himself, is created according to a dimension of totality prior to original sin. Gregory does not, however, mean to propose a temporal difference in speaking of

---

53. Cf. Philo of Alexandria, *La creazione del mondo* (Milan, 1978), 131-32 (*On the Creation of the Cosmos according to Moses*, trans. David T. Runia [Leiden and Boston: Brill, 2001]).

54. Cf. Gregory of Nyssa, "On the Making of Man," 16-17, in Nicene and Post-Nicene Fa-thers, 2nd ser., vol. 5, ed. Philip Schaff and Henry Wace (Grand Rapids: Eerdmans, 1954), 387-427, especially 405: "I think that by these words Holy Scripture conveys to us a great, lofty doc-trine; and the doctrine is this. While two natures — the Divine and incorporeal nature, and the irrational life of brutes — are separated from each other as extremes, human nature is the mean between them: for in the compound nature of man we may behold a part of each of the natures I have mentioned, — of the Divine, the rational and intelligent element, which does not admit the distinction male and female; of the irrational, our bodily form and structure, divided into male and female: for each of these elements is certainly to be found in all that partakes of hu-man life. That the intellectual element, however, precedes the other, we learn as from one who gives in order an account of the making of man; and we learn also that his community and kin-dred with the irrational is for man a provision for reproduction. For he says first that 'God cre-ated man in the image of God' (showing by these words, as the Apostle says, that in such a being there is no male or female): then he adds the peculiar attributes of human nature, 'male and fe-male he created them.'"

these two moments of creation, but rather an ontological one. He describes something that happens more in the dynamism of the prescience of God than in reality.

Origen's vision is even more clearly along this trajectory. For him and, in the final analysis, for Gregory as well, the *imago Dei* is located in the most elevated part of the soul.[55] It is this thesis that will be taken up and expanded in the Augustinian-Thomistic tradition, according to which the *imago* resides in the *mens*.[56] Consequently, just as in Christ, who is the perfect image, there is neither man nor woman (cf. Gal. 3:28), the archetypical Adam is asexual or androgynous. In the beginning, there stands before God the ideal of humanity incarnate in Adam.

Gregory of Nyssa affirms that since man as a creature had to decide freely for or against God, and since God foreknew that man would rebel, man was created with sexual traits in order to attain the total unification of humanity by means of sexual reproduction. That which can no longer be attained from the point of view of the archetypical value of Adam — according to a sort of multiplication of mankind in an angelic fashion unknown to us — is now laboriously attained in the sum total of the human race produced sexually.[57]

It is important to note, however, that for these authors sexuality is not a *consequence* but rather a "badge" of sin. In the authentic Judeo-Christian vision, sexuality is never seen from the point of view of a "phobia of sex." Thus, every causal link between sin and sex, which would present sex as the negative heritage of sin, is to be excluded. This position cannot be deduced either from Scripture or from the tradition. The position of the Cappadocian Fathers mentioned above did not derive from any such phobia; if anything, it arose from an attempt to elaborate the contents of a theology of the original state.

Such a theology requires the holding together of factors which, within the historical state of man as we know it, seem incompatible. In the original state there is a copresence of virginity and generation, and thus of virginity

55. Cf. H. C. Graef, "L'image de Dieu et la structure de l'âme d'après les Pères grecs," *La Vie spirituelle* 20 (1952): 331-39; A. G. Hamman, *L'homme, l'image de Dieu. Essai d'une anthropologie chrétienne dans l'Église des cinq premiers siècles* (Paris, 1987).

56. Cf. M. Dolby Mugica, "El hombre como imagen de Dios en la especulación augustiniana," *Augustinianum* 34 (1989): 119-54; M. L. Lamau, "L'homme à l'image de Dieu chez les théologiens et spirituals du XII siècle," *Mélanges de science religieuse* 48 (1991): 203-14; R. Moretti, "Con 'l'uomo imagine di Dio' al centro dell'antropologia teologica," in *Antropologia tomista. Atti del IX Congresso Tomistico Internazionale,* vol. 3 (Vatican City, 1991), 187-98; L. M. de Blibnieres, "La dignité de l'homme image de Dieu selon Saint Thomas d'Aquin," in *Antropologia tomista,* 199-220; M. Szell, "Facciamo l'uomo a nostra imagine, a nostra somiglianza (Gn 1:26)," in *Antropologia tomista,* 221-30.

57. Cf. Gregory of Nyssa, "On the Making of Man," 17.

and marriage, whereas in the historical state marriage and virginity are mutually exclusive from the point of view of physical generation.

Moreover, in the actual historical state of man, sexuality is linked to death
through generation. In nature, that which is born dies. For the Fathers just
cited, it was worth considering that if death appears to be a law of the species,
in Catholic dogma it is a consequence of sin.[58] In the original state man did
not die, at least not as he does in the historical state.[59] How, then, can sexuality be compatible with immortality? This is the profound reason that
prompted the Cappadocians to speak of a double creation, at least *in mente
Dei*. Their position, however — we repeat — cannot be confused with a fear
of sex.[60]

Without pausing on the teaching of the great Latin tradition relevant to
our problem (the relationship between sexual difference and the *imago Dei*),
we will make some observations on the thought of more recent theologians
on the subject. We mention in passing Scheeben and his attempt to formulate
an analogy between the relations of man, woman, and child and the relations
of the persons in the Trinity[61] — an analogy whose validity had been explicitly negated both by Thomas and Augustine.[62] This does not, however, directly involve our theme.

Barth's position, on the other hand, is directly related to the object of our
study. He affirms that the image and likeness of which Genesis 1:27 speaks indicates the reciprocity of man and woman.[63] Along these lines, though with

58. Cf. Rom. 5:12: "Therefore as sin came into the world through one man and death
through sin, and so death spread to all men because all men sinned." Cf. A. Pitta, "Quale
fondamento biblico per il 'peccato originale'? Un bilancio ermeneutico: il Nuovo Testamento," in *Questioni sul peccato originale*, ed. I. Sanna (Padua, 1996), 141-67, with an extensive
bibliography.

59. Cf. DS, 1511; *GS* 18; *CCC* 376, 1008.

60. It should not be forgotten that for other Greek Fathers — the Antiochenes, for example
— the image was not to be found so much in man's spirit (as the Cappadocian Fathers held,
hence running the risk of excluding the body and sexuality from the image) as in the dominion
exercised by man. In this sense man and woman (sexual difference) participate in the image. Cf.
S. Zincone, "Il tema dell'uomo-donna imagine di Dio nei commenti paolini a Genesi di area
antiochena," *Annali di Storia dell'Esegesi* 2 (1985): 103-13.

61. Cf. M. J. Scheeben, *Handbuch der katholischen Dogmatik*, vol. 1 (Freiburg im Breisgau,
1933), 877-81 (*A Manual of Catholic Theology* [New York: Catholic Publication Society, 1899]);
Scheeben, *The Mysteries of Christianity* (London: Herder, 1946), 181-89.

62. Cf. Augustine, *De Trinitate* 12.5.5–6.8; Thomas Aquinas, *Summa Theologiae* I, q. 93, a. 6,
ad 2um and, indirectly, I, q. 36, a. 3, ad 1um. Cf. B. Castilla y Cortázar, "La Trinidad como familia. Analogía humana de las procesiones divinas," *Annales Theologici* 10 (1996): 381-416.

63. Cf. K. Barth, *Kirchliche Dogmatik* III/1, 329-77 (*Church Dogmatics* [New York: Scribner,
1955-]).

important differences, moves Brunner as well.[64] According to this interpretation, masculinity and femininity are obviously a constitutive part of the *imago*. This position, however, stretches the text excessively, since sexual difference is not, theoretically speaking, necessary to found the reciprocity of man with another human being.

Pryzwara, too, has devoted much space to our theme. In his work *Mensch: Typologische Anthropologie*,[65] the text of Genesis 1:26-27 takes on more layers of meaning. Pryzwara says, among other things, that this text provides the basis for the spousal vision proper to the New Testament. In his judgment it is possible to construct a spousal theology of Catholic dogma; various biblical texts would justify this idea. This spousal theology would use the man-woman relation to interpret some fundamental mysteries of the faith. Moreover, it is the Old Testament itself — it is enough to think of Hosea and Jeremiah — which first interprets the relationship between God and his people in terms of marriage.[66]

Spousal theology is thus the amplification of a metaphor that asserts its strength and hermeneutical value already within the Scriptures themselves. For Pryzwara the symbolical function of nuptiality, paternity, and maternity for the relationship between God and his people can be drawn out of the verses of the first chapter of Genesis. However, in full consonance with the tradition,[67] the Hungarian theologian strongly insists on the radical dissimilarity between man and God. From this point of view, he sees sexuality as tied to intracosmic reality, inserted into the order of the creation of the animals.

In my opinion, Pryzwara's interpretation says, on the one hand, too much, and on the other too little. To draw the entire foundation of a spousal theology from that very important verse of Genesis is to force the text into saying more than it does. On the other hand, simultaneously to relegate the sexual element to the intracosmic world is to make the text say too little.

For Balthasar the claim that sexuality is part of the *imago Dei* is a theological affirmation which can clearly be drawn from the first, priestly account of creation.[68] The account contains an ascending creative dynamism: the narrative proceeds from the lower to the higher, according to an evolutionary

---

64. Cf. E. Brunner, *Der Mensch im Widerspruch* (Berlin, 1937), 102.

65. Cf. E. Pryzwara, *L'uomo. Antropologia Tipologica* (Milan, 1968), 177-202; originally *Mensch: Typologische Anthropologie* (Nürnberg: Glock und Lutz, 1959).

66. Cf. Hos. 2:4-25; Jer. 2:1ff.

67. Cf. DS, 806; *CCC* 43.

68. Cf. H. U. von Balthasar, *Theo-Drama II: Dramatis Personae: Man in God,* trans. Graham Harrison (San Francisco: Ignatius, 1990), 355-94; *The Christian State of Life,* trans. Sr. Mary Frances McCarthy (San Francisco: Ignatius, 1983), 224-49.

perspective, to the moment of the creation of man. At a certain point in this ascending perspective the narrative says, "Let us make man in our image, according to our likeness; and let them have dominion over the fish of the sea, and over the birds of the air, and over the cattle, and over all the earth, and over every creeping thing that creeps upon the earth" (Gen. 1:26). Verse 27's "assertion about the 'image of God' is interposed between the subhuman and the human fruitfulness, separating them."[69]

From this point of view, the second account confirms the first. The difference between human and animal fecundity is further confirmed by the possibility that Adam has of generating descendants "in his own likeness, after his image" (Gen. 5:3), not simply individuals of a species. This makes Eve, upon taking her first son into her arms, exclaim, "I have gotten a man with the help of the LORD" (4:1). Thus, for Balthasar, sexual difference is part of the *imago* precisely in its ordination to fruitfulness.

3.3. Sexuality, "One Flesh," and the *Imago Dei*

In conclusion, the interpretation of Genesis 1:26-27 which sees sexual difference (the man-woman pair) as part of the *imago Dei* appears balanced and sufficiently supported, both by exegesis and dogmatics. This interpretation allows us, on the one hand, to avoid locking the definition of man into the intracosmic sphere. On the other hand, it keeps us from limiting the meaning of the image to a purely spiritual element, which would relegate sexuality to an inferior level, considering it a dimension incapable of rising from the limits of animal nature. This vision of sexuality places it, moreover, beyond every shadow of Gnosticism, with its insoluble oscillation between bestiality (the body is so separated from the spirit that the spirit ends in behaving as an animal) and spiritualism (which gives rise to an asceticism of separation in a perpetual battle against all that reminds us of the body).

Once again it is Balthasar who clarifies the heart of our thesis, which we examine from the reference point of *Mulieris Dignitatem*. In discussing the teachings of the fathers of the church, Balthasar affirms,

> If we want to preserve what is of permanent value in their explanations, therefore, we will expressly emphasize that the difference of the sexes belonged beyond the shadow of a doubt to God's original intention in creating man. Consequently, it cannot be regarded as brought about by man's

69. Balthasar, *Theo-Drama II*, 369.

later fall into sin. Rather, the difference is part of the *imago Dei:* "Let us make man in our image and likeness. . . . In the image of God he created them. Male and female he created them" (Gen 1:26-27). If this were not so, Christ could neither have pointed to the relationship of the sexes to describe his mysterious union with the Church, nor have given the sacrament of marriage the power and the real possibility of symbolizing this perfect relationship in the relationship of the sexes.[70]

If man and woman, the essential substratum of the "one flesh," were not part of the *imago*, it would be impossible for Christ to use this double comparison. This affirmation shows how the thesis of *Mulieris Dignitatem* leads a reflection on sexuality toward a decisive "either-or." *Either* sexuality is part of the *imago* and the difference between masculine and feminine can find its ultimate and definitive foundation in the Christic, trinitarian, and ecclesiological heart of revelation, *or* sexuality is not part of the *imago*, and the rootedness of sexual difference in revealed truth does not go beyond the (still important) reference to human reproduction and the ethical imperative that flows from it.

In the second case, the celebrated passage of the Letter to the Ephesians[71] could be interpreted only minimalistically, with a purely symbolical reading of the connection between man and woman and Christ and the church. The passage would be deprived of that analogical "key" that makes it capable of founding a spousal theology. The masculine and the feminine would risk being seen in a solely functional light, and the same fate would befall the procreative dimension that belongs to its essence. Conversely, the interpretation that sees the man-woman pair as part of the *imago Dei* involves an understanding of human sexuality as a constitutive dimension of human nature.

---

70. Balthasar, *Christian State of Life*, 103.

71. Cf. Eph. 5:21-33: "Be subject to one another out of reverence for Christ. Wives, be subject to your husbands, as to the Lord. For the husband is the head of the wife as Christ is the head of the church, his body, and is himself its Savior. As the church is subject to Christ, so let wives also be subject in everything to their husbands. Husbands, love your wives, as Christ loved the church and gave himself up for her, that he might sanctify her, having cleansed her by the washing of water with the word, that he might present the church to himself in splendor, without spot or wrinkle or any such thing, that she might be holy and without blemish. Even so husbands should love their wives as their own bodies. He who loves his wife loves himself. For no man ever hates his own flesh, but nourishes and cherishes it, as Christ does the church, because we are members of his body. 'For this reason a man shall leave his father and mother and be joined to his wife, and the two shall become one.' This is a great mystery, and I mean in reference to Christ and the church; however, let each one of you love his wife as himself, and let the wife see that she respects her husband."

It is without a doubt that, through his body, man communicates and continually interacts with the cosmos and with cosmic reality, and yet he is not, in that same body, merely part of the cosmos. Man transcends the cosmos already in his body; his sexuality is qualitatively different from the sexuality of animals. This explains, too, why a child, the fruit of the reciprocal gift of the spouses, may not be treated as the individual result of animal reproduction.

Thus we can say that man is not only different from animals because he participates in dominating the cosmos, that is, because of his spiritual nature; he carries this difference also in his body. The pope carries out just such an exegetical and dogmatic interpretation of the Genesis text. Though remaining in continuity with animal sexuality, human sexuality does not exhaust itself in this latter, but participates in the *imago Dei*. If this is true, then one can truly say that the body "expresses the person,"[72] the whole person.

72. John Paul II, *Theology of the Body*, 61.

PART II

The Nuptial Mystery:
A Theological Perspective

CHAPTER 4

The Dynamisms of Nuptiality: Affection, Love, and Sexuality

4.1. Human Nuptiality

The human experience of love presents us with a paradox. As a fundamental experience, it is, in some way, within the reach of everyone; we have only to think of the relationship of an infant with its mother, or of a husband with his wife. And yet if we attempt to define love, we find ourselves faced with a most complicated reality. In fact, the Scholastics would say that all elementary natural phenomena are the most difficult to analyze. For example, nothing is easier than saying, "This is a watch," and yet how difficult it is to give a detailed account of what happens in the subject making this act of knowledge! With love we have an analogous experience: as soon as we seek to hold on to the phenomenon more closely, things get complicated.[1]

In his famous essay on love, Josef Pieper begins with a linguistic survey of the variety of terms which, in several classical (Greek and Latin) and modern (German, English, and Russian) languages, are used to describe the phenomenon of love.[2] He notes that the gamut of possible terms is extremely wide, and covers everything from the most uncouth sexuality to the most elevated spirituality. It is possible to identify what these terms have in common with regard to substance, notwithstanding the variety of their forms and manifes-

---

1. It is not by chance that Josef Pieper begins his reflection on love with the following affirmation: "There are more than enough considerations that might keep us from committing ourselves to the subject of love. After all, we need only leaf through a few magazines at the barber's to want not to let the word 'love' cross our lips for a good long time." "On Love," in J. Pieper, *Faith, Hope, Love*, trans. R. Winston and C. Winston (San Francisco: Ignatius, 1997), 145.

2. Cf. Pieper, "On Love," 145-62.

tations. In doing so, however, we cannot arrive at a definition of this substance, but must content ourselves with describing its salient dimensions and the meaning of its different manifestations.[3]

C. S. Lewis, on his part, confesses in his penetrating essay *The Four Loves* that at the beginning he thought he had found a "highroad" to confront his theme in the famous affirmation of the First Letter of John: "God is love" (1 John 4:8). He could then decide that human affections merit the name of love "just in so far as they resembled that love which is God."[4] The human experience of love could be distinguished into two broad genres, gift-love and need-love. This would allow us to conclude that only the first is truly worthy of God and, thus, that only the first is true love. It is Lewis himself who notes, "Every time I have tried to think the thing out along those lines I have ended in puzzles and contradictions. The reality is more complicated than I supposed."[5] In fact, one cannot deny the qualification of "love" to need-love; this would, among other things, do violence to many languages.

In an entirely other linguistic and cultural sphere, Vladimir Soloviev encounters no fewer difficulties in describing the deep value of love.[6] His intention, explicit from the beginning, to limit his theme to the love between man and woman (he calls it "sexual love") does not save him from the necessity of placing this form of love in relation to others, as well as plumbing more deeply the meaning of the relation between man and woman. He needs an integrated anthropology to define "sexual love" as the "form" of every love, since "spiritual love is false because a spirituality which denies the flesh is false."[7]

These references to authors so diverse is enough, here, to illustrate the

---

3. Pieper, "On Love," 147: "Thus we must once again wonder whether those seemingly disparate things referred to by the German word *Liebe* and the English word 'love' really 'have nothing to do with one another.' Sigmund Freud, on the one hand, also speaks of the 'carelessness' of language in applying the word *Liebe*. But, on the other hand, he points out, 'In all its whims linguistic usage remains faithful to some kind of reality.' Presumably, then, there may be a message hidden within the apparent or alleged 'poverty' of the German vocabulary of love. It may be that the language itself is telling us not to overlook the underlying unity in all the forms of love and to keep this broad common element in mind in the face of all the misuses that result from narrowing down the concept."

4. Cf. C. S. Lewis, *The Four Loves* (London: Fontana Books, 1960), 1: " 'God is love,' says St. John. When I first tried to write this book I thought that his maxim would provide me with a very plain highroad through the whole subject."

5. Lewis, *The Four Loves*, 2.

6. Cf. V. Soloviev, *Il significato dell'amore e altri scritti* (Milan, 1983), 75-86 (*The Meaning of Love* [London: Centenary Press, 1946]).

7. Soloviev, *Il significato dell'amore e altri scritti*, 86.

complexity of what we are trying to do.[8] How, then, are we to proceed in investigating the phenomenon of the inclination to love? It seems to me that the most plausible response is precisely that found in Soloviev's essay: in human experience, the love between man and woman constitutes the "form" of love. If it is preferable, one can say it is the *analogatum princeps* of all the various forms of love. Far from being arbitrary, such an affirmation expresses the constitutive and nonaccidental character of man's sexual nature.

The "unity of the two," or the nuptial character (spousal nature) of the human being, shows us the basic core of love. Pieper, who makes his own the affirmation of Pseudo-Dionysius, "love is a unitive and syncretive power," arrives at Soloviev's thesis: since, in order to unite, the two must remain two, the love between man and woman — sexual or erotic love — is the "paradigmatic form of love."[9] The affirmation of the paradigmatic character of the love between man and woman — we will use neither the term "sexual love" nor "erotic love," since these would need to be accompanied by continuous clarifications — obviously allows for much differentiation in the vast assortment of possible analogues. It also has the value of being very modern: it inseparably unites love to the affective sphere or, to be more clear, to the passions. In this regard, the weight of sexuality becomes evident. No manifestation of love in the person or between persons can prescind from the affective or the sexual spheres.

The thesis of the paradigmatic nature of nuptial love allows us to reach an important result. It offers us a high road to enter into the complex world of the inclination to love: this involves not only the study of love in itself, but also its affective and sexual roots.

It would be presumptuous, if not downright erroneous, to believe that we have thus found the way to conceptually deduce the existential simplicity of the experience of love. We have only opened a way toward understanding the phenomenon of love, which remains before us in all its splendid and elementary complexity. It does not take much to become aware of this. The intertwining of affection and sexuality in the manifestation of love, evident in the love between man and woman, immediately evokes a network of questions and problems so vast that it remains as discouraging as it is fascinating.

---

8. See also J. Guitton, *L'amore umano* (Milan, 1989), 11-27, especially 11: "The very word (love) is equivocal in all languages, as is demonstrated by the simple fact that it is used for God and for relationships between man and woman. Each person gives the word a different connotation, according to his spirit and personal inclinations. Love is also the sphere where sin, error, ambiguity reign, and, as far as we can see, have always reigned."

9. Pieper, *Faith, Hope, Love*, 247. The affirmation is followed by all the necessary clarifications.

To go immediately to the heart of the question, we can affirm that even a minimal understanding of the problem, limited to its philosophical and theological aspects, involves by its nature a discourse on man and his relation with the other.

Moreover, if the manifestations of love implicate the affective and sexual spheres, anthropological discourse must be carried out in an integral fashion, taking into account the dual nature of man as *synholon* of body and soul. As phenomenological evidence demonstrates, the affective and sexual spheres in man are rooted in his bodiliness. These two spheres interact, by means of psychology, with his spiritual dimension. Intelligence and will, or in a word, freedom, come into play together with factors which more commonly have to do with deep drives tied to the biological and psychic structures; these latter are, at least in themselves and for themselves, not free.

A great question still hovers over our discussion: that of the "place" of the other. To this question the "way" of love is tied par excellence. The human being's fundamental creatureliness points to it. What place is to be given to the other, even in the paradigmatic case of the love between man and woman? Who is this other, really? What is concealed behind this presence? From the little we can comprehend up till this point, dual unity does not mean an obvious symmetrical reciprocity of male and female. The other, the "place" of inalienable difference, is in fact never only male or female. He or she at the same time personifies other "states": mother, father, brother, sister, friend, and so on. But above all, the other-than-me, who is a finite creature, urges my freedom toward the dramatic question of the foundation of my finitude. I do not have this foundation in me, and yet paradoxically I cannot do without it, since my freedom (reflecting my being) is marked by the radical difference between finitude and the infinity of uni-total Being. The question regarding the foundation of the enigma of man, which constitutes the heart of my freedom and of my will, is inescapable. Freedom, in the manifestations of love, finds itself inevitably confronted with this question precisely because it cannot shy away from the question of the "place" of the other. This is true if I identify the question as the result in me of the presence of that Mystery who is *interior intimo me* (Augustine), and thus find a way to that Other who "in himself is no one else's 'other': he is the All-embracing One"[10] — the Non-Other of Nicholas of Cusa. But it is no less true even if I do not recognize the signs of the Mystery in the experience of being (which remains uni-total in the inevitable fragmentation of the indefinite acts of being of finite essences).

---

10. H. U. von Balthasar, *Theo-Drama II: Dramatis Personae: Man in God*, trans. Graham Harrison (San Francisco: Ignatius, 1990), 287.

These are simply examples, indicative of the quantity, but above all of the quality, of problems which rush to meet us as soon as we venture on to the "highroad" of spousal love. Obviously we cannot confront them directly.[11] It is, however, useful to have mentioned them as the context framing our central affirmation: that the dynamism of love implies the intertwining of the three important factors of affection, love, and sexuality.

This "intertwining" exists in the "I" as a dynamic and complex unity. It is our intention to demonstrate, in reference to an authentic personalistic vision, the meaning of each of these three factors, both considered in themselves and in their relations of interdependence with the other two. While never losing sight of this dynamic unity, it will be helpful, to reach the aim proposed, to examine each element separately. Distinguishing in unity allows for a better understanding of the profoundly personalistic nature of the many-faceted reality of human love.

4.2. Affection

In its most recent edition, Zingarelli, an Italian dictionary famous for its attention to the continual evolution of language, defines affection as "any modification of the consciousness resulting from the action of an agent external to the consciousness itself."[12] Notwithstanding a certain idealistic impoverishment — I refer to the limitation of the modification to the consciousness — the definition preserves the substance of the etymological meaning of the Latin word *affectio*. This derives from the verb *afficere*, to which is associated the passive voice *affici aliqua re* (to be affected by something) and which indicates, in its most basic meaning, being affected by something outside the "I" (e.g., *affici aegritudine*). The affective experience thus appears, on the phenomenological plane, as a modification of the subject resulting from an external provocation. We can ask ourselves: What, then, is the nature of the modification that happens in the subject when it is affected by love? In this way we have narrowed down the notion of affection from the extremely general level of the term to that which concerns our theme.

In the panorama of contemporary culture, we find the most adequate response to our question in the work of Sigmund Freud. This is not the place

---

11. The central anthropological questions evoked here find a certain organic development in A. Scola, *Questioni di antropologia teologica* (Rome, 1997), 85-102.

12. M. Dogliotti and L. Rosiello, eds., *Lo Zingarelli 1999. Vocabolario della lingua italiana* (Bologna, 1998), 51.

to discuss the merits or otherwise of such a predominant school of thought. Rather, we will consider a central thesis of Freud's thought regarding our theme: the modification produced by affection reveals the existence of an unconscious within the "I," understood as a determining, even if nonexclusive, factor of the affective life of that "I." The unconscious is the place of necessity; it is a world without freedom.[13] Such affirmations are of fundamental importance because of the widespread (and simplified) diffusion of the psychoanalytic sciences in the dominant culture; they are at the basis of the general opinion that the manifestations of the affective sphere, such as those pertaining to love, sexuality, and all that is connected to them, are facts which can only be passively received. According to this view, such manifestations are impulses arising from the depths of the constrained unconscious, outside the domain of freedom and thus of the consciousness and responsibility. If this is the case, the freedom of the person desiring happiness should limit itself to registering the multifarious array of affective drives and seconding them. In the opposite case, that is, if freedom attempts to interact with these drives to orient or to contest them, the person exposes himself to malaise.

This debased version of Freudianism, though far from the vision of things belonging to the "inventor" of psychoanalysis, contains a challenge which must be taken seriously: it prompts us toward a correct personalistic sensibility. A complete answer to the challenge would involve investigating the relationship between the unconscious and consciousness, between freedom and necessity in the affective experience. This is beyond our sphere of competence. It will be helpful, however, to examine the affective phenomenon as it appears in the complex world of the conscious.

The reader may be surprised by our decision to discuss the theme of affection by referring to the *Summa Theologiae* of Saint Thomas Aquinas. There are, however, *questiones* in the Angelic Doctor's well-known treatise on the passions which,[14] in the opinion of many authoritative scholars, remain impressively relevant. In these passages Thomas defines affection as a *passio*, a passion, because he considers it to be the particular effect of an agent on a "patient" ("passio est affectus agentis in patiente")[15] which a good, insofar as it is desirable, produces in the appetite. To say that affection is a passion — the term is extremely contemporary — is equivalent, for Thomas, to affirming that it is a modification of the appetite on the part of something that can

---

13. Cf. S. Freud, *Essais de psychanalyse* (Paris, 1973), 179-85.
14. Cf. Thomas Aquinas, *Summa Theologiae* I-II, qq. 22-48.
15. Thomas Aquinas, *Summa Theologiae* I-II, q. 26, a. 2.

be the object of appetite: "immutatio . . . appetitus ab appetibili." It is the modification of the desire on the part of a desirable good. If we analyze this fundamental definition of affection more closely, we will see that the phenomenon presents us with a high level of complexity. We will do this following Thomas's study.

Aquinas distinguishes a full five stages in affection, that is, in the *passio* that a lovable object provokes in the subject.[16] We will describe them briefly, though they merit a more accurate analysis, capable of demonstrating their great relevance even today.[17]

The first stage, already mentioned above, is *immutatio*,[18] an important modification in the subject. It is the characteristic, visible transformation which the lover suffers. This change will most often be the butt of his friends' jokes, but, as Lewis notes perceptively,[19] the interested party takes it very seriously.[20]

The second stage Aquinas identifies is *coaptatio*.[21] This is the recognition of the existence of a sort of harmony between the subject suffering the affective *passio* and the desirable object. What is involved here is not a casual correspondence, but an almost preestablished harmony, to borrow a phrase from Leibniz, an affinity and a correspondence of amorous sentiment between the lover and the beloved.[22] I believe this effectively corresponds to the profound psychological experience of those in love. One can say that for Thomas *coaptatio*, insofar as it refers to the sensible appetite, first springs up in man out of necessity but, in a second instance, gives rise to an *aliquid* of freedom.

The third — and principal — stage of the affective response is *com-*

---

16. Thomas Aquinas, *Summa Theologiae* I-II, q. 26, a. 2. "Reply: The term 'passion' denotes the effect produced in a thing when it is acted upon by some agent. Now where the natural agencies are in question, the effect is two-fold: first a form is produced, then a movement arising from that form: for instance, that which brings a body into existence gives it both weight, and the movement that results from weight. Since the weight is the cause of the body's moving towards its natural place, it may be called 'natural love.'" (All the English citations from Saint Thomas's *Summa Theologiae* are taken from the Blackfriars translation [Cambridge and New York: McGraw-Hill, 1964-].)

17. Cf. infra, pp. 314-30.

18. Cf. Thomas Aquinas, *Summa Theologiae* I-II, q. 26, a. 2.

19. Cf. Lewis, *The Four Loves*, 113.

20. A beautiful example of this affective *immutatio* can be found in the tragic description of falling in love in Thomas Mann's short story, "The Little Mr. Freidmann."

21. Cf. Thomas Aquinas, *Summa Theologiae* I-II, q. 26, a. 1.

22. Perhaps the most famous verse of all *stilnovismo* can convey the idea of *coaptatio:* "Amor che a nullo amato amar perdona" [Love that excuses no one loved from loving]. Dante, *The Divine Comedy, Inferno,* canto V, 103 (*Inferno,* trans. Mark Musa [Bloomington: Indiana University Press, 1971]).

placentia. That this term should be translated by the English word "desire" (unfortunately rather overused) indicates, without a doubt, the most salient characteristic of affection, to the point that Thomas uses it to define that most simple and elementary of affective responses: what he calls *amor naturalis.*[23] We will return to this point shortly. In speaking of desire, we find ourselves facing a main crux of the question of love as posed by the dominant contemporary mentality. The confusion regarding this aspect of the problem is enormous today, because the "desirous" nature of affection often masks coercion, violence, and force lurking under the disguise of love. If affection really implies desire, then we are to believe that all that love asks of us is always an expression of freedom and liberation.

From *complacentia* one passes to *intentio,* the effective tending to possess the desired reality.[24]

The last stage of the "process" of affection is *gaudium,*[25] or joy. This joy comes into being upon the possession of the desired object and represents, in a certain sense, the reestablishment of *quies,* of a situation of rest, thus resolving the *immutatio.* If this last represents a certain stirring up of the subject, joy is the reestablishment of the quiet which follows possession.

We have already alluded to the fact that Thomas calls this affective response to the provocation of a desirable being, that is, of a good, *amor naturalis.* This notion is of capital importance, and is often undervalued in Christian reflection on love. In *amor naturalis* we find ourselves confronted with the most immediate and natural level that the word "love" can have, a level which no form of love, not even the highest mystical union, can do without.

One might prefer, over this Thomistic description of the five stages of affection, a theory which adheres more phenomenologically to the data of the human sciences, and to psychology in particular. However, one cannot deny the existence of this elementary bipolar structure of the appetite and the desired object; affection in its natural and primary phase corresponds to this structure, and, again on this immediate and primary level, it is the source of *amor naturalis.* If we wish to know the meaning of this elementary level of affection, and in particular of *amor naturalis,* we are forced to introduce a second fundamental polarity (again, from the Thomistic vision of things) which is able to give a full account of the affective phenomenon.

23. At the end of our brief treatise, it is perhaps superfluous to enter into Thomas's distinction of the three forms of the appetite (natural, sensitive, intellective), to which correspond the three forms of love (cf. Thomas Aquinas, *Summa Theologiae* I-II, q. 26, a. 1). See also infra, pp. 325-28.

24. Cf. Thomas Aquinas, *Summa Theologiae* I-II, q. 26, a. 2.

25. Cf. Thomas Aquinas, *Summa Theologiae* I-II, q. 26, a. 2.

The will is the properly human form of appetite; in fact, it represents the rational appetite. And yet not every form of appetite can be reduced to the will. There are natural appetites connected to the natural inclinations that precede the will, even if in the rational creature these should not be lived outside the use of that *appetitus* informed by rationality which is, precisely, the will. Thomas assigns *amor naturalis* to the level of the natural appetites and, more precisely, makes it depend on what he calls *voluntas ut natura*.[26] This expression has not ceased, after so many centuries, to provoke debate among scholars, in part because it seems to contain a certain contradiction. Since it is posited in relation to the *voluntas ut ratio,* and since the will is informed by reason, it is difficult to understand what exactly Thomas means by such an expression. We can arrive at a fairly exact idea of its meaning by rising to that level in which the human appetite tends toward a good, a level which flows from the nature of man as *corpore et anima unus.* In virtue of the "givenness" proper to this nature, the natural appetite — which, inasmuch as it is an appetite informed by the intellect, precedes the work of the will — also precedes reason. This appetite, however, is not actualized without the help of reason.

The expression *voluntas ut natura* indicates, then, an extension that Thomas makes of the concept of the will, in order to express the existence in the human being of a system of appetites and inclinations which includes *amor naturalis* — understood as the manifestation of the elementary affective structure of the subject — and which is given to man before it is chosen by him. The consequences of such an affirmation are so weighty that forgetfulness of it has contributed to the production of that degenerate form of classical ethical theory which is modern casuistic ethics, critically analyzed by Pinckaers.[27] The modern theory is born from the erroneous conviction that the will as rational appetite is indifferent toward its subject. Rather, inclinations and natural appetites allow us to understand that the will is in fact always inclined to the good precisely because man originally, spontaneously, in the way he is made — and thus naturally (creaturely) — is inclined to the good. The possibility of choosing, which is what makes the human being properly human, is not exercised upon a tabula rasa but on a precise inclination to the good.

Regarding our theme, what we have called the "elementary structure of

---

26. Cf. Thomas Aquinas, *Summa Theologiae* I, q. 83, a. 4; III, q. 18, a. 3.

27. S. Pinckaers, *Les sources de la morale chrétienne* (Fribourg, 1985), 244-57 (*The Sources of Christian Ethics,* trans. Sr. Mary Thomas Noble [Washington, D.C.: Catholic University of America Press, 1995]).

affection," or *amor naturalis,* is to be found precisely on this level. Thomas rightly calls it the love of desire *(complacentia),* or affective love. On this foundation is grafted a second level of affection — and here we have the emergence of the other pole — which depends on a response to love that is willed, and thus free. This is the level of the *voluntas ut ratio,* in which love becomes the fruit of a free and conscious choice. Thomas calls this love *dilectio* or *benevolentia,* precisely because it follows upon an *electio.*[28] If the love of desire is an affective *passio,* the love of election is an effective choice.

The structure of love as affection — inasmuch as it concerns the subject — thus appears more clearly in its twofold dialectical polarity: the polarity between the desirable good and the natural appetite, and the second polarity built upon this, between *voluntas ut natura* and *voluntas ut ratio.* None of the elements of this twofold polarity can be obscured if we wish to comprehend in depth the nature of the inclination to love.

We must particularly take into account the fact that in human nature there exists a love of desire which precedes — that is, which arises independently of (hence *passio*) — free choice, even if this love must then be invested with choice. As such, this primary level *(voluntas ut natura)* can be found at the summit of the dilemma proper to every authentic human love: Do I love the other for himself (benevolence or the love of election), or do I love the other for myself (egoism or concupiscence)? That primary level, however, also conditions the solution. In extreme synthesis the natural love of desire is an inclination toward a good arising *(passio)* from the fact that every being, as such, is good and thus desirable; it is an affective conformation *(coaptatio)* prior to the choice between benevolence and egoism. In this way we reach the second stage of our "journey," which requires us to look at love in a strict sense, that is, considered in relation to its object.

4.3. Love

If we consider our problem beginning not with what occurs in the subject when it is surprised by a lovable object, but with the relation of the subject to the possible objects of love, we can sketch out our sphere of inquiry according to the classical tripartition of love into love of self, love of neighbor, and love of God. In a reflection as general as ours, however, these three "objects" can be compressed into two: love of self and love of God. On the one hand, the commandment tells us that we must love our neighbor as ourselves. On the other,

28. Cf. Thomas Aquinas, *Summa Theologiae* I-II, q. 26, a. 3.

the tradition teaches us that the "ratio diligendi proximi Deus est" ("God is the reason for the love of neighbor"). A study of the relation between love of self and love of God, therefore, offers us the key to an adequate interpretation of the meaning of and the relations between the three "objects" of love.

The widespread debate provoked by the famous work of Rousselot on the history of love in the Middle Ages[29] can offer us the starting point for identifying the central core of the question of love's "object," within the framework of our synthetic analysis of the dynamics of love. This starting point can be summarized in a question: Is there a continuity or a break between the love of self and the love of God? In other words, in loving God must I renounce myself, or can I find the love of God along the same lines of the love I bear for myself? The medievals posed the question directly: "Utrum homo naturaliter diligat Deum plus quam semetipsum" ("Whether man naturally loves God more than himself").[30] Without entering here into all the complex meanderings of this debate,[31] we can take up Rousselot's interpretation, which he in turn refers to two "dynasties" of medieval authors. The fame and vast influence had by Anders Nygren's book *Eros and Agape*[32] documents the (even scientific) relevance the question possesses, even for our day.[33]

Rousselot asserts that there are two responses to our question, each of which identifies a very precise understanding of love sustained by two thought-traditions stretching from antiquity to the Middle Ages. He calls the first, which implies a continuity between love of self and love of God, a "physical" conception of love. The second, on the other hand, postulates a radical break between the two objects of love. Rousselot terms this latter the "ecstatic" conception, because the love of God (and in God the love of the other) requires a total going-out-of-self, an *exstasis*.[34] Rousselot is partial to the

29. Cf. P. Rousselot, *Pour l'histoire du problème de l'amour au Moyen Age* (Münster, 1908).

30. A similar question arises from Aristotle's affirmation in the *Nicomachean Ethics* 9.4.

31. Cf. Geiger's critique of Rousselot in L. B. Geiger, *Le problème de l'amour chez Saint Thomas d'Aquin* (Montreal and Paris, 1952). The necessary bibliographical references can be found in J. J. Pérez Soba, "¿La interpersonalidad en el amor? La respuesta de santo Tomás" (Ph.D. diss., Pontifical John Paul II Institute for Studies on Marriage and the Family, 1996, currently published only in part, as an excerpt).

32. Cf. A. Nygren, *Eros and Agape*, trans. Philip S. Watson (Philadelphia: Westminster, 1953).

33. A further confirmation can be found in P. Scarafoni, "Descrizione dell'amore secondo la grande tradizione cristiana," in *Alfa Omega* I (1998), 193-215.

34. The following passage from Dionysius the Areopagite's *On the Divine Names* 4.13 is a masterful expression of the ecstatic conception of love: "This divine yearning brings ecstasy so that the lover belongs not to self but to the beloved. This is shown in the providence lavished by the superior on the subordinate. It is shown in the regard for one another demonstrated by

"physical" conception of love, which he believes can be found even in the works of Aquinas.[35] The love of self and the love of God are in continuity. His thesis, which we cannot here document in detail, is substantially articulated in three points.

1. The love of God is the total expansion of the love of the "I." If the appetite can be conceived only as the search for self-realization, one can say that all the inclinations, even those which are altruistic, derive from the love of self.

2. The motivating force of the appetite is its tending to the ultimate end: wherever the appetite (in a wide sense) turns toward an object, it is the ultimate end which moves it. From here flows the second point: Why does man naturally love God more than himself? Because God, as the ultimate end, is the *bonum totius universi,* and thus also of all its parts. Man realizes, with naturalness, that the whole is greater than the part, and thus admits that God, the *Ipsum esse subsistens,* is more than the beings which participate in his being. In this way man, in loving God, loves himself!

---

those of equal status. And it is shown by the subordinates in their divine return toward what is higher. This is why the great Paul, swept along by his yearning for God and seized of its ecstatic power, had the inspired word to say: 'It is no longer I who live, but Christ who lives in me.' Paul was truly a lover and, as he says, he was beside himself for God, possessing not his own life but the life of the One for whom he yearned, as exceptionally beloved. And, in truth, it must be said too that the very cause of the universe in the beautiful, good superabundance of his benign yearning for all is also carried outside of himself in the loving care he has for everything. He is, as it were, beguiled by goodness, by love, and by yearning and is enticed away from his transcendent dwelling place and comes to abide within all things, and he does so by virtue of his supernatural and ecstatic capacity to remain, nevertheless, within himself. This is why those possessed of spiritual insight describe him as 'zealous,' because his good yearning for all things is so great and because he stirs in men a deep yearning desire for zeal. In this way he proves himself to be zealous, because zeal is always felt for what is desired and because he is zealous for the creatures for whom he provides. In short, both the yearning and the object of that yearning belong to the Beautiful and the Good. They preexist in it, and because of it they exist and come to be." *Dionysius the Areopagite: Selected Works* (New York: Paulist, 1987).

35. Cf., for example, Thomas Aquinas, *Summa Theologiae* I-II, q. 5, a. 8 ("Unde appetere beatitudinem nihil aliud est quam appetere ut voluntas satietur"); II-II, q. 25, a. 4 (". . . unicuique autem ad seipsum est unitas, quae est potior unione. Unde sicut unitas est principium unionis, ita amor quo quis diligit seipsum, est forma et radix amicitiae: in hoc enim amicitiam habemus ad alios, quod ad eos nos habemus sicut ad nosipsos; dicitur enim in IX Ethic. quod amicabilia quae sunt ad alterum veniunt ex his quae sunt ad seipsum"). The motivating force of the will is its tending toward the ultimate end; wherever the will seizes upon something, it is the ultimate end which moves it.

3. In order to affirm totality, man is ready for sacrifice. This sacrifice, precisely because of its positive foundation, will never be self-repudiation or self-annihilation, but the path to the full realization of the self.[36]

Those who uphold an ecstatic conception of love pose a radical objection to such a vision: the problem is not to know whether the part loves the whole more than it loves itself, but rather to know if it loves with an interested or a disinterested love. Consequently, that love of the will informed by reason, which chooses to love the other for the other's sake, is truly worthy of man. The personalization of love by freedom means its detachment from every sensible appetite man has in common with every other being. Only in this way is love true, objective, truly disinterested, a love which can and knows how to give the good, which receives the other in his absolute value and offers him the pure homage he deserves. This is the position Geiger, in a clear polemic with the interpretation of Rousselot, holds to be the authentic interpretation of Saint Thomas.

Notwithstanding our great generalizations, we can seek out the limits of both these positions in order to integrate them, and thus surmount them in a more complete and harmonious vision of human love. To begin with, both authors affirm the analogical structure of love, which in its turn is based on other central analogical notions, *in primis* those of nature and appetite. Thus, according to Geiger, Rousselot postulates in Thomas a unity and absolute continuity between love of self and love of God, because he conceives of the Thomistic notions of nature and appetite univocally (downright monistically). It seems to us that Geiger emphasizes the difference between the sensible and rational appetites to such an extent as to break the analogy, and make of these separate notions. With such bases, one can understand how the love of self can come to be "ecstatically" opposed to the love of God.

The question consists, then, in vigorously maintaining the analogical structure of love, which in turn rests on the analogical structure of nature and appetite. In order to understand this, it is necessary to turn briefly to the distinction between the *voluntas ut natura* and the *voluntas ut ratio*, introduced with regard to the human affective dynamism. To these correspond, as we have said, respectively *amor naturalis*, which precedes the will, and *amor electivus*, which is the fruit of a choice of the will (always informed by reason)

36. This third passage, which affirms the historical necessity of sacrifice, is linked to the most problematic point in Rousselot's thesis. We refer to the fact of sin. How can sin exist if the love of God and the love of self are in continuity? Rousselot responds to this objection by a reflection on the nature of man as a being composed of body and soul; this nature makes such a negative choice possible.

and thus capable of benevolence and egoism. Though Rousselot clearly notes this complex structure, he ends in collapsing elective love into *amor naturalis* or desire. He is not able to consider the difference between the two in adequate terms. The accent he places on their profound unity leads him to undervalue the specific modality of human love, which implies freedom. Contrarily, Geiger so insists on the specificity of this second type of love (i.e., human love) as to fail to take *amor naturalis* into account. In this sense Geiger is not immune from Lewis's subtle criticism: "It would be a bold and silly creature that came before its Creator with the boast, 'I'm no beggar. I love you disinterestedly.'"[37]

If it is true that Rousselot risks making the structure of love monistic, it is just as true that his claim to have found a common and permanent foundation between the two objects of human love is valid, and, it seems to us, in perfect agreement with Thomas. When Aquinas speaks of *amor naturalis*, he wants to safeguard on the natural level the analogical structure of love between all beings, and for this reason he understands *amor naturalis* as preceding the intervention of the will informed by the reason: "inclinatio enim naturalis in his quae sunt sine ratione demonstrat inclinationem naturalem in voluntate intellectualis naturae."[38]

Our critique of Geiger takes on all of its weight when we are dealing with the *voluntas ut ratio*, on the level, thus, of elective love which freely directs itself toward a good recognized as such by the intelligence. On this level it must be realized that the love of the good of God in himself and for himself is different from the natural appetite with which every creature loves God and tends toward him, loving his own good. To say "different," however, is not the same as to say "exclusive of" and "opposite": this is Geiger's mistake. In man, in fact, the "genus" of love proper to the *voluntas ut ratio* is inevitably rooted in the *amor naturalis* proper to the *voluntas ut natura;* this *amor naturalis* expresses the natural appetite for the good-in-itself proper to all beings. Even on the level of the most disinterested spiritual love, man continues to follow his own good; in this he follows his ultimate objective end and his subjective beatitude. Notwithstanding this, the intentionality of such a love is not necessarily turned toward the self in a greedy egoism, but can be turned toward the beloved — a beloved who is loved disinterestedly. Rousselot's thesis seems to be in need of some adjustment, with the scope of making it more rigorous.

In order to respond correctly to the opening question regarding the object of love (whether man naturally loves God more than himself), we must

---

37. Lewis, *The Four Loves*, 4.
38. Cf. Thomas Aquinas, *Summa Theologiae* I, q. 60, a. 5 co.

distinguish between the love of one's own good and the love of self.[39] The love of one's own good is situated on the level of the *voluntas ut natura* — that is, of *amor naturalis* — while the love of self emerges at the level of the will, as a rational appetite. The mistake usually made in speaking of love is identifying the love of one's own good with the egotistical love of self. Thus the love of one's own good is eliminated, as a factor that makes love inauthentic.[40]

Doing this, however — even in the name of the search for authentic love — obstructs the adequate personalization of love, because it does not give enough weight to the biological-psychological-spiritual totality of the person. Looking at the consequences of such an exclusion as a whole, one can better understand the importance of this integration. Let us first of all consider the question of "interested or disinterested" love, which represents the crux of the opposition between sustaining a physical and sustaining an ecstatic conception of love. If tending toward one's own good *(amor naturalis)* is identified on all levels with egotistical love, there are two possibilities: either one rejects any relation between love and the appetite (desire), as do the supporters of ecstatic love, or one concedes that every love is egotistical. In this case the love of benevolence for the other and for God will never be possible. When Geiger criticizes Rousselot, he in fact brings to light what is lacking in this distinction between love of one's own good and the love of self, and the harm which flows from it, especially in connection with the Christian understanding of love as the gift of self. On the other hand, Geiger is absolutely mistaken when he affirms, "To be disinterested, love must exist outside the sphere of our own

---

39. Cf. A. Wohlman, "Amour du bien proper et amour de soi dans la doctrine thomiste de l'amour," *Revue Thomiste* 81 (1981): 204-34; Wohlman, "L'elaboration des elements aristo-téliciens dans la doctrine thomiste de l'amour," *Revue Thomiste* 82 (1982): 247-69. A solution to this question which follows Thomas's thought is also proposed in Soba, "¿La interpersonalidad en el amor?" 540-50.

40. Nygren founds his *destruktion* of the Catholic concept of love precisely on this erroneous presupposition: "Hence arises the problem that has made itself felt in different contexts and in the most varied forms through the whole of Christian history ever since: the problem of Eros and Agape. No long familiarity with this problem is needed to show that it is of a very peculiar kind. Its peculiarity can be plainly seen from the following facts: first, that in Eros and Agape we have two conceptions which have originally nothing whatsoever to do with one another; and, second, that in the course of history they have none the less become so thoroughly bound up and interwoven with one another that it is hardly possible for us to speak of either one without our thoughts being drawn to the other. . . . There cannot actually be any doubt that Eros and Agape belong originally to two entirely separate spiritual worlds, between which no direct communication is possible. They do not represent the same value in their respective contexts, so that they cannot in any circumstances be rightly substituted for one another" (*Eros and Agape*, 30-31).

good; this is the definition of disinterestedness. . . . If love-appetite is placed at the heart of disinterestedness, this disinterest is secretly corrupted and decays."[41] According to this logic, there is no longer any possibility for disinterested love; such a disinterest is structurally incompatible with the human being, who is a contingent creature and, as such, in a continuous, insuppressible tending toward his perfection and end through his every act. A creature that renounces tending toward its own good denies its very creatureliness. In the end, man seeks disinterested love in vain, following the path traced out by Geiger. Not even the creative love of God, though in him there is no sensible appetite, would escape such a vision: God himself cannot will anything outside of his own goodness, outside the pure love of his own Good. This means, in the concrete, that the sensible appetite (desire) in man is acknowledged in all its dignity. There is a continuity between the sensible and rational appetites: desire, in virtue of the unity of the "I," traverses both these territories. To deny this would mean to set out along the path of Lutheran pessimism, which led Nygren to his radically ecstatic vision of love in which neither Augustine nor Thomas can be salvaged. In affirming the *amor naturalis* of the creature toward God, asserts Nygren, both Augustine and Thomas leave Catholicism with the inheritance of the aberrant notion of an "egotistical charity."[42]

One must therefore recognize the possibility of a love-desire of one's own good which is a disinterested love (against Geiger), or if this is preferable, the possibility of a love of one's own good which is not the egotistical love of self (against Rousselot).

The above clarifications allow for the adequate conjunction of the love of one's own good, the love of self, and the love of God (and thus, derivatively, the love of one's neighbor). The love of self, says Rousselot, is the measure, root, and model of all loves. We can make this more precise: the love of one's own good, not the love of self! The love of one's own good, when perceived objectively, is this measure. It is right to say that every act of love, even the most radically disinterested, implies a certain "taking pleasure" *(complacentia)* of the subject in his own good. This *complacentia*, which is the profound expression of the love of desire on the level of the *voluntas ut natura*, seeks its actualization precisely through an act which marks the boundary between the *voluntas ut natura* and the *voluntas ut ratio*. It is an affective election implying a conscious intervention of the reason; Wohlmann calls it an act of "affective reflection." Only this reflexive act opens the way either toward benevolence or toward an egotistical love of self.

41. Geiger, *Le problème*, 25 n. 3.
42. Cf. Nygren, *Eros and Agape*, 681ff.

Thus, every love implies the subject's love for his own good. However, this love cannot be defined as egotistical because it is exercised before the question of interest or disinterest comes into play. It is an original "taking pleasure" which the subject cannot *not* encounter on the path toward his realization: it is a natural datum in the strong sense. This love of one's own good always takes place on the level of the natural appetite-desire for God. God is the terminus of desire, analogously with the fact that he is the end of the natural appetite of every creature. On this level, I love God as he who is the fullness of my own good, the Good who fulfills my nature. When, moreover, the act of affective reflection intervenes — that is, the *voluntas ut ratio* — then this *complacentia* can open itself to the conscious love of benevolence, or involve itself in egoism. At this point, and only at this point, I can love both God and myself either egotistically or with benevolence.

To verify our thesis, which in fact describes the dynamism of the personalization of the inclination to love, we can pose a radical question. What does that evangelical invitation to deny ourselves to follow Christ mean? It means losing oneself in order to find oneself! Poverty of spirit, too, and that radical form of the *sequela Christi* which is the choice for consecrated virginity are born from this "desiring" structure of the "I." Let us be more precise: love of self is illegitimate when it implies a choice of the self as ultimate end in the place of God, or against God. One must go as far as despising oneself, says Augustine. Thomas, in the perspective he traces out, meets Augustine when he affirms that sin consists in using what ought only to be enjoyed and in enjoying what ought only to be used. God can never be used, and nothing in the end can be enjoyed but God. For this reason every human good, however legitimate, must be enjoyed in the detachment of the poor in spirit.

With this said, it is clear that God is the ultimate "terminus" of a *complacentia* (desire) that must be fulfilled in conscious, lucid, and filial benevolence. For Thomas the most beautiful act of freedom in the love of God consists in adhering, fully, consciously, whatever the price, to the natural movement toward God inscribed in the desire of our created nature to realize its own good. In the face of the ontological impossibility of satisfying his desire for the infinite, which the consequences of sin have transformed into an open wound, man realizes that he is lacking and can, consciously, open himself to the gift of grace.

So we see that a profound correspondence exists between affection and love. It is along the lines of this correspondence that the natural dynamisms are personalized.

4.4. Sexuality

These observations regarding the subject (affection) and the object (love proper) of the dynamism of love represent the key for an adequate discussion of sexuality. We have already seen, beginning with *Mulieris Dignitatem*, how John Paul II's teaching has brought the salient characteristics of man and woman to light.[43] The pope's teaching draws on the tradition and the thought of numerous theologians and philosophers in order to focus on the conviction (confirmed by fundamental human experience) that sexual difference represents an original dimension of the human being.[44] This conviction rests upon two foundational affirmations which indicate the originality of John Paul II's teaching on the subject.

The first involves the principle that in the sphere of contingent reality, unity is always given within a polarization. Unity (like the rest of the transcendentals: the true, the good, the beautiful) is always *dual* unity. From this flow the meaning and the (asymmetrical) nature of that reciprocity proper to man and woman,[45] as well as a broadening of the doctrine of the *imago Dei*. The image of God no longer simply points to an analogy between the individual human being and God, but suggests an analogy between the communional *qualitas* which exists in the trinitarian God and the communion between man and woman.[46] From this basis arises the second affirmation, also indicated in *Mulieris Dignitatem:* human sexuality in itself is part of the *imago Dei*.[47]

Let us pause for a moment once again on this second thesis. The expression "we are made in God's image" must not deceive us: ours is a likeness which opens up within an abysmal unlikeness.[48] Since man, according to the nature of his origin, comes from nothing, the doctrine of the *imago Dei* defines him beginning with a twofold distance: from God and from nothingness. It is precisely in the humble recognition of his abysmal distance from God, that is, of his coming from nothing, that man realizes the highest possi-

---

43. Cf. above, pp. 3-20.
44. Cf. John Paul II, *The Theology of the Body: Human Love in the Divine Plan* (Boston: Daughters of St. Paul, 1997), 25-102; cf. *MD* 6-8.
45. Cf. infra, pp. 92-96.
46. Cf. above, pp. 21-31.
47. Cf. above, pp. 32-52.
48. Cf. Thomas Aquinas, *Scriptum super Sententiis* II, d. 16; Denzinger-Schönmetzer, *Enchiridion symbolorum*, 806 (hereafter DS). On man created in the image of God in the thought of Thomas, cf. A. Scola, *La fondazione teologica della legge naturale nello Scriptum super Sententiis di San Tommaso d'Aquino* (Freiburg, 1982), 213-56.

ble level of his likeness to God. This is the authentic meaning of man's being a creature, made *ad imaginem Dei.*

What is the nature of this creaturely relationship which marks the human "face" simultaneously with a likeness and an irreducible nonlikeness to his Creator? Where does creation come from? In good theology we must respond: from the Trinity. For this reason the relationship between the archetype (God) and the creaturely image (man) has its source in an intratrinitarian relationship. The Son originates from the Father in such a way that all the Son's being is in relation to the thought and will of the Father. The love (nexus) which establishes itself between the two co-spirates the Holy Spirit, the incandescent nucleus of the trinitarian life, the overflowing seal (the *Donum doni*) of the incommensurable love of the two.[49] In creating, the trinitarian God carries these intratrinitarian relations outside himself, through the missions of the Son and the Spirit.[50] Man, created within this distance, is however still "like," because he is created in the Son. In Him is impressed the light of God *(signatum est super nos lumen vultus tui, Domine)*, the sign of the trinitarian relations. If, then, the mainspring which moves the trinitarian life itself is the inexhaustible love between the Father and the Son which subsists in the Holy Spirit, love is the principle of creation. The creature, in all his expressions, cannot but be an echo of this original event of love which is the Trinity. Moreover, if intratrinitarian love is characterized by a constitutive fruitfulness — identified with the person of the Spirit who, with the Father and the Son, is equally God — the human creature, too, must in some way repropose that fruitfulness as a sign of the trinitarian fruitfulness. Here a reason emerges for the existence of sexual difference: we see why man is created as man and woman.

Nevertheless, precisely because the human being is created in a twofold distance, his fundamental vocation cannot but possess the character — or better yet, the interior form — of a dependence on God, full of reverence. The creature must maintain himself as such, that is, must distinguish himself ever more from God through the humility of a service full of zealous fear, in order to be truly like him. Human love must take up the divine will into a human will to realize it.

What has been said thus far is a foundation from which we can attempt to understand the nature of the sexual reciprocity[51] between man and woman, that is, of the "unity of the two."

49. Cf. *CCC* 253-56.
50. Cf. J. Prades López, "De la Trinidad económica a la Trinidad inmanente," *Rivista Española de Teología* 58 (1998): 1-59.
51. Cf. infra, pp. 92-96.

What does this mean, after all? The mystery of the man always, in some way, lies with his "counterimage," the woman, and vice versa, that of the woman with the man. And yet this "other" which the woman represents for the man and the man for the woman can never be dominated: there remains an element of difference between the two, which indicates their irreducibility. Within human nature, identical in each one, sexual difference emerges as the factor constituting the human being as a dual unity. The one is ordered to the other as to its fullness, so much so as to be inseparable from the other, and yet the one remains ungraspable for the other. The reciprocity of man and woman cannot be understood without an understanding of this insuppressible polarity. Man and woman cannot *not* tend toward one another in a constitutive tension, because the Creator has ordained them so, and yet the two remain diverse even when, having left father and mother, they become one flesh (cf. Gen. 2:24). This is the notion of asymmetrical reciprocity. Each human being thus experiences creatureliness and contingence even in his flesh.

At this point an important remark is necessary: one must not think that sexual union eliminates the radical experience of contingence, connatural to every human being, as if such a joining could produce an absolute, resting content in itself. Nothing could be more false! In fact, a child is normally (the adverb has here an ontological depth) born from this union, who obliges the two to leave the subjective sphere and reveals the fullness to which not only sexual union but reciprocity made up of polarity is ordered.

Here we find three factors, a natural trinity we cannot treat as casual. We must recognize it as the expression or, rather, the seal the Trinity leaves in man upon creating him, the imprint which makes man to be in the image of God. The copy of the original model, in this case man as sexually differentiated, does not only repropose the trinitarian structure (man-woman-child); rather, the very dynamism circulating among the lowercase three circulates among the uppercase Three: the *qualitas* of communion. We would like to indicate this with an expression which comes from the ancients, even though Christianity renewed it in freedom: *amor diffusivus sui.* Now we can clearly understand why the sexual nature of created man is part of his being in the image of God. Fecundity is an attribute the Creator attributed also to plants and animals. After creating plants and animals, God decided to make man in his image and likeness, so that man might rule over what had already been created. The expression "image of God," therefore, which includes sexual difference, is inserted as the discriminating element between subhuman and human fecundity. What is human fecundity? What is the content of human generation? Here the fracture between the fecundity of inframundane beings and human fecundity once again appears. Inframundane beings reproduce their whole nature in new exemplars of the species. And man? The response comes to us once again from the Bible. After the curse of the fall, Eve, giving birth to Cain, exclaims, "I have gotten a man with the help of the LORD" (Gen. 4:1). Beyond theological questions regarding the creation of body and soul, though these are very important, we note that the fruit of fecundity is represented by another man, singular and nonrepeatable, himself in the image of God.

In Eve, as in every woman and every couple who contemplate the mystery of generation, there is a clear feeling that the newborn child is not a "thing" belonging to the two parents, but is in immediate, strict dependence upon God. This means that the mystery of human conception contains within itself the insertion of the human being's procreative power within the creative power of God. Making himself available to the point of the creation of the first man, made in his image, God does not disdain a certain self-abasement by which, from the beginning, he makes his creation depend on a process (procreation) left in the hands of the creatures themselves.

On these bases we return yet again to the central core of our discussion, that is, to the question of masculinity-femininity as constitutive of the human being. We have already spoken of the limit of sexuality, tied to man's contingent nature. This contingence is the very foundation of the asymmetrical reciprocity between the two sexes. The man is constitutionally ordered to the woman precisely because the two remain so radically diverse as to be ungraspable.

The sin of origins adds a grave flaw to this original structure of sexuality — a structure which signifies nothing else than that man can realize himself, in this sphere, too, only by making the will of God the form of his own will. The fall produces a debilitation of sexuality: "the union of man and woman becomes subject to tensions, their relations henceforth marked by lust and domination."[52] Sexuality does not become evil in itself — it is important to stress this against the ever present temptation to Manicheism in this field — but it falls from purity and its original destination.

The book of Genesis tells us that before the fall, Adam and Eve were naked and not ashamed.[53] "In true love, the soul enfolds the body." This affirmation of Nietzsche's can describe how, in the original state, the sexual sphere enjoyed a particular situation of innocence. The intelligence and the will, too, possessed the same prerogative. The two were, as it were, veiled and polarized in the faith-dependence of Adam and Eve before God. Thus, when they disobeyed, they found themselves naked, in intellect and will even before the body. They began to distinguish between good and evil. They had been

---

52. *CCC* 400.
53. Cf. Gen. 2:25.

told that they were not to eat of the tree of the knowledge of good and evil. Eating of it, they experienced what it means to be able to distinguish between good and evil. At their own expense they learned the drama of critical freedom. Intelligence and will had been so involved in the act of faith that they did not need to be critically recognized, since the surrender involved in faith carried everything in it. When they disobeyed, the couple found themselves naked with respect to the critical intellect and free will.

Returning to the question of original nakedness, we can perhaps say that in Adam and Eve purity of soul invested their bodily nakedness with a particular light, without either of the two having to fear a concupiscent gaze arising in the other. In Eden the shadow of concupiscence did not exist, and love would have been fruitful with a fecundity different from the one we know. As a result of sin, the natural powers of the body *(virtutes)*, analogously to the natural powers of the soul (intelligence and will), were automatically emancipated or separated from loving fruitfulness — all the more so since love had already been betrayed in disobedience — and these, not without violence, seized upon sexual love. Original sin stains sexuality as it stains the exercise of freedom.

Thus, in the state of fallen man there emerges a difference between virginity and fecundity, which tends to place them in opposition. In the original state Eve's virginity was not threatened by motherhood; in her, love moved from the spirit and invested the body with its unifying power, bringing the body into its service. This happened according to the mode of an innocence that ultimately flowed from a radical obedience. This obedience can in itself be defined as virginity, as its root. What do those who choose the path of virginal consecration do when they renounce the exercise of their sexuality in a strict sense? They choose innocence. That is, they choose to offer this aspect of their "I" for the sake of an obedience full of love, when confronted with a specific call of God which promises, precisely in renunciation (detachment), an even fuller possession.

With the fall Adam renounces this loving and innocent abandonment to the Other and makes his will autonomous, contrasting it to the will of God. Every opposition is also an affirmation. In order to affirm himself Adam opposes himself, and therefore sets out with his descendants on the often sorrowful path of historical existence (sin radicalizes the drama of contingence).

Scripture documents the wound in fallen sexuality in two ways. First, "in pain you shall bring forth children" (Gen. 3:16). Sexuality is connected to pain, which is corruption, decay, an anticipation of death. For this reason sexuality in its destination (fecundity) is tied to death even more markedly than it is in the normal progression of the species. This is a fact that cannot be underestimated. Here death makes its metaphysical weight felt. It can no longer be thought of as the natural process of a cycle of life reaching an end. Death becomes a repellent tragedy. Catholic dogma has always posited a link of direct causality between original sin and death; this highlights the appearance of self-annihilation, which because of sin is connected to dying.[54]

The word of God to the woman, "your desire shall be for your husband, and he shall rule over you" (Gen. 3:16), reveals yet another distinctive sign of fallen sexuality: the affective power that lies at the origin of one of the greatest forms of human slavery. Sexuality is no longer freshly surrounded by the powers of the soul, which allow the body to radiate the beauty of the person, but can become an expression of the will to power, of the one human being's domination over another to the point of making the other a thing. With regard to this, Scripture seems to reveal a different way of relating of woman to man. The woman's power seems to be tied to an instinct of seduction, while that of the man is more directly, brutally expressive of a will to power.

Pain (death) and the will to power make of sexuality the dramatic "place" of the division within man and between men. As much as the dominant culture exerts itself, in a sort of merry nihilism, to reduce sexuality to a lucid level, sexuality does not cease dramatically to reveal man to man.

These are the consequences of original sin for human sexuality which, even after the redemption, are left to man in view of the struggle of freedom for its own truth.[55] If, however, sin is not the last word — because the last word is Jesus Christ, who has died and is risen — we are justified in asking ourselves how man is called to live his sexuality, beginning from the redemption. The redemption communicates a different quality of the man-woman relationship, established in the sacrament of marriage. Christ indissolubly joins the man-woman relation, proper to Christian marriage, to his own relation with the church, such that these two realities can no longer be interpreted separately from one another. The relationship between the man-woman and Christ-church pairs is now so closely linked that each of the two mysteries can be understood only in the light of the other.

4.5. Toward the Nuptial Mystery

What does sexuality become in the perspective of redemptive justification? Redemption is, before all else, incarnation. Let us pause for a moment on three fundamental aspects of the redemption worked by Christ.

---

54. Cf. Rom. 5:12; DS, 1512.
55. Cf. DS, 1515.

In the movement of the incarnation, the primary factor is, so to speak, the descent of God. The Absolute can encounter the creature only by stooping toward it, from his own initiative and in total freedom. In this *descensus* the absolute love of God can acquire nothing for itself; it can only give. The total gratuity of the redemption, and therefore also of the incarnation, leads us to say that the agape of the incarnate Son of God — made up of his *kenosis* — is not prompted by any covetous Eros on the part of the creature. Christ, who incarnates agape, is in no way controlled or regulated by Eros, but is rather a pure positive, the pure gift of self. This is the first aspect we will touch upon: in the redemptive incarnation there is the agapic descent of the absolute good, which does not correspond to any erotic ascent. It is an absolutely agapic *initiative*, not the agapic response to an erotic motive.

The second factor is this: in a certain sense the descent of God is never ending. It begins in the virginal conception in Mary's womb and continues to death on the cross; from there it continues in the descent into hell and, above all, continues after the resurrection in the breaking of the eucharistic bread, where his real presence remains silently given through time and space. There is no dis-incarnation in the resurrection and ascension. God who has given himself agapically does not take himself back. In reality, what is produced by the power of the Spirit of the Risen One is a transfiguration of all that the Word has encountered in his incarnation: *quod est assumptum, est servatum.* Christ, the one sent, sets out in the incarnation into all things human (except sin). In rising and ascending into heaven he does not take himself away, but takes what he has encountered and transposes it into a new dimension of being, the new era. This is the dynamism of the birth and growth of the new man. The Holy Spirit is the *energia* making this transformation possible.

The church — and here we have the third factor — in the structure of the seven sacraments, is the reality which allows for the permanence of the salvific presence of Jesus Christ, incorporating into herself all who adhere to him. If Christ had not assumed a body, he could perform no such incorporation. Christ incorporates us into himself through his body as food and his blood as drink.[56] In this way the movement of the incarnation is definitively actuated as an ecclesial-cosmic movement: cosmic because the novelty of incorporation is proposed to everyone, and ecclesial because, through faith and baptism, incorporation into the Head, Christ, comes about through the body, the church.

What do these three anthropological-soteriological elements tell us about human sexuality?

56. Cf. 1 Cor. 10:16ff.

The fact that the flesh is rooted in the spirit (the body in the soul) means that the spirit penetrates the whole body and elevates it to the sphere of the spirit. The resplendent strength of the body lies in the fact that its transcendence — its rootedness in the spiritual — is also a progressive penetration of the body by the spirit, and a progressive elevation of the body into the realm of the spirit. In the supernatural rhythm of God's incarnation into the farthest depths of man, an analogous penetration is accomplished on the part of the Spirit. All that is bodily is penetrated by the Spirit, transfigured and transferred into the Son's kingdom.[57] From the point of view of human sexuality, this transfiguring dynamism of the redemption inaugurates a new mode of relationship between love, sexual difference, and generation, because it establishes a new relation between love and death. The link between love and death is no longer tied to the implacable cycle of the generation of the species, marked, moreover, by the mystery of sin. Christ's love is a unique love; it descends agapically from on high and enters into the generative cycle in order, within this cycle, to suffer a free death, thus snatching from death its sting and victory.[58] The Word, like a meteorite, inserts himself from on high into the closed circle of the generation of the species oriented to death, and breaks it, because he chooses *(sponte)* a free and personal death to conquer death. All this has to do with sexuality, inasmuch as it reveals a fruitfulness of love no longer tied to the relation between generation and death. In this sense Balthasar speaks of a suprasexual, though not asexual, fruitfulness. We prefer to substitute the term "nuptial" for "suprasexual."

In the interpretative key of the death and resurrection of Christ, the sexual reciprocity and fecundity of Eden are surpassed: a new kind of fruitfulness is inaugurated. The reason Balthasar calls this fruitfulness suprasexual revolves around the fact that it is a sexuality which forms its partner of itself: Christ forms the church. An analogy remains with the sleep of Adam and the birth of Eve, but there is a radical difference between the two. The deep sleep of death on the cross and the extraction of the church out of Christ's wounded side (blood and water) is profoundly different from Adam's sleep, out of which Eve originates. Christ's sleep of death is the absolute opposite of passive unconsciousness; it is the voluntary embrace of death. It is the giving of self unto death for the sake of agape, the source of eucharistic fruitfulness. Therefore, the relation between Christ and the church can be thought of in terms of suprasexual fruitfulness because it is a relation that is not asexual. The Bible's nuptial

57. Cf. Col. 1:13.
58. Cf. 1 Cor. 15:55-56.

language confirms this: Christ the Bridegroom of the church-bride. Moreover, the church is the *body* of which Christ is the Head.

With the redemption worked by Christ, there appears in history a model of fruitfulness distinct from, even if related to, the model of fruitfulness presented by man and woman. Even more, the sexuality of man and woman is, as it were, taken into the dynamic of this new sexuality in order to become the symbol of this new fruitfulness. The concept of sexuality mysteriously widens into that of nuptiality. Nuptiality can no longer refer only to the modality of the relation between man and woman; it becomes a way of viewing the relationship between God and man. We repeat that it is the Bible itself that uses this logic: Revelation speaks of the wedding feast of the Lamb to describe the definitive nature of Paradise. Hosea and Jeremiah already made use of nuptial symbolism to describe the relationship between God and his people. What is interesting is that sexuality receives a new meaning from this new, suprasexual (but not asexual) form of fruitfulness expressed in the relation between Christ and the church.

This broadening of the notion of sexuality into the more ample notion of the nuptial mystery might seem abstruse if it could not be verified in a series of important consequences, which can be summarized in a word: virginity. It becomes possible for man to transcend the sexual as a function of the species in favor of a form of life in which the agape (nuptiality) of God becomes the full meaning of existence. The choice of virginity, though it implies a renunciation, is not an escape from, but a different answer to, the question of sexuality. A *different* response, but one that is real and practicable. Since this experience of nuptiality is entirely — agapically — given from on high, it is never the response to Eros arising in human nature. To whom it is given, it is given. He who can understand, understands.

Thus the spouses' leaving of father and mother for the sake of the "one flesh" poised to procreate a new man, becomes, by the one called to virginity, the abandonment of the very series of generation. One can understand how, before Christ, this was considered madness. But now, "There is no one who has left house or brothers or sisters or mother or father or children or lands, for my sake and for the gospel, who will not receive a hundredfold . . . and in the age to come eternal life" (Mark 10:29-30). This is a stepping out of the series of generations in order to enter into a new kind of supratemporal generation: that between the new Adam (Christ) and his bride (the church). "Then came one of the seven angels . . . and [he] spoke to me, saying, 'Come, I will show you the Bride, the wife of the Lamb'" (Rev. 21:9).

The natural dynamisms of love — affection, love in a strict sense, and sexuality — are seized by the power of Jesus Christ, Bridegroom of the church, and are opened to the depths of the nuptial mystery. This mystery contains a plurality of meanings held tightly in unity by the law of analogy. The plurality allows us to shed light on every possible form of nuptiality, passing from one term to another of the analogy (for example, from man-woman to Christ and the church, and vice versa, as is done in the Letter to the Ephesians). The unity between these various meanings is demonstrated by the fact that in each one, in obviously different ways, the inseparable intertwining of sexual difference (suprasexual or nuptial in God), love, and fruitfulness is preserved.

CHAPTER 5

A Description of the Nuptial Mystery

5.1. Nuptiality and the "Debate concerning the *Humanum*"

"The only analogy nature seems to offer to the intimacy with the divine truth is the union of the sexes, though the analogy holds only if we omit the time interval between the union of the two persons in one flesh and its result in the birth of a child."[1] The attempt to grasp this assertion by Balthasar — which at first seems paradoxical — gives us a way into our theme, namely, the nuptial mystery at the heart of the church.

The mystery of *nuptiality* indisputably constitutes one of the essential aspects of reality, considered both in itself and against the horizon of Christian revelation. Without attempting a complete definition, it is sufficient to note that the word "nuptiality" refers in the first instance to the relationship between man and woman. There are, however, broader meanings of the term documented in the history of Western thought, linked to the image of the "couple" seen from the point of view of eros: from the "sacred marriage" between heaven and earth[2] to the Judeo-Christian theme of the nuptial relationship between Yahweh and his people or between Christ-Bridegroom and the church-bride. Such an image has indirectly given rise to some of the boldest speculations on the spousal relation in the domain of Christology and even regarding the Trinity.[3] Incidentally, we may point out that the diversity

1. H. U. von Balthasar, *Prayer* (New York: Sheed and Ward, 1961), 64.
2. Cf. R. Graves, *I miti greci* (Milan, 1983), 21-28; G. Bataille, *Visions of Excess: Selected Writings, 1927-1939*, vol. 14 (Minneapolis, 1985), as cited in G. Loughlin, "Sexing the Trinity," *New Blackfriars* 79 (January 1998): 18-25.
3. Cf. L. A. Schoekel, *I nomi dell'amore: Simboli matrimoniali nella Bibbia* (Casale Monferrato, 1997).

and depth of the various meanings suggest one of the reasons we call the nuptial relation a mystery.

In today's society, our view of marriage and our behavior toward it have been profoundly affected by the astounding technological and scientific possibilities of genetic engineering. I am referring, for example, to the phenomenon of cloning,[4] which may lead in the not-too-distant future to the systematic dissociation of procreation from sexuality. In this context the citation from Balthasar that we began with would seem *ex abrupto* naive and at odds with popular thinking. In the mentality of today's man or woman, the Swiss theologian's theory would seem to express more an unrealistic fantasy than an examination of the real data in all of its even brutal facticity.

Allow me nevertheless to set out the terms of the challenge which Balthasar's statement raises to today's dominant mentality, even if I acknowledge that the battle is so disproportionate that it recalls that between David and Goliath. Balthasar proposes to look at nuptiality as the inseparable intertwining of three factors: sexual difference (man/woman or gender), love, and procreation. Current thinking, on the other hand, has for quite some time conceived of love and sexuality as two separate realities and is already heralding the separation of procreation from sexuality as a great victory.

On the one hand, we note from the outset that the text from Balthasar is a single affirmation drawn from the context of his work as a whole. Time and again over the course of his voluminous writings he returns to this general theme and to the organically unified vision of human sexuality in particular. The Swiss theologian articulated this bold thesis deliberately and with full awareness that it represents a radical departure from the dominant mentality.[5]

On the other hand, the positions and questions which sustain the opposing theses are well known.[6] If the dream of Goethe's Faust to produce man in

---

4. Cf. P. H. Caspar, "La pecora Dolly e lo statuto dell'embrione," *Nuntium* 3 (1997): 111-18.

5. Cf. H. U. von Balthasar, *Theologik III: Der Geist der Wahrheit* (Einsiedeln: Johannes Verlag, 1987), 147: "Imagine for a moment that the act of love between a man and woman did not include nine months pregnancy, that is, the aspect of time. In the parents' generative-receptive embrace, the child would already be immediately present; it would be at one and the same time their mutual love in action and something more, namely, its transcendent result"; see also Balthasar, *Theo-Drama II: Dramatis Personae: Man in God*, trans. Graham Harrison (San Francisco: Ignatius, 1990), 411ff.; Balthasar, *Theo-Drama V: The Last Act*, trans. Graham Harrison (San Francisco: Ignatius, 1998), 85ff.; Balthasar, *A Theological Anthropology* (New York: Sheed and Ward, 1967), 306-14.

6. It should be said that this mentality would seem nowadays to be singularly related to the utilitarianism referred to by famous authors in the Anglo-Saxon world (for example, P. Singer, *Practical Ethics* [Cambridge, 1993]), which is presented as the most effective revival of that

a laboratory[7] were to become technologically possible on a large scale, what would be the consequences for human sexuality and procreation? Would not the anthropological perspective that has always accepted the intrinsic link between sexuality and procreation show itself after all to have been an illusion, due solely to partial and limited scientific and technological knowledge? More specifically, would not the Catholic insistence, forcibly reasserted by Balthasar,[8] on the indissoluble connection between the unitive and procreative meaning of the conjugal act seem arbitrary precisely because it is incapable of taking into account the fact that procreation and sexuality can be separated? Will this not run the risk, as some have already maintained,[9] of making the church less credible when she announces the central propositions of the faith regarding the one and triune God, and Jesus Christ the savior and redeemer of mankind, precisely because the magisterium would venture to make assertions contrary to scientific data and invade the delicate sphere of individual freedom?

The mystery of nuptiality, which rests on the interconnection of sexual difference, love, and fruitfulness, thus appears at the center of the "debate concerning the *humanum.*"[10] Moreover, precisely because it involves delicate and decisive questions for our current historical situation, the nuptial mystery sheds new light on the church's own mission, the basic purpose of which is to show how Jesus Christ, the decisive paradigm of humanity, is contemporaneous with all people in every period of history.

---

which Heidegger called *the calculating thought* understood as the result of scientific mastery given in the various technologies now common (see M. Heidegger, *Che cos'è la metafisica: Poscritto*, 9th ed. [Florence, 1985], 50-57).

7. Cf. Goethe, *Faust II*, act 2, 6819ff.

8. This belief is found in its most concentrated form in Paul VI's prophetic and controversial encyclical *Humanae Vitae*, vigorously taken up and developed in its anthropological and ethical foundations in the various discourses of John Paul II (*Familiaris Consortio, Mulieris Dignitatem, Veritatis Splendor, Evangelium Vitae*, and *The Theology of the Body* [Boston: Daughters of St. Paul, 1997]). This has also been organically developed in important aspects by the Instruction of the Congregation for the Doctrine of the Faith, *Donum Vitae*. For useful references with regard to this subject, see *Humanae vitae 20 anni dopo: Atti del II Congresso Internazionale di Teologia Morale* (Milan, 1989), and A. Scola, "Imago Dei e la sessualità umana: a proposito di una tesi originale della *Mulieris dignitatem*," *Anthropotes* (1992): 61-73.

9. This objection is examined in L. Scheffczyk, "Responsabilità e autorità del teologo nel campo della teologia morale: il dissenso sull'enciclica *Humanae vitae*," in *Humanae vitae 20 anni dopo*, 273-86.

10. Cf. John Paul II, "On the Occasion of the Opening of the Academic Year 1996-1997 of the Pontifical Lateran University," *Nuntium* 1 (1997): 15.

84

5.2. Toward the Center of the Nuptial Mystery

In order to proceed further along this path in specifying the general content of the nuptial relation and its burning relevance today, we must address two questions.

5.2.1. Why "Mystery"?

First, wherein is the dimension of mystery in the relationship between sexual difference, love, and procreation that forms the foundation of the nuptial relation? It is not difficult to intuit this dimension, since each of us has some experience of it, even if as with all essential aspects of human existence, we find it justifiably difficult to articulate. In the same way, it is much easier to form an idea of what it means to know or to love than it is to explain how the dynamisms that constitute these elementary factors might reach their objective. In any case, humanity, throughout the whole of its history, has shown that it realizes that the word "mystery" does not first of all come into play in order to identify how much in these constituent factors it surpasses or escapes us.[11] Instead, the word "mystery" reveals that in this ensemble of factors, the infinite[12] in some way makes itself present in the most intimate experience of the "I." Thus the substance of the mystery, present even in the basic experience of nuptiality, does not in the first place refer either to the aspects of the phenomenon that are still unknown in themselves or to the subject who experiences them. I would like to quote a short passage from the last book written by one of the most influential Catholic thinkers of the twentieth century, the French philosopher Jean Guitton. With a stroke of genius full of subtle self-irony, he describes his death, his funeral, and God's judgment on his life. He imagines that his soul, now separated from his body, converses with philosophers, poets, popes, and politicians. In the conversation that turns to the theme of love, the philosopher speaks to his wife and the poet Dante. Here Guitton writes this brilliant dialogue: "'Some get married because they love each other, others end up loving each other because they are married. The best would be to have both occur in every marriage.' 'Why do they end up loving each other after they are married? Is it perhaps the need to keep the promise we made?'" asks Guitton. His wife answers: "'If we're talking about

---

11. Cf. M. Scheeben, *I misteri del cristianesimo* (Brescia, 1960), 8-15 (*The Mysteries of Christianity* [London: Herder, 1946]).

12. Cf. C. Bruaire, *L'affirmation de Dieu: Essai sur la logique de l'existence* (Paris, 1964).

love, there has to be something else to it.' 'Marie-Louise, what is this something else?' 'It has to do with time and eternity.'"[13] Love reveals, on the one hand, that the heart of man is "capable" of infinity, and on the other hand, that infinity communicates itself to man. In this sense love is an encounter between eternity and time.

Through nuptiality we perceive that someone calls to us and sets our freedom into motion. In this way the Mystery dons the face of a real presence, though it continues to remain veiled. It is the face of a "thou" that strives in some way to enter into dialogue with us. As Balthasar says, the deepest nature of man is *dramatic*.[14] The "I" experiences at every moment a constitutive tension between its openness to the infinite totality of Being (a capacity for the Infinite) and the insurmountable limit that constitutes it. Concretely, the nature of the "I" is revealed in the gift that the Mystery, understood as the "tenacious vigor"[15] that holds together all things, makes of himself to finite freedom, communicating existence to it and holding it in being. If every moment of human existence is marked by this positive dramatic tension, it finds heightened expression precisely in the constitutive dimensions of fundamental human experience. Thus, when we speak about sexual difference, love, and procreation, we perceive that something of the substance of the "I" is at stake, something of its integrity here and now, as a being that is at once capable of self-possession and relations with another — ultimately, we catch a glimpse of the very Infinite that gives it existence.

The main consequence of this state of affairs, that is, of man's very nature, becomes apparent in the fact that when we speak about the essential dimensions of our person, we are unable to consider them as so many static elements closed in on themselves, able to be minutely analyzed through the biological, psychological, and social sciences. Instead, we realize that these dimensions represent open and dynamic factors; they are pathways, invitations that open the "I" to the ways upon which it can expand its fundamental experience and bring to light all its natural and supernatural riches. I can explain myself better by taking some examples from Western culture. Sexual difference, love, and fruitfulness have always been the way religious man has read the nuptial relationship in general, on the basis of which he grasped the relation between heaven and earth, which is fundamental in any view of the cos-

---

13. J. Guitton, *Il mio testamento filosofico* (Milan, 1997), 154-55.

14. Cf. Balthasar, *Theo-Drama II*, 335: "If we want to ask about man's 'essence,' we can do so only in the midst of his dramatic performance of existence. There is no anthropology but the dramatic"; and A. Scola, *Hans Urs von Balthasar: A Theological Style* (Grand Rapids: Eerdmans, 1995), 84-100.

15. Cf. the beautiful liturgical hymn "Rerum Deus tenax vigor."

mos as divine.[16] As awareness developed, and God was eventually understood as a supreme being, nuptial categories became the expression of the relationship between God and man.[17] Very surprisingly, Jewish revelation represented the covenant itself (which includes creation) between Yahweh and the chosen people by putting forward the most loving and passionate instances of nuptiality: lover and beloved, husband and wife, father and mother.[18] It is enough to recall the touching words of the prophet Hosea: "I will betroth you to me for ever; I will betroth you to me in righteousness and in justice, in steadfast love and in mercy. I will betroth you to me in faithfulness; and you shall know the LORD. . . . I will have pity on Not pitied, and I will say to Not my people, 'You are my people'; and he shall say, 'Thou art my God'" (Hos. 2:21-22, 25).

The category of "nuptiality," considered in the perspective of mystery, properly understood, acquires therefore various levels of meaning which nevertheless converge in a single point.

5.2.2. The Various Levels of the Nuptial Mystery

We should endeavor to explore this a little further by posing the second question: In what sense does the nuptial mystery, which we have just sketched out, lie at the heart of the church? There are at least two explanations. The first, to which we have already indirectly referred, is linked to the Christian conception of existence as a mystery of grace and freedom. The dramatic nature of the "I," of which the nuptial experience (sexual difference, love, and procreation) is an essential part, is obviously the raison d'être of the church herself, who proclaims Jesus Christ head of creation and redeemer of man and of history. Therefore, all the human phenomena directly connected to the nuptial experience — emotions, love, marriage, the family, maternity, paternity, fraternity, friendship, preference, even celibacy and consecrated virginity — have always constituted a privileged factor through which the church, mother and teacher, cares for men and women, intermediate communities, and entire peoples.

There is however a second reason, perhaps not as immediately obvious as the first, which shows how nuptiality lies at the heart of the church. This rea-

16. A concise vision of these themes in Mediterranean civilizations is found in *Le civiltà del mediterraneo e il sacro* (Milan, 1992).

17. Cf. J. Ries, *Il rapporto uomo-Dio nelle grandi religioni precristiane* (Milan, 1992), 67-92.

18. For a development of this theme, see A. Scola, *Questioni di antropologia teologica* (Rome, 1997), 11-41.

son is linked to the nuptial language employed by Scripture, the fathers of the church, the holy doctors, and more generally by the whole tradition of Christian thought — even if it occurs with different qualitative and quantitative emphasis — to describe the most elevated mysteries of our faith. From the sacrament of the Eucharist, where there is question of the *body*, and of the body given and the blood poured out by Jesus Christ, who redeems us and makes us fully brothers and sisters, to the sacrament of baptism, which, *incorporating us* (again we see the theme of the corpus) into Christ within the church, makes us *sons in the Son* (the fundamental familial relationship appears here as connected to nuptiality!), and finally, the very relationship between Christ and his church. In the Letter to the Ephesians this relationship is presented as that of a Bridegroom (the crucified body is pierced, and blood and water pour forth) with his bride, without spot or wrinkle.[19] In this relationship the mystery of the marriage between Christ and humanity also finds expression.[20]

Moreover, through the mysterious union of the two natures in the person of Christ Jesus, nuptiality reveals to us how the Father and Author of all fatherhood[21] condescends to every human being, lovingly offering his powerful mercy in his own Son crucified and risen, whom the Spirit makes explicitly present today in the church, his spouse. He is the sacramental victim given to our wounded freedom so as to redeem it and bring it to completion.

Yet even this is not the ultimate meaning of nuptiality, if, as Balthasar shows us in profound and fascinating pages, spousal categories are the least inadequate for stammering a few words about the ineffable life of the Infinite Supreme Being who, by grace, revealed to us his face in Christ Jesus.[22] The perfect relationship of love between the Father and the Son sends forth the Holy Spirit, who is at once the bond and the fruit of that love.

Precisely this last powerful assertion of the Swiss theologian enables us to gather into a unity the plurality of aspects that describe the nuptial mystery. It begins from the natural experience of the relationship between mother, father, and child and ends in the relationship of perfect identity in difference which characterizes the mystery of the triune God.

We can thus understand a little better why we defined nuptiality as a

19. Cf. Schlier's commentary on Eph. 5:27 in H. Schlier, *Lettera agli Efesini*, 2nd ed. (Brescia, 1972).

20. Cf. C. Giuliodori, *Intelligenza teologica del maschile e femminile* (Rome, 1991), 163ff.

21. Cf. Eph. 4:6.

22. Cf. Balthasar, *Theo-Drama II*, 411ff.; Balthasar, *Theo-Drama V*, 85ff.; P. Evdokimov, *Woman and the Salvation of the World: A Christian Anthropology on the Charisms of Women*, trans. Anthony P. Gythiel (Crestwood, N.Y.: St. Vladimir's Seminary Press, 1994).

mystery, in the full sense of the term, as Scheeben affirms in speaking about the Christian mysteries. In this sense "mystery" does not designate the unknown, but rather the One who communicates himself in a real way, remaining veiled in order to involve human freedom in a dynamic of fruitful love. At the same time, it perhaps becomes clearer how central the nuptial mystery is for the life of man, of the Christian, and of the church.

In the present context, it is not possible to develop a full account of the *analogical* levels characteristic of the nuptial mystery. I will therefore limit myself to reflecting on several elements implicated by the nuptial mystery; but I will consider these on the basis of the daily experience of those who strive to live their lives in Christ, or if they have not yet received the grace of an explicit encounter with Christ, those who at the very least are permeated with a religious outlook on life.

First of all, I would like to dwell on the general meaning of nuptiality, understood as the interconnection of sexual difference, love, and procreation. Then I will endeavor to show how the human experience of nuptiality lies at the heart of the church according to God's original plan.

As a side note, it bears remarking that it matters little for our purposes whether we speak of male/female, sexual difference, or — to use the English word — "gender." These expressions are not altogether synonymous. In fact, there are nuances of difference implied in these variations in vocabulary. As has been recently pointed out, it is not the same thing to talk about gender rather than sexual difference or maleness/femaleness.[23] A difference in expression can be a way of insinuating an ideological reduction of the reality of things. Thus, for example, the category of gender, especially when transposed into the context of a Latin mentality, may lend itself more easily than that of maleness/femaleness to nullifying the weight of physiological evidence that establishes differences between masculinity and femininity.[24] Nonetheless, on a general level such as ours, these differences do not significantly affect the meaning of things, and we may thus use the terms interchangeably.

5.2.3. Sexual Difference, Love, and Procreation

We have already said that, by the expression "nuptial mystery," we mean first of all the concrete experience of the man-woman relationship that lies at the very origin of the phenomenon of nuptiality in all its various types, and thus

---

23. Cf. P. Donati, ed., *Uomo e Donna in Famiglia* (Cinisello Balsamo, 1997).
24. Cf. G. Rossi, "Genere e sesso: Chi ha paura dell'identità femminile?" *Nuntium* (1998).

forms its constitutive core. Using the language of analogy, we might say this relationship represents the *analogatum princeps*. We see in this affirmation one of the most fundamental exigencies of the history of thought in general and of the tradition of Christian thought in particular, namely, its realism.[25] Human thought is made to grasp reality. It therefore communicates with reality. It is on this basis that human thought becomes capable of knowledge and at the same time of language, that is to say, of communication with others.

Today, however, thought's elementary capacity to relate to reality is very often ignored. I am convinced that conversion *(metanoia) is* necessary also in this respect. I am referring to the urgency of turning *(cum-vertere)* to things just as they are, to reality in itself. What we need today is a conversion "to the real." Only thus will it be possible to grasp the mystery of which reality itself is always the *sign.* A *real sign* — it is exactly this! In more technical terms, we could say that reality presents itself as an event *(e-venio)*[26] that calls on our freedom to adhere to it. Allow me recourse to Chesterton to express this structural listening to the real which, as it happens to us (this is what "event" means!), sets in motion the creativity of the "I." In the novel *The Napoleon of Notting Hill* we find the following paradoxical dialogue:

> "And then something did happen. Buck, it's the solemn truth, that nothing has ever happened to you in your life. Nothing has ever happened to me in my life." "Nothing ever happened!" said Buck staring. "What do you mean?"
>
> "Nothing has ever happened," repeated Barker, with a morbid obstinacy. "You don't know what a thing happening means? You sit in your office expecting customers, and customers come; you walk in the street expecting friends, and friends meet you; you want a drink and get it; you feel inclined for a bet and make it. You expect either to win or lose, and you do either one or the other. But things happen!" and he shuddered ungovernably.

25. Saint Thomas reminds us that while divine knowledge is the measure of reality, reality is the measure of human knowledge: "Veritas autem quae est in intellectu humano . . . non comparatur ad res sicut mensura extrinseca et communis ad mensurata, sed vel sicut mensurata ad mensuram, ut est de veritate intellectus humani, et sic oportet eam variari secundum varietatem rerum" [But the truth that is in the human intellect . . . is not related to things as an exterior and universal measure to what is measured, but as what is measured is related to the measure, as it is in the case of the truth of the human intellect, and so this truth has to vary according to the variety of things] (Thomas Aquinas, *De veritate* 1.4.1).

26. In this regard one can speak of "symbolic ontology": cf. G. Colombo, *La ragione teologica* (Milan, 1995); A. Bertuletti, "La 'ragione teologica' di Giuseppe Colombo: Il significato storico-teoretico di una proposta teologica," *Teologia* (1996): 1, 18-36; Bertuletti, *Il concetto di esperienza,* in *L'evidenza e la fede* (Milan, 1988), 112-81.

"Go on," said Buck, shortly. "Get on."
"As we walked wearily round the corners, something happened. *When something happens, it happens first, and you see it* afterwards. . . . It happens of itself, and you have nothing to do with it."[27]

This is the primacy of reality as an event that calls on our freedom!

Entering now more directly into the mystery of the man-woman relationship, we once again set forth the question that — in a simple and unparalleled manner — John Paul II posed in the striking catecheses on spousal love (theology of the body) at the beginning of his pontificate. I am referring to the following assertion: "The definitive creation of mankind consists in the creation of unity of two beings. Their unity above all denotes the identity of human nature; the duality, on the other hand, manifests what, on the basis of this identity, constitutes the masculinity and femininity of created man."[28] John Paul II took up this theme again even more explicitly in *Mulieris Dignitatem:* "It is a question of understanding the reasons and the consequences of the decision of the Creator that the human being would always exist only as female or male" (1).

Going back to things in themselves — listening to the real — when speaking about nuptiality means answering the demand to welcome the data that offers itself directly to the consciousness of each one of us. Every human being in fact comes into the world as a sexual being (man or woman), in the context of a parental relationship, and in most cases, at least until recently,[29] born out of a conjugal act that involves the love of a man and a woman (two persons of a different sex), regardless of the couple's intention. Because I am born from a father and mother, I thus stand within a constitutive relationship which our tradition identifies with the term "marriage," as the basis of the reality of the family. What does all of this mean?[30]

---

27. G. K. Chesterton, *The Napoleon of Notting Hill* (London: Wordsworth, 1996), 80-82.

28. John Paul II, *Theology of the Body,* 45.

29. Cf. P. Morande, "La imagen del padre en la cultura de la postmodernidad," *Anthropotes,* 1996, 241-59.

30. A great difficulty undermines the educational capacity of parents toward their children, but also that of the ecclesial body — parish, diocesan church or the universal church — toward engaged couples preparing for marriage. It is a question of their incapacity to give good enough reasons for the moral injunction, the "ought." With respect to responsible procreation, contraception, and premarital relations, this incapacity often comes from not beginning with things as they are, which in our case means starting with the real experience of the man-woman relationship: we come into the world as a man or woman within a familial context. We are the children of a modernity which, having separated the individual dimension from the social dimension of ethics, has ended by bracketing the foundation of reality as it presents itself, sitting

I will respond briefly using a somewhat technical expression, but one that until now has seemed the most effective to bring to a point all the data concerning nuptiality. Nuptiality, in its interconnection of sexual difference, love, and fruitfulness, manifests a *reciprocity* between me and another. This reciprocity bears a very peculiar characteristic which I call *"asymmetry." Asymmetrical reciprocity* (this is the technical term!) is thus the meaning of nuptiality.[31]

Let us begin with the category of reciprocity: its immediate meaning is quite clear. There exists another modality other than my own for embodying the total identity *(corpore et anima unus)* of the human person, namely, that of the woman. My existence as a sexual being means, in some sense, that I am placed from the beginning in relation to another. The other is presented to me as being identical in her own being as a person, but at the same time, because of sexual difference, she reveals to me a radical difference that distinguishes her from me at all levels. Thus if my way of embodying the identity of

---

in its place and otherwise compensating for it by laying emphasis on the "ought," and having lost the capacity to give (ontological) reasons for acting. By contrast, in the inevitable weaving together of the "is" and the "ought," only the perception of how "things are" — the perception of being — can guarantee the truth and the creative freshness of the "ought." Moralism (whether in the form of laxity or rigorism) is a serious threat, particularly in the domain of nuptiality. I always say to my students who are priests that we are like the father who, not expecting his son's request to stay out late at night, tells him, "No, no you can't." And confronted with a son who responds, "Why can't I?" he does not know how to give any reason but what amounts to no reason at all, merely an arbitrary recourse to the principle of authority: "Because I say so" or "Because that's the way it is." But to be able to offer genuine reasons, we need above all to know things as they are. In order to be able to offer to the student convincing criteria for the "ought," it is necessary to link this with the very being of things. It is not by chance that education was defined as *"an introduction to total reality."* (Cf. J. A. Jungmann, *Christus als Mittelpunkt religiöser Erziehung* [Freiburg, 1939], 20.) Only thus will the "ought" appear as profoundly fitting (let us recall the medieval sense of the term *convenientia:* cf. Thomas Aquinas, *Summa Theologiae* 3.1.1: "Respondeo dicendum quod unicuique rei conveniens est illud quod competit sibi secundum rationem propriae naturae" [I answer that that suits each thing which belongs to it according to the intelligible structure of its own nature]) and capable of interpreting the objective desire of the freedom of the person being educated with the undeniable need for "satisfaction" which accompanies it. It will thus be possible to obey even with great sacrifice: "Why torment yourself, when it is so easy to obey?" (Paul Claudel, *The Tidings Brought to Mary,* trans Louise Morgan Sill [New Haven: Yale University Press, 1916], 158).

31. We return to this important theme, with some further developments, infra, pp. 116-21. P. Vanzan speaks of asymmetrical reciprocity ("Uomo e donna oltre la modernità," *Famiglia oggi* 10 [1997]: 25-31), and quotes Rosetta Stella ("Il Papa e la crisi della modernità: Una reciprocità asimmetrica," *Prospectiva Persona,* December 1996). I reached the same formulation myself around 1987 in the context of my teaching at the Pontifical John Paul II Institute for Studies on Marriage and the Family.

person is masculine, the feminine mode that stands before me is *a different way* of being a person. The reciprocity that springs from sexual difference thus shows that the "I" emerges into existence from within a kind of constitutive polarity.[32] In order to be able to say "I" in the fullest sense, I *need* to take the other into account; I have the possibility of (that is, the resource for) taking the other into account. Therefore, the expressions "male-female," "sexuality," and "gender" identify in concise terms wherein the difference lies. A difference that comes to light within a unity[33] never destroys the unity of human nature, which belongs to each of the two.

Hence we speak of a "unity of the two," or a "dual unity." It is worth saying that man, as he exists here and now *(Dasein)*, is not a purely spiritual subject. We do not find spiritual subjects walking in the street; when we look at our son or daughter, we always see a male or female human being. We are dealing with a relationship that is intrinsically connected with the fundamental experience of the self-awareness of our "I," to such an extent that it is coessential with it. There is no reason to waste words here: it suffices to recall our mother's smile when we were children and how decisive this smiling and friendly *"thou"* was for us to be able to say "I" with greater force and energy.[34] It happens, for example, when we enter into a friend's house, that a child who does not know us might hide in his mother's skirts. Then when a conversation begins between his parents and the "stranger," the child enters the circle of communication; he detaches himself from the mother and moves toward the friend. In a certain sense the child realizes that the other is quite different, and this at first puts him on his guard. But then this diversity is eventually revealed to him as something good, as a resource that makes the "I" grow. The example shows us in passing that the "other" is obviously a category broader than that of the "other sex." Nevertheless, it is undeniable that the original and basic experience of otherness is founded on sexual otherness. It is not necessary to get involved in depth psychology to see this.[35]

32. On constitutive polarities, see Balthasar, *Theo-Drama II*, 346-94; Scola, *Hans Urs von Balthasar*, 84-100; R. Guardini, *L'opposizione polare* (Brescia, 1998).

33. It is useful to note that the dramatic anthropology alluded to here might perfect, without destroying, the classical anthropological conception of the *individual*, only bringing out the influence of the man-woman and individual-community polarities, as coessential with the body-soul polarity, which, as in classical anthropology, maintains its own priority. Cf. Scola, *Hans Urs von Balthasar*, 89.

34. Cf. H. U. von Balthasar, *L'accesso alla realtà di Dio*, in *Mysterium salulatis*, ed. J. Feiner and M. Lohrer, vol. 2, 5th ed. (Brescia, 1980), 19-57; Balthasar, "A Resumé of My Thought," *Communio* 15 (winter 1988): 468-73.

35. With regard to psychoanalysis and the Christian Weltanschauung, it is remarkable how often those who accuse Christian education of inflicting severe psychological damage are not so

Why in fact do we qualify this reciprocity as *asymmetrical?* I will explain by referring to a significant passage from Plato's *Symposium,* in which Aristophanes imagines that sexual difference — the existence of people as male and female — is due to the jealousy of a god who cut into two halves a being who initially formed a unity. Sexual difference would therefore indicate the path that the two halves would have to follow in the almost always failed attempt to recover the much desired original unity.[36] This androgynous vision of things, widespread today, is profoundly erroneous.[37] The error lies in the fact that reciprocity is "thought" as simple complementarity. On the contrary, sexual reciprocity is not simple complementarity, but possesses, rather, an important asymmetry, and this for at least two reasons. The first reason is quite obvious: every male and female lives simultaneously, and as if in his or her very foundations, a plurality of relationships with the other sex. My "I" is simultaneously a point of reciprocity for different persons of the other sex, each of whom has a different *status.* I am immediately related to my mother, sister, a female friend, etc., and when I relate to someone of the other sex, I am not at all polarized in a search for a fictitious other half of myself.

It is important to see, however, that this is nothing but the macroscopic expression of the true, radical meaning of *asymmetry.* Asymmetry consists in the fact that sexual difference, in a significant and immediate way, testifies that the other always remains "other" for me. One can even say that "the aspiration to overcome the duality of the sexes is more than just a tragic illusion: it is the death of love itself and of those who love."[38] We find a confirmation of this point in depth psychology (which is certainly not likely to "connive" with the Christian vision of things). Psychoanalysis, for example, clearly affirms that sexual difference, in a certain sense, cannot be overcome. It cannot be deduced, that is, it cannot be translated into concepts, because it is precisely the decisive practical point in which the "I" experiences that the "other" always stands before him as "other." At the very moment in which the "other"

---

quick to recognize how similar the two approaches are in their assertion of the irreducibility of sexual difference. It seems to me that a similarly unobjective attitude can be seen in some of Beattie's reflections in T. Beattie, "A Man and Three Women — Hans, Adrienne, Mary and Luce," *New Blackfriars* 79 (February 1998): 97-105.

36. Cf. Plato, *Symposium* 189d.

37. This androgynous mentality which is dominant nowadays is not the least reason for the spread of homosexuality and transsexuality and explains at the same time why these might be presented as legitimate sexual alternatives. Our judgment here is ontological, not ethical (cf. *Antropologia cristiana e omossessualità* [Vatican City, 1997] with contributions from D. Tettamanzi, A. Di Berardino, E. Cortese, R. Penna, V. Grossi, G. Zuanazzi, A. Bissi, G. Berti, F. D'Agostino, P. Schlesinger, B. Kiely, L. Melina, and J. L. Breguès).

38. G. Zuanazzi, *Temi e simboli dell'eros* (Rome, 1991), 76.

presents himself as the condition and the occasion for the fulfillment of the "I," this same "other" leaves the "I" at a distance, by saying repeatedly, "I am another for you."[39] This occurs even in that special place of unity between man and woman, in marriage, which is called the conjugal act. In this instance, to use the great expression of the Judeo-Christian tradition, the "one flesh" comes into being; and even in the "one flesh" the "other" remains "other" for me (asymmetrical reciprocity). Why is this?

The reason lies in the fact that the *difference between the two* (the man and the woman) *makes space for a third,* and this once again bespeaks otherness. The reciprocity does not cancel the difference because it is asymmetrical, since it exists not for the sake of androgynous union of two halves, but for the procreation of the child. This is the fruit that is essentially connected to the love of the two persons. To avoid misunderstanding, this assertion requires a few words about love.[40] Asymmetrical reciprocity, which we have been discussing, is rooted in man's instinctive nature, draws this instinctive desire from the unconscious, accompanies it in the preconscious, and manifests it as the ontological value that leads Saint Thomas to define desire as *amor naturalis.*[41] Therefore asymmetrical sexual reciprocity forms the anthropological foundation that makes the experience of love possible.

On this theme, too, C. S. Lewis comes to our aid. In his beautiful style full of subtle irony, he presents the theme of love. I am referring to his wise and delightful essay *The Four Loves.*[42] Lewis rightly rebels against the idea of using different words to describe the complex forms of the phenomenon of love. According to many thinkers, even some Christian ones, we should not use the word "love" for describing physical love and at the same time for speaking about spiritual or ecstatic love, which implies a going out of oneself. By contrast, Lewis maintains that all expressions of love fall under the same category, "love." Even the most degraded form of commercialized love, which he calls *Venus,* no matter how debased and disfigured it may be, does not cease to possess the traits of love and should be called "love." The fact that love is realized in degrees that are enormously different does not prevent these different degrees from retaining the name "love."

Now, human love has to take into account the constitutive dimensions of

39. The publications of the Jesuit Beirnaert are noteworthy on this point (L. Beirnaert, *Aux frontières de l'acte analytique* [Paris, 1987]; Beirnaert, *Experience chrétienne et psychologie* [Paris, 1966]).

40. Cf. above, pp. 55-81.

41. Cf. Thomas Aquinas, *Summa Theologiae* 1–2.26.

42. C. S. Lewis, *The Four Loves* (London: Fontana Books, 1960); Lewis, *Mere Christianity* (London, 1996), 84-100.

human nature, which is made up both of soul and of body. Love should not be thought of as something angelic, any more than it should be reduced to mere animal instinct. There must always be a unity, even at its highest level, between the instinctual, psychological, and spiritual dimensions. Nature is not opposed to freedom, but, as Saint Thomas teaches us when he talks about natural inclinations as one of the orienting foundations of natural law and ethics,[43] it offers freedom guidelines that the latter is called on to choose, and thereby personalize them. This is why we cannot speak about love without involving sexual difference and what this objectively signifies, namely, the objective orientation of the conjugal act toward procreation! In this respect, sexual reciprocity means "love" and at the same time, by reason of its asymmetry, an openness to the fruits of love, to fecundity, and procreation. This is not the occasion to work out in detail the intrinsic link that connects sexual difference, love, and procreation;[44] it suffices to emphasize that the asymmetry that characterizes sexual reciprocity is necessary because of the fact that the two persons who come together in "one flesh," regardless of the degree of awareness with which the act occurs (although this is of course also important), are taken up into a dynamic that opens them to the procreation of a child who is the very fruit of love according to the vision that has quite rightly permeated the whole Western world: *amor est diffusivus sui.*[45]

5.2.4. The Foundation of the Nuptial Mystery

It is possible at this point to understand how the structure of human sexuality is part of a design in which we are called to participate. Welcoming this call belongs to the religious sense that characterizes humanity. The person who perceives the dimension of mystery connected to nuptiality recognizes in its constitutive factors signs through which Mystery itself calls on the person. Whoever, on the other hand, claims to deny this religious sense will be led to read the phenomenon of nuptiality (sexuality, love, fruitfulness) as something closed in on itself. This person will constantly be tempted to reduce nuptiality to the realm of the intracosmic and will not be able to see how our

43. Cf. Thomas Aquinas, *Summa Theologiae* 1–2.91.2; Scola, *Questioni di antropologia*, 131-38.

44. Cf. infra, pp. 110-26.

45. Cf. A. Scola, *Identidad y diferencia* (Madrid, 1989), 39f. The original axiom from Saint Thomas speaks of *bonum diffusivum sui*, for example in *Summa Theologiae* 1–2.1.4. Cf. J.-P. Jossua, "L'axiome *bonum diffusivum sui* chez saint Thomas d'Aquin," *Recherches de Science Religieuse*, 1966, 127-53.

nuptiality could contain in itself that remarkable openness of nature, with all its biological and psychological laws but also its reason, toward the transcendent. The experience of sexuality gives rise to an interaction between nature and culture which contributes to fulfilling not only the history of each "I," but at the same time the history of humanity as a whole, allowing also for an authentically ecological relationship, that is, a fully healthy relationship, with the universe.

Religious man finds it natural to let this threefold asymmetrical reciprocity call on him and provoke him to ask why things are as they are: we only need think of the amazement a newborn child stirs up in the hearts of its parents. This is an amazement full of humility because of the disproportion of such a gift, as it were. It is a humility that raises the heart toward the Author of life and causes us to fall on our knees in adoration and at the same time fills us with awe for being so unworthy of the gift received.

For the religious man who is a Christian, that is to say, for the one who has encountered in the person of Christ a powerful and adequate response to religious yearning, the provocation that arises from the asymmetrical reciprocity of sexuality marks only the beginning of an exhilarating road that leads, by grace, to the heart of the Mystery himself.

In this regard revelation, as manifest in Scripture and as abiding in "the place of practice and experience" that Blondel called tradition[46] — the place that joins us in unbroken continuity to the group of friends who lived with Jesus by the lake of Gennesaret, who participated in the important and dramatic final events in Jerusalem, and who were able to touch the wounds of the Risen One with their own hands — proposes the nuptial mystery as the key for understanding (by analogy, of course) the salient aspects, the dogma, of our faith.

It is useful here to list in order the three most fundamental aspects. First of all, there is the relationship between Christ and the church that is presented, particularly in chapter 5 of Ephesians, as a relationship between a bridegroom and a bride.[47] Then there is the existence of the two natures in the one person of Jesus Christ as the foundation[48] that makes possible the "one flesh" of the two spouses that stems from the sacrament of marriage.

---

46. Cf. M. Blondel's essay, "History and Dogma," in *The Letter on Apologetics and History and Dogma,* trans. Alexander Dru and Illtyd Trethowan (Grand Rapids: Eerdmans, 1994).

47. Cf. A. Vanhoye, "'Il grande mistero': La lettera di Ef 5, 21-33 nel nuovo documento pontificio," in *Dignità e vocazione della donna: Per una lettura della "Mulieris dignitatem"* (Vatican City, 1989), 146-53; H. U. von Balthasar, *Explorations in Theology,* vol. 2, *Spouse of the Word* (San Francisco: Ignatius, 1991), 143ff.

48. Cf. Giuliodori, *Intelligenza teologica,* 194-97.

Finally, there is the nuptial dimension within the Trinity,[49] where the difference between the divine persons dwells in perfect unity as the cause and reason for the possibility of unity in difference which is proper to the man-woman relationship.

We will return later in this volume to the various contents of the nuptial mystery. For now, we will limit ourselves to two anthropological considerations which carry an important practical significance. In the first place, it is worth repeating that when we speak about the nuptial mystery at the heart of the church, we are not only referring to the experience of asymmetrical reciprocity given to us in the love between a man and a woman, but we are moved by faith itself to inquire into the relationship between Christ and the church, the event of Christ, and the mystery of the Trinity. The mystery of nuptiality shows itself to be harmoniously unified and complex at the same time!

The question now arises: How is it possible to hold all these meanings in a unity and justify them, without becoming vulnerable to the objection that we have thereby left the field of the verifiable experience of human sexuality to end up prey to arbitrary constructions, perhaps the fruit of the fervent imagination of some particularly well versed theologian, but alien to everyday practical human existence? Here again we meet with David's battle with Goliath which we mentioned at the outset. To address this objection, we have to penetrate deeply into the logic of Christianity and grasp its profound nature. *This is the logic of the incarnation or of the sacrament.*[50] I believe that one of the most serious temptations that besets Christians today is spiritualism. What I mean is the often unintentional but nevertheless serious way some people have of looking at Christ's ascension as a disincarnation. It is fairly common, even among Christians, to find the practical belief that, ultimately, the event of Christ does not succeed in being present materially in the here and now of history. Jesus Christ is not considered effectively present to every person of every age. He is treated like a fact of the past! If this is so, then Jesus Christ ceases to be an event! Even if he could be considered the paradigmatic model for human behavior, he will invariably be reduced to a hypothesis. Thus his truth and his substance will be lost. In my opinion we have here one of the most insidious objections to Christianity. Arising with the Enlightenment, this unresolved challenge continues to surface, as forcefully as ever, in the experience of both the individual and the Christian community, especially in the interreligious and multicultural context which today characterizes the mission of the church. Christ is treated like a fact of the past, a noble

49. Cf. Giuliodori, *Intelligenza teologica*, 117-33.
50. Cf. Scola, *Questioni di antropologia*, 43-53.

98

metaphor that inspires our conduct. By contrast, the logic of the incarnation is the logic of the *real sign* which, according to *the form of the sacrament*, makes the event of Christ present to the freedom of modern man, calling him to follow. This logic leads us to read every circumstance, every relationship, as a sign of Christ's happening for me here and now. It is only in this perspective that the fundamental human experience is flooded with light at every level, including that of the asymmetrical reciprocity found in the man-woman relationship.

Here not only is the "I" called to make room for the "other" in order to say "I," but the two spouses are moreover led, in a certain sense, to transcend themselves as unity-of-two (a dual unity) so as to welcome a third person, the child. This reveals that in the reality of the very love that unites the two, there is an inherent moment of ascent toward a mysterious *"Quid."* Thus the question concerning what lies behind this ascending dynamism becomes even more acute. Balthasar helps us find an answer. He asks himself: "When the trinitarian God . . . creates the couple, what does he create? What is the original couple in the mind of God?" According to the theologian from Basel, God first had in mind the perfect archetype of the couple, namely, Christ the Bridegroom and the church his bride.[51] The experience of the man-woman relation thus encounters its fullest meaning, which is its final (eschatological) and for this reason primordial meaning, only in reference to this original relation. The truth of nuptiality is thus contained in the modality by which Christ generates his bride in the total self-gift of the cross, and continues his relationship with her according to the logic of the sacrament.

From this perspective, it becomes clearer what it means to speak of the family as the domestic church. In the first place, the expression does not mean that the family is a particular cell in a large diocesan community in the formal-juridical sense. If it did, we would be left with the difficult task of determining the particular prerogatives of this familial domestic church (Are the spouses the "ministers" of the domestic church? What is involved in such a ministry? Should the Eucharist be celebrated in the family?). The Council, referring to the fathers of the church, sought instead to call the members of the family to take joy in the creative depth of the relationship between a man and a woman founded on the sacrament of marriage.[52] What is at issue here is the possibility of living every day more deeply and thus participating in the sacramental sign of marriage, which is the total and joyous gift of oneself to the other, whose goodness and beauty redound back to and thus fulfill the "I."

51. Cf. Balthasar, *Theo-Drama II*, 413.
52. Cf. *Lumen Gentium* 11; *Familiaris Consortio* 21.

The sacrament of marriage, or rather marriage inasmuch as it is a sacrament,[53] puts at the disposal of the spouses' freedom the great resource of the perfect love by which Christ, who gave his life for his church, makes her his bride and preserves her from wrinkle or stain. As paradoxical as it may seem, on a pastoral level, the category of the domestic church emerges more, in its full effective reality, when we look at the church as a family[54] than at the family as a church. Here we see the great power of the vision of the Letter to the Ephesians where the relationship between Christ and the church is described in the light of the man-woman relationship and vice versa. Far from chasing after fantastic theories and abandoning the realm of experience, this choice permits an unparalleled concreteness which demonstrates the persuasive force of the experience and the logic of the incarnation. Balthasar affirms that the fullness of the mystery of man and woman "is only attained in the mystery of Christ and his Church (Eph 5:27, 33)."[55]

Now that we have opened the horizon of conjugal and family life to Christ's boundless love for his bride, we cannot help but pursue the question further. The asymmetrical logic of the reciprocity that characterizes nuptiality does not allow us to rest content; it prompts other questions. On what basis can we legitimately speak of Christ as the Bridegroom of his bride the church, without falling into a fruitless parody of the eros relationship, analogous to that which many writers see in the material world, if not even more dangerous since it is applied to the most noble reality of our faith, a reality we pray to and adore?[56] We are given the possibility of speaking in these terms because of the profound nature of the singular event of Jesus Christ. In him, two natures exist in one person, according to the modality wonderfully described by the Council of Chalcedon (inconfuse, immutabiliter, indivise, inseparabiliter).[57] With the revelation of Jesus Christ, the original experience of dual unity appears in history. The unity of the person of Christ (true God and true man) is communicated sacramentally through his powerful authority over

---

53. Cf. Scola, Questioni di antropologia, 51-52.

54. "According to the Council, the Church is the Bride of Christ and our mother, the holy city and the first fruits of the coming Kingdom. It will be necessary to take into account these suggestive images, according to the suggestions of the Synod, in order to develop an ecclesiology centered on the concept of the Church as the family of God" (John Paul II, Ecclesia in Africa, 63).

55. Cf. H. U. von Balthasar, Theo-Drama III: Dramatis Personae: Persons in Christ, trans. Graham Harrison (San Francisco: Ignatius, 1992), 289.

56. Cf. Loughlin, "Sexing the Trinity," 18-19.

57. Cf. Denzinger-Schönmetzer, Enchiridion symbolorum, 302 (hereafter DS).

humankind and the cosmos (miracles); moreover, there is Christ's greater Lordship over himself which enables his supreme, spontaneous ("*sponte,*" according to Saint Anselm) abandonment to the Father on the cross. "For the Son of Man came not to be served but to serve, and to give his life as a ransom for many" (Mark 10:45). Such is the self-mastery of the crucified Risen Lord! This powerful unity of the "I" of Jesus Christ (the perfect *Ich-Mitte*) is not sundered by the duality of natures. On the contrary, it is strengthened by virtue of their interconnectedness. Christ, in fact, is *one*, because he is the bearer of a single human nature — the unique and unrepeatable humanity of the Son of God.[58] As true man, he binds himself to a precise moment in time and to precise and particular circumstances, and becomes involved in the lives of certain men and women in particular. But inasmuch as his humanity is that of the Son of God, and through the power of the resurrection, Jesus Christ embraces all moments of time and all circumstances in space, thus making himself contemporary to every man and woman in every place and in every time. Concretely speaking, how can this be? Through the sacramental dynamism (an experience full of logos) by which the Risen Lord dwells bodily with the Trinity, and through all moments in time and space with his body, the church, which has her foundation in his mystical body (the Eucharist).[59] In this way the dual unity of the two natures in the one person of Christ appears as the source from which springs the dual unity between Christ the Bridegroom and his bride the church. The believer who has formed his thoughts in meditation on the nuptial mystery of the two natures in the one person of Jesus Christ will not be surprised that the four adverbs from the Council of Chalcedon serve to illuminate the meaning of the original biblical commandment to man and woman to become "one flesh." Thus a strict link is established between the man-woman relation, the Christ-church relation, and the man-God relation. Here our fragile freedom receives the unexpected possibility of finding a firm foundation in the experience of a tenacious and faithful love.

We said before that this represents the culmination of the experience of dual unity within the horizon of the human, but once again, the fruitful asymmetry by which the church-bride is born from the two natures in the one person of Jesus Christ requires a basis. Our ascent continues toward its final goal. Where does the unity of Jesus Christ come from and what is the reason for it? First of all, let us address its purpose. It comes from the mysterious

---

58. On the singularity of Jesus Christ, see G. Moioli, *Cristologica: Proposta sistematica* (Milan, 1978), 223-55; Scola, *Questioni di antropologia*, 11-27, 107-30.

59. Cf. H. de Lubac, *Corpus Mysticum* (Milan, 1982), 33-59.

decision of God the Father to send his only Son, and through him the Holy Spirit, to make men and women exist as autonomous creatures and nonetheless "capable" of participating at that supreme level of love which consists in being his adopted sons and daughters. We are called to be *sons in the Son* so that we can call on God as "Abba," an expression both tender and dramatic.[60] It is a name more familiar than "father" because of the tones of gentleness running through it.[61] The familiarity of God the Father with us is fulfilled in his unconditional fidelity to the original plan. Not even sin breaks this pact; instead, it becomes an occasion for the Father to reveal, in the crucified Risen Lord who pours out his Spirit on us, his true face: mercy. This is the bond (another nuptial word!) of perfect love. We can now see more precisely where the ultimate root of nuptiality lies, the root that illuminates every level of the reality because it reveals the full sense of the asymmetrical reciprocity that is the fruit of dual unity. It is the event of Jesus Christ that allows us to catch a glimpse, however inadequate, of the fact that the Trinity presents an experience of love in its most complete form, according to the perfection that consists in a difference between the three persons which does not destroy, but rather exalts, the unity of the one God. For this reason the triune God is the ultimate explanation of all possible difference, and therefore also of dual unity. God's triunity is the ultimate guarantee that difference does not do away with the contingent being. On the contrary, difference exists for the sake of its truth and fulfillment. In this sense difference within perfect unity, which characterizes the triune God, tells us who God truly is: he is purest love. The love of the Father for the Son is so perfect that the Holy Spirit is at once the bond (nexus) and the fruit of this love.[62]

We can now grasp the importance of Balthasar's striking analogy between the life of the Trinity and the conjugal act of man and woman in relation to the begetting of a child. Balthasar is not afraid to assert, even going against Augustine and Thomas,[63] that man, woman, and child are the most adequate natural analogy of the Trinity. In this sense, even in the Trinity there exists a nuptial relationship made up of a reciprocity. We are dealing here with a reciprocity which maintains, in a certain sense, the element of asym-

60. Cf. Gal. 4:6.

61. Cf. J. Jeremias, *Abbà* (Brescia, 1968).

62. Cf. Balthasar, *Theologik III*, 144-50.

63. "This spousal illustration of the mystery of the Trinity seems no less valid than that of St. Augustine (Father: *Mens;* Son: *Notitia;* Spirit: *Amor,* whose traces are fixed in the spirit of man as intellect, memory, and will) or that of Hugh of St. Victor, taken up again by St. Thomas who defines the Father as Power, the Son as Wisdom, and the Spirit as Love" (Giuliodori, *Intelligenza teologica,* 121).

metry because it rests on the exchange (each Person simultaneously relates to the other two) between the three in the one nature of God, but this perfect difference lies within perfect unity. The One-in-Three is the ultimate driving force of every nuptiality. In fact, in God, the third person is no longer hidden as he is in the various relationships between man/woman (child), Christ-Bridegroom/the church-bride (Jesus Christ), the divine and human nature of Jesus Christ (Father), because the Father, Son, and Spirit are identically manifest as the one God. At the same time, the dynamism of nuptiality is revealed in all its fullness: the reciprocal love between the Father and the Son is the perfect bond which begets a perfect fruit, the Holy Spirit, who is himself God. To bring the different aspects described in this section together, it is worth quoting in full a passage from Balthasar which shows the link between the Trinity and the family:

> We have already noted the impossibility of approaching the Holy Spirit except from two directions at once: as the (subjective) quintessence of the mutual love of Father and Son, hence, as the bond (nexus) between them; and as the (objective) fruit that stems from and attests to this love. This impossibility translates into a convergence of the poles. Imagine for a moment that the act of love between a man and woman did not include nine months pregnancy, that is, the aspect of time. In the parents' generative-receptive embrace, the child would already be immediately present; it would be at one and the same time their mutual love in action and something more, namely, its transcendent result. Nor would it be a valid objection to say that the diastasis we have described just now has to do simply with man's gendered nature, and that in some higher form of love there would be no reproduction (a view that turns up not only in today's common distinction between the ends of marriage, but also in the notion of eros that we find from Plato to Soloviev: cf., G3). We must say, in fact, that this form of exuberance and thus fruitfulness (which can be spiritual) is part of every love, and that includes precisely the higher kind of love. In this sense, it is precisely perfect creaturely love that is an authentic *imago Trinitatis*. . . . What follows from this, as Adrienne von Speyr explains (*Welt des Gebetes:* Einsiedeln, 1951), is mutual admiration, indeed, adoration, infinite mutual thanksgiving (the Father thanks the Son for allowing himself to be generated eternally, the Son thanks the Father for giving himself away eternally), mutual petition (the Father asks the Son to fulfill all of his, the Father's, wishes; the Son asks the Father for permission to carry out the Father's utmost wishes). This mutual indwelling would seem to be eternally self-sufficient, but it is intrinsically superabundant, so much so that it pro-

duces "unexpectedly" (one is tempted to say) and precisely *as* superabundance something that is once more One: the proof that the loving interpenetration has been a success, just as the human child is at once the proof of the reciprocal love of the parents and the fruit of their love. "The third," says Tertullian, "is the fruit from the root of the fruit tree" (*Adv. Prax.* 8 [PL 2, 163]).[64]

The ascent has reached its goal, and, well beyond the weak stammering of our poor concepts, the mystery of the Christian God at work in the lives of Christian spouses and the Christian family finds a way to become manifest in an attested manner. Supporting this assertion are not only the trinitarian prophecies in the Old Testament, where the Trinity's visit to a man or woman almost always leaves as a sign a son (for example, Sarah or Manoah), but also and especially the incomparable event of the annunciation with the gift of the Word, who became a child for us and for our salvation.

5.3. Nuptial Love and the Christian States of Life

If up until this point we have kept to the essential arguments, we can now ask ourselves how *nuptiality*, developed in the total vision of God's plan, enters concretely into Christian life. The church traditionally deals with this question by means of the theme of Christian states of life.[65] While referring the reader to the beautiful works of Balthasar and Adrienne von Speyr for a reflection on the genesis, meaning, and variety of the states of life,[66] I feel compelled on this occasion to highlight two often neglected aspects of nuptiality as a dynamic of the life of the faithful in the two states of marriage and virginity.

5.3.1. Nuptiality and the Indissolubility of Marriage

Indissolubility is ultimately what makes Christian marriage a sacrament, that is, an objective and subjective expression *(ex opere operato et ex opere*

---

64. Balthasar, *Theologik III*, 145-47.

65. Cf. C. Antoine, "États de vie," in *Dictionnaire de Théologie Catholique*, vol. 5 (Paris, 1913), 905-11; there is another bibliography in G. Lesage and G. Rocca, "Stato di perfezione," in *Dizionario degli Instituti di Perfezione*, ed. G. Pelliccia and G. Rocca, vol. 9 (Rome, 1997), 204-15.

66. Cf. H. U. von Balthasar, *The Christian State of Life*, trans. Sr. Mary Frances McCarthy (San Francisco: Ignatius, 1983); von Speyr, *The Christian State of Life* (San Francisco: Ignatius, 1986).

operantis) of *nuptiality.*[67] In fact, only by its being indissoluble does marriage participate in the nuptial sacrifice that the Word incarnate makes of himself on the cross to his immaculate bride, thereby revealing the essence of the spousal love that circulates in the Trinity. This offering is the absolute expression of the Father's fidelity to his plan of covenant with humankind precisely because it is irreversible. Here we have the root of the indissoluble nature of the Christian marriage (and ideally of "natural" marriage as an expression of the man-woman relationship).[68] This is possible for man and woman as a result of the grace of the sacrament (the objective dimension — *ex opere operato*) which calls on freedom (the subjective dimension — *ex opere operantis*) to adhere to it. The most elevated human sign of this subjective obedience in the objective grace of the sacrament is the fiat of Mary (the image of the church), who by her immaculate conception was able freely to receive the gift of the Word in the incarnation. The unconditional and immaculate "yes" of the Virgin Mary becomes the permanent guarantee of the reciprocity of the bride in relation to Christ the Bridegroom.[69] Incidentally, it should be noted that indissolubility, with all the dramatic trials of life it entails, corresponds to the constitutive desire of love as it is given in fundamental human experience.[70] A genuine declaration of love cannot keep from saying "forever." The sacrament of marriage, which by grace enables an act of indissoluble proportions, offers a sure and objective path for this deep-rooted exigence of the human heart.

5.3.2. Nuptiality and Virginity

The second observation I would like to make regarding nuptiality and the states of life lies in the somewhat provocative affirmation that virginity is the culmination of nuptiality — even for spouses.[71] In the end, virginity is the ultimate meaning of indissolubility. In fact, it is impossible to love the other as "other" if one does not love the other in his or her own destiny. There is no real love between a man and woman, between a husband and wife, if there is no detachment (which is traditionally called "chastity"), through which the other is welcomed as a sign of Mystery, a sign of the Trinity. In this *possession*

---

67. Cf. A. Scola, "Spiritualità coniugale nel contesto culturale contemporaneo," in *Cristo Sposo della Chiesa sposa*, ed. R. Bonetti (Rome, 1997), 49-52.

68. Cf. Scola, *Questioni di antropologia*, 51-52.

69. Cf. Scola, "Spiritualità coniugale," 49.

70. Cf. Balthasar, *Christian State of Life*, 58-60.

71. Cf. Scola, "Spiritualità coniugale," 52-54.

in detachment the husband and wife can live indissolubility, whose ultimate guarantee is forgiveness. Such a relationship has rightly been called Christian virginity.[72] We are dealing here with a virtue that is eminently Christlike, because it finds its most perfect expression in the way in which the God-man took possession of people and things. Christian virginity, which springs from baptism and develops as a virtue through sacramental grace, the gifts of the Holy Spirit, and ascetic effort, can find a point of reference in the Virgin Mary and Saint Joseph. Mary is a virgin precisely because she is a mother and a mother because she is a virgin. And the putative fatherhood of Joseph, far from being a disincarnate love, demonstrates that the ultimate depth of every human nuptiality is possession in detachment (virginal). This is the reason for the prophetic value of virginity in the life of the church, whose special value was reconfirmed by the Council of Trent.

This assertion, far from disincarnating marriage, shows its constitutive complementarity with the choice of virginity. The two states of life mutually recall the fullness of nuptiality.[73] The fact that love is always spousal illustrates the paradigmatic nature of marriage.[74] The other state of life, virginity, expressing the full modality of possession — possession in detachment — prevents love and the affective life from closing itself up in the intracosmic, and opens it beyond the implacable link between sexuality, begetting, and death.[75] We can now grasp the pedagogical force of the following assertion: "The more the charism of virginal life is present and affirmed in Christian life, the more marriage will be called to its true nature and will be helped to conform to its ideal."[76]

5.4. The Nuptial Mystery and Welcoming the Other

We may now ask ourselves: How does this exploration of the nuptial mystery reveal its fruitfulness? Why are married couples and consecrated people called to understand it more profoundly? In what sense are they transformed (metanoia) as a result of it and impelled with spontaneous joy to transmit this beauty to men and women of today, who are so wounded that they re-

---

72. Cf. L. Giussani, *Il tempo e il tempio* (Milan, 1995), 11-35.

73. Cf. A. Sicari, "Diversità e complementarità degli stati di vita nella Chiesa," *Communio* 135 (1994): 8-24. See also *Christifideles Laici*, 55.

74. Cf. John Paul II, *Theology of the Body*, 277ff.

75. Cf. DS, 1810. This concerns the fruitfulness which springs from consecrated virginity. See also Scola, *Hans Urs von Balthasar*, 115-16.

76. G. Biffi, *Matrimonio e famiglia: Note pastorale* (Bologna, 1990), 12.

main fundamentally skeptical toward nuptiality? In a word, how can the beauty of the nuptial mystery be communicated?

I express these ideas by having recourse to an apparently particular category, but one which in reality is capable of pointing out the privileged path for communicating the nuptial mystery. I am referring to the category of "giving welcome."

In "giving welcome" (solidarity and hospitality), an authentic experience of the culture of life, the Christian, but particularly the family, is invited to take as a starting point the memorable scene which took place on Calvary at the foot of the cross of Christ. This episode is described for us in John's Gospel. Jesus, dying on the cross, turned to his mother and said, pointing to John, "Woman, behold your son." Then he said to John, "Behold your mother." The Evangelist then comments: "The disciple welcomed her into his own home" (John 19:26-27). The relationship of flesh and blood is made true here, and the dimension of affection reaches amazing heights. A new relationship is born at the foot of the cross, and it is the relationship that constitutes the church itself. It is the communion of the church.

The fruitfulness of this new relationship (ecclesial communion) is based completely on a radical welcome that is intense and a little daunting. Think about how John must have looked at Mary at Jesus' invitation and how Mary must have treated John all during her earthly life after such an invitation! What power of affection; what truth in that affection! What a deep and radical level of purification of the possessiveness of the flesh and blood in an affection not based on domination, seduction, or the will to power, but rather on a pure and free welcome, on an openness to the other in his or her need as it presents itself.[77]

"And the disciple welcomed her into his own *home*." I would like in particular to emphasize the fact that John's home, the church, the Father's house, and the many rooms in the Father's house all form a unity. The word *"welcome"* thus reveals its enormous significance. One can understand why we will be judged according to our capacity to offer welcome (cf. Matt. 25). John makes physical space for this new and stronger relationship, and for this new motherhood. It is significant that in the scene we are describing, each of the three protagonists (Jesus, Mary, and John) receives a mission that involves welcoming.

---

77. "Out of the depths of his suffering, Jesus embraced in one look the two beings he had most loved in this world, and he confided them to one another. 'Woman behold thy son — Behold thy mother' — and ours, for eternity. Mary and John were never again to leave one another" (F. Mauriac, *Life of Jesus* [New York, 1939], 234).

At this point I would like to underscore the fact that giving welcome is always linked in some way to *bodiliness,* to a *materiality* which is the measure of the call of each of the three. *Jesus* strips himself of being God (Phil. 2) and takes a human *body.* He welcomes the plan of the Father who sends him: "You have prepared a body for me, here I am; send me" (cf. Heb. 10:5-7). By her "Yes," *Mary* makes space for Jesus in her body. And finally *John* offers his home — an extension of his body — as the material sign of his welcoming Mary. That gesture of welcome into his home takes him beyond the fact of not having been physically born of Mary and allows him to participate in the very same position as Jesus, in having been born, flesh and blood, of Mary.

John — let us not forget that the tradition of the church has always considered him a virgin — is the model for our way of welcoming. We can welcome someone in person inasmuch as we welcome him into our homes — we can welcome physically, by means of a mission, inasmuch as we welcome in our dwelling place. The figure of John is our measure, because the measure of Jesus and Mary is under the mystery of an absolutely extraordinary grace. In the case of Jesus, there is the divine sonship and identity with God. In the case of Mary, who was destined to give birth to the Son of God, there is the immaculate conception. But John is exactly the point in which this extraordinary, concrete, and indeed bodily experience of giving welcome passes into the history of ordinary men and women. In John's gesture — and perhaps it is significant that the Gospel says nothing about what Mary did for John, but only about what John did for Mary (he welcomed her into his home) — the act of welcoming a person into our home acquires an exemplary and fundamental significance for our faith.

How alien this impressive gesture, which once carried so much meaning and was so natural up through the Middle Ages, has become to the modern mentality! It still remains fundamental in some of the poorer countries of our time. I will always remember a touching episode that I witnessed in Brazil years ago, in an out-of-the-way area in the Amazon. I recall the scene: a missionary priest said a funeral for a lady who had had about ten children by different men. Coming out of the church, he gathered the ten children around him and began to ask a group of women who were there, "Who will take this one? Who will take that one?" Within a few minutes the ten had found new homes. This is truly a gesture born out of poverty, and one that stands within the welcome of John and Mary, lived in the Lord. How our mentality and civilization tend to treat as exceptional something that should be totally familiar to us as Christians!

Welcoming into one's own home (family) has an absolutely extraordinary power to build community and aid the common good (culture of life).

Moreover, it manifests in a remarkable way the intrinsic link between nuptiality and fruitfulness: it is not by chance that the Christian becomes Christian by being "welcomed," and adopted. For this reason he or she is rightly called, even on a supernatural level, a son or daughter. Indeed, we are God's children.

CHAPTER 6

The Nuptial Mystery and Fruitfulness

6.1. Freedom and "Satisfaction":
A Word on a Contemporary Malaise

An acute unease regarding freedom so often marks man's existence in the advanced societies of the Northern Hemisphere (freedom in much of the Southern Hemisphere is more often than not prey to the tragedy of survival). This unease is without a doubt linked to the question of *satisfaction*.[1] With this term I do not refer to the biological-psychic processes connected to the Freudian "pleasure principle" and all that lies behind it,[2] but rather to a dimension which, though not excluding the above, identifies a wider horizon.[3]

---

1. I dealt with the crisis of freedom in A. Scola, "Crisis de la liberdad, familia y evangelio de la vida," *Anthropotes* 11 (1995): 99-110; Scola, "Paternità e libertà," *Anthropotes* 12 (1996): 339-43.

2. Cf. S. Freud, *Beyond the Pleasure Principle*, trans. James Strachey (New York: Norton, 1975), especially chaps. 1–2, 5, and 7. It is well known that, ever since Freud, the link between satisfaction, pleasure, and enjoyment has been considered attentively by psychoanalysis.

3. Modernity has gone beyond the objective meaning of the term "satisfaction" ("to do something in a sufficient manner, or the result of this action"), and has begun to investigate the subjective meaning of the word, which binds it to the themes of desire and its fulfillment (cf. the entry "satisfaction" in A. Lalande, *Vocabulaire technique et critique de la philosophie*, 16th ed. [Paris, 1997], 943-47). In this way, through affection, the theme of satisfaction is tied to the question of love (cf. N. Malebranche, *Recherche de la Verité* [Paris, 1938], especially bk. 4, chap. 5), and more recently to the question of truth (cf. W. James, *The Meaning of Truth* [New York, 1932], 51-101). To link the category of satisfaction to that of freedom, as we propose to do, even in the most general terms, requires us to be aware of the modern origins of this possible meaning. Throughout the whole of Scholasticism, the term was tied exclusively to theological themes of Christology (the vicarious satisfaction of Christ) and of the sacrament of penance (cf. F. Deferrari et al., *A Latin-English Dictionary of St. Thomas Aquinas* [Boston, 1986], 936-37; J. F.

It is almost superfluous to point out how the search for satisfaction, understood as the fulfillment (well-being) of the "I" and tied to the constitutive aspiration to happiness, takes on particular features within the complex cultural climate of today.[4] This search is characterized not only by the results of the modern affirmation of the subject, with its related insistence on rights, particularly the freedom of conscience and expression, but by the practically unlimited possibility of choice in consumer goods — not only of a material nature — which the market places at the subject's disposition. Moreover, both affection and work, which have always constituted the pivotal points of the link between freedom and satisfaction, are generally confronted with the reigning principle of calculation. We refer not so much to the "calculating thought" criticized by Heidegger, but rather to the utilitarian model of thinking which, in its preferentialist variation, presents us with a formidable second edition of the classical vision of a Bentham or a Stuart Mill.[5] In this point of view, the previously calculated quantity of pleasure or pain linked to every human act appears as the only adequate path toward the satisfaction of desire, while the latter is made to coincide with the whole of freedom and is understood as a source of rights. Man spends his existence in the calculated

---

Niermeyer, *Mediae Latinitatis Lexicon minus* [Peiden, 1984], 940; cf. especially R. Busa, *Index Thomisticus. Concordantia prima,* 20:4-18). However, desire, affection, love, and truth in the contemporary sensibility seem to us to justify the use of the category of "satisfaction" in a broader sense, in terms of the fulfillment of freedom. This involves beginning with the subjective meaning of the term "freedom" (desire, love, but also the unconscious level in which these are rooted), with the awareness that we must reach a consideration of its objective value, ultimately with reference to reality and its foundation in truth (G. W. Leibniz, "Discorso di metafisica," in Leibniz, *Scritti filosofici* [Turin, 1967], 66-67).

4. Cf. P. Morandé, "Comprendere il nichilismo," *Nuntium* 1 (1997): 62-67.

5. Preferentialist utilitarianism claims to be the rigorous development of classical utilitarianism. The sum of the consequences connected to a human act would not directly influence the calculation of the quantity of pleasure or pain; rather, one begins with what is most favorable (preferential) to the beings involved by the action (cf. P. Singer, *Practical Ethics* [Cambridge, 1993], 14). In the end, however, if the utilitarian perspective is retained, it does not seem to me that these preferential interests can be established except by balancing out the consequences in terms of the pleasure and pain connected to a human act. It is enough to leaf through the accurate bibliography compiled by E. Sgreccia and M. B. Fino (*L'etica dell'ambiente* [Rome, 1997]) to see the enormous quantity of literature dedicated to utilitarianism in general and preferentialist utilitarianism in particular. It is worth noting that "environmental ethics," for these two authors, does not indicate a sector foreign to our theme, since it studies "the principles on the basis of which the relation between man and nature is regulated" (Sgreccia and Fino, 3). The term "ecology" has undergone a noteworthy evolution since it was introduced by Haeckel in 1866. Today one speaks of "human ecology" to refer to something that, once again, approaches the problem of freedom and satisfaction.

search of how affections and work, in which the inevitable I-thou relation takes its everyday form, can satisfy desire, generate pleasure, and limit (and if possible, eliminate) pain. In this laborious enterprise, modern man is sustained by a host of social agents full of advice and intent on persuasion, who do not hold back from transforming man's very rights — or, better, all that is felt to be a right — into merchandisable needs.

If the pursuit of satisfaction, understood as the integral fulfillment of the "I," is proper to the nature of freedom, then rather than denouncing the state of affairs just described and the utilitarian matrix of thought behind it, it seems more opportune to reveal an objective unease that accompanies modern man in his pursuit of happiness. This is precisely the unease of a freedom which seems encumbered, and cannot manage to find "satisfaction." This is not the place to describe the many indications of this crisis of freedom, in which freedom seems to be suspended and separated from the object adequate to its fulfillment. Here it is helpful to point out the reason for this paradox of a freedom that finds itself debilitated within a context, as ours today, where it is invoked at every step. This reason is in the end simple, because it is both ancient and ever new: *reality surpasses desire.* This is an affirmation analogous to one that is more easily accepted: reality surpasses the imagination! Desire, which is the first level of freedom, bespeaks an openness to the whole of reality, to the Infinite, which however it does not have at its disposal.[6] It may be said that it is good that things are so, that reality surpasses desire. If it did not, what could motivate desire? It is precisely reality, with its interweaving of relationships and circumstances, which puts desire into motion and offers it possible paths to the satisfaction that actualizes freedom. All one needs to know is how to make oneself content, weighing well the consequences of an action (in terms of pleasure and pain) before acting, and knowing how to choose the path that, with the greatest approximation, is the most convenient.

---

6. I refer to that level of desire that "has an ontological character, or rather, is constitutive of the subject's relation to reality and not extrinsically added on to this. The experience of freedom thus has its beginnings not in indifference, but in a polarization towards the subject's fulfillment. This can be called 'ontological desire,' which opens human freedom wide onto reality, by virtue of the lovability of the real. This desire possesses the nature of an openness to the whole of reality, even if, because of human nature, it must always be determined as the desire of this or that being" (A. Scola, *Questioni di antropologia teologica* [Rome, 1997], 90). Cf. also Scola, *L'alba della dignità umana* (Milan, 1985), 143-52. An accurate analysis of desire in its connection with freedom, language, and behavior can be found in the important text of Claude Bruaire: *L'affirmation de Dieu: Essai sur la logique de l'existence* (Paris, 1964). This text also examines the tie between desire, freedom, and the infinite. The category of the "infinite" is used here in an inevitably determined manner. To grasp the meaning of this choice, inevitably connected to the nature of the dialectic between desire and freedom, cf. Bruaire, 9-14.

The more reality increases the host of choices, the greater the possibilities of calculated satisfaction.

And yet, even a mildly thoughtful consideration of fundamental human experience reveals the inadequacy of this level of interpretation. Let us take circumstance: there are things that are inevitable, completely independent of me. Certain relationships possess the same characteristic: my mother precedes me, I do not choose her. Far from widening the field of calculation in the attempt to balance pleasure and pain, the affirmation "reality surpasses desire" implies, rather, a drastic reduction. One must recognize, at least, that for a wide range of actions calculation can in the best of cases concern only the containment of the quantity of pain that inevitable persons and circumstances can provoke. Here utilitarianism transforms itself into stoicism, an attitude to which, at first glance, it does not seem to be related. But the profound meaning of the principle "reality surpasses every desire" is deeper still, more radical, and that is what in the end explains the unease gripping freedom today on the decisive question of satisfaction. In what does this meaning consist?

Paradoxically, the answer appears clearly if one looks at the question from the side of the desiring "I." What do I desire, in the end, when I desire a person, a thing, or a circumstance? I desire everything. In a word perhaps more appropriate, I desire the infinite.[7] Particularly through the poetic genius, the whole history of humanity, as well as that of each individual human being, can offer us abundant documentation confirming the fact that desire is not placated except before the infinite.[8] This throwing itself open to the whole of reality explains the vital impulse prompting desire to rise up even out of its own ashes. The desire for the infinite clashes, however, with the inexorable finitude of individual acts of desire. I am capable of desiring the infinite, but this latter concedes itself to me through finite reality.[9] If it is consid-

---

7. Cf. Scola, *Questioni di antropolgia*, 97: "This is the real motivating force of our freedom; without this perspective, even our desire would ultimately remain unfulfilled and would be lost. The only goal adequate to our nature is the infinite."

8. Cf. C. Rebora, "Dall'immagine tesa" (The taut image), in Rebora, *Le poesie* (Milan, 1993), 151:

> From the taut image
> I watch the instant
> Imminent with waiting —
> And wait for no one.

Also C. Pavese, *Il mestiere di vivere* (Turin, 1973), 276: "How enormous is the thought that really nothing is owed to us. Did someone promise us something? Then why are we waiting?"

9. Cf. R. Guardini, "Fenomenologia e teoria della religione," in Guardini, *Scritti filosofici*, vol. 2 (Milan, 1964), 207: "All things call attention to themselves as directly real and essential; they

ered in its entirety, desire is necessarily shot through with an Augustinian inquietude of the heart.[10] The structure of desire, which in its full sense attests to itself through reason and the will, reproduces the modality with which these faculties encounter being. *They encounter it in the sign,* which simultaneously veils and unveils. Reality surpasses desire by revealing both desire's capacity for the infinite and its incapacity to reach it. The individual reality, precisely as it satisfies desire, mortifies or wounds it: the reality remains other, in some way external. Reality surpasses desire because it rouses desire and at the same time *wounds* it. In it the other says to the "I": "I am other than you, you cannot reduce me to yourself. The difference in which I remain and in which you see me cannot, ultimately, be suppressed." The misunderstanding of this constitutive structure of desire in relation to its object generates that unease of freedom which today has become macroscopic. The utilitarian criteria, seemingly so concrete and functional — to the point of having become popular opinion — misses the mark. It does not keep its promises.

The principle that reality surpasses every desire demonstrates the objective limit of the utilitarian mentality. If one wishes to defend the structure of desire, and with it utilitarianism's correct intuition that freedom also implies satisfaction, one must acknowledge that the calculated balance of the quantity of pleasure and pain connected to a given human act is not an adequate criterion for judging the goodness (and thus the *fittingness,* in terms of satisfaction) of that act.

6.2. Procreation without Sexuality?

The above premise takes on real weight when we turn our attention to several burning questions, today categorized under the heading "bioethics." The term can be misleading, since it is extremely difficult to sketch the boundaries of the object and method of bioethics.[11] In this discussion the

---

make me immediately sense that I am not the ultimate reality, but rather a point of passage through which the truly ultimate and authentic emerges: expressive forms that make it manifest."

10. Augustine, *Confessions* 1.1.1. "The thought of you stirs him so deeply that he cannot be content unless he praises you, because you made us for yourself and our hearts find no peace until they rest in you" (trans. R. S. Pine-Coffin [London: Penguin Books, 1961], 21).

11. Cf. L. Melina, "Riconoscere la vita. Problematiche epistemologiche della bioetica," in *Quale vita? La bioetica in questione,* ed. A. Scola (Milan, 1998), 75-115 and 359-66. Cf. also *Vent'anni di bioetica. Idee, protagonisti, istituzioni* (Padua, 1991); G. Russo, ed., *Bilancio di 25 anni di bioetica. Un rapporto dai pionieri* (Turin, 1997), with contributions from W. T. Reich, E. D. Pellegrino, V. R. Potter, H. T. Engelhardt, T. L. Beauchamp, D. Callahan, R. M. Veatch.

term "bioethics" will be employed in a very general sense, as a magnetic pole of sorts around which are grouped extremely contemporary questions, from (by way of example and not as an exhaustive list) genetic engineering to euthanasia, in vitro fertilization, and cloning. What connection exists between these problems, today the object of heated debate, and that unease of freedom mentioned above? It is almost too obvious to note how the hegemony of a utilitarian culture is clamorously revealed by the way these problems are lived and confronted on a popular level. This is because, in such extreme cases, freedom is forced to give an account of its relation to *satisfaction*. In these extreme cases the normal, everyday manner in which we risk our freedom is made manifest. In particular, these burning questions are a litmus test that shows how the affective dimension of the "I" — one of the two axes of every human being's daily fundamental experience (the other being work) — is generally lived and thought of today. Here, in a way that cannot be ignored, the game of freedom encounters the dimension of difference inherent in the real. The I-thou relation, in all its affective implications, is called into play in the perspective of freedom and satisfaction. This involves a concrete I and a concrete thou, made up of body and soul, who exist as man and woman, and who are individuals structurally poised toward community.

Without a doubt, one of the basic problems that runs through many bioethical questions and brings into play the relation between freedom and satisfaction, is that of the *link between sexuality and procreation*. With regard to this, and in the wake of astounding scientific discoveries that allow sexuality to be separated technically from procreation, the widely diffused utilitarian mentality seems to be convinced that this separation allows for a marked growth in the potentiality of satisfaction for the freedom not only of the individual, but of entire peoples (cf. demographic growth).

But will this really happen? And at what price? When this Faustian dream, which, thanks to modern biotechnology, is now within everyone's reach, is realized, what will its consequences be for human sexuality itself, and for procreation? How, in practice, will the person's and society's lifestyle be modified? These are disturbing questions that lead us, in synthesis, to a simple query: Does freedom, in its justifiable search for satisfaction, find in the technically practicable separation between sexuality and procreation an objective factor of growth?

In order to respond to these and other questions, we must examine the nature of human sexuality in its relation to procreation more closely, to see if the two factors do or do not *necessarily* imply one another. If they do imply one another, separating them only because it is technically possible to do so does not expand freedom. And this, in the long run, will manifest itself also through a lack of *satisfaction* and fittingness.[12]

6.3. Human Sexuality: Asymmetrical Reciprocity

During the span of his existence, everyone gives an answer, at least de facto, to the question of why the human being exists always and only as male and female.[13] As much as every human existence reflects the unique character of the "I," with its characteristic of unrepeatability, it would be impossible to not discern in it a central nucleus common to the experience of all. Even after having been sifted through numerous scientific disciplines, the category of *reciprocity* appears the least inadequate for comprehending the meaning of sexuality as it presents itself in its phenomenological immediacy. In fact, sexuality as a constitutive dimension of the person simultaneously indicates identity ("itselfness") and difference, unity and duality. This "dual unity" objectively opens onto the horizon of reciprocity. It is worth immediately posing a question which can at first glance seem as otiose as certain *quaestiones* of the medieval commentaries on the *Summa*, often recalled only to censure the nominalistic-sophistic decadence of late Scholasticism. I refer to questions such as that regarding the sex of the angels.[14] When we speak of reciprocity (dual unity) in regard to sexuality, do we identify a dimension proper — even according to the wide reach of analogy — to those beings which used to be called "animate" (possessing a soul), or only to those animate beings which possess a body? In other words, is the living body *(Leib)* an essential condition for the presence of sexuality? To be concrete, and disregarding here the forms both of vegetable life and the most elementary animal existence, can we speak of "sexuality" — obviously in an analogous sense — with regard to animals, man, and God?

---

12. It bears repeating that sexual difference and procreation, both in themselves and in their relation to one another, are the basic questions needed to confront many issues usually grouped under the heading of bioethics. Thus, a clarification in this regard helps us, at least indirectly, to better define the nature and the context of this epistemologically problematic scientific discipline.

13. Cf. H. U. von Balthasar, *A Theological Anthropology* (New York: Sheed and Ward, 1967), 306-14.

14. Cf. J. Auer, *Il mondo come creazione* (Assisi, 1977), 511: "At the beginning of the 14th century, the nominalist spirit prompted questions on how the angels moved and what space they occupied. Such questions may seem grotesque to us, but they had the function of illuminating, within the mentality of the time, the creatureliness and the immaterial spirituality of the angels."

The question is less artificial than it might seem. Normally, Christian thinkers exclude the possibility of speaking of "sexuality" in God.[15] The reason is obvious: God is pure spirit. Moreover, in God there is no species, and thus no necessity whatsoever of reproduction.

However, in the One and Three there is perfect reciprocity, as well as generation and creation *(potentia generandi et creandi)*.[16] Is this enough to widen the notion of sexuality according to analogy, as Evdokimov and Balthasar have done, and speak of a "suprasexuality" in the one and triune God?[17] In order to indicate the radical discontinuity between God and man, between him who is pure spirit and the being made *corpore et anima unus*, the term "nuptiality" is preferable to "suprasexuality." It is, however, useful at least once to refer the dimension of "suprasexuality" to God, for the sake of the light it sheds on the question of human sexuality. The analogy with nuptiality in God makes it easier to refrain from closing the consideration of human sexuality into the intracosmic plane, and to see in it an opening to the transcendent. Without separating human sexuality from genitalia, this opening keeps sexuality from being overly determined by the latter.[18] Here we catch a glimpse of the famous anthropological problem of the connection between

15. This depends on the assertion of the absolute immaterial spirituality of God: cf. Thomas Aquinas, *Summa Theologiae* I, q. 3, aa. 1-2: "Utrum Deus sit corpus" and "Utrum in Deo sit compositio formae et materiae." Cf. also C. Giuliodori, *Intelligenza teologica del maschile e femminile* (Rome, 1991), 130ff.; D. L. Schindler, *Heart of the World, Center of the Church* (Grand Rapids: Eerdmans, 1996), 237-74.

16. We cannot undervalue the fact that the Risen One is present with his "true body" in the Trinity: "In union with the whole Church we celebrate that day when Jesus Christ, our Lord, rose from the dead in his human body" (*Roman Missal*, Roman Canon: *Communicantes* from the Easter Vigil to the Second Sunday of Easter). This is not the place to draw out the consequences of the theme of nuptiality (suprasexuality) in God, if only because of the complexity of the question. If on the one hand it must be clearly affirmed that in the *kenosis* of the incarnation the Son humbled himself to the point of taking on a humanity of the male gender, on the other hand it must be kept in mind that Matt. 22:30 holds true in Paradise: "in the resurrection they neither marry nor are given in marriage." Sexuality is thus subjected to the "mysterious" anthropological change that implies a transfiguration of the body in the passage to eternity (cf. Thomas Aquinas, *Summa contra Gentiles* IV, 87: "De sexu et aetate resurgentium"). Therefore, even the meaning of sexuality and fruitfulness will change. We can, however, rationally suppose that this glorious transfiguration will bring human sexuality closer to divine nuptiality.

17. Cf., for example, H. U. von Balthasar, *Theo-Drama II: Dramatis Personae: Man in God*, trans. Graham Harrison (San Francisco: Ignatius, 1990), 413ff.; Balthasar, *Theo-Drama V: The Last Act*, trans. Graham Harrison (San Francisco: Ignatius, 1998), 85ff.; P. Evdokimov, *Woman and the Salvation of the World: A Christian Anthropology on the Charisms of Women*, trans. Anthony P. Gythiel (Crestwood, N.Y.: St. Vladimir's Seminary Press, 1994). Further references can be found in the work cited above of Claudio Giuliodori.

18. Cf. Balthasar, *Theo-Drama II*, 365-69.

human sexuality and the *imago Dei*, which, with the affirmation of Genesis 1:27, has occupied many exegetes, philosophers, and theologians, and is so classic as to be well known even in general cultural reflection.[19]

The analogy between human and animal sexuality, on the other hand, is immediately evident: this has its medium in the *Leib*, understood as the living body, which is precisely what allows for "itselfness" and difference, unity and duality.

Once reciprocity has been identified as the general meaning of human sexuality, we intend to keep it open to confrontation with both intracosmic animal sexuality and divine nuptiality.[20]

If we now examine more closely man's sexual reciprocity, we are immediately led by that same fundamental human experience to reveal its, so to speak, original or nonderivative character. It is not only the empirical sciences, in the everyday interpretations which reach us through the medical or psycho-pedagogical sciences (without limiting ourselves to those based on Freudian considerations of the unconscious and its possible pathologies), which draw our attention to the original character of sexuality. The anthropological sciences themselves do so, in their cultural,[21] philosophical,[22] and theological[23] dimensions. In particular, the invitation to make room for the dramatic nature of anthropology, by which it is possible for man to respond to the question regarding his essence only from within his existence,[24] is to be embraced without hesitation. It is only as *Dasein*, that is, as an "individual-being-already-situated-in-the-world," that man can pose the question, "What is man?" This question is structurally intertwined with another, more personal and original: "And *what* am I?" In fact, the former awakens only within the latter, as the poetic genius has demonstrated very well. The response to the original ontological question — "*What am I?*" — carries with it, in the fundamental experience of every man, the revelation of three polarities constitutive of the "I." Taking his inspiration from

19. Cf. Singer, *Practical Ethics*, 72ff.

20. It would be fairly easy, within this analogical framework, to take up the question of the sex of the angels. Interesting cues can be found already in Thomas Aquinas, *Summa Theologiae* I, q. 60: "De amore seu dilectione angelorum."

21. Cf. Levi-Strauss's affirmations in his *Le strutture elementari della parentela* (Milan, 1969), 50.

22. Cf., for example, G. Fessard, *Essai de conciliation anthropologique entre Libéralisme, Communisme et Nazisme grace à la dialectique de l'homme et de la femme*, vol. 2 of *Le mystère de la société. Recherches sur le sens de l'histoire* (Brussels, 1997), 203ff.

23. K. Wojtyla's reflections are original in this regard; they are taken up again in his papal writings.

24. Cf. Balthasar, *Theo-Drama II*, 335.

Fessard,[25] Balthasar has identified these as body-soul, man-woman, and individual-community.[26]

Sexuality (man and woman, sexual difference) thus demonstrates its coessentiality with human nature, through that polarity which indicates reciprocity. I, who exist as a man of the male gender, do not exhaust the whole of being man. I always have before me, almost as a counterimage, the other way of being man, which is inaccessible to me.[27] The nature of this reciprocity requires, however, already on the level of elementary phenomenological experience, important clarifications that will forestall equivocal readings of human sexuality.

Fundamental human experience demonstrates that *reciprocity is not complementarity.* It is not the search for an androgynous unity, as Aristophanes' mythical vision suggests in the *Symposium.*[28] Man and woman are not two halves of a lost whole, and sexual difference does not imply an incessant tending of each of these "halves" to seek the other with a view to a "recomposition" which would flow into the full peace of a mortal unity. Already on the level of primary relations, we can see that reciprocity is expressed in a plurality of interpersonal relations — motherhood, fatherhood, childhood, brotherhood, sisterhood, etc. — which interest each individual contemporaneously. The reciprocity in question is therefore *asymmetrical,* and cannot mean mere complementarity. Obviously, this asymmetry remains within reciprocity, just as the duality we are considering remains within unity.[29] A slightly more thorough examination of fundamental human experience demonstrates, moreover, that the constitutive polarity of man-woman, which the individual inexorably encounters when he responds to the question "What am I?" brings the question of difference to light as original and insuperable. Sexuality always presents itself in terms of difference. *Sexuality is sexual difference.*[30] We will not touch upon the fundamental conviction of the psychological sciences of the unconscious; these speak of a "fundamental situation" in order to describe the inescapable fact that man, inasmuch as he is born of a woman, remains constantly marked by this

25. On this subject cf. M. Sales, *Gaston Fessard (1897-1978). Genèse d'une pensée* (Brussels, 1997).

26. Cf. Balthasar, *Theo-Drama II,* 346-94.

27. Cf. Balthasar, *Theo-Drama II,* 365-82; Balthasar, *The Christian States of Life,* trans. Sr. Mary Frances McCarthy (San Francisco: Ignatius, 1983), 92-103.

28. Cf. Plato, *Symposium.*

29. In this sense asymmetrical reciprocity does not exclude a complementarity between man and woman: cf. *CCC* 372.

30. Cf. L. Beirnaert, *Aux frontières de l'acte analytique* (Paris, 1987), 142ff.

"original laceration."[31] In order to illustrate the raison d'être of sexual difference, it is more useful to have recourse to the dramatic nature of the "I." This allows us to see in *Dasein* (man-for-the-world) the ontological difference of which Heidegger spoke, or the real distinction (to use an expression which brings us indirectly back to Thomas)[32] characterizing contingent being. In every individual being, Being itself gives itself without thereby being exhausted. In giving itself, Being reveals *(re-velere)* itself. It is thus *event,* which in the final analysis cannot be deduced; reason cannot foresee it and the will cannot grasp it. Yet, in finite beings Being reveals itself as *promise* and *foretaste,* though remaining within an *insuperable difference.* The finite being is a real *sign* of Being. Because of this, the act of consciousness which intends (tends toward) the real appears as the locus of a reason whose ultimate (critical) form is faith, precisely because it depends on the fact that Being gives itself only as a promise or foretaste in the real sign which is the individual being.

The constitutive anthropological polarities cannot but reflect this ontological difference. These polarities are not accidental properties of being, but its essential dimensions; they represent the major axes of ontology.[33] If the difference of genders (sexual difference) allows itself to be defined in terms of reciprocity (that is, of dual unity), then we discover the weight of ontological difference on the level of the transcendental of unity. If contingent being in itself is in fact shot through with ontological difference *(essere-ente),* this difference will manifest itself in the transcendentals as well — in the one, the true, and the good — inasmuch as it is a property coextensive with Being itself: *ens (verum, bonum) et unum convertuntur.* The asymmetry proper to sexual reciprocity, which each person experiences concretely from his earliest familial relations, thus appears to be ontologically founded. Sexuality, as asymmetrical reciprocity, reveals the essential weight of difference. And inasmuch as this difference is essential, it is insuperable. On every level this is confirmed by the experience of the dual unity of man and woman: the claim to have overcome this difference can only be a tragic illusion. It has rightly been written, "Sexual difference as such es-

---

31. Cf. L. Beirnaert, *Expérience chrétienne et psychologie* (Paris, 1966), 323.

32. Cf. C. Fabro, *Tomismo e pensiero moderno* (Rome, 1966), 21-45.

33. It is worth noting that the dramatic anthropology mentioned above fulfills, without negating, the classical anthropological idea of the *synholon.* This dramatic anthropology limits itself, in a certain sense, to demonstrating the importance of man-woman and individual-community as polarities coessential to body-soul; the latter, as in classical anthropology, maintains a certain priority. Cf. A. Scola, *Hans Urs von Balthasar: A Theological Style* (Grand Rapids: Eerdmans, 1995), 91-92.

capes conceptualization. It is affirmed, but there is no discourse that can represent it."[34] Sexuality, existence as man and woman, indicates that in the human being alterity is constitutive and insuperable. Anthropologically speaking, human sexuality is the "high road" along which man experiences difference as internal to the "I" itself. This is so not because the "I" lacks its own autonomous ontological consistency, made up, as Maritain writes,[35] of constitutive elements and necessities. Rather, the polarity of the other at the same time constitutes the "I." There is not *first* a wholly autonomous "I" which *then* enters into relation with an other. The relation is not extrinsic and accidental, but intrinsic and constitutive. This particular man is a man inasmuch as he is a soul which informs a body, a man "polarized" toward woman, and an individual "polarized" toward community. By the very fact of existing as a man, he exists as a dual unity according to the threefold polarity mentioned above. We must immediately point out that the polarities of which we are speaking, as ontological, are not dependent in their essential nucleus on the dynamisms of the consciousness and self-consciousness of the individual person.

Before turning to the implications tied to sexual difference, we need to make one more clarification. The affirmation that through dual unity difference enters to define the human being's ontological structure does not mean that this difference destroys unity. We are speaking of *dual unity*, not of a unified duality. Though sexuality, like the other constitutive polarities, implies difference as constitutive, it remains within the unity of the "I" and does not break this unity.[36]

At this point it ought to be clearer why we have spoken of *asymmetrical reciprocity.* The categories of "itselfness" (identity) and difference, unity and duality, I and thou, describe this asymmetrical reciprocity proper to every human being's fundamental experience of sexuality.[37]

---

34. Beirnaert, *Aux frontières*, 144.

35. On this subject cf. J. Maritain, *La personne et le bien commun,* in Maritain, *Oeuvres 1940-1963* (Paris, 1978), 287ff. (*The Person and the Common Good,* trans. John J. Fitzgerald [New York: C. Scribner's Sons, 1947]); Scola, *L'alba della dignità umana,* 182ff.

36. Cf. Scola, *Hans Urs von Balthasar,* 90-91. The anthropology of the *synholon* was defended by the church's magisterium: cf. Denzinger-Schönmetzer, *Enchiridion symbolorum,* 372, 800, 1440, 2766, 2812, 3002 (hereafter DS).

37. Cf. G. Zuanazzi, *Temi e simboli dell'eros* (Rome, 1991), 9ff.

6.4. Love and Fruitfulness

Now we will turn to the further implications of asymmetrical reciprocity. History — and not only Western history — has associated sexuality with two other factors: *love* and *procreation*.[38] As asymmetrical, sexual reciprocity opens the way to love of the other, and in loving union the way is opened to procreation. In this perspective, taken for granted until the last few decades, sexuality, love, and procreation appeared as essentially related terms. Independently of the various levels of consciousness regarding its nature, love presents itself as the factor capable of founding the harmonious unity of these three elements.[39] The dialectic between "need love" and "gift love," *amor concupiscientiae* and *amor amicitiae*, eros and agape, "physical" love and "ecstatic" love, traverses the entire history of the problem, and is but the reflection, on the level of the transcendental of the good, of the law of dual unity proper to man and to every contingent being.[40] Even on the level of the transcendental of the good, contingence bespeaks, at the same time, both *limit* and *possibility*. Love, as the expression of a limit, draws man into the experience of a lack (need), but at the same time is also the "place" where the other reveals himself as a fascinating possibility (desire) which calls forth the gift of self. Thus the dynamic of satisfaction proper to freedom encounters one of its "high roads" in love. In this sense the many thinkers who refused to define love univocally, either by lowering physical love to the realm of the intracosmic or "angelicizing" the love of oblation, were right. One can immediately add, too, that asymmetrical reciprocity, inasmuch as it is the central nucleus of sexual difference taken up into the experience of love, demonstrates that the spousal dimension has every right to be considered the *analogatum princeps* of every love,[41] from physical love to that complete oblation of the mystical wedding feast of the Lamb, who is Christ the Bridegroom of the church-bride.[42] This understanding of love, which does not fear love's profanation and continues to call love "love" even when it is debased in behavior almost exclusively tied to instinctual drives, possesses an underlying realism; it is born of a correct vision of human contingence, inevitably tied as

38. Both factors can be found, for example, in the androgynous myth of Plato's *Symposium*.

39. Cf. D. de Rougemont, *L'amore e l'Occidente* (Milan, 1982).

40. Cf. above, pp. 21-31.

41. Cf. A. dell'Asta, "Dal cuore dell'unità. Note sull'estetica e l'erotica di Solov'ev," in V. Solov'ev, *Il significato dell'amore e altri scritti* (Milan, 1983).

42. Cf. A. Scola, "Spiritualità coniugale nel contesto culturale contemporaneo," in *Cristo Sposo della Chiesa sposa,* ed. R. Bonetti (Rome, 1997), 43ff.

it is to the dialectic (dual unity again shows itself on the scene!) of nature and freedom (culture).[43]

When Thomas speaks of inclinations with regard to the natural law, he offers us a teaching of inestimable value: human freedom (from *Dasein,* existence, hence a dramatic anthropology) is awakened by constitutive inclinations which emerge from man's bio-instinctuality and, through the unconscious and the spiritual preconsciousness,[44] press on toward his consciousness. However one wishes to define the complex question of nature, one cannot in the end deny that it has an objective regulating function on freedom. To turn again to Thomas and his famous treatise on the passions,[45] his definition of the tending of every being (including inanimate beings) toward its fulfillment is extremely provocative.[46] Love thus becomes the tenacious vigor which binds each reality to the whole, and which encounters in man the possibility of self-gift as the objective assumption of the physical level of love into the oblative. In the completion of the movement of this gift — which is not afraid of acknowledging the importance of nature — freedom discovers the object adequate to its desire. In fact, as *amor naturalis* (which has its source in bio-instinctual drives),[47] desire responds to the fascinating call of the real, choosing (free will)[48] to give itself and thereby turning *amor concupiscientiae* into *amor amicitiae.*[49] The single reality is then revealed as only a sign of the Infinite, which is the true motive of desire. And the Infinite of which we speak is not indistinct, uni-total (ontological, as Heidegger would say)[50] Being, but has the mysterious face of a *Someone.*

43. Cf. Scola, *L'alba della dignità umana,* 182-85.

44. Scola, *L'alba della dignità umana,* 145. On the notion of "spiritual preconsciousness," cf. J. Maritain, *Quattro saggi sullo spirito umano nella condizione di incarnazione* (Brescia, 1978).

45. Cf. Thomas Aquinas, *Summa Theologiae* I-II, qq. 22-48.

46. Cf. Thomas Aquinas, *Summa Theologiae* I-II, q. 26, a. 1.

47. Maritain refers to this reality when he speaks of "preconscious attraction." Cf. J. Maritain, "Freudianism and Psychoanalysis," in Maritain, *Quattro saggi sullo spirito.*

48. I dealt with the three levels of freedom (desire, free choice, and capacity for the infinite) in Scola, *Questioni di antropologia,* 85-102.

49. Cf. A. Scola, *Identidad y diferencia* (Madrid, 1989), 24-34.

50. In a polemic with Heidegger, Gilson writes, "In the metaphysics of being, the absolute transcendence of being over essence fully appears only in the moment in which the notion of being is theologized and identified with the philosophical notion of God" (E. Gilson, *Constantes philosophiques de l'être* [Paris, 1983], 206). The literature on the relationship between God and Being is endless, and includes both the perspectives in which God is Being and the recent attempts to speak of God without assimilating him to Being. This renewed interest doubtless finds its origin in Heidegger's critique of the onto-theo-logical constitution of metaphysics, with its corresponding forgetfulness of being (cf. M. Heidegger, *Identität und Differenz* [Pfullingen, 1957]; ET, *Identity and Difference,* trans. Joan Stambaugh [New York: Harper and

Thus, in *amor amicitiae* we see what desire truly seeks: not so much plea-sure as *gaudium* (joy, enjoyment) because one loves one's own good. This is very different from the egotistical love of self.[51]

Pleasure is not at all repressed, but it is not precisely what ontological desire seeks.[52] Pleasure is allowed to exist in its reality provided it is not in collusion with desire. Asymmetrical reciprocity, precisely because it is the expression of the insuperability of sexual difference, leads man and woman, as the subjects of desire, to the experience of an original *lack*. Man and woman discover this lack in the movement prompted by desire, because they realize that enjoyment is not immediately accessible to them. Instead of enjoyment they encounter plea-sure, which is always brief, whereas only enjoyment (joy) lasts. Unlike enjoy-ment, pleasure is characterized by a "before" and "after" which are not to be found along the same lines as the need to be loved forever. Rather, this need runs up against the lack mentioned above, and it is certainly not pleasure that can fill it.[53] Without wishing to force the point, we can say that these profound psychological data are not dissonant with respect to the central conviction of a dramatic anthropology: that man, though bearing a capacity for the infinite, is constrained to the finitude of not being able to dispose of it. In this sense, en-joyment depends in the end on the face of the Infinite making itself available. The desire to be loved definitively inexorably encounters that insuperable dif-ference which has its source in the unavailability of the other, and thus implies the painful experience of a lack. Undervaluing this structure of desire in rela-tion to the Infinite as its adequate object, with the relative articulations of en-joyment and pleasure, would mean failing to reach the proper sphere of love. In the perspective we have outlined, on the other hand, even the experience of re-fusal in love can be reabsorbed. Here one sees, in a certain sense, how the very structure of the "I" is open to the logic of forgiveness.

We cannot here delve more deeply into the relation between the capacity for the infinite, which characterizes desire, and the self-gift of the Infinite it-self, which possesses its own "face."[54] We can, however, affirm that an integral

---

Row, 1969]), and the succession of replies defending the necessity of an ontology. Gilson strongly affirmed that "There is but one God, and this God is Being, that is the corner-stone of all Christian philosophy" (E. Gilson, *The Spirit of Medieval Philosophy*, trans. A. H. C. Downes [New York: C. Scribner's Sons, 1946], 51).

51. Cf. K. Wojtyla, *Love and Responsibility*, trans. H. T. Willetts (San Francisco: Ignatius, 1993), 21-69. Cf. also pp. 64-71 above.

52. Cf. Beirnaert, *Aux frontières*, 147.

53. Cf. Beirnaert, *Aux frontières*, 147. Narcissism arises precisely from not seeing the differ-ence between desire's relation to enjoyment and to pleasure.

54. There is no lack of acute observations on this topic offered by psychology. I refer to the

vision of love is not afraid of maintaining, in a hierarchical unity, the physical (bio-instinctual), erotic,[55] and oblative dimensions of love, which objectively implies an opening to procreation. Need-love, the expression of the human limit, becomes the fertile ground for the building up of the love of friendship and of procreation. This latter is an even more acute expression of that same limit, in the insuperable circle of life and death,[56] and passes, always by virtue of oblation, into fruitfulness. The generation of a child, the fulfillment of the experience that love bears fruit, can be for man and woman the most normal confirmation of that characteristic of love which prompted the ancients to define it as *diffusivus sui*. As much as procreation — because of human limitation (and sin) — can take place without a conscious oblation or even be considered the undesired result of sexual union, it does not thereby lose its objective capacity to indicate love's fruitfulness as the locus where the asymmetrical reciprocity constitutive of human sexuality is actuated. Sexual difference as difference (duality) in unity, inscribing difference in the "I" itself, shows that *fruitfulness is the full "face" of asymmetrical reciprocity*. Spousal (conjugal) love reveals that sexuality has procreation as its essential (though obviously not exclusive) end.[57] This is not the place to enter into the debate — a classic one in moral theology — regarding the ends and goods of marriage, and their hierarchy.[58] It is enough to assert emphatically that sexuality, love, and procreation are essentially related, such that it is not possible in an objective and absolute sense to subtract one or another from the circumincession of the three without substantially changing the essence of each. The fact that a couple cannot have children means only that the fruitfulness of love in which their sexuality expresses itself can find other forms; it does not change the objective order of desire. Analogously, the fact that a man or

---

critique of the subject's narcissistic claim to give a "face" to the infinite without receiving it as a gratuitous event; the subject thus remains confined to an imaginary world populated with hallucinations that fascinate but lack reality. The subject can also remain in the obsessive claim of a "false infinite," conceived as the sum of all the parts. Such claims are always destined to collide with some*thing* which was not seen, spoken, or fulfilled; this thing alone is enough to declare the infinite unattained, and trigger obsessive mechanisms. Cf. Beirnaert, *Expérience chrétienne*, 311-12.

55. Cf. Zuanazzi, *Temi e simboli*, 86ff.

56. Zuanazzi, *Temi e simboli*, 68ff.

57. Cf. G. Martelet, *Amour conjugal et renouveau conciliaire* (Lyons, 1969), 33: "Even if the act need not be fruitful each time it is accomplished, it cannot be detached from sexual fruitfulness. The refusal to recognize this means to break the human being in two precisely in the act in which his most profound unity is made manifest."

58. On the ends of marriage, cf. C. Rochetta, *Il sacramento della coppia* (Bologna, 1996), 101ff.

woman is called to consecrated virginity demonstrates how the spousal nature of virginal love, which does not pass through the conjugal act and does not seek fruitfulness in procreation, is called to realize the person's sexuality and bear fruit in other ways.

Relation to the other is never constituted independently of sexuality.[59] This is an important affirmation, and one fairly easy to accept nowadays. What is more difficult to accept is the integral logic which requires that sexuality be open to fruitfulness, that is, to the welcoming of the child.[60] Procreation, seen in the logic of the fruit of love, overcomes in a bound the risk, perhaps a bit emphasized even by some Catholic authors in the last few years, of the instrumentalization of the person. Opposing "ends" to "fruit" in speaking of procreation, in order to refrain from subjecting love to procreation (understood as service to the species), might help liberate love from incongruous and heteronymous mechanisms. One can, however, in the logic of fruitfulness profitably maintain the category of "end."[61] Analogously, the claim that a "mechanistic" insistence on the link between sexuality and procreation has led to a denial to woman of the dignity of being a subject of desire and pleasure, transforming her into the pure object of masculine erotic inclination, is not a sufficient reason for negating the objective circumincession of sexuality, love, and procreation brought into play by the polarity of man and woman.[62]

6.5. The Challenge of Biotechnology

6.5.1. An Impossible Separation

The natural circumincession of love, sexuality, and procreation, peacefully accepted for centuries, clashes today with a new state of affairs. The techniques

59. Cf. Zuanazzi, *Temi e simboli*, 12ff.; M. Merleau-Ponty, *Fenomenologia della percezione* (Milan, 1965), 257.

60. Once more we find an indirect confirmation from depth psychology: "Although the child is not the cause of sexual desire, he is not for that reason extraneous to it. He comes, and can come, precisely in that place where the absence of enjoyment is revealed. . . . It is said and written that openness to the eventual child allows the spouses to not be closed into a twofold egoism. This is both true and false. It is true in the sense that the acceptance of the child can be the sign of the acceptance of the lack. It is false in the sense that it can also be interpreted as the sign of a non-acceptance of castration. Hence, in order not to be the object of substitution, the child, in relation to sexuality, must be the *fruit* of a sublimated love" (Beirnaert, *Aux frontières*, 148).

61. Cf. Zuanazzi, *Temi e simboli*, 82.

62. Cf. Beirnaert, *Aux frontières*, 142-243.

of in vitro fertilization and, even more, the possibility of cloning[63] have opened the path toward a radical separation of sexuality and procreation.

The widespread diffusion of a pragmatic mentality, in which preferentialist utilitarianism is coupled with scientific calculation, is more and more imposing a sort of technological imperative: *what we can do, we must do.*[64] Besides, does not the separation of procreation from sexuality mean liberating love from every naturalistic conditioning, opening it to a more complete freedom? At the same time, does not this separation grant us a more secure therapeutic and eugenic control, and a greater knowledge regarding procreation in its relation to the well-being of the person and society (cf. the demographic explosion)? "It is true," one hears, "the risks of violating the dignity of persons and peoples to which this asexual method of procreation can give rise are neither few nor small, but why live controlled by fear? Hasn't it always been so in the face of every scientific discovery? The material will need to be regulated through adequate laws, but it would be absurd to halt scientific progress." The link between sexuality and procreation which was gained in a vision of spousal love is laid aside, with the claim that it rests upon a biologistic conception of nature and its processes. An "open" vision of nature ought rather to receive, from *culture,* the fact that the sexual act and procreation are now separable.

It is easy to respond that this state of affairs, however novel in human history, does not change the order and objective meaning of the factors in play. If anything, it exalts human freedom, demonstrating, in a certain sense, its sovereign power: love must be chosen in its truth, and this implies that sexuality and procreation be maintained in an essential unity. Is not human freedom just as strongly challenged in other areas? Has not the use of atomic energy, after the tragedy of Hiroshima, and with its enormous risks, required a vigilant and responsible use of a freedom called, for the good of humanity, to make room for "no's"? Is it not true that "in the most dramatic situations of life, a 'no' emerges even before one knows the reason why. Its force depends on something other than the justifications advanced to sustain it,

63. Cf. G. Angelini, "Il dibattito teorico sull'embrione. Riflessioni per una diversa impostazione," *Teologia* 16 (1991). Cf. also R. Colombo, "Vita: dalla biologia all'etica," in *Quale vita?* 169-95 and 380-87.

64. On the relationship between ethics and science, cf. R. Buttiglione, "Etica e scienze umane," in *Persona, verità, morale. Atti del Congresso Internazionale di Teologia Morale* (Rome, 1987), 497ff.; B. Kiely, "Scienza e morale," in Congregation for the Doctrine of the Faith, *Donum Vitae. Istruzione e commenti* (Vatican City, 1990), 105-11; Scola, *Questioni di antropologia,* 215ff.; A. Serani Merlo, "La lógica de la técnica y la lógica de la ética en la procreación humana," in *Humanae vitae 20 anni dopo,* 673-75.

which can perhaps be criticized"?[65] This response is correct, and it is impossible to produce arguments, however convincing, that do not fall within this horizon. It is, however, worthwhile to try to clarify the *reasons* for opposing the alleged *reason* that the technological imperative has insinuated in us all, like a pragmatic doubt apparently full of good sense. This "alleged reason" consists in the practical refusal of all discourse regarding the (ontological) foundation of reality. It considers every ontological affirmation to be the undue transposition of a determined state of knowledge about things, always falsifiable, to the level of the essence of things in themselves. Thus, to affirm that love implies an essential link between sexuality and procreation becomes a way to disguise as a foundation what is in fact a provisional understanding of things. When procreation was in fact inseparable from sexuality, this opinion claims, a certain way of discussing love was constructed which transferred an insufficient knowledge to an ontological (theological) level. Now we must have the courage to accept that if sexuality and procreation are separable, this discourse is false. It reveals itself to be a myth, even if in the positive sense of the term (in which *mythos* does not directly oppose *aletheia*), and must be overcome.[66]

Let us try to accept this objection. What becomes of the triad sexuality-love-procreation? What happens to what we have called the "circumincession" of these three factors? The three break apart, and love can no longer be spoken of as an *unum* which, though in analogous terms, can be applied to all the possible variations of love, from *venere* to the circumincession of the persons in God himself. In fact, if sexuality and procreation (fruitfulness) are not objectively implied in one another but are considered two completely independent realities, spousal love ceases to be the *analogatum princeps* of love. This is so because the centrality of (sexual) difference is removed from such a perspective, and difference is the very mainspring of love. Difference points to that nondeducible difference which opens the way to desire (satisfaction) precisely by revealing, in the immediate lack of enjoyment, that a *third factor* always exists between two lovers. The child, as fruit, holds this place. To deny that this third factor is constitutive of sexual difference means, in reality, to abolish that difference. And to abolish sexual difference

---

65. Beirnaert, *Aux frontières*, 152.

66. Similar opinions, in the form of reflections on a more personalistic and less biological conception of paternity and maternity, can be found for example in M. de Vachter, "Une procréation à la mesure de l'homme," *Echanges* 115 (1974): 28-31. For an evaluation of the above, cf. D. Tettamanzi, "La fecondazione in vitro. Aspetti etici," in *Persona, verità, morale*, 89ff.; C. Caffarra, "*Humanae vitae*: venti anni dopo," in *Humanae vitae 20 anni dopo*, 183-95; A. Chapelle, "La dignità della procreazione umana," in *Donum vitae*, 127-36.

in its insuperable, dramatic otherness means, on the one hand, to reduce spousal love to the search for the fantasy of the androgynous whole, and on the other to demean procreation and transform it into mechanical "reproduction," analogous to any other marketable product. In the end, to separate sexuality from procreation means to deny the very possibility of spousal love, which, as the *analogatum princeps* of love, is the "high road" for learning about love (as is shown by the elementary experience of every human being who comes from a father and a mother). To break the circumincession of the three factors (love, sexuality, procreation) is equivalent to negating them. Nor can we delude ourselves into thinking that we avoid this consequence by moralistically inviting the spouses to permeate their decision to have a child, without having recourse to the conjugal act, with all the love of which they are capable. This attempt would reveal only the impossible claim of a freedom that does not want to reckon with nature. The human body would no longer be that sign (sacrament) of the whole "I" which allows for relation with others and with reality itself.[67] This even beyond the fact that a series of other decisions made by other subjects (doctors, technicians) intervene between the spouses' decision — however full of loving intention — not to have recourse to the conjugal act, and the conception of the child. The child as the *fruit* of the love of the two is in this case impossible. No one would ever be able to take away from that child the character of being a product.[68]

As for spousal love, the abolition of difference would appear clearly in the loss of asymmetry, which would transform reciprocity into pure complementarity, poised to pursue the phantom of androgyny. Only difference, inasmuch as it expresses an objective openness to fruit (procreative fecundity), indicates the place of the other to love: the "being there" of the man for the woman and vice versa. Without this, the two could not but conceive of themselves (androgynously) as two halves seeking a lost whole.

Separating sexuality and procreation, that is, the unitive and procreative dimensions of the conjugal act — the place in which the communion of persons is expressed through the joining of bodies — is equivalent to undervaluing the original, nonderived nature of sexual difference. This alters the man's "face," both in himself and in his constitutive relation to the other.

This choice, too, like that of harnessing atomic energy for the construction and use of the bomb, would be a mortal wound inflicted on all mankind. The most tragic consequence of this separation would make itself felt in the

---

67. Cf. Zuanazzi, *Temi e simboli,* 12ff.; C. Rocchetta, *Il sacramento della coppia* (Bologna: Dehoniane, 1996), 70ff.
68. Cf. Ph. I. André-Vincent, "La procréation artificielle," in *Persona, verità, morale,* 629ff.

practical impossibility for the majority of persons to find the path to the satisfaction of constitutive desire, and thus to the fulfillment of freedom. The human being would be placed in a situation of unbearable self-contradiction, precisely as regards his original vital energy: the infinite desire of totality which characterizes him in his constitutive impetus to be definitively loved. The abolition of what is really at stake in sexual difference would bind this ontological desire to narcissism, allowing the person momentary pleasures but depriving him of real and true enjoyment. Enjoyment is impossible where difference is abolished, and with it the experience of the lack of the *third factor,* which is a sign of the Infinite itself calling to human freedom. Breaking the "circumincession" of love, sexuality, and procreation leads, thus, to reducing procreation to mechanical reproduction, love to the search for an androgynous phantom, and condemns the "I" itself to narcissism.[69]

69. In the development of important magisterial texts in the past few decades, it is possible to find support, albeit indirect, for this approach to the problem of the relation between love, sexuality, and procreation. We have allowed ourselves to cite a possible path through recent magisterial pronouncements on this theme:

a. The element of the inseparability of the two aspects (unitive and procreative) of the conjugal act: "That teaching, often set forth by the magisterium, is founded upon the inseparable connection, willed by God and unable to be broken by man on his own initiative, between the two meanings of the conjugal act: the unitive meaning and the procreative meaning" (*Humanae Vitae* [hereafter *HV*] 12). "When couples, by means of recourse to contraception, separate these two meanings that God the Creator has inscribed in the being of man and woman and in the dynamism of their sexual communion, they act as 'arbiters' of the divine plan and they 'manipulate' and degrade human sexuality — and with it themselves and their married partner — by altering its value of 'total' self-giving. Thus the innate language that expresses the total reciprocal self-giving of husband and wife is overlaid, through contraception, by an objectively contradictory language, namely, that of not giving oneself totally to the other. This leads not only to a positive refusal to be open to life but also to a falsification of the inner truth of conjugal love, which is called upon to give itself in personal totality" (John Paul II, *Familiaris Consortio* 32).

b. The anthropology of dual unity (the unity of the two: body and soul, man and woman, individual and community) and the spousal and parental value of the gift of the body as sacrament of the whole person: "The moral value of the intimate link between the goods of marriage and between the meanings of the conjugal act is based upon the unity of the human being, a unity involving body and spiritual soul. Spouses mutually express their personal love in the 'language of the body,' which clearly involves both 'spousal meanings' and parental ones. The conjugal act by which the couple mutually expresses their self-gift at the same time expresses openness to the gift of life. It is an act that is inseparably corporal and spiritual. It is in their bodies and through their bodies that the spouses consummate their marriage and are able to become father and mother. In order to respect the language of their bodies and their natural generosity, the conjugal union must take place with respect for its openness and procreation; and the procreation of person must be the fruit

6.5.2. The Full Meaning of Spousal Love

We can now contemplate, in precise terms, the full meaning of love, one which maintains all its constitutive factors and dimensions in unity. In the end, what does this singular *mystery* (sexual difference cannot be directly represented in concepts!) of man and woman reveal to us? It is an echo, in the human creature, of that unfathomable mystery from which Jesus Christ has lifted a corner of the veil: the difference in perfect unity that exists in the Trinity, the three persons who are the one God.[70] The most appropriate word, coined by Christian thought, for indicating this impenetrable mystery is "communion." *Communio personarum* exists in its perfection in the Three in One, because the Father gives himself completely to the Son without keeping anything of his divine essence for himself. The Father generates the Son. The Son himself gives back the same, perennial divine essence. This exchange of love between the two is so perfect as to be *fruitful* in a pure state: it gives rise to another person, the Holy Spirit *(donum doni)*. Unity and difference coexist

---

and the result of married love. The origin of the human being thus follows from a procreation that is 'linked to the union, not only biological, but also spiritual, of the parents, made by one bond of marriage.' Fertilization achieved outside the bodies of the couple remains by this very fact deprived of the meanings and the values which are expressed in the language of the body and in the union of human persons" (*Donum Vitae* II B 4b).

c. The "communional quality" of the *imago Dei:* "The fact that man 'created as man and woman' is the image of God means not only that each of them individually is like God, as a rational and free being. It also means that man and woman, created as a 'unity of the two' in their common humanity, are called to live in a communion of love, and in this way to mirror in the world the communion of love that is in God, through which the Three Persons love each other in the intimate mystery of the one divine life. The Father, Son and Holy Spirit, one God through the unity of the divinity, exist as persons through the inscrutable divine relationship. Only in this way can we understand the truth that God in himself is love (cf. 1 Jn 4:16). The image and likeness of God in man, created as man and woman (in the analogy that can be presumed between Creator and creature), thus also expresses the 'unity of the two' in a common humanity. This 'unity of the two,' which is a sign of interpersonal communion, shows that the creation of man is also marked by a certain likeness to the divine communion *('communio')*. This likeness is a quality of the personal being of both man and woman, and is also a call and a task. The foundation of the whole human 'ethos' is rooted in the image and likeness of God which the human being bears within himself from the beginning. Both the Old and New Testament will develop that 'ethos,' which reaches its apex in the commandment of love" (John Paul II, *MD* 7).

N.B. These themes are in a certain sense anticipated in the Wednesday catecheses on human love (cf. John Paul II, *The Theology of the Body: Human Love in the Divine Plan* [Boston: Daughters of St. Paul, 1997], 42-48).

70. Cf. Scola, *Identidad y diferencia*, 6off.

in this perennial event of being and letting be, which (inconceivable to us) implies a difference in perfect identity.[71] This difference, the most radical possible even though it in no way threatens the identity of the Three who are one God, is also at the root of creation from God.[72]

The Judeo-Christian tradition, familiar even to secularized strains of Western thought, has recourse to the notion of the *imago Dei* in order to speak of the human being as created, and to document the imprint of the Trinity in him. In an original way John Paul II not only makes the *imago* consist in the human *mens,* that is, in the person's capacity to understand and to will, but widens the concept until a communional quality is unveiled within it.[73] Man is in the image of God not only as person but also insofar as he is capable of interpersonal communion. The difference in perfect identity proper to God leaves, through his creative act, its mark within the difference in nonidentity proper to man and woman. The first is perfectly fruitful: the Holy Spirit, the third person of the most holy Trinity, is at once expression and fruit of the love of the Father and the Son. The second echoes the first, though within a radical dissimilarity, in its structural openness to the child. In the first the love of communion which joins the Persons is purely spiritual, and yet exists within a reciprocity which realizes the transcendental of the One to perfection (there is no ontological difference in God). In the second, unity is realized under the sign of ontological difference, inasmuch as it is a dual unity from which flows that asymmetrical reciprocity proper to sexual love, oriented toward its fruit (a child). In this way sexuality, procreation, and love show a marvelous synthesis of nature and freedom, open to continuous refinements from authentic culture. The *communio personarum* of man and woman realizes the human person's being in the image of God. In its truth, human love is this communion between two persons of different sexes which is open to a third person. The communional *qualitas* of the *imago Dei* explains dual unity: it is a reciprocal fruitfulness, and fruitful because it is asymmetrical. This is why the unitive and procreative dimensions of love cannot be adequately considered separately!

The spiritual nature of God, the Three in One, does not contradict our positing — analogically — the profound meaning of (suprasexual) nuptiality in God himself. Neither can the link between sexuality and corporeity be seen as an objection to this analogy; it is no more an objection than the trinitarian

---

71. Cf. H. U. von Balthasar, *Theologik III: Der Geist der Wahrheit* (Einsiedeln: Johannes Verlag, 1987), 144-50.

72. Cf. Thomas Aquinas, *Summa Theologiae* I, q. 45, a. 6; Bonaventure, *Collationes in Hexaemeron* 11.9.

73. Cf. above, pp. 28-30.

level of man's creatureliness on the level of the analogy with God. The sciences which investigate the evolution of life help us understand the sacramental splendor of the body, which the Christian faith, precisely for this reason, sees as destined for the glory of the resurrection. Whether one speaks of "suprasexuality" in God or holds this to be inappropriate and irreverent, the substance of the analogy is not lost: the fruitfulness of perfect reciprocity made up of perfect difference and perfect identity in God is echoed, through the *imago Dei,* in the fruitfulness of the *communio personarum* of man and woman. In the latter communion we find an asymmetrical reciprocity, made up of difference and imperfect identity. This is the ultimate reason why sexuality, love, and procreation cannot be separated.

6.6. Generation, Procreation, and Reproduction

To bring the above discussion to a conclusion, we must pause on a last important point. This can be formulated in the following question: Does the fact that spousal-sexual reciprocity essentially implies fruitfulness say something about the specific nature of that fruitfulness? In other words, if we look at God, man, and animals, beginning with that reciprocity which characterizes, respectively, nuptial-suprasexual nature (God) and sexed nature (man and animals), can we identify a specific connotation of fruitfulness proper to each one?

The fruitfulness of the triune God is perfect. The loving reciprocity present in that Being who is the *Ipsum esse subsistens* gives rise to the third person of the Trinity, the Holy Spirit, who is from eternity identically God with the Father and the Son.[74] Without at this point entering into the complex problem of nuptial language (male and female) applied to the Trinity,[75] we can retain two facts. These are expressed, in an elementary fashion, in the creed: the Son is "begotten, not made" *(genitum, non factum),* and the humanity of the incarnate Son of God is *de Spiritu Sancto ex Maria Virgine.* He was "conceived by the power of the Holy Spirit," *concepit de Spiritu Sancto.*

---

74. Cf. *CCC* 238-67.

75. Cf. John Paul II, *MD* 6-7; H. U. von Balthasar, *Explorations in Theology,* vol. 2, *Spouse of the Word* (San Francisco: Ignatius, 1991), 147ff.; P. Evdokimov, *La donna e la salvezza del mondo* (Milan, 1980), 59ff. (ET, *Woman and the Salvation of the World*); I. de la Potterie, "Antropomorfismo e simbolismo nel linguaggio biblico sulla relazione uomo-donna," in *Dignità e vocazione della donna: Per una lettura della "Mulieris dignitatem"* (Vatican City, 1989), 110-16. An extensive bibliography on this subject can be found in Giuliodori, *Intelligenza teologica,* 263-74.

The Holy Spirit, the perfect love of the Father for the Son and the Son for the Father, and the perfect fruit of that love, presumes the generation of the Son from the Father and allows for Mary's virginal conception. Perfect fruitfulness flows from perfect nuptiality. In the suprasexual Being, the act of generating produces an Other but does not depend upon an Other. The Father does not generate the Son from a nature that precedes him. The Generator has no "eternal material" with which he enters into a nuptial relation in order to generate; reciprocity in God is not asymmetrical. The divine relations are in fact perfectly complementary. They do not cancel out difference, just as difference does not impair the common, identical being of the Three who are the one God. Every cosmogenic myth, with its relative divinization of the cosmos, falls to pieces in the face of the Christian God.[76]

Generation is the prerogative of the Father, inasmuch as he is *fons totius divinitatis* (cf. Eph. 4:6), and the Son is not "made." In him there is no degradation of being with respect to the Father, as the Gnostics and subordinationist theology would have it. The Holy Spirit, the fruit of their perfect love, is then at work in Mary's virginal conception. This last appears much less difficult to accept, however much it remains an inaccessible mystery, within the perspective of the (suprasexual) nuptial consideration of God himself, made possible by a unitary though analogical understanding of love.[77] Why could the Father's *potentia generandi* (generative power) and the *potentia creandi* (creative power)[78] not have found an exceptional meeting point in the conception of Jesus Christ in Mary, through the power of the Holy Spirit? Jesus Christ is procreated in his human nature from Mary, but in his divine nature he is conceived in continuity with being generated by the Father. For this reason Mary virginally conceives "by the power of the Holy Spirit."[79]

If we now pass to considering the analogies, we encounter man and woman. As we know by now, the reciprocity of love is in this case asymmetrical, because the contingent nature of the human being "polarizes" unity into a dual unity. The fruitfulness which flows from it participates in the anthropological, human condition. The constitutive polarity of body-soul[80] — in which

---

76. Cf. Balthasar, *Theo-Drama II*, 365-69. On theogenic and cosmogenic myths, cf. G. Reale, *Storia della filosofia antica*, vol. 1 (Milan, 1989), 47ff.

77. One cannot stress enough the abysmal "unlikeness" implied by this analogy: DS, 806.

78. Cf. G. Marengo, *Trinità e creazione* (Rome, 1990), 84ff.

79. Cf. *CCC* 484-86.

80. This is not the occasion to discuss the validity or nonvalidity of the critiques directed against this binomial, in which the West has seen the necessity of positing man's ultimate nature. Cf. Balthasar, *Theo-Drama II*, 355-64; J. Ratzinger, "Al di là della morte," *Communio* 3 (1972): 10-18.

is found the binomial nature-freedom — gives concrete witness to this. These polarities therefore imply a spousality which, passing through the body, involves the totality of both persons in love. The fruit of this love is, objectively, the child. The unitive and procreative dimensions exist in an intrinsic unity in the conjugal act, understood as a union of bodies which is the sign of the union of the lovers' whole persons.[81] The fruit of this is a personal subject. *We can, then, rigorously redefine the conjugal act as a procreative act.* It implies a *factum* which is nevertheless free of any "mechanism," not only and not primarily by virtue of the self-consciousness of the spouses — always desirable as the source of responsible parenthood — but because of the intrinsic meaning of freedom consonant with the spiritual dimension of the person, in which even the bio-instinctual aspect of the conjugal act is objectively anchored.[82] This last, which depends on the sacramental nature of the body,[83] is inserted into a spiritual horizon that impresses its form on all the conscious and unconscious biological processes which characterize it. In itself and independently of the self-consciousness at work in man and woman, the child is devoid of the character of being a product of reproduction, because it flows from human sexuality inasmuch as this is part of the *imago Dei*. It is this which confers on the conjugal act of man and woman the nature of a spiritual act (in the integral and not separate sense of the word, implying the body as sacrament of the person), as well as a communional quality. The fruit of such an act is another personal subject, not simply another individual of the same species. Thus, a human being must always be conceived in an act of love-gift constituted by the conjugal union of a man and a woman. The fact that new technologies offer the heretofore unheard-of possibility of procreation that does not pass through the sexual act perhaps makes this question more dramatic for every man and woman, and for all of society, but it does not objectively alter the nature of human procreation.

If we turn now to the animal sphere, what becomes of the analogy between God and man with regard to the themes of sexuality and reproduction? Up until recent decades, when no one thought to accuse those who thought animals lacking in self-consciousness, and even consciousness in its proper sense, of "speciesism,"[84] the question was easily answered. Without denying a certain analogy between the higher animal species and man in the bio-instinctual sphere of sexuality, and without excluding the presence of a "ves-

---

81. Cf. John Paul II, *Theology of the Body*, 395ff.; C. Caffarra, *Etica generale della sessualità* (Milan, 1992), 35ff.

82. Cf. Caffarra, *Etica generale della sessualità*, 51ff.

83. Cf. Rocchetta, *Il sacramento della coppia*, 30-34, 69ff.

84. Cf. Singer, *Practical Ethics*, 55ff.

tige" of the Trinity in animals,[85] it was affirmed that since animals did not, properly speaking, have the experience of love, animal sexuality could only be objectively ordered to the reproduction of the species. The coupling of the male and female animal is objectively poised to *reproduce* another individual of the same species. This anthropological vision perhaps led to an exaggerated anthropocentrism, responsible in large part for the ecological imbalance of which man has become aware in the last few decades. It is necessary to rethink not only the place of man in the cosmos, but his relations with other living beings and other species, animals in particular, as well. But must this rethinking lead, as some propose, to the recognition of certain higher primates as "non-human persons," or at least as subjects of consciousness?[86] Even more, can we, guided by utilitarian ethics, have recourse to the principle of pleasure and pain as the absolute criterion for establishing whether, in an individual animal, there exists the consciousness of its relation to its own and to other species? Can we therefore conclude that an anthropomorphism stemming from an exasperated anthropocentrism is all that lies at the basis of the conviction that only the human species is conscious, and that there is a difference of quality, not merely of degree, between the human and animal species?[87] It is worth remembering, first of all, how Western thought, which ultimately rests on the Aristotelian doctrine of the sensible soul of animals, has always recognized that animals have a place next to man, even though submitted to him. In this sense the results of scientific observation of animal behavior, with their penetrating description of "sensitivity," cannot be considered an absolute surprise, from a speculative point of view. Moreover, it seems very difficult to object to even very recent studies that, though they recognize an "intelligent behavior" in certain higher animals, distinguish this essentially from the intelligence proper to man. There remains an ontological difference between man and animal.[88] In any case, it is erroneous to hold that animals have a personal character in order to attribute to them the experience of love in the proper sense. However much a series of analogies with human behavior regarding sexuality, reproduction, and relationship with young can be discerned in some of these, the objective bases for discerning therein the *form of love* in its proper sense do not exist. This affirmation, which it is not

85. Cf. Thomas Aquinas, *Summa Theologiae* I, q. 45, a. 7.
86. Cf. Singer, *Practical Ethics,* 110ff.
87. Cf. Singer, *Practical Ethics,* 112.
88. G. Zuanazzi, "L'uomo e l'animale," *Anthropotes* 13 (1997): 91-106. In the same issue of *Anthropotes,* interesting developments for our theme can be found in Ph. Caspar, "La place centrale de l'homme dans les sciences biologiques contemporaines" (17-54), and H. Hude, "Présupposés philosophiques propres au biocentrisme ou anthropocentrisme" (69-90).

worth delving into here, leaves open a series of questions dear to animal rights proponents (from those regarding the legitimacy of man killing animals for food *if he can otherwise nourish himself,* to questions regarding vivisection). It is important to note, incidentally, how the perspective of a utilitarian ethics, so widely diffused nowadays because it is so consonant with the fashionable way of thinking, ends in the dissolution of man without leaving any space for God. The aberrant consequences which can result from such a system of ethics[89] depend on the fact that man as such is disfigured by it. In particular, the dignity and splendor connected to human sexuality are negated when one loses sight of the correct positions occupied by God, human beings, and animals in the hierarchy of beings. Far from leading to "speciesism," the affirmation of their essential difference allows each of these to be treated in the truth proper to them, for the good of all.

To return to the central question, it does not seem to us out of place to define the sexual act with which animals produce an individual of their species as an act of reproduction.

Generation, procreation, and reproduction identify, therefore, three different modes of fruitfulness connected, each in its turn, with various levels of suprasexual and sexual reciprocity. Thus we find generation in the perfect and purely spiritual reciprocity of God, procreation in the asymmetrical reciprocity proper to man, and reproduction in the reciprocity proper to animals.

The quality proper to the procreative act which is connected to the specific nature of human sexuality clearly shows the objective inadequacy of every act of human procreation which is not the fruit of the love expressed in the conjugal union of man and woman. The fact that another person, in the full and total sense of the word, can come into the world *technically,* through an act which is not procreative but reproductive, does not change the substance of things. On the contrary, it spurs us on to vigilance. Man produced by man — whom could he ever trust?

In the era of cloning, this appears more than ever to be a question of life or death.

---

89. For example, it would be immoral to kill a chicken for food while it would be moral to commit infanticide in the first months of life in the case of a severely handicapped child. Cf. Singer, *Practical Ethics,* 191.

PART III

The Nuptial Mystery and Cultural Changes: The Tasks of Marriage and the Family

CHAPTER 7

Marriage and the Family and the Crisis of Freedom

7.1. The Family and Contemporary Culture

7.1.1. A Crisis of the Couple

When we inquire into the life and vitality of marriage, we are not confronting a partial aspect of human experience, as if evaluating the condition of marriage and the family in a society were equivalent to touching upon one factor of civil society among many. Rather, we must speak of marriage as that dimension summarizing the condition of a society, as the determining characteristic of a culture.

Marriage and an understanding of nuptiality are in fact a constitutive dimension of man's self-consciousness, of his understanding of himself and his own task. Thus it is no exaggeration to say that a culture's understanding of the family and the health of married life are, effectively, the "litmus test" for a global evaluation of the state of a society.

It is not by chance that John Paul II, in his untiring teaching, has committed himself so strenuously — and with real innovation — to the relationship between man and woman, at once so difficult and so rich. The impressive bulk of his interventions, declarations, and documents testifies to his pastoral care and points to the family as "the way of the church."[1] The church herself,

---

1. John Paul II, *Letter to Families* 2: "The divine mystery of the incarnation of the word thus has an intimate connection with the human family. Not only with one family, that of Nazareth, but in some way with every family, analogously to what the Second Vatican Council says about the Son of God, who in the incarnation 'united himself in some sense with every man.' Follow-

in her new and permanent evangelization, cannot but keep the reality of married life particularly close to her heart. The truth of her pastoral action and, more generally, of her mission must inexorably pass this way.

Such a vast expenditure of energy on the part of the Holy Father can be explained in light of the signs of the times: marriage and the family, and the spousal relationship between man and woman, are fundamental realities of both society and the church (the Council documents speak of the "domestic church").[2] At the same time, however, these realities exhibit the symptoms of a grave crisis certainly connected to the changing sociocultural context in which we live and work. In this sense our cultural context urges us on to a task and a mission.

Before all else, I would say, with frank realism, we must recognize that a change is taking place. We can say without opposition that civilization, particularly in the European nations, has been rapidly de-Christianized, and that it is precisely the reality of marriage and the family that has paid the heaviest price. The decrease in the number of marriages, the rise in divorce, the increase of cases of so-called singles, the high number of abortions, a widely diffused contraceptive mentality, the phenomenon of homosexual couples, the incapacity and fear of a choice that involves a definitive tie — besides being morally blameworthy, these facts are above all symptoms of a shifting cultural horizon in which families find themselves placed.

We cannot, moreover, hide from the fact that one of the basic causes for this change has been the incapacity of the church — at least in many of its components — to transmit the reasons for faith to the men and women of the third millennium. What has been lacking is a real and reason-filled communication of the Christian life in its global and all-encompassing capability to respond to the questions that constitute the human heart.

The family is involved in this process in two ways. On the one hand, it is the object of a crisis, which can perhaps be more accurately identified as a crisis of the couple. On the other hand, the family is in some way also the subject of this crisis, inasmuch as it has revealed itself, with the complicity of its structure of education, to be incapable of transmitting a Christian vision of life.[3]

It cannot be denied that in the last thirty years a considerable opposition to the existence of the family has been raised on many sides, and an ideologi-

---

ing Christ who came into the world 'to serve' (Mt 20:28), the church considers serving the family to be one of her essential duties. In this sense both man and the family constitute 'the way of the church.'"

2. Cf. *Lumen Gentium* 11; *Gaudium et Spes* 48, 52; John Paul II, *Familiaris Consortio* 21, 85.

3. John Paul II, *Letter to Families* 6.

cal movement has developed to that effect. Surprisingly, and in spite of this, today all scholars in the human sciences recognize a widespread "desire for family." The family endures both in its *form* and in its *meaning*.

The *form* of the family endures: this continues to be understood in the collective consciousness as a couple oriented to the generation of children. Secondly, the *meaning* of the family endures. This is a "meaning" of humanization, that is, of the maturation of the couple through the experience of reciprocal love, which is accompanied in an essential way by an openness to the generation and education (humanization) of the child. Beyond the fact that when people think of the family they think of it in a complete and total sense — *sovereign,* as John Paul II would say[4] — a question nevertheless arises. What kind of family remains? What remains — one must acknowledge the evidence — is a weak family, as can be seen in both its *privacy* and its *fragility*.[5]

In revealing the crisis of the family to be at its root a crisis of the man-woman relation, we are also led to ascertain that one of the characteristics of our culture is, unmistakably, a widespread and marked individualism that is reflected on all levels of society, and before all else in the family.[6] In marriage and the family, this manifests itself in a somewhat paradoxical way.

4. John Paul II, *Letter to Families* 17: "As a community of love and life, the family is a firmly grounded social reality. It is also, in a way entirely its own, a sovereign society, albeit conditioned in certain ways. This affirmation of the family's sovereignty as an institution and the recognition of the various ways in which it is conditioned naturally leads to the subject of family rights."

5. On this subject the following can be consulted: J. E. Dizard and H. Gadlin, *La famiglia minima. Forme della vita familiare moderna* (Milan, 1996); G. Colombo, "Conclusa la ricerca sulla 'Famiglia,'" *La Gazzada* 12, no. 23 (1992): 9-13; W. O. Weyrauch and S. N. Catz, *American Family Law in Transition* (Washington, D.C.: Bureau of National Affairs, 1983), 2; E. Scabini and P. Donati, eds., *La famiglia 'luogo' del giovane adulto* (Milan, 1988); E. Scabini, *L'organizzazione famiglia tra crisi e sviluppo* (Milan, 1985).

6. The pope has highlighted the connection between individualism and the crisis of freedom: "We thus come to the very heart of the Gospel truth about freedom. The person realizes himself by the exercise of freedom in truth. Freedom cannot be understood as a license to do absolutely anything; it means a gift of self. Even more, it means an interior discipline of the gift. The idea of gift contains not only the free initiative of the subject, but also the aspect of duty. All this is made real in the 'communion of persons.' We find ourselves again at the very heart of each family. Continuing this line of thought, we also come upon the antithesis between individualism and personalism. Love, the civilization of love, is bound up with personalism. Why with personalism? And why does individualism threaten the civilization of love? We find a key to answering this in the council's expression, a 'sincere gift.' Individualism presupposes a use of freedom in which the subject does what he wants, in which he himself is the one to 'establish the truth' of whatever he finds pleasing or useful. He does not tolerate the fact that someone else 'wants' or demands something from him in the name of an objective truth. He does not want to 'give' to another on the basis of truth; he does not want to become a 'sincere gift.' Individualism

143

On the one hand, there exists an individualistic understanding which negates the value of the other-than-self. It is as if the other, the "thou," were not given with the "I." This other is considered, on the same level as objects, as something to be used for one's own advantage. He is recognized as merely extrinsic; he does not enter into the understanding the "I" has of itself, but is added on to this. Only with difficulty can the other be felt to be a friend or companion; he is much more easily perceived as either a useful means or an obstacle. Thus the two constitutive dimensions of the human being are reduced, both his nonrepeatability or uniqueness and his structural relationality, his being person. Today the second pole clearly seems to be sacrificed with respect to the first.

On the other hand, however, we cannot deny an emphasis on emotion and intimacy in the relationship of the couple. This relationship, sentimentally extolled, is in fact reduced to the private sphere. This nonpublic dimension of love, which in some respects resembles a continuation of the adolescent secrecy of one's first loves, goes hand in hand with a fundamentally individualistic way of conceiving the self in the face of society. Mutual entrustment takes on an official and public character with great difficulty. More often than not, it tends to conceal its nature as a public, socially relevant event (with all the judicial characteristics involved), in order to propose itself exclusively as a private fact, left to the choice of two freedoms. This is true to such an extent that in the United States, for example, there is no lack of courageous authors who reveal how modern jurisprudence treats marriage as an affair so privatized as to be reduced to a sort of "joint venture" project. This is easily seen in the society as such. In the end, the family tends to be reduced to the outcome of a private contract, welcomed only for the economic benefit — and this is not very significant — which the two contracting parties can receive from it. The governing institutions tend to perceive the family as something on the sidelines of civil society, when the latter is not directly thought of as an alternative to it.

These two elements, individualism and privatization of the tie, contribute, as we have said, to a sort of ephemeral emphasis on the couple itself. The couple is no longer positively experienced as the place of a mutual entrustment, responsible and calling forth responsibility, but as a sort of "hiding place." The couple takes on the identity almost of a third reality or entity, be-

---

thus remains egocentric and selfish. The real antithesis between individualism and selfishness emerges not only on the level of theory, but even more on that of ethos. The ethos of personalism is altruistic: It moves the person to become a gift for others and discovers joy in giving himself. This is the joy about which Christ speaks (cf. Jn 15:11; 16:20, 22)." John Paul II, *Letter to Families* 14.

yond that of the individuals involved, as if the first thing necessary were not the truth of each of the two as the indispensable condition for the truth and fruitfulness of a love.

In reality, the couple in a certain sense does not exist. What exists is an "I" and a "thou," a man and a woman, a husband and a wife; I exist and the other exists. The truth of each one is the necessary condition for the truth of the other. Being together, even becoming "one flesh," does not cancel out this requirement of the truth of each one as the condition for the truth of the family.

There is an undue exaltation of the couple when their "togetherness" becomes a way to hide themselves from truth, from their own need, fragility, and human inconstancy, when togetherness, rather than being a path to truth, becomes reductive sentimentalism. In this sense one can observe that the crisis of the couple goes hand in hand with the couple's mythical and therefore unreal exaltation. In a couple thus reduced, the other risks not being recognized in his (or her) destiny. Rather, each tends to affirm himself narcissistically as the meaning of the other.

After all, there are not a few marital crises that begin with the disillusionment following this quasi-mythical exaltation of the couple, and they often assume an even violent form. The spouses accuse each other of having fallen short of a promise — in fact utopian — made at the beginning of the relationship. Having been reduced in this way, the other becomes, sooner or later, a source of boredom or blackmail. Rather than offering companionship in the task and construction of a life, the relationship becomes a suffocating bond, so often full of mutual suspicion.

7.1.2. *Dichotomy between Personal and Civil Liberty*

Doubtless the unease of the family in contemporary culture, which we have touched upon, also depends on the substantial modification of the relation between the public and private spheres of existence, produced in Western democracies and radicalized in the postwar era.[7]

The modern evolution of law, perhaps beginning from the return to natural rights theory begun by Grotius and Pufendorf, can offer an interpretive key for considering this process. This return is also based on the separation,

---

7. We refer the reader to an attentive analysis (whose conclusions we do not fully share) of the phenomena linked to this transition, in R. Poole, *Morality and Modernity* (London and New York, 1991), 134-59. Also useful is V. Possenti, *Filosofia e società. Studi sui progetti etico-politici contemporanei* (Milan, 1983).

within ethics, of personal liberty and civil or juridical liberty, a separation borrowed precisely from law.[8] This dichotomy is tied to a precise modern conception of the state, born from the conviction that only a "contract" dependent on a system of conventional norms can found the ties of society.

Hobbes and Locke, followed by Kant, in a certain sense radicalized this vision. This rendered impracticable the idea introduced by Aristotle in the *Nicomachean Ethics* and taken up again by Thomas Aquinas at the beginning of the *Secunda Pars* of the *Summa Theologiae*, according to which human action, inasmuch as man is a rational animal, must be considered from the total horizon of his nature, and thus from the order to be given to ends and goods in life. This approach allows one to understand moral philosophy as a practical philosophy of human behavior, with a view to the good life.[9]

When this vision was abandoned, the dualistic figure of a public ethics, as opposed to a so-called private ethics, made its appearance, reflecting the division between personal and civil or juridical liberty. Such a public ethics is increasingly formal and norm-centered; as MacIntyre has accurately pointed out, the dimension of virtue is programmatically expelled from it and relegated to the purely private sphere of the individual. A closer look reveals that this radical dichotomy is made possible precisely by a loss of consciousness regarding the value of "intermediate social bodies," above all of marriage and the family, such that paradoxically the individual is not only reduced to a monad but the very articulation of civil society is reduced to a mere sum of individuals. On both levels, moreover, an incurable dialectic is produced between the spheres of the desires and interests of the subject and objective moral demands.

Notwithstanding its radical insistence on the subject, modern culture, without realizing it, is incapable of giving a reason for the constitutive polarity of the individual and society, and this precisely because it has lost sight of the constitutive polarity of man and woman, as we will see further on. This state of affairs, which we have defined as the first radical consequence of the modern vision of the state, was further radicalized by the accent given to the dialectic between economy and rights in contemporary Western societies after the Second World War.

It is unnecessary to touch on the current debate on welfare[10] to recognize that the relationship between economics and rights is radically confronta-

8. Cf. F. von Kutschera, *Fondamenti dell'etica* (Milan, 1991), 296-305, 351ff.

9. Cf. G. Abbà, *Quale impostazione per la filosofia morale?* (Rome, 1996).

10. Cf. M. Toso, *Welfare society. L'apporto dei pontefici da Leone XIII a Giovanni Paolo II* (Rome, 1995).

tional. Paradoxically, it is precisely the ever more pronounced reduction of the rights of the person to the purely individual sphere, as the result of a formalistic and Kantian reading of the Golden Rule — "Do not unto others what you would not have done unto you" — that can explain the nature of this conflict. The attempt to sustain the rights of the person while sundering freedom of conscience, understood as absolute, from its necessary reference to truth, ends in fact by favoring the application of a mercenary or monetary logic to any human need or desire.

On the practical level, basic rights become relevant only *if* and *when* they are articulated as needs to which the market can give a monetary response. In this view the conflict between economy and rights appears as a radicalization of the dichotomy between personal and civil liberty, which in turn reflects the divorce between public and private.[11]

7.1.3. Nihilism and the Absence of Family Relations

This state of affairs is but the reflection on the social plane of that inability of modern culture to remain faithful — though within a necessary critical evaluation — to the basic principle which classical and Christian thought has elaborated, in my opinion, in a perennial form. I refer to man's "capacity" to grasp reality. I intend to speak of that Christian and classical realism for which the truth, in its basic level, is *adaequatio intellectus et rei*.[12]

The first and inexorable consequence of this split between thought and the real can be identified in a sort of "unsatisfied Enlightenment" which characterizes the cultural climate of our times. It is an Enlightenment doubly unsatisfied since, though it began in claiming too much for reason throughout the whole of modernity — when it made the evidence of an absolute, sepa-

---

11. On the conflict between economy and rights, we recommend the dossier *Economia, diritti dell'uomo, cristianesimo*, with interventions from H. Kohl, M. Novak, G. Tremonti, S. Ricossa, S. Zamagni, P. J. Cordes, C. Cousiño, F. Marini, R. Buttiglione, S. D'Antoni, J. A. Sánchez Asiaín, A. Utz, and H. Hude in the cultural review of the Pontifical Lateran University, *Nuntium* 2 (1997): 26-113.

12. I present this in its essential core, to evoke the reservation of personalist philosophy: "Thomas Aquinas, as is well known, defined truth as the adequation of the intellect to reality. The personalistic philosophy of the inter- and post-war periods has been foremost in stressing quite sharply the inadequacy of this definition. Though it is certainly the case that this formula does not say everything that can be said, it does bring to light something of decisive importance: the perception of the truth is a process which brings man into conformity with being. It is a becoming one of the 'I' and the world, it is consonance, it is being gifted and purified." J. Ratzinger, *The Nature and Mission of Theology*, trans. Adrian Walker (San Francisco: Ignatius, 1995), 39.

rate, and abstract reason the *only* evidence — it has ended in demanding too little of reason, leaving it impotent and weak before the elementary affirmation of truth, understood as the *adaequatio* of the intellect to the real.

The programmatic and growing denaturalization of the family, too, has to do with this ontological "problem." There is an inevitable link between ontological unclarity, ethical relativism, and social relativism. This "denaturalization" in fact contradicts human nature on its most basic level, and represents a grave manipulation of the fundamental relationships of human nature in which the personality of each individual human being takes form.

No stratum of the human being escapes unscathed from this denaturalization. The identity of man (masculinity), that of woman (femininity), fatherhood, motherhood, childhood, and even the friendship proper to brotherhood and sisterhood are threatened at their very bases. We are witnessing a privatization of the family which in reality strikes not only at the dignity of the person, but at the very meaning of a common life.

Faced with the perspective just outlined, we cannot escape a question regarding another characteristic of contemporary culture. When man finds himself before that provocation of reality given in the I-thou relation, and specifically in that relation characterized by sexual difference, why does he stop right there rather than setting out on a quest for the ultimate foundation, the uni-total Being?

The fact that this path encounters such difficulty, when it is in itself inscribed in primordial human relationships, urges us to look even more deeply into the crisis of our culture. Here we approach one of the characteristics of the passage of the modern era into that which is now commonly called "postmodernity."[13]

We can say that something essential has changed in the fundamental experience of man's encounter with and comprehension of reality. The individualistic conception of the person makes him incapable of meaningful ties, and of esteem for difference. In a word, this reveals a crisis of freedom.

Freedom, understood according to the modern canon as the emblem of the "I," in fact appears to be shackled, embarrassed in its encounter with the real, so that man loses truth. I do not tire of quoting an affirmation of Augusto del Noce, the philosopher whose death we have recently mourned, because I consider it to be of unsurpassed timeliness and synthesis. He sus-

---

13. On the theme of modernity and postmodernity, cf. F. Botturi, *Modernità e crisi dell'universale; dalla secolarizzazione al nichilismo. Per una Filosofia* (Milan, 1992), 82-91; M. Ureña and J. Prades, *Hombre y Dios en la sociedad de fin de siglo* (Madrid, 1994); A. Scola, *Ospitare il reale. Per una 'idea' di Università* (Rome, 1999), 32-36.

tains that a fundamental characteristic of postmodernity is nihilism, described in the following incisive passage: "The nihilism that prevails today is a 'gay' nihilism, and this in two ways. It is without inquietude (one could perhaps even define it by the suppression of the Augustinian *inquietum cor meum*) — it seeks a sequence of superficial enjoyments with the intention of eliminating drama from the heart of man — and it has its symbol in homosexuality (one could in fact say that its intention is always a homosexual love, even when it maintains a man-woman relationship)."[14] The judgment which interests us here is anthropological, and not first ethical: a "gay" nihilism, in not "seeing" difference, even sexual difference, as a *sign* of the other, runs the risk of understanding love as merely a prolongation of the self (and thus as a homosexual love). It is striking how in this judgment one of the primary anthropological questions — that of the relation between man and woman — is accurately brought to our attention.

Now, what is this nihilism that today so often appears not tragic, but camouflaged under the false pretenses of a deceptive gaiety?[15] It is an understanding of things in which reality ends in nothingness; an ever more pervasive culture (media) has turned this into the dominant mentality. Since man is limited and experiences this limit each day in death and its sorrowful anticipations, so much more worthwhile is it to accept — over and above how much one is conscious of this — that nothingness is the true meaning of being.[16]

The nihilistic affirmation *denies reality any true consistency*. But if the real is not real, and if therefore it is impossible to establish a solid relationship of knowledge and love between the "I" (intelligence and freedom) and reality, then there is no truth. If man cannot "experience" reality to arrive at its truth, freedom remains completely disoriented. It becomes a capacity without an object, and therefore without meaning.[17]

Far from being merely an undifferentiated "tension," like the needle of a

14. A. del Noce, "Lettera a Rodolfo Quadrelli," unpublished, 1984.

15. On nihilism cf. G. Dalmasso, "Immagini della scienza. Dalla coscienza moderna al nichilismo," *Il Nuovo Areopago* 1 (1982): 106-13; T. Gadacz, "La provocazione del nichilismo," *Il Nuovo Areopago* 14 (1995): 5-17; P. Morandé, "Comprendere il nichilismo," *Nuntium* 1 (1997): 62-67.

16. In this sense nihilism, even while maintaining a painful coloring, ends by being in a certain sense desired: "Modern nihilism has a few fundamental dimensions: atheism, the absurdity of existence, political anarchy, and the tragic nature of history. Side by side with the many dimensions of nihilism, all of which interpenetrate one another, there exists a single unifying principle that Nietzsche formulated as follows: 'Nihilism is the desire for nothingness.'" Gadacz, "La provocazione del nichilismo," 7.

17. On the relation between truth and freedom, cf. F. Ratzinger, "Libertà e Verità," *Communio* 144 (1995): 9-28.

broken compass, human freedom is polarized to the fullness of desire, inevitably impressed upon us by our encounter with reality.

If, notwithstanding this, the nihilistic mentality denies the radical (ontological) question regarding the Infinite, then freedom renounces following the trajectory of desire, losing the very dynamic of human existence in the process. Augustine has brilliantly described this process: "Our life is a gymnasium of desire. . . . Therefore, what are you doing in this life if you have not attained the fullness of desire? In making us await Him, God intensifies our desire. With desire He widens the soul, and, widening it, makes it more capable of containing Him. When we say 'God,' what do we wish to express? This word is all that we are waiting for. Let us stretch ourselves towards Him so that He might fill us when He comes."[18]

Modern man runs the risk of so emphasizing freedom of choice that he begins to think it is the *whole of freedom*. Hence his frequent boredom, his incapacity to be stable or responsible. On the one hand, he does not uphold natural desire (inclination), and on the other he thinks himself able to do without God as the fulfillment of this desire. For a desire of the infinite, he substitutes an indefinite series of finite desires. With desire and the horizon of the infinite inhibited, the emphasis given to freedom is posited solely on the possibility of choice. This choice, however, is not exercised in the search for a path leading to a telos adequate to the whole of desire, but simply with a view to that which most instinctively pleases, from time to time.[19] In this way freedom as the capacity for choice becomes contradictory, because each step it takes, every decision it makes, must methodologically cancel out the preceding one. The nihilistic approach is thus a freedom without history.

It is precisely in this crisis of freedom that we can see how much the family is not only the object of a cultural change, but also its subject. This crisis of freedom is in fact tied to the crisis of fatherhood and motherhood, a crisis of family relations.[20] A first and telling symptom of this crisis can be seen in the more and more widely diffused manner of approaching the birth of a child *not* as an event to be welcomed with absolute gratitude, but as the calculated result of a choice. And, as we have seen, decisions made "on" persons end in reducing persons to things.[21]

On a more radical level, the crisis of freedom is the emblem of a "father-

---

18. Augustine, *Tractatus in 1 Johannem* 4.2008-9.

19. Cf. A. Scola, *Questioni di antropologia teologica* (Rome, 1997), 85-102.

20. Cf. T. Anatrella, "Crise de la paternité," *Anthropotes* 12 (1996): 219-34; P. Morandé, "La imagen del padre en la cultura de la postmodernidad," *Anthropotes* 12 (1996): 241-60; G. Zuanazzi, "Il padre tra realtà e finzione," *Anthropotes* 12 (1996): 235-40.

21. G. Colombo, "Osservazioni al II seminario," *La Gazzada* 14, no. 27 (1994): 77-78.

less" society.[22] The absence of paternity — understood here not only in the decisive sense of the male figure, but more globally as that function of generation which includes the mother — is simultaneously cause and effect of freedom's "illness," and therefore of the obscuring of the fundamental human experience of the relationship between the "I" and reality.

Before all else, it is clear that the lack of paternity is a symptom of the loss of a sense of origins. That which a child is, he receives from his parents.[23] The origin of one's own existence implies an absence of self, and suggests the presence of another from whom one comes.[24] But if the memory of origins is lost — and the story of a child's origins can be told him only by his parents! —

22. Kafka writes terrible reflections in this regard: "I was a fearful child, but also stubborn, as children are; mother surely spoiled me a bit, but I cannot believe that it would have been so difficult to have given me some direction. I cannot believe that a kind word, a wordless taking me by the hand, a loving glance would not have been able to obtain from me whatever was desired. You, too, were at heart a tender and good man (what follows is not a contradiction, since I am speaking only of the aspect that influences the child), but not all children have the endurance and the boldness to seek until they find this goodness. You knew how to treat a child as you yourself were made, with force, loudly and wrathfully; and in my specific case this approach seemed even more well-adapted, because you wanted to make me into a strong and courageous boy. Naturally, I am not able to describe directly your educational methods during my earliest years. . . . During the day I never saw you and so you made an even deeper impression on me, which did not dull with habit. From those first years, I remember directly only one episode. Perhaps you remember it as well. One night I was whimpering, asking for some water, certainly not because I was thirsty, but probably in part to make you angry and in part to amuse myself. After a few severe threats had no effect, you took me from my bed, carried me to the doorstep, and left me there awhile in my nightgown, in front of the locked door. I do not want to say that you were unjust; perhaps there really was no other way to recapture the pristine quiet of the night. I wish only to point out your educative methods and their effect on me. After that night, I was certainly more docile, but I carried with me an interior wound. Given my nature, I was never able to establish a right connection between the to me obvious element of my senseless begging for water and the exceptionally frightening experience of being deposited outside. For years afterwards I suffered agonizing pains at the thought that this giant of my father could, ultimately, come at night with no reason at all, snatch me from my bed and leave me on the doorstep, and that, consequently, I was nothing to him. This was a small beginning, but the feeling of nothingness which often overpowers me . . . flows abundantly from your influence. I needed a little encouragement, a little kindness, from someone who left my path a little open. Instead you blocked it, with the best intentions, surely: that of making me take another. But I was unable. . . . I felt miserable, not only in the face of you but in the face of the whole world, because you were for me the measure of all things." F. Kafka, *Lettera al Padre* (Rome, 1996), 29-31 (*Letter to His Father,* trans. Ernst Kaiser and Eithne Wilkins [New York: Schocken Books, 1966]).

23. Cf. B. Bertrand, "Essere figlio: ricevere un'origine," *Il Nuovo Areopago* 11 (1992): 21.

24. "The fact that man must posit himself as the child of a father means that he must recognize that he is given to himself from an absence of his own 'I.'" L. Beirnaert, *Esperienza cristiana e psicologia* (Turin, 1965), 218.

then freedom can no longer receive even the energy of desire while reality awakens in the subject.

The same absence inhibits the path and the meaning of destiny. The child, who grows up within a world with which he is not familiar, cannot orient himself without having someone to look to, who will give him a certainty of the goal and the meaning of his growth (thus the paternal figure is *auctoritas*, he who gives growth).

To this inhibition of growth is linked, a fortiori, a sense of loss in decision making.[25] Where there ought to be a daily exchange of love in which the father gives to his child a vision of life, and the child chooses because he is capable of judgment (of criticism, in the noble sense of the term), today we find uncertainty and absence.

This is why the crisis of freedom and the absence of paternity go hand in hand. If the human subject does not see himself as a being "received from" and "oriented toward," his freedom vanishes.[26]

In this analysis, parents today appear more easily as the companions, or even accomplices, of their children, rather than mothers or fathers.

The fundamental problem is that in order to be a parent, one must have had the experience of being a child. But this is possible only when such an experience remains present and real through the entirety of one's experience, that is, when one lives as a child of him whom the Letter to the Ephesians names as *fons totius paternitatis* (cf. Eph. 3:15).

That person who in his daily life does *not* have the experience of divine filiation — this apart from how he understands the great mystery of God — and who sees himself as the author of his own life, of his day, as the exclusive author of that which begins his own action and that which brings it to term, reveals that his own freedom, in its exercise, remains deprived of its tie to desire and to the infinite mystery. This cannot but lead to tragedy for the human person and for all of society.[27]

---

25. For an analysis of the act of freedom in its second constitutive factor, commonly called "free choice," cf. R. Guardini, *Libertà, grazia, destino* (Brescia, 1968), 74-84.

26. We can say in summary, with Balthasar, that finite freedom, in its experience of itself, finds itself irreducibly to be a being "from" *(woher)*, of being really given to itself, while its movement of self-opening makes it grasp its own existence as a "towards" *(wohin)*. Cf. H. U. von Balthasar, *Theo-Drama II: Dramatis Personae: Man in God*, trans. Graham Harrison (San Francisco: Ignatius, 1990), 110ff.

27. The exasperated denial of every tie is an example of this: "Western man is cultivating the myth of a total individual autonomy, in which the satisfaction of his own needs and humanity fears every bond that might introduce suffering (not just physical pain) and responsibility. But in order to affirm this radical autonomy, man has to be capable of producing himself, of

It may be useful to reflect on a biblical suggestion in this regard. It is signifi-cant that Saint Paul, in the fourth chapter of the Letter to the Galatians, posits the real alternative between existence as a slave and existence as a son, and dem-onstrates how the experience of freedom belongs only to the latter. The status of the slave is that of one who is deprived of his free subjectivity. Only the son pos-sesses freedom. Either freedom is filial or it does not exist at all.[28]

The relationship between mother and child, too, can suffer in this crisis. This relationship, which ought to be the place of affective maturation and the enabling of a critical exercise of reasonable freedom, can be corrupted into a bond which suffocates and enslaves.

It is interesting to note that such an occurrence has its roots in the lack of a real spousal relationship between husband and wife. Being spouses, as the place of a reciprocal gift of love, capable of not tying the other to oneself but of freeing the other within the relationship, of letting the other be, is the in-dispensable experience allowing mother-child and father-child relationships to be a constitutive factor of the child's identity, rather than being trans-formed into an almost unbreakable bond of affective slavery.[29]

With this we arrive at the conclusion that a real esteem of the relationship between man and woman inevitably has repercussions on one's being a par-

---

erasing from his mind and body those ties which constitute him — even those limitations of he-reditary and biological transmission that make him a 'son.'" A. Pessina, "Il controllo eugenetico. La clonazione tra desiderio e sperimentazione," *Vita e Pensiero* 81 (1998): 170-71.

28. "[T]he essential traits of the man who lives this childhood in God as an adult . . . are most evident in Christ himself, since he retained all the traits of the child of God even as he was entrusted with the difficult, superhuman task of leading the whole world back home to God. All his words and deeds reveal that he abides in looking up to the Father with eternal childlike amazement: 'The Father is greater than I' (Jn 14:28). Indeed, he is irretrievably greater in so far as he is the origin of all things, even of the Son, and the Son never thinks of trying to 'catch up' to this his Source: by so doing he would only destroy himself. He knows himself to be sheer gift that is given to itself and which would not exist without the Giver who is distinct from the Gift and who nonetheless gives himself within it. What the Father gives is the capacity to be a self, free-dom, and thus autonomy, but an autonomy which can only be understood as a surrender of self to the other. . . . But . . . when the Father hands over everything to the Son, this 'everything' in-cludes the Father's freedom. And precisely this handing over is the object of infinite amazement, wonderment and gratitude. For the act whereby the Father eternally hands everything over to the Son is always in the present: it is never something concluded, in the past, belonging to a previous epoch, or something obligatory and owed which exists outside the free outpouring of love. Even if it is something remembered from time immemorial, it also remains something offered ever anew, something hoped for with all the infinite trust of love." H. U. von Balthasar, *Unless You Be-come like This Child*, trans. Erasmo Leiva-Merikakis (San Francisco: Ignatius, 1991), 44-45.

29. See the observations on the reciprocal implication of motherhood and fatherhood as the fruit of dual unity in John Paul II, *Letter to Families* 7.

ent. The spousal relation — like that of acknowledging oneself as a son or daughter — is the condition of fatherhood and motherhood, understood as that capacity of generating and introducing the child into an experience of freedom in its confrontation with reality.

The spousal and filial relations seem, therefore, to be the focal points of the fragility of the man-woman relation in a culture characterized by individualism and a crisis of freedom.

7.2. Marriage and the Family and Society

The malaise described above, striking the vital nerve centers of marriage and the family, transforms the very features of society. Like a vigilant watchman, the church, whose specific and primary task is proposing the event of Christ as the concrete experience of salvation, does not tire of raising the alarm against this situation. She does not limit herself to denunciations, but does this positively, vigorously repeating the undeniable truth of things and proposing herself as a subject who questions standing policies. This is why the church does not hesitate to enter directly into a sphere — the civil and political — in which, beginning at least from the last century, she normally intervenes only through the autonomous responsibility of faithful laymen, even if these are organized into social bodies.

But we will proceed in order.

7.2.1. Family and Society

The church's social magisterium repeats incessantly that the family constitutes a fundamental dimension of society.[30] The family — today it must be defined — is understood as the union between a man and a woman; it necessarily refers to the generation of children and is publicly recognized through the *marriage contract*. It is clear that everyone does not share this definition of the family; the mass media often presents very different social and cultural parameters. We believe, however, that it is important to recover the anthropological foundations of the church's position, because we are convinced that only thus will a serene dialogue with each and every person be possible.

---

30. On the church's social doctrine, cf. P. de Laubier, *La pensée sociale de l'Eglise catholique. Un idéal historique de Léon XIII à Jean Paul II* (Fribourg, 1984); M. Cozzoli, *Chiesa, vangelo e società. Natura e metodo della dottrina sociale della Chiesa* (Cinisello Balsamo, 1996); M. Toso, *Dottrina sociale oggi* (Turin, 1996).

For this reason we will make a few brief observations on the reasons the family can be considered a fundamental dimension of society, on the consequences that flow from this, and on the criteria for an adequate relationship between the family and the state.

7.2.2. *The Sovereign Power of the Family*

The pope, in his *Letter to Families,* attributes a "sovereign power" to the family founded on an indissoluble marriage.[31] This sovereignty rests ultimately on the indissolubility of the marriage bond before God and men. Being *forever* belongs in fact to matrimonial consent. A "yes" that is not forever would be hardly credible; it would not seem completely true. If the *consent* of the spouses includes a temporal limit (even as a hypothetical possibility), a *dissent* is inevitably introduced which eventually corrupts the very nature of the marriage. We say "inevitably" because one finds at the basis of marriage the human experience of love, which structurally implies a *"forever."*

What are the implications of the affirmation of a "sovereign power" of the family?[32] First, there is a noninstrumental consideration which recognizes the value of the family in itself as a primordial given. It is anterior to the state and provides the bases for civil society. In this sense the expression "sovereign power" affirms that *possibility* of fullness that is found only in the family.

In the meaning assigned to it by the church, the "sovereignty of the family" refers to the family's position as a subject of fundamental rights. It is precisely the contract between the spouses, inasmuch as this is both a civil and a public factor, which is the source of marriage's weight within a society, and which makes the spouses the subjects of rights and responsibilities in this sphere. But the sovereignty of the family means, too, that the family has the possibility of humanizing its members. In order to grow, the human person needs to follow a path that moves from certainty to certainty: the crises of growth always also pose the question of a greater certainty. For the sake of

---

31. Cf. John Paul II, *Letter to Families* 17.

32. We cannot forget that the attribution of the term "sovereign" to families began with the magisterium of John Paul II. This term was ordinarily used in the church's social doctrine to refer to a *societas perfecta,* possessing total autonomy and independence. We cannot pause here on the debate provoked by the pope's use of the term "sovereign," nor on the consequences that might be involved in the rigid application of this term. (It has been said, for example, that such an affirmation reduces the principle of subsidiarity to mere substitution; and others have pointed out the risk of a society broken up into innumerable nuclear families.) Cf. C. Nardi, "Sovranità della famiglia?" *Vivens Homo* 2 (1996): 337-61.

this, the certainty of marriage's *"forever"* is posited at the origin of the adventure of conjugal life, which in its essence implies the education of children. Without that initial certainty, the objective bases of every other certainty in family life would falter.

7.2.3. The Man-Woman Polarity: A Paradigm of the Human Being's Social Character

A second point of reflection, which enables us to understand the importance of affirming the family as a fundamental dimension of society, refers to the polarity of man and woman, that is, to the fact that man cannot exist except as male and/or female. This polarity, which forms the basis of the family, opens onto another polarity: that of the *individual and society.* Balthasar affirms that the reciprocity between man and woman can be considered the "paradigm of that community dimension which characterizes man's entire nature."[33] Man, then, cannot be understood without a reference to the other mode of being man. This fundamental anthropological datum necessarily implies social reality as constitutive of personal being: the individual is not, in a certain sense, the *whole* of man. In this sense the man-woman polarity expresses the contingent character of being human. This contingence indicates, at the same time, both a limit and a possibility: a limit because the "I," to fulfill itself, needs the other; a possibility because contingence reveals that a capacity for self-transcendence and for opening to the other is a positive factor for the "I."

It is obvious that the family is the first "place" of this being in relation: in it, relation is a natural reality. Before encountering the primary social realities (neighborhood, school, or city), the child grows within the family environment into which it is born. We can say more: it is precisely through this family environment that it comes into contact with society. It is for this reason that the discourse on fundamental rights cannot be completely affirmed as long as the person is considered an isolated individual, on the margins of the family.[34] From the existential point of view, the person is first a husband, wife, father, mother, son, daughter, brother, or sister, and only secondly a citizen. As member of a family, he learns his personal identity and his being-with *(co-essere)* together with others. In the daily drama of family life, the person becomes conscious of his own dignity, and of his being a subject of rights; this awakening of consciousness naturally follows the law of love, the ideal setting of family life.

33. Cf. Balthasar, *Theo-Drama II,* 365.

34. And, as Balthasar says, not only as a spiritual subject: cf. A. Scola, *Hans Urs von Balthasar: A Theological Style* (Grand Rapids: Eerdmans, 1995).

Because of its ontological constitution, the family is the indispensable paradigm of the human being's social character.

7.2.4. The Family, Civil Society, and the State

The two affirmations we have tried to illustrate up to this point allow us to approach the concept of society, as proposed in the social doctrine of the church, with greater clarity. In this sense we believe it is possible to affirm that a reflection on the reality of the family founded on marriage is at the basis of an organic development of Catholic social thought. Certainly, both the concept of the family as a "sovereign reality" and its anthropological foundations (the man-woman polarity) allow us to elaborate an adequate understanding of society derived from the concept of the person. This latter, in its turn, cannot be rigorously thought out without reference to the family.

Man's social character is not first defined by his insertion into the state, which is not the original expression of the social dimension of human experience. The modern state, we repeat, is called to be only a function of civil society, formed in its turn by the persons who live out mutual relations in so-called intermediate bodies, the first of which is the family. Referring to these "intermediate bodies," John Paul II has spoken of the "subjectivity of society," highlighting its primacy over the state; the state constitutes an *objective* structure at the service of society. When, in an inversion of perspectives, the person, family, and intermediate bodies are instead thought of as a function of the state, the foundations are in place for an abolition of personal and social rights, and therefore for totalitarianism. In the perspective mentioned above, the principles of subsidiarity and solidarity, which it is not worthwhile entering into here, find their natural context. This is also the sphere of family politics, the content of which must embrace the widest range of possibilities: from debt relief to the promotion of young couples and large families, to the protection of maternity in the workplace, and school and university politics, according to a vision of the family as an authentic social protagonist. It is evident, in all this, how the family is a factor of civilization.

7.2.5. The Nature of Man and Culture

Perhaps a brief clarification is in order. I am aware that one of the possible criticisms of this approach can come from a certain theory of culture which excludes the possibility of elaborating a discourse on man as such, and which therefore is able to defend the essential unity of the human race without thereby negating the diversity of its cultural expressions. I think, for example, of the delicate problems of monogamy or of the conflicts resulting from ethnic-national tensions, both burning issues today. It goes without saying that, at least in large part, a discourse on the family is strictly tied to a model of culture, and to the varieties of cultures themselves. Notwithstanding this, we do not believe it possible to deny the existence of a "central core," which the classics identified with the concept "nature." This core is the expression of the metaphysical necessity and constitutive needs of the human being as such. Because of it, one can speak of "person" for the European as well as for the American, African, or Asian. Culture, in the most noble sense of the term — that is, the specific mode of man's being and existing as such — is an expression of this "central core."[35]

We will take a further step: monogamous and indissoluble marriage belongs to the original anthropological "given." This affirmation does not lose its force in the face of the various cultural and historical visions of marriage which do not keep within these two parameters. To affirm that monogamous and indissoluble marriage is an original anthropological given does not imply forgetting the human being's historical character. Thus, neither does it lose sight of the fact that in history the ideal is not always concretely lived.

35. Cf. John Paul II, speech to UNESCO (June 2, 1980).

CHAPTER 8

Marriage, the Family, and Life

8.1. Science Betrayed

The golden age of modernity, characterized by a growing exaltation of science, aroused a sort of delirium of omnipotence in man. In its wake, we discern in our so-called postmodern age[1] a sort of pernicious rebound effect: the threat of man's total self-elimination. We have encountered the possibility, that is, of laying hands directly on the origins of life and becoming, in a certain sense, its artificers, with the terrible power of extinguishing our own species.

We must have the courage to face this fact with objectivity, without a priori departmentalizing. The human being's capability to intervene so radically in the processes that determine his own birth is extremely disturbing, and marks a break with the preceding historical era.[2] Not even a comparison with

---

1. Cf. P. Morandé, "Vita e persona nella postmodernità," in *Quale vita? La bioetica in questione*, ed. A. Scola (Milan, 1998), 117-41.

2. "As far as concerns the cloning of entire human organisms, the following are presented as goals: (1) the 'production' of embryos not affected by pathologies of a mitochondrial origin . . . ; (2) the 'production' of embryos not affected by pathologies of a hereditary origin from parents who are both carriers of the same pathogenic gene; (3) the possibility of reproduction in cases of complete azoospermia, in order to satisfy the desire not only of having children, but that these children have the chromosomal inheritance of the person making the request. To these 'reasons' are appended others, all part of the now well-known list drawn up by Kass (L. Kass, "New Beginning in Life," in M. P. Hamilton [ed.], *The New Genetics and the Future of Man,* Grand Rapids, 1972, 14-63). According to Kass, 'semi-serious' reasons for requesting cloning might be: (1) the replication of individuals who possessed great genius or beauty for the betterment of the species, or to make life more enjoyable; (2) the replication of healthy individuals to avoid hereditary maladies inherent in the 'lottery' of sexual recombination; (3) to provide a large quantity of genetically identical subjects in order to conduct scientific studies on the rela-

the destructive potential of the atomic bomb suffices in the face of the phenomena tied to cloning, when these are applied on a large scale.

Such an unheard-of possibility did not spring from nothing. It was sown
and could strike solid root in the field of technological scientism, which
bases itself on the presupposition that the human being, like every other
form of life, can be completely manipulated and reduced to material.[3] Every
other dimension of human nature that escapes the control of scientific and
technological measure tends to be consigned to the limbo of insignificance
and forgotten.

It is not difficult to discern the relationship between this reduction and
the frequent demands for social equality, and for the power of man over man.
It makes a great difference whether personal dignity is something intrinsic to
the human being or is given to him by others or by the state, and is thus at the
mercy of their decisions. If man is reduced to mere material, capable of manipulation, death will always conquer in the end (the disturbing shadow of
nihilism again raises its head!); it would be the death of justice.

But "scientism" is not science. An example taken from an issue central to
the themes we are discussing is enough to make this clear. It is contradictory
that precisely in order to realize such a project of the total manipulability of
man, people refuse the evidence of biological research regarding the identity
of the human embryo.[4] Yet another paradoxical aspect of the strange contem-

---

tive importance of innate nature and environment for the various aspects of human performance; (4) to procure a child for a sterile couple; (5) to procure a child with a specifically chosen
genotype: of an admired celebrity, a deceased beloved, a spouse, or oneself; (6) to determine the
sex of the child who will be born, since the sex of the clone is the same as that of the person who
provides the transplanted nucleus; (7) to produce a series of identical subjects to carry out special tasks in times of war and peace (spying not excluded); (8) to produce embryo copies of each
person, to be kept frozen as a 'reserve' of organs that can be transplanted on its genetically identical twin; (9) to beat the Russians and Chinese, so that we not lag behind in the field of cloning." M. L. di Pietro, "Dalla clonazione dell'animale alla clonazione dell'uomo?" *Medicina e Morale* 47 (1997): 1105-7.

3. Cf. L. Melina, "Riconoscere la vita. Problematiche epistemologiche della bioetica," in
Quale vita? 75-115.

4. The logic of biology — as can be seen in the document *Identità e statuto dell'embrione
umano* of the Center for Bioethics of the Università Cattolica del Sacro Cuore, in *Medicina e
Morale* 39 (1989) supplement to no. 4 — tells us that as soon as egg and spermatozoa interact, a
new system arises with the characteristic of a combined system, not a mere sum of two underlying systems. This new system has a new genotype, which identifies the single-celled embryo
as biologically *human* and specifies its individuality, its biological center. The development of
this single-celled embryo will later be characterized by the three properties of coordination,
continuity, and graduality. Cf. also R. Colombo, "Vita: dalla biologia all'etica," in *Quale vita?*
169-95.

porary situation comes to light when practical and ideological interests, abusively brought forward "in the name of science," impede a simple and unprejudiced hearing of what science itself is capable of telling us.

In reality, to grasp the scientific truth about the human embryo, in its perspectives, limits, and requirements, one must first be open to the whole truth about man and his mystery. *Man, who are you?* This is the inescapable anthropological question which precedes and founds the moral question.[5]

8.2. The Urgent Need of a Foundation.
What Kind of Life? Bioethics at Trial

The observations made up to this point help explain why, in the course of a few years, bioethics has come to occupy, and continues to occupy, an enormous place in the cultural debate of our times. The themes tied to this discipline remain very uncertain both in terms of content and of method (that is, on an epistemological level), but at first glance their burning actuality seems to justify a multiplication of initiatives within the discipline. One cannot, however, deny that the proliferation of bioethical conferences and literature runs the risk of confusion, or at least of an ever greater difficulty in identifying the central core of the issues being discussed.

For this reason, and with absolute intellectual honesty — that is, obeying reason's inherent requirement not to obscure any of the factors at play — we ask ourselves: Has not bioethics, under the pressure of fixing (ethical) parameters of reference in extremely delicate and ever more complex questions, relegated an inquiry into the very thing to be regulated (life) into second place? Totally absorbed by the preoccupation of establishing ethical norms capable of ordering the phenomena connected to the origin and manipulation of life, the discipline has perhaps too quickly set aside the question: *What kind of life?*[6]

In recovering the centrality of this question, and before sketching out a response, I would like to make a number of comments which, in my judgment, have not always been adequately brought to light.

When dealing with life or the history of life, one cannot stop at calming explanations, often unequal to the questions really being asked. Nor, in order to deny this disequilibrium, can one refer to the growing, and oftentimes ob-

---

5. Cf. S. Grygiel, "Per guardare il cielo. Vita, vita umana e persona," in *Quale vita?* 43-73.

6. Cf. Scola, ed., *Quale vita?*; E. Agazzi, ed., *Bioetica e persona* (Milan, 1993); L. Melina, *Corso di bioetica: il Vangelo della vita* (Casale Monferrato, 1996); E. Sgreccia, ed., *Le radici della bioetica* (Milan, 1998).

jectively unbalanced, preoccupation for the animal and spirit worlds which increasingly characterizes the inhabitants of the Northern Hemisphere. It is not only a reference to the biological sciences, which are at the bases of bioethics, that demonstrates the complexity (but not the impossibility) of clearly defining the notion of "life" and the questions connected to it; the issue refers also to the disciplines of theology and philosophy. A rigorous and complete critical reflection is called for. As an example, one can point to the delicate problem of interpreting the relationship of the undeniable continuum that exists in the passage from the various forms of life (especially the superior ones) to that quality of human life that makes it ontologically "other." If some authors (like Singer), with their accusation of "speciesism," have been well enough received by the predominant cultural climate, and even strongly influenced it, this is a sign that the complex problems linked to the emergence of consciousness and self-consciousness must be faced without an attitude of simplistic self-sufficiency. One cannot limit oneself to a mechanical transposition, on the level of reflexive knowledge, of the syncretic perception with which common sense grasps the radical novelty of such phenomena! Personally, I am firmly convinced that this novelty exists, and that it can easily be demonstrated within the framework of a complete and scientifically articulated knowledge of man. However, this requires a considerable critical effort, and it is not at all obvious.

The singling out of *this individual man* (the expression is borrowed from Kierkegaard) gives us a further confirmation of this. It is certainly possible to demonstrate the founding principle of *personal difference* characterizing the single individual in the human species — in itself and in comparison with the principle of individuation within the animal species — but this is a very complex undertaking.

To set out on such a venture, with intellectual loyalty and without shying away from any of the questions posed by the various sciences dealing with life and its history, does not at all mean, however, that we advance into the famous "night in which all cows are black," making room for every definition of life without distinction. Human freedom cannot escape the moment of truth; in his every action the person is called to decide for or against truth. Nor can this be avoided by the simplistic thesis that in a multicultural and pluralistic society everyone has the right to his own truth, and is therefore limited, in the name of respect for his neighbor's liberty, to setting forth parallel truths which contradict his neighbor's. Reason and freedom cannot renounce the urge to wholeness contained in truth! In the light of all this, cloning, the emblem of our postmodern age that is exposed to self-annihilation, shows the inadequacy of an automatic transposition of the principle of the freedom of the individual conscience and of the Golden Rule (do not do unto others what you would not have them do unto you) to the level of civil society and juridical regulation, when that transposition is made without further theoretical and practical social development. In order to admit the necessity of confronting our opening question, without prejudice and in total openness, we need a critical attitude which is the exact opposite of the relativism that prevails today.

What, then, is the content of that truth tied to the notion of life and its history? There seem to me to be two incontestable facts.

The first begins with a limitation, and therefore, at first glance, with a negation. Man cannot be "deciphered" by pure biology. He breaks out of a closed temporal space in every direction. His identity, in fact, has its roots in a history (past) whose meaning must be read in the light of that *future* which is *present* in every instant of time, though it does not identify itself with any instant.

Hence the efforts to discover this identity only in the configuration of biological components or genetic codes will be in vain. In this sense the essential quality of personal human life cannot be understood without the recognition of a profound intertwining, in human nature, of the bio-instinctual level and the psycho-spiritual dimension which transcends it.

The poet Hölderlin writes,

Pure springing forth is a mystery,
Barely revealed even in song.
As you begin, so you shall remain;
So great and rigorous is misery that
Birth can do the most of it,
And the ray of light that greets the newborn child.[7]

An irreducible core can be discerned at the heart of human nature; no culture can ever create it from nothing. This simple affirmation reveals a contradiction at the heart of the current bioethical debate. If we wish truly to concern ourselves with the data that science, and first of all biology, provides, we cannot accept a theoretical perspective in which nature can be so formed by culture as to be ultimately produced by it. It is contradictory to invoke science to make an accusation of speciesism, and at the same time to postulate a concept of nature as created purely by culture (by pure human activity)!

"Birth can do the most of it," says Hölderlin, but he immediately adds,

7. Cf. F. Hölderlin, "The Rhine."

"and the ray of light that greets the newborn child." What is this "ray of light" if not a fundamental relation to the other, not understood as something extrinsic or juxtaposed to nature, nor as a by-product of human self-knowledge, but as an original and constitutive *quid* which traverses the bio-instinctual level to inaugurate the human life of this individual person? Man's life and identity imply this being present to the other which passes through the presence of the other. In this sense the most elementary revelation of *what* human life is, is its coming to be from the conjugal act of love of a mother and a father.

As the tradition of classical realism has taught us, human life is situated at the convergence of the spiritual and bodily dimensions. Without this convergence, which we have repeatedly called *dual unity,* it is impossible to speak of the whole of man. If we were at this point to make a stab at human destiny that would seriously compete with the nihilistic or "weak" tendencies of contemporary thought — which, as such, condemn themselves to discussions full of *aporia* — we could demonstrate that fundamental human experience is really well founded. On this level, at once prescientific and full of incontrovertible evidence, human life reveals itself to be ontologically inserted from the moment of conception into a nature made up of the dual unity of body and soul. But this is not the place for such an enterprise.

Since the second constitutive fact of the specific nature of human life has already been at a number of points the focus of discussion, only a brief reminder of it is necessary. This refers to man and woman, the second of the polarities in which the dual unity of human nature is expressed. The category of the nuptial mystery offers us an adequate understanding of this fact; this is the object of part I of the present work.

The tragedy of the contemporary age appears to be exploding onto the scene through the phenomena studied by bioethics; it consists in that break, prophetically denounced by Paul VI in *Humanae Vitae,* of the three constitutive components of nuptiality: sexual difference, reciprocity of love, and fruitfulness. (Now the perspective of a "human ecology" reveals all the cultural force of that denunciation!) The contraceptive mentality has ushered in the possibility of separating sexual relations from love and fruitfulness, and diffused the idea on a large scale. Today, with in vitro fertilization and especially cloning, sexuality and procreation can become completely separate realities, without the slightest reciprocal implication.

The mosaic of the response to the question, *What kind of life?* thus receives a new and decisive reinforcement: a life proportioned to the nature of human sexuality — qualitatively different from that of animals. As we know, the former reveals an asymmetrical reciprocity taken up into the oblation of love. This is no androgynous search for a lost whole, but the recognition, full of wonder, of the other as the condition of the truth of my "I," which has its guarantee in openness to a third.

8.3. Bioethics, the Religious Sense, and Religions

Here we find space for an inquiry into the ultimate foundation of the singular identity of human life, and of man himself, which, as we have seen, leads us to the trinitarian mystery. In this way the question, *What kind of life?* leads to the question of the foundation of reality, opening onto the religious dimension of human experience. It is therefore worthwhile to demonstrate the reciprocal, and in no way optional, implication between bioethics and religions.

The inextinguishable thirst for the Mystery which dwells in the human heart, even when buried under an endemic obscuring of the "I," constitutes the greatest resource of individuals and peoples. It appears more necessary than ever at the dawn of the third millennium. In *homo religiosus*, the religious man, the human being's rational nature is fulfilled.[8] In openness to the

---

8. "'What is man, of what worth is he? The good, the evil in him, what are these?' (Sir 18:8). The questions posed in the Book of Sirach, which we have just heard, questions which are echoed by all the biblical Wisdom literature that likewise reflected upon man's birth, death and frailty, these questions characterize a level of human experience that is absolutely common to all men. These questions are in the heart of every man, as is evident in the poetic genius of every age and people. Almost like a prophecy of mankind, this genius continually proposes the 'serious question' that makes man truly man. Such questions express the urgent need to find the 'why' of his existence, of his every moment, of his outstanding and decisive stages, as well as his most common moments. They attest to the profound reasonableness of human existence, since man's intellect and will are stimulated to search freely for the solution that can offer full meaning to life. These questions, therefore, constitute the greatest expression of man's nature: consequently, the answer to them measures the depth of his commitment with his own existence. Particularly, when the 'why of things' is investigated together with the search for the ultimate and exhaustive answer, then human reason reaches its apex and opens itself to religiousness. As a matter of fact, religiousness represents the loftiest expression of the human person, because it is the culmination of his rational nature. It springs from man's profound aspiration for truth and is at the basis of the free and personal search he makes for the divine." John Paul II, General Audience of the Holy Year, October 19, 1983, 1-2. In this audience John Paul II takes up a theme dear to him, which he developed during the council in at least five explicit interventions. A thorough investigation of the rational nature of the human person reveals that its culmination is *religio*, which consists "in liberam mentis humanae ad Deum adhaesionem, quae est omnino personalis et conscientiosa, et ex appetitu oritur veritatis." The inextinguishable religious attitude of man is thus the culmination of his reasonableness ("oportet ut persona humana appareat in reali sublimitate suae naturae rationalis, religio autem ut culmen istius naturae"). *Acta Syn.*, vol. 3, pars 2, 531-32.

165

transcendent Mystery which singles him out, man extends the arc of his reason to its fullest possible sweep. Precisely in this he encounters, in the recognition of the indestructible dignity of the human person, the adequate principle for the building up of society.

The reciprocal implication of bioethics and religions does not require
particular justifying clarifications. The important developments of science
and technology in the last century have unearthed new and grave ethical
questions regarding the place of man in the biosphere. On the other hand,
the great religious traditions of mankind are a point of reference in the human being's constant search for truth and the moral good. Thus contemporary bioethics challenges the religions, urging them to a more persuasive
search for the one true good that is their very reason for being. Moral experience, in its turn, is profoundly tied to the religious experience. Even if the
latter cannot be reduced to mere moral experience, a constant openness to
the transcendent which keeps man from acting on the level of this world
only and forms the basis of his yearning for salvation, is in strict relation
with the way he relates to the divine. A desire for salvation, involvement with
people and with the world order, religion, and morals are therefore intimately connected. It is in this context that the Catholic tradition's insistence
on the objective and intrinsic relation between the natural moral law and
salvation becomes understandable. Man discovers a natural capacity in himself regarding the knowledge of good and evil. In his *mens,* as the fathers and
doctors of the church transcribed the Hebrew notion of heart, there is a
mysterious spark — "signatum est super nos lumen vultus tui, Domine" (Ps.
4:7) — that admonishes him when he does evil and reminds him, beyond
the horizon of his own "I" and his relationship with the world, of the presence of the living God who transcends both. In the discovery of this divine
imprint, in the dramatic and exultant heart of the moral experience, man is
able to discover a law he has not given himself. Confronted by this moral urgency, his desire for salvation shows him his inadequacy, exacerbated by sin,
and opens him to the cry that invokes grace. The poetic genius has reminded
us of this: I think of Munch's *The Scream,* or of Dostoyevsky's profound
analysis of the stupor that so often characterizes us in the face of moral experience and its relationship with salvation.

Religious traditions, and particularly the monotheistic ones — the religions of the book — speak to us of a God who communicates the moral law,
as the signpost accompanying freedom in its path toward salvation. Human
life, in the reality of the world which surrounds it, is a primary and fundamental sign of this loving divine presence. In the face of grave threats to this
life, the religions defend its sacred character. The nature of life as gift must

be appreciated against every imperative technological claim that, in transforming the "it is possible" of science into a "we must," reveals a will to deadly power. The men and women of today, like Abraham, their father in faith, and even with all the peculiarities proper to their technological civilization, cannot prescind from the immemorial questions on the meaning of life and of technology. As we have said, there is in the human heart a desire for salvation that can come only from God; man discovers a moral norm within himself that approves when he acts well and reproves when he does evil. Salvation and the moral good, religion and ethics are the foundations with which man, whether he recognizes it or not, confronts the world to change it according to rational ends and appropriate means. Religion and ethics are thus inevitably implied in science and technology. Abraham sets out on a path in faith, basing himself on God's promise. Through the obedience of the patriarch of Ur, God's work of salvation is thus linked to the Jewish people and to the work of human hands, and thus, too, to science and technology, without being exhausted in these. To believers, contemporary bioethics is a challenge to this Abramic pilgrimage that does not cease on this earth, not even when the hope of salvation has come to pass through God's gratuitous initiative, as we Christians humbly believe when we confess Jesus Christ as Son of God made man.

8.4. For an Authentic Humanism

Being human possesses its own inalienable value. Human life, in fact, has value if the human being has value. As soon as he loses the existential perception of the infinite value of his person, his life, too, falls into meaninglessness. And no vitalism (we think of the innumerable health-centered practices that our societies engage in ever more obsessively) can mask the irremediable loss.

As Nietzsche has tragically revealed, every form of vitalism, whether naturalistic or beautifying, is nihilism in its larval stage. If man is nothing but "the shadow of a passing dream" (Shakespeare), life inexorably falls into a "being for death" (Heidegger).

As we proceed, it appears more and more obvious that the current, and often heated, controversy about life — for example, regarding the biological and ontological status of the human embryo, or the distinction between the "human" and "nonhuman person" — is but a chapter in the wider controversy about man.

The decisive match of this game is played in the answer to the question masterfully formulated by the poet Leopardi: "And I, what am I?"[9] Who is man, and what is the basis of his dignity?

A great part of modern culture claims to save man by detaching him from God, thus establishing a fundamental opposition between human fulfillment and faith, or else deluding itself into thinking it can continue to defend man while prescinding from all of this. But the failure of this claim stares us all in the face. And no one today speaks any more of humanism. In reality, as the pope writes in *Evangelium Vitae*, "man's revolt against God in the earthly paradise is followed by the deadly combat of man against man" (8), and even before this, of man with himself. As Cardinal de Lubac reminds us, "Man can organize society without God, but, without God, he cannot in the end help organizing it against man."

Torn from his belonging to God, man remains the victim of an insurmountable vulnerability. If the other in fact does not belong to God, I can do with him whatever I please. If, on the other hand, he does belong, I must respect this divine belonging. More, if belonging to God is the prerogative of each human being, as his creature, then I, too, am God's possession and tied to the other by a substantial and ontological bond. A common belonging to the same Father provides the basis for the equal dignity of every person, and for an indestructible solidarity with one's equals.

"What life have you if you have not life together?"[10] The burning truth of this question does not easily allow it to be silenced. But how is it possible to have a life in common if this communal nature is not already a principle of our being? In other words, how is this possible if the relation with the other and with life is not coessential and connatural to us?

8.5. The Light of *Evangelium Vitae:* Excursus

The encyclical *Evangelium Vitae* offers us an extraordinary panorama of the current debate about man. Negotiating its way through all the themes we have touched upon, the encyclical arrives at a penetrating social judgment and a powerful criticism of the socially dominant situations and forms of thought, at a time in which the greater part of the voices of the Western world are raised solely to defend the privileges and material well-being they have acquired and see threatened by other "worlds."

---

9. G. Leopardi, "Canto notturno di un pastore errante dell'Asia," v. 89, in *Canti,* ed. Mario Fubini (Turin, 1971), 183.

10. Cf. T. S. Eliot, *Choruses from the Rock,* in *The Complete Poems and Plays of T. S. Eliot* (London: Faber and Faber, 1969), 152.

The encyclical seizes upon an aspect of the attempts on human life which has not attracted much commentary until now; these attempts are multiplied particularly at the very beginning[11] and the end[12] of life, when it is weakest and most defenseless. What the encyclical underscores is the mass, or social dimension of these attempts. Such practices tend to be vindicated on the level of public opinion as the rights of individual liberty; they are perpetrated with a socially recognized recourse to medicine, and seek legitimization in the juridical codes of various nations, radically separating the civil law from the moral law.[13]

With this, something explosive is introduced into the democratic order regulated by law. At the center of this order is no longer a recognition of original and indisputable rights, valid for each and all, beginning from the right to life. The so-called democratic system has been struck to the heart, expropriated from its moral bases and assailed by a limitless ethical relativism. In the end it is used as a pure pretext for allowing the rights of the strong to prevail over those of the weak.

When human life is no longer a sacred and inviolable right, but a consumer good which can be appraised in terms of usefulness or pleasure, a "culture of death"[14] develops, threatening both man and his civilization. The single denominator of "quality of life" becomes the materialistic criterion. Suffering becomes useless, sacrifice for others unjustified, and the baby in its mother's womb a burden to be removed without remorse.

John Paul II has raised an alarm directed at the schizophrenia of a society that, as it promotes the inviolability of human rights, authorizes the manipulation of its fundamental presupposition: life.

This is the last link of that series of strictly connected *aporia* characterizing the development of modern ethics, which we have mentioned above in sketching its historical path. The key element is the dissociation between private and public ethics, the sphere of subjective desire/interest and objective moral requirements; its repercussions multiply in concentric circles, distorting the common life on all levels.

In the sphere of the family, the child is no longer considered a totally gratuitous event, the fruit of the spouses' love, but — both in the individual consciousness and the collective imagination, as the legislation of the more "ad-

---

11. *Evangelium Vitae* 58-63.

12. *Evangelium Vitae* 64-67.

13. *Evangelium Vitae* 68-75. In this regard cf. W. Waldstein, "Vita e vita sociale: pluralismo e regole sociali," in *Quale vita?* 323-47.

14. *Evangelium Vitae* 95. Cf. D. Schindler, "Sacralità della vita e cultura della morte," in *Quale vita?* 309-22.

vanced" democracies makes plain — as a variable totally dependent on the sovereign will of its parents. If it arrives undesired, they have recourse to abortion. If it does not arrive even if it is desired, they have recourse to any means whatsoever, so that their aspirations can be satisfied. Here it is enough to think of artificial fertilization, which transforms the child into the object of a process of production.

In the sphere of society, whose progressive "barbarization" is obvious to all, the divide between the social proclamation of respect for others and the absolute indifference with which people behave in the drama of personal relations continues to widen. One need only leaf through any given daily paper to find almost unbelievable examples.

In the economic sphere, the conflict between economics and rights has undergone a worrisome escalation in the last few decades. Since freedom of conscience has been absolutized and divorced from its essential relationship to the truth, the path has been cleared for the reduction of everything to market and monetary terms, the single interpretative key for all human needs and desires.

For the same reason the fundamental rights of peoples are invoked and defended only if the logic of the market permits it. We see dramatic evidence of this in the wars consuming vast areas of the third world; the "double measure" adopted by international peacekeeping forces, mobilized in massive numbers in some cases but completely lacking in others, is clear to all.

In the political sphere, the theoretical affirmation of utopian projects (marked by ideology, particularly of the Marxist variety) accompanies the pragmatic and unbiased defense of personal interests, or of the interests of a group, lobby, nation, people, or zone of world influence.

From this brief survey bearing witness to the dissociation between public and private ethics, it becomes more and more clear that modern culture, notwithstanding its radical insistence on the subject, is incapable either of thinking or of defending the subject in all of its depth.

Apart from an adequate anthropological discourse, founded on dual unity and the three polarities in which this is articulated, I believe that unity can be recovered by giving privileged attention to "intermediate bodies," and the family in particular. As John Paul II has reminded us, taking up the tradition of all the church's social doctrine, this involves realities (social, political, cultural, and economic groups) which have their origin in human nature, and which, in an obvious subordination to the common good, enjoy their own autonomy. These have absolute priority, because they constitute a "social subjectivity" with respect to the state, an "objectivity" which must always be at their service.

CHAPTER 9

Marriage, the Family, and Education

9.1. *Value* Education?

We have lost "the place of the spirit, that 'being at home' that comes of the knowledge of where we are and why we are there. We begin to suspect that there is no why in the 'what?' the 'now,' and the 'here': existence finds itself deprived of every basis. Thus there arises, in man, anxiety in the face of the world, fear in the face of the powers of nature: not merely because these can externally destroy, but because they erode the importance of his own being. Whereas before, all was seen in relationship to man, now it becomes clear to man's consciousness that this 'all' is indifferent."[1] Guardini's brilliant description of the origin of contemporary man's radical anxiety can help us understand how the concept of "value," so habitually employed in speaking of education, is today extremely problematic. "Problematic" does not mean "mistaken," but rather in need of an accurate critical foundation in order to avoid falling into ambiguity. Where does this "problematization" of the concept of value come from, and why did it arise? To limit ourselves to its more recent phase, there is no dearth of thinkers who identify its source in the passage from modernity to postmodernity.[2] Postmodern thought radically questions not only the values of modernity (linear and indefinite progress, a utopia of inevitable happiness, the absoluteness and autonomy of reason, absolute faith in science and its practical applications, the existence of a universal moral code), but the idea of "value" itself.

1. R. Guardini, *Pascal* (Brescia, 1957), 77-78 (*Pascal for Our Time*, trans. Brian Thompson [New York: Herder and Herder, 1966]).
2. A concise presentation with a good bibliography can be found in G. Penati, "Modernità e postmoderno nel pensiero filosofico attuale," *Communio* 110 (1990): 16-31.

If, with Gevaert, we define "value" as "all that which allows a meaning to be given to human existence, all that which permits us to be really human . . . (values do not exist without man, who, with them, is able to confer meaning upon his own existence),"[3] we realize that postmodernity challenges precisely the two key categories of this definition: man as subject, and totality. The widely diffused formula of the "death of the subject" as a self-conscious and personal being is without doubt most expressive of the predominant cultural climate today. The idea of the subject, both in its Cartesian, consciousness-centered, and atomistic-empiricist versions, has collapsed, the victim of an irreversible crisis.

Even alternative categories (I refer to relation, communication, altruism, sociality) which also indicate the the human being's inability to prescind from some necessary and fundamental pieces of evidence — and that of the subject is without a doubt one of the most important of these — demonstrate the problem mentioned above. This is confirmed by an inability to think in terms of totality and the whole, now even theorized by many. The death of the subject, its inability to grasp the whole and thus place itself in relation to totality, is precisely what some authors identify as the break between modernity and postmodernity.

It is important to note that this crisis of the very idea of "value" does not involve only the elite who create contemporary schools of thought, but affects the general mind-set as well. It is undeniable that the general population, though enjoying the benefits of technology, lives in a sort of growing torpor, in the twilight of so-called religious, moral, and spiritual values.

A lifestyle marked by indifference and laissez-faire has replaced the unity of a people understood as a belonging, a tradition that, at least in Europe, was tied to a precise notion of the person. Communion has given way to a commonality of homologous behavior. This new state of affairs makes use of an "emotional subjectivism" on the one hand and a "purely instrumental reason" on the other.

The Anglo-Saxon philosopher Alasdair MacIntyre has identified the three characteristics of the first in that individualism and relativism that give the individual the illusion of choice — thus becoming the "sovereign of his own moral authority" — among a multitude of orientations: the best according to one's will, preference, and pleasure. The result is that each person's moral assertions appear to him to be endowed with a universal force. By "instrumental reason," MacIntyre refers to a reason capable of operative strategy

3. J. Gevaert, *Il problema dell'uomo. Introduzione all'antropologia filosofica* (Turin, 1989), 7a, 147-54.

but powerless in identifying the ends of action or the criteria of choice; thus it renounces a serious consideration of the fundamental human questions. Efficiency, competence, aestheticism, and a manipulative control of facts and persons are for MacIntyre the masks used to obtain a consensus, utilized by the typical personalities of a subjectivistic culture tied to instrumental reason: the manager, the aesthete, and the therapist.[4]

Though we cannot in this study adequately evaluate this critique of "value" in the postmodern cultural context, we can certainly recognize that the category of value — originally borrowed from the sphere of economics — cannot continue to be thought of abstractly. Values are not things; they belong to that essential relationship between persons and things that marks the presence of a qualitative *depth* and always implies at least three fundamental properties: (a) a certain tension (dialectic) between the things which possess value and the persons on which these depend; (b) an interpersonal dimension: values are never only for me, but also for us; and (c) a question of transcendence which the value always poses to the subject, and which prohibits us from speaking of a "creation of values," because a value cannot but demand submission.[5]

To speak of "value education" (or an education to values) in the family or in schools is therefore impossible, and ultimately equivocal, if such an education is reduced to a list of things formulated in abstract concepts. The relationship between person and community, in themselves and in their relation to the (infinite) mystery, must always be brought to light, inasmuch as these constitute the adequate, personal, and communitarian subject within which a value maintains its capacity to give meaning to human existence and, above all, to be effectively communicated. It appears that in our discussion of the radical critique to which the category of "value" is subjected by postmodernity, we have arrived at the proper content of the concept of education: the introduction of the whole person to the whole of reality, through a communication that takes place from experience to experience. In this sense it is possible to speak of "values" only within an adequate educational relationship.

9.2. The Family: The "Educating Subject" Par Excellence

The primary and irreplaceable foundation of this educational relationship is the family. It is the first concrete possibility, for each man and woman that

---

4. Cf. A. MacIntyre, *Dopo la virtù* (Milan, 1993), 89ff. (*After Virtue: A Study in Moral Theory* [Notre Dame: University of Notre Dame Press, 1981]).

5. MacIntyre, *Dopo la virtù*, 148-49.

comes into the world, to be introduced to the whole of reality.[6] In this sense the specific task of *fatherhood* and *motherhood* — from which all other family relationships are derived and to which they are added — cannot be reduced to the mere *generation* of a new individual of the human species. Fatherhood and motherhood imply an educative dimension that cannot be renounced, and ultimately cannot be delegated.[7]

In the face of this evidence, suggested to us by the simple observation of fundamental human experience, the increasing absence of fatherhood (and parenthood in general)[8] in the contemporary cultural climate appears in all its disturbing gravity. If the parent-child relation is in fact the source and paradigm of the entire phenomenon of education,[9] the drying up of this source is at the same time the cause and effect of the malaise of freedom, and therefore of the growing fragility of that relationship between the "I" and reality, through which man has access to the truth. Unable to grow according to his full potential, the human person remains more and more at the mercy of the disorientation of nothingness. If, then, there is a difficulty in education as such today, it is that of acknowledging oneself a son or daughter, and therefore of being parents. It is as if the tie which binds parent and child along the whole of a person's life has been broken. A given individual's path is in fact the fruit of his relationship with his parents, and implies a continual exchange between parent and child and vice versa, even though this is carried out not in a symmetrical way but according to the principle of authority (*auctoritas:* that which makes grow).

In the history of the West, this dynamic of education has found its natural extension in the school.

6. John Paul II, *Letter to Families* 10: "The words of consent, then, express what is essential to the common good of the spouses, and they indicate what ought to be the common good of the future family. In order to bring this out, the church asks the spouses if they are prepared to accept the children God grants them and to raise the children as Christians. This question calls to mind the common good of the future family unit, evoking the genealogy of persons which is part of the constitution of marriage and of the family itself. The question about children and their education is profoundly linked to marital consent, with its solemn promise of love, conjugal respect and fidelity until death. The acceptance and education of children — two of the primary ends of the family — are conditioned by how that commitment will be fulfilled. Fatherhood and motherhood represent a responsibility which is not simply physical but spiritual in nature; indeed, through these realities there passes the genealogy of the person, which has its eternal beginning in God and which must lead back to him."

7. Cf. John Paul II, *Familiaris Consortio* 36-40.

8. This term refers not only to the prerogative proper to the male figure, but to the attitude of primary educator proper to the parent as such.

9. On the phenomenon of education, cf. M. Lena, "Educazione come ricerca dell'insperato," *Il Nuovo Areopago* 11, no. 2 (1992): 7.

9.3. *Paideia* and the School: Excursus

A school is the place of the communication of knowledge, which takes place concretely through the complex articulation of specific curricular programs that respond to differentiated and complex disciplines.

We ask ourselves: Does this, the school's very reason for being, retain a global pedagogical value, especially in the contemporary condition of the general fragmentation of knowledge? In other words: Can the teacher and member of a given educational institution — that delicate factor of mediation between person, family, and society — be the protagonist of an effective *paideia* (education to values) in the school? Is it possible to transmit the knowledge of mathematics or literature, to initiate young people into *seeing* Caravaggio's *Dormition of the Virgin,* or introduce them to the principles of chemical reactions, and so forth, within this perspective? In today's school, does an alternative exist to both *indoctrination* — the claim of the school as the exhaustive factor of a total education — and *abstention,* the illusion of a pedagogical neutrality? The question becomes all the more urgent now that the above-mentioned fragmentation of knowledge no longer refers only to the object of knowledge itself, nor is limited to the difficulty of establishing an organic link between the subject and object of knowledge, but seems to extend to a fragmentation within the subject itself. No one can be blind to how this last expression of fragmentation touches the heart of education *(paideia).*

However, posing the problem of whether the school must first be the place of instruction or imply the entire horizon described *(paideia)* is a misleading abstraction. It is in fact inevitable that "every form of knowledge — and the body of knowledge that is derived from it — tends to justify itself by demarcating its proper object and method in the most exact manner possible."[10]

Thus, even on the level of the object of knowledge, it is impossible to separate the communication of this object from the Weltanschauung with which the teacher concretely assimilates and proposes it. One cannot in any way entrench oneself behind a nonexistent neutrality of knowledge. As with every area that involves man, in the transmission of knowledge neutrality does not exist: it is the nature of the subject that is reflected in the characteristics of receptivity and integral openness proper to knowledge. Every act of knowledge, always the fruit of a reason set into motion or an affection which tends to judgment, implies the unfolding of all the properties of reason (memory, per-

10. A. Scola, "Frammentazione del sapere teologico ed unità dell'io. Note di metodo," in *La frammentazione del sapere teologico,* ed. G. Lorizio and S. Muratore (Rome, 1998), 253-54.

ception, projection, induction, deduction, speculation) in a confrontation with the whole of reality. Every act of knowledge, as the knowledge of the subject, reveals within itself an integral openness. This openness is obviously not to be confused with omnipotence, because it is well acquainted with the discursive limit of human reason, always constrained to pass from one object to another, without being able to embrace them all at the same time. In this way reason comes to know its own finitude: it is open to the infinite, but does not know how to rise to its level.

And yet the "knowing" at work in every act of knowledge cannot ever lose this aspect of integrality, just as it cannot renounce its character of being structurally receptive. Through it, the subject shows itself capable of receiving "another's being in one's own home" (capable, that is, of making room for this guest and receiving from it an element of truth).[11] This receptivity is not mere passivity but rather an expression of what Newman called the "wild and living intellect of man."[12] Reality testifies to itself: it is proper to every act of knowledge to receive this confession and in its turn testify to it. The dynamic of knowledge as gift is never definitively over precisely because it is in the end a dynamic of love in which the dialogue of the lover and the beloved never ceases.

Because of this, and beyond all the understandable difficulties and serious limitations of our schools, to which we are accustomed to associate the idea of crisis from that moment when we as children set our feet within the elementary school yard, a school without *paideia* is unthinkable. Rather, the specific reason for a school's existence — the methodical communication of well-defined bodies of knowledge through specific programs — becomes the normal and spontaneous path for a *paideia* born of the encounter between the freedom of the student with that of the teacher. Thus "the master must respond to the disciple's question by opening his own home, testifying to the unitary principle of his knowledge. The master is he who does not give the disciple prefabricated answers, but rather teaches him to think because he helps him ask the real questions. He does this through the witness of his personal history of involvement with these real questions."[13] In this sense one cannot undervalue the fact that the school of today, with all its belabored and sometimes contradictory changes, remains in continuity with the school of all times, in which the element of *communitas docentium et studentium* (the community of teachers and students) — that is, the element of *living-with* in a de-

11. Cf. H. U. von Balthasar, *Theo-Logic*, vol. 1, *Truth of the World*, trans. Adrian J. Walker (San Francisco: Ignatius, 2000), 45.

12. J. M. Hass, "La ragione nel suo posto," in *John Henry Newman. L'idea di ragione* (Milan, 1992), 102.

13. Scola, "Frammentazione del sapere teologico ed unità dell'io."

termined environment — cannot, in a certain sense, be overcome. A communication of knowledge inevitably gives rise to a community of life.[14]

9.4. Factors of Education

What, then, are the essential and indispensable factors of an authentic *paideia* in the family and school of today? In responding to this question, we do not fear falling into abstraction, since in the preceding paragraphs we have already traced out the general trajectory for a response to the postmodern objection to values. In so doing, we have also shown that what every *paideia* encounters in the specifics of a communication of knowledge is not an obstacle, but rather is its most powerful form of mediation.

14. In *The Idea of a University* (New York and London: Longmans, Green, 1907), Cardinal Newman offers suggestive intuitions on the theme of the common life in an academic environment: "It is a great point then to enlarge the range of studies which a University professes, even for the sake of the students; and, though they cannot pursue every subject which is open to them, they will be the gainers by living among those and under those who represent the whole circle. This I conceive to be the advantage of a seat of universal learning, considered as a place of education. An assemblage of learned men, zealous for their own sciences, and rivals of each other, are brought, by familiar intercourse and for the sake of intellectual peace, to adjust together the claims and relations of their respective subjects of investigation. They learn to respect, to consult, to aid each other. Thus is created a pure and clear atmosphere of thought, which the student also breathes, though in his own case he only pursues a few sciences out of the multitude. He profits by an intellectual tradition, which is independent of particular teachers, which guides him in his choice of subject, and duly interprets for him those which he chooses" (99). Newman goes so far as to formulate a paradox: if he had to choose between a university in which students were exempted from attendance at lectures and received diplomas once they passed exams, and a university in which a real community existed even in the absence of academic apparatus, he would not hesitate to choose the second: "When a multitude of young men, keen, open-hearted, sympathetic, and observant, as young men are, come together and freely mix with each other, they are sure to learn one from another, even if there be no one to teach them; the conversation of all is a series of lectures to each, and they gain for themselves new ideas and views, fresh matter of thought, and distinct principles for judging and acting, day by day. . . . Here then is a real teaching, whatever be its standards and principles, true or false; and it at least tends toward the cultivation of the intellect; it at least recognizes that knowledge is something more than a sort of passive reception of scraps and details; it is a something, and it does a something, which never will issue from the most strenuous efforts of a set of teachers, with no mutual sympathies and no inter-communion, of a set of examiners with no opinions which they dare profess, and with no common principles, who are teaching or questioning a set of youths who do not know them, and do not know each other, on a large number of subjects, different in kind, and connected by no wide philosophy, three times a week, or three times a year, or once in three years, in chill lecture-rooms or on a pompous anniversary" (147-48).

We will first of all take up the subject. An educational proposal requires a subject who is its protagonist: a father and mother for the children in a family, a community in a neighborhood, a civil reality (an interwoven structure of intermediate bodies) within a given society, an ecclesial community within the people of God, an educating community in a school. A subject is truly such when it lives its relationship with reality in terms of fundamental human experience, an experience that, because it is fundamental, can be easily communicated in the existing relation between persons and values. The communication of this experience takes place in the various primary realities, such as the family and school, more by means of osmosis than through theoretical discourse; it passes through the concrete circumstances and specific relationships that pinpoint a given institution's reason for being. In the school this occurs in the communication of bodies of knowledge adequate to the cognitive-affective development of the toddler, the child, the adolescent, or the young adult, in order to give the young person personal consistency and a life of relation freely and critically situated in the environment of today.

We now introduce the second factor of an authentic *paideia:* content, or that specific transmission of knowledge that "functions" as a conductor and not an insulator of the fulfillment of the whole person, through his encounter with the whole of reality. This involves helping the young person to discover — I will repeat this ad nauseam — that not only is reality not hostile (as Proust insinuates); to the contrary, it is the great school inviting the "I" to a comparison that can lead him to fulfillment. And this reality is made up of persons, relationships, circumstances, situations, facts, events, and more or less complex structures.

As the third factor we identify the method of this educational proposal: a communication that proceeds from experience to experience, from person to person. Education arises at the point of encounter between a "thou" who educates and a "thou" who is educated. Such a relationship requires two freedoms in action; it rests upon both freedoms. Only thus can the teacher help the student be an actor who is ever more free and creative on the stage of the "great theater of the world."

It is possible in this sense to see in the call of the first disciples an example of this. Jesus calls them by name. He turns to each of them as to a "thou," provoking their freedom; he forces no one. "'Master, where do you stay?' 'Come and see.'" In this exceptional educational experience, the Master and disciples stay together in the deepest and most realistic sense of the word. Together they confront life in all its aspects. Obviously, it will not do to take this style and mechanically apply it to the familial and scholastic environments: this would be to fall into acritical abstractions! And yet I would dare to say, in this context, that something of this style must be found in every act of education! The method implies an educating "thou" who addresses himself to a "thou" to be educated, communicating a specific knowledge that in fact carries the capacity to *see* and *enjoy* the real. Thus, for example, few things are so moving for a father or a mother as seeing their own child, with their help, discover some aspect of life. A loving "thou" is always a "thou" who awakens the beloved to life. One sees this in action when, for example, priests propose Jesus to the young and see that something lights up in their minds, or that something has been touched by this presence. There is no feeling of satisfaction (freedom) so great as that of seeing another discover the truth of his "I" and move a step closer to this. To my mind, for every educator as well as every father and mother, this represents the summit of human emotion.

9.5. Characteristics of an Educative Action

A last point can make our reflections more concrete. What prompts that encounter of freedoms between educator and educated, whose passionate meeting gives rise to those unforgettable hours which all of us, even if all too rarely, spent at school? Or those moments which engraved in our memories the faces of those adults to whom, we vividly perceive, we owe our *education?* An attempt to respond to this question allows me to suggest some essential characteristics of the educational relationship. I will list five.

9.5.1. Educating in the "Present"

The first highlights how the interpersonal exchange that constitutes education must know how to take into account the *present,* on which it is called to leave its mark. To my mind this is the neuralgic point that manifests the crisis of the traditional model of education: the proposed content no longer has any relation to the present. Now, if in a pedagogical exchange the value that one intends to communicate is not present, it cannot be received. This aspect is absolutely decisive, because the educational relationship is an event; it implies the acts of two freedoms which are by nature always determined, and which the calculations of another cannot capture. This is why education, properly speaking, is an art.[15] It is an art which can and must, certainly, imply

15. This contradicts Severinus's thesis that even art (and religion) is a variation of technique *(tecnica);* cf. E. Severino, "Quando la tecnica è suprema poesia," *Il Corriere della Sera,* April 11, 1999, 29.

much technique, but an art to which, at least in its minimal aspect, every educator has access, so long as he is capable of the risk involved: the risk of a freedom which goes forward to encounter an other. The verification of what we can call the "risk of education" is, then, the fact that it is a risk taken in the present: I must give you a reason why the proposal I make is good for you and for me, here and now. We all feel that we will never be able to sufficiently thank certain educators who have been witnesses of this unconditional openness of freedom. They are witnesses always open to the primacy of the other and his good, here and now, without calculations of time.

9.5.2. Following the Great Stream of Tradition

The more one is aware that the educational relationship takes place integrally in the present, the more one is able to convey all the riches of tradition. "Even when, as in revolutionary times, life undergoes stormy changes, much more is preserved from the past during a supposed change of everything than one might imagine. The old is grafted onto the new, acquiring a new vitality."[16] The structural curiosity of the infant, as well as that of the adolescent who, though perhaps through a thousand clues, poses a question about the knowledge and life of those dear to him, reveal that both of them feel themselves to be thrown into a tradition. Tradition, in the noble sense of the word, clearly emerges as the educative humus par excellence. Of course, it must pass through the critical scrutiny of the educator and the educated, demonstrating its validity and truth here and now. It is not enough to recall tradition theoretically; this can often be counterproductive.

9.5.3. Showing the Goodness of the Real

A "thou" who is present and who recovers the tradition demonstrates all the positive nature of reality. Here is the third characteristic of the education. The ultimate goal of all things and all relationships is a *good* destiny. And this is because — I say this leaving out all the steps to this conclusion — the ultimate nature of things is love. Friendship as perfect, reciprocal love is constitutive of God himself; there is this deep exchange of friendship even in God. And, as Dante brilliantly exclaimed, love "excuses no one loved from

---

16. H. G. Gadamer, *Verità e metodo* (Milan, 1996), 330 (*Truth and Method* [New York: Crossroad, 1982]).

loving."[17] Love calls to love; it calls inexorably, beyond all ambiguity and ambivalence of the response that must be improved (there is no education without ascesis!). To educate is to show that the ultimate fabric of reality is friendly. Reality is not an enemy. Its shadier elements cannot in the end cancel out its goodness. Being is the sign of that positive and friendly face who is God himself.

9.5.4. *Opening to Criticism*

To help this positive "face" of being to emerge, education must open itself to *criticism*, a term that derives from the Greek verb *krino* (judge). The fourth characteristic of the educational relationship consists, then, in giving reasons for what is communicated. This is poised toward generating knowledge, and therefore personalization, in the one educated. The educator is convincing only if he shows that he is continually learning from and with his student. Here we find ourselves confronting the great problem of the genesis and communication of knowledge. In fact, the problem of the school has its source here. One cannot speak of criticism without the systematic and, therefore, organic communication of a knowledge that founds it and makes it possible. But criticism itself will ultimately fail if it is not proposed by the educator in the form of witness.

9.5.5. *Communitarian Expression*

Although the educational relationship is ultimately personal, because it takes place only from experience to experience, the person is immersed in a people. It is never possible to separate person from community, just as it is impossible to separate male from female or, even more, soul from body. Soul-body, man-woman, person-community are the three constitutive polarities of an authentic anthropology, which, precisely for this reason, is always dramatic. By virtue of the polarity person-community, education is always simultaneously personal and communitarian. Even more, it is always a community who educates, in the proper sense. "The thou has its roots in the I. The thou is given to man with his humanity. It is given to man so that man carries within himself the yearning to be treated like a thou by others."[18]

---

17. *Inferno*, canto 5, 103.
18. J. Möller, "Menschen als dialogische Existenz," in Möller, *Verstehen und Vertrauen* (Stuttgart, 1968), 106.

9.6. *Erunt Semper Docibiles Dei*

There is a passage of the prophets quoted in John's Gospel which I prefer to cite in the realistic Latin of the Vulgate: "Erunt semper docibiles Dei."[19] What person would like to place himself outside the fascinating truth contained in this biblical affirmation? Is it not synonymous with every growth, the essential expression of education, because it is the unstoppable condition of life? Everything that does not grow dies. Who would deny that this wonderful dynamism of human freedom is not limited to perceiving the necessity of a discipleship with God — it would be better to say sonship — that extends in a certain sense from the cradle to the grave, but would also identify that truer attitude with which every parent looks at his child and every teacher faces his class in the morning, full of a delicate fear because he is conscious of the mysterious encounter of freedoms implied in that relationship?

19. Cf. Isa. 54:13; John 6:45.

CHAPTER 10

Marriage and the Family: A Communion of Generations

10.1. "... And the Life of Man Is the Vision of God"

"The glory of God is man fully alive."[1] Irenaeus's well-known declaration clashes shrilly with Guardini's (and Rahner's) definition of old age: "Old age is death prolonged over the course of years."[2] Only at first glance, however, do these words seem to contradict the praiseworthy efforts of all the social agents who, with systematic dedication, strive to give value to the final phase of life, in response to the growth explosion of elderly populations, especially in the Northern Hemisphere.

The second part of Irenaeus's famous affirmation — almost always forgotten — shows in what sense Guardini's definition can be positive. That is, "The glory of God is man fully alive, and the life of man is the vision of God." Here is the point: if man's consistency comes from the vision of God, then death no longer means ending in nothingness; whatever its origin, death loses the tone of a condemnation.[3] In the experience of Jesus Christ dead and risen *propter nos homines*, "for us men," life triumphs — *mors ero mors tua*[4] — and

1. Irenaeus, *Adversus haereses* 4.20.7.
2. R. Guardini, *Die Lebensalter* (Würzburg, 1967), 79.
3. Cf. H. U. von Balthasar, "Some Points of Eschatology," in *Explorations in Theology I: The Word Was Made Flesh* (San Francisco: Ignatius, 1989), 255-77. Balthasar, *Theo-Drama V: The Last Act*, trans. Graham Harrison (San Francisco: Ignatius, 1998), 19-54; J. Ratzinger, "'Perché Dio sia tutto in tutti.' La fede cristiana nella vita eterna," *Palestra del Clero* 71, nos. 1-2 (1992): 7-20; Ratzinger, *Eschatology, Death, and Eternal Life*, trans. Michael Waldstein (Washington, D.C.: Catholic University of America Press, 1988).
4. This expression is taken from Jerome's traditional reading of Hos. 13:14. It is cited, for example, by Augustine, *Sermo* 265, b.

the vision of God becomes possible in faith now, though *per speculum in aenigmate* ("in a mirror dimly").[5] The experience of death and of being-for death proper to every human being, though unaltered in its loathsomeness, is no longer one of a breaking off, or an unsurpassable abyss. To the contrary, "existence in Christ" inaugurates the concrete possibility of living from God through the whole of earthly existence, making old age the time when the approaching personal and definitive encounter with the Father allows the person to give the greatest value possible to personal and communitarian resources. In this radical perspective revealed by Jesus Christ, dying acquires its meaning: returning to the Father's house, "a house full of open doors, through which we are invited to walk."[6] So it is possible to confront the various phases of life of the elderly person — including that in which he bids farewell to life, sometimes marked by great physical pain — with the highest possible criteria. In an important study, Auer identifies these criteria in three levels: "taking advantage of opportunities, accepting as much as is required, and enjoying satisfaction."[7]

10.2. Family, *Care,* and *Inheritance*

The change of mentality required of the contemporary family in order to provide enough room for the elderly is only apparently obvious. This does not involve establishing the terms of a convention between the family and the elderly person, but of understanding the latter's situation in relation to the family, from a relational point of view. This naturally holds true even when the elderly person lives alone. From this perspective, the family appears as something much more than and very different from a group of persons living under the same roof. It cannot, that is, be reduced to mere cohabitation.

How are we to understand it, then? A sociological perspective that I am inclined to share defines the family as "a primordial environment of social relations." The adjective "primordial" points first of all to unavoidability. Human history begins with the family: it is, as we have already mentioned, the matrix of every process of civilization (which consists precisely in making the nonfamiliar familiar) and humanization.[8] To speak of social relations also

5. Cf. 1 Cor. 13:12.

6. H. U. von Balthasar, *You Crown the Year with Your Goodness,* trans. Graham Harrison (San Francisco: Ignatius, 1989), 144.

7. A. Auer, *Geglücktes Altern* (Freiburg, 1995), 277. On the theme of old age, the following is useful: R. Blestein, "Il tempo libero e la terza età," *La Civiltà Cattolica* 149, no. 3 (1998): 239-53.

8. P. Donati, *Manuale di sociologia della famiglia* (Bari, 1998), 7-8.

means identifying the family as an environment of meaningful ties which possess their own meaning. What is, then, their specific meaning? What distinguishes them from all other social ties? The fact that the family is the dynamic intertwining of two types of relations: that between the sexes (the conjugal relation) and that between generations (the relation between parents and children). In this sense the family is not only the couple who physically live together in a certain moment in time; it is all the persons tied to each member of the couple by a generational bond. This intergenerational aspect of the family has been strongly emphasized by John Paul II. In the *Letter to Families* he speaks of the family as a "communion of generations,"[9] whose importance for the civilization of love is referred to the "particular closeness and intensity of the bonds which come to be between persons and generations within the family."[10]

Each of the two relations forming the essence of the relational environment of the family presents a specific way of living out the code of love (of gratuity and gift) that is the basis for familial exchanges.

In our discussion until now, while investigating the many facets of the conjugal relation, we have spoken in terms of "asymmetrical reciprocity" and not of pure complementarity.

The relationship between the generations is characterized, on the other hand, by a *transmission* with a view to *transition*. Love, in the intergenerational relationships proper to a family, and without prescinding from sexual difference and fruitfulness — though these obviously have an importance different from that in the conjugal relation — is manifested in the pedagogical effort through which a vision of life passes *(traditio)* from one generation to another, thus securing the original character of the parent-child relation.[11]

Notwithstanding the unheard-of forms of family that continue to make their appearance on the social scene, and the fact that even the traditional families are undergoing profound internal modifications, this brief description serves to highlight the family's capability to face contemporary social challenges, renewing itself in the process, but without ceasing to be a primordial reality distinguished by the two fundamental relations outlined above. In this sense the family is foundational with respect to society.[12] In other words,

---

9. John Paul II, *Letter to Families* 10.

10. John Paul II, *Letter to Families* 13.

11. Cf. A. Scola, "Paternità e libertà," *Anthropotes* 12 (1996): 337-43.

12. The last few decades have been marked by a profound change in the relations between the sexes and the generations, which has affected the contours of the family. One of the phenomena attracting the attention of social observers is the shift of the bulk of the population to

an understanding of the family that takes into account its primordial nature and relational character reveals itself to be potentially capable of seeing the elderly person in all his or her worth. Analogously, a society that recognizes and appreciates the nature of the family in the terms just described will be able to retain the meaning and the richness of the family with and from elderly members even if these live alone.

It is not possible, in this place, to discuss in greater depth the teaching that the church, both in her magisterium and in the witness of concrete forms of life, has never ceased to offer humanity regarding the relationship between the elderly person and the family. It might be useful, however, to enucleate two limit cases of this relationship which, because of their paradigmatic character, allow us to verify Auer's criteria for the different phases and circumstances of life of the elderly ("taking advantage of opportunities, accepting as much as is required, and enjoying satisfactions"). We refer to the challenges faced by families with elderly members in situations of grave illness or death.

How can a satisfying familial equilibrium be attained while responding to these two challenges?

The task which confronts contemporary adults is twofold: on the one hand, they must promote the conservation of the family; in this perspective the idea of *care* becomes crucial. On the other hand, they must elaborate the aspects of the continuity of familial relations within the generations: here the idea of *inheritance* is central.[13]

Erikson has accurately observed that in the family the adult is the one who places himself as mediator between the two generations of grandparents and grandchildren. For this reason he is called upon to develop the "new virtue of care," which has as its aim the safeguarding of family ties and the history borne by them.[14] In the life of the family, the importance of care emerges in a particular way when there is a new birth: "Every birth inscribes itself within a family order which is both limit and resource, an order which is not the same for each member that is added to it."[15] Each birth is both positive and negative. Sexual generation, because of the connection between the individual and the species, in fact implies death. Socrates already remembered

---

the adult and elderly generations, in relation to the decrease in the younger generations caused by a shrinking birthrate.

13. Cf. E. Scabini and P. Donati, eds., *Identità adulta e relazioni familiari,* Studi interdisciplinari sulla famiglia, no. 10 (Milan, 1991).

14. Cf. E. Erikson, *I cicli della vita. Continuità e mutamenti* (Rome, 1984).

15. E. Scabini, "Affrontare l'ultima transizione: relazioni familiari alla prova," in *Tempo e transizioni familiari,* ed. E. Scabini and P. Donati, Studi interdisciplinari sulla famiglia, no. 13 (Milan, 1994), 89.

this, and Augustine takes it up again, placing in the mouths of newborn children these words addressed to their parents: "Away with you! It's time you thought about leaving. We, too, must play our part."[16] *Care* for the elderly finds its realistic criterion in the cycle of life tied to the procession of generations, which imposes an inexorable alternation of birth and death.

On the other hand, in family life death is not merely destruction or negativity. It leaves an inheritance that needs to be identified and brought into a living synthesis. In this synthesis one decides what must be let go of and what demands to be retained. This task falls to the adult member of the family. In this way care and inheritance identify two fundamental attitudes within the primordial environment of relations which is the family. Without these attitudes it is not only the family but its individual members who suffer.

Attachment and care, loyalty and inheritance: each of these dimensions acquires a crucial importance in the relationship between adult children and elderly parents. Caring for the elderly allows family members to settle the debts they have accrued, in various ways, with the elderly person. Already in the Old Testament we find indications of this.[17] It has been said in a felicitous expression that the form assumed by the tie in the parent-child relation, as this evolves in time, is that of a "care of recognition."

Family care can take on various forms according to the needs of the subject and the phase of the family's life cycle, but they are marked by a high degree of personalization, a global investment that goes beyond the time dedicated to single actions, and a minimum level of the organization of needs. Incidentally, sociologists inform us that the figure of the "caregiver" — that is, the subject who takes on the burden of the concrete responsibility of care, and also directs other resources — is, in the Western context, predominantly feminine.

It is important to note that, in these conditions, Auer's three criteria are realized even in the case of a severely dependent elderly person, and remain even in the face of the experience of death as an impending possibility. Within the perspective of "care" and "inheritance," the experience of the closure of earthly life can remain entirely within a perspective of eternal life, and no longer be understood as alienation in a doubtful future world. It can be an experience of life in God, already capable of changing the present. When care and heredity are assumed into an integral Christian perspective — which

---

16. Augustine, *Enarrationes in Psalmis* 127.15.

17. Very interesting is the work of M. Lorenzani, ed., *Gli anziani nella Bibbia* (L'Aquila, 1995), with contributions from M. Cimosa, V. D'Alario, A. Fanuli, M. Gilbert, G. Marconi, A. Mattioli, S. Pisano, J. L. Ska, U. Vanni, H. Simian Yofre.

leaves their value intact even for nonbelievers — they reveal themselves to be a form of the "hundredfold here below," a true anticipation of eternal life, even in an experience of pain that identifies the sufferer with the crucified and risen One. "If you have been raised with Christ," Paul says, not "if you rise."[18] Thus Irenaeus's affirmation, which served as our starting point, is made real.

10.3. Criteria for Family Policies

As we have already seen, the unquestionable role of the family as social protagonist is founded on the "sovereign power" of the "first and vital cell of society."[19] The intervention of the state must serve this role through appropriate social policies, within the guidelines of the two principles of subsidiarity and solidarity.[20]

The application of the principle of subsidiarity to social policies allows for the logic of colonization/assistance that has marked state and market actions until now to be overcome, in favor of a partnership between various actors, formed on a pluralistic model and capable of connecting general perspectives to particular needs.

The principle of subsidiarity, in its authentic formulation, has a twofold function with regard to the higher institutions in the area of social organization. It obliges them to act and to limit themselves, both to protect and promote in such a way as to sustain the subordinate entities — even the single citizen — without invading their field of action or taking away their responsibility, if they can carry out their own tasks autonomously. Only when these subordinate entities are unable to face the tasks they have assumed must the superior level intervene, out of respect for the principle of solidarity which always goes hand in hand with that of subsidiarity. But the principle of subsidiarity requires these superior levels to seek first to reinforce the energies and autonomous capabilities of the subordinate levels.

In order to establish a subsidiary and solidary social policy, "social subjectivity" must be placed at the center of society's life. By "social subjectivity" we mean the capacity of persons to respond to their own needs (economic, educational, health-related, etc.) through free association. The state's task is to promote, sustain, and order these forms of action; it must provide a legisla-

18. Cf. Col. 3:1.
19. *Apostolicam Actuositatem* 11.
20. Cf. A. Scola, "Familia, modernidad y nueva evangelización," *Anthropotes* 14 (1998): 19-30.

tive framework for them so that every autonomous subject, even the weakest, is cared for, and the free activity of competent subjects is guaranteed.

To join solidarity and subsidiarity in the development of social policy means, then, refusing every type of intrusive we'll-do-it-for-you-ism. It involves offering real help, promoting the autonomy of subjects, their capacity for self-governance, self-regulation, and self-development, in order to reach the authentic objective of subsidiarity: the disappearance of a relationship of dependence.

The relationships of subsidiarity/solidarity between the parts of society give society a precise ordering that is much more efficacious. Such a society operates on a relational dynamic, whereas modern society can easily be explained in the dichotomy between public and private, or between state and market. Contemporary society begs to be understood with the use of relational categories and not dichotomies; the first draws the active presence of the two autonomous social spheres other than state institutions out of the shadows: the organizations of the third sector and the family with the informal networks that characterize it.

Actualizing this perspective for families of elderly persons and/or families with elderly members implies an involvement of state institutions that extends from the *support* of families who are able to care for the elderly to the *development of services* for the elderly which keep them in their relational context. It involves, moreover, giving special attention to the value of *informal networks of care.*

In a Christian perspective, what has been said above allows us to appreciate the immense patrimony of religious orders, congregations, and volunteer associations, helping all of these to join charity and intelligence in a genuine respect for the great Christian tradition of sharing needs.

PART IV

The Nuptial *Mystery:*
Marriage and the Family
in the Light of the Christian *Mysteries*

CHAPTER 11

The Features of Marriage and the Family: From Past to Present

In the *Choruses from the Rock,* T. S. Eliot asks a probing question: "Has the Church failed mankind, or has mankind failed the Church?"[1] Though we keep this question in mind in order to avoid both a sterile sense of guilt when confronting the history of Christianity and a pessimistic moralism regarding the process of secularization in the societies of the Northern Hemisphere, it is important to observe that Christian thought has been at a loss to propose an organic, unified reflection on person, marriage, and the family. This is perhaps one of the chief causes of the weakening of the Christian subject, and its consequent inability to combat the progressive shadowing of God's design for these realities.

For the greater part of the history of Christianity, theological reflection on the concept of person[2] and reflection on marriage and the family have progressed along parallel paths. Moreover, reflection on the family has been so completely sidelined by the theology of marriage that it has not been able to attain a proper form of its own.[3] In this sense reflection on mar-

---

1. Cf. T. S. Eliot, *Choruses from the Rock,* in *The Complete Poems and Plays of T. S. Eliot* (London: Faber and Faber, 1969), 161.

2. Cf. A. Milano, *Persona in teologia* (Rome, 1996), 61-352.

3. As an example of this approach, we can cite the brief summary of the church's magisterium on marriage and the family compiled by Tettamanzi and Barberi. Although these authors had the explicit intention to confront the theme of marriage and the family, when they find themselves in the position of expounding the magisterium's teaching on the subject, they have as their sole point of reference — practically all the way to Vatican Council II — the realities of marriage and sexuality. An organic reference to the family does not appear even in a subordinate position. Cf P. Barberi and D. Tettamanzi, *Matrimonio e famiglia nel magistero della Chiesa* (Milan, 1986), 15-22.

riage, which considers the family as its presupposition and natural consequence, maintains the role of exclusive protagonist up to the twentieth century. We can therefore affirm that "in Christian tradition, a discussion of
marriage has emerged without a recognition of the necessity of its development into a theory of the family; it even positively precludes such a development."[4]

11.1. A Brief Overview of the History of
Reflection on Marriage and the Family

Setting aside for the moment the history of Christian reflection on the human person, emblematically summarized by the belabored and relatively recent emergence of an autonomous treatment of theological anthropology,[5] it
may be useful to sketch a broad outline of the history of Christian thought on
marriage and the family, beginning with the data of Scripture.[6] We will proceed by presenting in summary fashion the results of the (still scarce) existing
studies on the subject.[7] For clarity's sake we will distinguish three major
phases.[8]

In the first place, we refer to the reflection of the Fathers and ecclesiastical

4. G. Angelini, "La Chiesa e la Famiglia," *La Scuola Cattolica* 120 (1992): 467-68.

5. Cf. A. Scola, G. Marengo, and J. Prades, *La persona umana. Antropologia teologica* (Milan: Jaca Book, 2000).

6. A. M. Dubarle, *Amore e fecondità nella Bibbia* (Bari, 1969); P. Grelot, *La coppia umana
nella Sacra Scrittura* (Milan, 1968); A. Tosato, *Il matrimonio nel Giudaismo Antico e nel Nuovo
Testamento* (Rome, 1976); H. Baltensweiler, *Il matrimonio nel nuovo Testamento* (Brescia, 1981);
L. A. Schökel, *I nomi dell'amore: Simboli matrimoniali nella Bibbia* (Casale Monferrato, 1997);
A. Tosato, "L'istituto famigliare dell'antico Israele e della Chiesa primitiva," *Anthropotes* 13
(1997): 109-74.

7. The following are points of reference for the history of the theology of marriage and the
family: L. Godefroy, "Mariage. Le mariage au temps des pères," in A. Vacant and E. Mangenot,
Dictionnaire de Théologie Catholique, vol. 9/2, 2077-2123; G. Le Bras, "Mariage. Le doctrine du
mariage chez les théologiens et les canonistes depuis l'an mille," in *Dictionnaire de Théologie
Catholique*, vol. 9/2, 2123-2335. For specific studies see D. Tettamanzi, *Il Matrimonio cristiano.
Studio storico-teologico* (Venegono, 1979); D. Dacquino, *Storia del matrimonio cristiano alla luce
della Bibbia* (Turin, 1984); J. L. Larrabe, *El matrimonio cristiano y la familia* (Madrid, 1986); J. M.
Artadi, *Historia y teología del matrimonio* (Madrid, 1987). An extensive bibliography, particularly from the juridical-institutional point of view, can be found in J. Gaudemet, *Le mariage en
Occident* (Paris, 1987), 468-87. A more recent bibliography can be found in A. Sarmiento, *El
matrimonio cristiano* (Pamplona, 1997).

8. For the identification of historical phases, we follow Tettamanzi's proposal in
D. Tettamanzi, *La famiglia via della Chiesa* (Milan, 1991), 56-61.

writers of the first centuries of the church's life.[9] Patristic thought, characterized by a deep immersion in Scripture, reflects on marriage principally by exploring the theme of the Christ-church couple. References to the family, especially as regards the education of children, are included in this.[10] In this context, and in keeping with its authentically pastoral character, patristic thought is preoccupied with stressing the moral requirements of the married state (monogamy, indissolubility, fidelity), both in itself and in its relation to Christian virginity.[11] Considered thus, that is, strictly dependent on the theology of creation (which is the reason why the goodness of marriage is defended against every form of Gnosticism and Manicheism),[12] marriage is placed in a historical-salvific perspective. In this regard, Saint Anselm affirms, "primum in coniugio religio quaeritur."[13] In the progression we have traced out, the contribution of Saint Augustine is of particular importance; even today his influence is felt.[14] In combating the Manichean heresy, Jovinian's indifference, and Pelagianism, the bishop of Hippo emphasized three important doctrinal aspects: the original goodness of marriage, the consequences of sin on the matrimonial economy, and the necessity of its redemption by Christ (healing grace). In this context his famous doctrine of the three goods of marriage *(proles, fides, sacramentum)* took shape.[15]

Certain questions regarding the sacramentality of marriage can be considered the least common denominator of the three periods — identifying very distinct historical moments — which make up the second phase of our historical survey: medieval theology, the crisis of the Reformation, and the Council of Trent. This period engaged many Christian thinkers, from the

---

9. Cf. G. Oggioni, "Matrimonio e verginità presso i Padri," in *Matrimonio e verginità* (Venegono, 1963), 159-418; E. Saldón, *El matrimonio misterio y signo. Del siglo 1 a San Agustín* (Pamplona, 1971); Larrabe, *El matrimonio*, 79-106; D. Tettamanzi, *I due saranno una carne sola* (Turin, 1986), 12-23; Gaudemet, *Le mariage*, 49ff.; R. Lawler, J. Boyle, and W. E. May, *Catholic Sexual Ethics* (Huntington, 1985), 32-41; Godefroy, "Mariage. Le mariage au temps des pères," 2077-2123.

10. Cf. Tettamanzi, *La famiglia via della Chiesa*, 98-99.

11. Cf. John Chrysostom, *De virginitate* 7.8.

12. In this sense cf. Irenaeus, *Adversus haereses* 1.28.2; Clement of Alexandria, *Stromata* III, 12; Tertullian, *Ad uxorem* 1.2.1.

13. Ambrose, *De Abraham* 1.9.84.

14. Cf. L. Dattrino, *Il matrimonio secondo Agostino* (Milan, 1995).

15. Cf. E. Schmitt, *Le mariage chrétien dans l'oeuvre de saint Augustin. Une théologie baptismale de la vie coniugale* (Paris, 1983); E. Scalco, "'Sacramentum conubii' et institution nuptiale. Une lecture du 'De bono coniugali' et du 'De sancta virginitate' de S. Augustin," *Ephemerides Theologicae Lovanienses* 69 (1993): 22-47; Tettamanzi, *I due saranno*, 19-20; Larrabe, *El matrimonio*, 107-58.

High Middle Ages to the sixteenth century.[16] Reflection shifted, however, from marriage as a state of life to marriage as sacrament, with subsequent clarifications of some of its basic elements.[17] The central problem of this long historical period can perhaps be formulated as follows: Is Christian marriage simply a sign, or is it, properly speaking, a sacrament that efficaciously confers grace?[18] As an example, it is useful to recall the two greatest difficulties raised by canonists and medieval theologians regarding the full sacramentality of marriage. First, they held that marriage could not confer grace, because grace passes through the passion of Jesus Christ. What relationship could there be, they asked themselves, between the passion of Jesus Christ and sexual pleasure?[19] Secondly, given the frequent economic clauses tied to marriages, considering marriage as a sacrament created a risk of simony. Saint Thomas gives a response to these objections which gathers and synthesizes the thought of many medieval authors.[20] He leaves no room for doubt, and orients the whole of Catholic theology toward a recognition of the sacramentality of marriage: "quamvis matrimonium non conformet passioni Christi quantam ad poenam, conformat tamen ei quantum ad caritatem, per quam pro Ecclesia sibi in sponsam coniungendam passus est."[21] The church's magisterium makes this vision its own, proclaiming it in the Council of Florence (1438-45).[22] These important acquisitions were nevertheless called into question by the Reformation. The Reformers in effect reduced marriage to

16. Cf. Le Bras, "Mariage. La doctrine du mariage chez les théologiens et les canonists depuis l'an mille," 2123-2335; T. Rincon, *El matrimonio, misterio y signo. Siglos IX al XIII* (Pamplona, 1971); D. G. McCarthy and E. J. Bayer, *Handbook on Critical Sexual Issues* (St. Louis, 1983), 13-25; Larrabe, *El matrimonio,* 161-228.

17. See, for example, the controversy between Gratian and Peter Lombard regarding the factor constituting marriage: intercourse or consent. On this subject cf. Sarmiento, *El matrimonio cristiano,* 175-77. On the medieval theology of marriage, cf. A. Carpin, *Il sacramento del matrimonio nella teologia medievale. Da Isidoro di Siviglia a Tommaso D'Aquino* (Bologna, 1991).

18. Cf. Peter Lombard, *Libri quattuor sententiarum* IV, d. 26-42.

19. Cf. *Glossa ordinaria Decreti Gratiani* c. 1, q. 1, c. 101.

20. Cf. Hugo of St. Victor, *De Beata Maria Virgine* 1; Hugo of St. Victor, *De sacramentis* 2, p. 9, c. 8; Albert the Great, *De sacramentis* 9, q. 1, a. 6; Albert the Great, *In IV Sent.* d. 26, a. 8.14. The work of the theologian and bishop William of Auvergne merits particular attention for its reference to the concrete lives of Christian couples: cf. William of Auvergne, *De sacramento matrimonii.*

21. Thomas Aquinas, *Supplementum* q. 42, a. 1. Other texts in Aquinas, *Summa Theologiae* II-II, q. 100, a. 2 ad 6; Aquinas, *In IV Sent.* d. 2, q. 1 ad 2; Aquinas, *Contra Gentes* IV, q. 78.

22. Cf. Denzinger-Schönmetzer, *Enchiridion symbolorum,* 1327 (hereafter DS). The declaration of Florence was preceded by other conciliar declarations: Lateran Council II (DS, 718), the Council of Verona (DS, 761), and the Council of Lyons II (DS, 860).

the level of a natural institution, denying its sacramentality and therefore its indissolubility.[23] To such doctrine the church responded with the decree of the Council of Trent, which definitively confirmed both the sacramentality and the indissolubility of marriage.[24]

A third phase in this history can be identified in the period that stretches from the closing of the Council of Trent to the promulgation of the encyclical *Casti Conubii.*[25] The unifying element in this case is represented by a development of what Trent proposed dogmatically, particularly in a canonistic and moral perspective. The themes of the specific nature of the grace of marriage, and the minister of the sacrament, take on particular importance.[26] Given the progressive secularization of European society and the consequent emergence of the problem of church-state relations,[27] the *vexata quaestio* of the relationship between sacrament and contract merited attention. Leo XIII's *Arcanum Divinae Sapientiae* and Pius XII's *Casti Conubii* repropose theological doctrine on the connection between sacrament and contract.[28]

This very summary sketch confirms our opening hypothesis. From the patristic age to the beginning of the twentieth century, Christian reflection on marriage and the family was focused on decisive questions proper to a theology of marriage. Anthropological reflection, such as that on man as person, was in fact a presupposition taken for granted (canonists insisted on the full consciousness and total freedom necessary for the consent), while a specific consideration of the family remained substantially marginalized, limited to the theme of children as one of the *ends* and *goods* of marriage.

23. Cf. Luther, *Der Grosse Katechismus* 1, pp. 209ff.; *De captivitate Babylonica* 4; Calvin, *Institutes of the Christian Religion* 4.19.34; Melanchthon, *Apologia* 23.67. On this subject cf. Gaudemet, *Le mariage*, 277ff.

24. Cf. DS, 1801. On this subject cf. H. Jedin, "L'indissolubilità del matrimonio secondo il Concilio di Trento," in H. Jedin and K. Reinhardt, *Il matrimonio. Una ricerca storica e teologica* (Brescia, 1981), 7-87; G. Baldanza, "La grazia sacramentale del matrimonio al Concilio di Trento. Contributo per uno studio storico critico," *Ephemerides Liturgicae* 97 (1983): 88-140.

25. Cf. E. Ruffini, "Spunti per una rilettura della teologia del matrimonio," in *Evangelizzazione e matrimonio*, ed. S. Cipriani (Naples, 1975), 49-61.

26. Cf. S. Ardito, "Il matrimonio nella teologia posttridentina," in *Realtà e valori del sacramento del matrimonio*, ed. A. M. Triacca and G. Pianazzi (Rome, 1976), 155-72. Authors like Scheeben and Rosmini are an exception to this approach (cf. M. J. Scheeben, *The Mysteries of Christianity* [London: Herder, 1946], 593-610). On this subject cf. M. Valkovic, *L'uomo, la donna e il matrimonio nell teologia di Matthias Joseph Scheeben* (Rome, 1965); A. Auterio, *Amore e coniugalità. Antropologia e teologia del matrimonio in A. Rosmini* (Turin, 1980); D. Tettamanzi, "Il sacramento del matrimonio nel pensiero di Antonio Rosmini," in Tettamanzi, *I due saranno*, 40-71.

27. Cf. Gaudemet, *Le mariage*, 313ff.

28. Cf. Tettamanzi, *I due saranno*, 75-85.

This lack of an organic unity in reflection on the three constitutive factors of the nuptial mystery did not however keep these factors from being, for almost two millennia, the frame of reference for the Western world. But the moment these constitutive elements — sexuality (person), love (marriage), and fruitfulness (family) — were reduced to a purely biological level and lived out in radical separation,[29] beginning with the massive diffusion of chemical contraceptives, Christians found themselves lacking adequate reasons to explain the marvelous unity of the nuptial mystery.

The three phases of the crisis of the reception of the nuptial mystery, summarized in the expressions "ethical crisis," "the loss of the Christian subject," and "the abolition of man" (the eclipse of fundamental human experience), do not at all point to the sole responsibility of Christians. However, in the face of Eliot's question, one cannot be silent about the omissions in experience and reflection committed by the followers of Christ.

11.2. Factors of Renewal in Reflection on Marriage and the Family in the Twentieth Century

Christians have not remained entirely without initiative in the face of the dramatic changes in the sociocultural sphere. One must first of all recognize the many couples and thinkers who, already in the '40s and perhaps with a certain presentiment of how radical the impending change would be, began a process of renewal in the experience of and, in part, reflection on Christian marriage.[30] Some elements of this process are characteristic of the life of the church as such.[31] Others can be traced back to sociocultural circumstances or to new acquisitions of science, which, beginning in the second half of the nineteenth century, has left its decisive mark on the general experience of marriage and the family.[32]

29. Cf. above, pp. 126-30.

30. Both the historical development we have presented and the factors of renewal we will expound in the present section belong primarily to the experience of marriage and the family as this has been lived in the Christian West. We are well aware that such a perspective can be reductive. However, up until the end of the twentieth century, both Christian experience and theology have had their center in Europe (the category of the "West" includes, in our opinion, the Americas).

31. Extensive documentation can be found in F. Barbiero, *L'itinerario storico-dottrinale di una rivista di spiritualità coniugale: L'Anneau d'Or* (1945-67) (Rome, 1984).

32. Among these latter, we can cite the changes undergone by the institution of the family in the period indicated. A bibliography on this subject can be found in A. Mora, "Bibliografia," in *Le stagioni della famiglia,* ed. G. Campanini (Cinisello Balsamo, 1994), 335-64. For a study of

11.2.1. *Groups of Family Spirituality*

A first factor is tied to that maturation of the Catholic laity that had its center in Catholic Action, particularly in France and Italy.[33] Because of a new consciousness of the vocation and mission proper to the laity, marriage and the family acquired an essential importance. The various movements (liturgical, patristic, and biblical) born in the decades preceding Vatican Council II fed this flowering of the Catholic laity; with it came the recognition by couples and Christian families of their specific place in the life of the church.[34] In this sense there began to be talk of the ecclesial dimension of the family, taking up again the theme alluded to by some of the Fathers, who spoke of the family as a "miniature Church."[35] Krieg[36] and Noppel[37] made contributions in this regard. These two authors represent a significant exception in the field of Catholic theology in the first half of the twentieth century. At a time when the family was simply an "object" of pastoral care, Krieg and Noppel bear the distinction of having proposed the first properly theological reflection on it.[38]

The most important outcome of this springtime of the laity, in the area of marriage and the family, was without a doubt the birth of various family associations and movements. These "invented" specific formative means to promote a "conjugal spirituality."[39] Among the protagonists of this effort

---

this theme in the Italian context, cf. S. Tramontin, "Cattolici italiani e famiglie cristiane dall'unità ad oggi," in *Evangelizzazione e matrimonio*, ed. S. Cipriani (Naples, 1975), 202-13; A. Turchini, "Modelli famigliari, storia della mentalità e modernizzazione," in *Evangelizzazione e matrimonio*, 311-34. Also noteworthy is the birth of sexology as a science: cf. J. Hoenig, "Lo sviluppo della sessuologia dalla seconda metà del sec. XIX," in J. Money and H. Musaph, *Sessuologia*, vol. 1 (Rome, 1978), 55-101; L. Lombardi Vallauri, "Il pensiero moderno sulla sessualità umana," *Rivista di sessuologia* 8-9 (1984-85): 14-35.

33. Cf. Y. M. J. Congar, *Jalons pour une théologie du laïcat* (Paris, 1931); G. Garrone, *L'action catholique, son histoire, sa doctrine, son panorama, son destin* (Paris, 1958); A. Scola, C. Giuliodori, G. Marengo, P. A. De Proost, and G. Wagner, *Il laicato. Rassegna bibliografica in lingua italiana, tedesca e francese. In appendice complementi di bibliografia in lingua spagnola ed inglese* (Vatican City, 1987).

34. Cf. Barbiero, *L'itinerario storico-dottrinale*, 24-39, 222-32.

35. The expression "the family can be likened to a miniature church" can be found in Chrysostom. Cf. John Chrysostom, *In Genesi* 7.1.

36. C. Krieg, *Scienza Pastorale: Teologia Pastorale in tre libri*, vol. 1, *Cure d'anime speciale* (Turin and Rome, 1929).

37. K. Noppel, *Aedificatio Corporis Christi* (Brescia, 1939).

38. D. Tettamanzi, "La famiglia cristiana e la teologia pastorale: bilancio dell'attuale situazione in Italia," *La Scuola Cattolica* 108 (1980): 12-18.

39. Cf. Barbiero, *L'itinerario storico-dottrinale*, 63-81, 254-71, which contains an entensive bibliography on the subject.

were Father Caffarel and the Equipes Notre-Dame in France,[40] and the so-called "groups of family spirituality" in Italy.[41] The main contributions of these realities are grouped around three themes: marriage as a Christian "state of life" in the full sense, the necessity of promoting a conjugal spirituality, and the problem of family or conjugal "ministry."[42] Reflection within these family movements was nourished by an ample literature.[43] Already with Pius XII, the papal magisterium itself wasted no time in proposing an organic teaching on the subject.[44]

11.2.2. Stimuli from the Field of Philosophical Personalism

A second factor that aided the renewal of Christian reflection on person, marriage, and the family is tied to the strong development of philosophical

40. It was Fr. Caffarel who began the journal *L'Anneau d'Or*, a reference point for family movements and movements of conjugal spirituality in postwar Europe. On the movement Les Equipes, cf. "Les Equipes de Notre-Dame," *La Documentation Catholique* 64 (1967): 639-50.

41. Cf. G. Colombo, "Per una spiritualità della vita familiare," *La Scuola Cattolica* 79 (1952): 385-88; G. Colombo, A. Corti, and G. Moioli, "Per una 'spiritualità coniugale'. Analisi di un'esperienza: I 'Gruppi di spiritualità coniugale,'" *Communio* 16 (1974): 1052-66; U. Burroni, "Rassegna bibliografica teologico-pastorale sul matrimonio," in *Il matrimonio cristiano* (Turin, 1978), 463-543. We can cite, moreover, the following work, which we were not able to consult: A. Paiocchi, "I Gruppi di spiritualità familiari italiani e il loro 'Notiziario': 1948-1965. Per una valutazione teologica complessiva della ricerca" (license thesis for the Facoltà Teologica dell'Italia Settentrionale of Milan, 1985).

42. Cf. G. Colombo, "La teologia della famiglia," in *Chiesa e famiglia in Europa*, ed. A. Caprioli and L. Vaccaro (Brescia, 1995), 53-58. The spiritual reflection on marriage which arose in the postwar years was however limited by an a priori and mechanistic exaltation of the couple, as if the natural relationship between man and woman were as such the source of the entire Christian life. Rather, marriage, the couple, and the education of children are the place in which is realized the vocation of each of the members of the family. Though the family doubtless requires the greatest dedication and commitment, it is not exempt from a structural openness to communion, a locus of no less importance. In other words, while it is true that the sacrament of marriage creates a new unity and a new and clearly delineated space for the vocation and task of the spouses with regard to their children, it is also true that the sacraments of baptism and confirmation open a similar space of responsibility and work with regard to all their brethren.

43. Cf. Barbiero, *L'itinerario storico-dottrinale*, 264 n. 57.

44. Cf. Tettamanzi, *I due saranno*, 75-102. Speaking of the magisterium of Pius XII, Tettamanzi states, "it is not exaggerating to say that no major point pertaining to the theme of marriage and the family under its various profiles — from theological to ethical, social to juridical, medical, pastoral, and spiritual — was ignored."

personalism,[45] especially in France,[46] and its partial reception into Catholic sacramental theology.[47] In the same period the theme of love was at the center of debate between Protestant and Catholic theologians;[48] it is enough to recall the influence of Nygren's *Eros and Agape*[49] and the famous dispute between Rousselot[50] and Geiger.[51] Nor can one undervalue the fact that the field of philosophical personalism did not lack explicit studies on marriage.[52]

45. On personalism, see Ph. Delhaye, "Personalismo y trascendencia en el actuar moral y social," in J. L. Illanes, ed., *Etica y Teologia ante la crisis contemporánea* (Pamplona, 1980), 49-86; J. Lacroix, *Le personalisme. Sources, foundaments, actualité* (Lyons, 1981); A. Sarmiento, "El 'nosotros' del matrimonio. Una lectura personalista del matrimonio como comunidad de vida y amor," *Scripta Theologica* 31 (1999): 71-102. For a critique of the influence of a certain personalism on the theology of marriage, see C. Burke, "El matrimonio: ¿comprensión personalista o institucional?" *Scripta Theologica* 24 (1992): 569-94.

46. Among the authors who must be cited in this context are Max Scheler (cf. *L'idea cristiana dell'amore* [Rome, 1985]; *Amore e odio* [Carnago, 1993]; *Leibe und Erkenntnis* [Munich, 1952]; *La pudeur* [Paris, 1952]; on Scheler cf. G. Ferretti, *Max Scheler* [Milan, 1972]; it is worth noting that the young Karol Wojtyla wrote a thesis on Scheler; cf. K. Wojtyla, *Max Scheler* [Rome, 1980]); Emmanuel Mounier (cf. *Oeuvres I-IV* [Paris, 1961-63]; notes and bibliography on Mounier can be found in G. Goisis and L. Biaggi, *Mounier fra impegno e profezia* [Padua, 1990]); Gabriel Marcel (cf. *Homo viator* [Paris, 1945]; on Marcel cf. G. Giannantonio, *Gabriel Marcel e il problema della persona* [Vatican City, 1953]); Jean Lacroix (cf. *Personne et amour* [Lyons, 1942]; *Force e faiblesse de la famille* [Paris, 1948]; on Lacroix cf. H. Leclere, "J. Lacroix," in *Catholicisme* [1967], 1579-80); Gabriel Madinier (cf. *Conscience et amour. Essai sur le nous* [Paris, 1938]; *Nature et mystère de la famille* [Tournai, 1961]; Augusto Sarmiento considers this author to be particularly illuminating on the subject of *Gaudium et Spes'* affirmation of marriage as a "community of life and love"; cf. Sarmiento, "El 'nosotros,'" 76-102); Maurice Nédoncelle (cf. *La reciprocité de consciences. Essai sur la nature de la personne* [Paris, 1942]; on Nédoncelle see C. Valenziano, *Introduzione alla filosofia dell'amore di Maurice Nédoncelle* [Rome, 1965]). Each of these authors would merit an in-depth study in order to enucleate their particular contributions to the philosophy of love.

47. Cf. Larrabe, *El matrimonio*, 231-49; Tettamanzi, *La famiglia*, 60-61; Barbiero, *L'itinerario storico-dottrinale*, 40-61, 238-53.

48. Cf. above, pp. 64-71; A. Wohlman, "Amour du bien propre et amour de soi dans la doctrine thomiste de l'amour," *Revue Thomiste* 81 (1981): 204-34; Wohlman, "L'élaboration des elements aristotéliciens dans la doctrine thomiste de l'amour," *Revue Thomiste* 82 (1982): 247-69; J. J. Pérez Soba, "¿La interpersonalidad en el amor? La respuesta de santo Tomás" (Ph.D. diss., Pontifical John Paul II Institute for Studies on Marriage and the Family, 1996).

49. Cf. A. Nygren, *Eros and Agape,* trans. Philip S. Watson (Philadelphia: Westminster, 1953).

50. Cf. P. Rousselot, *Pour l'histoire du problème de l'amour au Moyen Age* (Münster, 1908).

51. Cf. L. B. Geiger, *Le problème de l'amour chez Saint Thomas d'Aquin* (Montreal and Paris, 1952).

52. Cf. Tettamanzi, *La famiglia,* 60: "The 'personalist' perspective that is increasingly affirmed in considerations of marriage prompted a noteworthy discussion regarding the traditional hierarchy of the ends of marriage, as well as conjugal ethics; it is also provoking a recon-

Dietrich von Hildebrand's, which takes its inspiration from Scheeben, is fa-mous among these.[53] The personalistic turn did not however favor a theolog-ical reflection on the family, which remained markedly subordinate to the theology of marriage.[54]

The efforts at renewal briefly described above converged in the Second Vatican Council. The constitution *Gaudium et Spes* gathered the best propos-als of this preconciliar theology,[55] while avoiding the risk of a predominance of the subjective factor in Christian reflection on marriage and the family.[56] In this reflection the council made an innovative and balanced use of the cat-egories of "person" and "dignity," privileging a consideration of the person and his acts over a purely juridical-institutional approach.[57] In this way we can say that the council provoked a development of the anthropological and theological dimensions of marriage (we think, for example, of the theme of

---

sideration of the various aspects of the sacramentality of marriage." Cf. H. Doms, *Vom Sinn und Zweck der Ehe* (Breslau, 1935); Doms, "Amorces d'une conception personnaliste du mariage d'après Saint Thomas," *Revue Thomiste* 45 (1939): 754-63; Doms, *Dieses Geheimnis ist Gross* (Co-logne, 1948); Doms, *Gatteneinheit und Nachkommenschaft* (Mainz, 1965). A bibliography of the polemic sparked by Doms, including magisterial interventions, can be found in Barbiero, *L'itinerario storico-dottrinale*, 245 n. 140. Also relevant is R. B. Arjonillo, *Conjugal Love and the Ends of Marriage: A Study of Dietrich von Hildebrand and Herbert Doms in the Light of the Pasto-ral Constitution "Gaudium et Spes"* (Bern, 1998).

53. Cf. D. von Hildebrand, *Marriage: The Mystery of Faithful Love* (Manchester, N.H.: Sophia Institute Press, 1984). In this regard see R. Dell'Oro, *Esperienza morale e persona. Per una reinterpretazione dell'etica fenomenologica di Dietrich von Hildebrand* (Rome, 1996).

54. Cf. E. Ruffini, "Per una rifondazione della teologia della famiglia," in *Un sinodo per la famiglia. Problemi e prospettive per gli anni 80*, ed. Ch. G. Vella (Milan, 1980), 97-100.

55. Cf. especially *GS* 47-48 and 51.

56. Cf. Ph. Dehaye, "La communauté conjugale et familiale d'après Vatican II," in J. Giblet and J. Etienne, *Aux sources de la morale conjugale* (Gembloux and Paris, 1967), 157-73; V. Fagiolo, "Essenza e fini del matrimonio nel magistero del Concilio Vaticano II," *Ephemerides Iuris Canonici* 23 (1967): 137-86; F. Gil Hellín, "Lugar proprio del amor conyugal en la estructura del matrimonio según la *Gaudium et spes*," *Anales Valentinos* 6 (1980): 1-35; A. Miralles, "Amor y matrimonio en la *'Gaudium et spes*,'" *Lateranum* 48 (1982): 295-354; E. Kaczynski, "Le mariage et la famille. La communion des personnes," *Divinitas* 26 (1982): 317-31; Tettamanzi, *I due saranno*, 103-21; A. Mattheeuws, *Les "dons" du mariage. Recherche de théologie morale et sacramentelle* (Brussels, 1996), 136-50, 260-63, 352-54, 465-68.

57. Mattheeuws, *Les "dons" du mariage*, 9: "Among the contributions of the Council, we note particularly the influence of personalist strains and the fruitful employment of the con-cepts of 'person' and 'dignity.' The guiding thread of the conciliar developments on marriage (GS 47, 48, 51) is neither juridical nor institutional. Rather, doctrinal reflection proceeds from a consideration of the person and the spouses, and of their actions. The person is a value in itself: more, it is at the summit of values in the natural order. The person may not be considered as a means used to obtain some other end."

interpersonal relations with regard to the first), particularly with reference to the relation between the church and the family.[58]

At the center of the postconciliar debate, as we have already mentioned, was the publication of the encyclical *Humanae Vitae*.[59] In it Paul VI prophetically defended the indissolubility of the procreative and unitive meanings of the conjugal act, without taking up the discussion of the ends of marriage.[60] We can say that it was *Humanae Vitae* which in great part polarized the (mainly moral) reflection on marriage after the council.[61]

11.2.3. An Impasse in Sacramental Theology

This admittedly generic overview gives us an idea of the attempt by Catholics to answer the deepening crisis of marriage. For thoroughness' sake, we should point to a decisive element of the theology of marriage that further helps us understand the serious difficulty encountered by Catholic thought in confronting contemporary culture in a way that is at all convincing, when marriage and its correlates are radically brought into question.

I refer to the fact that properly dogmatic reflection on marriage found itself, even after the '50s, at a serious impasse.[62] As we have seen, the themes connected to the sacramental nature of marriage have been a constant in the history of theological reflection. Notwithstanding this, such reflection showed itself in need of a new, more organic foundation that even the most recent the-

58. Cf. Tettamanzi, *La famiglia*, 60.

59. Cf. A. Scola and L. Melina, "Profezia del mistero nuziale. Tesi sull'insegnamento dell'*Humanae Vitae*," *Anthropotes* 14 (1998): 155-72 (here included as app. 5); Mattheeuws, *Les "dons" du mariage*, 150-54; *Humanae Vitae. Vent'anni dopo*.

60. "To speak of 'meaning' is to indicate, at one and the same time, what the spouses 'want to say to each other' in the conjugal act and that which the act 'says' in itself." Mattheeuws, *Les "dons" du mariage*, 12.

61. Cf. D. Tettamanzi, "La riflessione teologica sull'enciclica 'Humanae Vitae' nel decennio 1968-1978," in Tettamanzi, *I due saranno*, 233-66.

62. It is not by chance that in the 1970s O'Neill affirmed that "In order to evaluate the progress made in the area of sacramental theology, it is enough to ask oneself to what point single treatises freed themselves from an exclusively moralistic, not to say casuistic and juridical vision of things in order to adjust themselves and their formulations to that reality which constitutes their dogmatic foundation. As far as the sacrament of marriage is concerned, and in spite of all that has been written about it, particularly in recent years, this evolution made very little progress." E. O'Neill, "I sacramenti," in R. Vander Gucht and H. Vorgrimler, *Bilancio della teologia del XX secolo*, vol. 3 (Rome, 1972), 295. Palmer and Tettamanzi are of the same opinion: P. F. Palmer, "Necessità di una teologia del matrimonio," *Communio* 16 (1974): 1000-1009; D. Tettamanzi, "Matrimonio," *La Scuola Cattolica* 114 (1986): 585.

ology did not know how to produce. This perhaps explains why the many contributions of experience and reflection provided by so-called conjugal spirituality were unable to trigger a real renewal in the dogmatic consideration of marriage.[63] Thus the theme of the sacramental nature of marriage, as well as that of the link between matrimonial grace, the person of Jesus Christ, and the ecclesial dimension of marriage and the family, were left in the shadows.[64]

This impasse may have been born of a certain extrinsicism in understanding the connection between the sacrament of marriage and marriage as a natural phenomenon,[65] beginning with a certain way of understanding sacramentality as a pure *superadditum*.[66] This explains, as a consequence, why

---

63. Cf. Tettamanzi, "Linee di sviluppo della spiritualità coniugale in Italia," in Tettamanzi, *I due saranno*, 279-309.

64. For a bibliography on marriage compiled in the 1970s, cf. A. Pompei, "Saggio bibliografico sulla recente teologia del matrimonio," in *Evangelizzazione e matrimonio*, 244-63.

65. Cf. G. Marengo, "Creazione, alleanza, sacramentalità del matrimonio. Spunti di riflessione," *Anthropotes* 8 (1992): 27-39, with bibliography. The problem has been analyzed with reference to the famous theses of Schillebeeckx on the one hand and Rahner on the other: cf. E. Schillebeeckx, *Marriage: Secular Reality and Saving Mystery*, trans. N. D. Smith (London: Sheed and Ward, 1965); K. Rahner, "Il matrimonio come sacramento," in Rahner, *Nuovi saggi*, vol. 3 (Rome, 1969), 575-602. It is significant that these authors not only proposed important studies on marriage, but developed an organic reflection on the sacrament: cf. E. Schillebeeckx, *Cristo sacramento dell'incontro con Dio* (Rome, 1963); K. Rahner, *The Church and the Sacraments*, trans. W. J. O'Hara (Freiburg: Herder, 1963). For the evolution of modern and contemporary sacramental theology, even if this has yet to make its influence felt on the theology of marriage, see E. Ruffini, "I grandi temi della teologia contemporanea dei sacramenti," *Rivista Liturgica* 54 (1967): 39-52; G. Colombo, "Dove va la teologia sacramentaria," *Scuola Cattolica* 102 (1974): 673-717; A. Ganoczy, *Einführung in die katholische Sakramentenlehre* (Darmstadt, 1979); O'Neill, "I sacramenti," 263-313; J. Finkenzeller, *Die Lehre von den Sakramenten im allgemeinen. Von der Reformation bis zur Gegenwart* (Freiburg, Basel, and Vienna, 1981); L. M. Chauvet, *Linguaggio e simbolo. Saggio sui sacramenti* (Turin, 1982); U. Kühn, *Sakramente* (Gütersloh, 1985); J. Auer, *Il mistero dell'eucaristia. La dottrina generale dei sacramenti e il mistero dell'eucharistia* (Assisi, 1989); Auer, "Sacramento," in *Enciclopedia Teologica*, ed. P. Eicher and G. Francesconi (Brescia, 1989), 916-23; L. M. Chauvet, *Simbolo e sacramento. Una rilettura sacramentale dell'esistenza cristiana* (Turin, 1990); S. Ubbiali, *Il segno sacro. Teologia e sacramentaria nella dogmatica del secolo XVIII* (Milan, 1992); L. M. Chauvet, *I sacramenti* (Milan, 1997).

66. The following two citations suffice to clarify this position. Schillebeeckx proposes a "rigorously theological" examination of "that earthly reality which is marriage, and which, moreover, is precisely in its profane and earthly aspect the sacrament of a religious reality." *Il matrimonio. Realtà terrena e mistero di salvezza* (Milan, 1986), 28 (ET: *Marriage: Secular Reality and Saving Mystery*). "Every marriage, every civil marriage is Christian, either fully such or in a pre-Christian sense (as a marriage oriented towards Christ), or even negatively Christian (a deliberate refusal of this Christian aspect of marriage)!" Schillebeeckx, 349. Rahner, for his part, holds that "Marriage is not an event of grace only in those instances in which it is a sacrament. We might say, rather, that the event of grace which is marriage becomes a sacramental event of grace

so little attention was given to a direct consideration of the relationship of marriage to the mystery of Jesus Christ. It seemed that the only space open to the christological dimension was that of institution of marriage by Christ the Lord.[67] To better understand these two factors, Catholic theology used the idea of elevation with increasing success: Christ elevated marriage to a sacrament. This category, introduced to safeguard the unity between contract and sacrament, ran the risk of accentuating the extrinsicism mentioned above: that is to say, the view of marriage as an institution fulfilled in itself, to which the grace of the sacrament is added only in a second instance.[68] In such a perspective the event of Jesus Christ as such remains extrinsic to the nature of marriage itself.[69] The related discussion regarding the minister of the sacrament must also be recalled.[70] The Latin tradition, because of a privilege given to the category of *consent,* affirms that the spouses are the ministers of marriage.[71] Lastly, there was the risk of an excessive emphasis on the ministry of the spouses, such that these were ultimately divorced from a christological and trinitarian perspective.

To these increasingly evident attempts to reformulate the theology of marriage, a task to which various studies were dedicated in the '80s as well,[72]

---

as *opus operatum,* when it is celebrated in the Church as a marriage between two baptized persons." "Il matrimonio," 594.

67. Cf. Sarmiento, *El matrimonio cristiano,* 132-33.

68. This perspective has not entirely disappeared from current theological discussion.

69. It should be kept in mind that the (correct) insistence on the value of indissolubility, which arose in answer to the Lutheran challenge and grew with the growing secularization of modern society, has at times superficially given the impression that the specificity of Christian marriage coincided simply with increased ethical demands. Rather, as Inos Biffi writes, "the sacrament of marriage is not the 'elevation' of 'natural' marriage to the supernatural order, but the fulfillment of the objective 'intention' of every marriage, already ordered to Christ in the single supernatural order, even if it has been in reality 'deformed' because of the condition of sin." I. Biffi, "Per una teologia dell'uomo-donna: metologia e linguaggio. Appunti di metodologia," *Teologia* 14 (1989): 177.

70. Cf. E. Corecco, "Il sacerdote, ministro del matrimonio?" in *Ius et Communio,* ed. G. Borgonuovo and A. Cattaneo, vol. 2 (Casale Monferrato, 1997), 349-445; Sarmiento, *El matrimonio cristiano,* 184-88.

71. It is important to observe, however, that those who have seen the need to reexamine the question of the minister of the sacrament of marriage have justified this need more from an ecclesiological than from a christological horizon: the role of the consecrated minister would be decisive, in this approach, as the sign of the ecclesiality of the gesture with which the spouses exchange their consent.

72. We can cite as an example Tettamanzi, "Matrimonio," 572-86; E. Ruffini, "Il matrimonio-sacramento nella tradizione cattolica. Rilettura teologica," in *Nuova enciclopedia del matrimonio,* ed. T. Goffi (Brescia, 1988), 177-224; Ruffini, "Per una rifondazione della teologia della famiglia," 95-122.

were added the first attempts to elaborate a theology of the family.[73] Without question the celebration of the Assembly of the Synod of Bishops on the family favored this development. In the few examples of these attempts available to us, two elements emerge: attention to data from the human sciences[74] — an attention which nevertheless remained more or less tied to the dualistic perspective mentioned above[75] — and the development of a pastoral theology of the family,[76] as well as of the discussion of the so-called "ministeriality of marriage."[77]

We have thus arrived at the threshold of the question of content, which we have already alluded to through a contraposition with the three phases of the progressive eclipse of the design of God on person, marriage, and the family that characterizes the modern process of secularization.[78]

In order to gather some fundamental elements from this and proceed to the next chapter, we must turn once again — always in a critical comparison with the dominant culture — to the theme of the nuptial mystery. To do this adequately, we cannot ignore two important facts that allow us to complete the historical profile sketched above.

11.2.4. Further Horizons

We will refer first to the extraordinary contribution of John Paul II, who has opened new horizons in dogmatic reflection on person, marriage, and the family. Studies of his teaching, which includes the long pastoral experience

---

73. Cf. G. Campanini, "La spiritualità coniugale-familiare. Linee di sviluppo," *La Scuola Cattolica* 104 (1980): 126-39; Tettamanzi, "La famiglia cristiana e la teologia," 5-74.

74. Cf. G. Campanini, "Linee di evoluzione della famiglia," in *Un sinodo per la famiglia*, 33-50; G. Ambrosio, "La famiglia nella crisi della società italiana," *La Scuola Cattolica* 104 (1980): 74-91.

75. Even in 1995 an author such as Campanini was still dependent on Schillebeeckx's approach, in his attempt to justify a necessary reference to the human sciences: "It is impossible to engage in a theology of the family without a serious confrontation with the human sciences, since — to take up Schillebeeckx's basic thesis — the family is both 'human reality' and 'saving mystery.'" G. Campanini, *Il sacramento antico* (Bologna, 1995), 21.

76. Cf. G. Volta, "Indicazioni per una teologia pastorale della famiglia," *La Scuola Cattolica* 104 (1980): 92-125; D. Tettamanzi, "La fondazione teologica della pastorale famigliare," in *Un sinodo per la famiglia*, 149-86.

77. Cf. D. Tettamanzi, "Ciascuno ha il proprio dono da Dio: il ministero coniugale," in Tettamanzi, *La famiglia vita*, 92-113.

78. On the explosion of the "wild sacred" as a last phase of the process of secularization, cf. A. Scola, *Questioni di antropologia teologica* (Rome, 1997), 175-84.

and philosophical-theological reflection of Karol Wojtyla, are now more than can be counted.[79] It is enough, for now, to recall the pope's principal interventions. Among them all, the following merit particular attention: the Wednesday catecheses on the body and love (September 2, 1979–November 28, 1984);[80] the apostolic exhortation *Familiaris Consortio* (November 22, 1981);[81] the letter *Mulieris Dignitatem* (August 15, 1988);[82] *Redemptoris Mater* (March 25, 1987)[83] and the *Letter to Women* (June 30, 1995);[84] the instructions of the Congregation for the Doctrine of the Faith, *Donum Vitae* (February 22, 1987)[85] and

79. All the interventions of John Paul II up until December 30, 1988, can be consulted in A. Sarmiento and E. Escriva, eds., *Enchiridion Familiae* (Madrid, 1992). Cf. also above, chaps. 1–3; R. M. Hogan and J. Levoir, *Covenant of Love: Pope John Paul II on Sexuality, Marriage, and the Family in the Modern World* (Garden City, N.Y., 1986); M. Mroz, *Il principio sacramentale dell'uomo e del matrimonio alla luce dell'insegnamento di Giovanni Paolo II* (Rome, 1988). All these works contain substantial bibliographies. One can also consult the bibliography in J. M. Granados Termes, *La ética esponsal de Juan Pablo II* (Rome, 1998), 1-44.

80. The complete cycle of catecheses can be found in English in John Paul II, *The Theology of the Body: Human Love in the Divine Plan* (Boston: Daughters of St. Paul, 1997), and in Italian in *Uomo e donna lo creò. Catechesi sull'amore umano* (Rome, 1992). In the latter, see the introductions to the various cycles by Carlo Caffarra (5-24, 111-12, 255), Angelo Scola (27-29), Stanislaw Grygiel (289-91), Inos Biffi (339-41), Rocco Buttiglione (449-51). A related bibliography can be found in Mattheeuws, *Les "dons" du mariage*, 164-88, 359-74; L. Ciccone, *Uomo-donna. L'amore umano nel piano divino. La grande Catechesi del Mercoledì di Giovanni Paolo II (2 settembre 1979–28 novembre 1984)* (Turin, 1986).

81. Cf. *La "Familiaris consortio"* (Vatican City, 1982); C. Caffarra, "La verità del matrimonio e della famiglia nel Magistero di Giovanni Paolo II," *Communio* 89 (1986): 34-40; *La famiglia cristiana nell'insegnamento di Giovanni Paolo II* (Milan, 1988); D. Tettamanzi, "L'esortazione apostolica "Familiaris consortio" di Giovanni Paolo II. Introduzione alla lettura," in Tettamanzi, *I due saranno*, 153-74; Mattheeuws, *Les "dons" du mariage*, 188-203.

82. Cf. above, pp. 3-20. On this document cf. S. Maggiolini, ed., *Profezia della donna: Lettera apostolica 'Mulieris dignitatem.' Testo e commenti* (Rome, 1988); P. Vanzan, "'Mulieris dignitatem': reazioni, contenuti e prospettive," *La Civiltà Cattolica* 139, no. 4 (1988): 255-58; D. Tettamanzi, *Grandi cose ha fatto con me l'onnipotente: Meditando con il Papa la "Mulieris dignitatem"* (Rome, 1988); M. Toso, ed., *Essere donna: Studi sulla lettera apostolica "Mulieris dignitatem"* (Turin, 1989); *Dignità e vocazione della donna: Per una lettura della "Mulieris dignitatem"* (Vatican City, 1989); A. Serra, "La 'Mulieris dignitatem.' Consensi e dissensi," *Marianum* 53 (1991): 512-88. More recently, cf. S. Mader Brown, "*Mulieris Dignitatem*: A New Perspective on the Image of God," *Journal of Dharma* 23 (1998): 501-16.

83. M. Ponce et al., *La Redemptoris Mater de Juan Pablo II. Análisis y perspectives* (Sigüenza, 1995).

84. Cf. P. Vanzan and A. Auletta, *L'essere e l'agire della donna in Giovanni Paolo II* (Rome, 1996); J. Burggraf, "Juan Pablo II y la vocación de la mujer," *Scripta Theologica* 31 (1999): 139-55.

85. Cf. A. Chapelle, "Pour lire Donum vitae," *Nouvelle Revue Théologique* 109 (1987): 481-508; Congregation for the Doctrine of the Faith, *Donum vitae: Istruzioni e commenti* (Vatican City, 1990); Mattheeuws, *Les "dons" du mariage*, 203-8, 491-527; infra, pp. 331-36.

Ordinatio Sacerdotalis (May 24, 1994);[86] and the encyclical *Evangelium Vitae* (March 25, 1995).[87]

As is obvious, during his entire pontificate John Paul II has explored all the questions connected to our theme. In the face of the emerging challenges of the new millennium,[88] his magisterium has enabled the discussion to grow

86. Cf. Congregation for the Doctrine of the Faith, *Dall'Inter insignores all'Ordinatio sacerdotalis. Documenti e commenti* (Vatican City, 1996). Cf. moreover infra, pp. 307-13. Magisterial teaching is still far from receiving a peaceful reception; cf. A. Berlis, "L'ordination des femmes Pierre de touché de la conciliarité," *Concilium Revue International de Théologie* 299 (1999): 105-12.

87. Cf. E. Sgreccia and D. Sacchini, eds., *Evangelium vitae e bioetica. Un approccio interdisciplinare* (Milan, 1996); J. Vial Correa and E. Sgreccia, eds., *La causa della vita. Atti della Seconda Assemblea della Pontificia Accademia per la Vita sulla Evangelium vitae* (Vatican City, 1996).

88. On the challenges facing the family and pastoral work in its regard, cf. P. Donati, "Lo sviluppo di politiche europee per la protezione di famiglie e bambini: problemi e prospettive," *La Famiglia* 26, no. 153 (1992): 5-17; V. Iori, "Trasformazione di ruoli e identità di genere in famiglia," *Rivista di Sessuologia* 16, no. 4 (1992): 371-77; F. Altarejos Masota, "El papel de la familia en la humanización de la sociedad," *Scripta Theologica* 26 (1994): 1057-73; G. Angelini, "La Chiesa e la famiglia," in *Chiesa e famiglia in Europa*, 77-138; C. Bressolette, "Une pastorale de la famille aujourd'hui," in *Chiesa e famiglia in Europa*, 149-54; J. R. Flecha Andrés, "La famiglia en un mundo en cambio," in *Chiesa e famiglia in Europa*, 165-74; B. Laux and N. Klann, "Der Wandel der Familie und seine Interpretation," in *Chiesa e familia in Europa*, 205-14; "Dalla bioetica alla biopolitica: il 'caso embrione umano,'" *Rivista di Teologia Morale* 28, no. 112 (1996): 467-511; "Famiglia o famiglie? Sociologia, Diritto, Morale," *Rivista di Teologia Morale* 29, no. 113 (1997): 3-42; F. Masellis, "Famiglia e sessualità: un legame ambivalente," *Rivista di Sessuologia* 21, no. 1 (1997): 8-15; A. Scola, ed., *Quale vita? La bioetica in questione* (Milan, 1998); G. Schmid, "Ehe und Familie im Wandel," *Theologie und Glaube* 88 (1998): 342-53; B. Castilla Cortázar, "Familia y armonía social. Equipotencia entre varón y mujer," *Revista Augustiniana* 49 (1998): 661-94; R. Riedler-Singer, "Die neuen Familienformen im Wertediskurs," *Diakonia* 29 (1998): 327-31; M. A. Jiménez Tallón, "Familias monoparentales y clima familiar," *Carthaginensia* 15 (1999): 127-38. On the anthropological challenge underlying feminism, cf. J. Burggraf, "Madre de la Iglesia y mujer en la Iglesia. A propósito de la 'Teología feminista,'" *Scripta Theologica* 18 (1986): 575-93; M. Farina, "La questione donna: un'istanza critica per la teologia," *Ricerche Teologiche* 1 (1990): 91-120; "Teologia femminista. Teologie femministe nei diversi contesti," *Concilium Rivista Internazionale di Teologia* 32, no. 1 (1996): 13-226; P. Guietti, "Femminismo radicale negli Stati Uniti," *Vita e Pensiero* 80 (1997): 362-85; S. Grevel, "Bibliographie," in European Society of Women in Theological Research, *Jahrbuch der Europäischen Gesellschaft für die theologische Forschung von Frauen* 6 (1998): 143-52; K. Ramachandran Nair, "Women, Development and Policy: Changing Feminist Perspectives in India," *Journal of Dharma* 23 (1998): 430-53; F. Mathews, "From Epistemology to Spirituality: Feminist Perspectives," *Journal of Dharma* 23 (1998): 517-39; "Théologie féministe: Expérience des femmes et Saintes écritures," *Concilium Revue International de Théologie*, no. 276 (1998): 7-140; H. Häring and E. Schüssler Fiorenza, eds., "La non-ordinazione delle donne e la politica del potere," *Concilium* 35, no. 3 (1999): 413-592.

on an anthropological level, and has offered it a christological-trinitarian foundation.[89] In this way he has favored the development of a theology of the family that begins to make its weight felt within systematic theology, ceasing to be simply the appendix of a treatise on marriage.[90]

The second element that completes the framework described above involves a certain novelty, beginning in the early '90s, in the dogmatic reflection on marriage as a sacrament. The last decade saw the publication of several studies which were willing to risk a reinterpretation of traditional doctrine, while taking into account both the newness of magisterial teaching from *Familiaris Consortio* to *Evangelium Vitae*, and the burning problems tied to the theme of life and structurally inherent in reflection on marriage and the family.[91]

11.2.5. From the Perspective of the New Evangelization

More than ever before, modern man is called upon by faith to turn his gaze anew to God's revelation, in order to rediscover him who, as the divine Son, has introduced us into the mystery of divine fatherhood and, in carrying out his mission, has given himself as the Bridegroom of the church-bride. The

89. Among the publications that can serve as reference points for a more in-depth investigation of the theology of marriage and the family, we mention the repeatedly cited work of Mattheeuws, which contains an ample bibliography on the subject (cf. *Les "dons" du mariage*, 624-62), and the open perspective of integration proposed by Marc Ouellet (cf. "Pour une théologie des "dons" du mariage," *Anthropotes* 13 [1997]: 495-503). Cf. also C. Giuliodori, *Intelligenza teologica del maschile e femminile* (Rome, 1991); Colombo, "La teologia della famiglia," 45-75.

90. In this sense we can cite: Angelini, "La Chiesa e la famiglia," 422-71; S. Ubbiali, "La teologia della famiglia in Italia," *La Famiglia* 24, no. 155 (1992): 5-17; C. Caffarra, "Fondamenti dottrinali della famiglia," in *Famiglia: cuore della civiltà dell'amore*, ed. A. López Trujillo and E. Sgreccia (Vatican City, 1995), 41-51; A. Ruiz Retegui, "La famiglia alla luce della Parola di Dio," in *La famiglia alle soglie del III millennio*, ed. E. W. Volonté (Lugano, 1995), 14-26.

91. For example, the impressive work of Mattheeuws, *Les "dons" du mariage*, moves in this direction. The author's bold intention is that of integrating the Augustinian doctrine of the "good" of marriage and the Thomistic doctrine of its "ends" in a doctrine of "gifts." Seeking to join riches both old and new, Mattheeuws affirms that "before being 'ends' to be reached, the 'goods' are 'gifts' to be received." On this basis Mattheeuws develops an ontology of the gift; secondly, he systematically expands the theme of "goods." Thus he studies the sacrament of marriage in the context of a sacramental logic which emerges from the seven sacraments. Lastly, he confronts the theme of the "ends" of marriage by beginning with the gift of the child and the question of life. Cf. moreover: G. Baldanza, *La grazia del sacramento del matrimonio* (Rome, 1993); A. Miralles, *Il Matrimonio. Teologia e vita* (Cinisello Balsamo, 1996).

words of Genesis on man, as male and female, being in the image of God are thus made true in him. He is the source of the true light shed on the nature of marriage and the family in the context of the new evangelization.

In order to confront this theme correctly, a word on method is necessary. One of the gravest misunderstandings of the nature of the new evangelization is, without a doubt, that which makes it coincide immediately with an "activity." In such a perspective, speaking of the family as a subject of the new evangelization risks reducing to an itemized list what spouses, parents and children, or the family as a whole can do to make Christ be seen as the center of the cosmos and history.

As Saint Paul teaches us, the first work is faith ("For in Christ Jesus neither circumcision nor uncircumcision is of any avail, but faith working through love" [Gal. 5:6]), as a knowledge of reality *(fides quae)* and abandonment *(fides qua)* to the Lord Jesus Christ, who is the way to the Father in the Holy Spirit. For this reason the task of the new evangelization requires first of all that Christian families witness to how the anthropological reality of man and woman can be the place in which father, mother, and children find their personal and communitarian fulfillment. In this precise sense, the first evangelization is in the order of being and not of "doing."

The reference to the reflections developed in the first section of this work, on man and woman beginning from the archetype of Christ the Bridegroom and the church-bride, helps us understand in what sense the family is a subject of evangelization.

What we have affirmed thus far allows us the better to understand why John Paul II, in his untiring magisterium, returns prophetically and not without originality, with respect to his predecessors, to the importance of marriage and the family for society and for the church. The pope's teaching constantly refers to these themes as an essential dimension of the new evangelization: "The family is at the center of the Church's mission, and of her solicitude for mankind."[92] The awareness of this is translated by the Holy Father into a continual call to all the faithful to nourish a particular care for families.

This is an energetic indication of change that cannot be ignored by those who work in the area of pastoral care of the family: the family is not a "sector" of pastoral work, but a dimension that extends through the entire mission of the church, in both the content and method of evangelization.[93]

---

92. Cf. John Paul II, address after the prayer of the rosary, Saint Patrick's Cathedral, New York, October 4, 1995.

93. The Congregation for Catholic Education worked in this precise direction in develop-

In defining the family as "domestic church," Vatican Council II opened the way to a consideration of the family as a dimension of evangelization. The reality of the church as universal sacrament of salvation is present in the family, and is so with a particular concreteness and clarity that are not owed simply to the fact that the family is that reality which reaches farthest into the ultimate expressions of the human. (One thinks of the importance of the first years of life on the constitution of the personality.) The importance of the family as a "natural" reality goes without discussion.

Yet it is the sacramentality of marriage that makes the family objectively a "domestic church," and thus a dimension of evangelization. We will pause at length in what follows on the connection between the sacramentality of marriage and the reality of indissolubility.[94] For now, a few brief remarks suffice. We have said that the family is the most common, universal, and basic expression of the manner in which Christ is joined to the church (cf. Eph. 5: the sacramentality of marriage). Thus the family carries within itself the deep meaning that the church has for the world: the enduring presence of Christ. The church is sacrament because it realizes the possibility of God's encounter with contemporary man (*Lumen Gentium* 1). Marriage is sacrament because it realizes the possibility of the deep union in Christ of the two who love one another, and who thus become an ecclesial space (domestic church) for all. This sheds light on what is not yet the ultimate reason for indissolubility. In marriage and the family, human freedom can daily experience the humanity of Christ as the sacramental sign of his divinity.[95]

In the building up of the Christian family, the faithful respond to their ecclesial vocation. The holiness and fruitfulness of the family are understood as the expression and development of the task which flows from the sacrament.

To this is connected both the reciprocal gift of self and the duty to transmit life and educate children. Throughout the history of Christianity, many works born of an intelligent charity have emerged along this path; these have revealed even more clearly how the family, as a place of fruitful love, is a fundamental cell of the church and society. In and through the family, each person experiences the possibility of being educated in his twofold dimension of selfness (identity) and difference.

---

ing the document entitled *Directives for the Formation of Seminarians regarding Problems Relating to Marriage and the Family*, released March 19, 1995. This text represents an organic attempt to apply methodologically the central idea of papal teaching, on the level of seminary formation: marriage and the family are a dimension and not an aspect of the new evangelization.

94. Cf. infra, pp. 266-69.

95. Cf. *The Catechism of the Catholic Church* 515.

In living out its evangelizing vocation, the family founded upon marriage is a factor of civilization. In fact, as we have already mentioned, it is a primary expression of that "social subjectivity"[96] which is an indispensable element of the development of every society.

---

96. Cf. John Paul II, *Sollicitudo Rei Socialis* 15 and 28, and *Centesimus Annus* 13.

CHAPTER 12

The Insuperable Difference:
From Man and Woman to Marriage and the Family

Modern society, deeply confused about the fundamental terms both of man and woman and of marriage and the family such as God conceived them, runs the risk of the "abolition of man." How can this risk be avoided?

Keeping in mind the two critical factors which emerged from the history traced out above as causes of the weakening of the Christian proposal — an inability to conceive of the three factors of the nuptial mystery in an organic unity, and the lack of an adequate sacramental theology of marriage and the family — what contents ought our work to contain?

12.1. The Characteristics of the Nuptial Mystery

It is precisely the term "nuptial mystery," explored and deepened through various epistemological perspectives, that, to my mind, offers an adequate and synthetic perspective capable of responding to the sociocultural challenges facing us today. Since we have already amply discussed the theme in the first part of this work, we will limit ourselves here to a concise definition of terms.[1] On the one hand, the expression "nuptial mystery" refers to the organic unity of sexual difference, love (objective relation to the other), and fruitfulness; on the other hand it refers objectively, through the principle of analogy, to the various forms of love that characterize both the man-woman relation and all its derivatives (fatherhood, motherhood, brotherhood, sister-

---

1. Cf. above, pp. 82-109; A. Scola and L. Melina, "Profezia del mistero nuziale. Tesi sull'insegnamento dell'*Humanae Vitae*," *Anthropotes* 14 (1998): 155-72.

hood, etc.) and God's relationship with man in the sacrament, the church, and Jesus Christ, all the way to the Trinity itself. The expression, which has its foundation in the religious experience of individuals and peoples, from cosmogenic myths to the refined reflection of the Old and New Testaments,[2] is in this way able to identify, in terms both complete and unitary, the underlying contents of an inquiry into the original features of person, marriage, and the family in the divine plan.

It is not difficult to see how these three realities are taken up by the triad forming the nuptial mystery; by its very nature, this mystery also insists upon being thoroughly explored, with the criteria of the human sciences, philosophy, and theology. Nor can we undervalue that category of "mystery" which, rightly understood,[3] appears to be the most adequate for bringing the troubled contemporary sensibility into contact with the insuppressible and fascinating affective dimension of the "I."

At this point a number of unavoidable questions arise. In the climate of the loss of fundamental human experience, how does the expression "nuptial mystery" speak to the hearts of the men and women of today? And more: Does the nuptial mystery really point to an essential dimension of human experience, such that it can be proposed as a common point of reference for every man and woman? Lastly: According to what hierarchy ought we to illustrate its basic categories which, in their turn, involve all the facets of the affective dimension? To respond to these questions we must first return briefly to the sociocultural context already summarized above.

This context has undergone much recent evolution, beginning with the 1950s; beyond the three phases described in the preceding chapter, its development cannot be explained without a consideration of the relationship between modernity and the nuptial mystery. As a side note, we point out that already here the central role of the human sciences in our study becomes clear.[4]

---

2. Cf. J. Ries, *Il rapporto uomo-Dio nelle grandi religioni precristiane* (Milan, 1992), 67-92; A. Tosato, "L'istituto famigliare dell'antico Israele e della Chiesa primitiva," *Anthropotes* 13 (1997): 109-74.

3. Cf. M. J. Scheeben, *The Mysteries of Christianity* (London: Herder, 1946), 181-89.

4. Cf. in this regard: P. Miccoli, "Teologia e scienze umane," *Euntes Docete* 44 (1991): 381-417; J. H. Wright, "Theology, Philosophy and the Natural Sciences," *Theological Studies* 52 (1991): 651-68; I. Sanna, "Il ruolo delle scienze umane in teologia," *Lateranum* 58 (1992): 373-407; G. Gismondi, "Il dialogo fra teologia e sociologia: problematiche, limiti, possibilità," *Antonianum* 67 (1992): 3-38.

12.1.1. Scientific Universalism

The phenomenon which, perhaps more than any other, characterizes modernity is a so-called "scientific universalism." In the present era of globalization and of the television and Internet empires, this phenomenon enormously conditions man's self-consciousness, particularly as this is expressed in the nuptial mystery.[5] The expression "scientific universalism" identifies that predominant cultural trend which extends the claim of having constructed a universally valid objective discourse to all levels of the *humanum,* founding this discourse on the abolition of the subject. Incorporated into the narrow but impermeable fortress of scientific and technical language, scientific universalism is the concentration of a philosophical and anthropological way of thinking which holds fast to a double principle: first, that all that is knowable is reduced to the empirically measurable (physicalism), and second, an absolute subjectivism that permits anything, provided it can be done. The subject no longer experiences any limits;[6] he is struck by a radical sense of vertigo.

Every human experience — and its related discourse — rejects this imposition which political systems explicitly pursue, even through law. Real human experience and real discourse are tolerated on the condition that they box themselves into a particular space — a sort of Indian reservation — without ever daring to venture into the open sea of civil society. In the name of this falsely objective universalism, a logic of segregation is reinforced, in a sort of cultural barring of doors. In this enclosed space and only there, one is allowed to enjoy certain goods, even the most primary, with whomever one can find to share them.

The family, too, is similarly constrained — to return to the nuptial mystery as the effective place of the constitution of the person, in his reference to sexual difference and the possibility of marriage. The inability of our culture to abolish the family (we have pointed out that there is a crisis of the couple more than a crisis of the family)[7] leaves the state of segregational violence to

---

5. Cf. M. Binasco, "Un contributo clinico-psicoanalytico alla questione dell'omosessualità maschile," unpublished paper.

6. Cf. L. Lombardi Vallauri, "Il pensiero moderno sulla sessualità umana," *Rivista di sessuologia* 8-9 (1984-85): 15-16. The synthetic historical-cultural observations of the following paragraph take their inspiration from this article.

7. Cf. B. Barbero Avanzini, "Essere coppia oggi," *Rivista di Sessuologia* 8-9 (1984-85): 39-46; E. Scabini, *L'organizzazione famiglia tra crisi e sviluppo* (Milan, 1985); E. Scabini and P. Donati, eds., *La famiglia 'luogo' del giovane adulto* (Milan, 1988); G. Campanini, "'Persistenza' e 'marginalità' della famiglia," in *Chiesa e famiglia in Europa,* ed. A. Caprioli and L. Vaccaro (Brescia, 1995), 229-36.

which the family is relegated exposed to the eyes of all. This can be seen both in the attempt to define the family in such generic terms that it can refer to any kind of cohabitation, and in the reduction of its social relevance, particularly on the juridical-institutional level, to a simple "joint venture" between private citizens.[8]

12.1.2. From Libertinism to the Sexual Revolution

The development of modernity thus struck at the roots of the nuptial mystery, leaving deep scars. This began with libertinism, and proceeded from the first organic attempt to divorce sexuality from both biological and social fruitfulness, to the abolition of the difference of the sexes, and particularly the abolition of woman. The body thus lost its value as a sacrament of the whole person. One's own body and the body of others were reduced to a mechanism that must keep the fire of pleasure burning. The libertine perspective, which proclaimed licit every sexual relationship between the strong and the weak, was replaced by the liberal perspective, that variation which declared licit every sexual relationship between consenting adults. Romanticism reacted against the elimination of all passion and compassion in love, typical of both these views, proposing sexuality as an ecstasy following upon the fusion of the lovers. Sexuality, that place in which love finds itself related to death, took the mystic as its most meaningful figure. After the 1960s the so-called sexual revolution extended the libertine version of love to the masses, wisely combining it with elements of the other theories just mentioned.[9]

It is worth noting that this de-structured vision of eros, seen in an ecstatic key, does not attack the historical-sociological bourgeois version of Christianity, but rather strikes at a fundamental dimension of Christianity's very essence: the nuptial mystery. There is no lack of authors who, in the conflict between eroticism and Christianity, see the most radical conflict of the

8. A perceptive description of the condition of privacy to which the modern-day family is relegated can be found in C. Anderson, "La famiglia nella missione della Chiesa," *Il Nuovo Areopago* 13 (1991): 6-23.

9. Cf. L. Biswanger, *Grundformen und Erkenntnis menschlichen Daseins* (Zürich, 1942); G. Bataille, *L'erotisme* (Paris, 1957); M. Foucault, *Histoire de la sexualité* (Paris, 1976); V. Melchiorre, *Metacritica dell'eros* (Milan, 1977); T. Laquer, *Making Sex: Body and Gender from the Greeks to Freud* (Cambridge, 1990); G. Loughlin, "Sexing the Trinity," *New Blackfriars* 79 (January 1998): 18-25. In this regard the criticism of Balthasar's thought offered by certain Anglican theological circles can be of interest: L. Gardner and D. Moss, "Something Like Time, Something Like the Sexes: An Essay in Reception," in L. Gardner, D. Moss, B. Quash, and G. Ward, *Balthasar at the End of Modernity* (Edinburgh, 1999), 69-137.

present historical age — the dawn of the third millennium — as the replacement of the revolutionary perspective by a "lib-lab" culture, which at this point appears to have garnered unanimous consent. This makes an elaboration of the adequate contents of God's design on person, marriage, and the family even more urgent and necessary. The antithesis just mentioned suggests in fact that only Christianity can oppose the erotic distortion of love with love as a source of new life for the men and women of today.

The cultural development described above allows us to identify the weak link at the source of the attack on the nuptial mystery: the elimination of sexual difference. For this reason an attempt to understand the design of God means first of all exploring the meaning of this difference, while at the same time demonstrating its interaction with the other two factors of the nuptial mystery, as well as with all the categories proper to its underlying affective experience.

12.2. Sexual Difference

Scientific universalism, with its sociocultural connotations mentioned above, has eliminated all dimensions of mystery from among the fundamental characteristics of man and woman, and marriage and the family; it began this work by negating sexual difference. This affirmation can perhaps be more easily understood if we consider the fact that sexual difference in itself cannot be represented or deduced.[10] This illustrates that the man-woman polarity, which is both correlative to the body-soul polarity and understood as the background of the polarity between individual and community, is original and constitutive of man.

Both the magisterium of John Paul II and the reflections of authors such as Lewis, Soloviev, Evdokimov, Balthasar, Fessard, Pieper, and others have contributed to the building up of a considerable body of literature on the theme of man and woman.[11] Nor can we ignore the contribution of the various phases of feminist theology on this theme.

10. Cf. above, pp. 86-96.
11. Cf. J. Pieper, *Faith, Hope, Love,* trans. R. Winston and C. Winston (San Francisco: Ignatius, 1997); C. S. Lewis, *The Four Loves* (London: Fontana Books, 1960); P. Evdokimov, *Woman and the Salvation of the World: A Christian Anthropology on the Charisms of Women,* trans. Anthony P. Gythiel (Crestwood, N.Y.: St. Vladimir's Seminary Press, 1994); Evdokimov, *The Sacrament of Love* (Crestwood, N.Y.: St. Vladimir's Seminary Press, 1995); V. Soloviev, *The Meaning of Love,* trans. Jane Marshall (London: Geoffrey Bles, Centenary Press, 1946); J. Guitton, *L'amore umano* (Milan, 1989); G. Fessard, *Le mystère de la société. Recherches sur le sens de l'histoire* (Brussels, 1997).

We ask ourselves: How do the various feminist authors deal with sexual difference? Above all, do they really consider it? Even a rapid overview of this body of work leads us to the conclusion that the judgment made of difference, precisely because it is difference, remains substantially negative. Moreover, with the exception of the temptation to instrumentalize it in the struggle for women's liberation, difference is mentioned in the majority of cases in order to abolish it, as if one wished to exorcise the gap that every human being inexorably encounters within himself.

12.2.1. *Identity-Difference and Equality-Diversity*

In particular, we are witnessing the substitution of the terms "identity" and "difference," which, to my mind, adequately refer to man and woman, with those of "equality" and "diversity." The first pair bears the weight of mystery contained in its underlying *tremendum;* the second pair, in diffusing this mystery, ends by being completely innocuous. This evasion begins by making the meaning of sexual difference slide toward that of diversity. Thus we delude ourselves into thinking that we have transcended that which cannot be transcended — sexual difference — assimilating it to other differences (ethnic, religious, professional) that the human being normally experiences.

But sexual difference is not diversity. This latter, by its nature, has to do with multiplicity and plurality. As its etymology *(di-vertere)* tells us, the notion of diversity refers exclusively to *interindividual* relations, and is entirely extraneous to the relationship between identity and difference.[12] The etymology of "difference" *(dif-ferre)* suggests the idea of "bringing the self elsewhere," changing one's position. This is therefore structurally inherent to identity. It belongs to and indicates the belonging-together *(Zusammengehörigkeit)* of different things. It does not immediately have to do with multiplicity and plurality, but can be traced back to the person; it is first of all *within the individual.*

This evasion is prolonged in the surreptitious replacement of the concept of "identity" with "equality." But such an identity becomes an expression of inertia. "Equality" refers to a being incapable of relating to the other-than-self, because the loss of an irreducible individuality can mean only a deadly uniformity.

Once difference has abandoned the territory of identity in order to blend into diversity, it becomes impossible to think of man and woman in the biblical logic of the *imago Dei,* which Balthasar indicates so perceptively with the

12. Cf. Aristotle, *Metaphysics* 10.3; Hegel, *Scienza della logica*, II, 1.

double pair *Wort-Antwort* and *Litz-Antlitz*.[13] A consideration of man and woman in an adequately personal key, respecting the Christian sensibility rooted in the *imago Dei,* means — according to the terms "identity" and "difference" rightly interpreted — vigorously and fully affirming their essential originality.

12.2.2. The Path of the "I" in Sexual Difference

Sexual difference is a determining factor of fundamental human experience, precisely because in a certain sense it brings difference within the person himself while permanently maintaining its status of "other." The non-deducibility of sexual difference, however, keeps from it the character of the *already constituted.* More than explaining, it raises questions and calls for solutions; it forms a privileged path along which the individual is introduced to reality. Sexual difference possesses the character of an event and encounter, since the path of the individual's sexuality can never be reduced to a purely biological fact but is always placed within various forms of relationship to the other.

It is not worthwhile for us at this point to describe this path analytically, identifying its goal, object, and the manner of reaching them. It is the place of the human sciences to make us aware of these from time to time. Doubtless, however, a brief glance at the identity and difference of man and woman within the nuptial mystery cannot exempt us from calling to mind here, too — even if only in general outline — the key categories of fundamental human experience related to the subject.

Sexual difference allows the individual an access to the real that has to do, ultimately, with the fulfillment of his freedom in terms of *satisfaction.* It thus introduces him to the experience of *question, need, desire, pleasure,* and *enjoyment.* These are the terms in which human freedom discovers simultaneously its being *in itself, for itself,* and above all, *for the other,* thus grasping its creaturely condition.

In this way the individual person learns to join in himself nature and culture, recognizing his sexuality as something at once biological and spiritual — inasmuch as it is referred to the other along the entire gamut of social ties.

Through difference the individual's desire for satisfaction is above all

---

13. Cf. H. U. von Balthasar, *Theo-Drama III: Dramatis Personae: Persons in Christ,* trans. Graham Harrison (San Francisco: Ignatius, 1992), 284ff. On this theme see the interesting reflection of A. Bosi, "Il sito della differenza sessuale," *Rivista di Sessuologia* 15 (1991): 131-39.

called to reckon with the substantial difference between pleasure and enjoyment. The former unavoidably refers to the sphere of the useful, and by its nature points to a limited satisfaction in time. Enjoyment, however, beyond all possible pleasures, is where freedom is fulfilled, because satisfaction *habetur pro ultimo fine*. But precisely for this reason, if enjoyment reveals that desire cannot be reduced to need — because difference does not mean pure lack, but a demand of the other, and in the end the demand is always for love — there remains in its claim of definitivity an inexorable reference to the end (death).

The path of the constitution of the "I" in sexual difference — through its nondeducible nature — thus necessarily points to the fact that satisfaction is not within the reach of the desiring "I."[14] Sexual difference therefore objectively opens the path to love, whose fullness we encounter in fruitfulness. Here the various components of the nuptial mystery surface once again, in their indissoluble intertwining.

What identification of the "I" would be possible without the elaboration of sexual difference? But what path to this elaboration cannot be traced back to that love in which, from infancy, the "I" recognized the nature and law of desire? In this recognition the child discovers the father as a vehicle of freedom and, in this way learning *detachment* from the mother, opens himself to a recognition of the woman as other *(heteron)*.

Is not the full meaning of existing as man and woman thus identified, in its objective orientation to marriage? Man and woman tend by nature to the generation of the family as the normal environment in which procreation (education) exalts love and fulfills desire.

A forceful reproposal of the design of God for person, marriage, and the family to the men and women of today requires an adequate Christian subject who can testify to the attractiveness of the nuptial mystery. Only its beauty, visibly manifest in the lives of spouses, can unmask the lie of scientific universalism, which attacks marriage and the family by segregating and thus negating them. Christianity thus appears as the only effective antidote to the destructuring and perverse eroticism of today.

The contents of the nuptial mystery, thought through beginning with sexual difference, already at this point reveal a certain capacity for dialogue with the dominant mentality. We would, however, be at a far cry from the

---

14. Human experience in this regard tells us that enjoyment is present as fundamentally forbidden; hence it requires elaboration in the symbol. Freud's description of the infant's primary relationships to its father and mother according to the Oedipus and castration complexes is well known on this point. I owe these last intuitions also to Mario Binasco.

rigor and thoroughness required by our work if we did not open ourselves, at least in an introductory manner, to the philosophical and theological questions underlying the development outlined thus far.

What is the source of the enormous role played by sexual difference?

Even if we wished to respect the prohibition, so dear to psychoanalysts, of representing or defining sexual difference, on what grounds does this difference reveal itself in reference to the reality of things in themselves, or in the secret design with which the triune God, *tenax vigor,* holds all things in being?

12.3. The Principle of Difference and Ontology

12.3.1. Sexual Difference and Fundamental Human Experience

We have seen that sexual difference, always intimately connected to the other two components of the nuptial mystery (love and procreation), shows itself to be simultaneously original and incapable of deduction or representation. Precisely for this reason, it continues to provoke man throughout the entire span of his existence. This incessant interrogation cannot reach the foundation, because such an attainment would coincide with the claim of deducing (representing) sexual difference. And yet its very originality obliges man to think of it. The fact that sexual difference cannot be deduced does not mean it cannot be thought about.

How, then, are we to think of sexual difference? As a basic dimension of fundamental human experience, which today is exposed to the risk of a definitive eclipse. In brief: sexual difference is original, nonderived, nondeducible (capable of representation), because it presents itself as an immediate dimension of fundamental human experience.

To speak of fundamental human experience means to identify what lies at the origin of the human condition, within the larger frame of the original structure of all of reality. To think of sexual difference thus obliges us to think of the *whole.*

Here the tasks of the human sciences, philosophy, and theology emerge in the same place and at the same time. We must require all these disciplines to shed all the light possible on sexual difference, and thus on the entire nuptial mystery.

Since we have already indirectly referred to the perspective of the human sciences, let us now turn to that of philosophy. Philosophical reflection is capable of evaluating the whole history of thought and, at the same time, taking up the entire gamut of philosophical questions articulated by the Schoolmen in their various treatises. At what point does this reflection cross paths with the theme of sexual difference (the nuptial mystery)?

12.3.2. Sexual Difference and Ontological Difference

Situating ourselves within the contemporary debate, we can respond: at the horizon posited by the Heideggerian theme of *ontological difference*. It must be stressed that by using this reference we do not claim to lead all the complex and differentiated currents of Western thought back to this already overemphasized formula. Such a clarification is all the more necessary in view of the need for dialogue with Indian and African thought, whose roots certainly cannot be resolved into the Western mind-set, even though it would be superficial or downright ideological to underestimate the weight of the latter in these cultures; what has been said regarding scientific universalism is proof enough of this.

We cannot at this point engage in a technical exposition of the themes related to ontological difference, and can only refer to the abundant literature on the subject.[15] The following brief remarks, however, seem necessary to us.

12.3.3. The Difference between Being and Beings

The expression "ontological difference" in some way indicates the nature of the original structure of things (the foundation, *arché*). The whole of reality (Being) exists only in the fragment, in the individual being, which in its turn can exist only through the totality of the real (Being, the whole). The whole therefore attests to the existence of a *difference* (polarity) between *Being* and *beings,* a difference which itself can neither be deduced nor overcome. In every act of knowledge, we must in some way detach ourselves from the level of the individual being to open ourselves to Being as a whole, but Being as such does not present itself to us as an object. In order to discover a certain consistency in Being, we must then return to the existing being. Knowledge moves inexorably between these two poles: it cannot deduce Being because this would mean reducing it to the level of an object, and yet Being is the premise for every act of objective knowledge.[16] And yet the individual being, too, es-

---

15. Cf. A. Bertulleti, *Il concetto di esperienza,* in *L'evidenza e la fede* (Milan, 1988), 112-81; G. Colombo, *La ragione teologica* (Milan, 1995); A. Bertelluti, "La 'ragione teologica' di Giuseppe Colombo: Il significato storico-teoretico di una proposta teologica," *Teologia* (1996): 18-36.

16. Cf. Plato, *Republic* 7.1-2.

capes knowledge; it can be truly known only if it is seen in its necessary relationship with Being, thanks to which it *is*. This "gap" before which knowledge finds itself suspended is ontological difference.[17]

12.3.4. Heidegger's Unfounded Criticism of Thomas: The Fruitfulness of the Distinctio Realis

A second remark is imperative. As has been rightly pointed out,[18] Heidegger's criticism of onto-theologism inflicts no damage upon Thomas's thought. This latter, in fact, particularly through the doctrine of the *actus essendi*, "overcomes that forgetfulness of being that can be discerned in Aristotelianism and Platonism on the one hand, and in formalistic Scholasticism and an entire trajectory of subjectivist modern thought on the other."[19] We refer obviously to the ultimately Thomistic theme of the *distinctio realis*,[20] which shows itself capable of overcoming the difficulties into which Heidegger himself falls.[21] These difficulties arise because Heidegger in fact reduces difference to the (temporalized) identity of *Dasein*, and to its necessarily being the individual being in which Being is at stake.

Heidegger's inability to graft the essence of Christianity onto ontology

17. "Cognition has to be suspended between the two [Being and the finite thing]; accordingly, within the ontological difference found in indifference with respect to Being, cognition must allow Being to differentiate it in ever-new ways in relation to existing things — without ever attaining to being itself through indifference or ever reaching the necessary quality of the existent through differentiation. . . . It [ontological difference] is a void because thinking not only sees that it is not filled but understands that it cannot be filled." H. U. von Balthasar, *The Christian and Anxiety* (San Francisco: Ignatius, 2000), 126-28.

18. Cf. H. U. von Balthasar, *Epilog* (Einsiedeln, 1987), 35-66; P. Ricoeur, *La metafora viva* (Milan, 1976), 359-72.

19. Cf. P. Coda, "Dono e abbandono: con Heidegger sulle trace dell'essere," in *La Trinità e il pensare: figure, percorsi, prospetivve*, ed. P. Coda and A. Tapken (Rome, 1997), 123-59.

20. Thomas did not directly treat the problem of the *distinctio realis*, but today — after long discussion — there is no longer any doubt of the presence in his writings of the real distinction between the singular essence and Being. The expression *distinctio realis*, as such, does not occur in Aquinas, who sometimes uses the term *compositio realis* (cf. Thomas Aquinas, *De veritate* q. 27, a. 1 ad 8). Thomas and Heidegger share a common affirmation of the difference between Being and the individual being, but their interpretations of this difference diverge from the first instance. For Thomas difference is the expression of contingence, whereas Heidegger absolutizes difference, closing it in itself (cf. E. Pérez de Haro, *El Mistero del ser* [Barcelona, 1994], 152-62). Not a few authors have compared the positions of Thomas and Heidegger on the problem of metaphysics and, in particular, the concept of *esse*.

21. Cf. M. Heidegger, *Identität und Differenz* (Pfullingen, 1957).

derives from his failure to grasp that, in Thomas's decisive affirmation "esse significat aliquid completum et simplex, sed non subsistens,"[22] Aquinas already sees in substance the difference between Being and beings.

12.3.5. The Necessary Breadth of Philosophical Reflection

A third important note regarding philosophical reflection flows from this. Such reflection must draw nourishment, through an attentive study of Thomas, from the patrimony of Christian realism. From this basis it can engage in a free and critical confrontation with the whole of modern thought, and succeed in garnering all the promising stimuli emerging from contemporary philosophy. Even if contemporary philosophy seems to exhaust itself in all the problems inherited from modernity, it still offers no lack — particularly in certain strains — of decisive theoretical questions which deserve a response. This is the task which *Fides et Ratio* assigns to Christian philosophers and theologians; not, certainly, as the final critical act on the modern itinerary of thought, but rather as the explicit invitation to a new beginning.[23] Particularly in its invitation to move from "phenomenon to foundation," the encyclical shows faith and reason to be in a relationship that is both nuptial and fruitful.[24]

12.3.6. Symbolic Ontology

A fourth point. What contents for philosophical reflection can be derived from this "holistic" view? For convenience' sake I will summarize these in the expression "symbolic ontology." I will limit myself here to setting forth its general contours, with a necessary specification on method,[25] referring those readers who would like to grasp it more thoroughly to other sources.

Criticisms directed at the history of metaphysical and ontological thought have led many thinkers, even Christian ones, to exorcise the very expressions "metaphysical" and "ontological" from their vocabularies. This seems to us an attitude which is not only useless, but even dangerous. We must continue to speak of metaphysics and ontology, even if this must be

22. Thomas Aquinas, *Quaestiones disputatae de potentia* 1.1.

23. Cf. A. Scola, "Libertà umana e verità a partire dall'enciclica *Fides et ratio*," in *Fides et ratio*, ed. R. Fisichella (Cinisello Balsamo, 1999), 223-43.

24. Cf. *Fides et Ratio* 83.

25. Cf. A. Scola, *Questioni di antropologia teologica* (Rome, 1997), 164-65, 231-32.

done on objectively founded bases, and without fleeing from the burden of addressing the criticisms directed against them. Let us now seek to clarify what we mean by "symbolic ontology."

Being does not allow itself to be grasped by human concepts in an immediate manner. This does not mean that the act of consciousness which intends the real does not reach the real itself; it simply means that this act is complex. The original form of knowledge is not conceptual, but rather an intuition, symbolical in the Kantian (anti-predicative) sense! When a concept intervenes (predicative intellection), it is always preceded by knowledge which is in itself not a reflection, but rather that which makes reflection possible. This dialectic cannot be overcome by having recourse to a superior concept capable of seizing its object. Judgment comprehends its object through another object which functions as a sign. Only this object, which anticipates the original object, is immediate.[26] We understand why the foundation is event *(e-venio)* which gives itself, and shows itself only in giving itself, at the same time revealing the "subject."[27] In the sign (a real and, in a certain sense, sacramental sign),[28] Being actualizes freedom; it calls the subject immediately into play and gives consistency to his freedom. This freedom cannot be reduced to *a priori*, whether they be rational (a theory which justifies it) or "transcendental" (the self-positioning of the subjectivity). Reason and will/freedom are thus originally implied in knowledge, because Being shows itself only in giving itself.[29]

12.3.7. Gift and Freedom

While respecting the requirements of ontological difference, a symbolic ontology identifies the outline of the original structure in the relationship between gift and freedom. Contrary to what is asserted in the intellectualism and conceptualism proposed by many versions of postmodern philosophy, we need not pursue a region of objects (classical thought) or the transcendental structure of the "I" (modern thought) in order to ponder the original

---

26. Cf. A. Bertulleti, "Sapere e libertà," in *L'evidenza e la fede* (Milan, 1988), 448.

27. Jean-Luc Marion goes so far as to say that the subject never occupies the center of the scene, "since his function consists only in receiving that which is given." J. L. Marion, *Étant donné* (Paris, 1997), 442.

28. It is worth noting here that *Fides et Ratio* speaks of a sacramental logic. Cf. *Fides et Ratio* 13.

29. Cf. Scola, "Libertà umana," 234-35.

structure. We must rather place ourselves at the level of gift through which the (transcendental) foundation calls human freedom, always historically situated, to an act of decision.[30] Man's knowledge of the foundation from which he is constituted coincides with his experience, in act, of having to determine himself. The ungraspability of the (transcendent) foundation allows it to be known only under these conditions.[31] We see, then, how the individual act of freedom is possible precisely within the open space of *difference,* through which the (transcendent) foundation gives itself to man.

In a symbolic ontology the theme of difference is brought back to the level of the beginning. The theme thus shows itself capable of retaining the best of phenomenological and transcendental thought, as well as adequate instances of hermeneutical reflection. While doing this, it manages to identify the features of the original structure, without falling into relativism or the problems proper to these strains of thought. There is no dearth of thinkers seriously engaged in this enterprise, though it is beyond the scope of our work to identify them all.[32] Moreover, symbolic ontology is capable both of giving value to the great tradition of classical thought and of responding to *Fides et Ratio*'s call[33] for an opening to traditions as yet too often ignored: those of India, Africa, Latin America, and others.

We point out, incidentally, that the intertwining of the gift of the (transcendent) foundation with the freedom of the person allows symbolic ontology to open the field of discussion to both anthropology and ethics in a strict sense. The themes of *communio personarum* and sexual ethics already attest to this.

12.3.8. Ontological Difference and the Nuptial Mystery

The framework of the ontological principle of difference sheds light on the role of sexuality, in its nature as an insuperable invitation addressed to each individual human being for the constitution of his identity. With it, the entire nuptial mystery is illumined.[34] Sexuality exists always and only as insuperable

---

30. Cf. J. L. Marion, *Dieu sans l'être* (Paris, 1991); N. Reali, *La ragione e la forma* (Rome, 1999), 269-93.

31. Cf. Marion, *Étant donné,* 91-114.

32. Along with the reflection of Jean-Luc Marion, we can refer to that of Michel Henry: cf. M. Henry, *C'est moi la vérité* (Paris, 1996).

33. Cf. *Fides et Ratio* 72.

34. The following passage from Balthasar expresses this well: "The marriage union presupposes three things: (1) two persons, who, even in the union, remain 'unmixedly' *(asugchutos)*

sexual difference; the "one flesh" (marriage) is the normal expression of the love between man and woman; the difference which remains in the two who make up the "one flesh" is a sign of the third (the family), and bespeaks its intrinsic fruitfulness.

12.4. The Principle of Difference and Theology

12.4.1. Revelation and Theological Difference

To place ourselves within the perspective of the original structure and thus of fundamental human experience involves an openness simultaneously to the horizons of the human sciences, philosophy, and theology. The question of the whole is in fact simultaneously theoretical, practical, and religious.[35]

A discussion of sexual difference in reference to the principle of difference requires, then, a decisive step into the territory of theology.

On the other hand, there is no lack of voices which, going beyond the debate regarding the legitimacy of a Christian philosophy (as sterile as it is repetitive because it begins intellectualistically, with a formal definition of the two terms), conclude that a rigorous phenomenology is obliged to make room for theological discourse.[36] Nor can we ignore the fact that Heidegger's *destruktion* of metaphysics and ontology, with his critique of onto-theologism, culminated in the claim that God cannot be "constructed," either from or through the world. But what space can be given to the theological question, if not that which flows from a critical assumption of Christian revelation?

---

persons, and only so are in a condition to experience physical union as a rapturous encounter of their spirits or persons; (2) a physical union of such a kind as to make them both truly 'one flesh,' as is shown externally by the result, the child, in whom the share of both is not only physically but also metaphysically indistinguishable; (3) a physical opposition of the sexes that represents the opposition of the spiritual persons in the bodily sphere and at the same time makes possible their union in one flesh, this irreducible opposition being the basis of the irrefragable union." H. U. von Balthasar, *Explorations in Theology,* vol. 2, *Spouse of the Word* (San Francisco: Ignatius, 1991), 184-85.

35. Cf. John Paul II, General Audience of October 19, 1983, in his *Insegnamenti* VI/2 (1983), 814-16; H. U. von Balthasar, "Retrospective," in *My Work: In Retrospect* (San Francisco: Communion Books — Ignatius, 1993), 111-19; L. Giussani, *The Religious Sense* (Montreal and Buffalo: McGill-Queen's University Press, 1997).

36. Cf. Henry, *C'est moi la vérité,* 90-119.

12.4.2. Verbum Caro Factum

In its value as "concrete universal," the *Verbum caro factum* cannot be in any way reduced to general categories of human understanding. The mystery of God cannot be grasped outside of its free, historical self-manifestation: Jesus Christ. In this way alone does God's transcendent freedom continue to reveal its unfathomable mystery to human freedom. Precisely in the God-man relationship, the full weight of the principle of difference reappears and, with it, the intrinsic pertinence of the nuptial mystery in the theological sphere. As the gift of God to man's freedom, this relationship occurs only in a "distance" that — in maintaining a space between the two terms — makes communion possible and mediates the relation.[37] The correct relationship between God and man is thus founded precisely on the basis of their difference. This is the necessary condition to safeguard both the absolute gratuity of the gift God makes of himself and the nondeducible nature of every act of human freedom. We find traced out for us here the logic of the event, which is the logic of the incarnation. In it the dramatic nature of Adam sheds light on the dramatic nature of Christ, and vice versa. "This means that, on the one hand, Adam does not possess his own origin within himself. As created *(factus)* and not begotten *(genitus)*, he can realize himself only in an other-than-self. On the other hand, though, Christ, as the beginning of the beginning (Adam), is unthinkable without Adam, even if by His very essence He can only be free grace."[38] The only substantial analogy possible between God and man is thus christological. The incarnation bears witness to this: it consists in the exchange of places through which Jesus allowed himself to be bound, *propter nos homines,* to the ignominious wood of the cross. "God's anger strikes him instead of the countless sinners, shattering him as by lightning and distributing him among them. Thus God the Father, in the Holy Spirit, creates the Son's Eucharist. Only the Eucharist really completes the Incarnation."[39] The logic of the incarnation thus shows itself to be a sacramental logic. In it the trinitarian design for the human person reaches its fulfillment, because the encounter between the *Deus Trinitas* and man is realized in Jesus Christ.

---

37. Cf. Marion, *Dieu sans l'être,* 239.

38. Cf. A. Scola, "La logica dell'Incarnazione come logica sacramentale: avvenimento ecclesiale e libertà," in *Wer ist die Kirche? Symposium zum 10 Todesjahr von Hans Urs von Balthasar* (Einsiedeln, 1999), 109.

39. Cf. H. U. von Balthasar, *Theo-Drama IV: The Action,* trans. Graham Harrison (San Francisco: Ignatius, 1994), 348-49.

12.4.3. The Logic of the Incarnation as Sacramental Logic: Eucharistic Gift and the Attitude of Human Freedom

The sacrament of the Eucharist is the great testimony of this event. Paradoxically, the very poverty of the eucharistic sign guarantees that distance (difference) which allows for a relation between the God who gives himself and man who freely adheres.

> Human freedom, which, because it is historically determined, cannot at all be deduced, recognizes itself in the obligation to be-for-another. At the same time, by means of its transcendental nature, it knows itself to be essentially incapable of this. It needs an event, which itself cannot be deduced, to actuate this being for another. Through grace, this event presents itself in the fundamental form *(Gestalt)* of the self-communication of the Trinity. Jesus Christ shows himself, gives himself, speaks himself in the Church, as the radical sacrament which realizes itself in the sacraments. Jesus Christ perfectly corresponds *(Entsprechung)* to the will of the Father through the total gift of himself in his true body, the sacrament of his singular person. In the last supper and on the Cross, in Baptism and the Eucharist, Jesus Christ proleptically offers historically situated human freedom the possibility of performing a free act of correspondence to the Trinitarian foundation. In this act, man encounters Christ himself as his contemporary. In Christ, freely given and freely received in the sacramental sign, he enters dramatically, though not enigmatically, into the burning mystery of the *Deus Trinitas* who is all in all (cf. 1 Cor 15:28).[40]

In order to live according to the glorious novelty of the logic of the incarnation as sacramental logic, each one of us need only avoid the great peril of idolatry, in an attitude of incessant eucharistic praise. We must recognize that "a gift, and this above all, does not first of all give an explanation. It asks to be received. . . . If there must be an explanation, this must be understood in the sense of an explanation . . . of the kind that Jacob had from the angel at the ford of Yabboq. An explanation of this sort involves not so much speech as struggle; each adversary demands of the other, above all, confession or 'benediction,' and thus recognition."[41]

---

40. Scola, "La logica dell'Incarnazione," 126.
41. Cf. Marion, *Dieu sans l'être,* 226-27.

12.4.4. The Nuptial Mystery and the Sacramental Nature of Marriage

What has been said allows us to return to the nuptial mystery, and face the difficulties revealed above regarding the sacramental nature of marriage. In fact, an adequate understanding of the concept of sacrament leads to the affirmation that

> the fundamental law which governs all sacramental form in the Church . . . is that, in everything the Church, as the steward of the sacraments, does to give visible form, the manner and the measure of this form-giving is determined by the event which is to be made present in that form and which is itself the archetypal form of all revelation and, hence, also the primal sacrament. . . . The fundamental figure of grace is Jesus Christ himself, and all sacramental forms are grounded in his form in a most concrete sense. . . . They are distinguished from one another by the manner of this saving action, which is not primarily specified by man's universal sociological situations and the context in which the believer finds himself, but by the ways in which Christ has brought us his salvation, which are the ways of his life in human form.[42]

Man obviously intervenes to codetermine the form with which the sacrament mediates the event of Jesus Christ in time and space, offering expressive material which however must be redefined by God. Human freedom is thus more than ever called into play by the sacraments, which are in turn the concrete form in which this freedom can perform acts that are truly free.[43]

A nonextrinsic relationship between grace, freedom, and nature implies two important consequences. First, creation is not a reality which precedes the Father's design to communicate the eternal sonship of the Word outside himself, to have, in the Spirit, sons in the incarnate Son Jesus Christ. To the contrary, creation is the first moment of the unfolding of the saving covenant. As such, creation is essentially referred to the "concrete universal," Jesus Christ, made present in the *here* and *now* of history precisely through the sacrament. Secondly, from this flows a particular consideration for marriage as well.

Natural marriage is not something meaningful which prescinds from reference to Jesus Christ. In him alone, through the sacrament, the freedoms of

---

42. H. U. von Balthasar, *The Glory of the Lord I: Seeing the Form,* trans. Erasmo Leiva-Merikakis (San Francisco: Ignatius; New York: Crossroad, 1982), 576.

43. On this vision of the sacraments and sacramental logic, cf. Scola, "La logica dell'Incarnazione," 99-135.

the two spouses are allowed to communicate in the life of the Trinity. Since sacramentality is not something added on to a natural human given, but more precisely explains it, the nuptial relation between a man and a woman, when it does not share in sacramental fullness, can have consistency only through an indirect participation in this fullness.[44]

In the framework traced out above, it is possible to penetrate fully the meaning of marriage as sacrament. When it is authentic, human love reveals the insuppressible need to be for another, which implies a coming out of self *(ekstasis)*. The ecstatic dimension is coessential to love because in it the structure proper to human freedom is revealed. This consists not only in a being *in-oneself* and *for-oneself,* but above all in a *being for the other.* In the marriage-sacrament the human person's being for the other, *corpore et anima*

---

44. Cf. Scola, "Bases teológicas de la sexualidad, el matrimonio y la familia," in *El matrimonio y su expression canónica ante el III milenio. Actas del X Congreso Internacional de Derecho Canónico* (Pamplona, September 14-19, 1999), soon to be published: "Far from being a purely rhetorical exercise, the identification of this theological node sheds a singular light on certain problems present today in ecclesial practice. It is obvious that the ever-weighty question of the Christian celebration of marriage is accompanied by an oftentimes dramatic forgetfulness of the real sacramental dimensions of this gesture. The question is strictly connected to the theological uncertainty we have mentioned. An insufficient understanding of the sacrament of marriage inexorably leads to a progressive emptying out of the value of the sacramental gesture, which remains completely entrusted to the spouses' fragile intentions. In other words: the sacrament of marriage runs the risk of being reduced, for those contracting it, to an empty ritual, which merely records the will of a man and a woman to bind their relationship naturally, without posing the conscious question of the grace of God in Jesus Christ. What is needed, however, is not so much to ask ourselves if there is room in the life of the Church for a celebration of marriage — and thus an exchange of free assent — which does not always coincide with the sacrament, particularly in the case of baptized persons who are not consciously living out their belonging to the Church (cf. M. M. Bakermans, *The Sacramentality of the Marriage of Non-believing Baptized Persons. A Short Survey through Comparative Analyses of the Central Themes in the Literature 1965-1990,* licentiate thesis in manuscript form, Pontifical John Paul II Institute for Studies on Marriage and the Family, Rome 1993). Rather, the fact that the request for a Christian celebration of marriage still exists should catch the attention of the whole ecclesial body. It is a call to take up the task of evangelization with greater strength and clarity. What is needed is welcoming and giving value to the request for marriage, showing how only in incorporation into Christ is the human being made capable of an experience of love and of the other that is full, fruitful, and purified of the limits of human fragility. Only thus will the sacrament of Christian marriage be welcomed in its truth, and recognized as a gift of grace, the beginning and the fullness of the good." In this sense, Balthasar affirms, "In matrimony, for instance, it is not the event of a covenant entered into by husband and wife that specifies a grace which in itself is undifferentiated. Rather, this is effected by the nuptial relationship between Jesus Christ and the Church." Balthasar, *Glory of the Lord,* 1:576-77.

unus, becomes an indispensable norm.[45] As Ephesians 5 tells us, the natural reality of man and woman becomes the sign of the eucharistic union of Christ the Bridegroom with the church his bride.[46]

12.4.5. Ascending to the Source

The last step of our theological investigation of the principle of difference, capable of reckoning with the whole of the nuptial mystery, requires us to move in the direction of ecclesiology, Christology, and trinitarian theology. These developments will be able to explain why the intertwining of sexual difference, love, and procreation requires us, if it is to be understood, to traverse all the analogous forms of love.[47]

12.5. On Method: The Value and Limits of the Spousal Analogy

Our inquiry began with the ecclesial subject, carefully taking into account the radical challenge offered by the dominant contemporary culture regarding the nuptial mystery. We were able to identify at least two reasons for this culture's intrinsic weakness: the inability to think about sexual difference, love, and procreation in an organic unity, and the impasse in theology which prevented it from giving a reason for the sacramental nature of marriage.

In a second step we examined the major contents of the nuptial mystery, thus offering indirect proof for the necessity of investigating it according to the unified and articulated perspectives of the human sciences, philosophy, and theology. The question that now arises is that of method.

Without claiming to exhaust the subject or articulate all of its implications, I will limit myself to confronting what I judge to be a decisive problem. I refer to the value and the limits of the spousal analogy.

Obviously we cannot in this place take into account all the rhetorical, semantic, and hermeneutical implications of what Ricoeur, in his astute investigation of their affinities and differences, rightly defined as "modes of discourse," in order to show their inevitable plurality and reciprocal inter-

---

45. Cf. John Paul II, *The Theology of the Body: Human Love in the Divine Plan* (Boston: Daughters of St. Paul, 1997), 72-74; Balthasar, *Epilog,* 77-98.

46. Cf. H. U. von Balthasar, *Theo-Drama III: Dramatis Personae: Persons in Christ,* trans. Graham Harrison (San Francisco: Ignatius, 1992), 288-92.

47. On this subject see both above, pp. 55-81, and what I discuss in chap. 16 of the present work.

dependence, and to clarify the precise conditions under which one can speak of their continuity and discontinuity. Ricoeur's Toronto lectures on the living metaphor and the relation between the poetic and philosophical modes of discourse are emblematic in this regard.[48] Even less is it possible here to define "figures of discourse" and their relations. It is enough to be aware that, rigorously speaking, terms such as "comparison," "similarity," "symbol," "sign," "synecdoche," "metonymy," "allegory," "metaphor," and "analogy" are not synonyms.

An adequate foundation of the spousal (nuptial) analogy can exist only within the framework of these two premises,[49] which we simply call to mind. This is all the more true as there exists no lack of objections both to the use of the spousal analogy and, even more radically, to analogy itself.

A number of contemporary philosophers do not cease to remind us that the *ratio* of Thomas's *Summa,* analogy, has collapsed beyond repair due to the "lacerating effects of the critique carried out by the last great doctors, Dons Scotus and Ockham, and not because of modern philosophy."[50] The collapse was not triggered by an external assault, but by an internal inconsistency, and according to this viewpoint, *Fides et Ratio* succeeds only in hiding this tragic outcome of the audacity of Christian realism.[51]

As for the spousal analogy in the strict sense, it has been noted that "theology cannot limit itself to the repetition of narrative language (for example, that of the biblical account of the creation of man as male and female), but must engage itself in attaining and uttering what can be understood both from symbolic language and from cultural provenance. . . . When such a hermeneutic is lacking, a sort of short circuit is inevitable which . . . can only generate confusion and follow interrupted paths. . . . We retain as valid the question whether modern-day theology and the Magisterium have sufficiently carried out this task."[52]

On the other hand, the notion of the nuptial mystery makes direct and articulated use of this analogy. The unbreakable unity of the three aspects of

---

48. Cf. Ricoeur, *La metafora viva,* 9-61.

49. A comprehensive attempt to do just this can be found in C. Giuliodori, *Intelligenza teologica del maschile e femminile* (Rome, 1991), 81-116.

50. Cf. M. Cacciari, "Fides et ratio: il destino dell'analogia," *Humanitas* 54 (1999): 350-53.

51. Cf. R. Righetto, "I laici contro l'enciclica," *Avvenire,* November 27, 1998, 27, where reference is made to the positions of Paolo Flores d'Arcais, Eugenio Scalfari, Gianni Vattimo, Emanuele Severino, Carlo Bernardini, Salvatore Natoli, Giulio Giorello, Luc Ferry, Alain Finkielkraut, and Jean-Luc Marion.

52. I. Biffi, "Per una teologia dell'uomo-donna: metologia e linguaggio. Appunti di metodologia," *Teologia* 14 (1989): 172-78.

nuptiality must be founded (in ontology, sacramentality, ecclesiology, Christology, and the Trinity) in the God-man relationship, integrally conceived.

12.5.1. Factors of an Evolution

How can analogy be understood, in itself and in its spousal qualification, so as to avoid the *aporia* demonstrated by similar objections? Briefly, contemporary criticisms of the *analogia entis* have not taken into account the evolution of this decisive theme; the most farseeing figures of contemporary theology and philosophy have labored precisely in order to guarantee its capacity to attain to the real and, in some way, God himself.[53]

Thomas, taking up Plato, widens the Aristotelian concept of analogy, which had been notoriously limited in Aristotle to the horizontal level; the Stagyrite tended to formulate a mathematical relationship between substance and its attributes.[54]

In Aquinas's thought, attribution and proportionality allow analogy to say something about God without failing to uphold the principle of the Fourth Lateran Council: that of a *dissimilitudo semper maior*. But modern philosophy, too, makes an impressive use of analogy — even if, as with Kant, it does this secretly[55] — and Ricoeur's studies come to the conclusion that "the doctrine of the analogy of being arises from the desire to embrace, in a single theory, the horizontal relationship between category and substance and the vertical relationship that goes from created things to the Creator."[56] Though he fine-tunes the delicate relation between analogy and metaphor, Ricoeur defends analogy in a sharp debate not only with Nietzsche, Husserl, and Heidegger, but also with Derrida and other contemporaries.[57]

---

53. Among the most recent studies which take up the results of the decisive confrontation between Przywara, Barth, and Balthasar, it is worth noting: G. De Schrijver, *Le merveilleux accord de l'homme et Dieu; Etudes de l'analogie de l'être chez H. U. von Balthasar* (Louvain, 1983). In the area of philosophy, important justifications of the doctrine of analogy can be found in V. Melchiorre, *La via analogica* (Milan, 1983); F. Riva, *L'analogia metaforica. Una questione logico-metafisica nel tomismo* (Milan, 1989).

54. Cf. Giuliodori, *Intelligenza teologica*, 98; E. Berti, "L'analogia in Aristotele. Interpretazioni recenti e possibili sviluppi," in *Origine e sviluppi dell'analogia da Parmenide a S. Tommaso* (Rome, 1987), 98.

55. Cf. Melchiorre, *La via analogica*, 295-300.

56. Cf. Ricoeur, *La metafora viva*, 361.

57. Cf. Ricoeur, *La metafora viva*, 337-417.

12.5.2. Analogia Entis, Analogia Fidei, Analogia Libertatis, Analogia Relationis

It is more useful for our purposes to dedicate a few words to the dialogue between Przywara and Balthasar, which allowed the latter to develop an adequate concept of analogy.

According to Balthasar, Barth, through the concept of *analogia fidei*, manages to overcome the dialectic positively. However, the Protestant theologian lacks rigor in his criticism of the concept of *analogia entis;* he does not avoid a certain return to an idealistic reduction. For Barth, Jesus Christ is that obedient and indestructible principle which allows for the objective covenant of God with all of creation, but his triumphant understanding of glory leads him to empty the mystery of effectual human freedom; salvation ends by being almost imposed, automatically and extrinsically.[58] In an attempt to give value to the Barthian term of the *analogia fidei* and join it to the classical conception of the *analogia entis,* Balthasar uses the precious intuitions of the study of the Fathers carried out by Przywara, the master genius of his period of formation. In particular, the soteriological theme of the *admirabile commercium,* in connection with that of an "exchange of roles," proves decisive for Balthasar's doctrine of analogy. The Swiss theologian is however critical of Przywara because of what he terms an excessive emphasis on the principle of *Deus semper maior,* which impedes Przywara from reaching the *Gestalt* (form, figure) of the event of Jesus Christ. It thus becomes impossible to demonstrate how the *Verbum caro factum,* Jesus of Nazareth, can be the concrete locus of the analogy (correspondence, *Entsprechung*) between the trinitarian event and the individual man.[59] Overcoming an anthropocentric, idealistic vision of the God-man relation, Balthasar christologically deepens the *analogia entis,* turning it into what has been called an *analogia libertatis.*[60] In this latter the *analogia relationis*[61] has full rights of citizenship. It thus becomes possible to conceive of analogy beyond the contemporary criticisms,

---

58. Cf. De Schrijver, *Le merveilleux,* 180-83; H. U. von Balthasar, *The Theology of Karl Barth,* trans. Edward T. Oakes (San Francisco: Communio Books/Ignatius, 1992), 381-89.

59. Cf. E. Przywara, *Analogia entis. Metafisica. La struttura originaria e il ritmo cosmico* (Milan, 1995), 250-302; H. U. von Balthasar, *The Glory of the Lord IV: The Realm of Metaphysics in Antiquity,* trans. Brian McNeil et al. (Edinburgh: T. & T. Clark, 1989), 37; Balthasar, *Theo-Drama III,* 220-21.

60. Cf. Balthasar, *Theo-Drama III,* 206-14.

61. It is worth noting, on the side, that authors possessing sensibilities different from Balthasar's reach the same conclusions regarding the *analogia personalitatis et relationis.* Cf., for example, J. Galot, *La persona di Cristo* (Assisi, 1972), 30.

which targeted its idealistic version. At the same time, an adequate spousal analogy can be elaborated, making use of the category of relation.

Balthasar's position can be summarized in three steps. First, overcoming the conceptualist univocity still present in both Przywara and Barth, he affirms that

> Reflection on the analogous truth of being, far from getting lost in abstractions . . . forces us to face squarely the most vital questions of Christian faith and life. How, ontologically speaking, can God become man, or, to phrase the question differently: Does creaturely *logos* have the carrying capacity to harbor the divine Logos in itself? Presupposing that we have been able to disclose something of this fundamental mystery, we must still ask how things that do not themselves enact the incarnation of the Word can conceivably "follow Christ" within the world and its logic. Moving on to the indispensable framework of this *sequela Christi*, how can anything like a "Church" (understood as "body" and "bride" of Christ) make sense ontologically?[62]

Secondly, he elaborates an *analogia libertatis*, understood as the perfect correspondence *(Entsprechung)* between the historical self-manifestation of God in Jesus Christ and a human freedom which is truly free. The soteriological event of the incarnation, passion, death, and resurrection of Jesus Christ (the *admirabile commercium*) thus becomes the foundational locus of the analogy. In it "substitution" (*Stellvertretung,* the exchange of places) does not mean that Christ mechanically takes the place of man, fulfilling what the latter could not do on his own. Rather, the work of Christ opens up a space of effective — that is, not predetermined — freedom for man. Jesus Christ's free availability *(disponibilità)* to die on the cross *pro nobis* makes possible the liberation of human freedom.[63]

Lastly, the analogy of freedoms contains an *analogy of personalities,* and thus of *relations,* by virtue of which the single individual, in obedience to a call received from the personality of God, participates in his freedom. Man becomes more and more himself, a person, the more he dedicates himself assiduously to God's service.[64]

---

62. H. U. von Balthasar, *Theo-Logic,* vol. 1, *Truth of the World,* trans. Adrian J. Walker (San Francisco: Ignatius, 2000), 8.

63. A synthetic investigation of the christological *analogia entis* can be found in Balthasar, *Theo-Drama III,* 220-29.

64. Cf. Balthasar, *Science, Religion, and Christianity,* trans. Hilda Graef (London: Burns and Oates, 1958), 114.

12.5.3. An Unconditional Gift to the Act of Human Freedom

We ask ourselves: What is gained through Balthasar's widening of the concept of analogy? Briefly, this development further clarifies that conception of fundamental human experience, seen within the original structure, which we have already encountered in detailing the contents of our study. The unutterable event of the Trinity, who communicates himself in Jesus Christ to human freedom, is the *unconditional gift which calls man to obedient decision, in which the self is fulfilled and encounters total satisfaction*. This unconditional gift to the act of freedom unfolds within the principle of (ontological and theological) difference.[65]

12.5.4. Analogy and the Nuptial Mystery

Once the concept of analogy has received a foundation, we can move on to the spousal analogy, identifying the decisive gains this brings to the elaboration of the nuptial mystery. These are themes to which we have already referred here and elsewhere,[66] so we can limit ourselves at this point to recalling the main points.

- By virtue of analogy, sexual difference (male and female) ultimately rests upon the difference in perfect unity in the Trinity. "Seen thus, the fragmentation of nature through sexuality ceases to be tragic. Even nature differentiates in order to unite; how much more so does the bridal secret between heaven and earth, which gives us a share in the differentiation of the trinitarian unity. On all planes the truth and depth of union depend on preserving the differences."[67]
- It is possible to establish an important analogy between sexuality and

65. "The nonsubsistence of being, which is its self-dispossession, seems to be sheer poverty. And yet, it reveals that this poverty (as such!) is the plenitude of God's self-giving in essences, whose plurality both derives from being's 'self-renunciation' and, in accord with the divine exemplarity of the Logos, is also given to being as its end. The ontological difference thus originates both from nonsubsistent and from subsistent (divine) being; in that sense it reveals both a similitude (insofar as the multiplicity of creatures is one in esse) and a major dissimilitude, insofar as nondivine being necessarily cleaves in two and stands over against the divine identity in the form of a nonidentity." H. U. von Balthasar, *Theologic II: Truth of God,* trans. Adrian J. Walker (San Francisco: Ignatius, 2004), 183.

66. Cf. supra, pp. 55-137.

67. Cf. H. U. von Balthasar, *A Theological Anthropology* (New York: Sheed and Ward, 1967), 313.

fruitfulness. Reproduction corresponds to animal genitality, procreation to human sexuality, and generation to the suprasexuality of God.

- Again by virtue of the analogy, sexuality in the *imago Dei* is not limited to the relationship between creature and Creator, but can be extended to the *communio personarum*, to that communional *qualitas* of which John Paul II speaks in *Mulieris Dignitatem*.[68] From this flows the centrality of the theme of the family as *imago Trinitatis*.[69]

- To my mind, a further elaboration is needed of the application of the male-female analogy, with the consequent theme of bridegroom and bride, to its higher analogues, particularly in the area of christological and trinitarian doctrine. The analogical tie with ecclesiology is easier, in part because of Ephesians 5.[70] Here again we see the strength of the principle of the *maior dissimilitudo*.[71]

This seems to us to found a correct methodological use of the nuptial mystery.

68. Cf. *Mulieris Dignitatem* 7.

69. Cf. S. Giuliani, "La famiglia è immagine di Dio," *Angelicum* 38 (1961): 166-86; Giuliani, "La famiglia è immagine della Trinità," *Angelicum* 38 (1961): 257-310; A. Orbe, "La procession del Espíritu Santo y el origen de Eva," *Gregorianum* 46 (1964): 103-18; B. de Margerie, "L'analogie familiale de la Trinité," *Science et Esprit* 24 (1972): 77-92; A. Vásquez Fernández, "Los simbolos 'familiares' de la Trinidad según la psicología profunda," *Estudios Trinitarios* 14 (1980): 321-85; S. del Cura Elena, "Dios Padre/Madre. Significado e implicaciones de las imagines masculinas y femininas de Dios," *Estudios Trinitarios* 26 (1992): 117-54; M. Hauke, "La discusión sobre el simbolismo feminine de la imagen de Dios en la pneumatología," *Scripta Theologica* 24 (1992): 1005-27; P. Coda, "Familia y Trinidad. Reflexión teológica," *Estudios Trinitarios* 29 (1995): 187-219; B. Castilla Cortázar, "La Trinidad como familia. Analogía humana de las procesiones divinas," *Annales Theologici* 10 (1996): 381-416.

70. Cf. Giuliodori, *Intelligenza teologica*, 115-88; Loughlin, "Sexing the Trinity," 18-19.

71. "For God and man are related in a manner far different from man and woman: in no way do they complete one another." H. U. von Balthasar, *Heart of the World* (San Francisco: Ignatius, 1979), 39-40.

CHAPTER 13

Fatherhood, Motherhood, and the Mystery of the Father

13.1. The Eclipse of Fatherhood

"There are no good fathers: this is a rule. We bear no grudge against men, but against the bond of fatherhood, which is rotten. To make children? Nothing better. To *have* them? What iniquity! Had he lived, my father would have stretched himself out upon me and crushed me. Fortunately, he died young. In the midst of all the Aeneases carrying their Anchises on their shoulders, I move from one shore to the other, alone and hating these invisible parents weighing on their children all their lives. I left behind me a young man, dead, who did not have the time to be my father and who today could be my son. Was this for good or for ill? I do not know, but I willingly join in the verdict of a well-known psychoanalyst: I have no super-ego."[1] In this tragic declaration of Sartre, one of the keenest witnesses to the sense of loss permeating Western culture, we can identify the traits of the eclipse of parenthood that poisons the consciousness of the men and women of today, particularly in European societies. This is not the place for an analysis of the causes of such a crisis, or its main interpreters.[2] However, the affirmation of the French philosopher can provide us with extremely important clues.

---

1. J.-P. Sartre, *Les mots* (Paris, 1964), 11.
2. On this subject, see the well-done synthesis of Andrea Milano in A. Milano, "Padre," in *Nuovo Dizionario di Teologia*, ed. G. Barbaglio and S. Dianich (Rome, 1982), 1067-96.

13.1.1. The Eclipse of Fatherhood:
The Loss of the Relation of Origin and the Loss of Freedom

Sartre's words deny the goodness of the parental tie. The philosopher does not limit himself to questioning the moral quality of the father-son relationship ("the bond of fatherhood is rotten"); he goes as far as to suggest that the very fact of having been generated is an evil. This position, taken to its logical conclusion, ends in a contradiction. It is in fact impossible to deny that being is given to us, because we are not at the origin of our being-here. What sense, then, can there be in refuting the positive value of this relation?

What Sartre suggests in his affirmation that "there are no good fathers" is that every form of dependence — beginning with the primary, parental form — is always an evil.[3] The figure of the ideal man in this vision would be "he who makes himself": an autonomous individual, loosed from every tie and therefore infinitely "free."

This refusal of the father/parent damages not only social dynamics, but the very identity of the child. In depriving himself of this original experience of dependence and submission, the child can no longer recognize himself as son or daughter, and loses the supreme school of education in the real. He can no longer be helped to enter into reality as it is, but ends in confusing it with the object of his own dreams and the prolongation of his own desires.[4]

The first meaning of the term "father" identifies this figure as being at the origin.[5] This is an essential meaning, and one which cannot be suppressed, even if, as we shall see further on, it cannot define the whole mystery of fatherhood.[6]

---

3. Cf. the terrible pages of Kafka's *Lettera al Padre* (Rome, 1996), 29-31 (*Letter to His Father,* trans. Ernst Kaiser and Eithne Wilkins [New York: Schocken Books, 1966]).

4. Cf. R. Buttiglione, *L'uomo e la famiglia* (Rome, 1991), 48-50.

5. Cf. W. Kasper, *The God of Jesus Christ,* trans. Matthew J. O'Connell (London: SCM Press, 1984), 138: "The father is essentially the source on which the child indeed depends but to which it also owes its existence. He is the source that renders the child an independently existing entity and justifies that existence. The father-child relation is thus a symbol of the human condition as such; it gives expression to the fact that human freedom is a conditioned and finite freedom. The abolition of the father is made possible only by indulging in a hybrid utopianism that combines absolute freedom and an inhuman kind of human mastery. Since, however, the father-child relation is not only an inalienable aspect of being human but also cannot be replaced by other relation, 'father' is a primal word in the history of humanity and religion; it cannot be replaced by another concept and cannot be translated into another concept."

6. Andrea Milano distinguishes three levels of fatherhood: physiological (the one who generates); psychological (of affective responsibility); and symbolical (the figure of the father in the sociocultural context). Cf. Milano, "Padre," 1069. All three levels, however, can be led back to this consideration of fatherhood as *origin.*

The eclipse of fatherhood directly attacks the subject's perception of reality, generating a deadly anxiety which is the result of the child's Promethean claim.

A further element of the eclipse of fatherhood as the loss of the relation of origin can be gleaned from another phrase in Sartre's declaration: "To make children? Nothing better. To *have* them? What iniquity!" Even in its ambiguity, this affirmation involves a massive negation of the nuptial mystery. Breaking the circumincession of sexuality, love, and procreation leads to a reduction of procreation to mechanical reproduction, love to the search for the imaginary androgynous, and makes the "I" fall into narcissism.[7] We have already pointed out the disquieting results to which this disintegration has led in the last fifty years: we have moved from a defense of sexuality without procreation to the claim that procreation can be had without sexuality. Throughout these years, however, the church's magisterium has tirelessly repeated that the triad which constitutes the nuptial mystery is inseparable; now more than ever, this doctrine is being called into question by the new frontiers of science, as it investigates increasingly delicate ethical issues (for example, human cloning).[8]

The character of *origin* attributed to fatherhood needs a further important specification. It must be made clear that this "being at the origin" does not mean that the child is included as the parent's appendage. To the contrary, it means generating him as *another I*, unique, different from the self. The eclipse of fatherhood involves this aspect, too, and can easily lead to an inability to comprehend otherness as such. It is not by chance that many great voices of contemporary thought have attempted to recover this sense of the other precisely through a reflection on the originality of parental relations.

These brief considerations on the eclipse of fatherhood as a constitutive relation — being origin and positing the other in being as different from me, as person — urge us to recall the basic components of the link between paternity and freedom, which has already been explored in previous chapters.[9]

7. Cf. A. Scola, "Differenza sessuale e procreazione," in *Quale vita? La bioetica in questione,* ed. A. Scola (Milan, 1998), 161.

8. This term, often used generically, commonly means "the production, in a laboratory, of genetically identical individuals from other, pre-existent individuals. The only aspect this has in common with the scientific meaning of the term . . . is that this production would take place asexually, without recourse to the encounter between male and female gametes." R. Mordacci, "La clonazione: aspetti scientifici e problemi etici," *Aggiornamenti sociali* 48 (1997): 571-84. For a more accurate analysis of the various aspects of cloning, see M. L. Di Pietro, "Dalla clonazione dell'animale alla clonazione dell'uomo?" *Medicina e Morale* 47 (1997): 1099-1117; A. Serra, "La clonazione umana in prospettiva 'sapienziale,'" *La Civiltà Cattolica* 149 (1998): 329-39.

9. Cf. above, pp. 150-54, where I substantially take up again what I wrote in A. Scola, "Paternità e libertà," *Anthropotes* 12 (1996): 337-43.

The father does not stand before his child only as *origin;* he sustains him throughout life's *path* in order to lead him toward his ultimate *fulfillment.* If these three great aspects of fatherhood (origin, path, and destiny) are attentively explored, they reveal a precise correspondence with the three levels of freedom (ontological desire or *amor naturalis,* the capacity for choice, and adhesion to the infinite).[10] It will be useful for us to reflect briefly on the reasons for this.

Firstly, ontological desire reveals that human freedom is a gift. All that the human being is, he is originally — that is, according to the relation of origin — through gift. In receiving his being, he first of all receives freedom, as the innate tendency to self-fulfillment. Desire, or the energy with which the "I" enters into reality, adhering to it in truth, is primarily put into action by fatherhood.

Secondly, this desire leads man to fulfill the path of his life through a continuous series of decisions and choices: this is the second level of freedom. In their daily exchange of love, the parent gives his child a vision of life, and the child, because he is capable of judgment, chooses. The parent's educative task, which cannot be renounced, arises here, albeit in the diversity of functions which both experience and the human sciences invite us to consider. While the mother introduces the child into the gratuitous and unconditional dimension of being, allowing him to confront all of reality from a certainty of being loved, the father — inasmuch as he represents the principle of reality to the child — allows him to come out of himself to confront reality. He introduces the child to the path toward his own destiny, initiating him to the law of exchange (work) as the law of growth in life. Because of this law, no one has the right to receive something in exchange for nothing. Each person must earn a retribution in exchange for a work accomplished. In order to grow, man is called to learn both the law of gratuity and the law of exchange, which, in spite of their opposite formulations, are not contradictory.[11] This can be seen in God, in whom both laws exist contemporaneously, in a unity; there are both gratuity and exchange between the divine persons. It is, however, easy to intuit how this divine unity is reflected in human experience through the diversity of tasks of the father and mother.[12]

Thirdly, freedom is fulfilled in adhering to the Infinite. Only thus does man find complete satisfaction. In this sense it is possible to affirm that the fulfillment of freedom, too, must ultimately be given. Going to the heart of

---

10. Cf. A. Scola, *Questioni di antropologia teologica* (Rome, 1997), 89-98.

11. Cf. Buttiglione, *L'uomo e la famiglia,* 48-50, 136-38.

12. Cf. above, pp. 131-33.

human dignity, the Christian tradition defines man with an expression of incomparable simplicity: *capax Dei*. Each human being knows he must transcend himself in the direction of the mystery, but he does not know how to reach the face of God when left to his own efforts. Man perceives this twofold evidence within himself; in it lies the whole enigma of the human condition.

By virtue of the connection between the father and freedom, which we have touched on briefly, this enigma arises again in the experience of sonship, of being someone's child. This latter recalls a mystery and is in itself an enigma. We ask ourselves: Where can this enigma find an answer? And if the answer exists, what does it tell us of the experience of fatherhood which, now more than ever, runs the risk of total eclipse?

In the Father of our Lord Jesus Christ — who is origin, path, and destiny — the enigma of human fatherhood is resolved in the revelation of the very key of creation: adoptive sonship. Contemplation of the Father, made possible through the human history of the incarnate Son, shows that freedom's legitimate desire is far from being contrary to the Father. Rather, this desire, which is constitutive of human nature, finds its origin precisely in him.

It is thus necessary to consider, even if briefly, what the faith teaches us about fatherhood in order to then explore, in part 3 of this chapter, the reflections of the divine Fatherhood in Christian experience.

13.2. Fatherhood and the Mystery of the Father

13.2.1. A Methodological Premise: In Order to Believe in the Son of God, One Must First Encounter Him as the Son of God

Any theological reflection on God the Father cannot but take as its starting point the Son of God, who became incarnate in time and space to encounter man. "In order to believe in the Son of God, one must first encounter Him as the Son of God."[13] It must, then, be possible for man to encounter One who, in declaring himself to be in a singular relationship to the Father, can be recognized as Son.[14] When this happens, a way is revealed in faith to God the Father.

---

13. F. X. Durrwell, *Il Padre. Dio nel suo mistero* (Rome, 1998), 20.

14. Cf. R. Penna, *I ritratti originali di Gesù il Cristo* (Cinisello Balsamo, 1996), 153. In a commentary on Matt. 11:27/Luke 10:22, the author concludes, "an equality of nature is clearly suggested between the Father and the Son, as we see both from the exclusivity of the reciprocal relationship and from the Semitic-experiential connotation of the verb 'to know,' which indicates both the concepts of knowing and loving. The Son's relationship to the Father is not something accidental, but belongs to the ontology of the persons, however one interprets the 'all' that has

The New Testament clearly documents the existence of these two conditions. The Gospels propose, on the one hand, what has been called the "claim"
of Jesus of Nazareth (to be the Son of God). At the same time, they attest to a
perception, in Jesus' contemporaries, of at least the basic contents of this
claim (they encountered him as the Son of God). Laying out the proof of this
twofold affirmation would require a line-by-line investigation of the Gospels,
which is obviously impracticable here.[15]

In brief, it is precisely because Jesus is the Son that God can be recognized
as Father. This happens in a way different from (though obviously not contradictory to) that of other religions, and of the Old Covenant itself.[16] God is

been given to him. By way of conclusion, we can say that it is entirely legitimate to hold that Jesus thought of himself in terms of sonship with respect to God, and of a sonship which in practice had no parallels of the same type, and which was, thus, one of a kind."

15. It is enough to note several New Testament passages that can open the way to a consideration of Jesus Christ as the Son of God, and thus of God as Father. First, there is the prayer of
Jesus as this has been handed down by the Gospels (cf. Mark 14:36; Matt. 26:29) and Paul (Rom.
8:15; Gal. 4:6). The appellative *abba*, with which Jesus addresses the Father in an original manner, reveals the content of his self-knowledge: "the knowledge of a particular filiation which lies
at the heart of this prayer (Abba)" (Penna, *I ritratti originali*, 118). Secondly, a progressive contrast emerges between Jesus' claims and his adversaries, which develops throughout his public
ministry. When this tension reaches its apex, causing the condemnation of Jesus by the Sanhe-
drin, it becomes clear, in a certain sense, that the cause is blasphemy: "'I have shown you many
good works from the Father; for which of these do you stone me?' The Jews answered him, 'We
stone you for no good work but for blasphemy; because you, being a man, make yourself God'"
(John 10:32-33). Thirdly, there is the meaning of the category of *mission* as used in John's Gospel.
In the person of Jesus Christ, we see a clear identity between person and mission. Jesus' mission
rests on a radical expropriation of himself, by which even that which is the most his, his "I," ultimately does not belong to him. The Gospel of John — but also the *hapax legomenon* of Heb. 3:1
— is explicit in this regard. Jesus lives from the Father's will (cf. John 4:34), the search for continuity with this will ("I can do nothing on my own authority . . . my judgment is just, because I
seek not my own will but the will of him who sent me," John 5:30), and can do nothing other
than this will. In this identity between person and mission in Jesus, the ontological relation between Father and Son is made manifest. A last consideration should be added to these observations, which is decisive for a theology of the Father: Jesus never presents himself as the Father
and, nevertheless, claims to be equal to God. The rigid monotheism of the Jewish tradition
could not immediately and peacefully receive the fact that Jesus presented himself as the Son,
even if it was able to perceive the claim to divinity (blasphemy/condemnation).

16. On this topic cf. G. Schrenk and G. Quell, *"pater,"* in G. Kittel, *Grande Lessico del Nuovo
Testamento*, vol. 9 (Brescia, 1974), 1111-1306. In this sense the relationship between the Old and
New Testaments has been aptly described by Cardinal Ratzinger. He indicates, with particular
acuity, the way in which the Christian thinker must always look simultaneously toward the two
Testaments: "Thus it was that the Old Testament was opened up and became precious for me.
More and more I came to understand why the New Testament is not a different book of a differ-
ent religion that, for some reason or other, had appropriated the Holy Scriptures of the Jews as a

in fact not only father, but the Father of our Lord Jesus Christ, as the New Testament formula of blessing (eulogy) constantly affirms.[17]

13.2.2. The Paschal Mystery: The Supreme Revelation of the Father

Once we have established that we can speak of divine fatherhood only by beginning with Jesus Christ, we can inquire into the culmination of this revelation. We thus find ourselves before a consideration of the paschal mystery as the supreme revelation of the Father. In this discussion we are not interested in considering the mystery of the death and resurrection of Jesus Christ as a redemptive act; in other words, we will not look at this mystery from a soteriological point of view. We would like, rather, to respond to an absolutely theological question: What does the paschal mystery tell us about God? How does God reveal himself to man in the death and resurrection of Jesus Christ?

First of all, we must recognize that Jesus is condemned by Israel's highest religious authorities precisely because he claimed to be the Son of God. The death of Jesus — of him who claimed God as *Father* in an absolutely unique way — glaringly highlights the rejection of this claim on the part of men.[18] His resurrection, on the other hand, is the act by which the Father, so to speak, authenticates the truth of this claim.[19] Death and resurrection thus represent the heart of Jesus Christ's Sonship, and therefore, of the fatherhood of God with respect to him. Already at this level one intuits that the

---

preliminary structure. The New Testament is nothing other than an interpretation of 'the Law, the Prophets, and the Writings' found from or contained in the story of Jesus. Now, this 'Law, Prophets, and Writings' had not yet, at the time of Jesus, grown together to form a definitive canon; rather, they were still open-ended and, as such, offered themselves spontaneously to Jesus' disciples as a testimony to him, as the Sacred Scriptures that revealed his mystery. I have ever more come to the realization that Judaism (which, strictly speaking, begins with the end of the formation of the canon, that is, in the first century after Christ) and the Christian faith described in the New Testament are two ways of approaching Israel's Scriptures, two ways that, in the end, are both determined by the position one assumes with regard to the figure of Jesus of Nazareth. The Scripture we call today the Old Testament is in itself open to both ways." J. Ratzinger, *Milestones: Memoirs, 1927-1977*, trans. Erasmo Leiva-Merikakis (San Francisco: Ignatius, 1998), 53-54.

17. For example: Rom. 15:6; 2 Cor. 1:3 and 11:31; Eph. 1:3; 1 Pet. 1:3. On this topic cf. Schrenk and Quell, *"pater,"* 1287-88.

18. On the deeply paradoxical meaning that the death of Christ — on a cross between two *anomoi* (and the term used in Luke 22:37 means, literally, "one without law"; a lawless man in Israel was not an ordinary criminal!) — must have had for an observant Jew, it is enough to think of Paul's personal testimony. Cf. Gal. 1:13-14.

19. Cf. Acts 2:24; 1 Thess. 1:10; 2 Cor. 4:14.

face of the God of Jesus Christ is the face of the "Father" in an absolutely unique sense.

Let us look more closely at the event of Jesus Christ's death. Above all, it is a real death! And more, it is an ignominious death. When he experienced it, the cross was the most obscene of the means of execution. And yet this extreme death, which has all the traits of the most atrocious of punishments, is qualitatively singular. It is unique, cannot be repeated, and definitively conquers the sinister destiny of *total condemnation* which marked every other death, both before and after him. Why? Saint Anselm, who pondered this question deeply, offers two reasons. First of all, he says the death of Jesus of Nazareth is unmerited, the death of the perfectly innocent man.[20] In him there is no sin! The second reason Anselm gives is more marked by his genius, and is expressed in a single adverb: *sponte.* Jesus takes up his death *sponte,* that is, by a *free choice.* And yet these two characteristics would not on their own suffice to explain why, with his singular death, Jesus has vanquished the sinister destiny of total condemnation inherent in every death. Another fundamental point is necessary. The response to the terrible challenge of death shines forth in the free "Yes" of Jesus in agony in Gethsemane: "Father, if it is possible, let this cup pass from me! But let not my will, but thine be done" (Matt. 26:39).[21] The destiny of total condemnation that accompanied every death is "swallowed up" from underneath: "Death has been swallowed up in victory" (1 Cor. 15:54).[22] The human obedience of a divine person conquers death, and this obedience constitutes the supreme handing over of self of the Son to the Father.[23]

Groping our way forward into this mystery, we can be bold enough to think that the deep reason for the victory over death lies in the *kenosis* of the Son of God (cf. Phil. 2:6-7). This *kenosis* is found in his not considering his equality with God as if it were a treasure to be jealously guarded, and in stripping himself: "He must become man in free obedience if his death is to overcome death."[24] Jesus Christ is really the Innocent One, and this in a radical sense. He is the one who offers his completely unmerited death *sponte,* because he is the Son of God who allowed himself to be sent into the flesh to

---

20. "I have found in him no crime deserving death," says Pilate (Luke 23:22).

21. In this regard, see the interpretation that Maximus the Confessor makes of the human freedom of the Son of God, and its soteriological importance. Cf. F. M. Léthel, *Théologie de l'agonie du Christ* (Paris, 1979), with preface by Marie-Joseph Le Guillou.

22. H. U. von Balthasar, *Theo-Drama IV: The Action,* trans. Graham Harrison (San Francisco: Ignatius, 1994), 493.

23. Cf. H. U. von Balthasar, *Skizzen zur Theologie V: Homo Creatus Est* (Einsiedeln, 1986), 374-75.

24. Balthasar, *Theo-Drama IV,* 494.

conquer death. He could have not done this, and thus not have died. Balthasar rightly asserts, in this perspective, that Jesus' death is the expression of his eternal trinitarian vitality. For this reason, "when weighed in human terms, death is simply an end . . . and a pure simple being carried away. The folly of Christianity consists in making this limit a sort of center."[25] The death of the Crucified One is in fact the place of encounter with the Father in the Holy Spirit, and thus constitutes the supreme revelation of God as Father.

Such an affirmation is full of consequences for the concept of freedom. In the paschal mystery the Son presents himself as the One who has fully fulfilled his human freedom in his relationship with the Father. Through contemplation of the paschal mystery, which leads us back to the intimate life of the Trinity, we can intuit that freedom and dependence are not only not contradictory; in fact, each refers to the other. The Son reveals himself as Son in handing over his life to the Father, allowing himself to be sent "for us men and for our salvation." Jesus Christ receives his origin from the Father *(origin)*. He lived his human history in constant reference to the Father *(path)*. And finally, he fulfilled his destiny by handing himself over to the Father so that all might regain the freedom that had been lost through sin (the human destiny of Christ: *mission*). In this way the divine Fatherhood reveals itself to man in the event of the human freedom of the Son. We are face-to-face with the God of the Crucified and Risen One, and thus face-to-face with a Father!

13.2.3. The Three Levels of Divine Fatherhood

We will now attempt to deepen our understanding of the Father's countenance with a few brief considerations. Our decision to begin with the paschal mystery implies beginning with the consideration of God as Father of Jesus of Nazareth, the incarnate Word: this is the first level of divine fatherhood. From this basic level we move on to an understanding of divine fatherhood with respect to the faithful, who are called, by a predestinating and redemptive decision, to be sons and daughters in the Son: the second level. This leads, out of respect for a correct relationship between the immanent and economic Trinity,[26] to an understanding of the fatherhood of the Father with regard to the eternal Word as the origin of the possibility of the incarnation: the third level. These are the three

---

25. Balthasar, *Christen sind einfältig* (Einsiedeln, 1983), 59.

26. Cf. J. Prades López, "De la Trinidad económica a la Trinidad inmanente," *Rivista Española de Teología* 58 (1998): 285-344.

essential aspects of a theological discussion of God the Father:[27] God the Father of the incarnate Son, God the Father of the faithful and of all human beings in the incarnate Son, and God the Father of the eternal Word.

These three levels are all implied in the event of Jesus Christ. To consider them separately, therefore, will inevitably seem somewhat artificial. We will limit ourselves here to some general considerations.

The first level of divine fatherhood — God as Father of the incarnate Word — is, as we have seen, the basis of all Christian reflection on the fatherhood of God. In this way we avoid the temptation of "surpassing" or "going beyond" the event of Jesus Christ in theological reflection; the Johannine affirmation, "No one comes to the Father except through me" (John 14:6), constitutes an essential reference point. This warning is particularly necessary in a climate as multireligious and multicultural as our own, in which the faithful find themselves more and more frequently face-to-face with believers of other religions, with whom they must live and dialogue. The possibilities for enrichment which can flow from this encounter must not be confused with the search for a vague religious "common denominator";[28] this ought to be precluded from the beginning.

Human beings have access to divine filiation in the most holy humanity

27. "Hence the fatherhood of God, made explicit in the history of dogma as fatherhood with regard to the eternal Son, with regard to the incarnate Son and thus with regard to men, and in the precise sense which the Church gives to it, is indissolubly referred to the historical event of Christ. For this reason, it constituted the clearest refutation of every mythology. Christian theology of the fatherhood of God was not an inquiry made in the hopes of gaining knowledge about a metaphysical principle, but rather the effort to re-elaborate the historical experience of faith in Jesus of Nazareth, in all of its implications. The paradox of Jesus the God-man prompted the reflection that arrived at the formulation of the dogma of the Trinity, and consequently defined the threefold system of divine fatherhood as it is unveiled in faith." Milano, "Padre," 1091.

28. On the importance, at this time, of interreligious dialogue, cf. Scola, *Questioni di antropologia*, 155-73. An eventual "theology of the Father" which would claim to have gone beyond the event of Jesus Christ would radically abandon the area of Christian theology. The church's magisterium has issued an authoritative reminder of this: "There are also conceptions which deliberately emphasize the kingdom and which describe themselves as 'kingdom-centered.' They stress the image of a Church which is not concerned about herself, but which is totally concerned with bearing witness to and serving the kingdom. . . . Together with positive aspects, these conceptions often reveal negative aspects as well. First, they are silent about Christ: the kingdom of which they speak is 'theocentrically' based, since, according to them, Christ cannot be understood by those who lack Christian faith, whereas different peoples, cultures and religions are capable of finding common ground in the one divine reality, by whatever name it is called. This is not the kingdom of God as we know it from Revelation. The kingdom cannot be detached either from Christ or from the Church." John Paul II, *Redemptoris Missio* 17-18.

of Jesus Christ, the Son of God, in which the Word has in a certain sense united the whole of human nature to himself.[29] In this way we enter the second level of theological reflection on divine fatherhood: the adoptive filiation of the faithful.[30] Jesus himself referred to this, at once joining it to and distinguishing it from his own filiation. I refer to the distinction Jesus makes when he calls God "my Father" (cf. Matt. 7:21; 11:27; Luke 2:49; 22:29) and "your Father" (cf. Matt. 5:45; 6:1; 7:11; Luke 12:32). It is the specific task of theological anthropology to describe and reflect on the filial condition of the Christian from the moment of baptism, which marks the point of filial adoption, to its fulfillment at the end of time. One of the fundamental themes of this discipline is precisely a reflection on freedom, which, in the light of the doctrine of justification, shows itself to be always dependent upon the paschal mystery of Jesus Christ: it is a liberated freedom.[31]

The third level of our reflection — God the Father of the eternal Word — provides the decisive foundation, without which neither the first nor the second levels would have any meaning. In fact, man can call God Father only in Jesus Christ, who, properly speaking, is the Son of God, because his humanity has been personally assumed by the eternal Word generated by the Father.[32] The Son, whose identity is that of being the one *sent* from all eternity, can be grasped as Son only in reference to the Father who has eternally generated

---

29. Cf. *Gaudium et Spes* 22: "He Who is 'the image of the invisible God' (Col. 1:15), is Himself the perfect man. To the sons of Adam He restores the divine likeness which had been disfigured from the first sin onward. Since human nature as He assumed it was not annulled, by that very fact it has been raised up to a divine dignity in our respect too. For by His incarnation the Son of God has united Himself in some fashion with every man. He worked with human hands, He thought with a human mind, acted by human choice and loved with a human heart. Born of the Virgin Mary, He has truly been made one of us, like us in all things except sin."

30. We must immediately clarify, however, that the "second level" exists not because it comes *after* within the divine plan, but because it depends on an original level. This "not coming after" means that there is a single plan: the incarnate Son is the firstborn of many brethren (cf. Col. 1:13-20; Eph. 1:3-14).

31. A reflection on the adoptive filiation of the faithful, in relation to the classical principle that "what is last in execution is first in intention," throws new light on the mystery of creation. Creation in fact finds its theological justification in the original design of the predestination of all men to become sons in the son in Christ. This is the reason why the starting point for speaking of the fatherhood of God with regard to all men is the unique fatherhood of God with regard to the Christian.

32. The question of the inseparability of these three levels, which can also be considered an expression of the two fundamental dogmas of the faith — the redemptive incarnation and the Trinity — has been discussed in A. Scola, *Hans Urs von Balthasar: A Theological Style* (Grand Rapids: Eerdmans, 1995), 53-83.

him. Saint Cyril of Alexandria affirms, "The Father is, so to speak, the natural place of the Son."[33]

13.3. Marriage and the Family as an Education to Fatherhood

In the paschal mystery, as we have seen, the fatherhood of God is fully revealed. It is fatherhood not only with respect to the Son — God as Father of the Word, and God as Father of the incarnate Word Jesus of Nazareth — but also with respect to the human race, gratuitously called to filial adoption. At this point we ask: What is the concrete way for the faithful to learn about this fatherhood?

The scene of Mary and John at the foot of the cross is the preeminent example of how the fatherhood of God extends itself in history through the creation of a new human relationship. "Jesus, seeing his mother and, next to her, the disciple whom he loved, said to his mother, 'Woman, behold your son!' And to the disciple, 'Behold your mother!' From that moment, the disciple took her into his home" (John 19:26-27). In the supreme hour of his mission, that of the total handing over of his human freedom to the Father, Jesus brings his work to completion, establishing a new *familial relation* among men. Without denying natural relations, this new familial relationship, whose form (figure) is the church's motherhood, constitutes the (sacramental) sign of the fatherhood of God. The scene from John's Gospel brings all the factors implied in the nuptial mystery (sexual difference, love, and fruitfulness) to fulfillment, and in particular, precisely identifies the nature of the relations of fatherhood, motherhood, and sonship.

In the light of this, the third part of our reflection will be articulated in two points. First, we will reflect on the meaning of being children as the condition for becoming fathers or mothers. Second, we will see how the new familial relation introduced by Jesus in the supreme hour of the revelation of his Sonship sheds light on human experience and brings it to fulfillment.

13.3.1. Fatherhood, Motherhood, and Childhood

Fundamental human experience attests that being a child — that is, having an origin — is one of the primary contents of the self-consciousness of the "I." The

---

33. Cf. Cyril of Alexandria, *In Johannis Evangelium* 1.5; *Thesaurus* 7, cited in Durrwell, *Il Padre*, 192 n. 25. The consideration of the Father as the "place" of Jesus has been discussed particularly intelligently by Le Guillou: cf. M. J. Le Guillou, *L'Innocente* (Rome, 1976), 65-69.

human person cannot understand himself outside a concrete interweaving of familial relationships that are in fact identified with the family, which in its turn is the primary cell of a people and society. Undervaluing this truth always involves a certain violence, because it contradicts human nature itself. As we have stated above, filiation (being someone's child) does not only involve being originated, but being given origin as an *other*, as a free and unique person, different from one's parents. Very briefly, we can say that the meaning of being a child is revealed in the personal experience of a freedom that has been given (a relationship with the origin). In its relationship with its father and mother, the child learns the consistency of its personal identity, because it is led into the adventure of the encounter of its own "I" with reality, the other-than-self.

According to Christian revelation, the reason why childhood is a primary (original) experience must be sought in the mystery of creation. The human being is created in the image and likeness of God. Concretely, as the Fathers affirm, he is created in the image of the Image, who is the Son. We are not created in the image of the Father or of the Spirit; we are created in the image of the Son in order to become, through grace, *sons and daughters in the Son*. The ultimate reason why we must begin with being children in order to speak of parenthood lies in our having been created in the Son.

In filiation, the human person discovers he is a free and personal gift; fatherhood and motherhood consist in the communication of this gift through generation and education. Parents are called to accompany their children's freedom without ever claiming to be its substitute — such a claim would be illusory, since human freedom is personal and inalienable. Through the task of education the parents provide support for their children's freedom along the path of life, in order to accompany them to the fulfillment of their persons. No father or mother is allowed to avoid any of these three phases, in which freedom traces out its path.

We have already touched on these themes, just as we have already mentioned that the father, as origin, represents the principle of authority ("the principle of exchange"): the child's freedom is constantly reminded, through the father's presence, to confront reality and not to close in on itself. The father figure thus radically cancels out any claim of self-sufficiency on the part of the child. The latter, having been generated, must understand not only that he is not the "creator" of his own "I," but that he is not the source of reality. The mother, on the other hand, communicates a sense of gratuity that expresses the positivity of his own existence to the child, through a continual and unconditional welcoming. This is of course not to be taken rigidly, as if fatherhood did not imply gratuity and motherhood did not possess its own authority; we are dealing rather with different perspectives and starting points.

These brief comments allow us to understand the tragic consequences of the eclipse of the parental figures. Only a disincarnate and spiritualistic view of man, which does not recognize the constitutive character of the nuptial mystery, can confuse and ultimately deny the status of the father and mother as educators. As a side note, we can say that in this sense both the defense of cloning and certain strains of radical feminism unexpectedly reveal themselves to be incurably infected by spiritualism, because they do not respect the fundamental fact that every human being exists only and everywhere as a man or as a woman.[34]

Being parents is thus a dramatic task. The temptation to possess, not to allow the child to be, deep down, *other* and *free*, constantly threatens paternal and maternal love. As is often the case, it is a poet who best expresses the fascinating drama of human experience. I would like to cite Charles Péguy on this theme. As this poet tries to enter into the mind and heart of God contemplating human freedom, he expresses the dilemma with disarming ease:

> Like a father who teaches his son to swim
> In the flow of the river
> And who is torn between two feelings.
> Because on the one hand if he holds him up all the time and if he
>   holds him up too much,
> The child will depend on it, and will never learn how to swim.
> But if he does not hold him up at just the right moment
> The child will choke. . . .
> Such is the mystery of human freedom, says God,
> And of my government of man and of his freedom.
> If I sustain him too much, he isn't free any more.
> And if I don't sustain him, he falls.
> If I sustain him too much, I expose his freedom,
> And if I don't sustain him enough, I expose his salvation. . . .
> This freedom of this creature is the most beautiful reflection
>   there is in the world
> Of the Freedom of the Creator.[35]

To accept the risk of his children's freedom is the deepest trial of a parent's life; one would like to spare one's child any suffering, any evil. It is difficult to forget, in this respect, the figure of David weeping over the body of his son

34. Cf. above, pp. 22-24.

35. "Le Mystère des Saints Innocents," in C. Péguy, *Oeuvres poétiques complètes* (Paris, 1975), 714-15.

Absalom. After having received news of the death of the traitor-son, "the king was deeply moved, and went up to the chamber over the gate, and wept; and as he went, he said, 'O my son Absalom, my son, my son Absalom! Would that I had died instead of you, O Absalom, my son, my son!'" (2 Sam. 18:33). This lament for the death of the unfortunate son is perhaps one of the most beautiful expressions of fatherly love, undiminished even in the face of the most horrendous betrayal. Is this not perhaps also a reflection of the fatherhood of God with respect to sinful man?

There is a second aspect of the father-mother-child relation that merits attention: all filiation, concretely considered, is marked by sexual difference, which as such is insuperable.[36] Every human being lives only and exclusively as a son or as a daughter. From the perspective of the person's "status," this means that children can reflect either the mystery of the father (the origin of existence, authority, the principle of exchange) or the mystery of the mother (the mystery of intrinsic gratuity). The fundamental experience of the nuptial mystery always implies these two aspects: on the one hand, it is the experience of filiation as a freedom given to us, and on the other, it is the experience of being called to become a father or a mother.[37] These must be lived in a precise order. Every man and woman can be a father or a mother only as he or she is, in turn, a son or a daughter. This is not a banal fact to be taken for granted, but a constitutive aspect of the person which must be kept in mind in every instant of life. From the point of view of education, we can, then, affirm that only he who "recognizes" himself as a son (who recognizes that his freedom is constantly originated, supported along his path, and accompanied to his destiny) can be a father (be the origin of his child, sustain him along his path, and accompany him to his destiny). Only that man who recognizes his own father is able to reflect the mystery of fatherhood, giving the other his freedom. Only that woman who recognizes her husband and father is capable of maternally leading her child to this recognition.

What can sustain fathers and mothers in this great but dramatic task, particularly in a cultural climate like today's, so strongly marked by the eclipse of fatherhood?

---

36. Cf. M. J. Le Guillou, "Le Saint-Esprit, Marie et l'Église," *Études Mariales* 27 (1970): 95-104.

37. For the relationship between the trinitarian mystery and the dual unity of man and woman, cf. above, pp. 28-30.

13.3.2. *"Our Father, Who Art in Heaven,"* and the Church, Mother of Many Children

In considering the experience of new family relationships in Christ, we can identify three fundamental elements that shed light on what we have already said regarding the relationships of father, mother, and child.

The first is offered to us by the Christian prayer par excellence, the "Our Father." Each day the believer, alongside other Christians, addresses God as "Our Father, who art in heaven." The second element involves recognizing oneself as an *adoptive child of God*. The third is particularly vivid in Catholicism, and is the consciousness of having the church as mother: ecclesial maternity. In summary, one can say that the Christian, introduced into the virginal womb of mother church in baptism, is made a child of God, and can continuously turn to his Father who is in heaven. In these essential elements (divine paternity, the "sonship" of believers, and ecclesial maternity), we encounter the fulfilled *form* (figure) of the natural relationships of father, mother, and child. First of all, the Christian recognizes himself as one child among many: a child of the church and a child of God the Father. As a child is led to a recognition of his father through his natural mother, the Christian, through his belonging to the church, is helped to grasp the fatherhood of God.

Moreover, the fatherhood of God the Father is made present through the Son Jesus Christ, who is the head of the church, his bride. From the affirmations made up to this point, we can begin to intuit the "fittingness" of the fact that the Word became incarnate in a (male) man in order to represent the divine fatherhood. Jesus of Nazareth is the Son called in his humanity to be the sign (sacrament) of the Father. At the same time, we can intuit how the Son, in order to accomplish his mission, made the church his bride. Without her it would be impossible for us to have access to the fatherhood of God (analogously to natural relations, in which the mother opens the way to the father for the child). The fatherhood of God therefore makes itself present in history through the creation, by Jesus Christ, of a maternal womb, the church; through her the baptized, once conformed to the Son, can recognize God as Father. Saint Cyprian affirms this so powerfully that the phrase might scandalize some who are little used to the integrality of the logic of the incarnation: "No one can have God as Father who does not have the Church as mother." This means, too, that the church is mother only insofar as she continually refers to the Father. Her being the body of Christ the Head and bride of Christ the Bridegroom prevents her from seeing herself as autonomous with respect to the beginning and origin: the Father.

The implications of these reflections on the nuptial mystery — in the Trinity, in Jesus Christ, and in the church — for the mission of fathers and mothers should at this point be clear, as well as how all this affects every father and mother in his or her daily experience. Throughout our reflections various elements of human experience have emerged which ultimately, without Christian revelation, would remain enigmatic. I refer to the consideration of fatherhood as origin and as constitutive of the unique freedom of the child, as well as to the essential nature of childhood as a condition for the experience of fatherhood and motherhood (in the dual unity of man and woman). Only in the light of the Christian faith, and above all in the mysteries of redemptive incarnation and the Trinity, do these elements become completely intelligible.[38]

This same light can guide us toward a last important reflection on human freedom as experienced within the familial relationship.

13.3.3. Divine Fatherhood, Human Fatherhood, and Freedom

We have seen how every parent finds himself constantly face-to-face with his child's freedom. This is surely the most dramatic experience of a parent's life. This dramatic nature is not due only to the presence of the freedom of the other as other, which occurs in any human relationship and particularly between man and woman (and thus husband and wife). In every relationship *not* between parent and child, the other is more easily recognized as other, because one's own "I" is not at the origin of the other's "I." This is true of husband and wife, brother and sister, friend and friend, neighbor and neighbor, stranger and stranger, and enemy and enemy. In none of these cases does the relationship of reciprocity carry the weight it does in the relationship between parent and child. We are called to experience the vertiginous freedom of the other in every relationship, but only between parent and child does the tie unite to the point of giving me the perception that if I lose the other (my child), I lose myself, too. Even if parents were to consider themselves merely the instruments of procreation, the child's freedom in some way has its origin in the father and mother. If my child makes a mistake and gets lost, something in me is wounded! In this case, as everyone can experience, the drama of fatherhood and motherhood is called to increase geometrically in intensity along the whole of existence. With it grows the temptation to not leave room for the child's freedom, to substitute for it, to not recognize the child as such

---

38. Cf. above, pp. 96-104.

— that is, as a free and unique person, and thus one who is *other* than myself. The temptation is that of reducing my child to myself, making him a sort of prolongation of my own person.

In the face of this drama the church, our mother, educates us in two ways. On the one hand, she exalts the relationship of parenthood, making Christians, by virtue of the new "family" inaugurated at the foot of the cross, responsible for one another to the point of total self-offering. In a certain sense the *other* is generated by me to the extent that I am a member of the church and participate in her motherhood. For this reason Saint Paul speaks of Christians as *one (eis)* in Christ Jesus. The church's life offers two thousand years of examples of this: saints, founders, and spiritual fathers reflect a dynamic that is in reality proper to the whole of ecclesial life. Who among us cannot name that person or persons who have been our fathers or mothers in the faith? Virginal fruitfulness, in the image of the fruitfulness of Jesus Christ, gives rise to a fatherhood and motherhood not determined by flesh and blood, but by the objective relationship established by *being one* in Jesus Christ. This fatherhood and motherhood affirms the freedom of the other, living a *possession in detachment* with respect to him which allows the other to really be other. It exalts the "I," generating a love that liberates, not a love that enslaves.

On the other hand, the life of the church educates men and women to fatherhood and motherhood precisely because, within her womb, it is possible to live the experience of a redeemed freedom, and thus a freedom which ultimately is no longer determined by the possibility of sin. We ask ourselves: Why did God the Father create man so radically free? Because he was not afraid — if it is permitted to speak in such terms — of the eventuality of sin, of human freedom going astray. Because the Father creates us in Jesus Christ, the incarnate Son who died and is risen. Ultimately God creates us in the sacrificial mystery of the Lamb who was slain, through whom even the eventuality of sin is already included in his gratuitous and merciful design. God creates us in mercy; created freedom is a redeemed freedom in the sense that, in the eventuality of sin, forgiveness is already offered to it "in advance," as the ever renewed possibility of returning to the Father's house (though sin does not, for all that, lose the terrible character of an offense against God and a mortal wound). Every Christian experiences this mercy in the church, and particularly in the sacrament of reconciliation. Here the believer is considered not in function of his sin, but in the light of the redemption worked by Jesus Christ. Only thus is man truly free! Only the primacy of mercy allows us to contemplate our freedom with serenity, to see it as a positive fact and not as a threat or condemnation. Mercy allows freedom to retain its dramatic nature

— because nothing can "decide in advance" its final outcome, and man can always, mysteriously, refuse the salvation offered to him — and yet it keeps this freedom from falling headlong into tragedy, because redemption has been offered to it in advance.

All of this has a profound meaning for Christian parents: through their personal experience of forgiveness, parents learn to look at their children the way the church looks at them, to love them as God loves them. Christian parents can find the way to deepen their own fatherhood and motherhood if they authentically live as children — of the church and of the Father. These two things are, as we have seen, inseparable.

It would be extremely interesting to investigate whether, as it seems to me, a historical link exists between the loss of the experience of the church's motherhood and the eclipse of the sense of God's fatherhood. It was, in fact, only after the Protestant Reformation, which denied ecclesial maternity and thus the church's objective nature of sacramental mediation, that deism and later atheism found their way into the European consciousness. If this hypothesis can be proven, an important consequence follows for the church's mission at the dawn of the third Christian millennium: people will be able to recognize God's fatherhood in the measure in which they encounter, in the concrete circumstances of their lives, a church who is truly a mother.

But without Christian families, the place of a fruitful exchange between parents and children marked by the new relationships in Christ, how is the distracted man of today to encounter this ecclesial maternity, which admits of no substitute? Without this maternity, who will be able to attain, like the prodigal son, that deep penitence which requires an *unconditional surrender*? And yet only thus can one experience the sweet return to the Father's house.

CHAPTER 14

Christ, Bridegroom of the Church

14.1. Conjugal Spirituality Based on the Logic of the Incarnation

14.1.1. A Specific Vocation to Holiness

At the close of the 1940s, conjugal spirituality became a predominant and critically important theme in the Christian community. This was due in particular to certain people who were able to grasp the profound meaning of the Christian life and organically reflect upon it. We certainly do not lack studies that relate the rediscovery of this theme to both the teachings of the magisterium[1] and the development of the theology of the laity.[2] We have already expressed our opinion on this evolution elsewhere,[3] so without discussing it at length here, we simply point out that even from the time of the Council's preparatory phase, it is clear that an appreciation of the role of the laity in the church was gradually developing. The lay faithful were no longer viewed as *clients* of the church; rather, they were recognized as having an authentic ecclesial vocation and mission.[4] The call to holiness was organically

---

1. From the abundant literature on this subject, see D. Tettamanzi, *I due saranno una carne sola* (Turin, 1986); Pontifical Council for the Family, *La sacramentalità del matrimonio: La spiritualità coniugale e familiare* (Turin, 1989). These two books contain the relevant bibliographical references.

2. Cf. G. Colombo, *La "teologia del laicato": bilancio di una vicenda storica,* in *I laici nella Chiesa* (Turin, 1986).

3. Cf. above, pp. 193-212. See also A. Scola, *Questioni di antropologia teologica* (Rome, 1997), 69-81.

4. Cf. M. Vergottini, "La teologia e i 'laici': Una ipotesi interpretativa e la sua recezione nella letteratura," *Teologia* 2 (1993): 166-86; and "La missione di Cristo e del cristiano,"

applied for the first time to the conjugal relationship as it exists in the sacrament of marriage and the fullness of family life.[5] That call to holiness, as Augustine teaches, is based on the church's objective sanctity (given), but dramatically calls into play freedom's assent (subjective sanctity), through ascesis and ethical action.

It is very important that this deeply felt need for renewal did *not* begin first with a reelaboration of the theology of marriage and family — a task that has yet to be accomplished in a systematic way.[6] Rather, it began with Christian spouses themselves, with their urgent need to honestly face the circumstances and relationships that constitute their marital life.

There is no need to review the developmental stages of the various forms of conjugal spirituality at this time.[7] Rather, my focus in this first part of our reflection is to develop a precise understanding of the meaning of the term "spirituality."[8]

14.1.2. *Spirituality: An Ambiguous Notion*

Today's culture challenges Christianity to reclaim its own fundamental notions and to reappropriate their original meaning, for the broader culture has often arrogated those notions to itself and reproposed them in a context totally alien to their native soil. Even the category of spirituality was not spared such a fate, as we shall see.

Today we are the protagonists of a singular event. While many had anticipated a progressive secularization (or — in Bonhoeffer's terms — a worldliness) — that is, a redrafting of the Christian discourse in purely secular terms — we find ourselves face-to-face with nothing less than an explosion of the sacred. A sort of "savage sacred" is being imposed upon our whole society and culture, in both the Northern and Southern Hemispheres. (This is perhaps one of the few aspects of life in which there are no great differences between North and South. Consider, for example, the phenomenon of sects,

---

Communio 111 (1990), with contributions from H. U. von Balthasar, L. Gerosa, P. Gheddo, C. B. Massari, J. Servais, B. Testa, M. Waldstein.

5. For a fundamental reference on this point, see *Lumen Gentium,* chap. 5.

6. I sought to identify theological works that presuppose marriage and family as a dimension and not simply as themes to be developed: see pp. 337-56.

7. For an extensive bibliography on this subject, see C. Rocchetta, *Il sacramento della coppia* (Bologna: Dehoniane, 1996), 302-6.

8. Cf. the interventions of P. Coda, E. Guerriero, J. Ries, and A. Sicari in "La spiritualità del cristiano," *Communio* 135 (1994).

which are springing up not only in New York but also in Rio de Janeiro and Douala.)[9] This new religiosity is basically naturalistic in character; that is, it actually advocates a return to a pre-Christian or, perhaps better, neo-pagan vision of the sacred. In the final analysis, according to this conception, the cosmos itself is equated with the divine. Hence, this new religiosity tends to become a generic *pantheist spiritualism*. As a result, it is becoming a common conviction, not only of the mass media but also of the average citizen, that any form of religion is as valid as the next. Nevertheless, such phenomena do seem to reveal a genuine religious sense, for they express ultimate questions about the origin and destiny of man and the cosmos. They carry within themselves certain ethical and ascetical appeals and respond to questions about the meaning of life.

Spirituality lies at the heart of this "savage sacred." This is true despite the fact that today's consumeristic society tends to exalt the body and, in a kind of delirium of immortality, make it an object of excessive *care*, investing it with an abundance of material and spiritual resources. The *sacred* appears to coincide with a yearning for the spiritual, understood here as a sort of religion of the body. On the other hand, throughout the West a disincarnate spirituality, rooted in a Cartesian dualism between spirit and body, is ever more widely diffused. The body is understood as *paries animi*, a prison that prevents the soul from fully being itself.

Such a perspective challenges the very essence of Christianity.

What does the word "spirituality" really denote? As the church never tires of repeating,[10] it means *living according to the Spirit*. But life according to the Spirit has very little to do with the generic longing for spiritualistic religiosity! On the contrary, in the Christian experience it is a gift from above that summons man's freedom in objective and binding ways to assent in faith, hope, and charity. The Spirit is the Spirit of Jesus Christ who died and rose from the dead. He is the Holy Spirit, the third person of the Most Holy Trinity. The Spirit *sent* to us is intimately united with and shares the mission of the Son of God, who became man *propter nos homines et propter nostram salutem*. To understand this life in the Spirit — and thus Christian spirituality — it is absolutely necessary to examine how the Spirit of Jesus Christ is communicated to us.

---

9. Cf. Scola, *Questioni di antropologia*, 175-84.
10. Cf. *CCC* 735-36.

14.1.3. *The Method of the Incarnation*

In extreme synthesis, number 515 of the *Catechism of the Catholic Church* reaffirms that:

> The Gospels were written by men who were among the first to have the faith and wanted to share it with others. Having known in faith who Jesus is, they could see and make others see the traces of his mystery in all his earthly life. From the swaddling clothes of his birth to the vinegar of his Passion and the shroud of his Resurrection, everything in Jesus' life was a sign of his mystery. His deeds, miracles and words all revealed that "in him the whole fullness of deity dwells bodily." His humanity appeared as "sacrament," that is, the sign and instrument, of his divinity and of the salvation he brings: what was visible in his earthly life leads to the invisible mystery of his divine sonship and redemptive mission.

Here the *Catechism* clearly outlines how the Spirit of Christ is given to men: the method implied by the *logic of the incarnation*.[11] In it Jesus Christ appears as the way (from the Greek *metà-hodos:* "the road by which"). And Jesus, through the Spirit, becomes the way for us, in an analogous manner as he did for the apostles. Through his humanity they were led to discover his divinity.

In this regard, the following passage of the Letter to the Colossians is very significant: "For in him the whole fullness of deity dwells bodily" (Col. 2:9). This *bodiliness* refers to Jesus' physical humanity in the days of the apostles, and his eucharistic humanity in our day.[12] The logic of the incarnation coincides with the logic of the sacrament. Holy Thursday, in anticipating the death and resurrection of Jesus Christ, reveals the way we can encounter Christ in our time, and live a life according to the Spirit (spirituality) until the perfect fulfillment of our humanity (sanctity).

How does Christ really become present to me in the here and now? In the *sign*, the *sacrament*. In general we believe we clearly understand the significance of this affirmation when speaking of the Eucharist, that is, the sacrament in the strict sense of the term, understood as partaking of his body and blood, the actual sign of his passion, death, and resurrection, his total self-offering (sacrifice). Indeed, through our service of others we dispose our-

---

11. Cf. *Fides et Ratio* 94: "Human language thus embodies the language of God, who communicates his own truth with that wonderful 'condescension' which mirrors the logic of the Incarnation."

12. On this subject see A. Scola, "Eucaristia, fonte di comunione," *La Rivista* 2 (1994): 35-49.

selves to be conformed to Christ, who dwells among us as he who serves (in the washing of the feet). Here we become less certain of Christ's sacramental presence, and we work very hard to accept the decisive fact that Jesus, through the gift of the Holy Spirit, provokes our freedom to assent through the concrete circumstances, situations, and people we encounter in our daily existence. And among these everyday encounters are, *in primis,* those that give shape to the vocation of marriage and family. In the logic of the incarnation, the sacrament of matrimony, conjugal life and the reality of the family are the privileged factors that help us understand life as a vocation.

The logic of the incarnation allows us to experience Jesus Christ as an event and not as an abstract idea intended to satisfy a generic spiritual need. In other words, Jesus, in the mystery of his ascension into heaven, does not become disincarnate, but on the contrary, is revealed as the ultimate and constitutive end of reality. Thus, in the sign, everyone will always be able, by the grace of the Spirit and their own free response, to contemplate his face.[13]

This vision of things gives rise to a consequence primarily anthropological in nature. Spirit and body — the first polarity that presents the insuppressible unity of the "I," *corpore et anima unus* (*synholon:* composite, whole), both in itself and in its action — relate to each other according to the sacramental logic exhibited in the incarnation. Through this logic the body is the sign through which the Spirit can be perceived. Thus a proper understanding of life according to the Spirit (authentic spirituality) clearly requires this sacramental logic. For according to such logic, the "I" can never be considered in dualistic terms. There can never be a separation or opposition between spirit and body, whether direct or indirect.

This adequate anthropology finds one of its certain and original points of reference in John Paul II's *Theology of the Body,* a point taken up again in *Mulieris Dignitatem* (and was earlier applied as the criterion for ethical evaluation in *Donum Vitae*). Its decisive affirmation is precisely that *the body is the sacrament of the entire person.*

In truth, the only possible response to the relativism that dominates the fields of ontology and ethics — and thus religion and asceticism — is precisely an anthropological vision in which the sacramental logic enters into play as a principle of man's self-comprehension, inevitably understood from within his own existence.[14]

13. Cf. Scola, *Questioni di antropologia,* 51-52.
14. Cf. H. U. von Balthasar, *Theo-Drama II: Dramatis Personae: Man in God,* trans. Graham Harrison (San Francisco: Ignatius, 1990), 335.

14.2. The Relationship between Christ and the Church: Archetype of Conjugal Spirituality

14.2.1. Christ-Church, Archetype of Man-Woman

In order to identify the fundamental features of such anthropology, it will suffice to refer back to what was said in the first part of the present work on the meaning of the relationship between man and woman, which is fully revealed in the archetypal relationship between Christ and the church.[15]

In this sense Saint Paul's words in Ephesians 5:21-33 remain unparalleled. John Paul II comments upon them as follows:

The Church professes that marriage, as the sacrament of the covenant between husband and wife, is a great mystery, because it expresses the spousal love of Christ for his Church. . . . The confirmation and fulfilment of the spousal relationship between God and his people are realized in Christ, in the new covenant. Christ assures us that the bridegroom is with us (cf. Mt. 9:15). He is with all of us; he is with the Church. The Church becomes a bride, the bride of Christ. This bride, of whom the Letter to the Ephesians speaks, is present in each of the baptized and is like one who presents herself before her bridegroom. . . . St. Paul, after having said, "Husbands, love your wives" (Eph. 5:25), emphatically adds: "Even so husbands should love their wives as their own bodies. He who loves his wife loves himself. For no man ever hates his own flesh, but nourishes and cherishes it, as Christ does the Church, because we are members of his body" (Eph. 5:28-30). And he encourages spouses with the words: "Be subject to one another out of reverence for Christ" (Eph. 5:21). This is unquestionably a new presentation of the eternal truth about marriage and the family in the light of the new covenant. Christ has revealed this truth in the Gospel by his presence at Cana in Galilee, by the sacrifice of the cross and the sacraments of his Church. Husbands and wives thus discover in Christ the point of reference for their spousal love. In speaking of Christ as the bridegroom of the Church, St. Paul uses the analogy of spousal love, referring back to the Book of Genesis: "A man leaves his father and his mother and cleaves to his wife, and they become one flesh" (Gn. 2:24). This is the great mystery of that eternal love already present in creation, revealed in Christ and entrusted to the Church. "This mystery is a profound one," the apostle repeats, "and I am saying that it refers to Christ and the Church" (Eph. 5:32). The Church cannot therefore

---

15. Here we take up again in detail what was previously developed in pp. 3-52. This is further developed in John Paul II, *Letter to Families* 6, 19.

be understood as the mystical body of Christ, as the sign of man's covenant with God in Christ or as the universal sacrament of salvation unless we keep in mind the great mystery involved in the creation of man as male and female and the vocation of both to conjugal love, to fatherhood and to motherhood. The great mystery, which is the Church and humanity in Christ, does not exist apart from the great mystery expressed in the "one flesh" (cf. Gn. 2:24; Eph. 5:31-32), that is, in the reality of marriage and the family.[16]

If therefore the form of human spousal love is precisely Jesus Christ's love for his bride, then the tension contained within such love is ordered to the fulfillment of Christ's work of salvation.[17]

Creation itself is only the beginning of the actualization of the covenant, which finds its fulfillment in Christ. Thus there is no division between an understanding *in naturalibus* of marriage and the understanding derived from revelation. Everything concerning natural marriage finds its full light only in the sacrament which is the actual participation in the spousal relationship between Christ and the church. It is in this Christ-church union that the new and eternal covenant is consummated and thus the preestablished plan of the Father is fulfilled.

Therefore, it can be seen that the sacramentality of marriage contains within it the ultimate meaning of the relationship between man and woman.[18] To say that marriage is a sacrament is to say that it is an efficacious sign of the holy mystery, that is, of the Father's plan. And as such, it renders possible the highest exaltation of every element of conjugal life.

In fact, to affirm the sacramentality of the love between man and woman is to affirm that the mode of Christ's union with the church passes through the mode of union between the Christian husband and wife.

The union between man and woman, and therefore marriage and family, are the efficacious sign of the mystery of unity that exists between Christ and the church. Marriage and family is the most common, universal, and elementary expression of Christ's union with the church. As such, it bears within itself the profound significance that the church has for the world: the permanent presence of Christ, the possibility given to each and every one of us, even after two thousand years, to encounter him. The church is a sacrament because it makes the encounter with God himself, in Jesus Christ, possible for man.[19]

---

16. Cf. John Paul II, *Letter to Families* 19.

17. For a more in-depth treatment see C. Giuliodori, *Intelligenza teologica del maschile e femminile* (Rome, 1991), 163-90.

18. Cf. G. Biffi, *Matrimonio e famiglia: Note pastorale* (Bologna, 1990), n. 9.

19. Cf. *Lumen Gentium* 1 and *Gaudium et Spes* 45.

14.2.2. A Singular Self-Realization of the Church

Thus the sacrament of marriage, realizing the possibility of a profound union in Christ between the two spouses, becomes a locus of the church for everyone.[20]

In falling in love and receiving the sacrament of marriage, man and woman choose to root themselves so deeply in Christ that their love can properly be called a self-realization of the church. The relationship which exists between Christ and the church is actualized in a mysterious but real way in the unique modality of the communion of persons that constitutes the man-woman relationship.

We now turn to the theme of the family as a "domestic" church which we have previously touched upon. To speak of the family as a "miniature church" does not at all suggest that the reality of family life and of the couple can in its interior exhaust an adequate ecclesial horizon. Rather, in order in the end to be faithful to its vocation, the family must learn to live the whole horizon of the life of the Christian community, making its own the breath of the church as such.

At this point a vast field opens up before us which we cannot possibly exhaust at this time. In it, the family undoubtedly presents itself as the subject of a mission in which the church, as Christ's continuing presence on earth, is made sensibly present.

Above all, this is concretely actualized in fruitfulness, the welcoming and educating of children.[21] Parents, conformed to Christ, as living members of the church, participate in the church's own divine sonship *(sons in the Son)* and are therefore existentially enabled to be fathers and mothers.

These children will not simply be one of their parents' many *choices.* Viewing a child as an object of one's choice (and therefore inexorably reducing him to a thing) — as we have alluded to elsewhere[22] — is a very widespread notion in today's society. But if the child is in fact a person, and the parents have the task of collaborating in the development of his identity and freedom, it is necessary above all that he be welcomed, not chosen.

Authentically understood, the birth of a child always has the character of an event and ultimately of a surprise. It can never be the mere result of planning. The debate concerning the possibility or legality of human cloning is perhaps a tragic example of how one can undermine at its very roots the absolute gratuitousness of the natural experience of paternity and maternity, and replace it with the process of designing a preprogrammed product. One

20. Cf. *CCC* 1601-66.
21. Cf. *Gaudium et Spes* 50-51.
22. Cf. above, pp. 169-70.

can hardly imagine the psychological devastation which would have to occur in a human relationship to provoke such an experience![23]

It is not irrelevant to the particular cultural climate in which we are living to clarify, even if only briefly, the great and inalienable duty of the family to be the primary educator of its children.[24] A family is seen as an educating subject, organically connected to the entire people of God, and is called to defend its children's freedom of education.[25]

As we saw at the onset of this discussion, the profound crisis of society today is based both remotely and proximately upon the failure to present a comprehensive vision of the full meaning of life. Thus the specific task of every family today, inasmuch as it belongs to the church, is to be a place where one encounters for the first time the whole of reality. The family is a place in which the person may be welcomed and educated in true freedom. This freedom does not remain suspended over an empty abyss, but becomes capable of ties because in it man recognizes the desire for which every heart is made and cleaves to the infinite of which everything is a sign.

14.2.3. Indissolubility: A Condition of the Truth

In light of what we just said, we can make explicit mention of the characteristic which is, in a certain sense, foundational for the sacramental possibility of the man-woman relationship: its indissolubility.

23. "Cloning is one of the most aberrant forms of manipulating and objectifying human life. The scientist who wants to carry out such a project could not but be depicted as a *homo faber* whose only aim would be the advancement of research and knowledge without considering how he would use the results or thinking about the destiny of the man whom he created. This scientist would not be acting with a view towards healing the subject upon whom he was working. The act of cloning is certainly not a therapeutic one; one does not clone a human being in order to heal him. Rather, cloning would demonstrate the omnipotence of technology over man: Cloning would show that technology is able to artificially produce a human being (that is, beginning from an existing organism). . . . Not only is the unitive act of the heterosexual couple separated from procreation, but procreation is completely removed from the necessity of sexual complementarity. In other words, one produces a life in a laboratory without even using the masculine and feminine germinal cells, because the genetic property of the life that is reproduced is already integrally contained in the only somatic cell grafted in the oöcyte from which the nucleus was taken. This inevitably behaves as a cancellation of the parental and familial relations: the copy 'produced' in the laboratory by cloning would not be filially related to any genetically identical adult human organism." L. Palazzini, "L'uomo e le frontiere della genetica: la questione della clonazione," *La famiglia* 31, no. 183 (1997): 10-11.

24. Cf. A. Scola, *E tutti saranno ammaestrati da Dio* (Grosseto, 1993).

25. Cf. John Paul II, *Letter to Families* 16.

It is only in this context that marriage can properly and fully be a vocation. Christian marriage is indissoluble because it is a participation in Christ's total and irrevocable gift of self to the church. And the church has in her prototype, Mary, the perfect subject of reception of this love and revelation. The unconditional and immaculate *yes* of the Virgin guarantees the bride's reciprocal love for Christ, her Bridegroom.

Moreover, the church affirms the indissolubility of marriage because the mission entrusted to the spouses cannot but last their whole lives. Outside of the horizon of indissolubility, affection tends toward the infracosmic.

Today, right under our very eyes, the mass media from its various pulpits easily and "openly mocks the commitment of the spouses to fidelity."[26] Yet, in spite of this continual "preaching," men and women, since the time of their adolescence, have continued to declare their deep and everlasting love for each other.

In fact, it is impossible for two young people to reach the point of sincerely saying "I love you" without adding, implicitly or explicitly, "forever." It is a contradiction of terms to set, a priori, any temporal limit to love, because the very nature of love implies its totality. Characteristic of the experience of those who love is the desire to hand themselves entirely over, abandoning that false zone of indifference which would allow them to change their minds. In freedom the lover desires to commit his whole future to the beloved.

Balthasar affirms that every authentic love, in this sense, possesses the interior form of the *vow*, the decision to offer oneself, once and for all, to the beloved.[27]

If this has been the case since the dawn of this common and sincerely human experience of love, how much more, and explicitly so, must the *forever* be implied in the mutual love of the spouses, where the love between a man and woman reaches maturity in the choice to marry!

In terms of indissolubility, Christ's love for the church also becomes the criterion with which to judge any difficulties and contradictions, even the most dramatic and revolting ones that may occur throughout the course of the marriage. On an existential plane, indissolubility becomes a requisite of the truth and a dynamic of sanctity. It guarantees that each spouse is capable of loving the other for his own sake, for his destiny. In this way indissolubility is the spring from which flows a love that frees, not binds.[28]

26. John Paul II, *Familiaris Consortio* 20.

27. Cf. H. U. von Balthasar, *The Christian State of Life*, trans. Sr. Mary Frances McCarthy (San Francisco: Ignatius, 1983), 58-65.

28. Cf. John Paul II, *The Theology of the Body: Human Love in the Divine Plan* (Boston: Daughters of St. Paul, 1997), 48-52.

The truth about the love between man and woman requires them to be aware, at least at the level of a deep intention, that they themselves are not the origin of this highly human and personal affection tied to all the particular characteristics and contingencies which bring them together. In the sacrament of matrimony the spouses, once and for all, ground their affection in this foundation which lies beyond them. Thus the affection they have for each other is preserved from danger and precariousness and reestablished in the unifying flow of God the Father's unique initiative, which is full of love for man: Jesus Christ, the one who died and is risen.

Only the vocation to marriage transforms the love between man and woman, opening it up to its full potential. Therefore, indissolubility alone guarantees the channel within which the truth of conjugal love can find expression.

However, none of this is the result of a moralistic effort on the part of the spouses. Rather, such fascinating fullness is only possible to the extent that the spouses live out their relationship on a daily basis as a sacrament, a concrete circumstance of their existing as church. This is only possible if one is aware, from the outset, that this spousal affection is a gift whose essential feature is that the other may be true, that is, personally and seriously committed to the realization of his destiny.

At this point it is clear how indispensable it is for the growth of conjugal love to live an intense sacramental life, to continually be reminded of one's baptism, of one's objective belonging to Christ, and to always live a greater participation in the Eucharist, which is the center of the community of the faithful's life. The relationship between the Bridegroom and the bride, between Christ and the church becomes visible and can be verified under the veil of the sacrament of the Eucharist (the intrinsic culmination of baptism) in which the sacrificed Lamb celebrates the nuptials as the Bridegroom.

In such nuptials, which the church celebrates every day, it is Jesus who initiates the *communio* in his eucharistic offering: his dying and rising for our sake. And we, in eating his body, are *taken apart* and conformed to his likeness. The eucharistic command, *"Do this in memory of me"* (1 Cor. 11:24), encompasses the full definition of the raison d'être of the church and her mission. "Do this, allow yourselves to be eucharistically taken by me, because through the gift of the Holy Spirit, I generate the communion between you and the Father. In doing this, that is, in living this communion, you make Me present."[29] In following this command, the man and woman united in marriage rediscover the original form and sustenance of their spousal love.

29. On this point see Scola, "Eucaristia, fonte di comunione," 35-49.

This central source, from which the spouses draw the mystery of their utmost identity, extends to the great possibility for continual renewal of their mutual self-gift, by means of the *experience of forgiveness*.[30] The sacrament of reconciliation, which originates in the paschal mystery, likewise determines the interior rhythm of spousal love.

In the certainty of unfailing forgiveness, which flows from the cross of Christ, the relationship between the spouses is no longer conditioned by their limitations, resistances to each other, and sins. On the contrary, these factors themselves become part of the journey, a pedagogy of mutual surrender. The limitations of each spouse cease to be counter to love. Here every human measure gives way in order to make space for mercy as the ultimate form of the love relationship which is shaped by Christ's redeeming grace.

Nowhere else perhaps, as in the ability of the husband and wife to forgive each other, does the absolute novelty of Christianity emerge. This introduces a new and ever surprising factor to the man-woman relationship: the certainty that belonging to him who died and is risen is the ultimate truth of one's life, beyond every betrayal or hostility.

14.2.4. *Virginity as the Summit of Nuptiality*

The chosen title of this section is neither contradictory nor equivocal: it is paradoxical because Christianity itself is paradoxical. The theme of gratuitous forgiveness which the spouses are called to practice brings us to the final point in our reflection. It is here where forgiveness becomes the interior norm of the relationship, the ultimate *virtue*, because with it Christian nuptiality may be lived out in all its luminous newness.

The affection between man and woman is called to assume a new form, an imitation, above all, of the way Christ himself related to every human being. There will never be true self-giving in the union of two people, nor oblative love, as long as the other person is not understood from the outset within the horizon of his person, but rather only as an instrument of one's egoistical satisfaction.

The other is not loved unless he is loved in relation to his destiny. The *thou* is not the extension of the *I*. Rather, the *thou* is the mystery of the other who demands to be affirmed in his destiny.

True love will not exist between man and woman, nor authentic communion between husband and wife, unless a certain detachment is experienced,

---

30. Cf. J. Laffitte, *Le pardon transfiguré* (Paris, 1995).

even from within this intimate relationship which causes the two to become *one flesh*. If I am incapable of gazing upon the one I say I love so as to see her as she really is, in her metaphysical reality which may not correspond to what I think, want, or make her out to be, then there will never be true love. It is as if, within the physical reality of this affection, the presence of Another were called for to allow that detachment which teaches true love. It goes back to the sacramental logic of the incarnation in which the sign refers to an *Other* who is also a *Beyond*.

The mode of the relationship described can properly be called Christian virginity. It consists in the capacity, which grace confers upon man's freedom, *truly to possess reality in detachment*, by imitating the way Christ lived every relationship and how he now possesses the destiny of every man.[31]

Baptism, inasmuch as it is the sacrament of incorporation into Christ, offers this new manner of possession to all Christians. Therefore virginity can be understood neither as only a specific vocation within the church,[32] nor primarily as a renunciation of something. It is rather the manner of love characteristic of Jesus Christ, which all Christians, even spouses, are therefore called to live.[33] The virginal charism, as a specific vocation for some in the church, literally bears witness to this.

Living according to the virginal charism, and thus testifying in one's concrete existence that to live in the risen Christ is not only possible but is already actualized as a guarantee and bears much fruit even in this life, is the greatest gift virginity has to offer the world.

Christian virginity is definitively founded upon the paschal mystery. The cross gives birth to a new fruitfulness,[34] which is by no means asexual, but reveals the meaning of every true human fruitfulness.[35]

The Greek philosophers and some of the fathers of the church believed that every birth is linked to the necessity of replacing the parents who are des-

31. Cf. L. Giussani, *Il tempo e il tempio* (Milan, 1995), 11-35.

32. Cf. John Paul II, *Theology of the Body,* 263-303.

33. Cf. A. Sicari, "Diversità e complementarità degli stati di vita nella Chiesa," *Communio* 135 (1994): 8-24.

34. Cf. John 19:26-27, commented on above, pp. 106-9.

35. A. Scola, *Hans Urs von Balthasar: A Theological Style* (Grand Rapids: Eerdmans, 1995), 98: "The man-woman polarity is linked to the mystery of the Christ-Church relationship (Eph. 5), where nuptial love not only reaches its fullest form, but where at the same time its connection with death through the closed circle of generations for the sake of the species is broken. This is so not only because death is conquered in Christ, but also and more precisely because Christ inaugurates a new form of fruitfulness which is not limited to human procreation. This is a fecundity for the kingdom, which becomes the eschatological sign of the marriage between Christ and the Church; it is a virginal fecundity or nuptiality which is not at all asexual."

tined to die. This circle of generation and death is broken once and for all in the new fruitfulness which flows from the cross of Christ.

In the mystery of redemption death is overcome once and for all, and human flesh acquires an eternal destiny, based on the promise of the final resurrection of the transfigured body. It is this same mystery that frees the relationship between man and woman in the authentic spousal surrender.

In this sense the witness of those called to a specific virginal consecration cannot but enhance conjugal spirituality.[36] In fact, a virginal vocation lived with joy will be a point of constant reference for Christian couples and families. It is a strong reminder of the way in which those called to live in Christ are meant to relate to each other.

Thus the marvelous circumincession between the states of life, of which *Christifideles Laici* spoke with singular insight,[37] appears in all of its sanctifying fruitfulness. The nature of the love which exists in both states of life (virginity and marriage) is *spousal;*[38] the conjugal vocation has a paradigmatic character. At the same time the tension in virginity understood as possession in detachment lived in Jesus Christ, preserves, in turn, that *precedence (anteponendum)* affirmed by the Council of Trent.[39]

36. The more the charism of the virginity is present and affirmed in Christianity, the more marriage will be called to its true nature and helped to be conformed to its ideal." Biffi, *Matrimonio e famiglia,* n. 12.

37. John Paul II, *Christifideles Laici:* "In Church communion the states of life, by being ordered one to the other, are thus bound together among themselves. They all share in a deeply basic meaning: that of being *the manner of living out the commonly shared Christian dignity and the universal call to holiness in the perfection of love.* They are *different yet complementary,* in the sense that each of them has a basic and unmistakable character which sets each apart, while at the same time each of them is seen in relation to the other and placed at each other's service. Thus the *lay* state of life has its distinctive features in its secular character. It fulfills an ecclesial service in bearing witness and in its own way recalling for priests, woman and men Religious, the significance of the earthly and temporal realities in the salvific plan of God. In turn, the *ministerial* priesthood represents, in different times and places, the permanent guarantee of the sacramental presence of Christ, the Redeemer. The Religious state bears witness to the eschatological character of the Church, that is, the straining toward the Kingdom of God that is prefigured and in some way anticipated and experienced even now through the vows of chastity, poverty and obedience."

38. John Paul II, *Theology of the Body,* 277-78.

39. Cf. Denzinger-Schönmetzer, *Enchiridion symbolorum,* 1810: "If anyone says that the married state excels the state of virginity or celibacy, and that it is better and happier to be united in matrimony than to remain in virginity or celibacy, let him be *anathema.*"

CHAPTER 15

The Holy Spirit and the Truth about Marriage and the Family

15.1. Adam and the New Adam

One of the most marvelous consequences of the incarnation, the purpose of which is revealed in the death and resurrection of Jesus Christ, lies in the fact that the individual human being *(Dasein)* — made up of a soul that is the form of the body, placed within the man-woman polarity, and immersed as an individual person in a communitarian reality (the family and civil society) — can become *the way* to understanding something of the deep mystery of God. God, in his turn, whether probed by reason or received through revealed grace according to that critical form of knowledge which is faith, sheds the definitive light on the human being.

Chapter 15 of the First Letter to the Corinthians, which is based on one of the most ancient and solid accounts of the resurrection of Jesus Christ (15:3-5),[1] makes an extraordinary comparison between the first and second Adams. In this text we are shown how the new bodily existence of the Risen One (of which the apostles receive a foretaste in the transfiguration) retains the distinguishing characteristics of the true body of him who was crucified for our sins. Christ's resurrection is the firstfruits of the transformation of the body that awaits us all, according to the dogma of the resurrection of the flesh. This comparison between the two Adams shows how, in the singular (unique and unrepeatable) figure of Jesus of Nazareth, the *admirabile commercium* takes place between the human and divine natures, without the possibility of con-

---

1. Cf. H. Schlier, *La Risurrezione di Gesù Cristo* (Brescia, 1994); G. Ghiberti, *Resurrezione di Gesù* (Brescia, 1982), 34-40.

fusion between the two. Unlike the Hegelian attempt to posit a synthesis which would eliminate *(aufheben)* the human and divine natures, welding them into a third reality superior to both, the Catholic faith vehemently asserts the christological *analogia entis* as the highest application of the principle of analogy. In Pryzwara's debate with Barth, taken up again in the ongoing dialogue between the Protestant theologian and Balthasar, Pryzwara has demonstrated that the *analogia entis* is not at all an exclusively logical-formal principle.[2] As we have mentioned above,[3] it points rather to a high road from which man attempts to turn his eyes to his Maker, thereby understanding himself better as a historically situated *being-here*. Now this analogy — which proceeds both from the bottom up (*ana*-logy) and from the top down (*kata*-logy) — is not only an analogy of being, according to all the degrees in which Being is manifested in individual beings and in their transcendent properties. Once the event of Christ has by grace irrupted into history, this analogy becomes, through the action of the Spirit of the Risen One, a necessary method for understanding something of the unfathomable abyss of the countenance of the Father: Jesus Christ is the *Way*. Precisely at this point, and through analogy, fundamental human experience finds the path that grants access to the Mystery, and the Mystery in its turn sheds a new light on concrete human existence.

From this point of view, Scheeben's intuition bears mentioning. At the end of *The Mysteries of Christianity*, he describes the analogy at work in the fruitful exchange between faith and reason, through the twofold movement of *fides quaerens intellectum* and *intellectus quaerens fidem*, in terms of a wedding, or of nuptiality.[4] Faith and reason are thus wedded in a way analogous to the nuptial (spousal) relation between man and woman, to which every human being finds himself objectively referred from the moment of birth. In the tradition of all peoples, at least until now, birth in fact has its origin in the context of a family, however diverse its sociocultural configuration: the clan, the patriarchal family, the extended family, or the nuclear family.

---

2. Cf. H. U. von Balthasar, *The Theology of Karl Barth*, trans. Edward T. Oakes (San Francisco: Communio Books/Ignatius, 1992), 381-89.

3. Cf. above, pp. 235-37.

4. M. J. Scheeben, *The Mysteries of Christianity* (London: Herder, 1946), 783-85: "Because of this element of freedom, the relation [reason-faith] is conveyed far more profoundly, clearly, and adequately, and at the same time more nobly, if we describe it as the relation of a bride to her bridegroom. . . . Like the nuptials of nature with grace, the yoking of reason with faith in the theological sphere has its fairest and most sublime ideal in the espousals of the noblest of purely human beings, the Virgin of virgins, with the Holy Spirit, whereby she became the mother of Him who is personal Wisdom incarnate."

Nuptiality thus reveals itself to be an integral part of the analogy that rests ultimately on the logic of the incarnation, and — as we saw in the preceding chapter — it keeps spirituality, and especially conjugal spirituality, from falling into a spiritualistic equivocation.

15.2. The Spousal Nature of the Human Person

The logic of the incarnation allows the nuptiality which every man experiences to shed light, in analogy, on the mysteries of Christianity (marriage, the church, Mary, Jesus Christ, the Trinity).

Before all else, the sacrament of marriage becomes the sign rooted in human nature pointing to the eucharistic union of Christ the Bridegroom with the church-bride (cf. Eph. 5:21-33). How do we concretely explain this dynamism, which finds its supreme norm in the perfect nuptiality of Christ the Bridegroom with regard to the church his bride? This is made possible by the fact that the Holy Spirit, through the sacrament of marriage, makes the spouses participate in the nuptial relation of Christ the Bridegroom and the church-bride, helping them to integrate eros and agape. Here we already see the Spirit at work in the dimension of salvation history (the economy), that same Spirit who, immanent in the Trinity (theology), is at once the perfect expression of the bond (nexus) of love between the Father and the Son, and the fruit *(donum)* of that tie. We will return to this point. For now it is enough to observe that through the mission proper to the Holy Spirit, inseparably joined to that of the incarnate Son of God, the subjective love of man and woman is granted an objective dimension in the sacrament of marriage. The spouses are therefore called to live an experience of fidelity, in which freedom no longer has only subjective energies at its disposal. Rather, through existence in Christ, it is objectively called to an indissolubility that satisfies the demand intrinsic to every real love: that love be *forever.*

In this indissolubility, which is not afraid of mortification, Christian marriage encounters its true form as vocation. Through indissolubility, and by the power of the Holy Spirit, the spouses enter into the imitation of Christ, thereby revealing the common destiny of the married and virginal states of life: that *possession in detachment* that is the wise form through which the church has always educated her children in charity, the final end of every state of life.

The Holy Spirit — who, as the Spirit of the Risen One, can never be separated from Christ — shows in this way how the dynamism of fruitfulness is intrinsically part of the love of two persons. In the life of the Trinity, the Father and the Son love one another with an exchange of love that is the person of the Spirit (fruit). Analogously, in human love fruitfulness flows intrinsically from the difference between man and woman in their personal identity. For this reason the church has always taken care to show that the love between man and woman is directed toward marriage; this is the basis of the family, the place in which the love between man and woman develops its capacity for gift in the generation of the child. In Jesus the Bridegroom of the church-bride, the Holy Spirit leads the spouses into the fullness of love. This can take place because of the revelation of the trinitarian "face" of our Maker. With it we become fully conscious of what it means to say "God is love": "In this is love, not that we loved God but that he loved us and sent his Son to be the expiation for our sins" (1 John 4:10).

The Holy Spirit expounds the revelation of the Father in Jesus Christ, never advancing his own work but that of Christ; thus he provides proof of the insuperable goodness of the logic of the incarnation. In this logic, we can affirm with Tertullian, *"caro cardo salutis"* [the flesh is the hinge of salvation]. In a certain sense we can say that the affirmation of *Gaudium et Spes* which articulates the theme of the two Adams — "It is only in the mystery of the incarnate Word that the mystery of man takes on light"[5] — is fulfilled in a consideration of man as he concretely exists, in the dual unity of man and woman. Considered in the light of marriage understood as the foundation of the family, this anthropological datum fully explains what man is in himself and in his relation with the other. Marriage allows us to understand the meaning of the "I" and of the other, and the possibility of a relationship between the two. This relationship is a fruitful one of love, because it does not grasp the other as a lost half, but opens him to the generation of the child.

15.3. Postmodernity

We must once again add a few comments to the observations already made regarding the historical-cultural situation in which we are called to live the Christian proposal for marriage and the family. Notwithstanding an objective affirmation of the logic of the incarnation *(caro cardo salutis)*, we are in fact constantly tempted to see the depth of the mystery of nuptiality as abstract, both in its constitutive components (sexual difference, love, and fruitfulness) and in the various levels of its actuation (from the Trinity to conjugal love). At most we see it as a consoling escape from the drama of ordinary life, rather

---

5. *Gaudium et Spes* 22.

than as the possibility of living this drama to the point of its positive resolu-
tion in eschatology, letting ourselves be assimilated more and more, through
the power of the Spirit, to the Risen One. The Gospels testify to how Jesus,
with his body transfigured in the resurrection, reformulated human relationships on all levels, renewing them according to the law of virginal possession.
He encountered the Magdalene, the other women, and the disciples. In some
way he made them pass by way of the *law of detachment,* allowing fears and
doubts to arise in their minds and hearts before they could, by the grace of
faith, recognize him as the gift offered to them, the incorruptible anticipation
of their personal destiny of resurrection in the body. To think through the
logic of the incarnation and join, in analogy, the human experience of man
and woman to the nuptiality that exists between Christ and the church (the
admirabile commercium) is not an escape from reality!

How, then, do we face the situation of nuptiality in the cultural reality of
the Northern Hemisphere, which is already making itself felt in geo-cultural
universes so far away from us and yet already related to our experience? Two
absolutely challenging facts seem ultimately to destroy this vision of things,
rendering it abstract and powerless. The wealthy societies in which we are immersed present us with a radical break in the constitutive intertwining of
nuptiality. We are witnessing not only the separation of love from sexuality,
already a part of the common mentality, but in the measure in which cloning
can be pursued on a wide scale, the radical separation of sexuality from procreation. The three constitutive elements of the nuptial mystery which are, by
nature and grace, so intimately connected as to be objectively inseparable, are
now programmatically separated and disjoined. And much more: the mentality that reaches us every day through the mass media describes this project as
a progressive liberation from slavery to nature, in the name of culture and the
bodily, psychic, and spiritual well-being of the person, not to mention the
eugenicist and therapeutic well-being of the species. This twofold separation
— between love and sexuality, and sexuality and procreation — represents a
significant litmus test for modernity. The separation appears as the distinctive trait, so to speak, of the passage to postmodernity, to quote Deleuze's celebrated formula. Were we less intellectualistic and abstract in our way of
viewing the history of thought and culture, we would see in the practice of
contraception, introduced toward the end of the 1950s to separate sexuality
from love on a large scale, in the more recent possibility of separating sexuality from procreation in in vitro fertilization, and most recent of all, in cloning
the most important trait of postmodernity.

In what exactly does the difference between modernity and postmodernity consist? Notwithstanding its claim to construct itself without

God, who was reduced to a mere phantasm — either because God was seen to be the projection of man's neediness (Feuerbach) or because man pretended to be God (Hegel) — modernity did not reach the point of positing the premises for its radical self-destruction. Certainly, at the heart of the twentieth century (the "brief century"), the tragedy of Auschwitz and of the gulags demonstrated the barbarity of the programmatic extermination of races or masses. The Shoah in particular, which our Jewish brethren rightly claim to be unique, was the project for the systematic elimination of a race as such, because it aimed at eliminating all Jews born of Jewish grandparents. This experience was so tragic that, after Auschwitz, thought found itself entangled in a radical powerlessness, calling God himself into question. The grave affirmation of many contemporary Jewish thinkers and philosophers that it is impossible to speak of God after Auschwitz is well known. For those who, like Jews and Christians, hold that God acts in history, the theme of God's silence after Auschwitz has a theoretical force far superior to the Nietzschean declaration, "God is dead."[6]

If we consider, without defeatism and without constructing apocalyptic scenes, the possible effects of the separation of the three dimensions of the nuptial mystery, we must recognize that for the first time the techniques of genetic bioengineering have made the total self-elimination of the human species and of every species on earth concretely possible. For the first time man, in a way more subtle and more radical than what might have happened with the atomic bomb, possesses among his real possibilities eliminating the human race as such. From this point of view, if there is a gap between modernity and postmodernity, I see no other place where it might be situated, no other phenomenon with which to name it, than in this tremendous possibility of exposing the human race to the pure will to power.

---

6. We will not go into the meaning of the two formulae here. However, we must acknowledge, with Fackenheim, that they cannot be compared, because Nietzsche's "death of God" retains the taste of a metaphor whose level of truth would not go much beyond that of a slogan: cf. E. L. Fackenheim, *La presenza di Dio nella storia* (Brescia, 1977), 67, 72-73. For the theme of God's silence at Auschwitz, see the anthology compiled by M. Giuliani, *Auschwitz nel pensiero ebraico. Frammenti della teologia dell'Olocausto* (Brescia, 1998). This work presents the positions of leading contemporary Jewish thinkers on the subject of God after Auschwitz. Among the most important, we cite Fackenheim, R. Rubenstein, Maybaum, E. Wiesel, Berkovits, Jacobovits, Jonas, K. Shapiro.

15.4. For the Well-Being of Mankind

To conclude this first part, I would like to make two observations. At the distance of thirty years, we are able to evaluate the prophetic force of Paul VI's decision to promulgate the encyclical *Humanae Vitae,* with its vigorous affirmation of the intertwining of the three factors of nuptiality — love, sexuality, and procreation. This decision was absolutely countercultural and certainly brought suffering to the one who made it, but it was suggested by the Spirit who aids the successor of Peter. This is clear today not only because we can see that the natural methods of birth regulation, unlike the mechanical or chemical methods of contraception, respect the ecological well-being of man, of his health and body. Paul VI's intervention appears in all its momentous weight to those who are truly interested in the well-being of the human person, because it allowed a small remnant of the people of God, in the scandal of witness, to maintain the intertwining of the three inseparable dimensions of nuptiality. The "no" to such questions that arises spontaneously from the ecclesial body, even before it knows how to give all the convincing reasons for it, is really for the *well-being* of all mankind. In this case the "no" represented a defense for humanity, as well as a certain maturation, because it created a Weltanschauung capable of demonstrating the foolishness of having recourse to the technological imperative, which could lead to the destruction of life.

The magisterium of John Paul II (as can be well documented, from the famous catecheses on the body to *Familiaris Consortio* and *Mulieris Dignitatem,* and through the Congregation of the Faith, *Donum Vitae*) has deepened and developed the link between sexual difference, love, and fruitfulness, allowing the concept of nuptiality to flower in all its levels. From this point of view, the Spirit has accompanied the church's magisterium in shedding light upon spouses according to the spirituality of Christian incarnation, transforming them into actors on the stage of history.

From this arises a second observation. In the face of the tragic possibility of the self-destruction of the human race, how does one testify to the beauty of nuptiality, lived through a free and convinced choice within Christian families, in all of its threefold and inseparable intertwining? For this we must humbly recognize that the power of the Spirit of the Risen One is at work in the Christian family when, in the fruitful love of the spouses, there is present the logic of welcoming the other in his need. This welcome can be a perhaps unconscious expression of the human desire for plenitude. Christian families are called to be an open "home" in which, through the beauty of marriage, others can experience the goodness of human existence. In such families the *admirabile commercium* between the divine and human dimensions of nuptiality reveals itself to be the decisive resource for saving love from the ever more widely diffused risk of androgynism. This latter transforms the drama of homosexuality and transsexuality into a Promethean cultural project, insofar as it attributes to culture the impossible claim of producing nature, rather than letting culture be the powerful factor of positive interaction with nature.

But what is the factor at work in history that allows for this *admirabile commercium* between divine and human nuptiality? The Holy Spirit. We must now take a step that will allow us to see the nature of the relation that the Holy Spirit makes possible between marriage, the family, and the highest mysteries of Christianity.

15.5. The Spirit and Holiness

As we begin this second part of our reflection in terms that are concise and yet complete, we must have the patience to turn our necessarily inadequate gaze once again to the Holy Spirit, and to listen to what Christian doctrine teaches us about the third person of the Trinity. This will shed light on the affirmation at the heart of our discussion: the Holy Spirit is really the principle of the unity of family life, since he is the constitutive form of nuptiality in its threefold dimension of difference, love, and fruitfulness.

The most farseeing contemporary theology recognizes that in a consideration of the third person of the Trinity — independently of how this has been elaborated along the course of the history of theology in the East and West — we cannot fail to take a twofold aspect into consideration.[7] On the one hand, the Spirit is the quintessence of the love that circulates between the Father and the Son. On the other hand, the Spirit is the fruit of this deep love *(donum doni)*. The first dimension is *subjective* in that it considers the Spirit as the love with which the two hypostases (subjects), Father and Son, love one another in the perfect Good. The second dimension is *objective* because it shows the result, in a certain sense, of the love between the two. With regard to this, a twofold clarification is necessary. The first deals with method. To say that the *intellectus fidei* interprets the figure of the Spirit according to these two dimensions does not at all involve introducing some sort of separation

7. Cf. L. Bouyer, *Le Consolateur. L'Esprit Saint et vie de Grâce* (Paris, 1980); F. X. Durrwell, *L'Esprit Saint de Dieu* (Paris, 1983); J. Y. Lacoste, "La théologie et l'Esprit," *Nouvelle Revue Théologique* 109 (1987): 660-71; H. U. von Balthasar, *Theologik III: Der Geist der Wahrheit* (Einsiedeln: Johannes Verlag, 1987); M. Bordoni, *Cristologia nell'orizzonte dello Spirito* (Brescia, 1995); G. H. Müller, *Der Heilige Geist, Pneumatologie* (Graz, 1995).

into the Spirit himself. We are dealing only with a difficulty of our faith understanding, which must limit itself to stammering something about truths so real and at the same time so inaccessible.

Secondly — and this is a note on content — these objective and subjective dimensions of the Spirit are connected to the two dimensions that make up holiness within the church. What are they? The objective dimension of holiness, as Augustine calls it, coincides with those elements that make present in the church, here and now, the event of Christ dead and risen as a salvific event. These are the tradition, Scripture, and the minister, to which are linked the liturgical proclamation, the sacraments, canon law, and theology. The subjective dimension of the church's holiness indicates, on the other hand, those experiences of holiness that are more immediately connected to the freedom of the faithful: for example, prayer, forgiveness, the discernment of spirits, bearing witness in one's life, etc. This twofold and complementary dimension of ecclesial holiness, which maintains person and community in a dual unity within the church, is the fruit of the communication, on the level of the economic Trinity, of what is already lived on the level of the immanent Trinity, through the two dimensions of the Spirit. How does the Holy Spirit actuate this communication? The objective and subjective dimensions proper to the third person of the Trinity are communicated to the church through the objective and subjective dimensions of Christ's priesthood, which is expressed in the event of his death and resurrection.[8] Jesus Christ is the unique and unrepeatable priest because he is, at one and the same time, victim and priest. He is the one offered (subjective priesthood) and the one offering (objective priesthood). In him, the one who sacrifices and the one sacrificed, is found the indivisible unity of love and ministry. This priesthood[9] is mediated to us by the Spirit in the (objective and subjective) holiness of the church. The objective and subjective holiness of the church can also be described by referring to the Petrine dimension (objective holiness) and the Marian dimension (subjective holiness). The subjective element of total self-offering — the Marian element — must encounter and be verified by the Petrine element.

If we hold to this synthetic core, which allows us to join the Trinity, the event of Jesus Christ, the living dynamism of the church, and the relation of institutional and charismatic elements within the church, it becomes easier to understand in what sense the Spirit is the "expounder" of the love between the Son and the Father. He is the Spirit of truth (the whole truth) promised by

---

8. Cf. H. U. von Balthasar, *The Christian State of Life*, trans. Sr. Mary Frances McCarthy (San Francisco: Ignatius, 1983), 251ff.

9. Balthasar, *Christian State of Life*, 259ff.

Jesus to his own, which allowed them to bear witness to him fearlessly, notwithstanding the fact that for many of them this would imply martyrdom.

15.6. Divinization and Incorporation

We can take a further step and ask ourselves how, concretely, the Holy Spirit communicates himself to build up the holiness of the church in her children. We can then examine how he operates in the lives of spouses through the sacrament of matrimony. Taking up an ancient expression coined by Irenaeus, we can speak of the Son and the Spirit as the "two hands" with which the Father acts in history, making it salvation history. How do these hands work? He uses them, first of all, to communicate his design for man, for the community, and for peoples. In communicating himself through these two hands, the Father reveals the Mystery.

It is important to note that, from the beginning, we find in both the Old and New Covenants the idea that revelation is God's communication of himself. By entering into relation and by acting, God reveals something of his face. This is the *kabod Yahweh,* or *doxa Yahweh,* the glory of God who, while remaining profoundly other, holy, and inaccessible in his being, is communicated in the work par excellence of the death and resurrection of the Son. The Son, in his turn, gives us the Spirit. The unity of the missions of the Son and the Spirit allows us to glimpse the distinction between them, which in no way threatens the simultaneous action of the two hands.

How, then, does the action of the Spirit of the Risen One unfold as it continues in the "now" of history? In a general sense, as we have already seen, this occurs through the subjective and objective priesthood of Christ, which passes into the objective and subjective dimensions of the church. The latter is in turn echoed in the Marian and Petrine dimensions of the Christian community. To further clarify this point, it is useful to mention two categories that can describe the Spirit's way of acting in the "now" of his church, for the sake of the world. The first is dearer to the Eastern and Greek Fathers (though Augustine also uses it), and the second preferred by the Latin Fathers. I refer to the Eastern category of *divinization,*[10] and to the Latin category of *incorporation.*[11]

The Spirit of the Risen One accompanies the Christian, the Christian

---

10. Cf. "Divinisation," in M. Viller, A. Rayez, and C. Baumgarten, *Dictionnaire de Spiritualité,* vol. 3 (Paris, 1936ff.), 1370-1459.

11. Cf. L. Cerfaux, *Il cristiano nella teologia paolina* (Rome, 1969), 337-402.

community, and in a particular way, that original reality which is the family toward their true destiny: our Father who is in heaven. The true content of Satan's challenge to Adam — "You will be as God" (cf. Gen. 3:5) — is given to us by grace. We will be as God, but not because we will somehow be able to transform our human nature into divine nature; rather, as Thomas reminds us, the grace of the Spirit will make us capable in paradise of standing before the full glory of Christ. This will be the beginning of our unity with the Father. The action of the Spirit is therefore the progressive divinization of the person. This divinization is produced precisely through an *incorporation*.

This process represents the modality through which, in the sacramental dynamism, our freedom is called to take part in the glorious body of Christ; in this way the ecclesial gathering that the Fathers already saw as *forma mundi* is constituted, as the locus of the redeemed world. This is the way human beings, in the measure that their freedom does not obstinately oppose it, are called to glory — that is, to the full realization of themselves.

The indispensability of the logic of the incarnation as the logic of the sacrament returns here with all of its force. In this logic the glorified body of Christ is the transfiguration of his real, historical body. It is the firstfruits of our resurrection from the dead and the transformation of our real body into a glorified body.

The dynamism of divinization and incorporation points to the way in which the Spirit works in the church of God, showing himself to be the heart of the world. In marriage and the family, this work of the Spirit is carried out in a particular way. The gift of love, lived according to indissolubility and possession in detachment (virginity) — both expressions of the radical form by which the sacrament of marriage makes present the action of the Spirit — actualizes the offering of freedom and brings about divinization. Analogously (and this is an important observation) the logic of incorporation highlights the true meaning of the family as "domestic church." This theme has not yet been adequately developed in the history of theology, even after its energetic revival in the Council, because it has been (wrongly) thought of mainly in juridical-institutional terms, as if the idea involved reproducing the juridical-institutional model of the particular church within the family, through family "ministers," the celebration of the Eucharist in the family, etc. These are all secondary aspects. The true meaning of the family as domestic church lies, rather, in the more immediate possibility that the family offers of founding the Petrine (objective) dimension on the Marian (subjective) dimension. The expression "domestic church" thus indicates the modality with which both of these constitutive dimensions — Petrine (institution) and Marian (charisma) — should be lived within the church. In this sense, as we have understood from the great intuition of the special Synod on Africa when it addressed marriage and the family,[12] what is involved is bringing the logic of the family into the church, so that the influence of a kind of "business logic" is felt less and less.

15.7. The Holy Spirit, Principle of Nuptiality

Returning to our theme, we are now in the position to enucleate clearly in what sense the Holy Spirit is the principle of nuptiality, and, from this perspective, how he represents that inspiration of the organic unity between sexual difference, love, and fruitfulness that lies at the basis of marriage and the family. We will do this quoting Balthasar:

> We have already noted the impossibility of approaching the Holy Spirit except from two directions at once: as the (subjective) quintessence of the mutual love of Father and Son, hence, as the bond (nexus) between them; and as the (objective) fruit that stems from and attests to this love. This impossibility translates into a convergence of the poles. Imagine for a moment that the act of love between a man and woman did not include

---

12. Cf. *Ecclesia in Africa* 63: "Not only did the Synod speak of inculturation, but it also made use of it, taking the *Church as God's Family* as its guiding idea for the evangelization of Africa. The Synod Fathers acknowledged it as an expression of the Church's nature particularly appropriate for Africa. For this image emphasizes care for others, solidarity, warmth in human relationships, acceptance, dialogue and trust. The new evangelization will thus aim at *building up the Church as Family*, avoiding all ethnocentrism and excessive particularism, trying instead to encourage reconciliation and true communion between different ethnic groups, favoring solidarity and the sharing of personnel and resources among the particular Churches, without undue ethnic considerations. 'It is earnestly to be hoped that theologians in Africa will work out the theology of the Church as Family with all the riches contained in this concept, showing its complementarity with other images of the Church.' All this presupposes a profound study of the heritage of Scripture and Tradition which the Second Vatican Council presented in the Dogmatic Constitution *Lumen Gentium*. This admirable text expounds the doctrine on the Church using images drawn from Sacred Scripture such as the Mystical Body, People of God, Temple of the Holy Spirit, Flock and Sheepfold, the House in which God dwells with man. According to the Council, the Church is the Bride of Christ, our Mother, the Holy City and the first fruits of the coming Kingdom. These images will have to be taken into account when developing, according to the Synod's recommendation, an ecclesiology focused on the idea of the Church as the Family of God. It will then be possible to appreciate in all its richness and depth the statement which is the Dogmatic Constitution's point of departure: 'By her relationship with Christ, the Church is a kind of sacrament or sign of intimate union with God, and of the unity of all mankind.'"

nine months pregnancy, that is, the aspect of time. In the parents' generative-receptive embrace, the child would already be immediately present; it would be at one and the same time their mutual love in action and something more, namely, its transcendent result. Nor would it be a valid objection to say that the diastasis we have described just now has to do simply with man's gendered nature, and that in some higher form of love there would be no reproduction (a view that turns up not only in to-day's common distinction between the ends of marriage, but also in the notion of eros that we find from Plato to Soloviev . . .). We must say, in fact, that this form of exuberance and thus fruitfulness (which can be spiritual) is part of every love, and that includes precisely the higher kind of love. In this sense, it is precisely perfect creaturely love that is an authentic *imago Trinitatis.*[13]

Our initial theme resurfaces in this citation: substantial analogy, which expresses the design (logic) of the incarnation, especially inasmuch as it sees the reality of the nuptiality of man and woman as the way to grasp something of the inner life of the Trinity. From this flows Balthasar's final affirmation, that the natural love of mother, father, and child (the inseparable unity of sexual difference, love, and fruitfulness) is an authentic *imago Trinitatis.*

This is not an obvious affirmation. We know that it was contested by two great *auctoritates.*[14] First, Saint Augustine in *De Trinitate* explicitly denies the possibility that the father-mother-child triad can be considered an expression of the trinitarian God.[15] Saint Thomas further develops this Augustinian objection, going so far as to call the hypothesis absurd.[16] In the nineteenth cen-

13. Balthasar, *Theologik III*, 145-46.

14. Both Irenaeus (*Adversus haereses* 1.20.1) and Marius Victorinus (*Adversus Arium* I.57.7–58.14) were favorable to such an analogy.

15. Cf. Augustine, *De Trinitate* 12.5.5: "Accordingly they do not seem to me to advance a probable opinion, who lay it down that a trinity of the image of God in three persons, so far as regards human nature, can be so discovered as to be completed in the marriage of male and female, and in their offspring; in that the man himself, as it were, indicates the person of the Father, but that which has proceeded from him as to be born, that of the Son; and so the third person as of the Spirit, is, they say, the woman, who has proceeded from the man as not herself to be either son or daughter, although it was by her conception that the offspring was born. For the Lord hath said of the Holy Spirit that He proceedeth from the Father, and yet He is not a son. . . . For I pass over such a thing, as to think the Holy Spirit to be the mother of the Son of God, and the wife of the Father." (The English translation is taken from "On the Holy Trinity," in *St. Augustine*, ed. Philip Schaff, Nicene and Post-Nicene Fathers, vol. 3 [Grand Rapids: Eerdmans, 1980], 156.)

16. Cf. Thomas Aquinas, *Summa Theologiae* I, q. 93, a. 6: "As Augustine says, some took the image of the Trinity in man as something collective rather than individual, saying that *man*

284

tury Scheeben reacted to these objections.[17] A serious debate has arisen in contemporary literature which demonstrates that it is possible to hold, within the limits of the analogy, that the family is an image of the Trinity.[18] In defense of this thesis we can cite the authoritative suggestion of John Paul II in *Mulieris Dignitatem*, according to which the *communio personarum* is also a quality of the image of God.[19] This formula allows us to maintain the radical dissimilarity[20] between the triune God and the reality of the human family while, positively, seeing an element of similarity. Through this analogy we see how, through the action of the Spirit, the trinitarian mystery is at work in the family founded on Christian marriage.

To say that the family is an image of the Trinity is nothing other than the full development of a perception which still belongs to the experience of the great majority of people today. I refer to the fact that the love between a man and a woman, if it becomes the stable place of reciprocal edification and is open to the fruit of children, is the high road offered to man for learning himself, the other, the unity of the two, and the fruit of this unity. Just as in God there exists the one, the other, and the unity of the two in perfect equality, there can be in human experience (even if within an abysmal dissimilarity) the unity of two diverse beings. Difference represents for man, even in its inevitable mortification, a great resource and a great possibility. The child, the fruit of love (which is made possible by the dual unity, or endiad, of identity and difference), becomes the exalting and daily confirmation of the positivity of the life of the family.

It is imperative that Christians rediscover the strength to bear witness to the attractiveness and fittingness, for every human being, of confronting daily life from within the great resource of the family. Ours is a world tried to the deepest fibers of its being, because it is a world in which nuptiality has disintegrated, and its three constitutive dimensions are lived — for an

---

(male) represents the person of the Father; the person of the Son is represented by him who proceeds from man in such a way as to be born of him; and thus the third person, standing for the Holy Ghost, they say is woman, who proceeded from man in such a way as not to be his son or daughter. This is *prima facie* absurd, first, because it means that the Holy Ghost would be a source of the Son, just as woman is the source of the offspring which is born to man; secondly, because an individual man would only be in the image of one person; thirdly, because according to this view Scripture ought not to have mentioned God's image in man until offspring had been born to him."

17. Cf. Scheeben, *The Mysteries of Christianity*, 181-89.

18. Cf. B. Castilla Cortázar, "La Trinidad como familia. Analogía humana de las procesiones divinas," *Annales Theologici* 10 (1996): 381-416, with an extensive bibliography.

19. Cf. *Mulieris Dignitatem* 6-8.

20. Cf. Denzinger-Schönmetzer, *Enchiridion symbolorum*, 806; *CCC* 43.

ideology is always practiced — as separate. This world needs to encounter reasons to believe, in everyday life. These reasons do not come primarily from concepts, but from witness. A real witness to these reasons will allow the church's ontological and ethical invitation to keep the three dimensions of nuptiality united when facing the burning questions of the indissolubility of marriage, contraception, abortion, birth control, artificial fertilization, and cloning. It will permit the church's stand to be received not merely as a negative warning, but as the effective possibility of building up an adequate civilization.

15.8. The Holy Spirit and the Family

In conclusion, it is helpful to mention three dimensions that are in a certain sense the contents of the Spirit's action in the life of the family as *imago Trinitatis,* the place where an authentic nuptiality is realized. We can say briefly that the Spirit is *gift,* the Spirit is *freedom,* and the Spirit is *witness.*

15.8.1. The Spirit and the Gift

The Spirit is gift. He is *donum doni* because he is the fruit of the perfect, reciprocal love of the Father and the Son, communicated in the offering of Jesus on the cross (as victim and priest) and permanently proffered to our freedom in the sacrament of the Eucharist, font and culmination of the life of his holy church. If the Spirit is the principle of nuptiality because he actuates the family as *imago Trinitatis,* he will therefore open the family to the logic of the gift, to the gratuitous. The logic of the gift finds its objective verification within the family, in the insuppressible openness to the other that we find even in the "one flesh" (the conjugal act), where (sexual) difference as such is oriented toward the generation of the child. Procreation is in fact the self-gift of the father and the mother who, in the materiality of their existence, strip themselves of all egotism and allow themselves to be disposed of in their self-offering — not without renunciation — in order to affirm the other. And not only the other as husband or wife, but the other as the third, as a child. The child "constrains," so to speak, the two to redefine the *place of the other* in their daily existence, according to that modality proper to divinization. Through grace, and if our freedom does not resist, this divinization transforms the love that binds, eros, into the love that liberates, or agape.

15.8.2. *The Spirit and Freedom*

Secondly, the Spirit is always the place of the exaltation of freedom. "The wind blows where it wills" (John 3:8), we read, and "Where the Spirit of the Lord is, there is freedom" (2 Cor. 3:17). We are to see the mission of the Spirit of the Risen One from the perspective of the simultaneous action of the "two hands"; this is all the more necessary when we speak of the Spirit of freedom. It is absolutely unthinkable to separate the action of the Spirit in history from the singular event of Christ. Jesus himself says "the Holy Spirit, whom the Father will send in my name, he will teach you all things, and bring to your remembrance all that I have said to you" (John 14:26). The Spirit continues to announce and to expose the hidden treasures of wisdom and understanding which are nevertheless the treasures of Christ himself. How are these free actions of the Spirit reflected in the concrete life of the family as *imago Trinitatis*?

Here, certainly, we feel all the weight of a theme which makes itself felt even on a quantitative level. The crisis of the contemporary family is, as we shall see, a crisis of the couple, because the desire for family remains, even if the family involved is fragile; we must recognize that in large measure this crisis reveals itself in reality to be a crisis of freedom. From a certain point of view it is not difficult to understand this, since the family has been chosen, by nature and by grace, to be the place of love. How is it possible to say that a place of love is not a place of freedom? But a misunderstanding circulates in contemporary society regarding the nature of freedom. This misunderstanding tends to make freedom, in all things and for all things, coincide with pure freedom of choice. On the one hand, it fails to consider the fact that freedom of choice must give an account of the inclinations toward self-realization contained in the nature of every man; on the other hand, it forgets that in the ultimate analysis the will is moved by the Infinite. A freedom which does not begin with *amor naturalis*, as Thomas called it — that is, from the inclinations toward our fulfillment offered by nature — and which does not respect the movement toward the infinite that characterizes the human being, is a freedom in shackles. It will never actualize all the exigencies that motivate it. It thinks itself capable of producing its own good, on its own. To the contrary, father, mother, and child are called to learn what freedom is from within the family as the primary community. "The truth will make you free and you will be free indeed" (cf. John 8:32) must become a criterion each person can experience in the daily life of a family. It is an experience which passes, above all, through the acceptance of the other as other. Ultimately, it means obedience to the other's face as it is revealed in his human nature, with all its historical-temperamental traits. In his diversity with

THE NUPTIAL *MYSTERY*

respect to us, and in spite of the inevitable mortification involved, the other becomes a possibility of fulfillment, on the condition that he is lived as a sign and path toward concretely learning the love of God. This love can never be separated from the love of neighbor.

15.8.3. The Spirit and Witness

Lastly, the Spirit is the witness. Following the indications of Scripture, we can say that "the Spirit of truth . . . will bear witness to me; and you also are witnesses" (John 15:26ff.). In order to bear witness to the ends of the earth (cf. Acts 1:8), in order to be witnesses to all peoples — the reason for which conversion and the remission of sins have been granted to us (cf. Luke 24:47ff.) — in order to teach all of mankind everything that Jesus is and everything that Jesus taught (cf. Matt. 28:20), we must receive strength from on high (cf. Luke 24:49), the baptism of the Holy Spirit (cf. Acts 1:5), and the strength of the Holy Spirit (cf. Acts 1:8), so that all might be transformed into witnesses. It will be the Spirit who gives, each time, all that is necessary for this witness, because, as we read in John 16:13, "he will declare to you the things that are to come." The Spirit's task is really that of being the one who reveals, defends, and vindicates Jesus Christ in the "now" of history.

All this has repercussions on the interior life of the family as *imago Trinitatis*, since through the divinization and incorporation of its members the Holy Spirit actuates the principle of nuptiality. We do not intend here to touch upon that aspect of witness connected to personal life; we are concerned with the witness given by the family as such. The family is capable of bearing witness if it allows the consciousness of its being *imago Trinitatis* to shine through its members; if it becomes a place which testifies to a vital belonging to an ecclesial community (in the neighborhood, the home, the workplace, and anywhere man encounters man), against every tendency toward familial egoism; and — this is the point which must be stressed the most — if in the intense welcome and concrete assumption of the needs of the other it attains to the fullness of the new relationships proper to the *communio personarum* (Christ, John, and Mary at the foot of the cross: John 19:25-27).

15.8.4. The Spirit and Unity

The powerful capacity of the Spirit of Christ, according to the logic of the incarnation, thus consists in generating unity within the person, the family, and

288

human society. The Holy Spirit is the One who makes possible the experience of oneness. How beautiful it is to meet two faithful spouses toward the end of their lives, who, despite trials and fragility, bear clear witness to a reciprocal, purifying love, perhaps accompanied in the deterioration of their bodies by the care of children who have learned to become parents! It is easy to glimpse in their faces the expression of the unity of the "I" which has learned the *place of the other* precisely in the family lived as *ecclesia,* as the concrete sign of a love that is free and oblative, open wide to welcome the other. What a gaze these spouses sometimes have for one another, old and yet so young! It is as if each repeats to the other the extraordinary words of Ignatius of Antioch: "A living water murmurs in me, saying, 'Let us go to the Father.'"[21] Gift, freedom, and witness are the path the Spirit entrusts to Christian families for the task which coincides with the essence of the church: fully educating the human person through the indomitable comparison of the whole "I" with the whole of reality, with a view to encountering, in Jesus Christ, him who is the Father of all. "And they shall all be taught by God" (John 6:45).

---

21. Ignatius of Antioch, *Epistle to the Romans* 7.2.

CHAPTER 16

Marriage, Family, and the Eucharist

16.1. In the School of the *Mysteries of Christianity*

"Few persons, and these only recently, have begun to understand in what way Christ may be called the Bridegroom and the Church his betrothed and Bride."[1] Pascasius Radbertus, in writing these words with the clear awareness of the abyss that the believing intellect faces when it attempts to reflect upon revelation, reminds us of the extreme difficulty of our undertaking. The nuptial dimension of love, in fact, cannot be understood as one of the many *objects* that the *world* seems to place at its disposal. Thus, in order to speak of the phenomenon of nuptiality, we must have recourse to the term "mystery."[2]

Our discussion thus far has brought us to the point of considering the two dimensions of the nuptial mystery. If on the one hand a careful look at the nuptiality in the man-woman relationship has revealed that by its very nature there exists an inseparable connection between sexual difference, gift (love as objective relation to another), and fruitfulness, then on the other hand the inevitable question about the origin and end of this reality has led us, through analyzing the meaning of the difference, to recognize this same nuptiality as an essential property of love. This is proven by the fact that it is found in every manifestation or form of love, from the highest form, in which

---

1. Pascasius Radbertus, *Expositio in Matheo* 11.25.10: "Difficile et a paucis cognoscitur quomodo Christus sponsus et ecclesia uxor et sponsa vocetur."

2. Scheeben recognizes that "Then we have a mystery in its absolute form as a truth whose existence the creature cannot ascertain without belief in God's word, and whose subject matter he cannot represent and conceive directly, but only indirectly by comparison with the dissimilar." M.-J. Scheeben, *The Mysteries of Christianity*, trans. C. Vollert, S.J. (St. Louis: Herder, 1946), 11.

the three persons of the one God love each other, to the most degenerate form (*venere:* sensual).

Thus, in order to describe the forms (analogies) of love, we dwelled in particular on the christological and trinitarian components of the nuptial mystery. We began by considering nuptiality as manifested in the original event of Jesus Christ, that is, in his incarnation, life, passion, death, and resurrection. It is precisely in the paschal event that he is revealed as the Bridegroom of the church, his bride. To better understand the nuptiality of the paschal mystery we have thus uncovered its trinitarian roots, beginning with the incarnate Word. The reality of the Spirit likewise appeared before our eyes both as *donum doni* and as fruit of this perfect exchange between the Father and the Son. At last the Fatherhood of God is announced as *origo* and *fons* of every form of paternity and maternity that in turn relies upon human nuptiality. It is helpful here to underscore that this christological-trinitarian inquiry in itself already casts intense light on the nuptial dimension of the love between man and woman, as it is concretely realized in marriage and family.[3]

Nuptiality understood in its fundamental roots (Jesus Christ and the Trinity) presents us with a question which in a certain sense is the most provoking. How does this vision of things reach man in every age? In fact, because every man is situated in history, God himself came to encounter us *in history.* In order to enter into time and space and make himself an interlocutor of men, he assumed a body. But does this loving (nuptial) exchange between Jesus and man really perdure in the time of every human being? Is it evident in geographically displaced civilizations and cultures? And does it above all express the objective reality of things? Or when one speaks of the nuptial or spousal mystery, does it not rather deal with, as some modern authors have maintained (Bataille), the frantic attempt — already present in ancient cosmogony — to explain through the dynamic of the couple the elements of masculinity and femininity? Should this data not instead be accepted in its accidental biological arrangement, as an expression of *chance* — even if it is inexplicable within life as such and intelligent life in particular?

The response to this objection, which reproposes Lessing's challenge[4] at the

---

3. Cf. A. Scola, "Spiritualità coniugale nel contesto culturale contemporaneo," in *Cristo sposo della Chiesa sposa,* ed. R. Bonetti (Rome, 1997), 22-54; Scola, "Lo Spirito Santo rivela la verità tutta intera della famiglia cristiana," in *Il Matrimonio in Cristo è Matrimonio nello Spirito,* ed. R. Bonetti (Rome, 1998), 31-51; Scola, "Paternità e maternità nella cultura attuale," in *Padri e madri per crescere a immagine di Dio,* ed. R. Bonetti (Rome, 1999), 13-36.

4. How is it possible that "accidental historical truths can become proof of the truth of necessary reasons"? G. E. Lessing, "On the Proof of Spirit and Force," in M. F. Sciacca and M. Schiavone, *Grande antologia filosofica* t. 15 (Milan, 1968), 1557-59.

level of the relationship between man and woman (nuptial mystery), encounters in Christianity the path of reflecting on the church and the sacrament. According to Christ's will, the church is the subject who *from, in,* and *through* the sacrament allows for the encounter between the freedom of God and human freedom in the paschal event. The Eucharist, as a paradigmatic sacramental form, sheds light on all the sacraments with respect to their ability to *mediate* the event (paschal) of Christ to the act of human freedom in every age.

In its constitutive relationship to the Eucharist, marriage therefore adequately discloses the nexus between the relationship of man and woman — in its threefold dimension of sexual difference, gift, and fruitfulness — and the relationship between Christ the Bridegroom and his bride the church, which originates in the paschal event. The sacrament of matrimony and the family that flows from it are able to illuminate the origin of the man-woman relationship, its profound nature, and its end. And in turn this illumination of origins entirely reveals the raison d'être of marriage and family. The sacrament of the couple communicates love's nuptial character and, in turn, receives its full light by all the manifestations (forms) of nuptial love.

In the last part of our discussion we intend to delve more deeply, through the church-sacrament, into the connection that the paschal event establishes with marriage and family as an expression of the relationship between man and woman. We will do so by exploring such relationship in both senses. First of all we will show the nuptiality of the event of the death and resurrection of Jesus Christ as given in the church-sacrament. Thus the power of spousal theology will emerge, revealing to us in the man-woman relationship a surprising possibility of deepening the Christian mysteries. Secondly, we shall see how the ecclesiological-sacramental concentration of such mysteries, understood in a nuptial key, allows us to return to the man-woman relationship (marriage and the family) in order to penetrate its meaning more deeply.

16.2. The Paschal Mystery and Marriage and the Family

16.2.1. The Nuptiality of the Paschal Event of Jesus Christ in the Church-Sacrament

The soteriological (salvific) dimension of the paschal event has its condition of possibility and its interior tripersonal dynamic in the very life of the Trinity, as Love; the revelatory dimension of the paschal event (revelatory of the Trinity) is realized precisely "through" (in a strong ontological sense) the Word's assumption of flesh which is "destined for death." The revelatory dimension in some way comprehends in itself that soteriology: while the mystery remains, the substance that unifies them is love.[5]

To speak of the paschal mystery in the nuptial key is to recognize it as the eschatological *hour* of the revelation of the trinitarian God who is love. This is confirmed through the novelty of the terminology employed by the New Testament when speaking of love.[6]

In the event of the death and resurrection of the Son of God made man, therefore, the summit of love is gratuitously revealed to us: God who lives in triunity.

What then are the elements that come to light when we consider the paschal mystery in the context of nuptiality? In the New Testament perspective they can be recognized in the Father's initiative to which the Son responds, in the gift of the Spirit who proceeds from them, and finally in the birth of the church, which communicates love as nuptial mystery.[7]

We refer first to the free initiative of the Father who is rich in mercy.[8] The Father, as *fons et origo*, is in fact revealed, in the paschal mystery, as absolutely gratuitous love: no other reason exists for God's love than the fact that it is his very essence. For *"God is love"* (1 John 4:8), "he has loved us first" (4:19). Our salvation, however (and here is where the filial dimension of the revelation of God as love appears), had been *humanly* willed by a divine person.[9] In this way the Son's twofold love in relation to his Father and to his brothers (all men) is manifested. "The kenosis likewise points to the act of self-offering, the supreme gift of Christ's love which is his very life. He carries this all the way to the extreme humiliation of the sacrifice. It is the Son's love that fills the emptiness of this kenosis-humiliation."[10] The third factor is the gift of the Spirit. He, as the New Testament witnesses, is clearly tied both to the event of the cross — *"gave up his spirit"* (cf. Matt. 27:50) — and to the appearance of the risen Christ — *"receive the Holy Spirit"* (cf. John 20:22). Intrinsically tied to the paschal event of Jesus is the donation by the Father and the Son of the *Donum doni* (Spirit). This fact has been constantly confirmed.

---

5. P. Coda, *Evento pasquale. Trinità e storia* (Rome, 1984), 164.

6. Cf. C. Spicq, *Agapé dans le Nouveau Testament. Analyse des textes* (Paris, 1958-59).

7. "The revelation, in Christ, of absolutely gratuitous, unmotivated, divine love that shines in the initiative of the Father [first element], in the sacrifice of the Son [second element], in the donation of the Spirit [third element] by which a new community of salvation is constituted (the Church) [last element]." M. Bordoni, *Gesù di Nazaret Signore e Cristo*, vol. 3 (Perugia, 1986), 126.

8. Cf. F.-X. Durrwell, *Il Padre. Dio nel suo mistero* (Rome, 1998), 160-63.

9. On this subject see F.-M. Léthel, *Théologie de l'agonie du Christ* (Paris, 1979).

10. Bordoni, *Gesù di Nazaret*, 132.

The last element then emerges in clear dependence upon the gift of the Spirit: the birth of the church as the bride of the bridegroom Jesus Christ. From the Lord's open side on the cross pours forth, in fact, the new people of God, prophetically prefigured in the history of Israel and *anticipated* during the Last Supper in the institution of the Eucharist. The church's manifestation as the fruit of the paschal event is the mission. In fact, the superabundantly *fruitful* character of love revealed in the paschal event is perceived in the mission of the apostles. Infused with the gift of the Spirit, they are sent by the risen Christ to announce the gospel of the Father, and it is precisely by virtue of the actual fulfillment of their mission that we can call ourselves Christians today.

In the trinitarian relations and missions, which culminate with the genesis of the bride church in the paschal sacrifice of the bridegroom Christ, we discover *difference, gift,* and *fruitfulness,* the three constitutive factors of the nuptial mystery, inseparably interwoven. Scheeben summarizes what we have affirmed: "In the Godhead, the mutual love of the Son and the Father pours itself in the production of the Holy Spirit, who issues from their common heart, in whom both surrender their hearts' blood, and to whom they give themselves as the pledge of their infinite love."

Here the three interwoven elements constitutive of the nuptial mystery are delineated in the intratrinitarian life: the difference between Father and Son in the perfect identity that permits their divinely reciprocal and fruitful love in the spiration of the person of the Spirit. Scheeben continues:

> In order worthily to represent this infinitely perfect surrender to His Father, the Logos wished in His humanity to pour forth His blood from His heart to the last drop. . . . The Holy Spirit Himself is portrayed as the agent of the sacrifice. He is the agent in this sense, that in His capacity of *"amor sacerdos"* He urges on the God-man to His sacrifice, and brings the oblation itself into the presence of the Father, uniting it to the eternal homage of love which is He Himself. [But] the Holy Spirit proceeds from the love of the Father for the Son, and through the Son is to be poured over the whole world. . . . Thus the idea of Christ's sacrifice thrusts its roots deep into the abyss of the Trinity. As the incarnation itself was to be the prolongation and extension of the eternal generation and can be adequately comprehended only from this viewpoint, so the sacrificial surrender of the God-man was to be the most perfect expression of that divine love which, as God, He shows forth in the spiration and effusion of the Holy Spirit.[11]

11. Scheeben, *The Mysteries of Christianity,* 445-46.

16.2.2. Church/Eucharist/Marriage:
Sacrament and Sacramental Logic

We have already seen that in the nuptial contemplation of the Christian mysteries the gift of the Spirit and the reality of the church hold a privileged place, precisely in relation to the intrinsic fruitfulness of the nuptial mystery. The church, in fact, already inscribed in the Trinity's plan to make men live as *"sons and daughters in the Son,"* belongs to the *mystery* from the beginning.

We find ourselves facing the Catholic response to the challenge of the Enlightenment. The Enlightenment held that a fact of the past — in this case the paschal mystery — could not possibly be the foundation of necessary truths in all times.[12] The church, inasmuch as it is a historical event, constitutes the possibility of the permanence of the paschal mystery in the here and now, and therefore the possibility of a personal encounter between my freedom and the crucified Risen One in the present moment of my life. "The Church, as (an event of) an intrinsic mediation of the singular (original) event of Jesus Christ, is able to effectively propose him in the present, so that the encounter and relationship between Jesus Christ and man in the here and now means the real possibility of reaching him."[13]

This is, in the opinion of Balthasar, the fundamental ecclesiological question: "In what now follows we will discuss the Church only in so far as she can be and intends to be a medium of God's form of revelation in Christ. This is probably to pose the decisive question beyond which there is theologically speaking probably nothing more that can be asked of the Church."[14]

It is important, however, to understand how ecclesial mediation may be historically accomplished. In fact, to ask oneself about the possibility of encountering Jesus Christ today implies the attempt to make explicit the constitutive dimensions of the mystery by which, without losing his absolute salvific character, he can be truly present to every individual in every age.[15]

The experience of faith grasps in the sacraments, and above all in the Eucharist, the (symbolic) mediation that makes the event of the life, passion,

---

12. Cf. S. Ubbiali, "Il sacramento e la fede," *La Scuola Cattolica* 127 (1999): 313-44.

13. A. Scola, "La logica dell'Incarnazione come logica sacramentale: avvenimento ecclesiale e libertà," in *Wer ist die Kirche? Symposium zum 10 Todesjahr von Hans Urs von Balthasar* (Einsiedeln, 1999), 101.

14. H. U. von Balthasar, *The Glory of the Lord I: Seeing the Form*, trans. Erasmo Leiva-Merikakis (San Francisco: Ignatius; New York: Crossroad, 1982), 556.

15. Cf. P. Wegenaer, *Das Heilswerk Christi und die Virtus Divina in den Sakramenten unter besonderer Berücksichtigung von Eucharistie und Taufe* (Münster, 1958).

death, and resurrection of Jesus Christ contemporaneous to the existence of every man of every time.[16]

"Cujus latus perforatum fluxit aqua et sanguine."[17] As the verse of the *Ave Verum* reminds us, Catholic *traditio,* by referring baptism and the Eucharist to the pierced side of the Crucified One, has always strongly emphasized the direct relationship between Jesus Christ and sacramental action. In fact, the two principal sacraments represent two rites: the first sacrament, the *rite of incorporation,* and the second, the *rite of substitution* in Jewish worship in the temple.[18]

We cannot at this time address the complex questions tied to sacramental theology (for instance, the church as sacrament, and the seven sacraments, their institution by Jesus Christ, their material and form, their ministers and their efficacy).[19]

We will limit ourselves to examining, in the context of the nuptial mystery, the Eucharist, which by its nature is a figure of the sacramental dimension of the church. This is all the more so because the Eucharist is placed in direct relationship with the paschal mystery, the full revelation of God as love. In fact, at the Last Supper the Lord, in the institution of the sacrament of the altar, anticipates his paschal mystery and, by the work of the Spirit, freely gives himself so that all men of all times may be able to participate in this mystery *through the sacrament.*

The Eucharist, contemplated in the light of the nuptial mystery, is based on an exchange that, to use terminology we have used elsewhere, possesses the character of asymmetrical reciprocity. Speaking in these terms with respect to the relationship between man and woman, we have already shown how the difference between the two is never diminished even in the fecund *one-flesh* union that befits marriage. If we now consider the Eucharist, analogously to the man-woman relationship — *analogatum princeps* of love[20] — we can trace in the eucharistic *admirabile commercium* that *difference* from

16. It is necessary to examine the different positions on the so-called *real presence* of Jesus Christ in the Eucharist, which is obviously impossible to do at this time. On this subject see N. Slenczka, *Realpräsenz und Ontologie* (Gotinga, 1991), 583-602.

1y. Vesper Hymn for Holy Saturday, *Vexilla Regis prodeunt.*

18. G. Theissen and A. Merz, *Il Gesù storico: Un manuale* (Brescia, 1999), 534.

19. On sacramental theology in general, see S. Ubbiali, "La riflessione teologica sui sacramenti in epoca moderna e contemporanea," in *Celebrare il mistero di Cristo,* vol. 1 (Rome, 1993), 303-36.

20. One such analogy is permitted even with the awareness that "faith is not primarily discursive. It is constituted most fully in the body. It is to bodies that God gives his Spirit and communicates the power of the resurrection." H. Bourgeois, "La foi nait dans le Corps," *La Maison-Dieu,* no. 146 (1981): 141.

which flows the *gift* and *fecundity.* Thus we see again the intrinsically connected elements constitutive of the nuptiality of love. In the church, as in the Eucharist, it is the Bridegroom who, suprasexually, generates the bride: here is the asymmetry! In the interconnection of the three factors indicated, one can easily recognize how in the sacrament of the Eucharist the mystery of the crucified Risen One calls into play historically situated human freedom.

16.2.2.1. Given in Freedom

Only by contemplating, with awe, the radical character of the gift (love in the proper sense), can we discover the profound truth of the Eucharist and its fecundity for the life of the faithful.[21] In the sacrament of the altar the mysterious (asymmetrical) exchange of love between the gift of the Trinity and the believer's act of freedom is accomplished daily. Reflecting upon the dynamic of the gift likewise permits us to grasp all the dimensions of the eucharistic mystery that the Son of God made man, entering into the *hour* (cf. John 17:1) established by the Father, instituted during the Last Supper.

First of all, a gift does not exist without a giver. In fact, in its highest expression — that is, in the relationship between persons — a gift does not exist without One who gives *himself,* who surrenders *himself,* who generously donates *himself* to the other. In the Eucharist it is the Trinity who is self-given: the Father gives his very Self by sending his only begotten Son-made-man to die and to rise for us and for our sins; the Son, in his own free obedience to the trinitarian will, delivers himself into the hands of sinners and, being a priest, is made a victim; the Spirit of the Father and the Son is given so that the paschal offering may be perennially present to every individual in every age.

However, for there to be a gift there must also be One who receives: a gift is always given to someone, all the more when it coincides with the person who freely bestows it. The singular dimension of the gift proper to the sacraments was well received by the classical axiom of Catholic theology, *sacramenta propter homines.* Human freedom, in fact, is radically called into play by the gift offered in the Eucharist as in every sacrament. Without freedom, even if all its potential for grace is maintained *(ex opere operato),* the sacrament cannot become fruitful, that is, it cannot generate fruits in the faithful *(ex opere operantis).* When welcomed by freedom, the sacrament manifests all its fecundity in the work of incorporation and divinization of the Christian.

21. Cf. J.-L. Marion, *Étant donné* (Paris, 1997), I, §6.

The *pro vobis* of the formula of institution powerfully and efficaciously synthesizes these dimensions. In the *pro vobis* lies the secret of the eucharistic gift: it speaks to us, contemporaneously, of Him who gives Himself and of the freedom of him to whom He is given. This encounter between gift and freedom is realized in the Christian economy by the work of the Holy Spirit.[22]

Due to our weakness, we do not come into contact with any human experience outside the realm of an ineradicable drama: not even the gift is received by freedom without a component of struggle. But this, paradoxically, happens precisely so that the nature of the gift offered may be respected. Even the Christian faithful who, in the sacrament of the body given and the blood poured out, recognize the most radical gift they may ever be able to receive, are not spared the idolatrous temptation to possess what can only be received with gratitude. The mystery of unfathomable gratuitousness by which the Creator decides to offer himself, in the eucharistic bread and wine, to the creature's reach, runs the risk of being overtaken. The same Christians, in fact, can be tempted to take the eucharistic food and treat it as if it were any other food: to absorb it, instead of letting themselves be absorbed by it. Without *distance* the nature of the gift of the sacrament in the Christian economy would not be respected. Thus, we recognize the radical importance of the sacramental rite. The poverty of the material (a piece of bread, a drop of wine) that transmits the gift is inversely proportional to the greatness of the mystery that such a reality communicates: the permanence of the eucharistic *species* is always there to show us this.

The sacramental reality of the church, inasmuch as it is a gift offered to freedom through rites and sacramental symbols, requires an attitude of unceasing eucharistic praise on the part of man. This character of gift proper to the sacrament refers back, as its origin, to the reciprocal gift characteristic of the intratrinitarian life (theology of divine processions) and to the gift that life freely bestowed upon men (theology of mission — divinization of the baptized).

16.2.2.2. *Circumstances and Relationships in the Sacramental Horizon*

In the objective nature of the sacrament, the foundation is given, in an ontological and epistemological measure, that justifies the contemporaneousness

---

22. In fact, "the Spirit is the personal place of interpersonal communion between Christ and those who believe in him, he 'in whom' it is possible to encounter the Risen One." M. Bordoni, *Cristologia nell'orizzonte dello Spirito* (Brescia, 1995), 298.

of the redemptive event of Christ to every individual of every age. It is evident that this foundation fits the structure of a precise act of human freedom. One may ask, therefore, *if* and *how* the dynamic expressed in the sacrament can, analogously, fit every act that freedom is called to realize, in every circumstance and in every relationship the mediation of the actual event. In this way the sacramental dynamic would identify a true and proper *sacramental logic* as the *logic of the incarnation.*[23]

All the circumstances and relationships that concretely constitute the web of human existence are symbolic forms that attest to the transcendence of God who summons human freedom, and as such, they are analogously set within the paradigm of the sacramental logic.

With regard to relationships, the Christian himself, living the faith through the instituted forms of the sacraments, of Scripture, and of the hierarchically ordered ecclesial community, becomes an *occasion* of the symbolic manifestation (sacrament) of God's will. Existing *en Christoi* permits him to be an event of the truth which communicates itself through him. For this reason, even the ignorant and illiterate can be teachers and doctors of the faith.

As for the circumstances (understood here, in a broad sense, as facts or a set of facts implied by specific determining characteristics): one must primarily recognize that to affirm their character of symbolic mediation of the event is not to assert a mere pretext, because the circumstances do not ultimately come about by chance. Even without underestimating the autonomy of the many preexisting causes that enter into play in their coming to pass, they cannot in the end escape the play of the singular relationship of the freedom of God who calls the freedom of man. Even in this case, however, man left to his own does not recognize his circumstances to be a symbolic mediation: he needs to live within a community where faith is sensibly expressed, and permits him, ultimately, to grasp the character of those circumstances as an event.

The sacramental logic reveals, therefore, the true nature of human existence: life itself is a vocation. This is due to the fact that human freedom is called, in faith, to decide in favor of that foundation which in every circumstance and in every relationship is anticipated as a promise.

Such a conception of things gives rise to a vast number of consequences, beginning for example with the need to better understand the meaning of what today is often emphatically called "discernment." Indeed, this term must remain linked to the broader concept of "verification," in which the call to the specific *Christian state of life* may be subordinated, in turn, to *life itself under-*

---

23. For these expressions see *Fides et Ratio* 13, 94.

stood as a vocation. In fact, even if outside the sacrament and the relevant instituted forms of mediation of the christological event to human freedom, man cannot perceive the sacramental value of circumstances and relationships, nonetheless if this value has not become a concrete experience for the believer one can legitimately doubt that he has identified himself with the same eucharistic mystery and with the other instituted forms which mediate the event of Jesus Christ.

One can say that in the sacrament, and in the sacramental logic derived from it, the symbolic actualization of faith that constitutes the true form of knowledge is given. In it, in fact, the foundation or Truth is effectively communicated because by its nature it is an original event that continues in the event-mediation of the encounter of God's freedom with human freedom.

From what has been maintained thus far, a consequence arises that is certainly not irrelevant: Christ cannot be reduced to a pretext for the faith of someone who would in the end be, in the best of the hypotheses, either a visionary or an ingenious victim of fabulous beliefs. Christ is neither the product of human reasoning nor the culminating result of a particular religious sentiment. By virtue of the sacrament and sacramental logic, Jesus Christ is the original event who is mediated, symbolically, in every circumstance and in every relationship. He is the Savior present in my every act of freedom.

16.3. Marriage and the Family in Light of the Sacramental Logic

We have now reached the last part of our reflection. From considering the paschal mystery in the light of the nuptial mystery, we moved on to reflect upon the sacramental character of the paschal mystery's permanent offering to human freedom. From there we turned to a discussion of sacramental logic, always maintaining nuptiality as the backdrop. Now we would like to reread the sacrament of marriage and the family in light of the nuptiality proper to the sacramentality in the life of the church.

We have said that the sacrament as a (symbolic) realization of faith is the event of mediation in which the possibility of being fulfilled is offered to the freedom of every person, who adheres in faith to the original paschal event. Understood in this way, the sacrament, and the sacramental logic that derives from it, places the paschal mystery and the reality of marriage and the family in immediate relationship to one another, through the eucharistic mystery. In this sense it is possible to trace a connection between the humanity of the Redeemer, the eucharistic species, and the *one flesh* befitting of marriage-family.

The unifying factor is the *living body.* "The body represents that original level in which man experiences the necessity of being himself through an objective form other than himself. Ecclesial and sacramental corporeity are exactly placed within this perspective."[24]

From the living *body*[25] — as a sacrament of the whole person — prepared by the Trinity "before the creation of the world" (cf. 1 Pet. 1:20) so that the Son could become the sacrificed Lamb, flows (suprasexually) the *bride, incorporated* into her Head who is Jesus Christ. This *body* is perennially given in the bread and wine which become the *body* and *blood* of Jesus Christ, to the freedom of those who, by faith and baptism, are incorporated into the new people of God.[26] It is here where the reality of marriage and the family finds a sacramental foundation. Being an efficacious symbol of the fruitful nuptials between Christ and the church,[27] sacramental marriage — the full form of the man-woman relationship — makes the (anticipated) promise of the final fulfillment accessible in concrete existence.

The Trinity's loving plan of salvation (nuptiality) is effectively realized in the creation of man and woman in the image of the archetypical couple Christ-church. The original plan is fully accomplished in the death and resurrection of Jesus Christ — in the paschal mystery — from which the bride flows: the church. Saint Augustine marvelously illustrates this reality:

"One of the soldiers opened his side with his lance, and immediately blood and water flowed forth." The verb used by the evangelist is significant. He did not say struck, stabbed the side, or something of the like. He said: opened, to indicate that in the side of Christ the door of life was opened, from which flow the sacraments of the Church, without which one does not enter into that life which is true life. To announce this mystery at all times, the first woman was formed from the side of the man who was sleeping, and she was called life and mother of the living. Undoubtedly, this was the announcement of a great good, before the great evil of the transgression. Here the second Adam bowed his head and fell asleep on the

---

24. Scola, "La logica dell'Incarnazione," 123.

25. Cf. C. Rocchetta, *Sacramentaria fondamentale* (Bologna, 1990), 35-37; S. Spisanti, "Linguaggio del corpo nella comunicazione rituale," in *Comunicazione e ritualità*, ed. G. Ambrosio and L. Sartori (Padua, 1988), 303-11; G. Mazzocchi, "Il corpo e la liturgia," in *Liturgia e incarnazione*, ed. A. N. Terrin (Padua, 1997), 288-315.

26. "The Eucharist is represented as the foundation of the one body in Christ (Rm. 12:5)" and Baptism is the instrument through which the Spirit builds up the ecclesial body. H. U. von Balthasar, *Theologik III: Der Geist der Wahrheit* (Einsiedeln: Johannes Verlag, 1987), 268.

27. On spousal symbolism see J. Sanz Montes, *La simbología esponsal como clave hermenéutica del carisma de Santa Clara de Asís* (Rome, 2000), 27-96.

cross, so that his bride could be formed from the blood and water that gushed forth from his side.[28]

In marriage and the family the "one flesh" expresses the *fruitful gift,* which is made possible by the reciprocal surrender of the spouses based on their insuperable *difference* (also sexual). In this specific realization of the three dimensions of the nuptial mystery in marriage and the family we can thus identify the fulfillment of the characteristics proper to the sacramental logic: the freedom of the spouses and their children, clearly expressed by the intrinsic character of consent in the sacrament, is made effective by the gift of the paschal event of Jesus Christ, which passes through conjugal love. Thus, human love finds its full expression in nuptiality.

At the interior of the irreplaceable horizon of the Christian community, the path to an ever more fruitful fulfillment *(ex opere operantis)* of the efficaciously celebrated sacrament *(ex opere operato)* is laid open to the spouses.

The sacrament of marriage and the family, in the light of the nuptial mystery, requires therefore that the Christian spouses live the profundity of the sacramental logic on a daily basis. The same human experience of love between man and woman teaches us that the more the reciprocal gift grows, the more the other is allowed to be truly such, that is, properly *other;* the more the difference is respected and, therefore, its character of gift, the more likely there will be an equality of rights-duties. One can say in this sense that the best school of matrimonial life is the Eucharist/church. In fact, it becomes the primary path of *education in the gift,* and therefore of education in how to live reality. If in the encounter par excellence of man with the *"Author of life"* (cf. Acts 3:15) everything is marked by the dynamic of the gift — encounter between him who is given and the freedom of him who receives — every relationship, every circumstance, and every situation of the real, both in its temporal dimension and spatial, will find its *figure (Gestalt)* precisely in this dynamic.

Every part of reality, in this way, is recognized in its "sacramental" quality: every relationship with the other refers us back to the Other; every circumstance is seen as a trace of the Mystery that guides history. Employing this sacramental dynamic in the life of the couple all the way to its end, it is no longer possible to be scandalized — at least from the point of view of the *mens christiana* — by the triviality and apparent banality of everyday life or by the weakness of the bridegroom and the bride.

In opposition to this fascinating way of Christian life, human freedom is exposed to a twofold temptation. On the one hand, if one underestimates the

---

28. Augustine, *In Iohannis evangelium tractatus* 120.2.

nature of the gift proper to marriage, one risks falling into a sort of idolatry. And this can happen even where more importance is given to the necessary awareness of the reality of one's vocation than to the objective fact that constitutes it: marriage and the family as a sacramental gift (given) lived in the everyday. In a certain sense one ends up privileging one's own act of consciousness over the gift that Jesus Christ makes of himself in the sacrament. One can therefore be tempted to measure one's marital life by one's capacity to welcome the gift rather than by the virtue of the gift itself. Thus, for example, if one forgets that marriage is a gift, its indissolubility, above all when put to the test, will appear as an unbearable burden. This sort of idolatry surreptitiously transforms marriage into a pretext for one's own individual edification. Often, closing it up in the nostalgic memory of the past impedes the unfolding of its generating force of *communio* in the present.

The other part of the temptation confronting marriage is represented in the failure to live the sacrament as an expression of that *difference* in which Christ himself is offered to the freedom of the spouses and all the members of the family.

Therefore the inevitable element of repetition present in human relationships and circumstances causes them to no longer be lived as a necessary mediation symbolic of the unique event of Christ, but to be weakened in their force of being signs. In this way they become a source of obtuse habit that impedes every creative wonder.

In synthesis, the sacramental reality of marriage and the family is presented as the anthropological concentration of the eucharistic-ecclesial event. In it, in fact, the sacramental dynamic truly liberates the freedom of this husband and this wife. The beauty of so many Christian families bears witness to this!

The Christian life, eucharistically lived by the faithful in the reality of marriage and the family, thus becomes a paradigm for every type of human relationship, above all for those which constitute the ecclesial community. In the life of the people of God, the family educates all the faithful to understand their relationships — even those tied to the sacramental task of the presbyterial ministry — according to the nuptial dynamic of the sacrament.

Appendices

From Inter Insignores *to* Ordinatio Sacerdotalis

The Congregation for the Doctrine of the Faith has published a volume entitled *From "Inter Insignores" to "Ordinatio Sacerdotalis": Documents and Commentary,*[1] which traces a detailed itinerary through three magisterial interventions.

The first of these interventions consists of the *Declaration Inter Insignores
regarding the Question of the Admission of Women to the Priesthood;*[2] the second is John Paul II's apostolic letter *Ordinatio Sacerdotalis: On the Reservation
of the Ordained Priesthood to Men Only;*[3] and the third is the *Response to a
Doubt regarding the Apostolic Letter "Ordinatio Sacerdotalis."*[4] The Congregation's text presents two sets of commentaries. The first consists of three articles presenting the documents in question; these articles appeared in the
Osservatore Romano without a signature and were indicated by the Congregation. The second is a collection of two groups of articles (from 1977 and 1993,
respectively) on *Inter Insignores,* written by various theologians.

We are thus dealing with a volume which centers around the pronouncements of the magisterium regarding the nonadmissibility of women to the
ministerial priesthood. At the same time, the work seeks to provide, through

1. Congregation for the Doctrine of the Faith, *Dall'Inter insignores all'Ordinatio
sacerdotalis. Documenti e commenti* (Vatican City, 1996).

2. Published by the Congregation for the Doctrine of the Faith on October 15, 1976, with
the approval and by the disposition of Pope Paul VI.

3. Published May 22, 1994.

4. Made public, with the approval and by the disposition of John Paul II, by the Congregation for the Doctrine of the Faith on October 28, 1995.

This appendix refers directly to chapter 1, "A Theological Sketch of Man and Woman."

the responsibility of theologians and scholars, a further clarification of the reasons which prompted the magisterium to intervene three times in eighteen years on this delicate aspect of Christian doctrine and practice.[5]

The historical genesis of the first two magisterial interventions is linked to the initiative of three other Christian confessions to admit, in a differentiated manner, women to the exercise of the ministerial priesthood. The third seeks to respond to the question, present in Catholic and non-Catholic theological literature after the publication of *Ordinatio Sacerdotalis*, whether the doctrine proposed in this document was to be held definitively as belonging to the deposit of faith.[6]

In substance, what do these magisterial pronouncements propose?

They assert that the church does not have the power to modify the uninterrupted, two-thousand-year-long practice of calling only men to the ministerial priesthood, inasmuch as this is directly willed by Jesus. This is the core of the thesis sustained by *Inter Insignores* and reiterated by John Paul II,[7] as well as by the *Catechism of the Catholic Church*,[8] whose terminology is taken organically and authoritatively from *Ordinatio Sacerdotalis*.[9] In this latter the Holy Father, through the virtue of his ministry of confirming the brethren, affirms with a formal declaration that the Catholic Church in no way possesses the faculty of conferring priestly ordination on women. This phrase

---

5. For a complete analysis of the principal literature on the theme, the following texts are useful: M. Hauke, *Die Problematik um das Frauenpriestertum vor dem Hintergrund der Schöpfungs- und Erlösungsordung* (Paderborn, 1986); Hauke, "Il sacerdozio femminile nel recente dibattito teologico," *Rivista Teologica di Lugano* 1 (1996): 257-81.

6. Thus Paul VI explicitly asked the Congregation for the Doctrine of the Faith to elaborate what would later become the Declaration *Inter Insignores* after an epistolary exchange with the archbishop of Canterbury (Coggan). This latter, following the general Synod of the Anglican Church in Quebec in 1975, informed the pope that, slowly but surely, the conviction was spreading in the Anglican communion that objections did not exist on the level of principles to the priestly ordination of women. Analogously, *Ordinatio Sacerdotalis* was published by John Paul II on the solemnity of Pentecost as a definitive pronouncement on the impossibility of the admission of women to the ministerial priesthood, after the Anglican communion had made the opposite decision. We cannot forget, however, that this problematic in fact depends on the feminist question. On the feminist movement and its relevant themes, see, for example: *La donna nella Chiesa e nel mondo* (Naples, 1988); M. Farina, "La questione donna: un'istanza critica per la teologia," *Ricerche Teologiche* 1 (1990): 91-120; F. Martin, *The Feminist Question: Feminist Theology in the Light of Christian Tradition* (Grand Rapids: Eerdmans, 1994), with a substantial bibliography; M. Hauke, *God or Goddess? Feminist Theology: What Is It? Where Does It Lead?* trans. David Kipp (San Francisco: Ignatius, 1995).

7. Cf. *Mulieris Dignitatem* 26.

8. Cf. *CCC* 1577.

9. Cf. *Ordinatio Sacerdotalis* 2 (hereafter *OS*).

"has not merely a disciplinary, but doctrinal value, and is to be held definitively" because, as the Congregation for the Doctrine of the Faith specifies in the *Response to a Doubt,* it is infallibly proposed by the ordinary and universal magisterium inasmuch as it is founded in the written Word of God and constantly kept and applied in the tradition of the church.

I would like to limit myself here to taking up a few salient arguments contained in the volume in question, regarding the pronouncement of the magisterium and its objectively nondiscriminatory character with regard to women.

I refer to the article "The Meaning for Us, Today, of the Attitude of Christ and the Practice of the Apostles" by Descamps,[10] and that by Hans Urs von Balthasar entitled "The Uninterrupted Tradition."[11] I will only allude to their content, leaving the full development of their argumentation to an attentive reading of the volume. Descamps's article seeks to deepen the interpretation of Jesus' decision to choose the Twelve from among men only; Balthasar reflects on the indispensable anthropological dimension of our theme, beginning with the meaning of sexual difference. These are the chief points with which even those who resist the magisterial pronouncements begin, though in a different way.[12]

Descamps responds with acuity to the objection according to which Jesus — whose behavior with regard to women is unanimously held to have been innovative and countercultural — *could not have* definitively excluded women from the ministerial priesthood in his act of calling only men to be among the Twelve. Thus, according to the argument, the uninterrupted tradition could be changed without contradicting the will of Christ. It would be difficult to enter here into all the details of Descamps's response (his text is

---

10. Congregation, *Dall'Inter insignores,* 98-107.

11. Congregation, *Dall'Inter insignores,* 108-15.

12. Cf., for example: M. Alcalà, *Mujer, Iglesia, Sacerdocio* (Bilbao, 1995); W. Beinert, "Priestertum der Frau. Der Vorhang zu die Frage offen?" *Stimmen der Zeit* 212 (1994): 723-38; R. R. Gaillardetz, "Infallibility and the Ordination of Women," *Louvain Studies* 21 (1996): 3-24; G. Greshake, "Zur Erklärung der Glaubenskongregation über die im Apostolischen Schreiben *Ordinatio sacerdotalis* vorgelegte Lehre," *Pastoralblatt* 48 (1996): 56; W. Gross, *Frauenordination* (Munich, 1996); J. Moignt, "Sur un débat clos," *Recherches de Science Religieuse* 82/3 (1994): 321-33; the whole issue of *Theologische Quartalschrift* 3 (1993): 163-253, with articles by M. Jepsen, E. Schüssler Fiorenza, P. Hünermann, M. Theobald, A. A. Thiermyer, A. Jensen, D. Mieth; the issue of *Istina* 39 (1994): 113-224; F. A. Sullivan, "La strada della tradizione," *Il Regno* 9 (1996): 312ff.; P. Vallin, "Les ministères feminins," *Etudes* 382 (1995): 207-18. As a response to theological criticisms, cf. Hauke, "Il sacerdozio femminile nel recente dibattito teologico"; L. Scheffczyk, "Das Responsum der Glaubenskongregation zur Ordinationsfrage und eine theologische Replik," *Forum Katholische Theologie* 2 (1996): 127-33.

brief, and though it requires an attentive reading, is clear and accessible). He points out that it is not enough to ascertain the materiality of a fact which in itself needs no demonstration; one must discover its meaning. In the case at hand, this involves understanding the meaning that Jesus gave to his decision to call only (male) men to the College of the Twelve. In what measure did he will it? What did he really will? What is, moreover, the meaning of this decision? According to Descamps, in an accurate interpretation of the facts and indications available to us, one cannot interpret Jesus' choice by opposing the "circumstances" on the one hand and Jesus' "creative impact" (or genius) on the other, as if he were engaged in some kind of dilemma. Descamps has recourse to Guitton's distinction between "spirit" (the original contribution of a personality) and "mentality" (through which the circumstances mold, but are also surpassed by, the creativity of the spirit), and shows how the historical truth of Jesus' choice clearly expresses his positive intention to reserve the ministerial priesthood to men. Analogous considerations can be extended first to the decision of the apostles, and then to the constant practice of the Western and Eastern Church.

But how does one respond to the objection that all this does not necessarily imply that Jesus' and the apostles' understanding has a prescriptive value for all times? Descamps demonstrates that such practices possess a doctrinal character because they are elements which belong to revelation's coming-to-be. The plan of God is not a collection of abstract ideas, nor can it be reduced to a historical process in continual evolution. It is, rather, a *work*, an interweaving of event and Word which has its culmination in Jesus Christ himself. Jesus' choice is thus normative because it constitutes an essential element of revelation, objectively accomplished with the apostles. The church is well aware of this from the second century onward.

We do not need at this point to enter into the delicate argumentation with which Balthasar investigates the anthropological meaning of the man-woman pair and sexual difference.[13] He is very conscious of the fact that no historicist reading of the Scriptures can produce, by itself alone, a thesis for or against the admission of women to the priesthood. Scripture must be read within the living subject which is the church, with respect for tradition and, ultimately, through the authentic interpretation which the magisterium can provide. From this perspective Balthasar welcomes the central content of *Inter Insigniores* as based upon the will of Jesus Christ. His preoccupation, however, is that of deepening its anthropological dimensions. We are merely at the beginning of such a reflection; we can thus easily understand that

13. Cf. H. U. von Balthasar, "Solo la differenza produce la vita," *Jesus* 1 (1997): 57-58.

though the magisterium, from *Inter Insignores* on, makes reference to and encourages theologians engaged in this field of research, it rightly affirms that while the understanding of its pronouncement can be facilitated by such studies, magisterial authority is not based upon them. Balthasar nevertheless draws forth, in a manner which is to my mind profound and perhaps as yet unequaled except by the original magisterium of John Paul II on the subject, how, in order to make room for the equal dignity of man and woman, the movement for the promotion of women must take difference fully into consideration. This is so because, as the psychological sciences of the interior have demonstrated, it is precisely sexual difference which we find difficult to think of and even completely to represent. Balthasar gives particular consideration to the fact that woman always holds the "place of the other" and is thus always, more than the man, a sign of the presence of God within the human family. This fact limits the ministerial priesthood to the function of representation *in persona Christi,* without diminishing its sacramental-symbolic character. In this precise sense the ministerial priesthood is objectively linked to the male gender of Jesus. This priesthood exists, however, only for the sake of the people of God.

The feminine dimension, which Balthasar loves to call the Marian-Johannine dimension, belongs to the whole people of God. It explains the common priesthood *(sacrificium internum)* and possesses, in the end, an objective primacy with respect to the Petrine dimension, which is linked to the ministerial priesthood *(sacrificium externum).* The latter's meaning is comprehensible only in relation to the people of God.

The volume compiled by the Congregation therefore constitutes an obligatory point of reference for those who are interested in understanding a significant aspect of Catholic doctrine.

I would like to add a few considerations on the question of freedom, today more decisive than ever. To this question is intimately linked that of the dignity of the person, his rights, and his duties.

The documents in question affirm that the church "does not consider itself authorized to admit women to priestly ordination,"[14] or rather that it "does not in any way possess the faculty of conferring priestly ordination on women."[15] The magisterium has never said that the church *does not want* to make this choice; it has always affirmed that it *cannot* make it. She does not have the power to make it, if she wishes to remain faithful to herself.

The church thus does not have the *power* to admit women to participate

---

14. Congregation, *Dall'Inter insignores,* 31.
15. Cf. *OS* 4.

in the *power* proper to the ministerial priesthood. What does this statement imply? Does it not contain an invitation to ponder attentively the true nature of power, its genesis and its exercise? In the church, power arises from obedience to Jesus Christ, the Son of God, who made himself obedient to the Father through the power of the Spirit, to death on a cross. For the church, as for her Lord, power implies a freedom whose ultimate roots are not at her own disposition, not *in proprio potere*. We are here in the presence of a fact constitutive of finite freedom, and thus of power, in general. The human being and human communities are truly free only when they embrace the essential, preexistent and inalterable factors that constitute them. The genesis, nature, and exercise of freedom are rooted in the very nature of man and of the community. But today we are witnessing a paradox: freedom is on everyone's lips, and is in a certain sense emphasized as much as and perhaps more than the word "reason" in the nineteenth century. Yet at the same time, one cannot deny a grave crisis of freedom. Freedom seems to be suspended, almost incapable of grasping the object it desires and chooses. Contemporary man resembles an athlete attempting a high jump who, after a running start, remains suspended through a strange enchantment over the bar. Freedom seems today to be the victim of this structural incapacity, to the point that many philosophers have begun to theorize the necessity of "willing not to will." Let us ask ourselves: Does not this stalling of freedom flow from the fact that it is made to coincide with the ability to choose, as if man's free choice were absolute, exhausting the whole meaning of freedom? Is this not a way to negate the human being's original dependence on his Creator? This dependence is inscribed in human nature, but also in the objective precedence of reality over our "I." God and reality are factors which, through desire understood in its fullest sense (Saint Thomas's *amor naturalis*), spur freedom into action. Without this original level of dependence, it is impossible to speak of full freedom! Just how much these factors, which freedom does not produce but encounters as already given, form the basis of desire appears clearly when we consider pathologies such as autism or, on another level, the risk of self-destruction which today holds liberal democracies in its grasp.

Now the church in her understanding of herself — and in the end it is this which is at stake in the question of the nonadmissibility of women to the ministerial priesthood — accepts to limit herself, obeying her founder. Will this not bear fruit in positive repercussions on man and the community? How? By suggesting the necessity of thinking all the way through essential concepts like freedom and power. This, too, can be an element which can contribute to the interesting investigation taking place today, even in the "lay" world, on belief and the reasons for it.

These considerations are full of implications. I limit myself to indicating only one. The concept of freedom just suggested leads us to affirm the dignity of the person without making this dignity ultimately depend on the power of performing or not performing certain actions, of making or not making certain decisions: in a word, without tying it to a role. Why not see, in the church's fidelity to her Lord in the decision of choosing only men for the ordained ministry, an invitation to turn in other directions to promote the authentic dignity of women, in the church as well as elsewhere? I think the high road to this consists in the anthropological development of the true meaning of sexual difference.[16]

In conclusion, we observe that the definitive character of the magisterial pronouncement on the question of the nonadmissibility of women to the ministerial priesthood is based, in its turn, on the proper nature of freedom and power in the church. The authoritative and definitive proclamation of the truth by the church is possible precisely because of her original dependence. If we look closely, we find here a great and universal teaching regarding the necessity of a morality of thought. Perhaps it is precisely this morality of thought which often escapes some (even Catholic) cultivators of scientific disciplines. It ought rather to be recovered in a culture like that of today, so sensitive to the vast array of the meanings of freedom. Solidity of thought is not only linked to intuitive force and logical rigor, which represent in a certain sense the intrinsic conditions of its truth. It depends also on one's capacity to adjust oneself to reality, offering oneself — without illusory progressivism or defeatist preconceptions — to the service of that self-consciousness of the truth which men and peoples can elaborate in their journey on this earth.

16. It is thus a positive development that the current debate on the "woman question" is being carried out in terms of "reciprocity" (the use of this word is not always exempt from ambiguity, even in the church), having evolved from the earlier "phases of emancipation and separateness." Cf. Farina, "La questione donna," 111-12.

Affection in the Light of Several Articles of Saint Thomas Aquinas's De Passionibus: A Reading of the Summa Theologiae I-II, q. 22, aa. 1-3, and q. 26, aa. 1-2

One of the aspects of Saint Thomas's work which has perhaps been undervalued is his singular ability to describe the vital dynamisms of the subject in
psychological terms (we refer to a psychology that is obviously speculative
and not experimental). One generally tends to consider his analyses in a static
manner; the subject is not seen in action, and thus scrutinized in all the
dynamisms which constitute his working in the world. Saint Thomas seeks to
unearth the dynamism of the affective experience, describing the rational and
volitional motivations proper to the subject.

His treatise on the passions extends from question 22 to question 48 of
the *Prima Secundae*.[1] Prior to this section in the *Summa*, Aquinas had already
recognized the psychology of the subject: in following the vision of Aristotelian metaphysics, he had already studied the structure of the subject statically,
so to speak, in its capacity, faculty, or *virtus apprehensiva*, tied to the dimension of consciousness, and in its *virtus appetitiva*, tied to the dimension of the

---

1. With regard to the importance and timeliness of this treatise, the penetrating introduction by Fr. Tito S. Centi is useful: in Thomas Aquinas, *La Somma teologica*, vol. 1 (Bologna, 1988),
7-21.

This appendix offers a key, in the form of notes, to reading several passages from the tractate *De
Passionibus*, with the intent of shedding light on the affective phenomenon. In this sense the appendix can be directly referred to chapter 4 above.

will.[2] Beyond the structures of the intellect and will, he had already studied the roots of the will in instinct, and afterward occupied himself with the *habitus*, that is, with those permanent attitudes of the subject that can modify his action.[3] Now he is ready to evaluate the behavior of the subject in action and to study his dynamisms in the measure in which the subject is provoked, whether by external reality or by other persons. The tractate on the passions is placed in this context; it presupposes anthropological reflection in a strict sense, as well as reflection on rational psychology.[4]

A note on method. From the point of view of a theological investigation of the phenomenon of affection, a study of this treatise might be considered superfluous. On the one hand, many interpreters of Saint Thomas consider it to be a purely rational-philosophical investigation; on the other hand, we moderns already have precious contributions of this type in the areas of phenomenology and the human sciences (psychology and sociology). The response to this objection, which has a certain pertinence, must be made by reflecting on the fact that in Aquinas's thought it is never possible to separate the "philosophical" from the "theological." Modern Thomistic scholars have demonstrated this with sufficient solidity and clarity.[5] In this sense the problem of a distinction between philosophy and theology is a post-Thomistic problem, superimposed anachronistically onto Thomas's text beginning from the second Scholasticism — that is, after the rise of modern philosophy as an autonomous philosophy. Thomas's reflection was carried out in a historical context in which the known world was Christian, and in which man was contemplated in his entirety, according to the formal *ratio* of faith, even though Thomas clearly distinguishes between a natural dimension and philosophical reflection. For him, "nature" always means "creature." In Thomas it is never possible to receive the category of *physis* and its derivatives in purely Aristotelian terms.[6] In

2. Cf. Thomas Aquinas, *Summa Theologiae* (hereafter *ST*) I, qq. 77-89, and I-II, qq. 6-21.

3. Cf. Thomas Aquinas, *ST* I-II, qq. 50-54.

4. Cf. B. Gherardini, "Sintesi antropologico-tomasiana," in *San Tommaso d'Aquino Doctor humanitatis. Atti del IX Congresso Tomistico Internazionale,* vol. 1 (Vatican City, 1991), 333-45.

5. Cf. I. Biffi, *Tommaso d'Aquino. Il teologo. La teologia* (Milan, 1992); Biffi, *Teologia, storia e contemplazione in Tommaso d'Aquino* (Milan, 1995); O. H. Pesch, *Thomas von Aquin* (Mainz, 1988); J. P. Torrell, *Initiation à Saint Thomas d'Aquin* (Fribourg, 1993); J. A. Weisheipl, *Tommaso d'Aquino. Vita, pensiero, opere* (Milan, 1987).

6. Cf., for example, J. M. Petit Sulla, "La aportación tomista al concepto de naturaleza," in *Noetica, critica e metafisica in chiave tomistica. Atti del IX Congresso Tomistico Internazionale,* vol. 2 (Vatican City, 1991), 261-66. Regarding the question of the relationship between nature and supernature, cf. H. de Lubac, *Il mistero del soprannaturale. Opera omnia,* vol. 11 (Milan, 1978), 71-89 (*The Mystery of the Supernatural,* trans. Rosemary Sheed, introduction by David L. Schindler [New York: Crossroad, 1998]).

this sense, even in those places where our author considers the natural dynamisms proper to affection, which can be fundamentally distinguished into three factors (*passio, amor,* and *dilectio,* to which *caritas* must eventually be added), he never intends to describe an autonomous human being, severed from faith. In fact, the dynamisms in which man will progress in the overcoming of the passions, namely, the dynamism of the virtues (internal habits which modify the passions),[7] the gifts of the Holy Spirit (grace which modifies the structure of the subject),[8] and the law (the educational instrument for the modification of the passions),[9] are all always conceived of within the economy of salvation. The acting person Thomas takes into consideration is thus a person in whom the habits of nature (the natural moral virtues) and the habits derived from grace are considered to be at work simultaneously.

1. Affection as *Passio* (I-II, q. 22, aa. 1-3)

The first series of texts we will take into consideration can be found in question 22: *De subiecto passionum animae.* Already from the title, the question suggests two elements which merit attention. Firstly, Saint Thomas progressively widens his consideration from the soul to the subject. Secondly, even if the title speaks of the "passions of the soul," it is clear that in Aquinas's thought the passions do not inhere only in the soul. This is a symptom of a very modern attitude present in Thomas's thought. We must admit that a correct reading of the phenomenon of the unconscious as formulated in the contemporary age does not substantially threaten the rational psychology of our author; it does not bring it structurally into question.[10]

1.1. First Article: Utrum Aliqua Passio Sit in Anima

In this first article Thomas poses the question whether there are passions in the soul, and he gives the following response: "Respondeo dicendum quod pati dicitur tripliciter. Uno modo, communiter, secundum quod omne

7. Cf. Thomas Aquinas, *ST* I-II, qq. 55-67.
8. Cf. Thomas Aquinas, *ST* I-II, q. 68.
9. Cf. Thomas Aquinas, *ST* I-II, qq. 90-108.
10. Cf., for example, M. Binasco, "La tristezza: san Tommaso, Dante, Lacan," in *Documento di lavoro per il Congresso "Il rifiuto e la depressione. La tristezza tra clinica e forme del vivere"* (Naples, 1997), 56-66.

recipere est pati, etiam si nihil abiiciatur a re: sicut si dicatur aerem pati, quando illuminatur."[11] Here we find a first, completely generic idea of passion, according to which the word *passio* suggests only the idea of reception, and does not imply the elimination of anything by the subject. That is, it does not imply any modification of the subject.

"Alio modo dicitur pati proprie, quando aliquid recipitur cum alterius abiectione."[12] The adverb *proprie* reveals that the second manner of understanding passion refers to its more authentic sense. The verb *pati* is used, properly speaking, when something is received with the expulsion of something else. In its proper sense *pati* indicates an initiative which begins externally and which the subject receives but must, in order to receive it, eliminate something he already possesses. *Pati* is a *recipere* that implies an *abiicere*, a being touched that implies an *expellere*. Passion in its proper sense is not pure receptivity. As a side note, we observe that the category of *passio* is oftentimes not fully respected in common speech.

"Sed hoc contingit dupliciter. Quandoque enim abiicitur id quod non est conveniens rei: sicut cum corpus animalis sanatur, dicitur pati quia recipit sanitatem, aegritudine abiecta. Alio modo, quando e converso contingit: sicut aegrotare dicitur pati, quia recipitur infirmitas, sanitate abiecta. Et hic est propriissimus modus passionis. Nam pati dicitur ex eo quod aliquid trahitur ad agentem: quod autem recedit ab eo quod est sibi conveniens, maxime videtur ad aliud trahi. Et similiter in 1 De Generat. (c. 3, lect. 8) dicitur quod, quando ex ignobiliori generatur nobilius, est generatio simpliciter, et corruptio secundum quid: e converso autem, quando ex nobiliori ignobilius generatur."[13]

---

11. Thomas Aquinas, *ST* I-II, q. 22, a. 1: "Reply: The Latin verb *pati, to suffer* or *undergo* or *be acted upon,* is used in three ways. First, in a perfectly general sense, it is used whenever any quality is received, even if the recipient loses nothing in the process: for instance, one might say that the air 'suffers' or 'undergoes' illumination." (All English quotations from the *Summa Theologiae* are taken from the Blackfriars translation [Cambridge and New York: McGraw-Hill, 1964-].)

12. Thomas Aquinas, *ST* I-II, q. 22, a. 1: "More strictly, the word *pati* is used when a thing acquires one quality by losing another."

13. Thomas Aquinas, *ST* I-II, q. 22, a. 1: "And this may happen in two ways. Sometimes the quality lost is one whose presence was inappropriate in the subject: for example, when an animal is healed, it may be said to 'undergo' healing, for it recovers its health by shedding its illness. At other times, the opposite happens: for example, a sick man is called a 'patient' because he contracts some illness by losing his health. It is this last kind of case which is called *passio* in the most correct sense. For the word *pati* is used when a thing is drawn to some agent; and the more a thing is withdrawn from that which properly belongs to it, the more naturally is it said to be drawn to something other than itself. Aristotle makes a rather similar point: he says that when an entity of a higher order arises from one of a lower order, we call the process 'generation' pure and simple, and 'corruption' only in some qualified sense; and vice versa."

Sometimes what is eliminated is not fitting to the subject. At other times the opposite is true, and this is more proper to passion: something is eliminated which is fitting to the subject (for example, when one suffers an illness, health is expelled). Being forced to step back from what is fitting powerfully indicates that one is drawn by something else. If in fact the *ratio* of *pati* is this being attracted by the agent which provoked the "undergoing" or "suffering," this is all the more evident when one is drawn to something contrary to him. It is much more logical to say that someone "undergoes an illness" than that he "undergoes health" after having overcome the illness. Following the example of Aristotle, Saint Thomas calls more properly passion that sort of reception, with the modification of the subject, in which the agent draws the subject to itself in something not entirely *connatural* to that subject. Thus when passion arises, it always does so from the initiative of an external agent which the subject receives. The subject is then modified in the direction of the agent because he is attracted by it.

"Et his tribus modis contingit esse in anima passionem. Nam secundum receptionem tantum dicitur quod 'sentire et intelligere est quoddam pati' (cf. 1 De Anima, c. 5, lect. 12). Passio autem cum abiectione non est nisi secundum transmutationem corporalem: unde passio proprie dicta non potest competere animae nisi per accidens, inquantum scilicet compositum patitur."[14] According to the improper meaning of the term "passion," that is, when this latter is pure reception, one can for example say feeling and understanding are a certain type of *passio*. Here the great Thomistic principle is presupposed whereby there is no knowledge that does not come from reality, because the initial impetus of knowledge is a *pati*.[15] And the content of knowledge is in fact essence, that is, the *quidditas rei materialis*. Here we find ourselves in the face of the foundation of the classical understanding of feeling and knowledge, and thus in the face of what is at the basis of the principle by which, in the cognitive process, the intellect abstracts the *quidditas* from the material reality.

With regard to passion in the strict sense, this always implies an *abiectio*, a "throwing away": there is no passion without a bodily modification. This means that in a real experience of passion it is impossible for an external

14. Thomas Aquinas, *ST* I-II, q. 22, a. 1: "Now, *passio*, in each of these three senses, may be found in the soul. For first, the remark *thinking and understanding are in some sense passions* applies to that kind of passion which involves reception pure and simple. Those kinds of passion in which some quality is lost, however, always involve some bodily change; passion strictly so called cannot therefore be experienced by the soul except in the sense that the whole person, the matter-soul composite, undergoes it."

15. Cf. A. Contat, *Trois études sur la vérité selon saint Thomas d'Aquin* (Rome, 1994).

agent to modify only the soul: a modification of the body is always implied. Passion properly speaking touches the soul *per accidens;* what suffers or undergoes is always the composite subject. Here we see clearly how the development of thought surpasses the title of the article *(De subiecto passionum animae),* and how vigorously Thomas stresses that in speaking of passion, one involves the whole subject in its integrality.

Thomas proceeds by integrating the diversity of passions: "Sed et in hoc est diversitas: nam quando huiusmodi transmutatio fit in deterius, magis proprie habet rationem passionis, quam quando fit in melius. Unde tristitia magis proprie est passio quam laetitia."[16] The *ratio* of the passion is more present when the modification leads to a deterioration than when it leads to an improvement; we have said above that the force of the passive word *trahitur* is more evident when one is attracted by a force contrary to oneself, not fitting to the "I." This is why sadness is more properly considered a passion than is joy.

At the basis of this thought we find a conception of the subject which was lost in the interpretations of the great Thomistic commentators of the sixteenth century: the subject is structurally oriented to a good, to understanding and willing it. That which is *conveniens* to the subject, insofar as it is a good for him, is in some way connatural to that subject.[17] A thing is evil when, attracting the subject from another angle, it detaches the subject from that to which he is naturally inclined. These observations are of great importance for the Thomistic understanding of the will, which has nothing to do with the casuistic reduction of this category; this reduction began with modernity, and holds that the will is indifferent to good or evil.

According to Thomas, "suffering" or "undergoing" thus denotes both the greatness and the misery of the subject. It points to greatness because it shows the subject to be open, capable of welcoming, in a dynamic tension toward the all. But it also shows the subject's limitation because, despite the interaction implied by passion, the subject remains a permanent potentiality (capacity). "Suffering" or "undergoing" is thus the dynamism of interaction between the radical potentialities of being human and the factors that can fill these potentialities. In this way the individual passions are the actualization of the subject's potentiality, independently of whether the object of the passion is positive or negative and therefore actualizes a positive or negative potentiality in the subject. We draw attention once again to how Thomas's con-

---

16. Thomas Aquinas, *ST* I-II, q. 22, a. 1: "But here too we must distinguish: the bodily change may be for the better or for the worse; and it is in the latter case that the term *passion* is used more properly. Thus sorrow is more naturally called a passion than is joy."

17. Cf. Thomas Aquinas, *ST* III, q. 1, a. 1: "Respondeo dicendum quod unicuique rei conveniens est illud quod competit sibi secundum rationem propriae naturae."

ception implies the totality of the subject: it is not only the spiritual dimension which is at stake, but the totality of the "I." It is at stake precisely because passion, in its proper sense, does not refer only to the soul, but implies a *transmutatio corporis*, a modification of the whole "I."

1.2. Second Article: Utrum Passio Magis Sit in Parte Appetitiva quam in Apprehensiva

In this second article Saint Thomas asks whether passion is located more in the appetitive part (that is, in the capacity to will) than in the apprehensive part (the consciousness) of man. After having stated that the human subject is capable of passion, Thomas now seeks to identify the level of the human subject where passion begins its dynamism of an agent attracting the subject to itself. Where does this external agent touch man so as to spark *passio* in him? Does this involve more the volitive or the cognitive dimension?

"Respondeo dicendum quod, sicut iam (a. praeced.) dictum est, in nomine passionis importatur quod patiens trahatur ad id quod est agentis. Magis autem trahitur anima ad rem per vim appetitivam quam per vim apprehensivam. Nam per vim appetitivam anima habet ordinem ad ipsas res, prout in seipsis sunt: unde Philosophus dicit, in 6 Metaphys. (c. 4, lect. 4), quod 'bonum et malum,' quae sunt obiecta appetitivae potentiae, 'sunt in ipsis rebus.' Vis autem apprehensive non trahitur ad rem, secundum quod in seipsa est; sed cognoscit eam secundum intentionem rei, quam in se habet vel recipit secundum proprium modum. Unde et ibidem dicitur quod 'verum et falsum,' quae ad cognitionem pertinent, 'non sunt in rebus, sed in mente.'"[18]

Thomas affirms that the idea of passion entails that the *patiens* — the one experiencing the passion — is drawn toward the agent of the passion. The subject is, as we have seen, an interactive being. But in this movement the subject is attracted more by the force of appetite than of knowledge. Both appetite and knowledge are *virtutes* or faculties for Thomas, each with a specific capacity: through the appetite the subject is attracted to the real as it is in itself. Knowledge, on the other hand, knows reality through the power of *intentio*. What we

18. Thomas Aquinas, *ST* I-II, q. 22, a. 2: "Reply: The term 'passion' implies, as we have said, that the patient is drawn to something in the agent. But the soul is drawn to things by its oretic, rather than its cognitive faculties. For through its oretic faculties the soul is drawn to things as they are in themselves: as Aristotle says, good and bad (the objects of the oretic faculties) are in things themselves; it comes to know them by means of representations, which it either already has, or receives in the appropriate way: so Aristotle goes on to say, *true and false* (the objects of the cognitive powers) *are not things themselves, but in the mind.*"

have here is the theory of knowledge which belongs to Thomas and all of high Scholasticism:[19] knowledge comes about through *intentionality*. The word indicates that particular tension of the intellect toward the thing; this tension establishes a profound unity between the intellect and the essence of the thing such that it sparks the dynamism of knowledge. However, Thomas states that in the act of knowing (intentionality), the thing is not touched as it is in itself, outside the intellect, but is received by the intellect according to an abstraction, the proper modality by which the intellect can receive things into itself. Ideas are universal inasmuch as they are in the intellect, while reality is particular, inasmuch as it is outside the intellect. Thus, Aquinas appears to say that although there exists an undeniable apprehensive tension of knowledge toward the thing, the union obtained with the thing by virtue of knowledge is intentional. The intellect does not grasp the thing as it is in itself. It is therefore the idea of the thing that is in the intellect, and not the thing.[20]

The reason for passion is thus to be found more in the appetite, because here the attracting agent brings the subject really into contact with things as they are. We can say that the appetite implies a real interaction with things, whereas knowledge implies an intentional interaction.

A first nota bene. Saint Thomas chooses the expression *magis invenitur;* hence it cannot be affirmed that he holds passion to be a blind phenomenon that prescinds from knowledge. He merely says that in the dynamism of *passio,* the object touches the subject more on the level of the appetite than on the level of *apprehensio.* A similar vision, objectively open to the existence of the unconscious, has to do with a being's structural inclination to other beings, which is first manifested as attractiveness and then takes on the form of the free choice of good or evil. This is a profoundly unitary understanding, even if it involves a certain complexity which depends on the various levels of the appetite being interwoven with the levels of the understanding. It describes the nature of the human subject with extreme realism.

To conclude this article, we can ask ourselves: What factor leads Thomas to speak in this way about passion, in a certain sense inverting the Aristotelian tendency?[21] We must respond: it is the conviction that in original sin the will

19. Cf., for example, O. N. Derisi, "La aptitud de la mente humana para alcanzar el ser de las cosas, hasta el mismo *Esse subsistens,*" in *San Tommaso d'Aquino Doctor humanitatis,* 99-125; V. Possenti, "Intellectus e intuizione dell'essere," in *San Tommaso d'Aquino Doctor humanitatis,* 126-42.

20. In this sense truth can be defined as "adaequatio intellectus et rei": cf. Thomas Aquinas, *De veritate* q. 1, a. 1.

21. Thomas in fact inverts Aristotle's thesis (*Metaphysics* 1.2), which places *passio* more in the cognitive than in the appetitive (oretic) dimension.

was more damaged than the intellect, and that the *virtus appetitiva* is thus more fragile than the *virtus cognoscitiva.*

1.3. Third Article: Utrum Passio Sit Magis in Appetitu Sensitivo quam Intellectivo, Qui Dicitur Voluntas

The question which forms the title of the third article ("whether passion resides more in the sensitive appetite than in the intellective, called the will") allows Thomas to further specify the principle according to which a greater bodily modification indicates a greater passion, because it involves a greater passivity. This explains the reason why passion is stronger in the sensitive appetite than in the intellective (the will).

"Respondeo dicendum quod, sicut iam (a. 1) dictum est, passio proprie invenitur ubi est transmutatio corporalis. Quae quidem invenitur in actibus appetitus sensitivi; et non solum spiritualis, sicut est in apprehensione sensitiva, sed etiam naturalis."[22]

According to Thomas's conception, *passio* exists in its proper sense when there is a bodily modification: in the acts of the sensitive appetite. He makes the distinction, "et non solum spiritualis . . . sed etiam naturalis." In the structure of the appetite in the human subject, there exist acts of the sensitive appetite which imply a bodily modification. The sensitive appetite thus reveals itself to be, even in man, structurally connected to the natural appetite, whose characteristic is that *amor naturalis* which Thomas attributes to all creatures. Here we find an extremely articulated and complex understanding of the appetite in the human subject.

It is important not to lose sight of the unity of the subject, in whom the various levels of the appetitive and cognoscitive dynamisms find their unification. Thus, for example, it is true that man's animal nature conditions his spiritual nature. However, since it is the spiritual nature which is dominant in man, even the purely sensitive or natural acts of the appetitive dimension that are proper to animals are shot through with this spirituality. In modern, non-Thomistic terminology, we can say that the modality with which the spirit makes its demands felt on the animal or sensitive appetite is the "psyche."

---

22. Thomas Aquinas, *ST* I-II, q. 22, a. 3: "Reply: We have remarked that emotion always involves some physiological modification. Such a modification occurs in the functioning of the sensory orexis; and it is not the mere reception of a representation, the non-physical alteration which we have seen to be involved in sense-perception; it is a physical one." The pair "nonphysical"-"physical" does not seem to completely convey the Latin *spiritualis-naturalis.*

This latter immediately begins the work of spiritualization, in a certain sense, of the animal root of the appetite.

"In actu autem appetitus intellectivi non requiritur aliqua transmutatio corporalis: quia huiusmodi appetitus non est virtus alicuius organi. Unde patet quod ratio passionis magis proprie invenitur in actu appetitus sensitivi quam intellectivi; ut enim patet per definitiones Damasceni inductas."[23] This is the technical and complete answer to the preceding question: What does the modification of the body mean? Thomas says no modification of the body is required in the act of the intellective appetite, since this appetite is not the potency of some organ. While the sensible appetite is a potency of sensory organs, the intellect in fact has no organs through which it knows. Hence it involves no modification of the body.

For this reason we can conclude with Thomas that passion is stronger in the sensitive appetite than in the intellective, because the first involves the perception of organs to which correspond the *virtutes* (faculties) in the sensibility. The intelligence, on the other hand, lacks these organs.

2. Toward a Definition of Affection

In conclusion, we will attempt to reflect on the dynamism of affection from the data accumulated so far, bringing this data into dialogue with our sensibility and cultural formation. We will thus in some way broaden our reading of Thomas.

A first important affirmation: affectivity is a *passio*. It is not simply a generic modification provoked by attachment to something, but more properly a passion. We have learned from Thomas that in the human subject the structure of undergoing a passion is threefold. First there is an "undergoing" or "suffering" *(patire)* which qualifies the human potentiality in all its breadth (in this sense one even "undergoes" knowledge). Already and above all on this first level, we see both the indestructible originality of the human subject and its nature of being permanently in need of a fulfillment. The second level of *patire* is a manner of reacting proper to the appetite as such. Lastly, we can say that the level of *patire* that involves the body is the most intense, because it implies a bodily modification. The more intense the

---

23. Thomas Aquinas, *ST* I-II, q. 22, a. 3: "Nothing physical, however, is involved in the functioning of the intellectual orexis, which is not the faculty of a bodily organ. The emotions therefore belong rather to the functioning of the sensory orexis than to that of the intellectual: as the quotations from the Damascene suggest." ("Orexis" is the rendering, in the Blackfriars translation of the *Summa*, of the Latin *appetitus*.)

bodily modification, the more we are dealing with a passion. However, all three levels must be maintained.

We may ask ourselves at this point, with what kind of *passio* does affection come into play? The adequate level of affectivity lies on the second level indicated by Thomas: the manner of reacting proper to the appetite as such. This will become more understandable shortly, when we speak of *amor* as *passio;* the connection between affection and love will be clarified. Affectivity is thus a passion precisely because it involves the appetite.

When we are dealing with man *(corpore et anima unus)*, this level obviously exists in a continual relation with the other two. A connection in fact exists between this *passio* and the first level indicated above. Put simply, there is a connection between affection and knowledge, the two modes of the subject's *reaction*. They are inseparable from one another because knowledge, in a certain sense, generates affection. Without the perception of the object there can be no awakening of affection. Conversely, it is clear that affection in some way colors knowledge, granting it a thickness, a density it would not otherwise have. Thomas's theory of the threefold appetite (natural, sensitive, intellective) shows fairly well how knowledge interacts with the appetite already from the second level (here one ought to begin a discussion of knowledge by connaturality). On the other hand, all his discussion of the *conceptio naturalis* demonstrates the importance of the natural appetite in the dimension of knowledge.

The link with the third level, that of bodily modification, identifies the psycho-organic aspect which provides the substratum for affection in the proper sense. Saint Thomas clearly sees that affection, as the human appetite's capacity to react to every being insofar as it is desirable, possesses an inexorable tendency upward, toward knowledge, and an inexorable tendency downward, toward that place where nature leaves its mark on affection as such. Thus the sensible and spiritual appetites, to which affectivity in its proper sense is connected, are rooted in the psycho-organic substratum of the subject, through the sphere of the sensible. It is precisely this observation which prompts Thomas to speak of an ambivalence of affective movements (positive or negative).

While the tension toward the higher, cognoscitive-spiritual level allows for the purification of affection *(passio)*, its rootedness in the inferior and psycho-organic level more properly explains the polymorphic nature of *passio*. Passion is ambivalent, full of unpredictability, revealing in an unsettling quickness of succession a face that is either benevolent or destructive. The phenomenon of affection is thus sketched in all its breadth and possibilities.

What we have said thus far allows us to formulate a theological doctrine of the value of affection, which, along with sexuality and love properly so called, identifies the constitutive dynamisms of the whole phenomenon of love. By taking account of the modifications produced in the subject who is capable of affection, we will be able to address adequately the related ethical and ascetical issues. Affectivity is a decidedly complex experience which touches the subject at various levels, because it implies a fundamental tendency flowing from the subject's very nature; it implies instinctive forces and an élan of the spirit that becomes capable of orienting them. Lastly, it implies the production of acts and operations following upon the *passio* described. Above all, affectivity appears as a singular meeting point between the interior and exterior universes of man.

3. Affection as *Amor* (I-II, q. 26, aa. 1-2)

In an attempt to further clarify the general definition of affection as *passio* — as the subject's ability to react, through the appetite, to the provocation of a desirable object — we can take a step further and affirm that affection is that particular type of *passio* called *amor*. Thomas treats this explicitly in question 26: "De passionibus animae in speciali. Et primo, de amore."

3.1. A First Approximation of Love:
Utrum Amor Sit in Concupiscibili

The question Thomas poses in this first article (whether love is found in the concupiscible or irascible parts of the subject) does not directly interest us. More pertinent are the various elements he distinguishes in his analysis of the nature of love, in order to respond to the central question. He begins with an analysis, in a certain sense, of the phenomenon of love.

"Respondeo dicendum quod amor est aliquid ad appetitum pertinens: cum utriusque obiectum sit bonum. Unde secundum differentiam appetitus, est differentia amoris. Est enim quidam appetitus non consequens apprehensionem ipsius appetentis, sed alterius: et huiusmodi dicitur appetitus naturalis. Res enim naturales appetunt quod eis convenit secundum suam naturam, non per apprehensionem propriam, sed per apprehensionem instituentis naturam, ut in I libro (q. 6, a. 1, ad 2; q. 103, a. 1, ad 1, 3) dicitum est. — Alius autem est appetitus consequens apprehensionem ipsius appetentis, sed ex necessitate, non ex iudicio libero. Et talis est appetitus sensitivus in brutis: qui tamen in hominibus aliquid libertatis participat, inquantam obedit rationi. — Alius autem est appetitus consequens apprehensionem appetentis secundum liberum iudicium. Et talis est appetitus rationalis sive intellectivus, qui dicitur voluntas. In unoquoque autem horum appetituum, amor dicitur illud quod est principium motus tendentis in finem amatum. In appetitu autem naturali, principium huiusmodi motus est connaturalitas corporis gravis ad locum medium est per gravitatem, et potest dici amor naturalis. Et similiter coaptatio appetitus sensitivi, vel voluntatis, ad aliquod bonum, idest ipsa complacentia boni, dicitur amor sensitivus, vel intellectivus seu rationalis. Amor igitur sensitivus est in appetitu sensitivo, sicut amor intellectivus in appetitu intellectivo. Et pertinet ad concupiscibilem: quia dicitur per respectum ad bonum absolute, non per respectum ad arduum, quod est obiectum irascibilis."[24]

The object of love coincides with that of the appetite: it is a good. For this reason it is possible, in analyzing the various forms of the appetite, to identify the various forms of love.

A certain kind of appetite, which Thomas calls "natural appetite," is not derived from the subject's knowledge. In the human subject there are drives, tensions, desires, and inclinations which have their origin not in the subject's knowledge of something desirable, but from nature, from the subject's own constitution and by virtue of him who created nature. This is the famous *apprehensio alterius*. At this level the will and therefore morality are not yet at

---

24. Thomas Aquinas, *ST* I-II, q. 26, a. 1: "Reply: Love is essentially connected with the orexis, since they have the same object, viz., the good. There will therefore be as many kinds of love as there are kinds of orexis and wanting. Now one sort of orexis follows, not knowledge possessed by the subject, but knowledge possessed by someone else; this is called 'natural orexis.' For an inanimate entity 'wants' the things that accord with its nature, not through its own knowledge of them, but through that possessed by the Author of its nature: as we have shown. A second sort of orexis does indeed follow knowledge possessed by its own subject, but as a matter of necessity, not from free choice. The sensory orexis in dumb animals is like this; in men, however, there is something of freedom about it, to the extent namely that it is subject to rational control. Third, there is the orexis which arises both through consciousness and by free choice. These are the features of the rational or intellectual orexis, commonly called 'the will.' Now, in each of these cases, 'love' denotes that which produces the inclination to move towards the end in question. In the case of the natural orexis, this cause, which might be called 'natural love' is a sense of affinity with the object in question; thus a heavy body's sense of affinity with its natural place arises from its weight, and might be called 'natural love.' Similarly the terms 'sensory love' and 'intellectual or rational love' apply to the attachment, the sense of affinity with some good, the feeling of its attractiveness, felt respectively by the sensory orexis or the will: i.e. sensory love is seated in the sensory orexis, as intellectual love is seated in the will. More specifically, sensory love is seated in the affective faculty, for its object is sense-good sans plus: not sense-good difficult of attainment, which is the object of the spirited orexis." ("Spirited orexis" is the Blackfriars rendering of what we have called the "irascible appetite.")

play. A second kind of appetite follows the knowledge of the subject, but follows it necessarily and not by virtue of a free judgment. This is the "sensitive appetite," proper to animals. It involves tendencies sparked when a desirable object provokes the subject, but the tendencies are sparked out of necessity and without free judgment. As we have said, this appetite is proper to animals, and man participates in it inasmuch as he is an animal; in man, however, there is always a minimum of freedom, because in him the sensitive appetite obeys the reason. Thus the will enters into play, even if in a second instance. A third type of appetite follows the subject's apprehension, by virtue of his free judgment. This is the rational or intellective appetite, normally called the will.

Now that the phenomenology of the appetite has been roughly outlined, we can bring it to the level of *amor.* To do this we must begin with a general definition of love: love is that which constitutes the principle of movement tending toward a beloved end. There are three kinds of love, corresponding to the three kinds of appetite. The first level, which we can call *amor naturalis,* hinges on the idea of connaturality, that is, a likeness, a participation of nature between the subject with the appetite and that to which his appetite tends, what he wants or desires. Connaturality thus inevitably triggers *amor naturalis* before any attainment of knowledge or any choice by the subject. It is precisely a natural appetite. The second and third levels, of sensitive love and intellective love respectively, have in common an element of choice *(coaptatio)* through which the appetite adapts to a good, orienting itself to some good. Insofar as it is thus oriented, the appetite is normally called *complacentia* of the good. Saint Thomas remains on general terms when speaking of sensitive love because this is triggered *ex necessitate.* There is an aspect always present in it which we can call instinctive reaction, independent of freedom; this is so even if, in the human subject, a certain *aliquid* of freedom flourishes even on this level, because every appetite is dominated and governed by reason. Moreover, this *coaptatio* can become a real free choice in the case of intellective love. In brief, the three levels of love are: *amor naturalis,* characterized by connaturality; *amor sensitivus,* which implies a *complacentia boni;* and *amor intellectivus* or will, in which *coaptatio* becomes a choice.

A note on *amor naturalis:* this love is ultimately directed toward God, who creates nature, binds all things in some way to himself, and continues to attract them by virtue of a natural movement. The movement of natural love is originally impressed by the Creator. The creative act thus establishes a permanent relation of all things to God which cannot be understood only in the form of an extrinsic causality; it must be seen also under the form of an attraction implying a natural movement toward God. We can say that *amor naturalis* is the movement of return to God contained in every thing and every reality, in such a manner that it can neither be forced nor destroyed. It is, in a certain sense, something that precedes a given act of love, but is simultaneously the principle of every possible act of love. It is the indestructible and unstoppable yearning toward God which is triggered every time a desirable object, characterized in its turn by the same movement, resonates with the subject. This yearning can never stop at the particular good, since each time it is spurred once again into movement toward the Ultimate Good. In this sense *amor naturalis* is the relationship of every creature with its Creator,[25] and is present in man just as in every other creature. From this we draw an important conclusion: man is first nature before he is freedom.[26] This means that even in the human subject there is an original yearning, a movement of *amor naturalis* toward his Creator and Maker which is not subject to his freedom. Or better, the existence of this movement is given to freedom through nature. Freedom can consent to it or not, but cannot eliminate it. Human will, as *appetitus intellectivus,* finds within itself this inclination toward the Supreme good; it is not "neutral" or indifferent to good and evil. Moreover, it is in motion because the human subject is naturally oriented, inclined, desiring. Thus every act of love that the will succeeds in expressing — from the level of emotion *(amor sensitivus)* to that of *amor intellectivus* — always implies this participation in *amor naturalis* toward God. In the human subject there is no act of love possible outside this implication. One loves every object of love because one loves God. In this radical movement of *amor naturalis* in man there is not yet morality or freedom. But it is the foundation of every freedom and every morality.

3.2. The "Circularity" of Love: Utrum Amor Sit Passio

For a further investigation of the reality of love, we will take up the response offered by Saint Thomas in article 2 of question 26: "Whether love is a passion."

25. We find in this thesis of *amor naturalis* something of great importance, linked to other great classical scholastic themes regarding the definition of being. For example, this conception of *amor naturalis* is certainly a reflection of the definition of being in terms of participation in it, *Ipsum Esse Subsistens* — that is, in that being which subsists in itself, in which essence and existence coincide, or God. Thus the definition of being in terms of participation, according to the great idea that each creature, not *is* being, but *receives* being through participation, finds a very important correspondence here on the existential plane of the appetite; cf. L. B. Geiger, *La participation dans la philosophie de S. Thomas d'Aquin* (Paris, 1942), 496.

26. Cf. J. Mouroux, *L'esperienza cristiana* (Brescia, 1956), 228-64, especially 233.

"Respondeo dicendum quod passio est effectus agentis in patiente. Agens autem naturale duplicem effectum inducit in patiens: nam primo quidem dat formam, secundo autem dat motum consequentem formam; sicut generans dat corpori gravitatem, et motum consequentem ipsam. Et ipsa gravitas, quae est principium motus ad locum connaturalem propter gravitatem, potest quodammodo dici amor naturalis. Sic etiam ipsum appetibile dat appetitui, primo quidem, quondam coaptationem ad ipsum, quae est complacentia appetibilis; ex qua sequitur motus ad appetibile. Nam 'appetitivus motus circulo agitur,' ut dicitur in 3 De Anima (c. 10, lect. 15): appetibile enim movet appetitum, faciens se quodammodo in eius intentione; et appetitus tendit in appetibile realiter consequendum, ut sit ibi finis motus, ubi fuit principium. Prima ergo immutatio appetitus ab appetibili vocatur amor, qui nihil est aliud quam complacentia appetibilis; et ex hac complacentia sequitur motus in appetibile, qui est desiderium; et ultimo quies, quae est gaudium. Sic ergo, cum amor consistat in quadam immutatione appetitus ab appetibili, manifestum est quod amor est passio: proprie quidem, secundum quod est in concupiscibili; communiter autem, et extenso nomine, secundum quod est in voluntate."[27]

Passion is the effect of an agent on the patient; if there is no agent, there is no passion. Since love consists in a certain modification of the appetite by an agent, it is evident that love, as the external provocation of the subject, is a passion. The natural agent produces a twofold effect in the patient.[28] It con-

---

27. Thomas Aquinas, *ST* I-II, q. 26, a. 2: "Reply: The term 'passion' denotes the effect produced in a thing when it is acted upon by some agent. Now where natural agencies are in question, the effect is two-fold: first a form is produced, then a movement arising from that form: for instance, that which brings a body into existence gives it both weight, and the movement that results from weight. Since the weight is the cause of the body's moving towards its natural place it may be called a 'natural love.' Correspondingly, the effect produced in the orexis by a desirable object is a sense of affinity with it, a feeling of its attractiveness; then this gives rise to a movement of the orexis towards the object. For there is a certain circularity in the oretic process, as Aristotle remarks: first the object works on the orexis, imprinting itself there, as one might say; then the orexis moves towards the object, with the purpose of actually possessing it; so the process ends where it began. The first effect produced in the orexis by this object is called *love*, which is simply a feeling of the object's attractiveness; this feeling gives rise to an oretic movement towards the object, viz., *desire;* and finally this comes to rest in *joy.*"

28. It is important to stress that in Thomas the use of the word "natural" has various levels of possible meanings, when it is used to describe the elementary phenomenon of reality. As we have already had occasion to note, one must certainly not collapse the Thomistic idea of nature into the Aristotelian idea of *physis*. To avoid this error without giving the word "nature" a univocal meaning, one must always relate it to "creatural." For Thomas nature is the given, and the given is the creature who is to be contemplated not only statically, with regard to being, but also dynamically, with regard to action.

fers a form on the patient and impresses the corresponding movement in him. The desirable object first grants the patient's appetite an adjustment to itself *(coaptatio)*; the object requires this because it makes the patient feel that it corresponds to him, that it is fitting to him. This adaptation is a *complacentia* (it is not by chance that the word for pleasure, *placentia,* is included in this term). From this *complacentia* arises love, the movement toward the desired object. The appetitive movement is circular: the desirable object moves the appetite, making the latter in a certain sense intentional to itself. Thus the first change of the appetite provoked by the desirable object is *amor,* which, as we have seen, is *complacentia* in the desirable object. Once the appetite finds complacency in the desired object, a movement arises which is directed toward this object: desire. This movement reaches rest when the appetite is able to enjoy the thing desired. Here we find the third element: joy. This is the terminus of the circular movement of love, which is prompted by the desired object and ends by reaching it once again.

In Saint Thomas's response we find three elements which allow us to grasp the essential texture of the dynamism of affection. This dynamism begins and ends in the desired object. There is a first moment in which the appetite is provoked by this object. Hence, affection has the nature of passion *(immutatio)*. From this provocation arises a movement *(coaptatio)*. We can thus sketch a first and general outline of the dynamism of affection. *Amor* arises, which is *complacentia appetibilis,* a *cum-placere* or union, an involvement founded on a certain type of pleasure which triggers attraction. This is desire. Desire in turn provokes a positive search for the beloved object *(intentio):* an *intentio* of the appetite which, unlike intellective intention, brings man into direct contact with the real by modifying the appetite. This movement does not end until it reaches the desired object, where it began. The movement ends when there is in some way *gaudium,* the enjoyment of the desired object.

The Theological Principle of Human Procreation

1. The Originality of Human Procreation

"By comparison with the transmission of other forms of life in the universe, the transmission of human life has a special character of its own, which derives from the special nature of the human person."[1] This affirmation of the Instruction of the Congregation for the Doctrine of the Faith on "the respect for human life and the dignity of procreation" is of capital importance for the anthropological vision which lies at the basis of the magisterium's ethical directives.

It is in fact only through an adequate understanding of the originality of the transmission of human life that we can comprehend the foundations of the twofold affirmation contained in number II:4 of the Instruction. The text demonstrates the intrinsic nature of the moral tie between procreation and the conjugal act, and refers to two principles that can be called in a certain sense the cornerstone of the whole document. They are as follows: (1) from the moral point of view, procreation is deprived of its proper perfection when it is not willed as the fruit of the conjugal act, and thus of the spouses' specific gesture of union; (2) the moral relevance of the tie existing between the meanings of the conjugal act and the goods of marriage, the unity of the human being, and the dignity of his origin demand that the procreation of a human being must be pursued as the fruit of a specific conjugal act of love between spouses.

This twofold principle, taken up practically to the letter by the Instruc-

---

1. Congregation for the Doctrine of the Faith, Instruction *Donum Vitae*, intro. 4.

This appendix is a commentary on *Donum Vitae*. It is directly related to chapter 6, "The Nuptial Mystery and Fruitfulness."

tion, already opens the way to a reflection on the proper nature of the origi-nality of the transmission of human life. For the Instruction this originality appears to consist in the fact that human life is the fruit of the conjugal act, understood as a specific gesture of the union of the spouses. In this affirma-tion the identity of man in his unified totality is at stake.[2]

The conjugal act consists in the union of bodies which expresses or *signi-fies* the union of the persons. Precisely as the union of sexual bodies, this union is a union of persons, because of the sacramental meaning of the body. The expression is taken from the famous catecheses of John Paul II on the theology of the body: "The body, and only the body, is capable of making vis-ible that which is invisible."[3] In the language of the human body, in which the conjugal act is a fundamental *word*, the totality of the person is expressed be-cause the transcendence of the human person is written in his very body. Hence the union of bodies is a sign (sacrament) of the *communio personarum*, or the union of persons of the man and the woman. We will now look more closely at this vision of things.

A first foray into the theme requires an observation regarding the term "originality," which the Instruction uses to qualify the transmission of human life. The term inserts an analogical structure into the phenomenon of procre-ation among living beings, taken in a general sense. Among the higher spe-cies, and in particular the primates, to which man belongs, procreation comes about through the sexual conjunction of male and female. As the document's choice of terminology indicates, however, this conjunction takes on a qualita-tively different meaning in the case of man, even with respect to primates. The Catholic tradition, converging in recent papal teachings (from *Casti Conubii* to *Familiaris Consortio*) and also present in *Donum Vitae,* has consid-ered this qualitative difference to be established by consciousness, of which every other animal is structurally deprived. Man accomplishes the sexual act as a voluntary and therefore conscious act, and at the same time possesses the consciousness of the act he is accomplishing.[4] This fully corresponds to the scholastic principle by which man accomplishes all his acts, even those which proceed from the natural and sensitive appetites he has in common with the animals, according to the specific form of his nature, which is that of a ratio-nal being. Thus, for example, though the appetites of hunger and thirst, with their consequent inclinations to food and drink, are common both to men

2. Cf. *Gaudium et Spes* 14; *Familiaris Consortio* 11.

3. John Paul II, *The Theology of the Body: Human Love in the Divine Plan* (Boston: Daugh-ters of St. Paul, 1997), 78.

4. Cf. K. Wojtyla, *The Acting Person*, trans. Andrzej Potocki (Dordrecht, Boston, and Lon-don: D. Reidel, 1979), 25-59.

and animals, they are satisfied in man ultimately through reason and will, understood as rational appetites which cultivate the appetites and the natural and sensitive inclinations.

However, the Instruction *Donum Vitae* spurs us higher still in seeking this specific, qualitative difference of human procreation, in an even more profound direction. The document identifies this difference as a quality ontologically inherent to the conjugal act of the bodily union of the spouses. But this act of bodily union depends on man's sexual nature. This leads our investigation in the direction of the meaning of human sexuality understood precisely as the foundation of this specific union of the spouses. Human sexuality is ontologically oriented to the union of bodies, which is the sign of the communion of the persons. The originality of human procreation thus appears to be a consequence of the originality of human sexuality. We will set off in search of that originality, or rather, of the qualitative difference between human and animal sexuality.

2. The Specificity of Human Sexuality

The first account of creation contained in the book of Genesis (1:1–2:4a) is characterized by an ascending narrative structure because it describes an ascending perspective. It shows beings coming into existence in an order of increasing dignity, through the creative call of God. When man appears, the narrative introduces the idea of the image of God, taken up incessantly by the Catholic tradition. Man, and gendered man, is created in the image of God:[5] "in the image of God he created him, male and female he created them" (Gen. 1:27b). Sexuality reveals itself to be an original characteristic of the human creature, contrary to every temptation to attribute its genesis to original sin; this is also suggested by all the factors that constitute man.

Such a vision of things establishes a radical difference between man and the other animals, between human and animal sexuality. Human sexuality is not in fact relegated to the intracosmic, to the level of every other animal sexuality, but possesses a very different destiny! This thesis prompts a question. What does it mean that sexuality belongs to man's being in the image of God, and especially, how can this fact be theologically identified? The path we must take in order to respond to both questions has already been marked out. It involves further investigation of the relation between creature and Creator, in the light of the ancient doctrine of the *imago Dei*.

5. Cf. above, pp. 32-45.

We know that creation comes from the trinitarian God. In creating, the triune God impresses a trinitarian ontology in creation, which can be discerned on every level of creaturely existence. This is particularly true in man, created *ad imaginem Trinitatis* according to the paradigm of the perfect Image who is Jesus Christ. Such an eminently triune or triadic ontological structure shows that the Trinity is the profound and definitive consistency of being. Trinitarian ontology is not opposed to a Greek-inspired ontology of being, just as trinitarian logic is not opposed to the dual logic of an Aristotelian stamp. The first does, however, represent the latter's necessary and complete transformation.[6]

There are not many Christian philosophers and theologians who have attempted a thorough study of a trinitarian ontology and logic, both of which find so many points of support in the patristic, Scholastic, and particularly the great mystical traditions. Among those who have, we must mention the names of Balthasar and Hemmerle in theology, and Siewerth and Kaliba in philosophy. From the point of view of the content or the ultimate qualifications of such an ontology and logic, all these figures concentrate on the idea of love and its fruitfulness. This idea is, however, connected to fundamental ontological implications.

We will not carry out a full investigation of the content of such studies here, though they would be pertinent to the problem at hand (sexuality and procreation). For our limited scope, it is enough to ask ourselves whether and how to discern the triadic structure, the expression of trinitarian ontology, in man, and in man as sexually differentiated. If one speaks of trinitarian ontology, such a triadic structure must involve the whole of man (a unified totality), in all his constitutive spiritual and corporal dimensions. It must, therefore, also concern the body and sexuality in the body.

The question arises: How does this triadic structure of trinitarian ontology reveal itself in human sexuality? And most of all, what value does it have for man? To answer we must further investigate the meaning of sexuality. The existence of sexuality generates a constitutive original reciprocity between

---

6. We find a significant confirmation of this in the solutions Balthasar proposes in the area of trinitarian ontology to the problem of the *reflexio completa* in finite being: the latter becomes a "letting be of every co-being." This is shown to be the fruit of the trinitarian image, since in God each person is himself only insofar as he lets and makes others be in their own concrete essentiality, and in an infinite affirmation both of self-being and of co-being. In a second instance, this trinitarian ontology sheds new light on the great metaphysical problem of the real distinction of being. We will not in this place enter into Balthasar's solution to such a difficult problem (cf. H. U. von Balthasar, *Theo-Drama V: The Last Act*, trans. Graham Harrison [San Francisco: Ignatius, 1998], 61-98).

man and woman. This sexual reciprocity demonstrates that from the beginning the mystery of man is safeguarded with the image correlative to him who is the woman, and vice versa. The second account of creation highlights this being made for one another: "This at last is bone of my bones and flesh of my flesh" (Gen. 2:23). And yet man can exert no mastery over woman, as he is called to do with respect to the other animals. Although the two are made for one another because of their sexuality, they are exposed to a permanent and irreducible difference. Sexual difference thus emerges as a fact that cannot be eliminated, and it constitutes man as a dual reality within a single human nature. Contrary to Aristophanes' fantastic thesis in Plato's *Symposium,* no sexual union can eliminate, in an impossible and definitive androgyny, that radical difference which is the difference of the sexes.

Doubtless the asymmetrical structure of sexual reciprocity is one of the signs of creaturely contingence, but for the moment we wish to highlight another aspect, more pertinent to the theme at hand. The reason why sexual union cannot eliminate the difference between man and woman is that it is metaphysically open to the generation of another human being. It is the inherent destination of sexuality to procreation that reveals the full meaning of sexual difference and fully demonstrates the great dignity of human sexuality. Sexuality is a constitutive dimension of the human person's being in the image of the Trinity, and is therefore an expression of trinitarian ontology. In fact, by virtue of the *imago* the fruitfulness of human sexuality is linked, mysteriously but not accidentally, to the fruitfulness of the trinitarian life. Thus a trinity of being which reveals the ontological meaning of sexuality and procreation corresponds, even if within an abysmal dissimilarity, to the Trinity with a capital *T:* "Procreation is the proper end of the sexual urge which — as was said before — simultaneously furnishes material for love between persons, male and female."[7] In creating the human person in its image, the Trinity impresses even in his most elementary biological-instinctual dynamisms and the most hidden recesses of his natural affectivity, an ascending movement which opens him to his transcendent nature.

This ascending movement reveals that sexual union between man and woman is ontologically open to creation, because it is ordered through the union of bodies to the communion of persons. Through the union of bodies, sexual union thus becomes the principle of the *communio personarum* between man and woman. We can perhaps begin to see how the originality of the transmission of human life is connected to the originality of human sexu-

---

7. K. Wojtyla, *Love and Responsibility,* trans. H. T. Willetts (San Francisco: Ignatius, 1993), 55.

ality. This latter consists in the union of human bodies as the sign of the union of persons, with a view to the ontological scope of the union: procreation. The trinitarian structure of sexuality remains veiled even as it is ontologically clear, because it is inserted, as is every aspect of human nature, into the dimension of time. Creatureliness extends in time the appearance of the natural "trinity" of father-mother-child, in the specific union of bodies as a sacrament of the *communio personarum*.

From all that has been said thus far it is clear, first of all, that in the exercise of his sexuality the human person cannot prescind from this structural openness to procreation, lest he close himself to the creative initiative of God who impresses a seal of trinitarian fecundity in his heart.

We understand, too, that the child, the third subject of the triad, enjoys from the beginning the full dignity that flows from taking part in the *imago*. From the union between man and woman is born another human being, "this man" or "this woman," who must be respected as a person from the moment of conception.[8] The child is not simply another exemplar of the human species, as it would be if human sexuality were wholly identical to animal sexuality.

"I have gotten a man with the help of the Lord" (Gen. 4:1), says Eve after giving birth to Cain. This sentence contains the mystery of life in its coming to be, which essentially implies the specific act of conjugal love that is by its nature open to procreation. In this way the spouses cooperate with the creative action of God.[9]

We thus return to the twofold principle of *Donum Vitae* with which we began. The search for the theological meaning of human procreation has led us to the true meaning of human sexuality in its specific originality: the fruitful communion between man and woman through the union of sexually differentiated bodies. In its deepest essence this union is not only a bodily union between man and woman. It is — ontologically and inseparably — the union between a man and a woman open to the generation of another human being. Fatherhood-motherhood-childhood: this is the trinitarian form of man's being created in the image of the triune God. It is the meaning of his sexual originality, which also depends on the *imago Trinitatis*. In this originality is inscribed an orientation to the union of bodies as a sign of the communion of persons, inseparably connected with the capacity for procreation. For this reason the transmission of human life possesses a peculiar originality which clearly distinguishes it from the transmission of life in other living beings.

8. Cf. *Donum Vitae* 1:1.
9. Cf. *Donum Vitae* 2:4.

The Formation of Priests in the Pastoral Care of the Family

1. An Essential Dimension of the New Evangelization

There is no historical epoch whose salient characteristics cannot be interpreted by a glance at how it regards marriage and the family. Upon close examination, marriage and the family are not one aspect or sector of life, but an essential dimension without which it is impossible to understand man as an individual (identity) and personal being (relation). The whole of anthropology, then, is at stake in the understanding and experience of marriage and the family.

This objective fact becomes even more critical in light of how our Western societies look upon marriage and the family. We can list here only some characteristic traits that reveal the radical, critical change that is under way. While the "traditional" conception of the family (life together between man and woman that cannot not entertain, even if only to exclude, the question of children) is to a certain extent still present in the collective imagination, the couple as such finds itself in the midst of a serious crisis (common law unions, homosexual unions, etc.). This crisis is in its turn due to a weakening of freedom and is tied to the absence of paternity (maternity). These phenomena are interdependent and rest upon a widespread mentality that no longer acknowledges marriage as the root of the family or the family as the fundamental cell of society.

The tireless teaching of John Paul II's pontificate[1] has returned again and

---

1. All of John Paul II's interventions on matrimony and the family up until December 30, 1988, can be found in A. Sarmiento and J. Escriva, eds., *Enchiridion Familiae* (Madrid, 1992). Af-

again in a prophetic and, with respect to his predecessors, rather original way[2] to the importance of marriage and family for society and for the church. There is a constant reference in the pope's teaching to marriage and the family as essential dimensions of the new evangelization: "The family is at the center of the Church's mission and of its solicitude for mankind."[3] The Holy Father translates this awareness into a continuous appeal to all the faithful, and therefore also to priests, to maintain a very special concern for families. In this sense *Familiaris Consortio* states: "Their responsibility extends not only to moral and liturgical matters but to personal and social matters as well. They must support the family in its difficulties and sufferings, caring for its members and helping them to see their lives in the light of the Gospel. It is not superfluous to note that from this mission, if it is exercised with due discernment and with a truly apostolic spirit, the minister of the Church draws fresh encouragement and spiritual energy for his own vocation too and for the exercise of his ministry."[4] Nevertheless, this special concern is not something the priest can improvise. It is a dimension that has to be present at the origin of his formation. After all, the reality of marriage and the family occupies a fundamentally important place both in the personal configuration of his priesthood and in the necessary preparation for his future ministry.

It is precisely to this end that the Congregation for Catholic Education has directed its efforts in producing the document entitled *Directives on the Formation of Seminarians concerning Problems Related to Marriage and the Family*, of March 19, 1995. This document is an organic attempt to give effective expression, at the level of methodology, to the central idea of the pope's teaching: marriage and family are a dimension, not an aspect, of the new evangelization.

The document has the considerable merit of beginning with a synthetic but precise overview of the state of formation on marriage and the family. In

---

ter that date it is necessary to refer at least to the following documents: *Letter to Families* (February 2, 1994), *Evangelium Vitae* (March 25, 1995), *Letter to Women* (June 29, 1995).

2. The importance of this question was already seen by the council fathers. Both the decree *Optatam Totius*, whose fundamental principles govern all seminaries and theological studies up to our day, as well as numbers 47-52 of the constitution *Gaudium et Spes* have constituted an authoritative impulse for both theological reflection and the disciplinary practice of the particular churches. A number of magisterial documents follow the conciliar texts. They have taken up the tradition once again and form the immediate precedent for the teaching of the present pontificate. For a useful consultation of all the documents, see Sarmiento and Escriva, *Enchiridion Familiae.*

3. John Paul II, remarks after the recitation of the rosary, New York, Saint Patrick's Cathedral, October 4, 1995.

4. *Familiaris Consortio* 73.

this way it stresses the necessity of such formation and forcefully defines the lines along which it has to be renewed. Let me outline briefly the content of the document.

After a very brief introduction which cites some passages of the pope's teaching regarding the decisive importance of marriage and family in the context of the new evangelization (nos. 1-2), there follows a description of the present-day system of formation (nos. 3-12). This description can be summarized as follows:

- The subject of marriage and family is not neglected in ecclesiastical studies, even though the quality and effectiveness of what is taught are not always satisfactory.
- Indeed, there seems to be a lack of balance and of a clear perception of the goals and principles of the sort of authentic theological research that should govern the teaching of these subjects.
- Added to this situation is the objective complexity of the ethical, medical, juridical, scientific, and economic problems that mark the reality of marriage and the family today.
- As positive factors, on the other hand, the document cites the significant and sustained body of guidelines given by the pontifical magisterium, as well as the development of a more organic family apostolate that is able to offer new proposals for formation in the area of marriage and the family.

What conclusion can be drawn from this examination? The document states forcefully: "It follows that this aspect of the formation program must be accurately revised and, if necessary, qualitatively improved" (no. 13). To encourage this revision the text sets forth some guidelines concerning intellectual (nos. 20-30), spiritual (nos. 31-37), and pastoral formation (nos. 38-54). Following these guidelines, the document adds, by way of conclusion, a few practical recommendations (nos. 55-63).

I am especially concerned here to bring out the affirmation which is the key to the whole document. This affirmation is a clarion call for change, and it cannot be disregarded by bishops and those entrusted with the formation of seminarians. The key affirmation can be stated as follows: It is not a question of adding individual courses or disciplines dealing with marriage and the family in the field of theology or spirituality or pastoral ministry to the courses of formation already existing in seminaries. Rather, it is necessary to ensure that marriage and the family become "an internal dimension of pastoral and intellectual formation" (no. 16).

2. A Concept of Education

The centrality of marriage and family in the formation of future priests is affirmed by John Paul II and restated by the directives of the congregation at the level of methodology. This centrality implies a very definite conception of education. It is necessary to discuss, albeit briefly, the salient features of this understanding of education, whose roots lie in the church's great tradition. This will enable us to see more clearly why, when we speak of marriage and the family, we are dealing with a dimension of the entire educative proposal, and not simply with the addition of a further subject of scholarly research.

The phenomenon of education can be defined, in elementary terms, as an introduction of the person to the totality of reality.[5] The introduction of man to reality always requires a relationship between master and disciple, teacher and pupil. Since the relationship of education involves the person in all the phases of his development and reality in its entire evolution, education is something that concerns man throughout his entire life: he can always be educated.[6]

Within the horizon set by this general though precise definition, which is the fruit of centuries of Christian experience,[7] we can go on to distinguish the subject, the method, and the goal of the process of pedagogy. The subject, that is, the agent of education, is the Christian community itself; the goal is a convinced faith, which is to say, a faith that can give the reasons for believing; the method, finally, consists in the progressive and free involvement of the entire existence of both educator and educated with the event of Jesus Christ, which is present in a tangible way in his church.[8] Education is at one and the

---

5. "Eine Einführung in die Wirklichkeit" (J. A. Jungmann, *Christus als Mittelpunkt religiöser Erziehung* [Freiburg, 1939], 20).

6. "Erunt semper docibiles Dei" (John 6:45; cf. Isa. 54:13 and Jer. 31–33).

7. We cite as an example a well-known passage of Augustine: "And so, they benefit many by preaching what they do not practice, but they would benefit far greater numbers by practicing what they preach. For, there are many who seek a defense of their own evil lives in their directors and teachers, replying in their hearts, or even with their lips (if they give vent to this extent), saying: 'Why do you not practice yourself what you are preaching to me?' The result is that they do not listen with submission to a man who does not listen to himself. They despise the word of God which is being preached to them, and at the same time they despise the preacher himself. In fact, when the Apostle, writing to Timothy, had said: 'Let no man despise thy youth,' and added how he was to avoid being despised, he said: 'but be thou an example to the faithful in speech, in conduct, in charity, in faith, in chastity'" (*Writings of St. Augustine* [*De doctrina Christiana* 4.27.60], vol. 2, *The Fathers of the Church*, trans. John J. Gavigin, O.S.A. [New York: CIMA Publishing Co., 1947], 230-31).

8. See A. Scola, *E tutti saranno ammaestrati da Dio* (Grosseto, 1993), 9-12.

same time a matter of freedom and of obedience, an experience of the person and of the community.

This conception, which shows even more clearly how valid it is when we apply it to seminaries and the formation of priests, is the fruit of the nature of Christianity itself. Indeed, the essence of Christianity, to use one of Guardini's expressions,[9] hinges on three factors: event, encounter, and freedom:

> An event changes my life; this event occurs through an encounter; and this encounter calls my freedom to a response. And my life becomes comprehensible in my eyes and the eyes of others only within the context of these three factors: event, encounter and freedom. None of us, whether he be a Christian by conviction or by name only, can evade this basic fact. No one can imagine it possible to grasp the identity of Christianity differently from this elementary structure, which adequately contains the truths of doctrine, the precepts of morality and the action of the liturgy and the sacraments.[10]

To create space for the new dimension in the formation of seminarians called for by the document of the congregation, we must avoid three major risks that are present in any work of education. Before entering into the question at hand, it will be useful to say a word concerning these risks.[11]

The first and most pernicious of the three is "intellectualism." In this context I mean by intellectualism the imparting of academic knowledge in an abstract way, that is, separately from the concrete life of the subject who teaches and the subject who learns. In the final analysis this separation amounts to separation from the Christian community. This situation contradicts the reality of education as we have described it, not only because the educator ends up by substituting himself for the church,[12] but above all because the person being educated is no longer able genuinely to verify the *intellectus fidei*. Such verification is in fact hindered by the separation of that which is transmitted from lived faith. In this way the educational relationship ceases to be a teacher-disciple relation analogous to the relation between father and son, and becomes a relationship between a specialist and an apprentice which fails to take account of all the constitutive needs of the "I" in relation to the whole of reality. The inevitable result is that education is conceived as a pro-

---

9. Cf. R. Guardini, *L'essenza del cristianesimo* (Brescia, 1980).

10. Cf. A. Scola, *Lettera Pastorale: "Sarete liberi davvero"* (Grosseto, 1992), no. 13.

11. Cf. Scola, *E tutti saranno*, 14-15.

12. In this context a reflection on the role of the professor of theology and his relationship with those responsible for seminary formation would be quite useful.

cess that comes to an end at a set time. An intellectualistic conception of education leaves no real place for permanent education. Needless to say, the critique of intellectualism is not in any way meant to undervalue either the importance of solid scholarly competence or the need for places devoted primarily and specifically to education in a man's life (the seminary is obviously among these).

There are two further risks that are also foreign to the nature of an authentic relationship of education. I mean what could be called "sociologism" (which substitutes a collection of "relevant issues" for the transmission of the content of faith) and what we might call "sentimentalism" (which can at most call forth "good feelings" but does not call forth freedom). Both attitudes undermine education. The first is an obstacle to an organic and critical assimilation of the reasons for faith, while the second prevents the involvement of the whole person in relation to reality.

These remarks affect the way we understand the seminary as an educational environment. Inasmuch as the church is the true agent of Christian education at every level, seminaries must be considered above all a reflection (self-realization) of the church. This implies the immanence of the seminary within the life of the people of God. The core of its pedagogical proposal can only be the person of Jesus Christ present in the church, whom it understands as the synthetic and existential principle of the assimilation of reality. Every other type of proposal is doomed to remain mired in secondary matters and to produce a weak pedagogical result.

3. Marriage and the Family in Their Essential Content for the Formation of Priests

We will now present some of the basic features of marriage and the family understood as an essential dimension of evangelization. In doing so, we would like to bring out the relation which by the nature of the case links them to the concept of education referred to above. For obvious reasons it will be necessary to limit our exposition to a few points only.

3.1. The Man-Woman Relationship and Its Constitutive Relations

One of the most typical themes of the anthropology, be it philosophical or theological, of John Paul II's magisterium is reflection on man-woman relationships as the expression of the ontological principle of dual unity. Let us begin with a text from *Mulieris Dignitatem:* "Man cannot exist 'alone' (cf. Gn 2:18); he can exist only as a 'unity of two,' and thus in relation to another human person. . . . To be a person in the image and likeness of God therefore entails an existence in relationship, in relationship to the other 'I.'"[13] Since we already developed these themes in the first part of this work,[14] we confine ourselves here to outlining by major headings some facts which are not only central to the theological literature, but which we also believe are fundamental for the renewal hoped for in the document of the congregation.

- Man exists as male and female, and no man (or woman) can be by himself (or herself) alone the totality of man. Instead, he has always before him the other mode of being human, and this other mode is beyond his reach.
- We can characterize the relationship between male and female as a relationship both of identity and of difference.
- From a more strictly theological point of view, human sexuality and, therefore, the difference between the genders belong to man's being as the image of God.
- What we have said makes it possible to locate in spousal love the *analogatum princeps* of every type of love, and at the same time to regard it as a privileged metaphor for man's relationship to reality.[15] In this regard the pope makes the following affirmation: "[T]he nature of one and the other love [virginity and marriage] is 'conjugal,' that is, expressed through the total gift of oneself. Both types of love tend to express that conjugal meaning of the body which from the beginning has been inscribed in the personal makeup of man and woman."[16]
- Let me conclude these schematic theses by mentioning the fundamental *status* instituted on the basis of the man-woman relationship. I am speaking of the relationships of fatherhood, motherhood, childhood, brotherhood, and sisterhood.[17]

---

13. *MD* 7.

14. Cf. above, pp. 6-31.

15. Cf. M. J. Scheeben, *The Mysteries of Christianity* (London: Herder, 1946), 783-85.

16. John Paul II, *The Theology of the Body: Human Love in the Divine Plan* (Boston: Daughters of St. Paul, 1997), 277-78.

17. The following reflection of the pope sheds much light on the relation between physical and spiritual fatherhood and motherhood: "On the other hand, conjugal love which finds its expression in continence for the kingdom of heaven must lead in its normal development to paternity or maternity in a spiritual sense (in other words, precisely to that fruitfulness of the Holy Spirit that we have already spoken about), in a way analogous to conjugal love, which matures

These points are far from exhausting the essential themes relating to Christian teaching on marriage and the family. Nonetheless, they are the basic elements that found both a theology of marriage and an organic reflection on the family. In fact, without these elements it would be impossible to give an organic, that is, systematic and critical, account of God's design for marriage and the family. In this sense these points traverse all the major headings of a theological discussion of marriage and the family. Inasmuch as the theological perspective is the one that interests us here, and in view of the enormous breadth of this subject, I will limit myself to the points that are in my opinion necessary and sufficient.

3.2. The Impact of These Themes on Formation in Seminaries

How can these considerations have an impact on the way we conceive the educational itinerary of future priests? We will speak first of the educational relationship that characterizes seminaries.

As regards houses of formation, they cannot but encourage the seminarian to remain within the people of God, which is the locus of the lived experience of the man-woman relationship. The point, then, is to consider the figure of the priest as intrinsically related to the Christian people. It is necessary to do so while maintaining continuity with fundamental human experience, which is necessarily one of being-in-communion. Seminary formation must therefore help the candidate for the priesthood to discover Jesus Christ as the affective center of the "I" which can include every authentic human relationship. Ideally the seminary community is the sign of the newness of relationships which are both in continuity with family life and at the same time an image of the church.

It is particularly necessary to highlight the question of priestly celibacy. Although called into question even today, it is de facto the way in which Catholic priests of the Latin rite are called to live virginity. The Latin Church regards as particularly fitting the practice of choosing its priests from among those who freely adhere to the *sequela Christi* in the form of virginity. It is indispensable that seminaries educate the conscience of candidates for the priesthood in virginity, which enables them by grace to have the freedom of a

---

in physical paternity and maternity, and in this way confirms itself as conjugal love. For its part, physical procreation also fully corresponds to its meaning only if it is completed by paternity and maternity in the spirit, whose expression and fruit is all the educative work of the parents in regard to the children born of their conjugal corporeal union." John Paul II, *Theology of the Body*, 278.

true possession of reality in detachment.[18] This experience is made possible by identification with Jesus Christ, the one and definitive priest.

Education in celibacy, on the other hand, is the key factor in the development of the spousal character of the priesthood:

> The sacrament of orders makes the priest participate not only in the mystery of Christ as Priest, Teacher, Head and Shepherd, but also, in some sense, in Christ as "Servant and Spouse of the Church." This Church is His Body which He loved and continues to love to the point of giving Himself for her (Eph 5:25); He regenerates and purifies the Church continuously (Eph 5:26); He strives to make her ever more beautiful (Eph 5:27); finally, He nourishes her and cares for her (Eph 5:29). . . . Priests, who within "the individual local communities of the faithful make present, so to speak, the Bishop, to whom they are united with a trusting and generous spirit," must be faithful to the Bride, and, as it were, living icons of Christ the Bridegroom. They must make effective Christ's multiform gift to His Church. By this communion with Christ the Bridegroom, even the ministerial priesthood is established — like Christ, with Christ and in Christ — in that saving mystery of love of which marriage between Christians is a participation. Called by a supernatural, absolutely gratuitous, act of love, the priest must love the Church as Christ loved her. He must, that is, devote all of his energies to the Church and make a gift of himself with pastoral charity, even to the point of daily giving his very own life.[19]

A virginal vocation lived with joy will always remain a constant point of reference for couples and Christian families, which in their turn help the priest deepen the spousal character of his vocation.

3.3. The Renewal of Philosophical and Theological Studies

The rigorous integration into the curriculum of certain themes connected with man and woman and marriage and the family as a full-fledged dimension of ecclesiastical studies could even become the starting point for a new systematic vision of theology. We will limit ourselves to highlighting a few points regarding the various thematic areas. These are obviously merely fragmentary notes; to document them I will take the liberty of incorporating sev-

18. Cf. L. Giussani, *Il tempo e il tempio* (Milan, 1995), 11-35.
19. Congregation for the Clergy, *Directory on the Ministry and Life of Priests* (January 31, 1994), no. 13.

eral (long) passages taken from some of my earlier writings. Any claim of completeness in such an endeavor would be absurd. Thus the notes that follow are simply a stimulus for reflection.

a. In the field of philosophy and fundamental theology, a consideration of the man-woman relation can suggest a twofold renewal. On the one hand, reflection on dual unity as the distinctive characteristic of contingent reality leads to a discussion of the ontological difference, indeed, of theological difference. The ontology at the basis of these developments, which can be called *symbolic ontology* (since it speaks of the manifestation of being in the sign), rests upon a deepening of the realist tradition proper to Christian thought. In this regard it is fitting to say a few words at the outset about the necessity of overcoming the extrinsicism of faith-reason and nature-supernature that characterizes the modern age.

We cannot develop here the analytical method characteristic of this ontology.[20] We must limit ourselves to listing its principles. Being is of such a character as to be ultimately beyond man's reach. Technically, this is to affirm that being is indeducible. And yet being communicates itself. How? It communicates itself in the sign. Being is *event (e-venio)*. Being *reveals* ("re-veils") itself in the sign, calling to the subject whom it addresses, in order that the subject may assent to it. As event, being always gives itself in a sign; as revelation, the event of being always calls to a consciousness capable of welcoming it. Human freedom must necessarily work together with reason in the assent to being. Still, man cannot autonomously know how the call that being addresses to him will be fulfilled. In technical terms we have to say that man cannot resolve the difference of the origin, which nonetheless communicates itself to him. In this sense we are forced to acknowledge that ultimately the structure of the act of knowledge in its (intentional) relation to reality has the form of faith (but not of a generic concept of belief). Thus, faith conceived in this way is not extrinsic to reason, but in a certain sense constitutes its truth. In fact, far from being confused with reason, faith is its critical foundation. This compels us to rethink the modern history of the relation between philosophy and theology. Christian faith now appears as the actuation, by grace, of this original structure of faith. In fact, God's unconditional devotion to men (made fully visible in the event of Jesus Christ) manifests the pure gratuity of God's decision to communicate himself. So much so that biblical revelation could discover that the communication of

---

20. Cf. G. Colombo, *La ragione teologica* (Milan, 1995), 191ff.; A. Bertulleti, "La legittimazione della teologia," in *Il teologo* (Milan, 1989), 164-200; Bertulleti, "La ragione teologica," in *L'evidenza e la fede,* ed. G. Colombo (Milan, 1988).

truth to man (revelation) implies the very creation of man, and thus the constitution of history. The gratuitous character of God's dedication to man explains why God reveals himself in the sign and thus appeals to freedom. In technical terms this means that "according to the self-understanding of Christian faith, the possibility of access to the original meaning of transcendence is subordinate to the event which manifests it historically."[21] The event is Jesus Christ who asks for faith. In this sense, and this point is decisive for the matter at hand, Christian faith is the critical instance of religious experience, which, as we have already said, manifests the transcendent foundation of the relation of consciousness and reality.

Event, revelation, and the act of consciousness thus appear ontologically indistinguishable. In particular, the act by which consciousness intends the real, grasping it as the sign (trace) of Being which calls on freedom to decide, belongs intrinsically to the concept of revelation. Revelation would not be revelation if it were not an appeal addressed to someone capable of receiving it. The lines of this ontology, which has rightly been defined as symbolic precisely because being reveals itself in the sign, enable us better to understand, if we take the path glimpsed by Vatican II, the correct theological concept of revelation. This concept includes both the manifestation of being (event) and the response of reason and freedom on the part of man.[22] Once the

21. A. Bertelluti, "Fede e religione: la singolarità cristiana e l'esperienza religiosa universale," in *Cristianesimo, religione e religioni* (Milan, 1993), 99.

22. In his well-known study on Saint Bonaventure, Joseph Ratzinger shows how the Seraphic Doctor's understanding of faith includes an understanding of revelation: "From this, we understand the identification between Sacred Scripture and theology in a new way: only Scripture understood in faith is truly Sacred Scripture. In this way, Scripture is theology in the full sense, that is to say, the book and the comprehension of the book in the Church's faith. Theology can also call itself Scripture, because it is nothing but a comprehension of Scripture which gives this Scripture, for the first time, a fruitfulness conformed to revelation. Thus we understand the motive that prompted Bonaventure, in his programmatic preface to the Commentary on the Sentences, to define the theologian as *revelator absconditorum,* and, correspondingly, theology as *revelatio absconditorum.* The determination of the current false interpretation ought to appear clearly now. In brief, it is based on the fact that understanding, elevated for the first time by Scripture and revelation, cannot be conceived as an affair of the individual reader, but as capable of being verified only within the living understanding of Scripture on the part of the Church. The objectivity of the requirement of faith is in this way guaranteed beyond any doubt. If we keep this in mind, we can nevertheless affirm that, while this objectivity remains, the true meaning of Scripture is reached only when it is explained beyond the letter, and therefore that its understanding requires, on the part of every reader, something more than mere objective consciousness. It requires an attitude that we might definitively call mystical: the faith through which man enters into the Church's living understanding of the Scriptures. In this way, and only in this way, can he receive revelation." J. Ratzinger, *San Bonaventura. La teologia della storia* (Florence, 1991), 141-42.

extrinsicism of reason and faith has been overcome, we see that this response consists in faith. There will thus be no revelation without a response: response is required by revelation and, in this sense, belongs to the event of revelation.[23]

b. What we have said about ontology is intrinsically related to the issues and developments of fundamental theology. In fact, the consideration of truth as event, an affirmation we can consider as the result of a properly developed symbolic ontology, is part of the renewal of the concept of revelation brought about by the constitution *Dei Verbum.*

An invaluable contribution of Vatican II to theological reflection is without doubt the renewal of the concept of revelation with respect to Vatican I's *Dei Filius.* There is no antithesis between Vatican I and Vatican II on this point. Nevertheless, *Dei Verbum* effects an essential development.

Borrowing the words of de Lubac, we can say that the Second Vatican Council replaces an "abstract idea of truth with the idea of a truth that is as concrete as can be imagined. I mean the idea of personal truth that has appeared in history, works in history and, from within the womb of history, is capable of sustaining all of history; I mean the idea of that truth in person which is Jesus Christ, the fullness of revelation."[24] This centrality of revelation as *truth in person,* however, does not lead to a concept of truth which is not addressed to man's reason. In this sense an "anti-intellectualist" position that undermines the necessity of dogmatic formulation can find no support in the conciliar texts.[25] The true renewal consists in the intuition of the profound unity between absoluteness and historicity, between necessity and freedom, that is implied in the notion of *truth in person.* The unity of these elements is possible because *Dei Verbum* proposes truth as an event.[26] This consideration is, upon close examination, the fruit of the council's christological focus.[27] In fact, in the language of Vatican II, truth and Jesus Christ are identified: in this way "Vatican II frees the notion of truth from

23. The preceding two paragraphs were originally included in A. Scola, *Questioni di antropologia teologica* (Rome, 1997), 164-66.

24. H. de Lubac, *La rivelazione divina e il senso dell'uomo* (Milan: Jaca Book, 1985), 49.

25. De Lubac, *La rivelazione divina e il senso dell'uomo,* 31: "There is thus no antagonism between a revelation as knowledge and a revelation as event. The Council itself removed this danger, by, in the same sentence, following the phrase *'doctrinam et res'* with the phrase *'gesta verbaque.'* The intellectual sense of 'doctrine' leaves no room for doubt."

26. J. Ratzinger, *Natura e compito della teologia* (Milan, 1993), 119 (*The Nature and Mission of Theology* [San Francisco: Ignatius, 1995]).

27. Cf. Colombo, *La ragione teologica,* 91ff.

the ahistorical precomprehension that tends to reify it, thus restoring truth to its identity as a historical event. Truth is in fact inseparable from event; otherwise we drift into formalism."[28] The consideration of revelation as an "event which occurred in the past and continues to occur in faith, the event of a new relation between God and man,"[29] presupposes a renewed approach to revealed truth.[30]

c. Another starting point for renewal in philosophy in the context of the ecclesiastical disciplines is the bringing to light of the dramatic character of an adequate anthropology.[31] A reflection on man must take into account the essential datum of sexual difference, not as derivative but as original (man/woman); this also leads us, through the ontological difference, to the fact that man, insofar as he is historically situated *(Dasein)*, can reflect upon himself only as already placed on the stage of the great theater of the world: "If we want to ask about man's 'essence,' we can do so only in the midst of his dramatic performance of existence. There is no other anthropology but the dramatic."[32]

d. Moving now to the field of dogmatic theology, which, I repeat, we can treat only in outline, we can conceive of the *historia salutis* as the history of the nuptial union between God and man:

> The analogy we are dealing with (the analogy of spousal love) allows us to understand, to a certain degree, the revealed mystery of the living God who is Creator and Redeemer (as such, he is at the same time the God of the Covenant). It allows us to understand this mystery in terms of a spousal love, at the same time as it allows us to understand it also in terms of a "merciful" love (according to the passage of the book of Isaiah), or a "paternal" love (according to the letter to the Ephesians, especially in the first chapter). . . . The analogy of the love of the spouses (or spousal love) stresses particularly the moment of the gift of himself on the part of God to man, who is chosen "from all ages" in Christ (literally "to Israel," "to the

28. Colombo, *La ragione teologica,* 80.

29. Ratzinger, *Natura e compito della teologia,* 120.

30. The preceding two paragraphs were originally included in Scola, *Questioni di antropologia,* 163-64.

31. On dramatic anthropology cf. A. Scola, *Hans Urs von Balthasar: A Theological Style* (Grand Rapids: Eerdmans, 1995), 84-100.

32. H. U. von Balthasar, *Theo-Drama II: Dramatis Personae: Man in God,* trans. Graham Harrison (San Francisco: Ignatius, 1990), 335.

Church"); a total (or "radical") and irrevocable gift in its essential character as gift.[33]

e. From this point of view, trinitarian theology could be developed by bringing out points that are by no means of secondary importance. Man and woman can be considered to be the traces of the Trinity in the created world. As the primordial expression of all possible communion among men, communion between man and woman can be seen — always within the laws of analogy — as an integral part of a reflection on man as *imago Trinitatis*.

f. The event of Jesus Christ (Christology), in whom divine nature and human nature are hypostatically united in one person, is the point of reference for every "unity of two," which always ultimately derives from him. Man, in his concrete existence as male or female, was created in the image of the Image, which is Jesus Christ. Man's being *imago Trinitatis* consists in this fact.

> To say that Jesus Christ is the center of the cosmos and of history, or more properly, to speak of creation in Christ, signifies that Christ's freedom becomes the central axis for the understanding of human freedom and that the person of Christ, in his singular humanity, is the form for understanding man. This person is the exemplar and norm of freedom and the form of all those who are predestined to be sons of God in him. In Christ, by the mystery of the hypostatic union, finite freedom is enveloped, *"indivise et inconfuse,"* in the infinite freedom of the Son of God. In this way, through the grace of the Incarnation, the great story of God's accompaniment of man in the bond of love with the Holy Spirit is placed before our eyes. The freedom of Christ turns towards the freedom of man, which, it must not be forgotten, is a given which has to "conspire" with the grace-filled will of God to bring about the actuation of the economy of predestination: without freedom the full participation of created being in trinitarian life would not be possible, since man can oppose his free refusal to Christ's universal saving will. What is the relationship between the freedom of Christ and the dramatic freedom of man? What is Christ's relationship to man? Putting it synthetically, we could say that Christ, through the events of his life and resurrection, in which he reveals himself to be true God and true man, resolves the enigma of man yet without settling the drama in advance.[34]

---

33. John Paul II, *Uomo e donna lo creò. Catechesi sull'amore umano* (Rome, 1992), 500.
34. Scola, *Hans Urs von Balthasar*, 96-97.

g. What has been said about Christology has consequences for Mariology, ecclesiology, and theological anthropology as well. Mariology, as set forth in *Redemptoris Mater*[35] and *Mulieris Dignitatem*,[36] presents Mary as the first of the predestined in Christ and, therefore, the model of the Christian and of the woman (by her nuptial character, her maternity, and her prophetic genius).[37]

In the light of Christology, and thanks to the renewal of Mariology brought about by the council, the consideration of the church (ecclesiology) as *sponsa Christi* gains new importance: "The synthesis is established in the personal unity of Christ, in which unity the duality of humanity/divinity perdures. This duality is also recognizable in the new structuring of his one ecclesial body, in the way that the members of the Church-Bride are fitted to the head who is Christ the Bridegroom."[38]

A word about theological anthropology. It is renewed by the incorporation of the dramatic character to which we have already referred, by its christological starting point, and by the development of new contents. I am referring, first of all, to the consideration of human sexuality as an essential component of man as the image of God,[39] and secondly, to the constitutive tensions or polarities of man: in the event of Jesus, which unravels the enigma of man without eliminating its drama, these polarities find a certain stability.

The man-woman polarity is linked to the mystery of the Christ-Church relationship (cf. Eph 5), where nuptial love not only reaches its fullest form, but where at the same time its connection with death through the closed circle of generation for the sake of the species is broken. This is so not only because death is conquered in Christ, but also and more precisely because Christ inaugurates a new form of fruitfulness which is not identical to human procreation. This is a fecundity for the kingdom, which becomes the eschatological sign of the marriage between Christ and the Church; it is a virginal fecundity or nuptiality which is not at all asexual.[40]

h. Even sacramental theology can be renewed by taking up this approach. Let us simply touch upon a few elements: The dual unity of man and woman must receive a more organic, in-depth study in the theological treatment of marriage. The principal advances that we have mentioned must all flow to-

---

35. Cf. *RM* 46.
36. Cf. *MD* 6-7, 18, 21, 29-30.
37. Cf. above, pp. 14-20.
38. C. Giuliodori, *Intelligenza teologica del maschile e femminile* (Rome, 1991), 175.
39. Cf. above, pp. 32-52.
40. Scola, *Hans Urs von Balthasar*, 98.

gether to enrich the theology of marriage: the analogy between trinitarian communion and spousal communion; the "one flesh" in analogy to the union of two natures in the single person of Jesus Christ; the relationship of Christ the Bridegroom to the church-bride (whose basis is Mariological) must reveal its character as the ontological symbol of the union between man and woman in the sacrament.[41]

This relationship between the bride and the Bridegroom, between Christ and the church, can be seen under the veil of the sacrament of the Eucharist (the intrinsic culmination of baptism), in which the immolated Lamb, as the Bridegroom, celebrates his nuptials.

In this wedding, celebrated daily in the church, the primary factor is Jesus, who gives identity to the *communio* in his eucharistic offering — which is death and resurrection for us. The secondary factor is that we are "set apart" while we eat his body; that is, we are truly assimilated to him. The third factor is established by Jesus when he says, "Do this in memory of me" (1 Cor. 11:24). The eucharistic "do this" fills out the definition of the church's raison d'être and mission. "Do this, let yourselves be taken eucharistically by me, because I generate through the gift of the Spirit the communion between the Father and you. Doing this, that is, living this communion, you make me present."[42]

As for the sacrament of orders, it would be possible to develop a reflection around the incorporation of the ordained ministers into the unique priesthood of Christ (which is definitive and unrepeatable inasmuch as victim and priest are identical in it), and thus their incorporation into Christ's being bridegroom of the church. In this sense it would be desirable to delve more deeply into the relationship between the sacrificial giving of self and spousal love.

i. A final point regarding eschatology. Eschatology can be described as the consummation of the marriage of the Word with redeemed humanity. This marriage took place in the redemptive incarnation, which remains in the life of the church as the pledge of the good things to come.

---

41. In this sense I feel it necessary to stress that natural marriage is not something meaningful which prescinds from any reference to Jesus Christ, in whom alone the freedom of the two are made capable of communicating, through the sacrament, in the trinitarian life. Sacramentality is not something added on to a natural human datum, but is that which explains it; hence the stable relationship between a man and a woman, when this does not attain to sacramental fullness, can have a certain consistency only if it participates, albeit indirectly, in this fullness.

42. This paragraph was originally part of A. Scola, "Eucharistia, fonte di comunione," *La Rivista* 2 (1994): 45-46.

The resurrection of Christ as the firstfruits, and thus the pledge of our future resurrection, is what makes possible our fulfillment, the integral realization of our human existence. This fulfillment is given us already now, in baptism, above all in the Eucharist, and in the other sacraments. It occurs in the living and life-giving place which is the church. The church, generated by the sacraments and by listening to and following Christ, is the community animated by the Holy Spirit, in which even now we are allowed to experience, at least in germ, this fullness of new life. In belonging to Christ in his body which is the church, the Christian already experiences an inchoate life of resurrection which is like a prolepsis, an anticipation in time, of what will be in the definitive reality, in the "new heavens and new earth." In this way the "new creation" is reconnected to its original beginning, to Jesus Christ, the Word of the Father in whom and for whom everything was created. Beginning with Christ, this new creation integrates all things and all men so that, in the end, God may be all in all (cf. 1 Cor. 15:28).[43]

j. Let us now mention a few trajectories of development in the domain of so-called practical theology.

With regard to moral theology, the approach outlined here impels us to overcome a double extrinsicism. On the one hand, we must recover a more intimate link between anthropology and morality, pushing moral theology in the direction of a deeper search for unity between the inward attitude and the outward act. In fact, the interiorization of the norm is, to say it once and for all, more important than the mere outward observance of the norm. This must not be understood as a relativization of the norm, but rather as necessarily including the *lex naturae* in its objective normativity *(lex personae)*. Indeed, the inward attitude molds and gives shape to the outward act, just as the outward act embodies the inward attitude. We cannot forget Thomas's great affirmation, which is already present in the *Scriptum,* of the high moral value attained by those persons who "ipsi sibi sunt lex," an affirmation he applies to those who have succeeded in interiorizing the norm.[44]

On the other hand, it is necessary to overcome the even graver extrinsicism between Christocentrism and the natural law. Nor will the overcoming of this extrinsicism entail the loss either of the objectivity of the norm or of its universal validity.

We are referring here to a Christ-centered anthropology which affirms

43. This paragraph was originally included in Scola, *Questioni di antropologia,* 67.

44. Cf. Thomas Aquinas, *In III Sententiarum,* d. 3, q. 1, a. 1 ra 5. The bulk of this paragraph was originally included in Scola, *Questioni di antropologia,* 129.

that man has one supernatural end. This anthropology can reflect on the logic of the history of salvation and distinguish that logic from its chronology. This implies a type of theological reflection that proceeds in an integral perspective based on a whole which contains, without confusion and without separation, nature and supernature, creation and redemption, essence and history. Indeed, to speak of the supernatural end as the one end of man in the concrete historical order (which end, being gratuitous, could have been otherwise)[45] necessarily leads us to see creation as creation-elevation. It leads us to conceive of the creature, in the terms of its constitutive metaphysical necessities, within the covenant realized in the history of salvation. In the perspective of such an anthropology, the right kind of ontology and history appear as inseparably united from the very beginning.

This anthropology is opposed to the anthropology of the twofold end, which conceives of nature as de facto separated from the supernatural, and which, precisely because nature is separate, regards it as capable of furnishing a neutral common ground as the locus of universal and immutable contents. In this perspective creation establishes nature as a reality that is more or less implicitly juxtaposed to redemption and underlies it. Nature is then conceived as the essence of man, while redemption is seen as what adds history to essence. In consequence, nature offers the metaphysical, the immutable, the universal, while redemption offers the historical, the mutable, and the contingent.[46] As we will see further on, this position is full of negative consequences for how we understand natural law.

If we now return, after this clarification, to the field of moral theology, we could say that at bottom creative predestination coincides, on the level of ethics, with what the theological tradition has called eternal law. Eternal law is the practical dimension of the great trinitarian design which is creative predestination.

We could therefore conclude as follows: since all laws, including the divine law, are nothing other than the translation of predestination in Christ, to which the eternal law objectively reduces, then natural law loses none of its density and is no longer perceived as extrinsic to the christocentric perspective; it is objectively included in it. Such a christological and anthropological focus in moral theology will not at all threaten the universality of ethics. To the contrary, it is precisely in its rootedness in Christology, anthropology, and ecclesiology that ethics will take on a universality which is not purely formal.

---

45. Cf. *DS* 2318.

46. Cf. I. Biffi, "Integralità cristiana e fondazione morale," *La Scuola Cattolica* 115 (1987): 582-83.

It is always possible to show a nonbeliever the intrinsic reasonableness of a norm which can also be known naturally, without a priori forgoing the presentation of it as an ingredient of a whole that receives its complete foundation only in the perspective of Christ.[47]

In this way Jesus Christ becomes the living and personal law, and Christian morality is founded on an event which gathers around itself a people that traverses history and, at the same time, is the pledge of eternal life (*Veritatis Splendor* 23).[48] All the burning questions related to marriage and the family (responsible parenthood, contraception, abortion, in vitro fertilization, etc.), which we cannot discuss here, can find the right solutions in this general approach.

k. In the field of canon law, the theology of canon law could be deepened as a reflection on the "juridical" nature of the bride of Christ. The constitution of the church would thus reveal a more properly institutional dimension, one more distinctively charismatic.[49] Within this reflection the relationship between vocation and mission, ministries and charisma, would provide a fitting key for understanding canonical legislation on matrimony.

l. As for pastoral theology, I wish to highlight, in the first place, the urgency of a correct theology of the vocation of the baptized faithful (which includes a reflection on the states of life). This reflection could be articulated around two elements: communion and mission.[50] Secondly, it is important to work out a catechesis which gives primacy in education to Christian experience in all of its integrity and which subordinates to this experience the use of the necessary psycho-pedagogical methods and techniques.

Whether in pastoral theology or in the context of moral theology, we cannot fail to mention the importance of the social doctrine of the church, which confronts some of the most burning questions of our difficult historical situation.

m. With respect to the theology of the liturgy, we can say that the whole structure of the church's sacraments and, consequently, of her celebration is born of the mystery of the redemptive incarnation. As we mentioned previously, this mystery can be read as a mystery of marriage between divine nature and human nature in the person of the Word. Christian liturgy, in this sense, al-

47. The preceding four paragraphs were originally included in Scola, *Questioni di antropologia,* 133-37.

48. The bulk of this sentence is taken from Scola, *Questioni di antropologia,* 106.

49. Cf. E. Corecco, *Ius et communio. Scritti di Diritto Canonico* (Casale Monferrato, 1997).

50. Cf. Scola, *Questioni di antropologia,* 55-68.

ways has a nuptial structure which is readily seen in the ordinary of the Mass and in the liturgy of the hours.[51]

n. In conclusion, we should bear in mind two facts. First of all, the so-called human sciences (psychology, medicine, sociology, bioethics, etc.) make a necessary contribution to theology today:

> For its own inquiry, it [theology] makes use of contributions from the human and positive sciences (biology, medicine, psychology, economy, ethnology), as well as of such results of various sociological and demographic analyses and investigations. In the use of such data, one must avoid "falling into the trap of ideologies that manipulate the interpretation of the data, or into positivism which overrates empirical data to the detriment of the overall understanding of man and the world" (Congregation for Catholic Education, *Orientations for the Study and the Teaching of Social Doctrine of the Church,* no. 68. Cf. no. 10).[52]

Secondly, appeal to the spousal dimension in the presentation of philosophical-theological subjects must not in any way cancel out the requisite scholarly rigor. Still, this appeal can suggest many ways to avoid both the fragmentation of knowledge, under which theology itself suffers, and the unattractiveness which often characterizes the business of theology. It is by no means true, as many theological styles in the history of the church have shown, that scientific rigor and beauty necessarily exclude one another.

---

51. Cf. H. U. von Balthasar, *Explorations in Theology,* vol. 2, *Spouse of the Word* (San Francisco: Ignatius, 1991), 193-288.

52. Congregation for Catholic Education, *Directives on the Formation of Seminarians concerning Problems Related to Marriage and the Family,* no. 30.

A Prophecy of the Nuptial Mystery: Reflections on the Teaching of Humanae Vitae

In the thirty years that have passed since the publication of *Humanae Vitae*, the turbulent period traversed both by the Church and the whole cultural fabric of society has demonstrated that Paul VI's encyclical touched a neuralgic point, not only for conjugal ethics but for the very conception of the human person. This point is neuralgic and decisive for today as for yesterday: it is not an exaggeration to affirm that the question of the meaning of sexuality and the transmission of human life is the discriminating point of various anthropologies, which clash and confront one another on the stage on which the future of mankind will be decided. The prophetic response offered by the Successor of Peter thirty years ago, in 1968, went against the grain of so much of public opinion, both inside and outside the ecclesial community, and yet was profoundly coherent with the tradition of the Church. Its proclamation triggered the explosion of a series of other and increasingly radical questions, regarding which the Magisterium has not failed to make its voice heard. It will be useful to follow this development, gradually shedding light on the strong anthropological core of Catholic teaching: the nuptial mystery, along with the ethical consequences and pastoral perspectives that this opens up.

This appendix reproduces an article written in collaboration with Prof. Livio Melina on the occasion of the thirtieth anniversary of the publication of the encyclical *Humanae Vitae*. While aware of the repetitions caused by its inclusion (some passages include sentences found verbatim in preceding chapters), I thought it useful to insert the article as it was originally published in the journal *Anthropotes*, because of its synthetic-didactic character.

1. The Path of Magisterial Teaching

In response to the problems of ecclesial life, pastoral work, and theological reflection, the Magisterium has progressively developed the implications of *Humanae Vitae*, bringing to light its anthropological, ethical, and ecclesiological foundations. It is precisely on these three levels that the major objections to the Church's teachings have been raised. Awareness has grown, with increasing evidence, that "it is no longer a matter of limited or occasional dissent, but of an overall and systematic calling into question of traditional moral doctrine, on the basis of certain anthropological and ethical presuppositions" (*Veritatis Splendor*, n. 4).

1.1. The Personalistic Dignity of Love and Procreation

On the level of anthropology, the core of *Humanae Vitae*'s teaching regarding the inseparability of the unitive and procreative meanings of the conjugal act (n. 12) shows itself to be a defense of the personalistic dignity of human love and procreation.

In the face of various hedonistic and functionalistic reductions, the post-synodal Apostolic Exhortation *Familiaris consortio*, and especially the cycle of Wednesday catecheses (1979-1984), clarified and deepened the integrally personal dimension of sexuality as the place where the "language of the body" is called to express itself, signifying the complete gift of the person of the man and of the woman. The body is never situated on a merely biological level, as matter that can be manipulated, but is a "sacrament of the person,"[1] a visible sign expressing the invisible reality of the gift of the persons who love one another.

Developing the anthropology of the conciliar constitution *Gaudium et Spes*, John Paul II affirms, "Man is precisely a person because he is master of himself and has self-control. Indeed, in so far as he is master of himself he can 'give himself' to the other. This dimension — the dimension of the liberty of the gift — becomes essential and decisive for that 'language of the body,' in which man and woman reciprocally express themselves in the conjugal union. Granted that this is communion of persons, the 'language of the body' should be judged according to the criterion of truth."[2] For this reason, "the

---

1. John Paul II, *The Theology of the Body: Human Love in the Divine Plan* (Boston: Daughters of St. Paul, 1997), 75-77.
2. John Paul II, *Theology of the Body*, 398. Also on this theme, see C. Caffarra, *Etica generale della sessualità* (Milan, 1992), 9-19.

essential evil of the contraceptive act" consists in the "violation of the interior order of conjugal union, which is rooted in the very order of the person."[3] When it is artificially deprived of its procreative capacity, the conjugal act is also stripped of its interior truth of the complete gift of self and welcoming of the other person, and ceases to be an act of love. We can say, then, that the teaching of *Humanae Vitae* is "the formulation of the conditions required in order for conjugal sexuality to be an expression of true love. It is a defense of sexuality as the true expression of spousal and personal love."[4]

On the other hand, the dignity of human procreation, which cannot be reduced to the "reproduction" of an individual of the species, is safeguarded in its originality by having its origin precisely in an act of love, at once spiritual and corporal, of a man and a woman joined by the nuptial bond.[5] The Instruction of the Congregation for the Doctrine of the Faith, *Donum Vitae,* specifies the conditions ethically necessary for the beginning of human life, in the face of various methods of medically assisted procreation. The life of a new human being is willed and sought after rightly when it is awaited and welcomed as a "gift from a gift," when medical intervention aids but does not substitute the physical and spiritual gift that the spouses make of themselves in the conjugal act. The encyclical *Evangelium Vitae* reaffirms the unique and inviolable worth of human life, in the wider horizon of a meditation on the Christian message. Thus a coherent response has been offered to the other facet of the problem.

The connection of the unitive and procreative meanings of the conjugal act is thus the guarantee of the personalistic truth of both these meanings: when the conjugal act is deliberately removed from the perspective of the transmission of life, it is no longer an authentic act of love on a personalistic level. And when it is removed from the context of conjugal love, procreation violates the dignity of the person of the child, who must be welcomed and affirmed for its own sake and not produced as it he were a thing, through the domination of technology.

1.2. The Absolute Nature of Moral Truth and Conscience

On a properly ethical level, we find much discussion regarding the absolute nature of the moral norm prohibiting contraception as an "intrinsically dis-

---

3. John Paul II, *Theology of the Body,* 398.

4. M. Rhonheimer, *Sexualität und Verantwortung. Empfängnisverhütung als ethisches Problem* (Vienna, 1995), 63.

5. Cf. J. Ratzinger, "Uno sgaurdo teologico sulla procreazione umana," in *La via della fede. Le ragioni dell'etica nell'epoca presente* (Milan, 1996), 133-51.

honest" act (*Humanae Vitae*, n. 14).[6] What sort of universality and immutability can claim to prohibit specific behaviors? Are such norms really absolute, independently of circumstances and cultures? Does not personal conscience, called to apply the universality of the precept to the singularity of the situation, have the right and the duty to further evaluate the pertinence of indications proposed by the Magisterium?

As we can see, this discussion involves themes that have to do with the very foundations of moral theology, calling its identity into question. The Encyclical *Veritatis Splendor*, in the doctrinal core of its teaching, reaffirms "the universality and immutability of the moral commandments, especially those which prohibit always and without exception intrinsically evil acts" (n. 115). In these "we find ourselves faced with the question of man himself, of his truth and of the moral consequences flowing from that truth" (n. 83). If human existence is always found within a particular culture, that culture does not exhaust man; something in him transcends culture, and this something is precisely his nature. Thus, with Vatican Council II, "the Church also maintains that beneath all changes there are many realities which do not change and which have their ultimate foundation in Christ, who is the same yesterday and today, yes and forever" (*Gaudium et Spes*, n. 10).

The relationship between human freedom and God's law has its living center in the heart of the person, or his conscience. When it is a right conscience, the conscience becomes the faithful interpreter of the objective moral order established by God (*Humanae Vitae* 10). The theme of the conscience, often equivocated and misunderstood, has become in the last few decades the Trojan horse through which a practical evacuation of the moral norm of Paul VI's encyclical has been introduced into the heart of conjugal morality. An arbitrarily "creative" interpretation of the role of conscience, its identification with an autonomous and non-governable faculty of decision-making, a unilateral value attributed to its existential originality have all led in practice to making the conscience an instance ultimately independent of moral norms, as these are authoritatively taught by the Church's Magisterium. *Veritatis Splendor* (nn. 54-56) clearly reminds us of the two reference points of an authentic Christian conception of conscience: dependence on truth and a configuration of communion. Definitively resolving the perplexity heightened by the so-called "Washington case,"[7] the encyclical of John Paul II affirms that "circum-

---

6. For a critical overview of this discussion, see W. E. May, *Moral Absolutes: Catholic Tradition, Current Trends, and the Truth* (Milwaukee, 1989).

7. [This involved the public rejection, on the part of several proponents of proportionalist theology in the United States, of Magisterial teaching on certain moral questions following the

stances or intentions can never transform an act intrinsically evil by virtue of its object into an act 'subjectively' good or defensible as a choice" (n. 81).

1.3. The Authority of the Magisterium in the Moral Sphere

On the level of ecclesiology, the teaching of *Humanae Vitae* claims Magisterial authority in offering an authentic interpretation of the moral law. This authority was entrusted by Jesus Christ to Peter and the Apostles for what pertains both to evangelical and to natural law (*Veritatis Splendor*, n. 4).

Disputes regarding the correctness of the relationship between the conclusions of the study commission created by John XXIII in March 1963 and the Pope's pronouncement have resurfaced continually, most recently on the occasion of the encyclical's thirtieth anniversary.[8] At times a lack of agreement with the *sensus fidelium* and with the prevailing opinion of theologians is opposed to a teaching of the Magisterium, which is therefore held to be a merely ordinary and non-infallible papal teaching. This is exacerbated to the point of denying the possibility of an authentic Magisterial teaching in the realm of the determinate norms of the natural moral law.[9]

In fact, the extraordinary firmness and constancy of papal teaching in these years; the substantial unanimity of the Episcopal college, made manifest in the declarations of Episcopal conferences and in the Synod of 1980; and, above all, the coherence of the great moral tradition of the Church throughout the centuries, permit us to have no doubts regarding the fact that the doctrine of *Humanae Vitae* belongs to the ordinary universal Magisterium of the Church.[10]

The necessary presuppositions for this affirmation and its consequences in both theology and pastoral practice have been amply stated in the course of the debate that arose around the position of the American theologian Charles Curran, and the successive clarifications made by the Congregation

---

publication of the encyclical *Humanae Vitae*. The most prominent of these theologians, Fr. Charles Curran, was dismissed from the theological faculty at the Catholic University of America in Washington, D.C. — Tr.] Cf. L. Melina, *Morale: tra crisi e rinnovamento. Gli assoluti morali, l'opzione fondamentale, la formazione della coscienza* (Milan, 1993), 87-88.

8. Cf. N. J. Rigali, "On the *Humanae Vitae* Process: Ethics of Teaching Morality," *Louvain Studies* 23 (1998): 3-21. For an objective look at the preparatory phase, see J. E. Smith, *Humanae Vitae: A Generation Later* (Washington, D.C., 1991), 1-35.

9. Cf. C. Caffarra, "La competenza del Magistero nell'insegnamento di normi morali determinate," *Anthropotes* 4 (1988): 7-23; L. Melina, "The Role of the Ordinary Magisterium: On Francis Sullivan's Creative Fidelity," *Thomist* 61 (1997): 605-15.

10. See F. Ocáriz, "La nota teologica dell'insegnamento dell'*Humanae vitae* sulla contracezione," *Anthropotes* 4 (1988): 25-43.

for the Doctrine of the Faith, above all in the Instruction *Donum Veritatis,* *Professio Fidei* (the Doctrinal Note of the same Congregation), and the recent Apostolic Letter of John Paul II, *Ad Tuendam Fidem.* Already in 1987, John Paul II affirmed, "The Church's teaching on contraception does not belong to that material open to disputation among theologians. To teach the contrary is equivalent to leading the moral consciences of married persons into error."[11]

The doctrinal development of the Magisterium which took place following *Humanae Vitae* and in connection with the problems and disputes which arose in the ecclesial community does not, however, exempt theological reflection from a further and specific effort. Theologians must take up the task of an anthropological deepening of the nuptial mystery, such as to shed more light on — and even to find terms that are humanly more persuasive for — the reasons for Catholic teaching.

2. The Nuptial Mystery

2.1. Humanae Vitae *and the Nuptial Mystery*

The principal teaching[12] of *Humanae Vitae* consists in the affirmation of the *indissolubilis nexus* [indissoluble tie] willed by God, which man therefore cannot break on his own initiative, between the two meanings of the conjugal act: unitive and procreative (cf. *HV* 12). Such an affirmation reveals a precise understanding of the conjugal act which brings into play a whole series of specific anthropological questions. To limit ourselves to the main ones, we indicate three.

First, *sexual difference* as the ontological manifestation of God's decision to create man always and only as male or as female.[13]

Second, *love,* understood as an objective relation to the other. It is based on subjective love *(affectio),* understood as the ensemble of bio-instinctual and spiritual modifications — unconscious, pre-conscious, and conscious — which arise in the subject as lover or as beloved.

Third, *fruitfulness:* the procreation of children as the fruit of the love of the two spouses.

The thesis of the "indissoluble unity" of the two meanings of the conjugal act requires that the three factors mentioned above be intrinsically and in-

---

11. *L'Osservatore Romano,* June 6, 1987.

12. This expression is taken from a particularly authoritative source on the subject: C. Colombo, *L'insegnamento fondamentale di Humanae vitae* (Milan, 1989), 411-12.

13. Cf. *Mulieris Dignitatem* 1.

separably united in an indissoluble intertwining. Basing ourselves on foundations in the history of culture and biblical revelation,[14] we can have recourse to the term "nuptial mystery"[15] to indicate this indissoluble intertwining of sexual difference, love, and fruitfulness (procreation). All the more does the nuptial mystery appear to be configured to the phenomenological consideration of the fundamental human experience of the encounter, in love, between a man and a woman. Moreover, the term is able, through a discerning use of the principle of analogy, to shed light on all the possible forms of love, from *venere* all the way to the manner in which the three Persons love one another in the one God.[16] All the principal dogmas of the faith can be represented in the key of the nuptial mystery (spousal theology). In fact, a spousal (supra-sexual)[17] dimension is present in God himself, albeit in an abysmal difference; in him we find, obviously, love in its proper sense, and fruitfulness. Thus the basest love, the lowest point on the analogical scale, retains in spite of its animalistic traits that yearning for fulfillment which the other can be for the "I," at least as a disfigured echo.[18]

The nuptial mystery allows us, first of all, to grasp the true nature of conjugal love and of marriage, seen in their supreme source. God, who is love, is the Father "from whom every family in heaven and on earth is named" (Eph. 3:15; *HV* 8).

---

14. Cf. for example: R. Graves, *I miti greci* (Milan, 1983), 21-28; J. Reis, *Il rapporto uomo-Dio nelle grandi religioni precristiane* (Milan, 1992), 67-92; L. A. Schökel, *I nomi dell'amore: Simboli matrimoniali nella Bibbia* (Casale Monferrato, 1997); the entries for love (35-64), the Song of Songs (237-45), corporeity (308-21), woman (416-29), marriage (920-30), man (1590-1609), and virginity (1639-54) in P. Rossano, G. Ravasi, and A. Girlanda, eds., *Nuovo Dizionario di Teologia Biblica* (Cinisello Balsamo, 1989).

15. Cf. above, pp. 82-87.

16. C. S. Lewis, *The Four Loves* (London: Fontana Books, 1960), 1-9.

17. In employing this expression we are not borrowing the term, used by both Balthasar and Evdokimov, "suprasexuality," although it is worthwhile to make reference to it. The expression, at least in Balthasar, indicates the absolutely agapic nature of love which, unlike erotic love, does not need the beloved to preexist the lover: cf. H. U. von Balthasar, *Theo-Drama II: Dramatis Personae: Man in God,* trans. Graham Harrison (San Francisco: Ignatius, 1990), 413ff.; Balthasar, *Theo-Drama V: The Last Act,* trans. Graham Harrison (San Francisco: Ignatius, 1998), 85ff.; P. Evdokimov, *La donna e la salvezza del mondo* (Milan, 1980), 21ff. (*Woman and the Salvation of the World: A Christian Anthropology on the Charisms of Women,* trans. Anthony P. Gythiel [Crestwood, N.Y.: St. Vladimir's Seminary Press, 1994]). In this regard see also D. L. Schindler, "Catholic Theology, Gender, and the Future of Western Civilization," in Schindler, *Heart of the World, Center of the Church* (Grand Rapids: Eerdmans, 1996), 237-74.

18. The intertwining of the three constitutive factors of the nuptial mystery can be applied analogically even to the higher animals. In these, one can speak of love only in an improper sense, and yet Thomas would not exclude them from *amor naturalis.*

Secondly, it is clear, in the light of the nuptial mystery, why the spouses are free and responsible collaborators of God the Creator in the most serious task of transmitting human life (cf. *HV* 1).

Lastly, an attentive exploration of the nuptial mystery can provide the adequate context for understanding the chief teaching of *Humanae Vitae* (the indissoluble tie of the two meanings of the conjugal act). It represents the necessary link between this latter and the "integral vision of man and his vocation, not only his natural and earthly, but also his supernatural and eternal vocation" (*HV* 7).

It will be useful to take up once again the three factors of the nuptial mystery.

2.2. Sexual Difference

A phenomenologically attentive glance at things in themselves reveals that sexuality is sexual difference. Through sexual difference, difference is not exhausted by the other who is face-to-face with the "I"; it is, in a certain sense, inscribed within the "I" itself. Without breaking the unity of the "I," difference urges it to reciprocity, not as the integration of a lack, but as the condition for free self-realization.

Man, who, as *corpore et anima unus*, is always determined in sexual difference, encounters the other in his body, understood as the "sacrament of the whole person" and as the necessary medium both for one's own individuation and for relationship to the other.[19] The reciprocity that flows from this is not mere complementarity — it is not the androgynous recomposition of two halves, as Aristophanes' story would have it — because it possesses an *asymmetrical* character. This asymmetry can already be discerned on the level of common sense, since reciprocity is given to man within a plurality of simultaneous interpersonal relations, all of which bring sexual difference into play as something constitutive. Thus the male man is in relation at once to a plurality of figures of the opposite sex (mother, sister, etc.) without being exclusively polarized by one of these, in a search for a supposed other half of himself.

On a deeper level, however, the *raison d'être* of asymmetry can be found on the level of ontology. Sexual difference (man-woman) identifies a constitutive anthropological polarity (the others being body-soul and individual-community). These polarities express the law that, within contingent reality,

19. Cf. H. U. von Balthasar, *Epilog* (Einsiedeln, 1987), 81.

being and its transcendentals (the one, the true, and the good) always exist in a dual unity. This dual unity is ultimately that between being and essence (*distinctio realis,* ontological difference), and encounters its summit in an ontological anthropology in which human freedom yearns to transcend itself and yet cannot realize this "capacity" through its own powers. For this reason, we must affirm that sexual difference, like human freedom, cannot be deduced.

In pointing to asymmetrical reciprocity, sexual difference shows conjugal love (the one flesh, marriage) and fruitfulness (the family) to be intrinsically connected. The one flesh indicates both the fusion of the two in their fruit (the child) and the fact that, even in the conjugal act, the difference between man and woman remains insuperable. This difference is, in fact, the place of the third (the child).

2.3. Spousal Love

As the peculiar expression of that difference (polarity) characteristic of beings in the world, sexual difference is the "ontic step towards that which, between free beings, is love."[20] It is the condition for the exchange of beings among themselves, and, in the case of conscious and self-conscious beings, of their reciprocal inhabitation. Love thus possesses a natural foundation[21] which in man is assumed (but not cancelled out) by freedom. In being-for-the-other, human freedom encounters its own meaning. The manner in which the human person can live love necessarily passes through his sexually differentiated body, understood as that original level where the person experiences the necessity of being himself through an objective form different from himself. Through the body thus conceived, man "collides" with other beings in the world.[22] When a human being "collides" against another creature like himself, he discovers the limit of his freedom and the positive reality of the other. From this mutual discovery of one another shines that reciprocity which founds the dialogue of love.

Here we find the elementary meaning of the biblical "one flesh" which is the foundation of marriage.

20. Balthasar, *Epilog,* 44-45.
21. It is in this sense that for Thomas and the Scholastics, *amor naturalis* is proper to all creatures, even inanimate ones.
22. "Thoughts dwell lightly with one another, but space knows the harsh collision of things" (Goethe).

Spouses mutually express their personal love in the 'language of the body,' which clearly involves both 'sponsal meanings' and parental ones. The conjugal act by which the couple mutually expresses their self-gift at the same time expresses openness to the gift of life. It is an act that is inseparably corporal and spiritual. It is in their bodies and through their bodies that the spouses consummate their marriage and are able to become father and mother. (*Dona Vitae* II B 4 b)

2.4. Procreation

The "one flesh" demonstrates what integral vision of man is expressed in the conjugal act. This act consists of a bodily union which makes of the two one flesh, as can be seen in the fruit, the child, in whom the participation of the two is inseparable on a biological, psychic, and spiritual level. And yet the two remain *inconfuse*, distinct, and precisely for this reason can experience their union as a union of persons. This is possible because the body, the sacrament of the person, is univocally sexed in an irreducible manner. Polarity, which bespeaks difference, cannot be suppressed precisely because it is ontologically oriented to the child. We can say that in the conjugal act, man emerges as the summit of creation. At the same time, the nuptial mystery appears as the deepest mystery on the natural level. In the conjugal act, we witness the singular encounter between nature and spirit. The creative complementarity of these two factors illumines the meaning of human procreation: an encounter between two spiritual bodies under the sign of fruitful bodily union. This encounter is superior to, and yet in some way participates in, that incomplete individuation by which animals reproduce in an act of multiplication sealed by death. It also participates, however, in that sort of spiritual fruitfulness proper to the angels, who cannot "multiply" through the experience of self-dissolution for the survival of the species.

The specific nature of the nuptiality proper to man and woman determines the specific nature of their fecundity. This latter must be grasped, as procreation, in its qualitative difference both with respect to animal reproduction and to generation (in God).

In order to respect the language of their bodies and their natural generosity, the conjugal union must take place with respect for its openness and procreation; and the procreation of persons must be the fruit and the result of married love. The origin of the human being thus follows from a procreation that is 'linked to the union, not only biological, but also spiritual, of the parents, made by one bond of marriage.' Fertilization achieved outside the bodies of the couple remains by this very fact deprived of the meanings and the values which are expressed in the language of the body and in the union of human persons. (*Dona Vitae* II B 4 b)

2.5. The Nuptial Mystery and the Imago Dei

Balthasar writes with great profundity, "The only analogy nature seems to offer to the intimacy with the divine truth is the union of the sexes, though the analogy holds only if we omit the time interval between the union of the two persons in one flesh and its result in the birth of a child."[23] Here the nuptial mystery is expressed in all its force: the indivisible and articulate unity of sexual difference, love, and fruitfulness in which the person, marriage, and the family take on their full form. This profound natural mystery thus reveals man's figure, or *Gestalt*, to be essentially dramatic. Inasmuch as he can reflect on his existence only from within this existence, every human being lives the law of dual unity, through which he experiences the original and insuperable unity of the "I" as polarized: in spirit and body, man and woman, individual and community. As with every other essential difference in human existence, the nuptial mystery brings into play all three of these polarities, showing *the other to be coessential to the "I"* through a consideration of the body as sacrament of the whole *person*, the condition of the "one flesh" (marriage) which is essentially ordered to fruit (the family). Without threatening the autonomous consistency of the "I," difference does not appear to be extrinsic, and therefore does not run the risk of being considered accidental. Marriage and the family become essential factors for the spiritual subject's fulfillment as *person*.[24]

Mulieris Dignitatem takes up the task of suggesting a significant broadening of the classical doctrine of the *imago Dei*, to make room for this articulate anthropological vision. While remaining solidly rooted in the most significant gains of the classical tradition, the document opens itself to the modern sensibility while proposing a way to overcome its limiting conceptualistic prejudice:[25]

23. H. U. von Balthasar, *Prayer* (New York: Sheed and Ward, 1961), 64.

24. The case of virginity for the kingdom does not diminish the validity of this statement precisely because it represents the most significant "variant" of the nuptial mystery, in which, through grace, a form of spousal love is actuated. Cf. above, pp. 105-6.

25. Cf. A. Scola, "La logica dell'Incarnazione come logica sacramentale: avvenimento ecclesiale e libertà," in *Wer ist die Kirche? Symposium zum 10 Todesjahr von Hans Urs von Balthasar* (Einsiedeln, 1999), 99-135.

The fact that man 'created as man and woman' is the image of God means not only that each of them individually is like God, as a rational and free being. It also means that man and woman, created as a 'unity of the two' in their common humanity, are called to live in a communion of love, and in this way to mirror in the world the communion of love that is in God, through which the Three Persons love each other in the intimate mystery of the one divine life. The Father, Son and Holy Spirit, one God through the unity of the divinity, exist as persons through the inscrutable divine relationship. Only in this way can we understand the truth that God in himself is love (cf. 1 Jn 4:16). The image and likeness of God in man, created as man and woman (in the analogy that can be presumed between Creator and creature), thus also expresses the 'unity of the two' in a common humanity. This 'unity of the two,' which is a sign of interpersonal communion, shows that the creation of man is also marked by a certain likeness to the divine communion *('communio')*. This likeness is a quality of the personal being of both man and woman.[26]

In this text, the Holy Father points to the communional quality of the *imago Dei,* and introduces the link between the nuptial mystery and the divine communion.

Presented in this way, the doctrine of the *imago* allows us to grasp the nuptial mystery in all of its fullness. Through the law of ascending (analogical) analogy, the intertwining of sexual difference, love, and fruitfulness which shines through man and woman throws a singular light on ecclesiology (Christ the Bridegroom of the Church-Bride: cf. Eph 5:21-33) and, through the immolated flesh and blood poured out of the crucified Christ (Christology), on the life of the Trinity itself. These central mysteries of Christianity, in turn, allow us the better to comprehend the nuptial mystery as it is lived out by man and woman, through the descending (katalogical) law of analogy. The high point of the analogy is objectively encountered in the relation between the Trinity and the family. Insofar as it is the expression of perfect creaturely love, the family is an authentic *imago trinitatis.*[27]

A striking consequence of this theological vision of the human person can be found in its confirmation of the fundamental thesis of *Humanae Vitae* regarding the inseparability of the unitive and procreative meanings of the conjugal act. Moreover, it shows the important link with the central thesis of *Donum Vitae,* in which affirmation of *Humanae Vitae* is objectively included:

26. *Mulieris Dignitatem* 7.
27. The affirmations of Augustine (cf. *De Trinitate* 12.5-7) and Thomas (cf. *Summa Theologiae* I, q. 93, a. 6, ad 2) cannot be opposed to this reading.

The origin of the human being thus follows from a procreation that is 'linked to the union, not only biological, but also spiritual, of the parents, made by one bond of marriage.' Fertilization achieved outside the bodies of the couple remains by this very fact deprived of the meanings and the values which are expressed in the language of the body and in the union of human persons. (*DV* II B 4 b).

3. Ethical Perspectives

The ethical reflection of the past decade, especially in North America, has highlighted the restrictions of a norm-centered morality which observes human acts from the point of view of an observer, and claims to regulate them from the outside (a "third-person" approach to ethics).[28] Moreover, moral theology has sought to overcome the extrinsicism of its reference to Christology and to rework the theological framework of action. The perspectives revealed by an anthropology centered on the nuptial mystery are rich in consequences for ethics, in its triple level of act, moral subject, and communion.

3.1. The Eucharistic Dimension of Action

The human act, grasped in its original dimension, is essentially an act of love. It arises from an initial promise of fulfillment which it then tends to realize through a communion of persons, in an anticipation of the happiness of the Kingdom and as a human reflection of the glory of the Trinitarian life of God. In conversion and the following of Christ, the Christian's action is called to be, in history, a gesture of free correspondence to the supreme act of love of Christ on the Cross: the glorification of the Father through the gift of himself to the Church and to mankind.

The whole of Christ's gift of love remains permanently present and available in the Eucharist, which thus becomes the paradigmatic form and condition of the Christian's free action.[29] In the Eucharist, Christ the Bridegroom gives himself to the Bride, involving her in the dynamic of the sacrificial gift,

---

28. Cf. G. Abbà, *Felicità, vita buona e virtù. Saggio di filosofia morale* (Rome, 1989), 76-132.

29. The value of the Eucharist as the supreme act par excellence of human freedom, in which the gift anticipates death, can be found in the work of M. Blondel, *L'Action (1893). Essai d'une critique de la vie et d'une science de la pratique* (Paris, 1973), V, 1-2; this has been recently brought to light by M. Antonelli, *L'Eucharistia ne 'L'Action' (1893) de Blondel. La chiave di volta di un'antropologia filosofica* (Milan, 1993).

to the praise and glory of God. The Christian's action is a consent to love: "We have believed the love God has for us" (1 Jn 4:16).

Acts of conjugal love in particular are called to be rooted in the Eucharist, in order to be manifestations and actualizations of Christ's love for his Church: an integral gift of self, without reserve, which always implies body and soul and which must necessarily remain open to the fruitfulness of a communication of life as the superabundance of love.

3.2. Participating in the Virtues of Christ

In this way, the problem of ethics is located in the perspective of the subject (the "first person" perspective) who, as the author of his acts, perfects himself in love. Attention to the interior principles of action orients moral discourse to the virtues and to their root: charity as the union of love with Christ in the Spirit.[30]

Virtue is something "totally different from a habit":[31] it is an increase in freedom, a spiritual energy which forms the faculties and the inclinations and allows for excellent action. Far from being a mere repression of the passions, it realizes their "truthful integration"[32] in the light of the truth about the good of the person, called to the gift of himself in love. Impulse, emotion, passion, and affection are received in all their promise and raised to the spiritual level of encounter with another person. In this approach, moral rule is no longer an exterior control over natural dynamisms, but rather an education to virtue, or to the growth of freedom in love (St. Thomas Aquinas).[33]

In the Christian dimension, the virtues are "participations in the virtues of Christ" (St. Bonaventure),[34] who, through the Spirit, associates the Christian to his perfect love for the Father. The virtues are the wedding gift Christ makes to his Church in the Spirit, to make her perfect and "present the church to himself in splendor, without spot or wrinkle or any such thing, that

---

30. This perspective has been developed in L. Melina, *Sharing in Christ's Virtues: For a Renewal of Moral Theology in the Light of "Veritatis Splendor,"* trans. William E. May (Washington, D.C.: Catholic University of America Press, 2001).

31. Cf. S. Pinckaers, *Le renouveau de la morale* (Paris, 1979).

32. Cf. K. Wojtyla, *The Acting Person,* trans. Andrzej Potocki (Dordrecht, Boston, and London: D. Reidel, 1979), pt. 3 ("The Integration of the Person in the Action").

33. Cf. Thomas Aquinas, *Summa Theologiae* I-II, q. 92, a. 1; G. Abbà, *Lex et virtus. Studi sull'evoluzione della dottrina morale di san Tommaso d'Aquino* (Rome, 1983), 226-64.

34. Cf. Bonaventure, *III Sent.,* d. 34, p. 1, a. 1 (III, 737); A. Nguyen Van Si, *Seguire e imitare Cristo secondo san Bonaventura* (Milan, 1995), 179-203.

she might be holy and without blemish" (Eph. 5:27). The spousal charity of Christ, in which the Christian participates, is the mother and form of all the other virtues, which are like its strategies of actualization (St. Augustine).[35]

Conjugal morality is thus the expression of Christ's spousal charity for the Church. Chastity is not reduced to continence, but is the virtue of true love, strengthened in the spouses by the Spirit.

3.3. The Ecclesial Dwelling Place of Ethics

The question regarding the moral subject is also a question regarding the place of his genesis, the Church. Far from claiming autonomy or reducing himself to heteronomy, the Christian is a *son,* a son or daughter in the Son, generated into a new filial freedom by Christ's love for the Church.

The Church, the Bride of Christ, is also his Mother. In her, the Christian is born and formed in the virtues. In her his conscience is formed in an ecclesial "sense," which is the polar opposite of every autonomous presumption and every servile conformity. "He who wishes to live has a place to live, has a place from which to live. Come near, believe, let yourself be incorporated so that you may be made alive. Do not flee from the cohesion of the members."[36] The ecclesial communion becomes the *morum regula* not from an exterior and juridical point of view, as a limit, but as the interior reference of the heart and the mind.

If these are the essential outlines of the ethical development of a nuptial anthropology, the pastoral question becomes fundamentally the problem of the genesis and education of the Christian subject.

4. The Pastoral Dimension

4.1. The Work of Education

The prophecy of the nuptial mystery contained in *Humanae Vitae* has been much developed in the past thirty years. These developments reveal how the delicate matter which formed the encyclical's specific content actually im-

---

35. Cf. Augustine, *De moribus ecclesiae catholicae* 1.15.25. For Saint Thomas see P. J. Wadell, *The Primacy of Love: An Introduction to the Ethics of Thomas Aquinas* (New York and Mahwah, N.J., 1992), 125-41.

36. Augustine, *In Johannis evangelium tractatus* 26.13.

plied a whole conception of man and society, upon which civilization ultimately depends. In this framework, the work of education appears to be the
primary task of the Church. The "new evangelization" and the "third millennium," to cite two central terms of John Paul II's Magisterium, are inseparable
from the awareness that every human being is always *docibilis Dei* (cf. Jn
6:45). "Venerable brothers, beloved sons, all men of good will, great indeed is
the work of education . . . to which we now summon you" (*HV* 31).

This task requires, first of all, an adequate subject: the Church must be
born in the person as a response to the initiative of Jesus Christ, who generates his Bride in the sacrament (Holy Thursday) and on the Cross (blood and
water). For this reason, the Fathers spoke of Mary as the *Ecclesia immaculata.*
Around her are gathered the people of the baptized, incorporated into the
one body through faith and baptism, from which flows their personal mission. The ecclesial subject must express itself tangibly in all the realms of human existence (family, neighborhood, work), so that the salvific event of Jesus
Christ can be made present, open to sacramental encounter.

The ecclesial subject thus conceived is called to evangelize with full respect for the "method" proposed by Christ himself: "I am the *way,* the truth
and the life." This is the method of the incarnation, and it consists in opening
man to the whole of reality, involving him in a common journey towards the
Father.

Both subject and educational method require witnesses convinced of the
event of Jesus Christ as the principle of new life, free human beings who
know how to propose Jesus Christ to another's freedom. This holistic educational perspective draws the attention to "creat[ing] an atmosphere favorable
to the growth of chastity" (*HV* 22). In the context of the "observance and respect of the divine law regarding matrimony" (*HV* 19), "the teaching of the
Church regarding the proper regulation of birth is a promulgation of the law
of God Himself. And yet there is no doubt that to many it will appear not
merely difficult but even impossible to observe. . . . But to those who consider
the matter diligently it will indeed be evident that this endurance enhances
man's dignity and confers benefits on human society" (*HV* 20).

The Church, mother and teacher, treats man with the same attitude as
the redeemer: "She knows their weaknesses, she has compassion on the multitude, she welcomes sinners. But at the same time she cannot do otherwise
than teach the law. For it is in fact the law of human life restored to its native
truth and guided by the Spirit of God" (*HV* 19).

"Jesus Christ is the living and personal law" (*Veritatis Splendor* 15). Following him is not an "exterior imitation," but requires "becoming conformed to
him" (*VS* 21). As much as fragility may mark the human journey, that grace is

never lacking which gives the full freedom of the children of God. In his identification with Christ, the disciple discovers with amazement that his every action contains a breath of his relationship to the Father. Thus he is grateful that, in this identification, his wounded freedom is guided and sustained by the commandment: whoever hopes in God "purifies himself as he is pure" (1 Jn 3:3).

4.2. The Dominant Culture and the Temptations of the Christian

"In preserving intact the whole moral law of marriage, the Church is convinced that she is contributing to the creation of a truly human civilization" (*HV* 18).

Today's dominant culture invades even the lives of many Christians and puts them to the test ("temptation" in the evangelical sense); as we consider several of its primary characteristics, we will perhaps find it easier to see the prophetic force of the encyclical and its message, oriented as these are to tracing out the nuptial mystery.

4.2.1. Spiritualism

With its objective recognition of the full value of the body as sacrament of the whole person, *Humanae Vitae* points out the way to overcome the serious temptation of a disembodied spiritualism, very widespread today even among Christians. Such spiritualism ignores the method of the incarnation, by which Christ "appeared as a 'sacrament,' that is, the sign and instrument, of his divinity and of the salvation he brings: what was visible in his earthly life leads to the invisible mystery of his divine sonship and redemptive mission" (*CCC* 515). Thus, spiritualism ends in the materialistic logic of modern "health-consciousness," promising our mortal bodies an impossible eternity in the sense of the pure conservation of its biological functions. Both of these attitudes deprive the body of its sacramental meaning, thereby also impeding, in a faith perspective, a real grasp of the value of the ecclesial and eucharistic body as the place of the greatest freedom offered to man.

4.2.2. Androgynism

In the framework of the Magisterial developments of the past thirty years, the encyclical shows us how to overcome yet another macroscopic "temptation" of today's culture: androgynism. The term refers to the claim that the individual man is "capable" of both sexes (bisexual). By abolishing the insuperability of sexual difference, androgynism regards man and woman as two structurally unfulfilled halves, driven to search for an imaginary original unity. The fulfillment of the "I" is thought to be found in this illusory perspective of reuniting two halves in one, in the quest for an impossible lost peace. This perspective makes more and more room for the tragic illusion that sexuality can be reduced to a mere option; each person has the possibility of choosing his place in the sexual sphere, according to his personal sensibility.

Against the claim that culture can entirely "produce" nature, *Humanae Vitae* and successive Magisterial pronouncements have shown that in the framework of the nuptial mystery, sexual difference — when completely thought through — introduces difference not as something extraneous to the "I," but as the expression of the "I's" being for another. The body (as sacrament of the whole person) is defined all the way through by its insuperable sexual difference. This body is the basis of that human *dia-logos* which would otherwise be impossible; it is what makes possible actions (even the conjugal act) that are truly free.

4.2.3. Dualism

The prophecy of the nuptial mystery helps us, moreover, to counter the widespread temptation of a dichotomy between the personal and social dimensions of action. This dualism arises from the modern refusal of an Aristotelian concept taken up again by St. Thomas at the beginning of the *Secunda Pars* of the *Summa Theologiae:* insofar as man is a rational creature, his action must be considered from life taken as a whole, and thus ordered according to ends and goods that essentially characterize it. This approach allows for an understanding of human behavior as the practice of a good life, made up of personal and social behaviors with both private and public relevance, and without an artificial separation between individual and community. Sociopolitical reflection (moral philosophy) can then be understood as the practical philosophy of such behavior.[37]

Today, to the contrary, we find ourselves faced with an image of public ethics as opposed to a so-called private ethics, the faithful reflection of a preexistent division between personal freedom and civil and juridical freedom. Public ethics appears increasingly formal and based upon norms. As Alasdair MacIntyre rightly observes,[38] the dimension of the virtues is ex-

---

37. Cf. G. Abbà, *Quale impostazione per la filosofia morale?* (Rome, 1996), 33-203.

38. Cf. A. MacIntyre, *After Virtue: A Study in Moral Theory* (Notre Dame: University of Notre Dame Press, 1981).

cluded and ethics is abandoned to the pure free choice of the individual, separate from society. An incurable dialectic is thus generated between the sphere of subjective interests and the field of objective moral demands, creating an artificial opposition between desire and fulfillment, will and duty.

In the sphere of the family, for example, we find this dualism in the opposition between the desire for fatherhood and motherhood, on the one hand, and the child as a personal subject capable of socio-juridical autonomy on the other. The child is no longer considered to be the gratuitous fruit of the love of the spouses, but becomes an "object" subjected to the sovereign will of its parents (cf. *Evangelium Vitae* 42).

Thus we are witnesses to an ever greater accentuation of personal rights in the individualistic sphere — the consequence of a formalistic reading of the Golden Rule, "Do not do unto others what you would not have done unto you" — and a conception of freedom of conscience that claims to be absolute, loosed from the necessary reference to truth which, in its fullest sense, is Jesus Christ himself (*Veritatis Splendor* 15). Against these reductions, *Humanae Vitae's* prophecy of the nuptial mystery points to a highroad: living and documenting the attraction, and thus the *cumvenientia* [fittingness] for man (even for the man of today) of following the law of Christ as it presents itself in the indissoluble intertwining of sexual difference, love, and fruitfulness (the nuptial mystery). The inevitable experience of *detachment* (mortification) offers man the possibility of completely *possessing* the affective dimension of his own being, as the place of effective freedom. This cannot but influence all the other dimensions of his existence (work and social life).

The Engagement Period:
A Gift and a Task in the Preparation for Marriage

1. A Methodological Premise

In realities such as the engagement period, love, and marriage, concepts tend inevitably to meet and intertwine, not without risks of ambiguity and equivocation. Facing such realities in the contemporary cultural climate requires us not to lose sight of a fundamental criterion for a healthy critical faculty: to adhere as closely as possible to reality. To borrow a phrase from Husserl, one of the most influential philosophers in the history of Western thought, we need to make the effort today to "return to things in themselves." In this sense we find the great contribution of classical realism to be extremely pertinent: it defines the fundamental level of truth as thought's capacity to grasp reality and adjust to it (Thomas's *adaequatio intellectus ad rem*).

Nietzsche, too — the greatest, albeit tragic, genius among the interpreters of the contemporary conscience — stresses the same things: Husserl's demand to return to reality in itself, and the classical affirmation that the concept must tend toward reality. He uses a particularly felicitous expression: "I call a lie not wanting to see what is seen, and not wanting to see it as it is seen."[1] He makes the comment precisely in *The Antichrist*, the most severe reproach ever written against Christianity.

---

1. F. W. Nietzsche, *L'Anticristo* (Milan, 1981), 79-80 (*The Antichrist*, trans. Anthony M. Ludovici [Amherst, N.Y.: Prometheus Books, 2000]).

This text presents the greater part of a conversation held during the second national encounter for those responsible for pastoral work for the family, organized by the Italian Bishops Conference's office for the family (Rome, February 12-15, 1998).

In order to avoid the lie — not wanting to see something as it is seen — one must, then, turn to the thing in itself, to the res. This methodological criterion is more necessary than ever if we are to take up the constitutive terms of the Christian experience.

2. Betrothal, a Pledge of Fidelity

What, then, is the reality of the engagement period, or betrothal?

The term "betrothal" comes from "troth" or "treuth," the obsolete forms of "truth," and indicates a pledge of faith which involves giving something in token of the promise. One pledges one's troth, or entrusts oneself (promising to be true), because one knows that the person receiving the trust is true, or trustworthy. Concretely, engagement or betrothal coincides with an act — which can be formal, sealed by the exchange of rings — expressing the reciprocal entrustment of a man and a woman.

If, then, the *res* of a betrothal is the pledge, this pledge signifies the binding in advance of something else. The pledge is the anticipatory sign of an accomplished reality. From the point of view of the history of Western thought and of all cultures, from the most ancient to the most evolved, the pledge of faith given at the moment of betrothal is a sign and anticipation of that total and reciprocal gift of self called marriage. Our human and cultural fragility can relativize this elementary factor of experience as much as it pleases, but can never entirely eliminate it from the human heart. I never tire of repeating to young people: When you are really in love, I challenge you to say to your boyfriend or girlfriend, "I love you," without adding the "forever." You might even be intimately convinced that you do not know how to avoid falling short of this affirmation, but when the heart says in truth, "I love you," to someone, the "forever" comes naturally. This "forever" is part of the essence of the question. Marriage — and indissoluble marriage — is thus inexorably anticipated at the moment of betrothal.

What has been said thus far seems to me to be decisive. I am convinced that moralism, both in its rigorist and lax forms, constitutes the most fundamentally unfitting way to propose marriage to the young. Moralism arises precisely from the incapacity to present things — marriage — as they are, or from a lack of faith that the other's intelligence can grasp this reality. But things are the way they are according to God's design, and this design has implicated man's capacity to grasp its profound nature.

We, on the other hand, often imitate that father who, fuming at his daughter who announces, "I'm going out," says only, "No. Don't go." And when she asks, "Why not?" he responds, "Because I say so!" He does not know how to give reasons, how to convince. In a similar way we affirm (and rightly so!), "Marriage must be indissoluble," but allow ourselves to get caught in the "must" without ever advancing into the "why." If man does not grasp the nature of things, he cannot find a reason which convinces his freedom, that synthesis of intelligence and will, to adhere to reality as it presents itself. In that inseparable intertwining of being (ontology) and having-to-be (ethics) which marks human experience in its every act, it is the gaze at being — to things as they are — which transforms having-to-be into something creative and fresh. A similar gaze, beyond all fragility and incoherence, grants a certain ease to that supreme moral figure which Kierkegaard calls "starting over." Morality consists above all in this "starting over" which flows from repentance, and not in a presumptuous perfection.

3. Verification: Adhering, in Freedom, to a Constellation of Objective Signs

If we consider the fundamental experience of love simply and without prejudices, we must acknowledge the inseparability of the "I love you" and the "forever." Fidelity is not an accessory, but belongs to the very essence of love.

This fact brings us to the glowing heart of the question. We give the word once more to Balthasar. In *The Grain of Wheat: Aphorisms,* a series of real flashes of Christian intelligence, he writes, "Where there is infidelity, love was never present. Where there is fidelity, love does not yet necessarily exist. The heart can say: 'Even if I cannot love you, I want at least to be faithful to you.' But the bond of fidelity either leads to love or contains deep within itself, unknown to feeling, the knot of love, which is tied outside of time."[2]

The fidelity which is within love is in reality the culmination of love because it is what guarantees love's perpetual rebirth, even when it seems to be lost to one's self-consciousness and immediate perception. Fidelity has already bound the two in a tie that defies even time.

It is possible, from this affirmation, to trace out the history of love in the West. We could show, for example, the effects of romanticism's equivocal interpretation of love in the eighteenth and nineteenth centuries, which fatalistically linked love to death and thus destroyed it in its presupposition of responsibility.

The engagement period, on the other hand, is a time of verification; it is

---

2. H. U. von Balthasar, *The Grain of Wheat: Aphorisms,* trans Erasmo Leiva-Merikakis (San Francisco: Ignatius, 1995), 83.

the time when responsibility is brought increasingly into play. Because of it, the freedom of the two individuals is led to the *res* of marriage, and within this state to indissolubility, the supreme form of matrimonial fidelity. Indissolubility and fidelity are the reasons why marriage is, properly speaking, a vocation. What kind of vocation can there be in two people taking one another and then allowing themselves to be determined by their own instinct?

Only in its achieved form in the sacrament of the intimate and primordial nuptiality of Christ and the church does marriage attain indissolubility and reach its vocational summit. With respect for the clarifications made by the Council of Trent, this vocation is not qualitatively different from that of the vocation to virginity or consecrated life.

From the concept of fidelity as the supreme form of love, as Balthasar suggests, we understand the concept of verification. Some clarifications appear necessary with regard to this latter.

There is today a very widespread concept of vocational "verification" which identifies it entirely with "trying out" a way of life, with the illusion that the more "experiences" one amasses, the more one has a clear idea of one's vocation. To the contrary, the word "verification," from the Latin expression *verum facere*, has to do with a fact. At the origin of all the vocations of the Old and New Testaments is a surprise: something happens that is unforeseen and unforeseeable, sometimes downright resisted (think of the vocation of Jonah!).

I have sometimes said in speaking to youth, "Imagine that one of you, hearing a Franciscan brother who came to speak at your parish about his missionary work, is filled with enthusiasm and decides to leave for missionary work in Colombia. Imagine this young man seriously preparing himself for a couple of years, convincing mom and dad who were opposed to the idea, asking his fiancée to marry earlier than planned so that they can go together. Suppose he does all these things, and the evening before leaving, when everything has been prepared and he has the airplane ticket in his hands, Colombia suffers a coup d'état and the borders are closed. That young man did not have the vocation to be a missionary in Colombia. It is a fact. Obviously, this does not mean that his urge to dedicate himself to people in the developing world should be extinguished. It will find another outlet, which the eternal Father will show him."

Verification means seeing how life, step-by-step and through the constellation of signs that Providence offers to my free and public obedience, unveils the progressive story of my vocation in time. The verification of a vocation thus implies adherence to a constellation of signs, objectively identifiable traces in the life of someone who is free, and who for this reason is not afraid of the public and binding dimension of his choice.

Have you never asked yourself why so many young people flee from this public dimension of their affective relationships? (By this I refer not so much to letting themselves be seen together as presenting their companion to their parents or to the community.) In my opinion, it is because they have lost the idea of verification. We have already observed how a freedom which is reduced to free choice avoids every sort of bond.

When verification does not imply a total commitment of one's freedom and is carried out in a series of "trials," the path of obedience to facts, the only way to construct the history of one's personality and fulfill it, is lost.

After having accomplished the whole process of verification, one can rediscover the value of "discernment," liberating the word (so fashionable today!) from an ambiguous interpretation that would make it some sort of previous analysis made in the safety of one's home. The word originally meant a conscious and critical scrutiny. Were it placed at the beginning, discernment would not be able to avoid falling into one of two traps: a total and totally illusory self-determination or alienation in another's judgment, both of which destroy the Christian idea of vocation.

To decide autonomously, without listening to the voice of the One who calls, means not to respect the nature of vocation, much less of mission. No one sends himself, not even the Son or the Spirit! The most fundamental and rigorous concept of mission implies this impossibility of sending oneself. But he who calls (vocation), calls me: no one can substitute for my responsibility, nor can I cede it to anyone, no matter how holy or how wise they might be.

4. Affection: The Great School of the "Thou" as the Condition for the Realization of the "I"

The marrow of the engagement period and marriage is, obviously, affection. Affection and work are the two great dimensions in which the human person fulfills his personality. On this point Freud utters a great truth when he says that the psychologically healthy person is the one who knows how to work and to love.[3]

The affective dimension is thus one of the two great axes along which man fulfills his existence and realizes his personality in an integral way. Saint John's great affirmation, echoing the prophets, can be applied here: we will always be capable of being taught by God.[4] In the dimensions of affection and

---

3. This idea can be found in the first chapters (especially chaps. 2 and 4) of his essay *The Unease of Civilization.*

4. John 6:45, "They shall all be taught be God," which takes up Isa. 54:13 and Jer. 31:33ff.

work, understood in their fullest sense, we will always be capable of learning, "from the cradle to the grave." Each phase of our lives is a possibility of growth.

So what is affection? Once again we find the etymology of the word to be the most limpid source of the connection between concept and reality. As we have already seen, *affici aliqua re* is the Latin passive verbal form meaning "to be struck by something."[5] Something happens to you, and you must first of all register the blow. We can therefore define affection as a phenomenon by which man is "taken" by something or someone. He is driven to direct all the energies of his person — intelligence, will, and freedom — to the other who provokes him, because he feels this pro-vocation to be the possibility of a previously unimagined fulfillment.

Falling in love as the root of betrothal has in this sense a strong pedagogical force: the nature of things (that is, God's plan for them) always accompanies this provocation from the other with an attraction. The path of human affection — falling in love, engagement, marriage — thus begins in a *passio* which fills the presence of the other with attraction for me, and provokes me to a response. This response is at the same time (even if at the beginning the two things can be distinguished only with difficulty) a desire for the good of the other and a desire for the good for me.

Thus the affective dimension, and the man-woman relationship in a privileged way, is the great school of the "I." It is the place where one learns that without the other it is impossible really to say "I." In other words, it is the school of the "thou" as the condition for saying "I," for learning the weight and the place of the other in my own life.

You, woman, are as fully person as I, man. Yet you are this in a way that is radically different from my own, so decisive and so inaccessible. You are, precisely, *other.* Here we see all the force of the originality of man and woman. Or, in psychoanalytic terms confirmed unawares by the Christian vision of life, sexual difference is insuperable. So it is that if even today, at the turn of the millennium, we can still find forms of discrimination between men and women, this is not due to the fact that people are not thinking enough about equality. It is because they are not thinking deeply enough about difference. Unfortunately, even the most perceptive forms of feminism have yet to realize this.

This is why I prefer the expression "asymmetrical reciprocity" to the more widespread "complementarity" to describe the "quality" of the relationship between man and woman. Even in the most intimate form of the unity

5. Cf. above, pp. 59-64.

between husband and wife — the biblical "one flesh" — difference is not abolished. The other remains irreducibly "other." And this insuperable difference between the two is the sign and place of the third: it points to the place of the child.

It is not for nothing that Balthasar, one of those who have thought these things all the way through, affirms in his work on contemplative prayer, "The only analogy nature seems to offer to the intimacy with the divine truth is the union of the sexes, though the analogy holds only if we omit the time interval between the union of the two persons in one flesh and its result in the birth of a child."[6]

At this point we can grasp the full meaning of the relation between man and woman in all its breadth, as God designed it and as Scripture describes it: the nuptial mystery is an indissoluble intertwining of sexual difference (the thing in itself), love (the I-thou relation), and fruitfulness (procreation).

To return to the main theme, we can say in summary that the engagement period is the place of fidelity where, with a singular attraction, the "I" is called to the great school of the other in order to learn itself. In this sense we remember the commandment, "Love your neighbor as yourself." In the great debate about the nature of true love, we must accept neither the position of exaggerated and suspicious altruism nor that which is too hurriedly egotistic. Even in the most complete forgetfulness of self, the natural drive to the fulfillment of one's own "I" cannot be avoided. The love of God, the love of the other, and the love of self are three dimensions of love. Obviously the love of self is understood here as the love of one's objective good, and not as an egotistical self-love.

If this is the case, the profound root of the affection between a man and a woman lies in a value judgment.

Young people seem to stir themselves awake when they hear such things, because they are very open to the truth of things, to things as they are in themselves. The tragedy lies in ourselves, who often veil the truth of things with abstract discourse. It is true that some subjects are difficult and even hard to take — this is undeniable — but that is different. Difficulty is one thing, abstraction another. That which is abstract is separated from life.

Thus a value judgment lies at the root of affection: Why does the other deserve to be loved completely? Because I see that to love the other's destiny completely is also something good for me, because in so doing I accomplish

---

6. H. U. von Balthasar, *Prayer* (New York: Sheed and Ward, 1961), 64. It is important that Balthasar reaches such an affirmation by meditating on the Trinity, so faithful is his approach to the constitutive structure of being!

my own good? These questions touch the deepest recesses of the "I"; a response to them involves the Christian proposal. Someone let himself freely (*sponte,* says Saint Anselm with an even greater acuity) be annihilated on the ignominious gallows of the cross for our good, and did not disdain to cry, "Why have you forsaken me?" putting the whole fulfillment of his own good at stake: he is the measure of the other's destiny and my destiny, of the other's fulfillment and my own.

He is my contemporary, and I can follow him in that constellation of relationships that he has built up, and which, without a break in continuity, has reached even me. It is called the church. Even I have entered, by grace, into the company of his friends which stretches generation after generation.

Christ is the root of the affection which blossoms between man and woman because he generated his bride on the cross and keeps her alive, fresh, without stain or wrinkle, beyond all the sins of the faithful, including pastors and ecclesial authorities, beyond (to borrow an expression from Maritain) the sins of the *persons* of the church, which are not to be confused with the *Person* of the church.

Young people must be helped to understand that the ideal for which they are being prepared by the attraction of falling in love and by the engagement period is this nuptiality between Christ and the church, the original and eschatological couple that the Father had in mind when he created man and woman.

Man and woman are the great path that educates us to this ultimate level of nuptiality, the wedding feast of the Lamb.

The Nuptial Mystery:
A Perspective for Systematic Theology?

1. Beyond a Classical Prohibition

We have already noted the impossibility of approaching the Holy Spirit except from two directions at once: as the (subjective) quintessence of the mutual love of Father and Son, hence, as the bond *(nexus)* between them; and as the (objective) fruit that stems from and attests to this love. This impossibility translates into a convergence of the poles. Imagine for a moment that the act of love between a man and woman did not include nine months of pregnancy, that is, the aspect of time. In the parents' generative-receptive embrace, the child would already be immediately present; it would be at one and the same time their mutual love in action and something more, namely, its transcendent result. . . . In this sense, it is precisely perfect creaturely love that is an authentic *imago Trinitatis*.[1]

Balthasar's affirmation, which dares to go beyond the radical objections of the two greatest authorities of Catholic theology, Augustine and Thomas,[2] can serve as an introduction both to the nature of the "nuptial mystery" and

---

1. Hans Urs von Balthasar, *Theologik,* vol. 3, *Der Geist der Wahrheit* (Einsiedeln: Johannes Verlag, 1987), 145-46.
2. Cf. Augustine, *De Trinitate* 12.5.5; Thomas Aquinas, *Summa Theologiae* I, q. 93, a. 6.

Original title, "Lezione di congedo. Il mistero nuziale: una prospettiva di teologia sistematica?" given at the Lateran University, December 10, 2002. This document was Cardinal Scola's farewell address to the Pontifical John Paul II Institute for Studies on Marriage and Family, where he served as president from 1996 to 2002.

to the range of its systematic possibilities.[3] Both of these factors immediately place the themes of marriage and the family — for centuries, and partly still today, relegated to theological isolation — at the heart of the knowledge of faith as such.[4] Through the use of analogy, Balthasar simultaneously brings into play both the mystery of the Trinity and the "nuptial mystery," thus going beyond the "prohibition" against seeing the natural triad of father, mother, and child as an image of the Trinity. This decision amounts to a claim that the nuptial mystery has objective implications for working out the elaboration of the *intellectus fidei* of revelation (theology). In order to justify this systematic claim, we must first briefly explain the content of the "nuptial mystery."

2. Theology's Openness to the Themes of the Nuptial Mystery

The Second Vatican Council, and the Pastoral Constitution *Gaudium et Spes* in particular,[5] gave the discussion of the questions surrounding marriage a new anthropological depth, without thereby succumbing to the temptation of an excessive emphasis on the subjective in Christian reflection on marriage and the family.[6] In this way the council favored a certain recuperation of these themes from the margins of theology. Until then, they had essentially been the preserve of canon law (consent-contract), moral theology (the sixth and ninth commandments), spirituality (the value of the couple), and pastoral theology (which saw marriage and the family as worthy of greater attention by the Christian community).

On the other hand, we must acknowledge that theological reflection on

---

3. Given the nature of the present article, many of the footnotes refer to other publications of mine. In these the reader will be able to find many pertinent bibliographical references.

4. Cf. Chapter 12 above.

5. Cf. *GS* 47-52.

6. Cf. Ph. Dehaye, "La communauté conjugale et familiale d'après Vatican II," in J. Giblet and J. Etienne, *Aux sources de la morale conjugale* (Gembloux and Paris, 1967), 157-73; V. Fagiolo, "Essenza e fini del matrimonio nel magistero del Concilio Vaticano II," *Ephemerides Iuris Canonici* 23 (1967): 137-86; F. Gil Hellín, "El lugar proprio del amor conyugal en la estructura del matrimonio según la *Gaudium et spes*," *Anales Valentinos* 6 (1980): 1-35; A. Miralles, "Amor y matrimonio en la *Gaudium et spes*," *Lateranum* 48 (1982): 295-354; E. Kaczynski, "Le mariage et la famille. La communion des personnes," *Divinitas* 26 (1982): 317-31; D. Tettamanzi, *I due saranno una carne sola. Saggi teologici su matrimonio e famiglia* (Leumann-Turin: Elle Di Ci, 1986), 103-21; A. Mattheeuws, *Les "dons" du mariage. Recherche de théologie morale et sacramentelle* (Brussels, 1996), 136-50, 260-63, 352-54, 465-68.

marriage is perhaps only now finding a way out of the long-standing impasse created by an unclear theology of the sacrament.[7] Critics have highlighted the objective underdevelopment of a theology of the family, which was treated as an appendix to the theology of marriage.[8]

It is without doubt the merit of John Paul II's teaching to have brought "nuptial language" (and not merely "spousal vocabulary")[9] to general attention.[10] (It is noteworthy that the "catecheses on human love" of the beginning of his pontificate repeat the conclusions of his work on the subject as Karol Wojtyla.)[11] While we do not claim to expound, or even to summarize, the pope's detailed teaching on this matter,[12] it will be helpful to draw attention to two fundamental elements of nuptial language.

The first element, whose privileged locus is chapter 3 of *Mulieris Dignitatem*,[13] consists in an original development of the notion of the *imago Dei*. John Paul II does not limit himself, in the footsteps of the Judeo-Christian tradition, which continues to leave its mark even on secularized Western thought, to identifying the content of the image of God with the human being's rational

7. Cf. E. O'Neill, "I sacramenti," in R. Vander Gucht and H. Vorgrimler, *Bilancio della teologia del XX secolo*, vol. 3 (Rome: Città Nuova, 1972), 295; P. F. Palmer, "Necessità di una teologia del matrimonio," *Communio* (Italian) 16 (1974): 1000-1009; D. Tettamanzi, "Matrimonio," *La Scuola Cattolica* 114 (1986): 585; G. Marengo, "Creazione, alleanza, sacramentalità del matrimonio," *Anthropotes* 8 (1992): 27-39.

8. One writer has gone so far as to say that "In the Christian tradition, discourse about marriage has proceeded without awareness of the need to prolong it into a theory of the family; it has even positively precluded such a development" (G. Angelini, "La Chiesa e la Famiglia," *La Scuola Cattolica* 120 [1992]: 467-68).

9. For clarity's sake, it may be useful to distinguish between "spousal vocabulary," "nuptial language," and the "nuptial mystery." By "spousal vocabulary" I refer to concrete spousal images (bride-bridegroom, the wedding feast, adultery, etc.), of which the Scriptures offer numerous examples. By the term "nuptial language" I mean the hermeneutical elaboration of spousal categories. The most outstanding example of this occurs in Eph. 5:21-33; here the use of the comparison Christ-church/husband-wife led the Council of Trent to affirm that in this passage the author of the letter "*innuit* [hints at]" the sacramentality of marriage (cf. Denzinger-Schönmetzer, *Enchiridion symbolorum*, 1799 [hereafter DS]). Lastly, the expression "nuptial mystery" indicates a critical and organic elaboration of nuptial language for the sake of the *intellectus fidei*.

10. Among the authors who have dealt with these themes, we can cite Matthias-Joseph Scheeben, Vladimir Soloviev, Gaston Fessard, Martin Buber, Emmanuel Lévinas, and Hans Urs von Balthasar.

11. The complete catecheses on human love have been collected in English in John Paul II, *The Theology of the Body: Human Love in the Divine Plan* (Boston: Daughters of St. Paul, 1997).

12. Cf. above, pp. 3-52.

13. *MD* 6-8. The pope explores the theme of the image particularly in catecheses 8 and 9 of the first cycle: "The Original Unity of Man and Woman" and "Through the Communion of Persons Man Becomes the Image of God."

and free nature. The pope highlights the communional *qualitas* of the image.[14] Man and woman are the image of God not only as individuals, but also insofar as they are capable of interpersonal communion. This brilliant development builds in a novel way upon the important passage in *Gaudium et Spes* 24,[15] which hinges on what amounts to an anthropological broadening of the notion of *communio*. Following one company of a school of phenomenological thought (Scheler, Ingarden) and relying to a certain extent on personalist philosophy,[16] the pope frees the theological notion of *communio* from an inevitable provincialism resulting from its relegation to a few chapters of eucharistic theology, ecclesiology, and eschatology. Indeed, he makes *communio* an integral anthropological category that can tackle the central question about man, in terms of the elementary datum of the Creator's decision that "the human being should always and only exist as a woman or as a man."[17]

In the space opened by the exploration of this unique "unity of the two,"[18] the second innovative element of Wojtyla–John Paul II's thought takes shape: the theology of the body — the body which exists only in sexual differ-

---

14. A detailed example of this would require a complete citation of *MD* 7, but we can limit ourselves for now to the text's central affirmation: "The fact that man 'created as man and woman' is the image of God means not only that each of them individually is like God, as a rational and free being. It also means that man and woman, created as a 'unity of the two' in their common humanity, are called to live in a communion of love, and in this way to mirror in the world the communion of love that is in God, through which the Three Persons love each other in the intimate mystery of the one divine life. The Father, Son, and Holy Spirit, one God through the unity of the divinity, exist as persons through the inscrutable divine relations. Only in this way can we understand the truth that God in himself is love (cf. 1 Jn 4:16). The image and likeness of God in man, created as man and woman (in the analogy that can be presumed between Creator and creature), thus also expresses the 'unity of the two' in their common humanity. This 'unity of the two,' which is a sign of interpersonal communion, *shows that the creation of man* is also marked by a certain likeness to the divine communion *('communio')*. This likeness is a quality of the personal being of both man and woman, and is also a call and a task."

15. "Indeed, the Lord Jesus, when He prayed to the Father, 'that all may be one . . . as we are one' (Jn 17:21-22) opened up vistas closed to human reason, for He implied a certain likeness between the union of the divine Persons, and the unity of God's sons in truth and charity. This likeness reveals that man, who is the only creature on earth which God willed for itself, cannot fully find himself except through a sincere gift of himself" (*GS* 24).

16. Cf. A. Wierzbicki, "La persona e la morale. Presentazione," in K. Wojtyla, *L'uomo nel campo della responsabilità* (Milan, 2002), 7-16; P. Jobert, "Jean-Paul II. Philosophe de la transition de l'anthropologie classique à l'anthropologie moderne," in *Karol Wojtyla: Filosofo, Teologo, Poeta* (Vatican City: Libreria Editrice Vaticana, 1984), 47-52; A. Poltawski, "The Epistemological Basis of Karol Wojtyla's Philosophy," in *Karol Wojtyla,* 79-91; T. Styczen, "Responsabilità dell'uomo nei confronti di sè e dell'altro," in *Karol Wojtyla,* 107-27.

17. *MD* 1.

18. Cf. *MD* 7.

ence — as a sacrament of the whole person.[19] This decisive point is the backbone of the pivotal argument of the Congregation of the Doctrine of the Faith's *Donum Vitae*.[20]

3. Nuptial Language and Dramatic Anthropology

This twofold development — the communional quality of the image of God and the sexually differentiated body as the sacrament of the whole person — incorporates the best developments of theological anthropology. Notwithstanding its relatively recent emergence as a material of study (even today one encounters difficulties in introducing it as a separate subject in many faculties),[21] theological anthropology has produced a number of important results, while avoiding both the risk of an erroneous interpretation of the anthropological turn[22] and a capitulation to a system à la Hegel.[23]

The term "dramatic," which Balthasar uses to describe an adequate anthropology, can be taken as standing for a whole maturation of the *intellectus fidei* regarding man. The process is the fruit of numerous contributions, which we cannot list exhaustively here.[24] One thing is certain, however: "drama" goes right to the heart of the ex-centric nature of man. Man is an enigma ("he exists but does not have the foundation of his existence in himself") that finds its explanation key in Christ — the key, but not the predetermination of his own drama (Christology does not absorb anthropology).[25]

19. Particularly important in this regard is catechesis 19 of the first cycle, "Man Enters the World as a Subject of Truth and Love."

20. "Spouses mutually express their personal love in the 'language of the body,' which clearly involves both 'sponsal meanings' and parental ones. The conjugal act by which the couple mutually expresses their self-gift at the same time expresses openness to the gift of life. It is an act that is inseparably corporal and spiritual. It is in their bodies and through their bodies that the spouses consummate their marriage and are able to become father and mother" (Congregation for the Doctrine of the Faith, *Donum Vitae* II, B 4b). Cf. Scola, *Il mistero nuziale*, 1:171-76.

21. Cf. A. Scola, G. Marengo, and J. Prades, *La persona umana. Antropologia teologica* (Milan: Jaca Book, 2000), 26-37.

22. Cf. Scola, Marengo, and Prades, *La persona umana*, 34-36, 48-49.

23. In this regard, cf. G. Colombo, "Sull'antropologia teologica," *Teologia* 20 (1995): 223-60.

24. Among the major postconciliar contributions in the area of theological anthropology, see M. Flick and Z. Alszeghy, *Fondamenti di una antropologia teologica* (Florence: Libreria Ed. Fiorentina, 1970); K. Rahner, *La grazia come libertà* (Rome: Paoline, 1970); J. Alfaro, *Cristologia e antropologia* (Assisi: Cittadella, 1973); O. H. Pesch, *Liberi per grazia* (Brescia: Queriniana, 1988).

25. Cf. A. Scola, *Hans Urs von Balthasar: A Theological Style* (Grand Rapids: Eerdmans, 1995), 84-100; Scola, *Questioni di antropologia teologica* (Rome: PUL-Mursia, 1997), 29-41.

Now the enigma-drama of man is rendered clamorously present in the experience of every individual precisely through sexual difference. Each child which comes into being through the encounter of father and mother experiences in himself, deeply, what it means to exist without having one's foundation in oneself (man as enigma). The child experiences this particularly in having to deal with sexual difference along the whole span of his life (man as drama).[26]

4. Spousal Vocabulary, Nuptial Language, and the Nuptial Mystery

Nuptial language, which is already a theological elaboration of spousal categories,[27] demands a critical, organic work of the *intellectus fidei*. We have given the result of this work the name "nuptial mystery" — a formula that remains provisional.

Why "mystery" (taken, obviously, in the sense that Scheeben gives to the word)?[28] Because its objective link to the foundation gives it a share in the latter's ungraspability, which can be fittingly described in the ultimately Augustinian formula *incomprehensibiliter comprehendere incomprehensibile* [incomprehensibly to comprehend the incomprehensible].[29] In other words, the

---

26. In my writings I have generally tried to avoid the more abstract term "sexuality," and to speak instead of "sexual difference," precisely in order to show that it is impossible to speak of sexuality without speaking concretely of sexual difference. It would be more rigorous to say that the individual always exists in sexual difference. The neologism "sexuation" employed by depth psychology better expresses the dynamic character of sexual difference, which brings into play the constitutive nucleus of this individual's personality (including the deep dynamisms of the unconscious), from the beginning to the end of his life. Contrary to a widespread superficial opinion, this open, process character of "sexuation" fully expresses the fact that the individual, in every one of his actions, remains within an insuperable and nondeducible sexual difference. In this regard cf. M. Binasco, "Sulla sessualità femminile," in Scuola Europea di Psicoanalasi, *Madre Donna*, G.I.S.E.P. (Rome, 1993), 9-22.

27. On spousal vocabulary, see the lectures of B. Ognibeni, *Il matrimonio nell'Antico Testamento* and *Il matrimonio nel nuovo Testamento*, in manuscript form (Rome, 2002). More specifically on marriage, cf. A. Tosato, *Il matrimonio israelitico* (Rome: Biblical Institute Press, 1982). A careful study of the use of spousal categories in the key of a nuptial language can be found in J. Sanz, *La simología esponsal como clave hermenéutica del carisma de santa Clara de Asís* (Rome: Pontificium Athenaeum Antonianum, 2000). The author studies the linguistic and anthropological presuppositions of nuptial language (27-96) and then discusses its use in the biblical tradition (97-180) and in patristic and medieval theology (181-313).

28. Cf. M. J. Scheeben, *The Mysteries of Christianity* (London: Herder, 1946), §2-3.

29. This paradoxical formula was coined by Jean-Luc Marion (cf. J. L. Marion, "A Discussion between Jacques Derrida and Jean-Luc Marion," in *God, Gift, and Post-Modernism*,

originality of sexual difference constantly brings the experience-thought of nuptiality into play in each individual. It is here that we find a preeminent witness to the dramatic character of human existence. Since we exist necessarily only within sexual difference, each one of us is driven onto the path of love, whose unitive and procreative tension — since man is a *synholon* of body and soul[30] — objectively tends toward the fruit of new life. In this way nuptiality reveals to the individual the ontological impossibility of realizing oneself within sexual difference without simultaneously bringing into play the experience of love as capacity for procreation.

We should not be confused by the fact that the exercise of sexuality can take place outside of the horizon of an authentic act of love, or that for some decades now contraception has enabled the separation of sexuality from its objective openness to procreation, or that in the ever-nearer future, technology may make commonplace a type of procreation that prescinds from sexuality. The insidious "technological imperative" which the dominant mentality infers from this state of affairs — "since it can be done, it has to be done!" — has nothing scientific about it.[31] It is the idolatrous expression of a utopian madness, to which, particularly in the popular understanding, the achievements of science and technology remain exposed. In order to unmask the idolatry (that is, the lie) present in this "imperative," we can draw once again upon the fundamental truth of the *nuptial mystery* as expressed by Balthasar: "Perhaps the only natural analogy for our intimacy with divine truth is that of the union of the sexes; but to be a fruitful analogy it must be taken together with the fruit of this union, the child, ignoring the temporal hiatus between the two."[32]

The unity of the three constituents of the nuptial mystery is, so to speak, ontological. The difficulty in winning this unity a hearing among our contemporaries is no different from the difficulties we encounter in speaking of any other aspect of fundamental human experience. Just think of "knowledge" and of the stubborn resistance that greets the conviction that one can, under precise conditions, attain a true and certain knowledge of realities such as God, good, and evil.[33]

---

ed. J. D. Caputo and M. J. Scanlon [Bloomington and Indianapolis: Indiana University Press, 1999], 75). Marion draws the term from a passage of Augustine's *De Trinitate* (15.2.2), which is echoed by both Anselm (*Monologion* 64) and Thomas (*Summa Theologiae* I q. 12, a. 7).

30. Cf. *Gaudium et Spes* 14.

31. Cf. A. Scola, "Differenza sessuale e procreazione," in *Quale vita? La bioetica in questione* (Milan: Mondadori, 1998), 143-68, 368-80.

32. Hans Urs von Balthasar, *Prayer*, trans. Graham Harrison (San Francisco: Ignatius, 1986), 78.

33. These difficulties are pointed out in *Fides et Ratio* 5. Cf. on this subject A. Scola, "The

5. The *Nuptial Mystery* and the Event of the Foundation

At this point in our discussion, how are we to understand the extension in time *(diastasis)* of the procreative fruit of the unitive act made possible by sexual difference? The answer can be found precisely in a consideration of man's dramatic nature. In the original, nonderived character of sexual difference, love, and procreation — the expression of man's "flesh" that both places him firmly in the world and opens him to the other/the beyond — the individual is faced with the inescapable question, "And I, what am I?"[34] Because it powerfully unveils the fundamental anthropological question, the nuptial mystery opens the human being to the event of the foundation. For now, rejecting every formal *epoché* that excludes everything revealed, and Christian revelation in particular, from the horizon of the phenomena, we can simply say that the threefold nuptial mystery finds its confirmation in the gratuitous self-gift of the trinitarian foundation. Difference, love, and fruitfulness can be discerned in God himself.[35] Even in the immanent Trinity, in which there is neither temporal *diastasis* nor sexed body, the unitive and generative dimension of love brought about by perfect personal difference within absolute identity of substance[36] is still present. The person of the Holy Spirit is the fruit of the nexus of fruitful unity between the Father and the Son. Both generative-receptive embrace and its fruit are present primarily in the superior (spiritual) form of love.[37] Under precise conditions this integral vision of the nuptial mystery, which involves other analogates connected to the central mysteries of Christianity, unveils the full meaning of the individual's experience. Nor need we underestimate the weight of time. The *diastasis* mentioned above, far from underwriting the separation of the three dimensions of the nuptial mystery (difference, love, and procreation), expresses the created and inevitably contingent modality in which the *imago Trinitatis* is enacted. In the footsteps of Blondel, Balthasar affirms that "[This *imago Trinitatis*] is perma-

---

Integrity of Human Experience: Cultural Dimensions and Implications of the Encyclical *Fides et Ratio*," in L. P. Hemming and S. F. Parsons, *Restoring Faith in Reason* (London: SCM Press, 2002), 256-76.

34. G. Leopardi, "Canto notturno del pastore errante dell'Asia," v. 89 in *Canti*, ed, Mario Fubini (Turin, 1971), 183.

35. Cf. above, pp. 96-104; David L. Schindler, "Catholic Theology, Gender, and the Future of Western Civilization," in *Heart of the World, Center of the Church* (Grand Rapids and Edinburgh: Eerdmans and T. & T. Clark, 1996), 237-74.

36. Cf. *Catechism of the Catholic Church* 252-55.

37. Cf. M. Ouellet, "Lo Spirito Santo sigillo dell'alleanza coniugale," in *Il Matrimonio in Cristo è Matrimonio nello Spirito*, ed. R. Bonetti (Rome, 1998), 73-96.

nent proof of the triadic structure of creaturely logic. It shows that, when creatures attempt to introduce abstract logical principles — the axiom of the excluded middle — into real life (in the form of contraception), they contradict the law of that life."[38]

St. Thierry ### 6. "Amor a Quo Omnis Amor . . ."

As a perspective from which to do the work of the *intellectus fidei,* the nuptial mystery sheds light on the fundamental experience of human love in all its expressions, even in the degraded form that C. S. Lewis terms *Venus.*[39] In the face of the "abolition of man" threatening our society today, the capacity to hold together all of the manifestations of love in a single analogical unity is of decisive importance. Now more than ever, a witness to the nuptial mystery is needed for the church's task (which can no longer be put off for the future) of (pastorally) regenerating the subject. The nuptial witness, in fact, bears out the depth of Guillaume de Saint-Thierry's exclamation, "O Amor, a quo omnis amor cognominatur etiam carnalis ac degener!" [Love, from which every love is named — even carnal and degenerate loves].[40] To realize that this is a relevant aspect of the Christian mission, we need only reflect on how the dominant culture at any rate still uses the word "love" to describe a vast array of manifestations, including disfigured ones, of the I-thou relationship. The personal experience of the nuptial mystery, transcending the long dispute between physical and ecstatic love,[41] allows the Christian to discover, even in its most aberrant forms, the need for love that cannot be removed from the human heart. And to establish how things really stand with love: to say "love," one must always also imply sexual difference and fruitfulness.[42]

It is beyond the scope of this study to show how the nuptial mystery, integrally understood, might open interesting possibilities for understanding man's relationship to all living beings and to the cosmos, through the use and development of the highly differentiated scholastic notion of *amor naturalis.*[43]

---

38. H. U. von Balthasar, *Theo-logic II: Truth of God,* trans. Adrian J. Walker (San Francisco: Ignatius, 2004), 62.

39. Cf. C. S. Lewis, *The Four Loves* (London: Fontana Books, 1960), 7-14.

40. Guillaume de Saint-Thierry, *Expositio super Cantica,* preface, 25.

41. Cf. above, pp. 64-71.

42. Cf. above, pp. 110-37.

43. Cf. above, pp. 59-64; Scola, "Freedom, Grace, and Destiny," *Communio* 25, no. 3 (fall 1995): 439-61.

7. A Synthetic Description

It is helpful at this point to give a synthetic description of the nuptial mystery. The expression indicates the organic unity of sexual difference, love (objective relation to the other), and fruitfulness. Beginning from the man-woman relation (paternity, maternity, fraternity, sorority), it opens out onto all the manifestations of love. Because it indicates an essential property of love, the nuptial mystery is present in every form of love, whether human or divine: in the man-woman relation, friendship, charity, the sacrament, the church, Jesus Christ, and the Trinity.[44]

8. A Perspective for Systematic Theology?

Can we now eliminate the question mark in the title of this essay and recognize the legitimacy of the nuptial mystery as a key to the *intellectus fidei* of revelation? Can we claim that the nuptial mystery opens a perspective for systematic theology? Before definitively answering this question, we must critically examine two positions that appear to prevent a "Yes": one by way of excess and the other by way of deficiency. Both have to do with the use of analogy which, as in every theological exercise, is intrinsic to the proposal of the nuptial mystery. We cannot enter into this decisive and delicate methodological point, which has already been subjected to much scrutiny and yet is always begging for new and expanded study.[45] We must limit ourselves to the affirmation that the nuptial mystery presupposes a knowledge of the Trinity and so claims to take account of the twofold movement of analogy, understood in the fullest sense as *analogia libertatis*:[46] the movement from below upwards (ana-logic), and the movement from above downwards (kata-logic).[47]

---

44. Cf. Scola, *Uomo-donna. Il "caso serio" dell'amore* (Genoa: Marietti, 2002).

45. I limit myself to referring the reader to my summary account of this matter in Chapter 12 above.

46. Cf. H. U. von Balthasar, *Theo-Drama*, vol. 3, *Dramatis Personae: Persons in Christ*, trans. Graham Harrison (San Francisco: Ignatius, 1992), 220-29.

47. Balthasar takes the expression from Gerken; cf. A. Gerken, *Theologie des Wortes, das Verhältnis von Schöpfung und Inkarnation bei Bonaventura* (Düsseldorf: Patmos, 1963), 323. Cf. Balthasar, *Theo-logic II*, 169. With regard to the spousal analogy, Claudio Giuliodori is an obligatory reference: C. Giuliodori, *Intelligenza teologica del maschile e del femminile* (Rome: Città Nuova, 1991), especially 81-112.

9. A Maximalist Interpretation

As for the so-called "maximalist" interpretation of the nuptial mystery, I would say from the outset that it runs the risk of turning it into a Hegelian-type "system."[48] While aiming at a modern, conceptualistic foundation for the nuptial mystery, it ultimately tends toward an anthropomorphic deformation of our understanding of God, and even introducing sexuality into God himself.[49] Recent theological explorations in this direction have rightly triggered great perplexity. Some have even gone so far as to try to "sex" the Trinity, in an effort to find an argument in favor of homosexuality.[50] This maximalistic temptation abandons analogy for univocity. Its underlying logic, whether its proponents intend it to or not, ultimately makes the claim that spousal categories are the only categories capable of elaborating the *intellectus fidei* of the mysteries of Christianity, and are therefore the only categories fit to illuminate Christian dogma. To move in this direction is to engage in bad theology. As is the case with every other theological language, nuptial language must remain analogical, limiting itself to uncovering yet another point of view that can enrich the great tradition of Christian thought. If we take our cue from the spousal vocabulary from the Bible, we can opportunely integrate the language of being, substance, causality, the transcendentals, and gift with the nuptial mystery.

In any case, I must stress that this reflection remains open regarding the possibility of a rigorous, analytical use of the categories of "male" and "female" — and the related themes of bridegroom-bride, father-mother-child — to penetrate the higher analogates (the Trinity, Christ, and the church). This is an undertaking in which authors who cannot be suspected of superficiality, such as Scheeben[51] or Balthasar,[52] have proceeded with great care, always affirming the substance of Lateran IV's characterization of the analogy

48. Cf. Hans Urs von Balthasar, *The Theology of Karl Barth*, trans. Edward T. Oakes (San Francisco: Ignatius, 1992), 220-24.

49. I. Biffi, "Per una teologia dell' 'uomo-donna': metodologia e linguaggio," *Teologia* 14 (1989): 172-78, here 176. As debatable as they may be, Balthasar's claims about "suprasexuality" in the Trinity and in Christ's generation of the church have nothing to do with the above-mentioned position.

50. See, for example, the "theological integration" of homosexuality proposed by Gerard Loughlin in *Radical Orthodoxy: A New Theology*, ed. J. Milbank, C. Pickstock, and G. Ward (London: Routledge, 1999), 143-62. Also G. Loughlin, "Sexing the Trinity," *New Blackfriars* 79, no. 923 (1998): 18-25; R. Williams, "Afterword: Making Differences," in *Balthasar and the End of Modernity*, ed. L. Gardner, D. Moss, B. Quash, and G. Ward (Edinburgh: T. & T. Clark, 1999), 173-79.

51. Cf. Scheeben, *The Mysteries of Christianity*, §56.

52. Cf. Balthasar, *Theo-Drama*, 3:137-43.

between God and man as involving a *maior dissimilitudo*.[53] This is one of the reasons why the nuptial mystery remains a work in progress. Though the building has begun, only the foundations have been laid.

10. The Evisceration of Analogy

Perhaps in an attempt to avoid the maximalist surrender to a "system," others — more or less consciously — run the opposite risk. They fight every attempt to give the nuptial mystery theological weight. This group includes a wide range of positions. There are those who refuse to go beyond pure biblical exegesis, and for whom spousal vocabulary could at most be likened to the language of the parables (and thus would not have even a symbolic value): nuptial images would be on a par with many other biblical images, for example those of the shepherd and his sheep. Others marshal theoretical arguments to deny the nuptial category any systematic weight. Representatives of this approach invoke the impossibility of drawing rigorous concepts out of nuptial language, especially with regard to the fundamental mysteries of Christianity, and argue that doing so would generate confusion and lead to dead ends.[54]

11. Nuptial Testimony

Is there a way past this Scylla and Charybdis? Does analogy warrant the claim that the nuptial mystery is a fully legitimate component of the knowledge of faith as such, without falling into systems that reek of gnosticism[55] and threaten to transgress the limits of analogy that theology lays down for us? Is it good theology to refuse to take the findings of exegetical research into

---

53. "Quia inter creatorem et creaturam non potest tanta similitude notari, quin inter eos maior sit dissimilitudo notanda" [Because no likeness between creator and creature can be identified without a greater unlikeness having to be identified between them]. DS, 806.

54. Cf. Biffi, "Per una teologia dell' 'uomo-donna': metodo e linguaggio," 173.

55. "If something of this vertical mystery were to appear in the course of history, then it could only be a continually more deeply experienced union in a continually more deeply and finally experienced differentiation. If, therefore, Paul says that in Christ there is neither man nor woman, then that does not mean that the difference between God and the creature is effaced (in the sense of a pantheistic interpretation of 'that God may be everything to everyone' 1 Cor 15:28), nor that the earthly sexes become eternalized (as in the Gnostic doctrine)" (Hans Urs von Balthasar, *A Theological Anthropology* [New York: Sheed and Ward, 1967], 314).

spousal vocabulary as a sort of "prohibition" against going forward? Does the "labor of the concept," which the theology of the nuptial mystery certainly cannot avoid, fall prey to the conceptualistic blackmail[56] — no longer naive after modernity — that can't keep the *intellectus fidei* from "laying hands" on the foundation?

In order to respond to these questions, we must turn humbly to the actualization of the nuptial mystery in the experience of the individual.

What "language" does this mystery speak? First of all, it requires the individual to make the *movement* demanded by sexual difference (*dif-ferre:* to carry the same elsewhere).[57] In order to realize itself within sexual difference, the "I" is constantly called to carry itself (*dif-ferre*) toward the "thou" of another sex with respect to itself. In fact, sexual difference is a direct echo of the ontological difference in which every human being constitutively exists (*Dasein*). In its noninferable, ungraspable, indefinable nature, sexual difference is the original place of transcendent truth's singular mode of communication to human freedom. The event of truth conveys its promise to the act of freedom in a (symbolically) evident way through the individual's existence in sexual difference. In the concrete, the sexual difference is a privileged *symbol* through which the transcendent Absolute (the foundation) simultaneously gives itself to human freedom and calls this freedom to a decision. Thus, at this decisive level of fundamental human experience, we find a confirmation of the dynamism that constitutes the act of freedom. Every act of human freedom is necessary, yet cannot be reduced to itself alone: to fulfill itself it must go out of itself. This necessarily involves the "I," but equally necessarily it points the "I" to the gift of the transcendent Absolute which allows the "I's" very act of freedom to be posited.[58] For this reason we have elsewhere characterized the act of freedom as essentially testimonial.[59] Though the truth is not the fruit of the decision of the act of freedom, it nevertheless passes through it in order to give itself. In this way every act of freedom is, for man, the place where the transcendent foundation is communicated. The self-*attestation* of

---

56. In conceptualism, "the act by which consciousness intends the *res*, that is, the affirmation of the truth, is a representation produced by a merely conceptual operation, and action is the putting into practice of this representation, the execution of a previously recognized idea" (A. Scola, "Ecclesiologia in prospettiva ecumenica: qualche linea di metodo," in *Studi Ecumenici* 20 [2002]). Much of modern theology has performed a *doctrinalistic* reduction of revelation, which is linked to an *intellectualistic* conception of faith and a *conceptualistic* vision of theology.

57. Cf. above, pp. 218-21.

58. Cf. Scola, "Which Foundation? Introductory Notes," *Communio* 28, no. 3 (2001): 560-61.

59. Cf. ibid., 552-67. On this subject cf. P. Martinelli, *La testimonianza. Verità di Dio e libertà dell'uomo* (Milan: Paoline, 2002), with a substantial bibliography.

the foundation to the act of freedom calls man to expose himself in his turn, in a decision: he is urged to *bear witness.*

The intertwining of transcendence, freedom, and testimony which is realized concretely in the performance of the very act of human freedom prompts us to say that the language of the nuptial mystery cannot but be that of *nuptial testimony,* or witness.

12. The Dynamic of Desire

Practically speaking, what is the content of this testimony? The unitive drive to procreative love put into motion by sexual difference has always been placed in strict correspondence with the desire for happiness in the heart of man, and rightly so.[60] As the primary relations (motherhood, fatherhood, marriage, brotherhood, and sisterhood) make clear, to love *forever* and to be *definitively* loved are how the individual desires/needs to "be in relationship with."[61] This desire to love forever and to be definitively loved expresses itself in everything from the infant's at once loving and egotistical impulse to seek its mother's breasts to the purest self-immolation — which Jesus Christ, the supremely innocent one, makes of himself on the cross. This desire is the first "word" of nuptial language.

But the "forever" of love-desire is not obvious. In contemporary society it has been so widely denied as to have practically disappeared; the reason for this lies hidden in the culture's incapacity to hear the full language of nuptial testimony. What does this "forever" have to say? It echoes the promise which the foundation unceasingly makes to the act of freedom, urging it each time to a decision. That which is continuously proposed to this act of freedom is the ineradicable root of fidelity. So the second word of the language of nuptial testimony is precisely *fidelity.* Since we are speaking of the nuptial mystery, in order to be rigorous we must speak of *indissolubility.*

By marking every individual in his flesh, indissolubility fully expresses the paradox of human freedom. In the man-woman relationship, fidelity-indissolubility is the reciprocal promise that my "I" hands itself over to you to become in some way yours. If we take into account the element of time, essential to the idea of fidelity, this reciprocal handing over reveals a paradox: I

---

60. Cf. G. Zuanazzi, *Temi e simboli dell'eros* (Rome: Città Nuova, 1991), 86-97; L. Melina, "Amore, desiderio e azione," in *Cristo e il dinamismo dell'agire* (Rome: PUL-Mursia, 2001), 19-35.

61. Cf. S. Grygiel, *Extra Communio Personarum nulla Philosophia* (Rome: Lateran University Press, 2002).

can decide *only for me, and not for you,* to promise that I will no longer have a *my* time apart from *yours.* Moreover, this time is not in the power of the two spouses; they cannot objectively know how long it will last. Fidelity-indissolubility requires the individual to give a definitive commitment to something, time, whose quality and quantity is not within the exclusive control of the "I." This gap gives *difference* the full space due it. Difference reveals that the insuppressible desire to love and be loved forever must, in order to be fulfilled, pass through the strange necessity of sacrifice:[62] "he who wishes to save his life will lose it; but he who loses his life for my sake will find it" (Matt. 16:25). The desire to love forever and to be definitively loved which the "I" is capable of is not — we repeat — within the exclusive control of the "I." Sexual difference, which urges the individual toward the other, is there to bring this fact home again and again. The other is, precisely, *other* to me. This brings desire objectively face-to-face with the necessity of sacrifice. And in fact, sexual reciprocity is not a symmetrical complementarity, because the insuppressible difference expressed even in the one flesh of the conjugal act holds the place of the third,[63] the child. Here we have yet another instance of the indivisibility of the three dimensions of the nuptial mystery: no account of sexual difference can speak of love between man and woman without an opening to procreation.[64] Parenthood is coessential to the man-woman pair, which therefore cannot close itself off in a pure sponsality. "Nuptial language," then, includes the one, the other, the unity of the two, the fruit of their union, and an indissolubility that brings into play the inevitable necessity of sacrifice as an essential part of love-desire. By the same token, it is more complete than a "spousal vocabulary," and can be considered the latter's fruitful development.

The nuptial mystery is the privileged symbol of the gift of the transcendent foundation because of its universality and singularity. It is the path along which freedom is lovingly called to fulfill itself. In order to do this, freedom must expose itself and utter a "yes" that must constantly be renewed within time. This "yes" can be full of exciting adventure: other times it can appear as praiseworthy abnegation or be marked by the weariness due to burdensome habit. It can appear to be contradicted by fragility and perhaps even by betrayal. It can ask for, receive, and give forgiveness.[65] It will experience the regenerative power of a second try. It will marvel at the miracle of birth. It will bear the intense and affectionate gaze of an enduring bond. It will express

62. Cf. L. Giussani, *L'attrattiva Gesù* (Milan: BUR, 1999), 29.
63. Cf. above, pp. 95-104, as well as Chapter 6.
64. Cf. Appendix 5, above.
65. Cf. J. Laffitte, *Il perdono trasfigurato* (Bologna: EDB, 2001).

the fearful and lacerating surrender of the beloved to death and the certain hope of being together again in the resurrection of the flesh. In every case this "yes," taking up all the time of existence, becomes the fulfilled form of love and of being loved forever. Why should we be surprised if this "yes," like the innumerable acts of freedom we make every day, stands before us as a task or, better, as a duty we must decide for? This is a duty that I want to have, the exalting duty of testimony.

13. Irreversible Fate or Beneficent Plan?

What can make this duty perennially light and truly life-giving; what can make faithfulness the defining mark of a love that finally *is* love, because it keeps the promise of the "forever" written in its fundamental core? The fact that I receive it as a proposal from the absolute and transcendent foundation. This foundation gives itself to me in the very act of my freedom, allowing me to participate in the goodness of *its* design, which contemplates *my* good. It is this positive proposal which calls for indissolubility by opening the space of difference in which the relationship between truth and freedom is played out for the individual. By itself human freedom would be impotent and incapable of indissolubility (the space of difference) — and thus could not fulfill itself and be "free indeed" (cf. John 8:36) — if it did not take over as a *duty* the *power* the transcendent absolute gives it to decide for indissolubility in every act, in circumstance after circumstance, throughout the whole of one's existence.

The secret that motivates every act of freedom and gives it back to itself fulfilled is this: *life is the response owed to vocation.* This is what enables the individual to pursue his own well-being. Also and especially through the nuptial mystery freedom is invited to follow the path on which there is no longer any opposition between power and duty.[66] Nuptial testimony is an intense expression of *life as vocation.* It thus turns out to be the place where reality — and not primarily reasoning or discourse about it — is received for what it is and needs no system which might justify it.

The alternative to this thrilling experience of freedom is condemnation to a tyrannical fate *(anánkē);* to a fatalism that can only be passively endured and that makes inevitable the attempt to lay hands on the foundation in order to construct a system to justify everything that happens. To fulfill a design or plan, on the other hand, means to be open and to embrace everything that

---

66. Cf. N. Reali, "L'erede e i suoi beni. Note teologiche sulla libertà in Galati 4:1-7," in *Soggetto e libertà nella condizione postmoderna,* ed. F. Botturi (Milan: Vita e Pensiero, 2003).

happens, in fidelity to what is given us. What is given us is given lovingly by the ungraspable transcendent foundation. It therefore really corresponds to us, even if it should demand the sacrifice of fidelity at the limit of the impossible (as it does, for example, when one spouse abandons another). Shakespeare penetratingly writes, "Love is not love / Which alters when it alteration finds, / Or bends with the remover to remove."[67] Perhaps with even greater acuity, Balthasar observes in a brilliant aphorism, "Where there is infidelity, love was never present. Where there is fidelity, love does not yet necessarily exist. The heart can say: 'Even if I cannot love you, I want at least to be faithful to you.' But the bond of fidelity either leads to love or contains deep within itself, unknown to feeling, the knot of love, which is tied outside of time."[68]

In the Eucharist the foundation (the Trinity), which is perennially lavished on us in the offering of the Lamb who was slain, gives itself to freedom and calls it to a physical involvement. The Eucharist thus sheds light on the sacramental logic implied in nuptial testimony, which is normally called upon to actuate itself in the sacrament of marriage.[69]

Precisely in the radical difference between the dead and risen Jesus Christ and the species of the bread and wine — a difference that replicates the "hiatus" between the Father and the crucified Son, which in its turn takes place within the space of perfect difference between the persons of the Trinity — pure and sacrificial love calls the believer's free act of faith to a deeply fruitful exchange. The event of Jesus Christ addresses itself unmistakably to the act of my freedom in the Eucharist. The three dimensions of the nuptial mystery at work in the eucharistic event shed further katalogical light on the nuptial mystery: they show that nuptial testimony is totally sacramental. Thus, for example, the Eucharist helps the spouses to understand that their relationship and its circumstances correspond to them precisely because these things are given to them, and not vice versa. This specifically katalogical aspect is balanced by a no less significant analogical dimension, which takes up every circumstance and every relationship into nuptial testimony. The spouses' free act of faith thus helps them to understand ever more deeply how the living and personal Word gives himself over in the Eucharist, the marvelous encounter and exchange between the freedom of God and the freedom of man.

Literary imagination can bring home the radical alternative which the

---

67. William Shakespeare, "Sonnet 116," 2-4.

68. Hans Urs von Balthasar, *The Grain of Wheat: Aphorisms*, trans. Erasmo Leiva-Merikakis (San Francisco: Ignatius, 1995), 83.

69. Cf. P. Martinelli, *Vocazione e stati di vita del cristiano* (Rome: Laurentianum, 2001), as well as the integration proposed with respect to marriage in G. Richi Alberti, "Lógica sacramental y estados de vida. A propósito de una obra reciente," *Anthropotes* 17 (2001): 369-78.

nuptial mystery places before each and every human being, whatever his state of life: to undergo fate or to fulfill a plan. In Thomas Mann's *Buddenbrooks,* Tony Buddenbrook, the paladin of faithfulness to the family's name and honor, faced with the ruin of his house consummated in the death of his young heir, says, "Yes — they say so. — Oh, there are times . . . when that is no consolation, God forgive me! When one begins to doubt — doubt justice and goodness — and everything. Life crushes so much in us, it destroys so many of our beliefs — ! A reunion — if that were so — ."

At this point the old family governess leaps to her feet, slams her fist on the table, and cries, "It *is* so!"[70] This conclusion leaves a bitter aftertaste, because we sense that it is a purely voluntaristic affirmation of a principle by someone saying the opposite of what he feels: "We know that it's not true that we will see each other again, but to console ourselves, we have to say it's true." It is as if man has to face up to the implacable fate of his annihilation with the sheer force of his naked will.

The atmosphere is entirely different in Paul Claudel's *The Tidings Brought to Mary.* Upon returning from the Holy Land, the father, Anne Vercors, finds the body of his daughter and learns of the death of his wife: "Is the object of life only to live? Will the feet of God's children be fastened to this wretched earth? It is not to live, but to die, and not to hew the cross, but to mount upon it, and to give all that we have, laughing! There is joy, there is freedom, there is grace, there is eternal youth! . . . What is the worth of the world compared to life? And what is the worth of life if not to be given? And why torment ourselves when it is so simple to obey?"[71]

Where a plan is embraced, not even death is a defeat. It, too, becomes a call to freedom.

14. Nuptial Testimony and Theology

Nuptial testimony in the actualization of the individual's faith thus stands forth as one of the main sources of the regeneration of the subject to which John Paul II continuously invites us in his invocation of the "new evangelization." The contemporary world is confused; with incredible speed it has moved in the last thirty years from severing the unity of the three di-

70. Thomas Mann, *Buddenbrooks,* trans. H. T. Lowe-Porter (New York: Vintage Books, 1984), 604.
71. Paul Claudel, *The Tidings Brought to Mary,* trans. Louise Morgan Sill (New Haven: Yale University Press, 1916), 157-58.

mensions of the nuptial mystery to claiming to abolish sexual difference itself, to erase it in favor of a culture of androgynism and pervasive eroticism.[72] Is the fragile and wounded freedom of Christians ready to propose, once again, this nuptial testimony to the world in an exciting and compelling way?

Christ immolated himself on the cross and generated the church to enable them to do so. In his faithful "yes" to the Father in extreme abandonment (hiatus, difference), he reached the apex of love. He, the chaste Bridegroom, generated his holy bride. From this perspective, the three parts of the nuptial triad katalogically express the full significance of the family as domestic church.[73] Analogously, the domestic church allows us better to penetrate the nature of the *new family relationship* proper to ecclesial communion, which we witness in Jesus' command to Mary and John at the foot of the cross (cf. John 19:26-27).[74]

But in order to speak of Christ the Bridegroom who generates and unites himself to the church his bride (cf. Eph. 5:21-33) without unfruitfully aping the couple's erotic dynamism,[75] we must turn our attention to the singular event of Jesus Christ.[76] In him, according to the teaching of the Council of Chalcedon, two natures exist in one Person. The four adverbs of the Chalcedonian definition, *inconfuse, immutabiliter, indivise, inseparabiliter,* shed light katalogically on the "one flesh" of man and woman. The latter, too, at least according to Scheeben,[77] sheds light analogically on the hypostatic union of the two natures in the single person of the Man-God,[78] not to men-

72. Cf. A. Scola, *Chi è il cristiano? Duemila anni, un ideale senza fine* (Siena: Edizioni Cantagalli, 2000), 36-39.

73. Cf. *Lumen Gentium* 11; *Familiaris Consortio* 21, 38, 48, 49, 51-55, 59, 61, 65, and 86; *Ecclesia in Africa* 63. On this subject cf. above, pp. 265-66; D. Tettamanzi, *La famiglia via della Chiesa* (Milan: Massimo, 1991), 70-91.

74. Cf. above, pp. 107-9.

75. Cf. G. Bataille, *L'Erotisme* (Paris: Ed. de Minuit, 1957).

76. Cf. Giuliodori, *Intelligenza*, 163-74.

77. Cf. Scheeben, *The Mysteries of Christianity*, §56. However, other authors criticize what they take to be the improper application of the nuptial metaphor to the hypostatic union. Cf. G. Mazzanti, *Teologia sponsale e sacramento delle nozze* (Bologna: EDB, 2001), 44-45.

78. Another example of the analogical use of nuptial language in speaking of the incarnation of the Word is offered by the first patriarch of Venice, Saint Lorenzo Giustiniani: "Sub hoc quidem sponsi ac sponsae vocabulo sanctus Spiritus, divinam ad hominem genus voluit commendare charitatem, et Verbi ad animam spiritus unitatem. Si enim relinquens homo patrem et matrem, et uxori adhaerens fit unum cum ea, et sic efficuntur duo in carne una, quanto magis humana divinae adhaerando naturae in unitate personali, unum fient? Sed et si quis adhaerens meretrici unum efficitur corpus, nonne amplius, si Ecclesia adhaeret Christo, unum corpus sunt? Sacramenta magna haec sunt, profunda mysteria, spirituales nuptiae, et spiritualiter perscrutandae. Sponsus nacque Verbum est, sponsa humana natura; sponsa sancta

tion the importance of the categories of father and son, which we have all directly experienced, in the groping attempt to penetrate the mystery of Fatherhood and Sonship in both the economic and the immanent Trinity.[79] And how could we fail to mention the motherhood of Mary and the awakening "thou" that she, like every mother, utters to her infant, proper to every relationship between a mother and child, as we attempt to stammer something about the self-consciousness of Jesus Christ?[80]

The nuptial mystery thus helps us to understand the Eucharist, Christ and the church, the Man-God, and the Trinity, and conversely, these holy mysteries shed light on the nuptial mystery in its three dimensions. All of this is safe from the temptation to elaborate a Hegelian-type system precisely because, in the twofold movement of the analogy (from above and from below), every utterance of nuptial language must pass through a new act of testimony on the part of this particular individual, because the individual cannot capture the act of his freedom a priori. Hence nuptial language urges us to keep our thought in motion, because it constantly demands that thought become experience. The fact of dealing with mystery places the person before a task for which he must decide, always and ever anew. No systematic perspective can grasp the foundation, which unceasingly gives itself by urging freedom to testimony. On the other hand, if nuptial testimony is possible — as it in fact is

---

Ecclesia; sponsa fidelis anima: non qualiscunque, sed talis, quae meritis et dilectione sponsae vocabulo digna sit. Ut autem Verbum, Deique sapientia suas cum filiis hominum delitias esse notificaret, humanam, homo factus, assumpsit naturam, sibique copulavit Ecclesiam: atque in fide et charitate desponsavit, et quotidie desponsat devotam sibi animam semper caste, semper misericorditer" [The Holy Spirit, indeed, used the terms bridegroom and bride in order to commend God's charity to the human race. He used the term Word in order to commend the unity of spirit to the soul. For if, leaving mother and father, and cleaving to his wife, a man becomes one with her, so that the two become one flesh, how much more will not the human and divine natures become one when the human nature cleaves to the divine nature in unity of person? But if even someone who cleaves to a prostitute becomes one with her, won't it be even more true that, if the Church cleaves to Christ, they are one body? These are great sacraments, deep mysteries, spiritual nuptials, and they need to be investigated spiritually. For the Word is the bridegroom, and the bride is human nature. The bride is the holy Church. The bride is the faithful soul; not just any soul, but one whose merits and love make her worthy of the title bride. But that the Word and Wisdom of God might make known that his delights are among the sons of men, he became man; he took on human nature and joined to himself his Church, and in faith and charity he espoused to himself, and continues to do so every day, always chastely, always mercifully, the soul devoted to him] (Lorenzo Giustiniani, *De spirituali et casto Verbi animaeque connubio*, caput IX: *De unione in Christo celebrata divinae et humanae naturae in unitate personali*).

79. Cf. Chapter 13 above.
80. Cf. Balthasar, *Theo-Drama*, 3:175-76.

— for many men and women in many families, it is so because of the grace of God. The "source of all fatherhood" (Eph. 3:15), step by step, reveals his design to humble and obedient freedom. So we see that the nuptial mystery offers a systematic perspective — but one never taken for granted or possessed — for the *intellectus fidei*.

15. Farewell

At this moment when, after twenty years of teaching, I bid an official farewell to the chair of theological anthropology I have occupied at the John Paul II Institute at the Pontifical Lateran University, the presentation of the nuptial mystery I have just laid out reminds me of my efforts as a boy to climb Mount Grigna near my home. That was before real mountain-climbing shoes existed, but I would find a few nails here and there, left by previous climbers, which made the way up safer. There were not very many of these nails, because it was an inflexible law that the climber's skill was measured by his capacity to remove the nails he had used, not least so as to allow the next person to demonstrate his ability. Moreover, since the nails might have been there for a long time, each one had to be tested for stability before the climber hooked his grip onto it. This is how it will be for those of you, students and teachers, who want to continue the ascent, at once exciting and dangerous, up the sheer face of the nuptial mystery. But this is the excitement of theology and the raison d'être of a university like our alma mater.

In any case, as a possible perspective for systematic theology, the nuptial mystery expresses the singular wedding between the pontifical magisterium and the ecclesiastical sciences that is the distinctive note of the *Scuola Romana*, with its long and often glorious tradition. Through the Pontifical John Paul II Institute for Studies on Marriage and the Family, our alma mater, the Lateran University, shows us that this *Scuola* continues to play an indispensable, fruitful role in debate about the *humanum* which contemporary thought has no choice but to participate in.

Deepening our understanding of the nuptial mystery, as well as of every other aspect of the Christian mystery, through research, teaching, and study of the ecclesiastical sciences, is also an eminently pastoral way of supporting the testimonial nature of faith. Such faith means to stand firmly in the One who opened the way for us and did not consider his equality with God as something to be grasped at (cf. Phil. 2:6), but passed through the eye of the needle at Golgotha so that the mercy of the heavenly Father could shine forth in his glorious humanity. How do we set out to follow him in the work of a university?

The Spirit of the Crucified and Risen One gives us, in baptism and the Eucharist, the grace of belonging to his holy church, which guides, sustains, and corrects our freedom in the task (which no one can perform in our place) of deciding for the truth, always anew in every act.

In Paul Claudel's *The Satin Slipper*, Camillo addresses Prouheze with the words, "If I am void of everything it is the better to wait for you." To her perfect but all too doctrinal response of "God alone fills such a void," Camillo opposes the logic of testimony: "And this God — who knows if you alone are not the one to bring me Him?"[81]

How do we communicate love except by giving ourselves to love?

81. Paul Claudel, *The Satin Slipper,* trans. Fr. John O'Connor (New York: Sheed and Ward, 1945), 12-13.

Index of Names

Index of Names

Campanini, G., 206n.75
Chesterton, G. K., 90
Chrysostom, John, 23n.4, 199n.35
Claudel, Paul, 92n.30, 401, 405
Colombo, Giuseppe, 37n.14
Cottini, G., xxii n.1
Curran, Charles, 361
Cyprian, 254
Cyril of Alexandria, 250

Dante, 61n.22, 85, 180
Deleuze, G., 276
Denzinger-Schönmetzer, 37n.13, 121n.36,
   271n.39, 386n.9, 395n.53
Derrida, J., 234
Descamps, A. L., 309-10
Dionysius the Areopagite, 65n.34
Dostoyevsky, F., 166
Duns Scotus, 233

Eliot, T. S., 168n.10, 193, 198
Erikson, E., 186
Evdokimov, P., xix, 117, 217, 363n.17
Eve: creation of, 23, 39, 46, 79; and Mary,
   15, 18; as mother, 19, 41, 44, 50, 75-76,
   336

Faust, 83, 115
Fessard, G., 119, 217
Feuerbach, L., 277
Fino, M. B., 111n.5
Freud, Sigmund, 56n.3, 59-60, 110, 118,
   220n.14, 380

Gadamer, H. G., 180n.16
Geiger, L. B., 67-70, 201
Gerken, A., 30, 393n.47
Gevaert, J., 172
Gilson, E., 123n.50
Giuliodori, C., 11nn.22-24, 102n.63,
   393n.47
Giustiniani, Lorenzo, 402n.78
Goethe, J. W., 83, 365n.22
Gregory of Nyssa, 46-47
Grotius, H., 145
Guardini, R., 113n.9, 171, 183, 341

Guitton, J., 57n.8, 85, 86n.13, 310

Haeckel, E., 111n.5
Harper, M. F., 42n.33
Hegel, G. W. F., 24, 273, 277, 388, 394, 403
Heidegger, M., 8, 84n.6, 111, 120, 123, 167,
   222-24, 227, 234
Hemmerle, 334
Hildebrand, Dietrich von, 202
Hobbes, T., 146
Hölderlin, F., 163
Hugh of St. Victor, 102n.63
Husserl, E., xxvi, 234, 376

Ignatius of Antioch, 289
Ingarden, R., 387
Irenaeus, 32n.1, 183, 188, 281

John, Mary presented to as his mother,
   107-8, 250, 288, 402
John XXIII, 361
John Damascene, 21, 46
John Paul II, on: absolute moral order,
   360-62; the family, 141-43, 155, 174n.6,
   185, 206-10, 337-40, 386; *imago Dei* as
   communional, 33-34, 132, 271n.37, 285,
   386-88; "intermediate social bodies,"
   146, 157, 170, 178; Mary, 15-20; modern
   society, 168-70; the new
   evangelization, 209-10, 283n.12, 337-39,
   372, 401; sexuality, 3-7, 33-34, 118n.23,
   217, 278, 342-43; theology of the body,
   22, 28, 39-41, 91, 262, 332, 358, 387
Jungmann, J. A., 92n.30, 340n.5

Kafka, F., 151n.22
Kaliba, 334
Kant, I., 146, 225, 234
Kasper, W., 240n.5
Kass, L., 159n.2
Kierkegaard, S., 162, 378
Krieg, C., 199

Leibniz, G. W., 61, 111n.3
Leo XIII, 197
Leopardi, G., 168

407

Index of Subjects